The Boeing B-47
Stratojet

The Boeing B-47 Stratojet
Strategic Air Command's Transitional Bomber

C Mike Habermehl & Robert S Hopkins III

www.crecy.co.uk

Crécy Publishing Ltd

www.crecy.co.uk

First published in 2018 by Crécy Publishing Ltd

Copyright © Robert S Hopkins III and C Mike Habermehl 2018

Layout by Russell Strong

A CIP record for this book is available from the British Library

ISBN 9781910 809082

Printed in Malta by Gutenberg Press Ltd

Crécy Publishing Limited
1a Ringway Trading Estate, Shadowmoss Road, Manchester
M22 5LH

www.crecy.co.uk

Front cover: Following an accident on 15th September 1951, B-47B 50-0011 transferred to the 3320th TTW at Amarillo AFB as a ground trainer. Curiously, it was redesignated as a TB-47B in 1953 but was never physically modified. It was finally scrapped in situ on 8th August 1957. *Courtesy Boeing*

Rear cover: The TEE TOWN modification provided an ECM capability for 100 B-47Es roughly equivalent to Phase V ECM EB-47Es. This example, B-47E 52-0487 from the 830th BS, 509th BW is seen on REFLEX alert in 1963 at RAF Brize Norton. *via Steve Hill/EMCS*

Rear cover, top inset: Early B-47B 51-2094 carries the A-2 twin 0.50 caliber tail turret and has yet to receive anti-flash paint. It served with the 306th BW from 28th November 1952, and was in the initial B-47 deployment to the UK as part of the 369th BS during June 1953. *Author's collection*

Rear cover, middle inset: RB-47E 52-0725 is one of the rare PETER PAN jets assigned to the 26th SRW at Lockbourne AFB. It is seen here at Goose AB, Labrador, during Operation SNOWFLURRY during March 1958. *Augustine Letto*

Rear cover, bottom inset: On REFLEX alert and ready for launch from RAF Brize Norton during August 1963, 301st BW B-47E 53-4229 has a full complement of ATO and the penultimate ECM configuration. *via Steve Hill/EMCS*

Half title page: A 306th BW B-47B at RAF Fairford on a rare sunny day during the unit's 1953 UK deployment. Bad weather and unsatisfactory facilities hampered the type's initial visit to the UK. *Harold Siegfried*

Title page: XB-47 46-0066 finishes engine start prior to a test flight from Renton. In this configuration the airplane could not fulfill its military mission, but displays the uncluttered simplicity and elegance of a beautiful airplane. *Gordon S Williams via Jay Miller*

Contents

Acknowledgements

This project began so long ago, has been to so many places, and encountered so many people that it is impossible to name them all. For those unwittingly omitted from the names that follow your knowledge, expertise, and encouragement are nonetheless graciously remembered. I trust that this book properly reflects the history of the B-47 that you entrusted me to tell.

The Boeing Company played a crucial role in reconstructing the B-47 story. Although Boeing has, at times, seemed ambivalent about its groundbreaking airplane, the employees who were directly involved with the airplane had no doubts about its importance. They enthusiastically supported my work with photos, documents, memories, and encouragement. N D Showalter – Chief of Flight Test in the early B-47 days – first responded to my humble pleas for assistance. He put me in contact with Robert M 'Bob' Robbins, who flew the XB-47 on its first flight, and who invited me to Wichita to share precious days of his time. By then Bob was the B-52 Project Manager, but he never tired of recounting the first Stratojet flight and the days of preparation leading up to it. Bob supported my research until his death in 2005. He was always encouraging and helpful, even if understandably somewhat defensive about Boeing's role in the difficult B-47 production process.

At Boeing-Wichita I enjoyed the wonderful assistance of Public Relations Manager Herb Hollinger, Jack Wecker, John Freeden, and Jerry Gordon. Help from Boeing-Seattle was abundant thanks to Harl Bracken, iconic Boeing photographer Gordon S 'Gordy' Williams, and the legendary Marilyn Phipps (who went above and beyond more than once). Ed Wells, Boeing's quintessential engineer, and test pilots Guy Townsend, Richard Taylor, and Roy McPherson provided critical insights. Jim Fraser, who was in the back seat when the XB-47 canopy took test pilot Scott Osler's life, became a good friend and shared a deeply personal viewpoint of the early test days. The late Al Lloyd, author of a previous B-47 history, provided important materials.

Boeing's generous support did not end with those who were 'present at the creation' of the B-47. Michael Lombardi, current Boeing Corporate Archivist, provided access to the vast repository of documents and photographs which he deftly preserves, as well as extraordinary insights into the Boeing Company and the B-47's legacy. His assistant Tom Lubbesmeyer and volunteer John Fredrickson ferreted out both rare images and documents. Our memorable lunches proved much brighter than the Seattle weather!

Two other aerospace giants produced B-47s. Jess Hightower, Public Relations Manager at McDonnell-Douglas Tulsa, was helpful with photos, documents and unbelievable access to technical details. He also set up an appointment with the late A P 'Whit' Whitmore, who directed the EB-47Es flown for the US Navy until the mid-1970s. Whit had more B-47 experience than other pilot, having flown them from 1951 until 1976. The two Navy EB-47Es were in the hangar at Tulsa when I visited and I'll never forget my personal tour of the airplanes. Lockheed-Marietta was equally helpful in the persons of Jeff Rhoades and Lee Rogers, and Robert Ferguson from Lockheed-California provided great photos of the S-3 Viking testbed.

Several museums played critical roles in my research. The National Museum of the United States Air Force allowed access to their library along with help from Dave Menard. They also loaned rare documents in the early days of my work, something that is no longer done. Dennis Jenkins and Dan Hagedorn, retired curators of the Museum of Flight in Seattle, allowed access to documents,

photos, and a rare first person encounter with George Schairer's watershed letter from Germany. John Little, the Museum's Assistant Curator, provided a virtual ton of material, and Archivist Jessica Jones was equally helpful in accessing the Museum's photo collection.

Numerous historians aided my work over the years, including Bonnie Olson, Chief Historian at McClellan AFB, Robert E Trevathan, Chief Historian at Tinker AFB, Robert J Smith, Chief Historian at AFLC, Wright-Patterson AFB, and Judi Endicott and Maranda Gilmore at the Albert F Simpson Historical Research Center (renamed the Air Force Historical Research Center). Archie DiFante at AFHRA oversaw SAFE PAPER efforts to accelerate access of relevant material. Master researcher and friend George Cully waded through endless pages of documents to find the missing details that tied together so many previously unknown operations or incomplete records. Other USAF historians and public information personnel who assisted over the years included J T Bear, M E Bodington, John T Bohn, Michael H Brown, John R Burton, Robert T Cossaboom, Myron L Donald, Royal D Frey, Gladys Graves, Albert E Misenko, Robert E Morgan, James A Morrow, Patricia Shafts, Lester S Smith, and William C Woodrum. Matthew Aid and Doug Keeney provided invaluable source material, including declassified histories and documents, as did Bill Burr and the late Jeffery Richelson from the National Security Archives. Gregory Graves found crucial documents amid the endless stacks at the Library of Congress and National Archives and Research Agency. Dave Forster and Chris Gibson shared similar research from the National Archives (formerly the Public Records Office at Kew) in the UK. Chris Gibson is also responsible for cleaning up old drawings and preparing new drawings and the many maps. Tony Buttler provided invaluable assistance on the initial B-47 replacement program. R Cargill Hall championed the need to tell the real story behind Western overflights of the USSR. Although his conclusions differ markedly from those of Hall, Paul Lashmar deserves equal credit for uncovering much of the early history of overflight operations. Simon Watson of The Aviation Bookshop ferreted rare and interesting monographs.

Great photographs make or break this research and I enjoyed the gracious support of a number of people. Howard Hendry shared his wonderful slides from his vantage point as a KC-97 boom operator, as did John Bessette, Knox Bishop, Ben Knowles, Mauno Salo, Wayne Mutza, Stephen Miller, Norm Crocker, Geoff Hayes, Steve Hill/EMCS, Toshio Tagaya, Harold Siegfried, Larry D First, Angelo Romano, Gordon Macadie, Mark Natola, Dean Abrams, Frederick Johnsen, Robert L Lawson, and Paul Stevens. John Kovacs shared images and memories of his EB-47E(TT) TELL TWO experiences. The late David Anderton provided both photos and documents and insight into the workings of SAC. Colin Smith graciously shared his encyclopedic knowledge of the B-47 and SAC operations, correcting and clarifying many long-established misconceptions about B-47 operations in the UK, Spain, and North Africa. His detailed accounting of SAC operations proved invaluable in recounting the legacy of mass deployments and REFLEX. Lindsay Peacock, who wrote the first book on the B-47 (following the brief B-47 Profile by Peter Bowers), graciously reviewed material and provided thoughtful commentary, not least of which was 'cracking the code' on RB-47H tail numbers passing through RAF Brize Norton.

Individuals with specific knowledge of various programs took time to share their memories. Charles G Kohler was invaluable in describing the QB-47E program as was engineer James Hannigan (for both the QB-47E program and the nuclear-powered bomber), the late Chuck Hansen (nuclear weapons), Michael Binder (BOLD ORION), John Towson (MONTICELLO), Canadair Test Pilot Michael Cooper-Slipper (the CL-52), Terry Panopalis (CL-52), Wai Yip (ECM and aircraft records), Tom Lebar, and Kenneth D Wilson.

I am deeply indebted to John McKone and Bruce Olmstead, both now deceased, for sharing the story of their fateful experience in an RB-47 on 1st July 1960 and their subsequent incarceration in the Lubyanka Prison. They are true American heroes and I am honored to have called them friends. The other four members of their crew were not so fortunate, as were three other fliers who perished in another Soviet attack on an RB-47 in international airspace. Similarly, Don Hillman and John Timmins, son of then-Major Edward Timmins – navigator on the airplane, provided photos and insights into the first B-47 overflight of the USSR in October 1952. Hal Austin recalled his overflight of the USSR in 1954. The 26th SRW at Lockbourne AFB was involved in some very interesting reconnaissance programs and several of their former crewmembers related their memories, including Dave Nicholson, Barney Calligan, and Bob Waltz. Special thanks go to Walter Savage for recounting the tragic loss of the TELL TWO at Incirlik AB, as well as Bob Bumen, Jim Cover, and Earl Crowson. Bruce Bailey provided materials on RB-47H operations. 55th SRW legend and RB-47 pilot Reggie Urschler reviewed the reconnaissance material and held our feet to the fire to 'get it right.' Colonel Johnny Drost, via his son Gary, provided the photos for the NEW BREED and IRON LUNG RB-47H. He also took the MiG-19 photo on page 128. B-47 Stratojet Association members who have provided memories and insights over the years include Don Cassiday, Dick Purdum, Jim Diamond, Andy Labosky, and Bob Griffiths. U-2 expert Chris Pocock was also an early contributor.

Jeremy Pratt and Gill Richardson at Crécy graciously supported this book. Russell Strong did the magnificent layout work. In the absence of endnotes, material in 'quotes' reflects attribution of verbatim content or ideas by other writers or sources.

The vast majority of people provided help via mail, email, and/or telephone calls. A few of these developed into friendships that provided not only material but emotional support as well. Paul Swendrowski probably gave up on me long ago but continued to offer years of help and support that will never be forgotten. William T 'Tom' Y'Blood published the Squadron/Signal B-47 history and flew RB-47s, offering first-hand insight. We exchanged Stratojet-related material for many years and I eventually ended up with his collection. Sigmund 'Alex' Alexander, President Emeritus B-47 Stratojet Association and tireless recorder of B-47 history, was a constant source of inspiration (both spiritual and material). Augustine 'Gus' Letto flew RB-47Es and EB-47Es out of Lockbourne AFB and has shared my passion for recounting the Stratojet story. Gus was dedicated to tracking the B-47 service in SAC with his camera and he got away with it very well. He has been most generous in sharing his images with writers around the globe. I have a thick folder of his many letters, helping me uncover the story of the ROMAN I airplanes, the PETER PAN AN/APQ-56 SLAR installations, REFLEX operations to the UK, and many other aspects of the operational and testbed Stratojets.

And then there is Jay Miller, whose friendship extends back further than either of us cares to remember. We once talked of airplanes and

wives, then of airplanes and kids, and now of airplanes and grandkids. What a wonderful friend, supporter, and relationship! He provided the very first bit of help I had in my research and he has refused to let this project die. Jay led me first to Neil Lewis who never gave up on bringing this B-47 history to realization. And then to Robert Hopkins, my co-author, whose expertise in research and writing made it all happen. Robert is respected the world over for his depth of knowledge in reconnaissance, overflight history, and all things KC/EC/RC-135. But to me he is one of the most gracious individuals I have ever known and I am proud to call him my friend.

David Mills, to whom this volume is dedicated, was my cousin, my hero, and the inspiration of my love for the B-47. His wife, Bobbie Ruth, and he hosted me for a wonderful two weeks in 1956 in Roswell NM where I was immersed in the world of SAC, the 509th BW, Walker AFB and the B-47.

There are more important things in this life than airplanes and I am blessed to have experienced that. Robert's family has supported (more like tolerated) his own research efforts as well as our collaboration on this book. His father, Robert 'Hop' Hopkins, was a B-47E pilot who related his own experiences, as did his mother Eula Mae who was among the silent wives who waited (and worried) as their husbands flew an airplane with an atrocious safety record or who sat alert at home or away. Robert's children Sarah, Mike and his daughter Olivia, Robert IV, Emily, and Christopher have grown up with airplanes but lack their father's passion (or obsession) for them. His wife Amy patiently transcribed thousands of Julian dates, oversaw household duties while Robert was visiting archives or researchers across the US and Europe, and reminded him if the B-47 story was important enough to be part of their family then it was important enough to get it right. Amy, I trust this book meets with your approval.

Judy Habermehl has been by my side for over fifty years now and she has loved me through it all (I will never repay the hours she spent scanning documents at the archives). C M and Erich, our sons, travelled with us to archives, manufacturing plants, and air force bases as they grew up. Today, they have homes and families of their own and I am sure they thought their Dad would never finish this work. In the meantime, they gave us two wonderful daughters-in-law, Faylinn and Amanda, and six beloved grandchildren, Mitchell, Addison, Parker, Tyler, Davis, and Reid. The late Carl and Blanche Habermehl and Billie Jean DelHomme (my sister) will always be a part of everything I do. I am richly blessed.

Mike Habermehl
Brenham, Texas
May 2018

From first to last. Bob Robbins (r) was pilot for the first XB-47 flight on 17th December 1947, while Major General John D 'JD' Moore (l) was pilot for the last B-47E flight on 17th June 1986. Colonel Richard 'Dick' Purdum (c) shares the spotlight. *via Dick Purdum*

Foreword

On the evening of 22nd October 1962 my B-47 Crew, S-86, was watching TV in the alert barracks at Forbes AFB near Topeka, KS. Our B-47 was loaded and cocked, sitting a few yards from the facility. Our viewing was interrupted when President John F Kennedy, our Commander-in-Chief, came on to tell the nation that the USSR had missiles in nearby Cuba. This of course grabbed our attention and began one of the most stressful periods in our young lives. The Defense Condition (DEFCON) was immediately raised and the remainder of our wing joined us on alert within 24 hours. Our stress might have been all the worse had we known then what we've learned since – our nation came closer to nuclear war than at any other time in our history.

I had been flying the B-47 for four years and had stood alert many times and flew multiple simulated attack missions. We all knew that the B-47 was a major part of the mailed fist on SAC's emblem. We 'knew' that our airplane was the 'best' and that we could do the job we were assigned. And we firmly believed that our capability was a key element in America's posture of deterrence.

Despite an accident rate that was horrendous (we lost 30 B-47s in my first year in the airplane) we loved flying it and took great pride in our role in America's defense. We thought little of the losses, unless they were close friends. We knew that SAC relied on us and we were ready to do what we had to, if we were launched.

As the airplane was retired we discovered more and more about the B-47. We learned that it was the granddaddy of Boeing's subsequent fleet of swept-wing airplanes. Those of us who were strictly bomber crews learned that our bird had undertaken all sorts of other types of missions such as electronic countermeasures and very successful strategic reconnaissance. Later we watched as the weather service used our airplane and the Navy put it to work. Yet, in most of our cases, the comprehensive picture of the B-47, its development, and its multiple missions eluded us.

This book has thrown light on that darkness. The authors have provided us the most comprehensive picture of our beloved airplane yet published. From its development, through its deployments and

Don Cassiday and the nose of B-47A 49-1901 at the Pima Air & Space Museum. *C Mike Habermehl*

its many missions and finally retirement, they present it all. The 'warts' are not avoided and the many problems of both development and operations are openly discussed. They delve into aspects of the bird and its missions that many of us who flew it didn't realize existed. Their research sheds light on where we and our airplane fit into the national defense during the years of the Cold War. Their technological expertise answers questions that many of us had, despite our hours and hours of flying the B-47.

Our war, the Cold One, has been studied and covered in numerous volumes. Mike and Robert provide insight into a small but fascinating and highly significant chapter in that war. As we who flew the '47 are fond of saying, 'That's the war we won!' This book helps clarify why, despite many foibles, we did indeed win.

Don Cassiday, Colonel, USAF (Retired)
President, B-47 Stratojet Association

CHAPTER ONE

An Unlikely Beginning

Lieutenant General Curtis Emerson LeMay, the second Commanding General of Strategic Air Command (SAC), hated the Boeing B-47 Stratojet. When asked during Congressional hearings on the viability of the Convair B-36 Peacemaker if he would prefer the B-36 or the B-47, LeMay replied 'I would choose a B-36.' When pressed why he would sacrifice the speed of the Stratojet, LeMay noted that the 'B-47 won't go where I want it to go' – the Soviet Union. Maligned as the perfect bomber should war break out with Canada or Mexico, the B-47 was limited by its poor range, widespread production difficulties, and its fair-weather bombing capabilities. It acquired a reputation as a demanding – if not downright lethal – airplane, totally unforgiving of any pilot who failed to respect its sluggish jet engines or its tendency to stall or spin during critical phases of flight. It is surprising, then, that the B-47 became SAC's most numerous bomber with nearly 2,000 in service, and pioneered SAC's transition from piston-powered B-36s and Boeing B-50s to the Boeing B-52 Stratofortress. Despite its critical role as SAC's transitional bomber, LeMay never did change his opinion of the B-47. Every modification program to mitigate its shortcomings, LeMay warned, would detract from SAC's ultimate bomber – the B-52. However apocryphal, LeMay reportedly told every briefing officer who pitched some upgrade to the B-47, 'How deep do we have to bury this thing before you dumb SOBs stop digging it up?'

Throughout its operational lifetime the B-47 served in a variety of operational roles: medium bomber, electronic warfare 'jammer', strategic reconnaissance platform, testbed, and even as a drone configured to carry a hydrogen bomb. Its lifespan as a bomber, however, was short by modern standards. The 306th Bombardment Wing (BW) at MacDill Air Force Base (AFB) undertook its first operational deployment in April 1953, signaling the B-47's initial readiness for its Emergency War Plan (EWP) mission. The final B-47 came off alert on 31st December 1965, and the last two B-47Es flew to storage at the Military Aircraft Storage and Disposition Center (MASDC) at Davis-Monthan AFB on 11th February 1966. In just a dozen years, B-47s had gone from the backbone of SAC's jet bomber force to an endless supply of aluminum beer cans. To be sure, other variants lasted longer. SAC's RB-47 reconnaissance force was retired in December 1967, and the Military Airlift Command's (MAC) WB-47E weather fleet was finally grounded in October 1969. During October 1977 the last two operational Stratojets, two EB-47Es flown by McDonnell Douglas-Tulsa on behalf of the US Navy, were retired to become static display aircraft.

The many successes and failures of the B-47's design, production, and operational service effectively smoothed the way for the B-52.
Courtesy Boeing

Opinions about flying the B-47 were contentious. Many veterans of World War II and the Korean War who had flown Convair B-24 Liberators or Boeing B-17 Flying Fortresses or Boeing B-29s in combat over Europe or Asia failed to make the cut as B-47 pilots. The B-47 was intolerant of errors and demanded thinking 'ahead of the jet' with faster reaction times that were unknown to many 'Old

Heads.' SAC desperately needed pilots with jet experience, and free-spirited 'kick a tire, light the fire' fighter pilots were dragooned into LeMay's 'by the book' command built on rigid adherence to rules and regulations. More than a few copilots posted to the B-47 viewed their assignment as 'SAC from the Bottom.' Instead of 'yanking and banking' in the latest jet fighters, these would-be Thunderbirds hauled flight manuals, managed the fuel panel, took celestial navigation shots for the navigator, fired the tail guns, and very rarely got to fly the airplane until ready for upgrade to aircraft commander (AC). Indeed many B-47 copilots opted for reassignment to the KC-135 as a faster route to upgrade.

Conversely the B-47 was the ultimate technical challenge to fly. Calculating airspeed on final approach based on fuel weight was an intellectual exercise of the highest order. Refueling at heavy weight behind the piston-powered Boeing KC-97 required skill and finesse to avoid stalling and spinning. During the 1950s and early 1960s SAC was the Air Force's elite command, with 'spot' promotions in rank to crews that distinguished themselves in annual competitions or Unit Simulated Combat Missions (USCM). With the world seemingly on the verge of nuclear war between the United States and the Soviet Union, SAC was viewed as the primary deterrent to a surprise Russian attack. However unpleasant alert might have been, B-47 crews justifiably felt they were doing their share to maintain global peace. Overseas deployments meant that crews could visit England, Spain, Guam, or French Morocco, seeing the world and stocking up on furniture and liquor otherwise not available at home bases in Ohio, Georgia, or Oklahoma.

The history of the B-47 is a study in contradictions. It was designed to carry only conventional bombs but spent its operational career hauling nuclear weapons. It was designed by arguably the world's foremost bomber company but its production was so poorly executed that it took years (and multiple builders) to resolve the problems. Despite LeMay's disdain for the B-47, he worked tirelessly to get as many into service as fast as possible even if they were not operationally capable, and he unsuccessfully opposed efforts to retire them just as quickly in order to maintain a credible bomber force. Understanding these many contradictions is the key to appreciating the history of the B-47. The Stratojet was never intended to be anything more than SAC's transitional bomber, facilitating the evolution of strategic airpower from the age of piston-powered, conventionally armed bombers flying in mass formations at high altitudes to the design, production, and operations of jet-powered, nuclear armed strike aircraft skimming the earth at low altitudes and bristling with electronic countermeasures. To ascribe any other achievements to the B-47 fails to recognize its limits and inadequacies.

A World at War
On 17th August 1943 US Army Air Forces (USAAF) B-17s undertook the dual air raids on Schweinfurt and Regensburg. The goal was to destroy the German ball bearing production centers there, which the Americans believed would cripple the German aircraft industry. The group which attacked Regensburg, led by 4th BW

Top: LeMay despised the B-47 due to its inadequate range, many technical shortcomings, and initial inability to fulfill its mission. Over time he grudgingly accepted the airplane as an interim solution pending delivery of the B-52. This caricature was the cover drawing for the scrapbook of LeMay's 1954 familiarization checkout in the B-47. *Author's collection*

Left: Colonel Elliott Vandevanter (l) gives a preflight equipment briefing to General LeMay prior to his qualification flight at MacDill AFB. LeMay passed his check ride on 9th February 1954 after a 1+10 hour flight and two landings. *USAF*

Commander Colonel Curtis LeMay, achieved reasonable results before heading south to recover at bases in North Africa. The 1st BW, led by Brigadier General Robert B Williams, was less fortunate. Although both groups lacked fighter escort over the targets, the Schweinfurt group was badly mauled and the results of its mission were an utter failure, necessitating a second raid on 14th October with equally dismal results.

The airplane that would eventually become the B-47 was born between these two disappointing missions, and the tactics SAC would eventually use with the B-47 were influenced by the successes and failures of Schweinfurt and Regensburg. On 20th September 1943 the Development Engineering Branch in Washington, DC, asked Air Materiel Command's (AMC) Engineering Division at Wright Field, OH, to assess the 'design of an experimental airplane which utilized one or more TG-180 (J35) turbojet engines.' With no funds available for yet another bomber (the last prototype XB-29 Superfortress had been delivered on 27th June 1943), this resulted in a USAAF request for proposal (RFP) for 'Military Characteristics for Photographic and Reconnaissance Type Aircraft' that was approved on 15th October 1943.

Boeing quickly began studies and the Army was quite impressed with the results. After seeing some penciled curves of projected performances and sketches of airplane designs, Brigadier General Franklin O Carroll, commander of the Engineering Division of the AAF Materiel Command, wrote the following to the General of the Armies Henry H 'Hap' Arnold, Commanding General of the Army Air Forces: 'Contrary to the existing belief that jet-propelled aircraft are limited to short ranges and fighter type aircraft, the Boeing studies indicate that for equal takeoff distances, the range of jet-propelled aircraft may exceed that of conventional aircraft. Also, the studies indicate that if a speed of approximately 600mph [966kph] is attained, the specific fuel consumption of jet-propelled aircraft may approach that of conventional airplanes. This opens up the attractive possibilities of developing at least medium range jet propelled bombardment airplanes.'

As Boeing engineers were no longer employed on design work for the B-29 and were finishing work on plans for yet another long-range bomber (the Boeing Model 384), Carroll suggested that the design work for a jet bomber be given to them, expressing fear that if they were not engaged in this work they might be 'allowed to drift to Navy projects.'

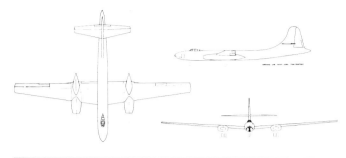

Top: The Model 413 was Boeing's initial response to the 1943 request for a jet-powered reconnaissance airplane. It was liberally based on the B-29 but with two turbojet engines mounted in a single nacelle under each wing.

Below: During early 1944 Boeing proposed two turboprop and two turbojet designs for the USAAF request for a jet-propelled medium bomber. All were essentially straight-wing variations similar to other manufacturer's proposals. None was selected for further development.

The initial Boeing design was, for all practical purposes, a jet-powered B-29 known as the Model 413. The four jet engines were in twin nacelles mounted on the underside of the wings much like the soon-to-appear North American B-45. Mounting jet engines in nacelles was possible because of work being done by General Electric on an axial-flow engine. Although the new jet design produced 250lbf (0.1kN) less thrust than the earlier centrifugal flow engines, its diameter was 10in (25cm) smaller. Unfortunately for Boeing by the time Model 413 had been submitted for consideration in January of 1944 the USAAF had closed its photo-recon competition, leading to a final competition between the Hughes XF-11 and Republic XF-12 Rainbow. Moreover, the Model 413 was rejected because of 'lack of requirement.' The engineers from Wright Field did make it clear, however, that they wanted Boeing to continue with its research on large jet aircraft. Between January and March 1944 Boeing engineers developed four designs, two jets (Models 424 and 425) and two turboprops (Models 422 and 426), all with straight wings. Planners in Washington sent Boeing a statement of characteristics on 22nd April 1944, intent on beginning an industry wide competition for a 'jet propelled medium bomber.'

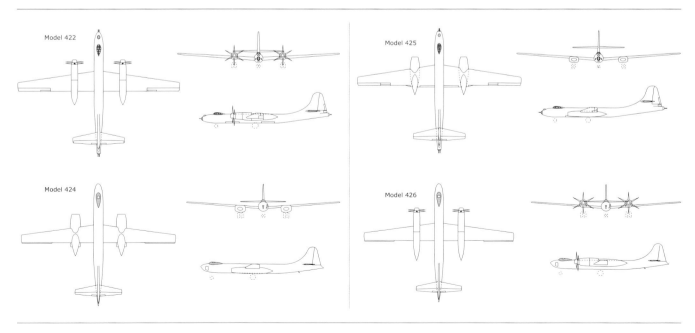

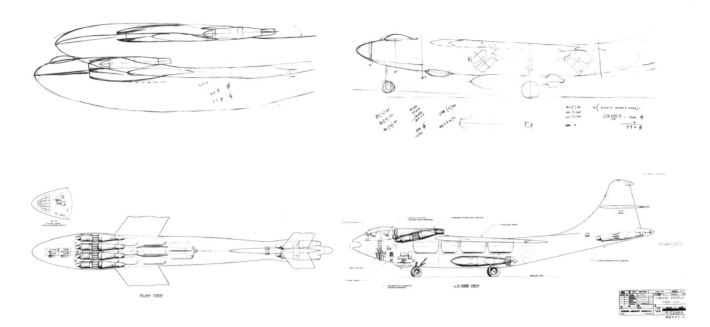

After considerable revisions the final requirements were approved on 17th November 1944. These called for an aircraft with a top speed of 550mph (885kph), tactical operating altitude of 35,000-40,000ft (10,668-12,192m), range of 2,172-3,041nm (4,022-5,632km), takeoff distance (without assist devices) over a 50ft (15m) obstacle of 5,000-6,000ft (1,524-1,829m), and a landing distance over a 50ft obstacle of 3,500-4,500ft (1,067-1,372m). Defensive armament would be either a nose or tail remote-controlled 0.50 caliber turret, although the USAAF would consider 20mm or 0.60 caliber guns. The bomber was to carry a load of 16 x 500 lb (227kg) bombs or alternate combinations of 1,000 lb, 2,000 lb, or 4,000 lb (454kg, 907kg, or

1,814kg) bombs. The minimum crew would be the pilot, copilot/radioman, bombardier/navigator, and the necessary turret operators. The airplane would be pressurized and provide for window, wing, and tail de-icing. On-board radios and radar would be suitable for all-weather 'bombing, navigation, routine communications, and countermeasures.' Finally, the airplane design would 'emphasize reliability and ease of maintenance.'

Boeing's Model 425 was, again, essentially a jet-powered B-29, with the four engines paired in single underwing nacelles on each wing with a much thinner cross-section. The horizontal stabilizer was moved higher on the tail and a bubble canopy covered the cockpit. A subsequent iteration, the Model 432, had a clean wing with the four jet engines buried in the upper fuselage behind the cockpit, with air intakes on either side of the forward fuselage known as 'elephant ears'.

The Model 432 was fat and dumpy, but it did free the wing of considerable drag. On 16th December 1944 Boeing submitted the design to the USAAF. It was awarded a Phase I contract (Letter Contract W33-038ac-8429) on 31st January 1945 for preliminary engineering, wind tunnel tests, and structural tests. The original proposal also called for Phase II (mock-up, three experimental airplanes, static test article, and spares) but this was deleted. Boeing was authorized to spend up to $150,000 but the company estimated that at least $1,429,884.56 – ten times the money authorized – would be needed. This figure was later renegotiated to $1,319,968. On 31st January 1945 Model 432 was given the military designation XB-47 (Project MX-584).

All five entries in the medium bomber competition were awarded Phase I contracts, approved on 9th March 1945. North American had submitted its XB-45 (Project MX-553), Convair proposed its XB-46

Above: Boeing's Chief Engineer Ed Wells sketched a number of designs showing unorthodox landing gear retraction (a variation would be used on the Model 450-1-1), and what later became the Boeing Model 432. Interior sketch of the 448 shows the unusual engine arrangement ahead of the wing root and in the tail. *Courtesy Boeing*

Left: Wind tunnel variations of the Boeing Model 432 show similarities to the eventual nose of the B-47, but the additional TG-180 turbojets mounted on the horizontal stabilizer and in the tail proved ineffective. Moreover, the USAAF was unimpressed by any of these designs. *Courtesy Boeing*

(Project MX-583), Martin entered the XB-48 (Project MX-598), and Curtiss-Wright pitched the XA-43 (Project MX-582) – which had the lightest weight (60,000 lb – 27,216kg) of the five proposals. The Douglas XB-43, the first American jet bomber was also built during this period but was not competitive with the others. By the summer of 1945, however, the USAAF Engineering Division was not impressed by either Boeing submission, noting that neither offered 'substantial advantage over aircraft currently being considered by other manufacturers.'

The Letter

By early April 1945 American and British forces were advancing along a broad front inside Germany. Fighting was light, as all but German elite troops were surrendering piecemeal to Western forces rather than face the certainty of Soviet captivity (or worse) should they return to their homes in the eastern half of Germany. Still, the grim task of defeating the Third Reich continued. On 11th April American forces liberated the Nazi concentration camp at Buchenwald. Among the inmates freed was Marcel Bloch, later known as Marcel Dassault, famed French aviation designer. The following day American troops reached the small German town of Völkenrode. Located a short distance from Braunschweig, it escaped that town's horrific bombing on 15th October 1944, after which American and British target planners considered the destruction of this important arms manufacturing region to be sufficiently complete that no further raids on the area were planned, ensuring that Völkenrode – an utterly inconspicuous assemblage of nondescript buildings – remained unscathed. A week after this tiny community fell into Allied hands, a small group of American scientists, aerodynamicists, and engineers of the 125th Liaison Squadron arrived on an urgent mission ordered by Hap Arnold: investigate the *Luftfahrtforschungsanstalt* – the Hermann Göring Research Institute – a top secret aviation research facility located at Völkenrode. Among the American visitors of Operation LUSTY (LUftwaffe Secret TechnologY) – including Hugh L Dryden and Theodore von Kármán – was a quiet aerodynamicist from Boeing, George S Schairer. What he would find there would lead directly to the B-47 and play a defining role in the adolescence of the jet age.

Schairer observed cutting-edge German aerodynamics research, both theoretical and practical. He saw supersonic wind tunnels which produced considerable data on high-speed and transonic air flows. He examined testing facilities for various types of turbine blades used in jet engines. Perhaps most importantly, he studied research notes on the *Pfeilflüge* ('arrow wing'), better known as the swept wing first introduced by Adolf Busemann at the 1935 Volta Conference in

 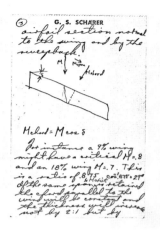

Rome and explored by a few aerodynamicists in the following years, including Robert T Jones from the US National Advisory Committee on Aeronautics (NACA). In a famous 10th May 1945 letter hastily scrawled on seven small sheets of paper imprinted with his misspelled name – 'G S Scharer' – Schairer told fellow Boeing aerodynamicist Benjamin Cohn about the 'extensive work on high speed aerodynamics.' Illustrated by a drawing on page three, Schairer then 'did the math' to show that sweeping the wing resulted in an increase in critical Mach number, allowing a commensurate increase in maximum airspeed. On page five he presciently noted that this benefit would be negated by anything disrupting the continuity of the wing leading edge. 'This is not complicated by adding a body at the center [ie, a fuselage between swept wings] but is badly effected [*sic*] by most nacelles.'

As part of Operation LUSTY, Schairer was acting on behalf of all US aviation companies hoping to benefit from Nazi research. Keenly aware of the implications of swept wings for future designs, he asked Cohn: 'I do not know how soon this info will get around to other manufacturers so will you write letters to Ozzie [Williams, Senior Aerodynamicist for Republic], C[larence] L ['Kelly'] Johnson [at Lockheed], R[alph L] Bayless [Chief Engineer for Convair at San Diego], E[d] Horky [at North American], E[arl] Sheafer [Vice President of Stearman], & [R A] Darby [Chief Research Engineer at Fairchild] quoting pages 2-5 for their information.' Excited about the potential of swept-wing designs, Schairer nonetheless wanted to make sure that Boeing would be among the first, if not *the* first, American airplane companies to benefit from this research. Confident in the theory behind swept wings, it remained for Schairer to convince

Above: The first and third pages of Schairer's famous missive from Germany. The third page shows the critical data that changed the evolution of the B-47 and its successors, illustrating the advantages of the swept wing. *Courtesy Boeing*

Right: Boeing's Edmund T Allen Memorial Aeronautical Laboratories housed the Boeing Transonic Wind Tunnel. This verified the efficiencies of the swept wing and the podded engine design. *Drawing 47868 courtesy Boeing*

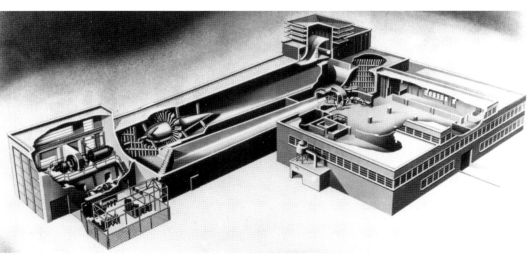

Above: The Boeing Model 448 seen on 20th September 1945 emphasized the clean, swept wing design that would prove effective on the B-47 and its many successors once the podded engines were validated. *Photo 94135-B courtesy Boeing*

Below: At first glance the Martin XB-48 shared many similarities with the B-47: bicycle landing gear, outrigger wheels, and six engines. The critical differences were the B-47's swept wings and tail, and engines suspended beneath the wings rather than attached directly to the wing. *Author's collection*

Bottom left: The North American B-45 bears a striking resemblance to the German Arado Ar 234C. Although the Tornado won the USAAF bomber competition, it was quickly supplanted by the B-47. *Author's collection*

Bottom right: Convair's XB-46 did not fully benefit from Schairer's report on the advantages of swept wings. Moreover, without a transonic wind tunnel the company was unable to test engine arrangements that did not compromise the wing leading edge. *Author's collection*

others at Boeing of their value and to determine the optimum design. That required a shift from theoretical to empirical research, and that meant the need for a suitable high-speed wind tunnel.

Most corporate test pilots consider themselves lucky if they are fortunate enough to take one airplane on its maiden flight, and only a few can claim credit for more than a single first flight. Edmund T 'Eddie' Allen, however, was the pilot on the inaugural flight for multiple airplanes built by Northrop, Stearman, Douglas, North American, Sikorsky, and of course, Boeing with its B-17s and the XB-29. Considered by many to be one of the greatest test pilots in history along with Charles E 'Chuck' Yeager and Eric 'Winkle' Brown, he was first and foremost an accomplished aeronautical engineer. Hired by Boeing in 1939 to lead the Flight Research Department, Allen recognized the importance of empirical research in improving airplane design and performance. To achieve this, he urged Boeing to invest an estimated $1 million to build its own wind tunnel, a rare commodity among airplane manufacturers. In August 1941 Boeing's President Philip G Johnson was willing to take that risk and approved the construction of a wind tunnel which could reach speeds as high as Mach 0.9, approximately 625mph (1,000kph). Sadly, Allen would not see completion of the wind tunnel, as he and 29 others perished in the crash of the second XB-29 on 18th February 1943. Thanks to efforts by Boeing aerodynamicists William 'Bill' Cook and Bob Withington, the Boeing Transonic Wind Tunnel (BTWT) was finally finished at Plant 2 in Seattle. On 2nd April 1944, Allen's widow Florence officially started the tunnel for the first time as part of the Edmund T Allen Memorial Aeronautical Laboratories.

Armed with Schairer's new-found aerodynamic insights and the resources of the Allen wind tunnel, Boeing representatives 'appeared at the project office at Wright Field to propose major changes' to their previously rejected proposals. By 6th September 1945 they submitted the Model 446, which appeared to be a swept-wing version

of the Model 432. They also submitted the Model 448 (referred to as the Model 433 in some documents) which included swept tail surfaces. Boeing touted the Model 448's 555mph (893kph) airspeed at 35,000ft (10,668m), a marginal improvement over the earlier 550mph top speed. This increased speed came with a price, however, as the Model 448 had two additional turbojets buried in the aft fuselage, although the 'elephant ears' were now gone. Previous models could not take advantage of the power available; now even more power was needed to take advantage of the high-speed wing. The two rear engines were placed inside the back of the fuselage with flush air inlets. The swept wing also played havoc with the fuselage arrangement. The new wings produced a calculated 20% increase in speed but they also moved the mean aerodynamic chord (MAC) back some 15ft (4.6m), making the fuselage arrangement effectively unusable. Small changes to improve visibility resulted in Model 448-2-2.

Despite these new designs, the USAAF was unimpressed, especially with the engines in the fuselage (for obvious reasons). Engine malfunctions, battle damage, or even regular maintenance were all complicated by the buried engines. Tests were carried out using an early jet engine in a partial mock-up of the proposed design and quickly identified crucial weaknesses. The engines would be too close to the fuel supply, requiring stainless steel along the upper wing and fuselage where fuel cells were located. The tail surfaces would be in the hot exhaust of the four front engines, seriously reducing their efficiency. Probably the greatest difficulty, with the most far-reaching implications, was the consideration for future growth. As jet engines developed and improved, a completely redesigned fuselage would be necessary to incorporate any of them in the XB-47. Other shortcomings were noted in a fairly critical report: 'Pilot ejection is a must; means of dropping bombs without opening up a hole in the fuselage must be developed; …dive control flaps are needed. In addition, it was requested that Boeing study the possibility of utilizing boundary layer air supplied through flush intake ducts to the two aft engines as a means of cleaning up the airplane and minimizing drag. Boeing was also requested to study methods of preventing airflow through the aft engines as a means of eliminating windmilling drag and increasing partial power range.'

AMC considered the newest Boeing submission, even with swept wings, to have too many 'undesirable features', and by the end of September it appeared that Boeing would be excluded from the final competition for a medium jet bomber. After eliminating the XA-43 the designs were divided into pairs with the XB-45 competing directly with the XB-46 (each with four J-35 engines), leaving the XB-47 and XB-48 (each with six J-35s) as rivals. Both the XB-45 and XB-46 were in more advanced design stages than the XB-47 and XB-48, so they were chosen to proceed in trials for the initial production contract. If, during subsequent testing and evaluation either the XB-47 or XB-48 proved to be a superior airplane to the winner of the XB-45 or XB-46 competition, then it would supersede the earlier winner. NACA was also asked at this time to develop a minimum drag configuration for twinjet air inlets in nacelles. This work was done at Moffett Field, CA, but only North American and Convair made use of it.

Although the XB-47 did not win the jet bomber competition (North American's B-45 did), the USAAF believed that Boeing should devote more time to its wind tunnel research in an attempt to solve the problems associated with high-speed jet bombardment

aircraft. The Boeing design team was led by Edward C Wells as chief engineer and George C Martin, project engineer.

Success at Last

Wells and Martin went back to their drawing boards and, more importantly, to their wind tunnel. They tried almost every conceivable powerplant location (over 50 in all) until tests indicated that engines mounted on pylons ahead of and below the wing detracted minimally from overall wing efficiency, and also brought the center-of-gravity (cg) within the allowable limits of the airfoil center-of-pressure travel. As Wellwood Beall, Boeing's Vice President for Engineering recalled, 'We did not arrive at the [engine] pod without experimentation, for it is the least obvious configuration; and, as a matter of fact, it was more or less of an accident that we tried it at all.' Now known as the Boeing Model 450-1-1, the XB-47's wings benefitted from the work of Victor Ganzer, a graduate student at the University of Washington, who determined that a wing sweep angle of 37.5° was optimal. Coupled with a Boeing-derived airfoil of about 12% thickness ratio and a rather high aspect ratio of 9.6, this created grave structural problems for engineers faced with a very flexible wing. The location of the inboard engine pods along the wing relieved the wing-fuselage fittings of their loads and helped to tame wing flexure in both bending and torsion. Single engine pods were mounted on the wingtips, further reducing the minimal wing flutter. The pylons would also prove beneficial to ground maintenance personnel. The vertical tail was now also swept. A tricycle landing gear folded into the fuselage. This design was committed to mock-up form and made ready for inspection.

On 6th November 1945 the USAAF Engineering Division at Wright Field described the Boeing Model 450 as a 'step beyond the present jet bombers (XB-45, XB-46, and XB-48) by applying a swept back wing to bomber design.' They requested that Washington authorize the procurement of two 'flight article XB-47s' with the understanding that these would not 'jeopardize the concurrent development of other types of bombardment aircraft.' Three days later, on 9th November, Boeing proposed that for the sum of $9,357,800 it could build two prototypes with the completion date for the first airplane to be one year from date of the contract and the second airplane delivered two months later. This was approved on 6th December 1945 with a fixed-price contract for two XB-47s (Boeing Model 450-3-3).

The two prototypes differed from the original proposal by having an increased wing area, pylon-mounted outboard nacelles, and bicycle landing gear. It had a design gross weight of 125,000 lb (56,699kg) which could increase to 140,000 lb (63,503kg) when

Boeing's B-47 'brain trust' gathers around a model of the XB-47 (l) to (r) George Schairer, Chief Aerodynamicist, Ed Wells, Boeing Senior Vice President-Engineering, George Martin, and Bob Jewitt. *Photo P6260 courtesy Boeing*

Left: The penultimate B-47 design, the Model 450-1-1 had wingtip outboard engines and the inboard pairs mounted in a single nacelle, as well as fuselage-mounted tricycle landing gear. The USAAF liked what it saw, and in December 1945 approved development of the XB-47. *Courtesy Boeing*

Below: Wind tunnel images show the degree of wing flexure on the B-47. Left undampened this would result in failure of the wing and loss of the airplane. The engine pylon/pod combination helped mitigate this, but the B-47 nonetheless suffered from wing problems throughout its career. *USAF*

Center: Full-scale mockup of the Model 450-1-1 shows the original engine arrangement and the complex landing gear. USAAF inspectors insisted that both of these be revised. *Photo 96181-B courtesy Boeing*

Bottom: Photo sequence showing the gear retraction on the Model 450-1-1 mockup. This proved needlessly complex, so Boeing and the USAAF settled on a bicycle-style landing gear, which brought its own set of problems. *Photos 96548-B, 96459-B, 96550-B, and 96551-B courtesy Boeing*

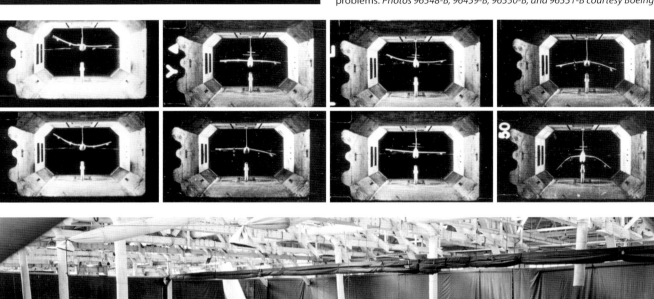

carrying a 20,000 lb (9,072kg) bomb, and a ferry gross weight of 165,000 lb (74,843kg). Its crew of three all had ejection seats. Defensive armament included a tail turret equipped with two 0.50 caliber machine guns using a 'split-periscope sight' for aiming (with the provision for the later installation of a radar-directed fire control system). Offensive systems included the AN/ASP-23 search radar, as well as the AN/APA-59 computer and AN/APQ-31 bombing-navigation system which combined to form a radar-optical bombsight. All fuel tanks were contained within the fuselage and were self-sealing. Multi-segment bomb bay doors would 'sweep bombs into the airstream as they were opened'. Performance estimates anticipated a top speed of 578mph (930kph) at 30,000ft (9,144m), a service ceiling of 36,000ft (10,973m), a takeoff run to clear a 50ft obstacle of 7,500ft (2,286m) and a landing roll of 6,600ft (2,102m). Unfortunately, the XB-47 still did not reach the specified range which USAAF required. The definitive contract (W33-038ac-8429) was approved on 10th July 1947, with Boeing receiving $9,668,483.52 for its work. The Price Control Branch at Wright Field noted the cost of $95 per airframe pound as 'fair and reasonable' as it was 'considerably lower' than the XB-45 or XB-48.

From Drawing Board to Reality

The mockup inspection was on 16th April 1946, and the Army generally approved of the design. The landing gear, however, presented a significant problem. The main gear were located in the fuselage and used a very complicated and bulky door mechanism, leading to complications in the retraction sequence. As the gear moved up and back into the fuselage the wheels rotated so that they were briefly broadside to the airstream (a mechanism perfected in the B-52). Should the airplane lose an engine (and hence thrust) during takeoff, retracting the landing gear would actually increase, rather than decrease, the amount of drag. Tests undertaken by the Martin Company with a tandem-gear XB-26H 44-68221 known as the '*Middle River Stump Jumper*' prompted Boeing to send its XB-47 test pilots to evaluate the arrangement. Robert M 'Bob' Robbins and E Scott Osler went to Freeman Field in Indiana to fly the XB-26H, providing valuable experience in handling an airplane with bicycle landing gear. The Model 450 was soon modified with a tandem main gear retracting into the fuselage and small outrigger wheels that folded into each twin nacelle, saving 1,500 lb (680kg) in the process.

Other studies showed that the XB-47 needed more wing area, so the wings were extended by 8ft (2.4m) on each side. The outboard engine nacelles were now located approximately 15ft (4.6m) inboard of the wingtip. This reduced the potential hazard for asymmetric thrust should either the #1 or #6 engine fail, which allowed the reduction in size of the vertical stabilizer. The greater wing area reduced the takeoff distance by 1,000ft (305m), increased the service

Above: Boeing test pilots Bob Robbins and Scott Osler flew the Martin XB-26H to determine if the bicycle landing gear arrangement was feasible for the B-47 – it was, and the design was changed. *Author's collection*

Below left: The Model 450-1-1 mockup had the crew entry door on the starboard side and the throttles on the port side. Why this was reversed has not been determined. *Photo A23863 courtesy Boeing*

Below: Among the many innovative designs used in the XB-47 was a bomb bay where the bombs were attached to the doors. This limited the XB-47's load capability and was never implemented.

ceiling by 2,000ft (610m), and extended the range by 70nm (130km). Additional changes moved the crew entry door and cockpit aisle from the right to the left side, added a rotatable copilot's seat, and returned to a more conventional design for the bomb bay. The original bomb bay doors were eight small, individually snap-opening devices with attached bomb racks. However, the USAAF review board felt that these would restrict the type of loads the XB-47 could carry. Formal start of the XB-47 Phase II design was 4th June 1946.

The first airplane was to be ready by 31st May 1947 with the second one rolling out two months later. Production and development delays occurred and these dates were repeatedly revised. Some of the major problems involved the control surfaces, power boost systems, powerplant installation, and the landing gear. Boeing was breaking new ground not only with the design but also in the fabrication and assembly techniques they used. The Air Force and Boeing agreed on 27th May 1947 that the XB-47, as designed, could undertake its first flight when ready, and the 'definitive contract' for the airplane was signed on 10th July 1947.

The first XB-47 (46-0065) rolled out on 12th September 1947. It had been constructed under the supervision of Fred P Laudan, his assistant A W Jacobson, and W W Rutledge, production manager of the Experimental Division. Although the event was a rather subdued affair, the airplane would later be greeted with considerable enthusiasm by both the military and the press. They had already seen the XB-45, XB-46, and XB-48, but here was something truly new.

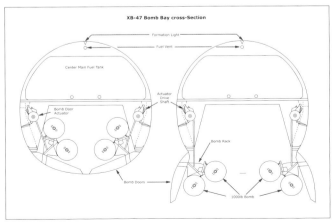

The two XB-47s began assembly in Plant 1, site of Boeing's famous 'Red Barn.' The top photo shows 46-0066 ready to move. Each fuselage and wing section was then shipped by barge up the Duwamish River and then trucked along Federal Way to Plant 2 for final assembly. The two men on the right in the bottom photo are working with the fittings held by the 'milk bottle' pin, an area that would cause Boeing and the Air Force considerable grief and money in later years. *Photos P7428, H6058, H6064, and H6068 courtesy Boeing*

AN EARLY REPLACEMENT

Interestingly, plans were underway as early as 1947 for the follow-on to the B-47 known as Project MX-948. The USAAF asked Boeing, Convair, Curtiss, Douglas, Lockheed, North American, Northrop, and Republic for proposals during FY48.

Convair proposed a conventional 'straight wing four-engine turboprop design' using Pratt & Whitney PT-2C or PT-2D engines. It had a maximum speed of 434KIAS and a service ceiling of 40,000ft (12,192m). The maximum bomb load was 25,000 lb (11,340kg), including eight 500 lb (227kg) bombs or a single 12,000 lb (5,443kg) bomb. Defensive armament was a four-gun 20mm tail turret.

The Douglas Model 1126 was similar to the Boeing Model 450-1-1, although it was larger with an overall span of slightly more than 140ft (42.7m) and length of 128ft (39m). Estimated performance data has not been identified. It had a crew of seven, including two gunners.

Lockheed proposed the L-173-15, with its final design based on six Westinghouse KJ40 turbojet engines, a high wing for bomb bay clearance, bicycle landing gear to reduce weight, and pressurization only in the forward crew cabin and tail gunner's position. It had a cruise speed of 413KIAS (less than the 430 KIAS specified), a service ceiling of 45,000ft (13,716m), and an operating radius of 1,737nm (3,217km).

It should not be surprising that Northrop's MX-948 proposal was based on its extensive prior experience with flying wings, and included multiple versions of the same airframe. The N-31 used six Westinghouse X40-E2 jet engines, four mounted in the inner wing with another in a nacelle at each wingtip. Bomb load included 20 x 500 lb, eight 2,000 lb (907kg), three 4,000 lb (1,814kg), or a single 22,000 lb (9,980kg) bomb. The N-31A had only two Turbodyne XT37-1 turboprop engines with six-blade contra-rotating propellers capable of up to 7,500shp (5,593kW) and designed for 10,000hp (7,457kW). The N-31B looked similar to the jet N-31 but had just the four wing-mounted engines. Bomb load was a single 22,000 lb (9,980kg) bomb mounted externally

on an underwing pylon just to the right of center. The N-31F was a photographic reconnaissance version of the jet-powered N-31B.

Project MX-948 did not result in any prototypes, let along production, but it did influence the development of the B-47's true successor, the B-52.

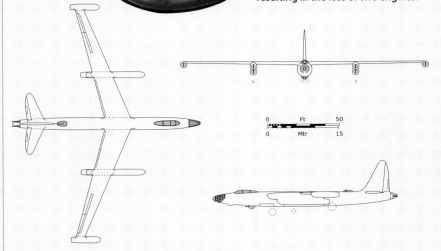

Left: **The Douglas Model 1126 resembled the Boeing Model 450-1-1, and its nose was comparable to the IL-28** *Beagle*. *Via Tony Buttler*

Below: **Lockheed's L-173-15 was also a six-engine design with wingtip engines. The 'stacked' inboard engines would be a nightmare if the upper engine caught fire or disintegrated, resulting in the loss of two engines.**

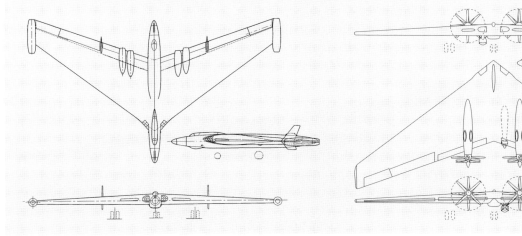

Below left: **Northrop also considered using wingtip engines in the N-31. Boeing's work with pylons quashed engines mounted within wings or the fuselage on heavy bombers, at least until the B-2.**

Below right: **Many aircraft designers on both sides of the Iron Curtain believed that turboprops were the ultimate solution to the shortcomings of range with turbojets. Northrop's N-31A used contra-rotating props much like the Tupolev Tu-95** *Bear*.

The XB-47's rollout on 12th September 1947 was underwhelming. The small crowd symbolized Boeing's general uncertainty about the Stratojet's future. *Courtesy Boeing*

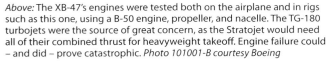

Above: The XB-47's engines were tested both on the airplane and in rigs such as this one, using a B-50 engine, propeller, and nacelle. The TG-180 turbojets were the source of great concern, as the Stratojet would need all of their combined thrust for heavyweight takeoff. Engine failure could – and did – prove catastrophic. *Photo 101001-B courtesy Boeing*

Above right: Much like the B-36, the XB-47s had inlet doors on each engine to prevent windmilling in flight after shutdown. These proved needlessly complex (as did engine screens to prevent foreign object damage) and were deleted. *Courtesy Boeing*

Below: Boeing towed the XB-47 through a number of obstacles and uneven terrain to determine if the outrigger gear caused any adverse effects on the engine pylons. *Photo 7566 courtesy Boeing*

There were similarities with the others. All had crews seated in tandem under bubble canopies and all were jet-powered. But those features were mostly cosmetic. The XB-47 was the beginning of a new era in large aircraft design and everyone seemed to know it. As one writer said, 'Even special gun mounts were blueprinted, to prevent any gun muzzle projection from causing air turbulence and drag in the otherwise sleek lines of the bomber.' Not all writers were so kind. One description said the bomber looked like a 'torpedo on a roller skate with wings added as a sort of afterthought, and six jet engines hung in clusters under the wings.' Another writer dubbed the new bird 'Old Droopy' with its wings tapering toward the ground. As aviation writer Bill Gunston noted, 'the wing had zero dihedral

and the droop stemmed from the combination of sweepback and a 5° angle of incidence which had the effect of rotating the wingtips downward. Parked, the wing really did have anhedral because it simply sagged.' The flexible wings carried no fuel, and the engine mass was distributed evenly along the span of each wing, which could arc through a range of 20ft (6.1m) at the wingtips during flight.

The airplane was moved from the manufacturing plant to the Pre-Flight Group of the Flight Test Section on 26th September 1947. Engine and ground tests were conducted during October and November. The General Electric TG-180-B1s (J35-GE-7) proved to be the source of several difficulties. The engines were originally to have been supplied by Chevrolet but it suffered from production difficulties. There was also a compatibility problem. The J35-GE-7 (TG-180-B1) had a 60in (152cm) tailcone, whereas the J35-GE-9 (TG-180-C1) – to be installed on the second XB-47 – had a 30in (76cm) tailcone. Boeing decided to modify the J35-GE-7 to the shorter version instead of waiting for more J35-GE-9s to be delivered. The TG-180s/J35s produced only 4,125 lbf (18.3kN) of thrust at 7,700rpm. Their fuel consumption was quite high – 1,026 lb/hr (465kg/hr) – and there was only a 25-hour period between overhauls. Fortunately the placement of the engines in pods rather than embedded within the fuselage meant that newer, more powerful and more efficient engines could soon take their place. Engine air inlet screens also caused headaches. On the ground these screens would help prevent Foreign Object Damage (FOD). During tests, however, the screens failed often. Tests without the screens resulted in a 4.4% increase in thrust and a 1.9% decrease in specific fuel consumption. The screens were left on the two XB-47s, but they failed so often during flight tests that they were removed and not installed on all future Stratojets. These screens should not be confused with the inlet doors installed on the B-47As and some early B-47Bs. These were developed at the request of the Air Force to close off an engine after shutdown to eliminate the windmilling of its turbine (similar to the design on the J47 engines of the Convair B-36). As with the screens, these proved to be ineffective and were deleted from production aircraft.

The bicycle landing gear prompted special taxi tests. For example, as a tractor towed the XB-47, small blocks of wood were placed in front of the outrigger wheels to assess outboard engine clearance when taxiing over uneven surfaces. During later tests trenches 10in (25cm) deep were dug alongside the ramp for the outriggers to test the sway of the gear. Final ground tests included a series of low- and high-speed taxi runs. The low speed runs were characterized by performing a series of sharp 'S' turns. The high-speed portion called for the bomber to be accelerated to speeds of up to 90mph (145kmh) – the maximum refusal speed for the initial takeoff – and then stopped using maximum braking.

In October an AMC Engineering Division representative visited Seattle and pronounced the XB-47 as 'the most promising of the Air Force jet bombers, its development prospects are far greater than for any of the Forty series [i.e., the XB-45, XB-46, etc].' Following a safety inspection, AMC released 46-0065 for Phase I flight testing on 27th October.

Preparation for Flight
In mid-1946 Boeing asked Bob Robbins to serve as a liaison between the flight test department and the B-47 design project. He was an aeronautical engineer graduate from the Massachusetts Institute of Technology (MIT) and had flown Boeing 314 Clippers as a flight engineer from 1939 to 1941. He came to Boeing in 1942 and flew B-17s and the experimental Boeing XPBB-1 flying boat built for the Navy. After Eddie Allen was killed, Robbins became project test pilot on the XB-29 program. Robbins reported to Noah D Showalter, the

assistant chief engineer for the B-47 program, who offered Robbins the job as XB-47 project test pilot. They chose E Scott Osler, an engineering graduate of the University of Washington, as the copilot.

The two had almost a year to prepare for the first flight following an extensive training program. Robbins remembers taking drawings of the XB-47 to his home at night and spreading them out on the floor to study the aircraft's systems. As flight consultant to the project, he had already participated in many of the design decisions. Robbins' first exposure to a jet engine came in B-29 44-84043 that General Electric had modified with a TG-180 installed in the bomb bay. The engine could be extended below the fuselage and operated during flight. Robbins logged at least an hour and a half of flight time experimenting with air starts and engine acceleration from various power settings. Boeing also had a B-29 with electric props that could adjust the pitch more effectively to simulate approach profiles in the new airplane, and Robbins' final B-29 flights were spent landing it like the XB-47. The USAAF provided Lockheed P-80 44-85085 at Muroc Army Air Field (AAF), CA, for further indoctrination in turbojet operation. Both Robbins and Osler practiced takeoffs and landings, with and without assisted takeoff (ATO), with each logging about five hours in the jet fighter. Both pilots rode an ejection seat simulator at Wright Field to get a feel for the then-new method of emergency egress.

Perhaps the most beneficial training took place at the NACA wind tunnel at Moffett Field, CA. Scale models flown in Boeing's tunnel had already provided clues as to how the B-47's controls would react in flight. The huge Ames tunnel allowed room for the entire empennage of the number two XB-47, and it was there that Robbins first 'flew' the Stratojet while seated inside the tail section. While the pilots got their feel for the airplane, the engineers got a wealth of data on the power boost system and coordination and aerodynamic balance of the control surfaces.

Plans for the first flight proved to be somewhat contentious, especially as to where it would take place. The runway at Boeing Field was relatively short at 6,700ft (2,042m), and the proposed flight path would take the airplane over residential areas in Renton and

Boeing's XB-47 test pilots Scott Osler (l) and Bob Robbins (c) discuss the planned first flight with Major General Emmett 'Rosie' O'Donnell (r), the Deputy Director of Public Affairs for the newly created US Air Force. All three were aware that the B-47 would be a 'tough sell'. *Photo 7417 courtesy Boeing*

Seattle. Concerns about possible emergencies – loss of an engine on takeoff or even a crash – prompted alternative plans. Some of these called for shipping the XB-47 to another location, including nearby Whidbey Island Naval Air Station (NAS) and even to Muroc AAF, which would have required a very long overland trip after shipping it down the coast.

Full of confidence in its new design, Boeing instead developed a very careful flight plan from Boeing Field. Takeoff would be to the south so as not to overfly the populated Georgetown area. The XB-47 would then fly east over the Cascade Mountains about 150nm (278km) to Moses Lake Army Air Base (AAB). The runways at

Moses Lake AAB were about 4,000ft (1,219m) longer than the one at Boeing Field and the base was largely unused (it had been used previously for B-17 testing, and later for B-29 gross weight trials). The approaches were also clear without nearby residential areas. The XB-47 would carry only enough fuel for the trip in the event the landing gear or flaps might not retract. Moreover, it would be as light as possible should an emergency landing have to be made on Boeing's short runway after takeoff.

XB-47 46-0065 was ready for its first flight on 14th December. Each day the road on the east side of Boeing field was crowded with people waiting to watch the first flight. Bad weather prevented flight

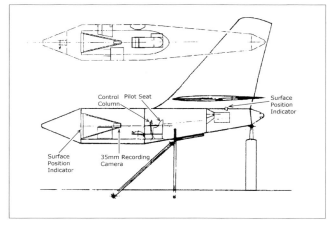

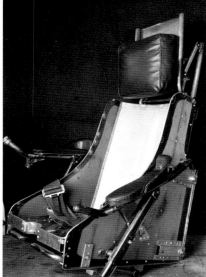

Above: Prior to the first flight Robbins and Osler practiced turbojet air starting procedures and evaluated response parameters in the GE B-29 testbed. *Photo 209970 courtesy General Electric*

Upper and lower far left: Both Robbins (in P-80) and Osler flew 44-85085 to gain jet and ATO experience. Robbins made his first flight at Muroc AAF on 17th July 1947. *Courtesy Boeing*

Left: Robbins and Osler traveled to Wright Field to train in the ejection seat rig, which Robbins described as a 'thrill'. The XB-47 ejection seat hardly inspired confidence due to its general lack of post-war development. In a controversial decision, the Air Force removed ejection seats from the B-47B to save weight, an option that was later reversed. *Photo 98916-B courtesy Boeing*

Bottom left and right: Robbins sat inside the tail section to 'fly' XB-47 46-0066 positioned in the NACA wind tunnel at Ames Aeronautical Laboratory, gaining experience in the 'feel' of the airplane. *NASA photo A-11732*

Above: After an aborted attempt due to a false fire warning light, XB-47 46-0065 took to the skies on its inaugural flight on 17th December 1947. The southern departure avoided populated areas in case of emergency. *Photo P7788 courtesy Boeing*

Right: After a successful 52-minute first flight, 46-0065 landed at Moses Lake AAB. Other than minor shimmy with one of the outrigger gear, the flight was uneventful. *Courtesy Boeing*

operations for three days, and on 17th December it appeared that another day would pass without the first flight, especially as Showalter had decreed that 2:00 PM would be the cutoff time for the day's attempt. As the morning progressed, however, local conditions improved to marginal and the ice had melted from the runways at Moses Lake AAB. All other stations along the flight route reported dense fog, however, with no improvement in the forecast. After lunch, Ben Werner, the XB-47 Flight Engineer, called from Moses Lake AAB and reported that the skies there had cleared. With this good news about the destination, Captain James 'Jim' Fitzgerald – who had come to photograph the flight for the people back at Wright Field, took off in his P-80 45-8406 to assess the situation. When Fitzgerald returned 27 minutes later, Robbins and Osler were already in their seats in the XB-47. With the positive weather report from Fitzgerald, Robbins taxied the airplane to the end of the runway.

Although many pilots had flown jets before, and some had even flown swept-wing jets, no one had ever flown a large, swept-wing, multi-jet aircraft. After a few brief moments – during which Robbins remembers asking for Divine help – the airplane began its takeoff roll. As the airspeed hit 90KIAS the fire warning light for #2 engine suddenly flashed on. Robbins quickly closed the throttles and the Stratojet slowly came to a halt. Local news accounts called this aborted takeoff a 'taxi test', and noted that the XB-47 had two rocket motors near the tail for 'emergency bursts of power.'

While taxiing back to the ramp, Osler determined from back-up instrumentation that the warning had been a false alarm. Robbins decided to try again. Once again, the fire warning came on, but this time the airplane left the ground, slowly rose a few feet, and then pulled sharply into a steep climb. The XB-47 became airborne at 2:02:50 PM, nearly three minutes after Showalter's deadline. The sharp pull-up caused some concern among observers on the ground, including Mrs Ann Robbins. Robbins did this to avoid the flap limit speed as the flaps were slower in retracting than expected. He could have reduced power but had cautiously decided against that. Bob had told Ann that if anything went seriously wrong, he would fire the ATO, climb steeply for altitude, and then eject. The black smoke trail coming from the six engines – later taken for granted at all B-47s bases – made it appear as though the ATO had been fired. Many spectators thought the flight was in trouble and the airplane was indeed climbing to allow the pilots extra altitude to eject!

Robbins and Osler managed to retract the errant flaps with a back-up system and then headed toward Moses Lake AAB, climbing to 16,500ft (5,029m). The flaps were subsequently redesigned to minimize chronic failures due to high-intensity sonic vibration, leading to their honeycomb construction. During the brief flight Robbins and Osler undertook basic controllability tests, preliminary stall characteristics, and simulated landings at altitude. The trip was uneventful, and the XB-47 landed at 2:54 PM, 52 minutes after takeoff. On rollout one of the outrigger wheels started to shimmy, but otherwise there was little to indicate that this was the initial flight of a radically new aircraft. Ironically, 45 minutes later the fog rolled back in and Moses Field AAB was closed.

Lieutenant Colonel Henry E 'Pete' Warden, Chief of AMC's Bomber Section flew a B-26 as a chase plane for the first flight. One Seattle newspaper quoted him as saying the XB-47 is the 'airplane of the future… We reached a long way with the XB-47…but the post-flight conference made it evident that we achieved our goal.' Unfortunately Captain Fitzgerald, who had figured so prominently in the decision to make the first flight, did not get to witness the landing. While taxiing back at Boeing Field after his weather sortie his P-80 struck a runway light and was disabled. Despite the threat of bad weather, Boeing's public relations people could not have picked a better day for the first flight of their new airplane. It came on the 44th anniversary of the first powered flight by Orville and Wilbur Wright. It also enabled the XB-47, the last of the proposed medium bombers – the 'Forty Series' – to finally fly (the XB-45 had flown on 17th March, the XB-46 on 2nd April, the XB-48 on 14th June, and the YB-49 on 21st October).

Although Boeing had demonstrated that its swept-wing multi-engine medium bomber could fly, it still had two profoundly challenging jobs ahead. The first was to prove the airplane, to show that it performed up to specifications and that it would be a capable medium bomber if placed into production. The second, and arguably more difficult, was the larger problem of selling the airplane to the newly constituted Air Force and Strategic Air Command.

Proving the XB-47

The B-47 mockup was approved less than a month after the establishment of SAC on 21st March 1946. This Army Air Force command was responsible for all strategic bombardment, and included airplanes like the B-29 which would be replaced by the B-47 medium bomber. President Harry S Truman signed the National Security Act of 1947, authorizing the establishment of an independent US Air Force effective 18th September 1947. Three months later the XB-47 made its first flight. It would now have to prove its effectiveness in meeting SAC's long-range bombing requirement. In the early days of the Cold War, there were few illusions that this meant the ability to strike targets in the Soviet Union. On paper the XB-47 met all of the Army's original requirements except this critical issue of range. Boeing had to convince the new Air Force and SAC leadership (nearly all of whom were Army holdovers), that it could develop the XB-47 into a bomber that could reach the USSR. In December 1947 there were few 'true believers' in the suitability of the medium jet bomber to fulfill the mission which many in SAC believed could only be accomplished by the B-36.

There was no doubt that the XB-47 was impressive. It looked good, it flew well, and it was fast. None of this could alter the fact that Boeing's new bomber was terribly short on range. As one official was heard to say, 'It's a helluva plane for a war with Canada or Mexico.' The Air Force and SAC shared this concern. They had ordered a few B-45s but still had their operational hopes pinned to the B-47 to fulfill future requirements, though it might prove totally useless. LeMay, who had just left the Pentagon as the Air Staff's Deputy Chief of Research and Development, would have preferred spending the XB-47 funds on more B-36s, but he was transferred to command the US Air Forces – Europe (USAFE) before he could influence any decision in Convair's favor.

Meanwhile, Robbins and Osler continued their tests. The second flight of the XB-47 was on 20th December and lasted a little more than an hour. Again, the fire warning light came on and the flaps would not retract. Both of these problems would remain as minor irritants until late in Phase I testing. During the second flight, Robbins and Osler more fully investigated the XB-47 stall characteristics and the airplane behaved very well. The first stall warning was felt at 127KIAS, with moderate buffeting at 121KIAS. The stall came with

a slight pitch-up, then a moderate pitch down at 120KIAS with good lateral control through the entire sequence. The second flight also turned up a problem that was not solved for some time – moderate to severe airframe buffeting with the gear extended. The culprit was narrowed down to the front gear. On later tests the gear doors were removed but the vibrations continued. Finally, through a combination of baffles in the wheel well and a strengthening of the doors, the problem was eliminated.

A third flight took place before 1947 drew to a close. On 30th December Robbins and Osler again investigated stall characteristics and found that the aileron boost was too slow to correct the roll (the flaperons had already been adjusted to act more quickly). Each control was checked for its performance with the boost turned off, and Robbins satisfactorily landed the XB-47 with the elevator boost completely off to test the back-up control system. After the landing, however, post-flight inspection revealed a hole in the inlet duct screen of #4 engine. After the pieces were discovered in the compressor, the engine was removed and replaced, reinforcing the decision to remove the screens from all of the engines.

More ominously, during the 30th December flight a new problem was identified: Dutch roll. This is a phenomenon of most large high-performance aircraft, especially those with swept wings, where the pilot sees a gentle rolling and yawing motion much like the rhythmic motion of an ice skater. Boeing engineers had anticipated it but Robbins and Osler were somewhat surprised by the extent of its appearance, although they considered the mild oscillation more of a nuisance than anything serious. In later tests, however, Dutch roll proved to be a definite obstacle to full utilization of the airplane. As Robbins reported to the post-flight conference after the fifth test flight, '…In rough air in clear weather, it may be a problem; and I am quite certain that on a let down with [an Instrument Landing System] ILS instrument system or flying the airplane manually at these speeds in rough air, it would be quite objectionable.' Boeing engineer Bill Cook suggested that a yaw damper be used to control the Dutch roll problem as a better, easier, faster, and more effective solution than complex (and costly) aerodynamic changes. The damper consisted of a sensing device to detect yaw and a mechanical linkage to the rudder to correct the yaw. After searching for basic components among hardware stores in Moses Lake, Cook finally rigged the device from components taken from a B-29. It had an on-off switch in the cockpit along with a rheostat to select sensitivity. Installation was completed by 11th March, and the first trials were conducted on the 38th flight, but it turned out to be a very temperamental device. Nicknamed 'Little Herbie' by Cook, the damper almost acquired a mind of its own. Every attempt at adjustment made it either too sensitive or not sensitive enough. The problems were finally overcome, but not before one very interesting flight. On 30th June 1948 during test flight #41, Robbins turned off the rudder boost to check the trim coordination and the airplane yawed violently to the left. As Robbins later recalled: 'I glanced down at the yawmeter, and I am pretty sure I saw it hit 20 inches of H2O [pressure deflection]. I don't know whether it was going up or down at the time. I have a feeling that that is close to the peak, but the airplane sure turned fast… We slowed down to 250 then, and most of the flight back was made at speeds below 250 or 270 and did not use any appreciable yaw at all from there on in. I was afraid that we might have damaged the tail… That is as close as we have come to losing this airplane.'

Two flights took place on 3rd January 1948, with Osler making the first landing from the back seat. Recalling his days of backseat flying in North American AT-6s, Osler found forward visibility was nil but was able to make the landing by looking out to the side. A number of people had been concerned about backseat landings and

Osler's success helped to allay their fears. Osler made his first backseat takeoff the following day with no difficulty. He then did a stall series and practiced engine-out conditions. On 5th January the takeoff was made without the front gear doors to determine the cause and possible solutions to the buffeting that occurred with the gear extended. Surprisingly, this dampened the Dutch roll somewhat. In addition, these flights explored asymmetric thrust conditions, and both Robbins and Osler emphasized the necessity for using the rudder to maintain zero yaw to prevent the high rolling moment due to yaw characteristic of swept wings. They worried that pilots coming from B-29s might be 'rudder lazy.' Robbins wanted some kind of yaw indicator for the pilot and decided upon a simple but ingenious solution. He took a length of parachute chord and attached it in front of the windshield. It was installed on every subsequent B-47.

Two days later Boeing test pilot James 'Jim' Fraser was checked out in the airplane, finally flying in the copilot's seat as Osler had come down with a severe cold. Robbins took advantage of this flight to do a number of touch-and-go landings. Everyone at Boeing was impressed with the XB-47's ability to do this, and felt that the Air Force would appreciate that capability in its trainer version. The next two days were spent doing landings with a forward cg. Because of the necessity to carry all fuel in the B-47's fuselage, proper cg was of great concern during the tests and would remain so for the rest of the airplane's history. During the final landing on 8th January, the XB-47 experienced a minor mishap with the disintegration of the right rear tire.

The 13th flight on 1st February 1948 was especially noteworthy. After a 120,500 lb (54,658kg) takeoff, the emergency gear extension system was tried. The rear wheels would not retract, but finally did so when the gear was cycled using the normal system. Robbins brought the XB-47 back over the field at an altitude of 4,500ft (1,372m) and fired six of the ATO rockets. He reported no sensation except for noting a 300fpm (91mpm) increase in the climb rate. On the next pass, Robbins made a touch-and-go and fired the remaining twelve ATO, resulting in a 30-35° climb-out, which Robbins described as quite a 'kick in the pants.' The pilots also noted that the smoke stayed over the runway for a long time, portending a problem for ATO operations in combat situations. The pressurization system had not been tried as yet, but the heating/cooling system had. The pilot's report noted that in the full 'cold' position, white fog and occasional snow came from the outlets. In the 'warm' positions air distribution was uneven, causing half of the body to roast while the other half froze. SAC navigators later complained that they were freezing while the pilots were comfortable, but the pilots griped that they were baking while they thought the navigators were comfortable!

During these early tests Senator Millard E Tydings (D-Maryland) seemed to let the cat out of the Air Force's bag. Tydings, who encouraged the US to lead the world in nuclear disarmament, announced that America had a bomber that could carry a 10,000 lb (4,536kg) bomb load from Maine to Moscow in five hours, and he identified it as the XB-47. Amazingly, the Air Force denied that such an airplane existed despite its public presence in unclassified Congressional budgets, general knowledge among aerospace writers and correspondents, and the Boeing press releases from the first flight on 17th December! Meanwhile, testing continued nicely. The front gear buffet problem was corrected, and boost response was increased for better action on the ailerons and rudder.

During a test flight on 19th March, control surface flutter was checked and no problems were found, clearing the way for structural integrity tests. At 20,000ft (6,096m), an approximate weight of 98,000 lb (44,452kg) and an airspeed of 424mph (682kph), the pilot made a 2.03g turn. The next maneuver took place at the same weight,

Concerned about 'lazy rudder skills' among pilots transitioning to the B-47, Robbins added the 'yaw string' found on gliders to the XB-47. It was installed on every production Stratojet along with a white line to show the aircraft centerline. *via Robert M Robbins*

but with an airspeed of 485mph (780kph) at an altitude of 13,000ft (3,962m). The final 2.0g turn occurred at 490mph (789kph) at 12,000ft (3,658m). In each case, the XB-47 behaved as predicted by wind tunnel and engineering models. Another performance and handling flight took place on 22nd March to determine if there was any 'buzz' in the control surfaces. At 0.7 Mach the pilots noted a slight 'roughness' in the elevators similar to that observed on an earlier flight. Tests to conduct performance at 35,000ft (10,668m) were not completed as Dutch roll and unstable air resulted in inconsistent data.

The first full ATO takeoff was a spectacular sight, with the XB-47 reaching some 60° nose up, unheard of at the time. The smoke lingered on the runway, however, which would create problems for multiple operational launches in SAC. *Photo courtesy Boeing*

An impressive group of test pilots examine 46-0065 at Moses Lake on 14th July 1948 (l) to (r): Captain Jack Ridley, Captain Chuck Yeager, Major Guy Townsend, Bob Robbins, and Scott Osler. Yeager was not part of the XB-47 test program. *Photo P8333 courtesy Boeing*

Air Force officials came to see the new XB-47 on 27th March. After Robbins had taken Lieutenant General Howard A Craig for a short flight, Robbins decided to demonstrate one of the Stratojet's spectacular ATO takeoffs and, after landing, left the inboard engines running for a quick turn-around. At the end of the runway he was still going about 50mph (80kph), made a high-speed turnoff, and nearly ran over one of the ground crew. Osler jokingly accused Robbins of acting like a cowboy, but in fact Robbins had discovered a major problem with the brake design. There was insufficient hydraulic fluid flowing through the brake deboost valve into the expander tubes to push the brake pads against the hot expanded drums. In retrospect Robbins realized that if he had been required to abort his initial takeoff from Boeing Field there would not have been enough braking power to stop the XB-47.

Tests during the spring and early summer of 1948 were interrupted by a strike at Boeing. The last few tests were mainly for trim coordination and flap operation. Phase I ended on 13th April 1948 after 42 hours of flying. Overall the testing had gone quite well, and by the first week in July preparations were underway to turn the airplane over to the Air Force.

The flight which 'sold' the B-47 to the Air Force. On 25th July 1948 Townsend gave Brigadier General Kenneth Wolfe the 'ride of a lifetime' in XB-47 46-0065. From (l) to (r) are Wolfe, Boeing's Wellwood Beall, Captain Jack Ridley, George Martin, Major General Joseph McNarney, Townsend, and Boeing President Bill Allen. *Photo P8351 courtesy Boeing*

Phase II and Phase III Testing

The Air Force accepted 46-0065 on 8th July 1948, and immediately began Phase II tests. These covered much of the same ground as the Boeing Phase I tests. Major Guy M Townsend and Captain Jack L Ridley (formerly project engineer on the Bell X-1) were the pilots for this portion of the flying. On 19th July General Joseph T McNarney, Commander of Air Materiel Command, and Brigadier General Kenneth B Wolfe, AMC's Director of Procurement and Industrial Mobilization Planning, were at Boeing headquarters in Seattle for a meeting on the B-50 with Boeing President William 'Bill' Allen. At the time, a number of senior and mid-level Boeing officials and engineers were 'less than enthusiastic' about the entire B-47 program. Most were 'traditionalists' who believed that the company's economic future lay with B-50 and C-97 derivatives for the Air Force and the 377 for the airlines. Having the XB-47 flight test program at Moses Lake AFB was an effective way of keeping it 'out of sight, out of mind' and not interfering with the serious business of designing and building the next generation of Second World War era bombers. Allen, however, understood that the Air Force preferred a future powered by jet engines, and he and Pete Warden prevailed upon McNarney and Wolfe to stop at Moses Lake AFB to see the Stratojet despite their tight schedule to return to Dayton. Brigadier General Albert 'Al' Boyd, had already flown the XB-47 from the front seat as acting Chief of Flight Test at Wright Field, but getting McNarney and Wolfe to support the B-47 would be crucial to the program's viability, with the Air Force currently inclined to end its support.

As Townsend recounts the story, Wolfe (who had never flown in a jet) was telling Warden that 'he did not want to buy the [B-47] because it was a medium bomber and it was not a heavy bomber and did not have any place in the force structure… He finally ended up telling Pete, "Damn you, I'll go ride in the airplane just to get rid of you."' After takeoff Townsend let Wolfe fly the B-47. Wolfe was reportedly 'impressed with the light aileron forces, high climb speed, and rate of roll.' After buzzing the field and landing, Wolfe got out and Townsend demonstrated an ATO takeoff. Wolfe turned to Warden and said, 'You'd better come to see me in the morning,' Townsend added, 'Pete did and the next day [Wolfe] ordered the B-47A.'

Boeing historian Harold Mansfield considered this as the flight that 'sold' the B-47. Less than two months later, on 3rd September the Air Force asked Boeing to build 10 B-47As and an unspecified number of later models. This was confirmed in a 22nd November contract (W33-038 ac-22413) that called for 13 B-47As and 41 B-47Bs. A later amendment, dated 28th February 1949, finalized the number at 10 B-47As and 55 B-47Bs with deliveries beginning in September 1950 and running through March 1951. A third amendment also ordered the design and construction of a ground test rig to test the prototype ATO system. On 28th February 1949 a subsequent contract provided for both XB-47s to be re-engined with more powerful J47s, with the first flight using J47s on 8th October 1949 in XB-47 46-0065.

This 'semi-official' endorsement of the XB-47 as the 'winner' of the medium jet bomber competition merits explanation. During a 23rd March 1949 meeting LeMay and AMC commanders explained to Secretary of the Air Force W Stuart Symington that the original decision to produce the B-45, drop the B-46, and have the B-47 compete with the B-48 was made prior to the test flights of the B-47. Senior AF and SAC officials then determined that the B-47 was sufficiently more advanced than the B-45 in all respects to justify acquisition of the B-47 to replace the B-45 and to serve as SAC's new medium bomber. As with the KC-135 and the jet tanker competition in the mid-1950s, Boeing's B-47 'lost' the Forty Series competition to the B-45 but was produced in quantity as the de facto 'winner'.

Table 1-1. **B-47 Contract Information**

FY49 procurement	FY51 procurement	FY52 procurement	FY53 procurement
W33-038ac-22413 – Work Order 387	AF33(038)-21407 – Work Order 300	AF33(600)-5148 – Work Order 301	AF33(600)-22284 – Work Order 302
22nd November 1948	9th July 1950	26th November 1951	15th September 1952
10 B-47A (Units 1-10)	312 B-47B (Units 88-399)	227 B-47E (Units 617-843)	247 B-47E (Units 844-1090)
87 B-47B (Units 1-87)	217 B-47E (Units 400-616)	168 RB-47E (Units 53-220)	20 RB-47E (Units 221-240)
25 months from contract to first delivery	52 RB-47E (Units 1-52)	21 months from contract to first delivery	15 RB-47K (Units 1-15)
	18 months from contract to first delivery		35 RB-47H (Units 1-35)
			23 months from contract to first delivery

The second XB-47 (46-0066) had its first flight on 21st July 1948. Again, Robbins and Osler were at the controls. This was Robbins' last flight as project test pilot. He went on to play major engineering and management roles throughout the B-47 production program and later with the B-52 and KC-135. To make his final XB-47 flight 'something special' he made the takeoff from Boeing Field using all 18 ATO units, resulting in a spectacular end to building B-47s in Seattle. Although Boeing had originally intended to build B-47s in Seattle, this changed in 1948. Labor troubles hit the Seattle plant early that year and Bill Allen's hard line resulted in a strike. His court fight with the union was successful, and Allen considered building the B-47s in Seattle as a way to help his plant recover. He also saw the end coming for the piston-powered aircraft being produced in his Washington factories. The Air Force did not share his view about building the B-47 in Seattle, however, and the new contract specified that the majority of B-47 production would be in the government-owned facility at Wichita. However, a significant number of other B-47s were built under contract at Tulsa, OK, and Marietta, GA.

The two XB-47s participated in Phase III tests (referred to as 'Phase Ia' in some documents). This included deceleration chute tests. Because of its bicycle gear, the B-47 had a fairly high angle of attack on the ground and braking effectiveness was very low until the airplane slowed down. During earlier minimum stopping distance tests Robbins had blown all four main tires because he could not get good braking without skidding. Because the XB-47 did not meet braking specifications, Major Townsend suggested the use of a parachute to help bring the airplane to a stop. He had been involved in similar tests on the B-17 during the Second World War. The chute would help take some of the pressure off the brakes and relieve worries over runway conditions. Both 30ft and 32ft (9m and 9.8m) diameter canopies were evaluated, with the larger size chosen as standard equipment. In addition, Boeing developed their own brake anti-skid system (actually invented by Dunlop), one of the many lasting contributions that the B-47 design made to later high performance aircraft.

The Air Force officially accepted 46-0065 on 29th November 1948 and 46-0066 on 18th December. They wasted little time in touting the XB-47's abilities. During early testing the Stratojet had already shown it could easily outrun and turn more tightly than existing jet fighters. Robbins was fond of telling a story about leaving a Republic F-84 Thunderjet flown by legendary aviator Charles 'Chuck' Yeager 'in the dust'. Fraser recounted a similar story involving a P-80 chase plane. There were few believers among the 'fighter jocks' that a bomber could fly faster than a fighter, however, but the B-47 quickly verified its 'speedy' reputation. On 20th December 1948, 46-0065 flew from Moses Lake AFB to Kirtland AFB, a distance of 869nm (1,609km) at an average speed of 500mph (804kph). Air Force Secretary Symington announced this to the public and confirmed that the bomber was in the '600 mph class'. In an even more dramatic demonstration of the B-47's speed and capability, XB-47 46-0065 completed a transcontinental speed dash on 8th February 1949. At the controls were Major Russell E Schleeh, Deputy Chief of AMC's bomber branch and Major Joseph

The two XB-47s seen together in the hangar at Moses Lake AFB. 46-0066 shows the extended slats to good advantage. These were bolted shut and later omitted on production aircraft. *Photo P8767 courtesy Boeing*

Majors Russell Schleeh and Joseph Howell set a record for a flight between Moses Lake AFB and Andrews AFB. Just before landing the #3 engine intake nose cone fell off. Note the 'sporty' white wall tires. *Courtesy Boeing*

W Howell, neither of whom had much time in the airplane. They left Moses Lake AFB at 10:22 AM Eastern Standard Time (EST), and arrived at Andrews AFB, MD, 3 hours and 46 minutes later at 2:08 PM EST, cruising at altitudes between 32,000-37,000ft (9,754-11,278m). This resulted in an average speed of 607mph (977kph), a new coast-to-coast speed record. The event also caused the crew some embarrassment. As the airplane approached the runway at Andrews AFB, the intake nose cone on the #3 engine fell off followed by a landing short of the runway (on the overrun) but with no real damage (see Appendix IV). Although the Air Force maintained that no special attempt was made to set a record, the flight took place while Congress was in session. There was still no guarantee that they would buy the B-47 in the quantities desired by Boeing and the AMC. A good impression on the gentlemen of Capitol Hill and those in the Pentagon would certainly not hurt the new bomber's chances when the time came to appropriate defense funds.

The airplane stayed at Andrews AFB to participate in the 'Progress of Air Power' airshow. Firing its full complement of ATO bottles, the XB-47's noise and smoke won many admirers. President Truman inspected the new bomber, and when asked if he wanted a ride in a new two-seat P-80 he replied that he preferred the faster XB-47. Perhaps this dazzling display helped, for soon after the Andrews AFB show the president released funds that had been earmarked for other projects (notably the Boeing B-54 – based on the YB-50C – which

was canceled on 6th April 1949) so that they could be applied to the procurement of 45 additional B-47Bs. By the end of the year, 32 extra B-47Bs had been added to the total on contract.

By February 1950, however, the price tag for the XB-47 had risen by over $1.5 million due to changes resulting from the flight test program, with the final cost of $11,944,043.09. This increase was due to many things, including (1) changing the test site from Seattle to Moses Lake; (2) wind tunnel tests for a 1/20th scale flutter model and a full-size empennage; (3) installation of 18 x rocket assisted takeoff (RATO) units; (4) use of J35-GE-7 instead of J35-GE-9 engines and the addition of an oil heating system; (5) bomb racks in the second airplane; (6) flight testing the number one airplane beyond Phase I and Boeing maintenance during Phase II testing; (7) installation of an inhabited tail gunner's enclosure and Emerson Model 161 turret in the number two airplane plus a mock-up (neither of which was adopted); and (8) addition of deceleration chutes.

The End of the Beginning

Over the next two years the XB-47s served as testbeds for the B-47A and B-47B production aircraft, participating in weapons tests and other suitability projects (see Chapter 7). Tragedy struck, however, on 11th May 1949 during an autopilot test in 46-0065 over Moses Lake AFB. Osler was in the front seat, Fraser in the copilot's seat, the new Chief of Flight Test John Fornasero was in the observer's seat, and the autopilot company representative was on board as well. While flying at about 10,000ft (3,048m) and making a gentle climbing turn at 350mph (563kph), the airplane experienced an explosive decompression. As Fraser recalls, 'the chain of interlinked retaining clamps that held the canopy secure in flight had become unlatched and the canopy had blown up, over, and back to the two foot open position used for ventilation when on the ground.' The canopy hit Osler on the head, killing him instantly. As Fornasero and the autopilot representative tried to remove Osler's body from the front seat, Fraser was now fighting the autopilot as it continued the climbing turn set by Osler. The only autopilot controls were in the front seat and the XB-47 was now at risk of continuing to bank and climb, eventually rolling over. Loss of the airplane would almost certainly mean an end to the B-47 program. Fornasero had climbed into the pilot's seat after moving Osler. After seeing Fraser waving his arms wildly Fornasero understood and quickly cut off the autopilot, allowing Fraser to regain control of the airplane. Some accounts report that Fornasero made the

President Harry S Truman (with binoculars) toured the XB-47 during its stay at the Progress of Airpower show. Soon thereafter he released funds for the procurement of additional B-47Bs. *Author's collection*

landing, but this is almost certainly incorrect. This was Fornasero's first flight in the B-47, and as Fraser recounts in his memoirs, he quickly moved to the front seat for the landing. In an effort to stop as soon as possible to get Osler to medical treatment Fraser blew all four main tires. Unfortunately, it was too late.

Osler's death cast a serious chill over the entire flight test program. Former Bell test pilot A M 'Tex' Johnston had been hired to become Fraser's copilot after he was projected to move to the front seat. Fraser, however, never flew again. Osler's absence was always remembered. During a 2002 B-47 Stratojet Association symposium panel of B-47 designers and flight crew, Fraser put an empty chair between himself and Bob Robbins in honor of Edward Scott Osler.

The two XB-47s ended their days rather ingloriously. 46-0065 logged a total of 410 hours before it was flown to Wright-Patterson AFB, OH, on 31st December 1953. In early 1954 it was cut up by the USAF Orientation Group, the fuselage mounted on a trailer, and the first Stratojet became a traveling recruiter for the Air Force at county fairs and other gatherings around the country. Today nothing remains of the airplane. XB-47 46-0066, which logged 338 hours, flew to Chanute AFB, IL, on 14th December 1954, and ended its career as a training airframe for new mechanics of the 4455th Training Squadron (TS). For many years it was on display at the Octave Chanute Aerospace Museum at Rantoul, IL, modified to represent B-47E '2278', the damaged airplane which First Lieutenant James Obenauf successfully landed from the back seat after his aircraft commander ejected but the navigator was unconscious. In September 2016, 46-0066 was disassembled and trucked to the Air Force Flight Test Museum at Edwards AFB for restoration to appear as 46-0065 did when it made its first flight.

However impressive the XB-47 was as an innovative swept-wing jet-powered medium bomber, it had yet to prove that it could actually accomplish its mission, and there were still many doubters among senior Air Force and SAC commanders. Moreover, no company had previously built an airplane as complex as the XB-47. Despite Boeing's track record in mass producing B-17s and B-29s, the B-47 would nearly fail because Boeing could not adapt its production methods to deliver combat-ready B-47s in the quantity and limited time demanded by SAC. As one official history noted, 'the production-development effort which followed, particularly after the outbreak of the Korean War [which began on 25th June 1950, the same day that the initial B-47A 49-1900 flew for the first time], was more an experimental engineering program than a development

During a routine flight in 46-0065 on 11th May 1949, an explosive decompression caused the canopy to open, killing Scott Osler (l). Copilot Jim Fraser (r), with the help of test engineer John Fornasero, moved to the front seat for the landing. Fraser never flew again. *Photo P8864 courtesy Boeing*

engineering program.' 'The XB-47 aircraft,' the history continued, 'had been constructed with little thought for production problems.' This was echoed by W H Rowley, Boeing Chief of Flight Test and later the B-47 Project Engineer on engine development, 'We were far ahead of everyone else [in aircraft design], but the problems we encountered with the B-47 were due to our own inabilities to understand and handle such new and magnificent designs.'

The Air Force was not without fault, as it constantly changed the requirements and specifications for the B-47, forcing Boeing to build airplanes that required extensive retrofit of new equipment. The impact of the Korean War cannot be minimized. On 14th April 1950, two months before the war erupted, the top secret National Security Council (NSC) policy paper NSC-68 called for a massive increase in spending on conventional weapons. Once the war broke out US manufacturing again began to shift toward weapon production. Boeing was suddenly asked to build B-47s without the requisite components from its suppliers amid competition for the mass production of other airplanes, tanks, and armaments in response to the North Korean invasion of South Korea.

For all of its strengths, the B-47 remained permanently hampered by its insufficient range, even with the addition of air refueling. For all its weaknesses, the B-47 served as the 'trial by fire' for modern jet production that would enable airplanes like the B-52 and Boeing KC-135 to be built and delivered ready for duty, and pioneered the operational and combat procedures which SAC would use for decades to come. That success, however, would be a long time in coming.

Both wings of XB-47 46-0065 were removed and the fuselage cut in half. The front portion was mounted onto a trailer as a mobile recruiter, and was eventually scrapped. *USAF*

CHAPTER TWO

Not Ready for Prime Time

Following the successful flight tests of the XB-47, on 10th September 1948 the Air Force authorized up to $35,000,000 for Boeing to build 10 B-47As at its Wichita, KS, plant. By 22nd November this initial agreement expanded via contract W33-038-ac-22413 to include the 10 original B-47As plus three additional B-47As and 41 B-47Bs, although maximum payment for the B-47As decreased to $28,500,000. Air Materiel Command (AMC) recommended against buying any B-47As, however, arguing they were little more than 'shells' and at best would be non-combat ready test vehicles. Instead, AMC urged that production begin with B-47Bs. The Air Force wisely chose to reject AMC's proposal and directed Boeing to proceed with building the B-47A. Never intended to be combat aircraft, the B-47As became the core of a small but invaluable fleet responsible for developing and testing the many various subsystems including the bombing-navigation system (BNS), assisted takeoff (ATO), the fire control system, as well as 'special weapons' (meaning atomic and nuclear weapons) programs.

The first B-47A (49-1900) rolled out from the Boeing factory at Wichita on 1st March 1950 and took to the air nearly four months later on 25th June. Only 10 B-47As were built (the latter three were canceled), and all 10 were initially assigned to AMC and Air Proving Ground Command (APGC) with the first (49-1904) handed over on 13th December 1950. Ordinarily these would have been YB-47As, but for some unknown reason AMC chose not to use this designation.

Despite the difference in age between this Parker Pusher/Curtiss D and the first B-47E, production methods were unable to adjust to the new complexities of the B-47, leading to a fleet of jet bombers incapable of fulfilling their mission. This B-47E inexplicably has the long bomb bay doors. *Photo courtesy Boeing*

Other agencies including SAC, Air Training Command (ATC), Air Research and Development Command (ARDC), the Atomic Energy Commission (AEC), and the Air Force Special Weapons Center (AFSWC) also sought to use the B-47As to assess their own unique requirements, leading to a handful of organizations conducting tests without any sense of integration. The standard Air Force evaluation program, traditionally undertaken by the manufacturer, APGC, and the Wright Air Development Center (WADC), no longer applied. Multiple agencies, often with conflicting priorities, each wanted to be the 'prime mover' in the B-47 program with SAC's claim as the loudest. Not surprisingly, this led to widespread confusion, delays, and cost increases in the ongoing development and production. Most significantly, Boeing was simply not prepared to produce in bulk an airplane as complex as the B-47, especially with constantly changing directives from multiple agencies. Boeing failed to deliver an

Table 2-1. **Standard Air Force Phase Testing Program circa 1950**

Phase I	Contractor compliance to determine if the aircraft would fly. This lasted about 20 hours and the aircraft was usually held to about 80% of its design limits.
Phase II	Initial performance similar to Phase I but with USAF pilots.
Phase III	Contractor development to fix major problems.
Phase IV	Performance and stability tests over the entire envelope. Data for the aircraft handbook was obtained during approximately 200 flight hours.
Phase V	All-weather testing done by WADC at Eglin AFB, FL, and Ladd Field/Eielson AFB, AK.
Phase VI	Functional development.
Phase VII	Operational suitability.
Phase VIII	Unit operational employment testing by the using command under the supervision of APGC.

Top: Rollout of B-47A 49-1900 on 1st March 1950 was only slightly better attended than that of the XB-47 in September 1947. All 10 B-47As were used for test and evaluation programs associated with improving the B-47 fleet. *Photo BW4407 courtesy Boeing*

Center: 49-1904 was the first B-47A handed over to the USAF for testing on 13th December 1950. Some four years later it was retired to Amarillo AFB as a ground trainer. This view clearly shows the 'long' bomb bay extending from the front gear to the aft gear. *Author's collection*

Bottom: The Air Force's insistence on building the B-47 at Wichita assumed there would be sufficient existing hangar space but this proved illusory, necessitating additional construction to meet the planned production. 51-2056 in the lower left later became a YRB-47B and then a TB-47B. *Photo BW60411 courtesy Boeing*

operational – let alone combat ready – B-47, and the Air Force was unable to decide what such a B-47 would look like. In short, the early B-47 effort was a program imbued with considerable speed but very little direction.

Battle of Kansas

Something as simple as *where* the B-47 would be built and tested had a profound effect on the program. According to the SAC history of the B-47 development, the assignment of interceptors to Moses Lake AFB 'necessitated movement of the [Boeing] test facilities to Wichita in late 1949. This was in line with the decision to move production of the bomber to the same place.' Brigadier General Wolfe's directive that the B-47 assembly line move inland to Wichita was highly contentious, and not merely because of the sudden presence of fighters at Moses Lake AFB. Wolfe argued that Boeing's new jet

bomber facility had to relocate from Seattle to protect it from Soviet espionage or attack by Soviet bombers or submarines. Boeing President Bill Allen wanted the B-47 production to stay in Seattle, however, to ameliorate the after effects of a nasty labor strike and very few Boeing employees wanted to leave Seattle and relocate to what they called 'Siberia'. The Air Force not only insisted that Wichita would be the manufacturing site but that the first B-47A should be delivered in January 1950, barely 16 months after the production order had been issued. Although B-29 manufacturing at Wichita had ceased shortly after the end of the war and the plant put up for sale, Brigadier General Wolfe reopened it in March of 1948 for the purpose of modifying B-29s with air refueling equipment and B-50s for reconnaissance work. The Air Force argued that Wichita had the advantage of an existing labor pool (as did Seattle), multiple factory buildings from its days as a B-29 production plant, and longer

runways [the runway at Wichita required lengthening to 10,000ft (3,048m) prior to the arrival of the XB-47 in October 1949].

Despite these appearances, the reality of the Wichita move was far more problematic. A TOP SECRET 1954 Air Force report noted that the 'Boeing factory at Wichita…was not designed for the type of airplane that is now being built there.' The B-47 required far more assembly stations than the B-29, and the existing physical plant layout at Wichita could not accommodate this increase. This meant that 'a large number of installations had to be made or completed outside of the factory,' a real problem given Wichita's hot, rainy summers and cold, snowy winters. Wichita quickly earned the label of a 'fair weather' operation. The parking aprons were filled to capacity with incomplete airframes pending the construction of shelters, resulting in 'lost time, lost man-hours, and increased costs.' Boeing historian Harold Mansfield called this period of B-47 production the 'second Battle of Kansas' (the first had been the start of the B-29 program there). This battle extended well beyond disagreements with the Air Force, and included major problems with tooling, materials, and labor.

The two XB-47s had been largely hand built, and now Boeing was expected to produce hundreds of B-47As and B-47Bs en masse. New tooling had to be designed and moved into Wichita. Manufacturing tolerances were tighter than any industry – aerospace or otherwise –

had previously attempted. Boeing made close to 60,000 tools and jigs, including a wing jig with a concrete foundation that extended 15ft (4.6m) below the factory floor. Specialized maintenance tools and ground handling equipment had to be designed and built for the technicians in the field. The B-29 required 140 of these special items but Boeing was able to keep the number at 87 for the Stratojet.

Unlike the B-29 days, Boeing had no priority claim on raw materials or equipment. The B-47 needed large quantities of the new 75S-T aluminum alloy, but it had to be purchased in competition with other industrial users, both military and civilian. This was no small problem, as aviation writer Bill Gunston recorded in his 1973 book *Bombers of the West*, given that the B-47 required '64,000 lb of light alloy, including 415 forgings; 20,000 lb of steel, mostly forgings; 2,000 lb of copper, brass, and bronze; and 1,000 lb of magnesium.' In September of 1950 defective extrusions were found in some aluminum fabrications. The necessity for complete inspections compounded the delay in an already lagging production schedule. Then, in February of 1951, deficiencies in the Emergency Landing Gear Extension (ELGE) system surfaced after several instances of control cable failures. It was not until October 1951 that a fix was accomplished.

Each B-47 was made of some 70,000 parts, with over half of these contracted to 432 other companies in 34 states outside of Kansas. In addition there was Government Furnished Equipment (GFE) which

The lack of indoor hangar space at Wichita led to creative solutions for weather protection for crews working on the nose section and engine pods. Interestingly, the three B-47Bs in the background lack serial numbers. *Photo 45583-B USAF*

Manufacturing the B-47's wings required tools and jigs that had not been previously considered, let alone developed. One can easily imagine the cacophony of sound on the production line. *Photo BW-75706 courtesy Boeing*

The Air Force was equally to blame for the many delays in getting the B-47A off the assembly floor and into the air, with many changes demanded and little consideration for the production-line consequences. The first two B-47As are seen here in front of the two XB-47s. *Photo P10410 Courtesy Boeing*

the Air Force contracted for separately and supplied directly to Boeing, including tail turrets, bombing-navigation systems, and autopilots. Boeing faced a daunting management task, something which it had generally resolved at its Seattle plant but which was unproven at Wichita. With so many parts and suppliers in the pipeline the potential for trouble was overwhelming, and the supply problem became worse before it improved. Seat belts, inertia reels, structurally unsound copilot and navigator seats (the Republic seats would eventually be replaced by Weber and Stanley units), and the K-2 BNS were just some of the problem areas. An ARDC report revealed 'A seemingly unbroken cycle of deficiencies – fixes – retrofits – deficiencies – fixes – retrofits – deficiencies – fixes – retrofits etc characterized the B-47 program…Countless directives and projected modifications led to a complicated planning schedule.'

A 'TOP SECRET' Report

These shortcomings in B-47 production, deliveries, and initial operations attracted LeMay's unwanted wrath following a presentation on 4th October 1950. Boeing responded by noting that when the B-47 program was approved in September 1948 the Air Force had requested that Boeing build 'a group of airplanes essentially similar to the XB-47.' These were 'primarily to set up the manufacturing facilities for and turn out a limited number of B-47A airplanes at the earliest possible date,' and none of these would be equipped with the A-2 tail turret or the K-2 bombing system. During a Summer 1949 review, however, the Air Force changed its mind and directed that the B-47As should include 'additional tactical items to bring them up to limited tactical status,' including solid ATO, the K-2 systems, and the A-2 turret. By March 1950 the list of additions had grown substantially to 'several hundred', affecting the B-47As on the assembly line and those already delivered. Boeing flight tests of the first two B-47As revealed 'certain troubles and deficiencies,' all of which necessitated time-consuming changes. Boeing placed the blame for the delay delivery of the B-47 squarely on the Air Force: 'Fundamentally, the principal reason for the slippage in the delivery of the B-47As is because the concept of both the 'A' airplane configuration and the overall program have changed since September 1948' when the program began.

The Air Force responded in typical bureaucratic fashion by appointing Major General Samuel R Brentnall as Special Assistant to the Chief of Staff to monitor the B-47 program (Brigadier General

Oscar F Carlson replaced Brentnall in April 1951). Brentnall operated in an advisory capacity only, and could not suggest or require changes in the program. Indeed, the Air Staff largely ignored reports on problems with B-47 production. At a 1st October 1951 Pentagon meeting on the B-47, for example, in spite of overwhelming evidence to the contrary the Air Staff decreed that the B-47 program was 'adequate' and its 'directives were sufficient and clear.' LeMay remained dissatisfied with the lack of progress on the B-47 and asked Air Force Chief of Staff General Hoyt S Vandenberg to intercede. Vandenberg ordered the Air Force Deputy Inspector General (IG) at Norton AFB, CA, to conduct a special survey to 'evaluate the entire [B-47] program to determine deficiencies, develop possible solutions, and recommend the most suitable corrective measures.' Between 9th September and 6th October 1951 Brigadier General Thomas O Hardin and his staff visited, interviewed, or observed senior officials at Boeing-Wichita, each of the Air Force major commands (MAJCOMs) involved – SAC, ATC, AMC, and WADC, and operational venues such as Wichita AFB and Pinecastle AFB. The IG team was especially interested in 'program planning and production, operational capability of the current production B-47, provisions for training of air and ground crews, and provisions for operational support.'

Not surprisingly, results of the TOP SECRET report were a scathing critique of existing B-47 production and early operations. The IG concluded that 'the B-47 is still in the experimental stage, suitable for only limited "fair weather" flying only, by the most highly skilled and experienced pilots.' All completed B-47s and those currently on the assembly line would require 'extensive modification…to make them acceptable to the using agencies for both Training and Tactical purposes.' Existing and proposed modifications that were needed to 'correct basic engineering, tooling, and manufacturing deficiencies' of the B-47 were inadequate, and were 'directed at the effects rather than the causes of the difficulty.' Plans to continue accelerated production of B-47 production in the current configuration were 'ill advised' and 'not justified in light of increased cost and the inevitable lowering of quality.' Hardin warned that the B-47 program was 'of such magnitude and importance as to require that it be made a matter of primary concern of all Directorates and agencies involved.' Program schedules established jointly by Boeing and the Air Force in November 1948 for production, training, support, and operational use were 'overoptimistic and unrealistic,' with the expectation that Boeing would deliver 108 B-47s to SAC by 1951. It also found that producing

the B-47 and its components as a 'fully operational airplane concurrent with the development and service testing, the training of maintenance and operational personnel, the development and production of support equipment, the acquisition and development of necessary training and operational bases, all on an accelerated plan,' was beyond the capabilities of Air Force organizational competency. The B-47 was too radical a design and configuration to fall within existing airplane procurement processes, many of which were used during the Second World War. In short, the B-47 was nowhere near where it needed to be in terms of development and operational readiness as stipulated in the B-47 contracts, and this inadequacy directly and adversely affected US national security.

During his visit to Offutt AFB, SAC planners told Hardin that based on the existing contract with Boeing they expected to receive B-47s

'in quantity, commencing about September 1950,' sufficient to start preparations to have two full B-47 wings (the 301st BW and the 43rd BW) operationally ready by the end of 1951, although the final list of units to be converted changed to the 306th BW, 307th BW, 301st BW, 99th BW, and 2nd BW, in that order. By July 1951, however, only 17 B-47s were available to SAC and ATC to start the initial cadre of flight training (other commands had 11 B-47Bs, eight B-47As, and one YRB-47B). As of 30th September 1951 'only 26 marginally flyable airplanes – 10 Model A and 16 Model B production airplanes' – had been delivered. Of these, just eight were available for training, hardly an auspicious start for SAC's new signature bomber.

There were multiple reasons for this production shortfall, and plenty of blame for everyone involved. Production at the Boeing Wichita plant was comingled with a 'program of concurrent experimentation and service testing,' and suffered from the outset due to 'inadequate facilities, poor management, untrained personnel, inadequate quality control, insufficient and defective tooling, Government Furnished Property (GFP) and Contractor Furnished Equipment (CFE) shortages, and lack of priorities.' Buildings were incomplete and many of those that were finished were inadequate or insufficient. A substantial amount of complex and delicate work had to be undertaken outdoors in extreme heat and cold, wind, rain, and snow. Air Force planners 'took for granted' the operational

Above: Early B-47Bs were hampered by the lack of sufficient parts, with only 16 barely flyable in September 1951, hardly enough to meet SAC's expectation of two fully operational wings by the end of 1951. This image shows the rollout of 49-2642 – the first B-47B – on 9th January 1951. *Photo courtesy Boeing*

Left: By the end of 1951 SAC leaders feared that some '250-500' B-47s would be built 'devoid of the equipment which makes a plane a bomber,' as this view of the ramp at Wichita shows. The Air Force pointed an accusing finger at Boeing for engineering, production, and inspection 'deficiencies.' Boeing responded with justifiable complaints of its own. *Photo BW55335 courtesy Boeing*

Opposite, left: Boeing struggled with employee morale issues as AMC imposed a 6½-day work week to catch up with production plans. This did little more than alienate employees as they built B-47s that were incomplete and often unflyable. *Photo BW91074 courtesy Boeing*

Opposite, far left: The Air Force could not decide if the corrections and revisions should be incorporated on the production line or after rollout. This indecision exacerbated the already problematic delivery schedule. *Photo P11116 courtesy Boeing*

effectiveness and capabilities of the 'new and complex equipment' needed to build and to be installed in the B-47. According to Holdin, however, 'most of the engineering was still in the design or highly experimental stages.' There were no plans for temporary alternative components, leading to a 'complete breakdown' in coordinating the various installation processes. The entire B-47 production program 'was totally out of phase.'

In an effort to produce the requisite number of airplanes, AMC directed that the Wichita factory institute a 6½-day workweek. Boeing objected strenuously, warning that shortage of subassemblies would cause costly out-of-sequence problems, would require overtime on airplanes which could then not be delivered due to missing components, and would have an adverse effect on the morale of Boeing workers. AMC dismissed these concerns, arguing that the need to build airplanes in large numbers outweighed these temporary inexpediencies. Moreover, AMC did not insist that Air Force B-47 engineering groups at WADC, ARDC, and its own staff within AMC also work the same extended hours. Consequently, engineering and production efforts were further out of phase, widening the gap between the production airplane and the operational airplane. As incomplete B-47s left the assembly line they were parked outdoors on the adjacent ramp awaiting completion to an undetermined configuration at some unspecified future date. This led to significant problems in quality, workmanship, continuity of production, interchangeability of parts, as well as increased costs and significant delays – some B-47s sat on the ramp for '6 months or more awaiting completion.' B-47B 50-0002, for example, rolled off the assembly line on 26th January 1951 but did not make its first flight until 27th February 1952 – a delay of 13 months. Similarly, B-47B 50-0018 rolled out on 11th May 1951 and made its first flight five months later on 3rd October 1951. By September 1951 'more than 60' B-47s were parked unfinished and unflyable at Wichita as a result of 'production deficiencies, engineering deficiencies, and inspection deficiencies.' Of these, only engineering deficiencies could not have been 'foreseen and prevented.' SAC planners were deeply concerned that '250 to 500 B-47s [would] become available to the Air Force devoid of the equipment which makes a plane a bomber.'

The IG report faulted Boeing for 'inefficient management and supervision throughout the Boeing Wichita organization,' but also condemned AMC's despised 6½-day workweek, recommending that returning to a traditional 40-hour week 'would allow the contractor to perfect his organization and would result in a marked savings to the Government with little loss in actual production of B-47s.' Another significant management issue was the physical division of

engineering work between Boeing's Seattle facility and the Wichita factory. Engineers wasted considerable time traveling between the two sites to resolve issues, and 'few, if any, final decisions could or were being made at Wichita.' The IG recommended consolidating all B-47 engineering personnel at Wichita, but many Boeing personnel balked at being transferred from the idyllic Pacific Northwest to the Plains of Kansas.

The Air Force choice to procure B-47s using concurrent development and production of an operational aircraft was intended to provide a 'force in being' at the same time as the airplane was being tested and refined. Despite this acquisition jargon, there was no 'force in being.' B-47s that had been delivered (as well as those with impending hand-over dates) were 'unable to operate safely in extremes of temperature, at night, or in even marginal weather conditions. They had no operational capability as they lacked defensive armament, had an incomplete and unreliable bombing system, had no effective means of navigation, and could not be abandoned in case of emergency.' At best, the existing and projected fleet of B-47s could be used 'only for limited pilot transition [conversion] training.'

The airplanes lacked the performance guaranteed by Boeing, falling 'considerably short' of what SAC required and expected. The report noted that 92 major deficiencies had been identified, 'many of which have yet to be resolved and which prevent the B-47 from achieving the "force in being" required by SAC. These included communications, bombing and navigation systems, the fire control system, the landing gear, ejection seats, fuel cell difficulties, the autopilot, and engines.' Some unresolved problems were critical 'safety of flight' items, such as wing anti-icing, windshield wipers, the flight gyro, the instrument landing system, and engine anti-ice. Of these, 52 could not be incorporated into current production aircraft, largely because of the Air Force's continued insistence on the unrealistic and counterproductive accelerated production program. The Air Force was knowingly requiring Boeing to build unusable airplanes simply to meet unrealistic production schedules. Boeing and Air Force engineers had identified corrective solutions to many of the deficiencies, but the Air Force program office refused to decide between incorporating them on the production line or through modification at a refinement center after completion of the basic airplane.

This was not merely an exercise in project management gone wrong. For example, fixing 36 of the required changes would entail between 15,000 and 20,000 man-hours *per airplane*. An additional 14 improvements would require and additional 18,000 to 20,000 man-hours *per airplane*. Installation of ejection seats alone needed an

additional 30,000 man-hours, at a cost of $500,000, again, *per airplane*. A further 5,000 man-hours would be required to install the tail turret and fire control system but only *after* a suitable system had been selected and developed. Each B-47 nominally required 33,000 to 36,000 man-hours per airplane to build. The extra changes necessary to bring each completed B-47 up to minimal operational standards required 68,000 to 75,000 additional man-hours, nearly double the time it took to build it from scratch. When asked to determine the cause of these out-of-sequence changes resulting in massive man-hour overruns, Boeing told the Air Force such a study 'would take two weeks and cost $3,000', and refused to proceed without payment of this fee. The Air Force scoffed at this comparatively 'insignificant' demand, telling Boeing to absorb the study's cost due to its complicity in the problem. Boeing countered by saying that the $3,000 exercise was 'unnecessary because the situation was correcting itself,' citing improved data for recently produced airplanes. These rosy figures failed to account for unimplemented changes which were not discovered until *after* Boeing had presented the airplane to the Air Force for inspection for acceptance. Rather than an attempt to deceive the Air Force, these last-minute discoveries were the result of 'serious deficiencies in the Boeing quality control organization.' Inspectors were 'poorly trained' and procedures 'were frequently not followed.' In one example, a wire was found to be improperly routed during final assembly. No corrective action was taken for more than 60 days,

during which time the wire was still being improperly installed on every B-47 still on the assembly line.

Boeing was equally concerned that any slow-down or temporary stoppage of the production schedule to accommodate changes while the airplanes were still on the assembly line might lead to the dismissal of skilled personnel needed to build portions of the airplane assembled in phases after the improvements were added. Corporate officials warned the Air Force that it could not pay workers to do nothing while waiting for upgraded airplanes, and the IG report noted that there was already 'much idleness' on the shop floors. Boeing was able to retain some of the highly experienced supervisory personnel and workers who had contributed to the success of its B-29 production at Wichita, but demand for personnel with 'ability and know how' exceeded the supply, and many skilled employees had left Boeing-Wichita for greener and more lucrative pastures in Southern California's burgeoning aircraft industry. This left a large number of 'new and inexperienced' personnel to build the B-47 with its extraordinarily steep learning curve. Boeing aggressively sought to fill these gaps in skilled labor. One headline in its in-house newspaper *Plane Talk* read 'Urge Employees to Aid in B-47 Hiring Program' to find '40 special project mechanics for general pre-flight mechanical work.'

Surprisingly, Air Force planners were sensitive to the labor issue and recommended that Boeing continue to build incomplete

airframes at its Wichita plant (keeping its workers busy), while upgrade and modification to these B-47s would be accomplished elsewhere. The Grand Central Aircraft Company (GCAC) at Tucson, AZ, would finish each B-47 as a subcontract to Boeing. Under the GRAND CANYON program (see Chapter 3), an Air Force crew would fly the airplane from Wichita to Tucson where GCAC would implement 55 of the required changes over an additional three to four months per airplane. This would still not result in a fully operational B-47, but instead an airplane which AMC disingenuously called 'the best potential tactical configuration,' requiring still more modifications. Ultimately each airplane would need at least three upgrades, with a minimum total 'in process' time of eight months, a figure which the IG report regarded with a healthy dose of skepticism, warning that 'a time lag of eight months *or more* must be added to the factory acceptance schedules to arrive at the earliest probable delivery' of tactically operational airplanes [emphasis in original].

The IG report was also highly critical of the Air Force for permitting Boeing 'to rely upon modification as a panacea' for the many shortcomings in the B-47's production and operation. Modification was being used as a 'substitute for timely and complete engineering, efficient management, and as a ready remedy for defective tooling.' Boeing was building and delivering master tooling, jigs, and fixtures to Douglas-Tulsa and Lockheed-Marietta to build B-47s which were 'known to be unsatisfactory', resulting in production deficiencies that were 'being perpetuated and magnified' rather than corrected. Boeing was simply drowning trying to keep up with the B-47 program – the company was ill prepared to adapt the essentially handcrafted B-47 to large-scale production. The Air Force was partly to blame, however, through its indecisiveness in articulating specific quantities and production rates. This meant that Boeing could not adapt production tooling fast enough to meet the rapid changes required in the still-evolving B-47. Even something as esoteric as the production Block Numbers contributed to poor quality production. The first B-47Bs were built in a block of four, followed by two blocks of 12 aircraft, typical of new aircraft production to allow for major changes to be incorporated at the earliest possible opportunity. By the time the seventh and subsequent blocks were in production this number had risen to 54 aircraft, a figure far too large to be upgraded. To resolve this the IG recommended discontinuing work on completed but substandard B-47s at Wichita, Tulsa, and Marietta, and instead recommended finishing those airplanes currently on the assembly line. Once the backlog of deficient airplanes cleared, Boeing would then make the necessary engineering and tooling changes to the three assembly lines with the intent that, once restarted, each would at last produce B-47s in the operational configuration. By that time some 150 B-47As and B-47Bs would be available for 'necessary testing and crew training.'

Top left: Boeing's greatest asset in building B-47s was its skilled work force at Wichita. Production delays meant that many opted for the warmer climate and better wages paid by aerospace firms in Southern California, adding to Boeing's B-47 woes. *Photo P10825 courtesy Boeing*

Top right: Suppliers of subassemblies, such as Hudson Motor Car which made B-47 noses, were equally culpable in production problems due to late deliveries and substandard quality. This image shows the slipway door open on the left two and partially assembled optical periscope nose fairings. *Photo RD 3499 courtesy Lockheed Martin*

Bottom: Ford Motors was contracted to build B-47 wings, but failed to meet contract deadlines. Boeing-Wichita took over but this added to existing delays. Congress eventually investigated Ford's performance. *Photo BW45689 Courtesy Boeing*

Boeing Responds

Criticism of the early B-47 program pointed a damning finger at Boeing for administrative incompetence, inadequate program oversight and management, and insufficient resources devoted to a new and incredibly complex production line. The company certainly merits criticism for its many management and quality control missteps. In fact, however, Boeing was not alone in failing to meet the expectations of B-47 production and performance. The Air Force continually changed existing or added new requirements and specifications, many of which required substantial lead time to incorporate. Suppliers failed to appreciate the heavy demand for components that were yet to be proven.

Even before the IG's 1951 report, Boeing was aware of SAC's dissatisfaction with B-47 production. Writing to then-Lieutenant General LeMay, Boeing Vice President for Engineering and Sales Wellwood E Beall complained on 18th October 1950 about the constraints placed on Boeing in meeting demand for the B-47As. 'Dear Curt,' he began, 'It has come to my attention' that SAC was not happy with the 'tardy delivery of B-47A airplanes intended for use by Project WIBAC' (described below). Beall reviewed the B-47 program from 1948 onward. He noted that aside from changing Air Force requirements, 'defective aluminum extrusions were discovered', necessitating time-consuming inspections not only of the parts but of the airplanes which were already completed. He criticized the K-2 bombing system as 'still in a period of engineering development' rather than ready for installation in test – let alone operational – aircraft.

The B-47 had some 70,000 parts, most of which were not made by Boeing, and subcontractors struggled to adapt their own acquisition and production schedules to meet Boeing's requirements. Subcontractors with whom Boeing had worked previously now required 14 months to produce key components whereas they had previously only needed 10, leaving incomplete B-47s on the assembly line (or on the ramp) for four months. In other cases, subcontractors could not deliver parts that met the new stringent quality controls required. For example, the Hudson Motor Car Company built B-47 nose sections, mainly for Douglas-Tulsa. From the outset deliveries were late and the parts suffered from multiple deficiencies. Despite assistance – and threats – from the Air Force and Boeing, Hudson was unable to perform as guaranteed. Finally, in August 1953 their contract was terminated and Chance-Vought (which had been building nose sections for Boeing) took over their work. In another case, the A O Smith Corporation delivered faulty landing gear struts to Lockheed-Marietta and Douglas-Tulsa. The contract was finally terminated and given to Cleveland Pneumatic and Bendix Corporation. Finally, a 21st October 1953 telegram from Boeing-Wichita to Boeing-Seattle blasted the Ford Motor Company's Kansas City plant for being unable to deliver wing sets. Wichita managers pleaded with Seattle: 'We feel it very necessary for Boeing-Wichita to start immediately to build wings for Boeing use because without help our estimate is' that even after implementing production improvements, Ford could deliver only 12 sets by 31st January 1954, 14 fewer than required. This eventually led to a major congressional investigation and the Ford contract ended.

Boeing had to compete for raw materials with other manufacturers during the Korean War, and many of the competing demands were commercial with no connection to defense (especially aluminum). Large industrial presses needed to make key structural components simply did not exist. Normal procurement time for critical aluminum alloy landing gear forgings ranged from 32-40 weeks – nearly a year – inducing delays in installing the gear and associated components. Magnesium sheets needed 64 weeks of lead time given the 'national condition of supply and demand, not to be influenced in the least by

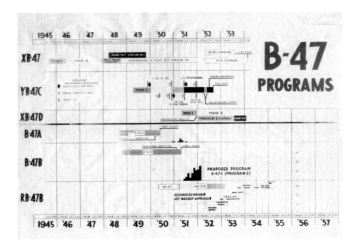

Boeing planning document shows the projected simultaneous development of the YB-47C, the XB-47D, and two reconnaissance variants (RB-47B and RB-47C). This led to competition for scarce resources and engineering talent, compromising the B-47B bomber effort. *Courtesy Boeing*

urgent needs at Boeing.' The increased use of electronics proved troublesome, as this burgeoning new industry had yet to achieve any meaningful degree of quality control and tolerable mean-time-between failure (MTBF) rates. The autopilot required 24 months from initial contract to high-rate delivery. In addition to dealing with the many complexities of the B-47 bomber program, Boeing had to divert resources to support initial development work on the YB-47C, as well as Phase I and II efforts for the XB-47D and the RB-47B.

Ultimately, no one was prepared to build the radically new B-47 or introduce it into service. Boeing and its suppliers were 'over their heads' in meeting the demands of the B-47 production – especially in light of concurrent aerospace requirements associated with the Korean War and National Security Council Memorandum NSC-68, which called for a substantial increase in the acquisition of conventional weapons. As one instrument subcontractor noted, 'The suddenly accelerated demand for [our] devices which followed the Korean action found the existing small scale production facilities inadequate to the [B-47] programs…this has imposed a situation of extreme pressure and shortages.' Moreover, the Air Force could not make up its mind about what an operational B-47 should look like in terms of design and capability.

Project WIBAC

Few people appreciated the unique complexities of bringing the B-47 from initial development to introduction in service, particularly in light of the many challenges experienced during the development of the Convair B-36. One of those was Colonel Paul W Tibbets, best known as the aircraft commander and pilot of the B-29 *Enola Gay*, which dropped the first atom bomb on Hiroshima, Japan, on 6th August 1945. As Chief of the Strategic Air Division in the Air Staff Requirements Division at the Pentagon, Tibbets was part of the effort to convince the Air Force to buy the B-47. Whether or not it was he who was 'finally able to sell the Air Force on the idea of buying a limited number of B-47s' as he claimed in his 1978 biography *The Tibbets Story*, he would become intimately linked to the early development of the new jet bomber.

Testing the B-47 created a critical organizational problem as SAC, AMC, APGC, and even Boeing all claimed ownership of the program. SAC's Vice Commander, Major General Thomas S Power, insisted that B-47 tests 'should be controlled by SAC to the extent that it should be staffed and commanded by SAC personnel,

augmented by such other technicians as the test program actually required.' Not surprisingly, other commands balked as this usurpation of their traditional prerogative. Tibbets, speaking for Air Force Chief of Staff General Vandenberg, told SAC officials on 23rd March 1950 in no uncertain terms that B-47 testing would be led by AMC and APGC, and that participation by 'SAC personnel will be welcome but SAC control will not be permitted.' Tibbets was equally concerned that traditional flight tests by Boeing would 'show only the best side of the plane,' and AMC would hardly 'be expected to find serious fault with its own specifications.' Having test facilities, pilots, and engineers all at the same location and under a single organization would mitigate these concerns and accelerate the evaluation process. A conference held at Wright-Patterson AFB less than a week later, on 29th March, sealed the deal. APGC would 'expeditiously and adequately test the B-47 aircraft to determine its operational suitability prior to its delivery' to SAC. Engineering work would be the domain of AMC in conjunction with Boeing. Despite being invited 'to aid in the test program,' SAC was essentially a non-voting bystander in the test and evaluation of its new flagship jet bomber.

The Air Staff decreed on 7th April 1950 that a special project, known as WIBAC (for **WI**chita **B**oeing **A**irplane **C**ompany), be formed at Wichita on behalf of APGC to 'investigate and analyze the ground handling, flight, and maintenance characteristics of the Stratojet.' To no one's surprise, Tibbets was assigned as Project Officer for WIBAC, and his first action as Project Officer was to qualify as a B-47 pilot. After a few T-33 flights to learn about jet handling, he completed a month of B-47 ground training. His initial flight in the B-47 was with none other than Boeing's newest test pilot 'Tex' Johnston, hired after the death of Scott Osler. Johnston demonstrated 'slow rolls, loops, Immelmans' and other acrobatics in the B-47. He also showed Tibbets the airplane's notorious aileron reversal, its 'coffin corner' at high altitudes, and the need for precise speed and altitude control during approach and landing.

WIBAC was given the highest 1-A (Precedence 1 Group 1) priority for operational requirements and an S-1 priority for supplies, underscoring the B-47's unequalled importance for the Air Force. WIBAC was tasked to 'thoroughly test the airplane and its equipment prior to delivery to operating units within Strategic Air Command,' and its mission was clearly defined: '1) Development and operational suitability testing of the B-47, 2) Obtaining necessary statistics, such as parts consumption data, parts failures engine life, etc, and 3) Establishing an organization, plans, policies, and procedures for

Table 2-2. **Project WIBAC Test Aircraft Planned Allocations**

MDS	Serial	Command	Purpose
XB-47	46-0065	AMC	Automatic Pilot
XB-47	46-0066	AMC	MX1113 Special Weapons
B-47A	49-1900	AMC	Performance, RATO, A-2
B-47A	49-1901	AMC	Performance, RATO, A-2
B-47A	49-1902	AMC	Performance, RATO, A-2
B-47A	49-1903	APGC	K-2
B-47A	49-1904	AMC	Special Project
B-47A	49-1905	APGC	Operational Suitability Test
B-47A	49-1906	APGC	Operational Suitability Test
B-47A	49-1907	APGC	Operational Suitability Test
B-47A	49-1908	APGC	Operational Suitability Test
B-47A	49-1909	APGC	A-2
B-47B	49-2642	AMC	Performance
B-47B	49-2643	AMC	Performance
B-47B	49-2644	APGC	Operational Suitability Test
B-47B	49-2645	APGC	Operational Suitability Test
B-47B	49-2646	AMC	Special Project
B-47B	50-0001	AMC	Special Project
B-47B	50-0002	AMC	Phase V Test

service testing new aircraft.' Moreover, WIBAC would determine the ability of the B-47 to 'execute its role as a Strategic Air Command medium bomber, such as range, navigational ability, bombing accuracy, and defensive action,' as well as refueling, command communications, and 'all aspects of the employment of atomic weapons.' Additional tests would assess the need for 'special tools required for maintaining the airplane,' as well as 'consideration of training needs, both flight and maintenance.' As Tibbets noted, 'if there were any bugs in the airplane, the people who were going to use it could work them out.' Ironically, those people were predominantly *not* from SAC. On 16th May 1950 Tibbets asked SAC for just two aircraft commanders, a supply officer, an engineering officer, four crew chiefs, eight engine specialists, and nine airplane and engine mechanics, electrical and hydraulic specialists, and supply technicians for a total of four officers and 21 airmen. These 25 SAC personnel would be on indefinite temporary duty (TDY) to Wichita and, in the absence of any government-furnished lodging or messing, would be paid per diem to cover daily motel and restaurant expenses, reflecting the appalling lack of infrastructure at WIBAC.

Of the 500 personnel assigned to WIBAC, many were simply chosen because they would be part of an operational B-47 unit, would be expected to learn everything about the new airplane from scratch, and would, according to a Boeing publication, help 'determine what type of flyer made the best jet bomber pilot and how much transitional training a crew required to successfully operate the airplane.' Pilots developed emergency procedures and an in-flight checklist to ensure they were carried out correctly. Maintenance personnel helped determine the 'real world' life expectancy of 'tires, parachutes, generators' and other key components, as well as develop standardized procedures for preventive maintenance. For example, if WIBAC determined that generators typically failed after 60 hours of use, then they should be replaced at 55 hours to prevent failure during flight. Supply personnel calculated spare parts requirements to ensure that each base would have adequate stock on hand. Manning specialists determined how many parachute riggers and hydraulic specialists were needed at each base. WIBAC personnel completed bombing tests at Eglin AFB, FL, as well as Edwards AFB for 'special weapons', the euphemism for atomic bombs. All-weather tests were carried out at Wright Patterson AFB, OH.

WIBAC's noble intentions, however, were severely constrained by the lack of airplanes. Original plans called for the first B-47s to be available on 12th September 1950, with flight tests beginning 1st October. The second XB-47 (46-0066) was slated for 'solving the armament problems' through mid-December. Aircraft performance testing using the sixth airplane would begin 29th December and run through February 1951. Slippages interfered, however, and the first B-47A was not assigned to WIBAC until 13th December and then only as a temporary loan aircraft. The second B-47A was assigned on 15th February 1951, the third airplane on 6th March, the fourth on 14th April, the fifth on 11th May, and the sixth on 25th May. By June 1951 WIBAC averaged only 3.3 available airplanes per month, hardly the 19 called for in the original charter. Moreover, the flying hours were paltry – only 34+10 during February, although this increased to 201 hours in May. Even more frustrating was the near irrelevance of the results. All of the flying and evaluations were done in B-47As, while WIBAC was set up specifically to assess the B-47B. Given the dramatic differences in design, components, and capabilities, the test results were often of questionable applicability to the planned B-47B rollout for SAC. In the absence of airplanes, personnel were compelled to take repeated training courses simply to 'keep WIBAC personnel occupied'.

Pilots had 'a high opinion' of the B-47, and WIBAC compiled a pilot's handbook which provided 'all necessary information as the takeoff and landing characteristics, use of ATO, cruise control, range, speeds, loads, flight characteristics, etc.' The B-47 had yet to

Above: Colonel Paul W Tibbets (left), famous for piloting the B-29 *Enola Gay* on its fateful mission, became the WIBAC Project Officer. He was checked out as a B-47 pilot by none other than A M 'Tex' Johnston (right), seen here with Major Guy Townsend (center). All three proved critical to the eventual success of the B-47. *Photos courtesy Boeing*

Left: WIBAC pilots (Tibbets at left) gave high marks to the B-47A, but cautioned that it was a very different airplane to fly and that many 'old heads' might not make the transition. Even more problematic was that WIBAC was charged with evaluating the B-47B, but had few to fly. *Photo courtesy Boeing*

Table 2-3. **Comparison of XB-47, B-47A, and B-47B Equipment**

Equipment	XB-47	B-47A	B-47B
Engines	J35	J47-11	J47-23
Fire Control*	None	A-2	B-4
Bomb-Nav System	None	K-2A	K-4A
Crew	3	3	3
Water Injection	No	No	No
Autopilot	None	E-6 (MH-7)	E-4 (A-12D)
Ejection Seats	Yes	Yes	No
In-flight Refueling*	No	Yes	Yes
Special Weapons*	Yes	No	Yes

* - Not all XB-47s or B-47As were so configured

demonstrate a range of approximately 4,000nm (7,408km) at 425KIAS, and WIBAC finessed this issue by ascribing the shortcomings to the many variables involved. Perhaps the most controversial WIBAC test finding was that 'experience to date in the B-47 has indicated that the copilot in the B-47 performs no function that requires him to hold a pilot's rating.' WIBAC argued that 'the copilot can perform no flying duties in the air that the automatic pilot cannot perform better,' warning that from 'the rear seat it is virtually impossible to align the plane with the runway when landing or taking off' (no doubt every B-47 copilot felt irrelevant while sitting in the back seat – see Chapter 4). A flight engineer could accomplish the same job without the experience required as a pilot. Needless to say, SAC rejected this recommendation outright.

WIBAC also told SAC that its proposed plan to train each B-47 crewman in all three positions – the 'triple-headed monster' – was a mistake. Each crew position required 100% effort, and flying the B-47 was 'too big a job to expect one man to handle all three qualifications.' In addition to the disastrous SAC 'cross training' program in 1947-1948, those airplanes currently in operation where multi-position qualification proved acceptable were simply not in the same league as the B-47. As Tibbets recalled in a 22nd August 1951 interview, 'The B-47 is not just another airplane. It is a plane in a category all by itself. And it has become apparent that all pilots cannot fly it. No matter how much flying time a man may have in other planes that is no guarantee that he can fly the 47. A number of excellent pilots have been forced to accept this fact, most of them of their own free will. It is just too much airplane for some.'

Maintenance tests at WIBAC were less controversial. Most problems related to B-47A non-production parts, many of which were

hand tooled. Other tests revealed many of the obvious problems in the new jet bomber. Although concluding that the B-47 was an 'excellent airplane' and that the 'airframe design and power plants are years ahead of the component systems installed in the bomber,' Boeing was forced to use the very same equipment in the B-47 that proved troublesome in the B-29 and B-50. Unless the subsystems were brought up to the same modern standards the B-47 would ultimately be a failure.

Despite its obvious appeal Project WIBAC was short lived. Its original contract expired in October 1951, well before any operational suitability tests for SAC were undertaken. Only a single B-47B had been assigned to WIBAC in July, and at least a half-dozen airplanes were needed to validate operational readiness expectations. WIBAC's contract was eventually extended to 28th February 1952 for a grand a total of only 18 months. To its credit, WIBAC accomplished quite a bit in terms of cost and time savings. Indeed, according to Tibbets, Project WIBAC reduced the normal procurement-to-operational time from seven to three years. He added, with no little pride, that a Boeing engineer told him that WIBAC 'was one of the best things that ever happened in aircraft testing and procurement'. SAC and Curtis LeMay, however, disagreed in this rosy assessment of the benefits of WIBAC, which shut down before providing SAC with any meaningful data about 'an operationally reliable aircraft at the earliest possible date.'

Early Problems and Solutions

Service trials with the WIBAC B-47As soon turned up a variety of problems. Some were seemingly small, such as the brake chute bags being torn up by ground contact. At first, it was recommended that the chute be deployed when the aircraft was 3-6ft (0.9-1.8m) off the ground. Since this early deployment caused a rather dramatic arrival on the ground, especially when the pilot misjudged the final flare distance, a better solution involved simply modifying the chute containers.

Other trials illuminated problems that would always plague the aircraft. The crew compartment was cramped and the layout made coordination between the three crew members difficult. The oft-repeated story about Colonel Mike McCoy, the colorful Wing Commander selected to introduce the B-47 into SAC service, illustrates the point with a touch of humor. During initial tests by the 306th BW, the colonel decided to ride in the nose of his new

B-47A 49-1908 served as the test platform for the brake chute to identify the optimal procedure for deployment, allowing maximum braking with minimum damage to the chute from ground contact. *Photo courtesy Boeing*

Boeing installed three small spoilers on B-47A 49-1903 in front of the bomb bay to reduce buffeting when the doors were open. This helped, but weapons delivery remained a problem for months, raising LeMay's ire and leading to extensive testing of both conventional and 'special' weapons. *Photo P11221 courtesy Boeing*

bomber to fiddle with the BNS and other electronic gadgets. When he tired of this he announced over the intercom that he was coming back up and for 'the pilot' to get out of the seat. As he reached the narrow walkway all three crewmen confronted each other face-to-face as both pilots had left their station to allow McCoy to take their place!

These things were minor, however, when compared to others that seriously questioned the new design's ability to do the job for which it was designed. One month before the first B-47B was flown, Air Force Major General Carl A Brandt warned SAC, 'The truth is that we can't drop a bomb from the B-47. Either the airplane must drop bombs effectively and soon, or there is no need for it.' The Stratojet had a potential capacity for carrying any type of bomb then in service but tests pointed up difficulty in delivering any of them. The bomb bay doors opened and closed quickly, but in the short time they were open an unacceptable buffet developed. It was early in 1952 before a combination of bomb bay tuners and small retractable spoilers resolved the problem.

Along with the other operational testing difficulties, the issue of range remained arguably the most intractable. Removing superfluous equipment (such as ejection seats!) helped somewhat but failed to offer more than an incremental – and marginal – improvement, hardly the extra 2,000nm (3,704km) radius specified in the original contract. The nascent field of in-flight refueling offered the promise of unlimited range, but equipping the B-47 for this capability proved troublesome.

Boeing initially considered the probe-and-drogue method but fuel flow rates and drogue stabilization presented some big problems (see Chapter 7). Boeing's proprietary 'flying boom' eliminated these problems but raised design issues for the B-47 – where to place the refueling receptacle. At first it seemed logical to place this aft of the

49-2642 was the first B-47 configured for aerial refueling, and the first transfer took place on 10th January 1951. It is seen here with KC-97E 51-0214 during heavyweight onload trials with wing tanks. *Photo BW60093 courtesy Boeing*

The jet-powered B-47's performance was a poor match for the piston-powered tankers of the day, including KB-29P 44-83896 used in refueling trials with B-47B 50-0014 at Edwards AFB. B-47s often flew at the edge of a stall during air refueling. *USAF*

cockpit, eliminating a lot of plumbing that traversed the crew compartment. Test flights with the XB-47 in close trail behind a Boeing KB-29P tanker indicated that, with the receptacle behind the canopy, receiver pilots tended to fly into the boom. Consequently Boeing engineers decided it would be better to place the receptacle in front of the pilot. Despite the 'plumbing' running through the crew area, this position led to greater safety, especially in the event of an emergency breakaway during refueling.

B-47B 49-2642 was soon modified with receiver gear in the nose and piping routed to the 3,000gal (11,356 liters) bomb bay fuel tank. The first transfer of fuel took place on 10th January 1951 when a KC-97 transferred 19,000lb (8,618kg) of fuel at a rate of 500gpm (1,893lpm). Over the rest of the month an additional 44 day and night contacts were made at altitudes ranging from 3,000-25,000ft (914-7,620m) under all weather conditions. Results of these tests were kept secret until 15th March 1951 when Boeing announced that its KC-97 had successfully refueled a B-47 using the flying boom. Subsequent tests with B-47A 49-1902 and B-47B 50-0014, however, were less than impressive. Boeing tried to refuel a B-47 to its maximum in-flight weight of 202,000lb (91,626kg), but experienced the performance mismatch between the piston-powered KC-97 and the jet-powered B-47. Brigadier General Oscar F Carlson, the Air Force Deputy Chief of Staff for Materiel, expressed concerned about the

Above: High-pressure altitude tests for the ATO system took place at Kirtland AFB using XB-47 46-0066 during its modification for atomic weapons tests in the Pacific. Both Boeing and the Air Force were interested in improving the system by increasing thrust, reducing cost, and improving maintenance reliability, leading to extensive trials. *Photo courtesy Boeing*

Below left: Phase IV tests were undertaken at Edwards AFB using B-47B 50-0014 (seen here) and 50-0056, including a 24-hour flight. The airplanes were configured with wingtip pitot tubes for more accurate data collection. *USAF*

Below right: Boeing pilot Ed Bracher (l), observer Gerald Simmons (c), and copilot Ed Hartz (r) flew a single B-47B to accrue 1,000 hours of flight time over the course of 121 missions. This provided invaluable 'lead the fleet' data for both operations and maintenance planning. *Photo BW65706 courtesy Boeing*

adequacy of the KC-97 for the job. A month later these fears were somewhat attenuated when a KC-97E refueled a B-47B to a maximum weight of 202,150 lb (91,694kg). The refueling took place at altitudes between 13,200-14,000ft (4,023-4,267m), which was nowhere near the desired higher altitudes where refueling would preserve the B-47's jet efficiency but it got the job done.

It is interesting to note that some consideration had been given to towing the B-47. A study by the ARDC Aircraft Laboratory's Engineering Division concluded that a 140,000 lb (63,503kg) B-47 was capable of delivering a 10,000 lb (4,536kg) bomb to a target some 2,225nm (4,121km) distant when towed by two Boeing B-50Cs for the first 1,700nm (3,148km). The B-47's engines would be shut off after takeoff and then restarted prior to release from the tow aircraft. After the strike the B-47 would proceed to its recovery base.

From the very beginning, fuel management was a critical problem for the B-47. One issue was fuel 'boil off' at high altitude. As much as 20% of the desired 1,860nm (3,445km) combat radius – 372nm (689km) – could be lost during a typical flight. The Air Force and Boeing solved this by using JP-4, a lower vapor pressure fuel, instead of JP-3. The nylon bladder fuel cells in the center wing section were

equally troublesome. Although many fuel cells were damaged during installation by mishandling, an Air Force investigation disclosed that cells from the B F Goodrich Company were defective. This allowed the cell walls to split and the rubber particles and residual sealant clogged the fuel filters. These fuel cells were soon replaced by those made by U S Rubber. Even as late as 1953, the 306th BW suffered from fuel cell problems in their operational testing. Boeing had already supplied the USAF with a better tank (the so-called 'White Dot') but the problem persisted. Improved quality control, the addition of thicker inner liners, better handling techniques, and more frequent inspections all eventually led to the resolution of ongoing fuel tank leaks.

Development of the Bombing-Navigation System

American radar bombing systems used during the Second World War were fairly simple, so were not well suited for use with the jet bombers under development. This prompted plans for a bombing-navigation system (BNS) that combined radar, altitude, heading, airspeed, and the specific bombing technique (offset, etc). The first components of the new BNS concept slated for the B-47 were the Western Electric AN/APS-23 radar, Sperry SRC-1 (AN/APA-59) computer, and an optical periscope. Working together these determined the relative position of a recognizable landmark and tracked it either optically or by radar. Wind correction was then entered into the computer and 'remembered' for all subsequent maneuvers. This new equipment was flight tested in XB-47 46-0065 for the first time on 3rd February 1948. Performance was satisfactory even without an optical periscope installed. By March the periscope was installed and the complete system was designated K-1. It passed its functional flight test on 28th May 1948.

Although flight tests progressed well, development of the full system was still incomplete. Both AMC and SAC were anxious to get the new BNS installed in operational aircraft. Surprisingly, funds were not guaranteed for future BNS units for the hundreds of B-47s already purchased, so AMC hurriedly bought 118 BNS systems. The end result of this accelerated procurement was that 71 of these BNS units were simply unusable. These were later replaced, but the 'K' system, as it was called, would be subject to a long series of modifications and improvements that all stemmed from this hasty push to procure an untested product.

When the horizontal periscope was finally installed the BNS became known as the K-2, and it was this variant that was initially slated for use in the B-47. The first K-2 was installed in XB-47 46-0066 in late 1949 at Wichita. Very few K-2s were actually built as a number of changes in 1950 resulted in the K-4A. Most notable among these was the addition of the Y-4 horizontal periscope, developed by Perkin-Elmer, Inc, which incorporated camera mounts to photograph either radar or optical displays. Boeing struggled to fit all of the components into the airframe, however, and the system proved to be extremely unreliable. Tests at WIBAC showed that

trying to make the B-47 and K system work together was nearly impossible. Beginning in February 1952 Project RELIABLE (see Chapter 3) sought to resolve this situation by relocating BNS components and adding access panels on the starboard fuselage. Moreover, updated system parts were tested and installed. By 1953 the K system was at least usable.

Despite these improvements the BNS suffered from a critical weakness: its vulnerability to enemy jamming. Ideally this could be solved by using an inertial system but this technology was still unproven and risky. Instead, Boeing elected to use the AN/APS-64 tunable radar system, allowing the navigator to switch from the jammed frequency to a clear one. The K-4A was redesignated as the MA-7A, and this became the final version of the B-47 BNS.

Testing Continues

Long after WIBAC ended in February 1952, early B-47s participated in traditional Phase tests at Edwards AFB, CA, Eglin AFB, FL, Kirtland AFB, NM, and Wright-Patterson AFB. These included crosswind tests, which the Air Force considered critical due to the airplane's bicycle landing gear. On one memorable flight a B-47 landed at Kirtland AFB in a 60 knot crosswind at a 45° angle to the runway. The pilot's report noted that the B-47 could be 'a bit touchy' under these extreme conditions! Despite this capability, SAC and the Air Force wisely decided that a 25 knot crosswind at a 90° angle to the runway was the most a typical pilot could handle. Indeed, even this limit seemed too great at times given the number of airplanes lost or damaged in crosswind takeoffs and landings.

Phase IV tests took place at the Air Force Flight Test Center (AFFTC) at Edwards AFB from 29th August 1951 through 15th April 1952 using B-47B 50-0014. The airplane accumulated 250 hours conducting longitudinal stability and lateral and directional control and stability tests. These established the maximum forward center of gravity (cg) limit for takeoff and landing as well as a technique for landing the aircraft with an unbalanced fuel load in the external tanks (the final report recommended against landing with unbalanced external fuel tanks). Unfortunately, the 306th BW did not know this when it evaluated the same technique under operational conditions during the same time span, leading to some 'tense' landings!

Heavyweight air refueling tests were also conducted as part of Phase IV. On 23rd March 1952 now-Lieutenant Colonel Russell Schleeh took 50-0014 on a mission that lasted 24 hours and one minute. Carrying a 10,000 lb dummy bomb, the B-47B left Edwards AFB and flew to Mobile, AL, back to Edwards AFB, then to

Childress, TX, back to Edwards AFB to drop the bomb, to Memphis, TN, and finally back to Edwards AFB via Wichita and Denver, CO. No autopilot was installed and, as Lieutenant Colonel Schleeh recalled, 'The first eight hours were the worst. After that we were numb.' B-47B 50-0056 also flew some of the Phase IV tests. In February 1952 it was released to the Aberdeen Bombing Mission for installation of Short Range Navigation (SHORAN) equipment, after which it flew in support of tests at the White Sands Missile Range in New Mexico. The 3200th Test Squadron (TS) conducted Arctic refueling trials, with an unidentified B-47B and KC-97 completing a rendezvous over the North Pole on 19th February 1953. B-47B 51-2137 completed a 1,000hr Accelerated Service Test (AST) on 26th February following 121 flights. Boeing pilots Ed Bracher and Ed Hartz became the first pilots to log 1,000hr of Stratojet time, with Gerald Simmons the first observer to do so.

By late 1953 Operational Suitability Tests were under way at several bases, including YRB-47B 51-2266 assigned to the 320th BW at March AFB, CA. High gross weight takeoffs and warm climate air refueling tests took place at Ramey AFB, PR. Eielson AFB was used for cold weather tests. Biggs AFB was the site of the high altitude takeoff tests while Eglin AFB was used for routine data. Heavyweight takeoff tests at Edwards AFB revealed a crucial limit for the new B-47E, which had a planned takeoff weight of 216,700 lb (98,293kg). Handling characteristics at weights approaching 220,000 lb (99,790kg) were sufficiently poor that Boeing recommended that the airplane use an additional 2,000ft (610m) of runway to increase its takeoff speed and hence controllability. Unfortunately SAC did not have any 12,000ft (3,658m) runways, and the B-47E taxi weight was already 224,000 lb (101,605kg). The solution, as with many of the other problems associated with the early B-47 development and production, would come as part of an extensive and ongoing series of upgrade programs.

Above: A B-47B was used for Phase V all-weather evaluation in the 'deep freeze' facility at Eglin AFB. Early B-47s were hardly suited for extremes in weather, both on the ground and in flight. *USAF*

Right: SAC planned to operate its new B-47s and its dedicated ground tug in locations known for snow and ice. On 10th December 1951 Boeing pushed B-47 49-2642 across a taxiway covered with dry ice to assess steering and braking effectiveness of the proposed tug. *Photo P11735 courtesy Boeing*

CHAPTER THREE

The 'Ultimate' Bomber

Boeing, AMC, and SAC were determined to resolve the many production and operational issues that had crippled early B-47s. This required time, money, and resolve, all of which were in short supply. Nonetheless, the B-47 eventually acquired assisted takeoff capability (ATO), ejection seats in all airplanes, a usable tail gun, improvements to alleviate structural fatigue, an increasingly sophisticated electronic warfare (EW) capability, and even an expansion of its mission into a radio relay platform.

Assisted Takeoff

Considering the early state of jet engine development in the 1940s, it should not be surprising that even with six engines the B-47 was underpowered. What is surprising, however, is that it was intentionally underpowered. The majority of the airplane's flight regime was high-speed, high-altitude cruise, which required far less thrust than the engine was capable of producing. However, the B-47 was sorely lacking in thrust during initial takeoff when it was at its highest gross weight and needed to accelerate from a standstill. An engine capable of producing sufficient takeoff thrust was far too powerful, not to mention too large and too heavy, for cruise flight.

Above: Overproduction of incomplete airplanes led to a massive backlog of B-47s of all variants. It would take several years and a number of specialized programs to resolve these shortcomings. Two RB-47Hs, one RB-47E, and five B-47Es fill the ramp outside the final delivery area at Wichita. *Photo courtesy Boeing*

Right: Boeing planned to use 18 internal ATO canisters to augment the B-47's marginal takeoff thrust. The logistics of this configuration were problematic as the canisters added to the airplane's weight which detracted from its already insufficient range. *Photo P8861 courtesy Boeing*

Consequently, Boeing opted for the General Electric J47 engine instead of more powerful proposals. Efforts to resolve the inadequate thrust during takeoff led to assisted-takeoff (ATO) research, most notably the use of solid-fuel canisters and liquid-fueled rocket engines.

Boeing initially planned for the B-47 to use 18 solid-propellant rockets mounted in the fuselage just above the aft landing gear. Made by Aerojet Engineering, these would provide some 18,000 lbf (8kN) of additional thrust. This was intended only as an interim measure, however, as both Boeing and the Air Force preferred a liquid fuel ATO using white fuming nitric acid (WFNA) and JP-3 fuel, eliminating the need to carry the 18 empty rocket bottles which added 2,160 lb (980kg) to the airplane, reducing payload or fuel commensurately. Also under consideration was a jettisonable

'horsecollar' rack aft of the rear landing gear with 33 solid-propellant rockets yielding 33,000 lbf (14.7kN) of thrust. Two versions of this horsecollar were evaluated, with one simply dropping off when jettisoned and the other 'more forcefully guided away' from the aft fuselage. In any case, the solid-propellant ATO provided just 15 seconds of additional thrust and produced a dense smoke exhaust which made visibility for aircraft following down the runway extremely poor. Moreover, the solid ATO, once fired, could not be shut off, meaning that it would continue to produce thrust in the event of an aborted takeoff.

To mitigate these undesirable effects, Boeing explored a liquid-propellant ATO configuration to be incorporated beginning with the first B-47C and retrofitted to all B-47Bs. Two contracts were let in 1948 to Aerojet (which also manufactured the solid propellant canisters) and the W M Kellogg Company to develop liquid ATO utilizing non-hypergolic (non self-igniting) WFNA oxidizer and JP-3 (later JP-4) jet fuel as propellants. Kellogg's proposal ended in 1951, most likely due to a series of explosions that damaged their test cell. Only the Aerojet design reached a prototype stage and underwent flight testing at Edwards AFB.

The Aerojet YLR45-AJ-1 engines were expected to operate 100 times without maintenance. In late 1949 Boeing advised AMC and Aerojet that their rockets would have to be retractable so that aircraft skin temperatures would not be excessive. Other design challenges included the addition of necessary plumbing from the aircraft's fuel tank for the JP-3/4 (and requisite boost pumps), finding space for the two 200gal (757 liters) WFNA tanks plus preventing contamination of the WFNA. Kellogg was not alone in experiencing explosions during ground tests. In 1952 a thrust chamber ruptured on the Aerojet design installed in a fuselage mockup, breaking a fuel line and igniting an intense fire, certainly an undesirable event on a B-47 during takeoff. Tests revealed that only 4oz (118ml) of the liquid fuel would lead to detonation, necessitating a delicate engineering solution. Pump seal leakage was an equally frustrating and ongoing problem.

Ground tests began in 1952 at Edwards AFB using EB-47B 49-2644 which Boeing had built specifically to incorporate liquid ATO. During one ground test, the EB-47B was parked adjacent to the Bell X-1B which was also scheduled for a ground rocket motor test. Normal propellant streaming from the X-1B's XLR11-RM engine caused considerable alarm for the EB-47B test personnel, who scrambled to safety. The X-1B start was entirely normal, and the fire crew then moved to the EB-47B for its start. With crews back in place the YLR45 fired normally, clearing the airplane for flight tests.

Flight tests consisted of 59 ATO takeoffs with gross weights varying from 130,000 lbs to 181,000 lb (58, 967kg to 82,100kg) with full flaps, 100% engine power (7,950rpm), and standard day conditions. Heavy weight takeoffs necessitated the EB-47B flying around 'dirty' to burn off excessive fuel to reach the maximum landing weight. Colonel Frank 'Pete' Everest and Captain Fitzhugh 'Fitz' Fulton were among the pilots who conducted these test. Initial plans to film the ignition and burn sequence relied on two Lockheed T-33s with cameramen in the back seats. The EB-47B, however, could out-climb the T-33s. Instead, 16mm gun cameras were installed in the ATO compartments and on the aft gear door. The tests were not without some excitement. In one case the pilot pulled the EB-47B into a steep climb as the ATO stopped, leading to a stall. The pilot recovered just 500ft (152m) above the ground. Flight tests ended on 25th August 1954.

Results showed generally improved performance. Takeoff distances ranged from 2,425ft to 5,445ft (739m to 1,660m) compared to 9,400ft (2,865m) with no ATO, 7,300ft (2,225m) with 18 internal bottles, and 4,725ft (1,440m) with the 33 bottle horsecollar Given the reduction in smoke and ability to abort a takeoff, the liquid-fuel

Above: The solid ATO produced dense smoke and could not be shut off once started. Consequently, Boeing, SAC, and AMC explored a liquid-fueled system. *Photo P7703 courtesy Boeing*

Below: Liquid-fueled ATO eliminated the main problems with solid ATO but used highly volatile fuel. The door and ATO engine closed after use, but still added weight and complexity to the airframe, neither of which SAC would accept. *Aerojet-General Corporation*

ATO solution appeared to offer greater performance and reduced side effects. Operational data collected by SAC concurrently with the ATO tests revealed, however, that at least 75% of B-47 combat takeoffs would be possible without ATO. Coupled with changes to load requirements on the airframe, water injection, and the cost tradeoff of simply extending runways versus installing the liquid ATO rocket in all airplanes plus producing and storing the WFNA, Boeing and the Air Force did not approve the YLR45 for production.

Instead Boeing recommended the horsecollar external ATO racks. By 30th June 1953 – while the liquid ATO tests were still underway – all B-47Es beginning with the 665th Boeing unit (52-0442) were configured to carry the horsecollar, and earlier aircraft were subsequently modified. This new design freed up space for 1,248gal (4,724 liters) of additional fuel. Dropping the used ATO bottles was a clear advantage for the external rack but early tests did not go well. During the first two months of 1954 the rack often struck the aft fuselage and turret when it was released at speeds in excess of 200KIAS. SAC pilots were instructed not to jettison the rack at speeds greater than 195KIAS. Brigadier General Albert Boyd at WADC was clearly displeased with this solution, and Boeing eventually designed simple displacing gear to force the rack down and clear of the fuselage.

Above: EB-47B 49-2644 was the sole airplane configured with the liquid ATO system (camera mount is discernable on the aft gear door). Despite modest improvements in takeoff performance compared with solid ATO, the liquid system was not adopted. *USAF*

Below: Two different external ATO configurations were eventually adopted, both were jettisonable. The 33-bottle 'horsecollar' rack offered the most increase in thrust but the commensurate increase in heat adversely affected the fuselage skin. *Photo BW91061 courtesy Boeing*

Using all 33 bottles on the horsecollar rack caused extremely high skin temperatures and generally prohibited the full complement of rockets being used at once.

Boeing developed an improved ATO rack – known as the split rack – using the same fuselage attachment fittings as the horsecollar. The split-rack allowed for 15 bottles to be arranged on each side, avoiding the areas affected by high temperatures. Both types of racks were used on operational SAC bombers (see Chapter 4). By mid-1956, the cost of each ATO bottle had dropped from $450 to $160 per unit, with the cost of each ATO takeoff – using 30 bottles – reduced from $13,500 to $4,800.

Punching Out

A Secret 1952 study on 'Human Factors in B-47 Operation' found that B-47 crews – 'among the Air Force's most experienced at their age level' – exhibited a 'somewhat fatalistic philosophy' to 'emergency escape from the non-ejection seat [B-47].' It noted that crews felt that 'since each B-47 flight may be their last one why even bother to discuss such an impossible situation.' From the beginning the B-47 was designed to carry ejection seats for the crew of three. The pilot and copilot would use upward-firing seats and the navigator would use a downward firing seat. During the initial mock-up inspection in April 1946 the Air Force approved the installation of ejection seats, and by June Boeing expected the seats to be government-furnished equipment (GFE), meaning they would be manufactured elsewhere and delivered ready for Boeing to install in the B-47. The two XB-47s and all 10 B-47As were delivered with ejection seats, but the ensuing 388 B-47Bs were delivered without ejection seats, a controversial decision driven, in large part, by the need to remove weight to enable the B-47 to reach its promised 8,000nm (14,816km) range.

A special Weight Reduction Board met in September 1946 and eliminated some 15 items from the B-47 to meet the range requirement. Removing the three ejection seats would, according to the Board, decrease the overall weight of the B-47 by 4,200lb (1,905kg), reduce the cost of each B-47 by $250,000, and add a modest 350nm (648km) to the airplane's range. The Air Staff approved these changes on 28th September. SAC's new Commanding General Lieutenant General Curtis LeMay and other senior Air Force procurement leaders endorsed these changes, and on 28th October they were made official. Protests fell on deaf ears. As the Assistant Deputy Chief of Staff for Materiel wrote, 'until our high speed bomber range approximates 8,000 nautical miles, it may be assumed that the ejection seat will not be standard bomber equipment.' The figure of 8,000nm was itself the subject of contention, as the Weight Reduction Board had considered the range issue to be 2,000nm (3,704km) radius of action, equating to some 4,000nm (7,408km), exactly half of the final 8,000nm requirement. Moreover, the issue was not merely the removal of ejection seats to improve range, but concern that in the late 1940s ejection seat technology and reliability were too immature to insist they be installed. In short, the Board believed that despite pilot protestations it was still safer to bail out manually than to use unreliable ejection seats, although tests in 1948 suggested that the proposed B-47 seat was more reliable than existing seats, hardly a ringing endorsement.

Boeing responded in 1950 by installing a bailout spoiler which would extend outside, providing an airflow barrier that allowed crewmembers to drop sufficiently before entering the airstream so they could clear the airplane safely. This added 100 lb (45kg) to the overall weight, meaning that eliminating the ejection seats would result in a grand total weight reduction of 4,100 lb (1,860kg). Unfortunately, the spoiler was totally inadequate in design and operation.

Using the spoiler meant that the aircraft commander (AC) first had to sound the alarm bell and depressurize the airplane, then someone (most likely the navigator) had to manually open and jettison the crew entry door and crew entry ladder, and then deploy the airstream spoiler. The AC and copilot each had to remove their parachutes before they could leave their seats due to the extremely narrow clearances inside the airplane. Additional time would be required to put the parachutes back on in the narrow walkway before they could actually bail out, creating congestion at the bailout area. The crawlway aisle was itself a problem, as crewmembers repeatedly complained of equipment and/or metal structures snagging their clothing, helmet and parachutes. The walkway was only 13in (33cm) wide at the floor and 19.5in (50cm) wide at the shoulder. Large crewmembers, especially if wearing winter clothing, could barely fit through the bailout hatch. At speeds in excess of 280 KIAS a person would strike his head on the spoiler. Moreover, the landing gear doors and the bomb bay doors were in alignment with the bailout exit, meaning that no one could bail out from the hatch if the gear was down or the doors were open. Efforts to crawl to the bomb bay for emergency egress were limited, and even then this was difficult while wearing a parachute (granted, Ravens did this on every flight, but not while under duress). In addition, bailout from the bomb bay was prohibited with the aft gear extended. Bailing out of the canopy opening could result in the crewman striking the leading edge of the wing or falling along the leading edge to an engine strut or intake and was considered a 'last resort'. There was no method for crewmembers to bail out if the airplane was in a spin or otherwise uncontrollable, nor could the AC leave his station to reach the bailout area without risking loss of control.

As of 17th November 1952 no one had ever bailed out of a B-47. The first successful bailout of all four crewmembers from a B-47 without ejection seats took place on 10th December 1954, when B-47B 51-2100 flamed out due to inadequate navigation aids. AC Captain Dale H Cooper slowed the airplane to 130 KIAS, descended to 5,000ft (1,524m), allowed the copilot, navigator, and crew chief to bail out, and then finally bailed out himself (see Appendix II). In short, the spoiler system worked correctly only if the B-47 was in essentially straight-and-level flight and in clean configuration. Boeing finessed this issue by arguing that 'the incidence of uncontrolled flight in bombardment aircraft was well below that encountered in fighters, and that the possibilities of utilizing normal crew escape methods were substantially more favorable in bombardment types.' On 18th July 1950 Major General Thomas S Power, SAC's Deputy Commander, noted that at the time the seats were eliminated, 'there was no evidence of equipment dependability and no flight test proof of practicality.' He added, 'It was thought that an alternate exit plan would be satisfactory.'

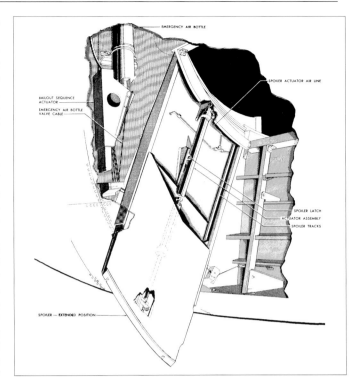

The bailout spoiler was designed to allow crewmembers to extend their egress from the airplane sufficiently before entering the slipstream, hopefully avoiding contact with the fuselage and empennage.

The copilot's ejection seat had its own share of difficulties. If the copilot seat was turned around to use the tail armament (or radio relay gear in the case of the PIPECLEANER EB-47L), he had to first tip the seat forward, then rotate the 400 lb (181kg) seat through 180° by his own effort, tip the seat back, arm the seat (waiting for the control column to stow automatically and the seat drop to the bottom firing position), and then fire the seat.

For the navigator, the April 1946 plan was to have the navigator ditching position aft of the copilot's seat, but this was moved to a position in the aisle next to the copilot's seat. The installed crash harness proved unsatisfactory. A redesigned harness easily handled the extreme forces associated with a crash landing or ditching, but could not be installed in the walkway because there was no place to attach the right vertical strap! When B-47B 50-0038 ditched in Tampa Bay on 11th April 1952 the navigator was sitting in the area aft of the copilot's seat. Bail out was through the crew entry chute as previously noted.

The 1952 report concluded that the cabin depressurization valve be relocated to a point accessible to all crewmembers rather than just the AC, that operation of the copilot's seat be improved, including the possibility of ejecting with the seat facing in either direction, that B-47A ejection seats be installed in B-47Bs prior to the 400th airplane (the first B-47E) when fully operational seats would be incorporated, an improved ditching harness for the observer be installed, and that projecting items in the walkway be 'relocated, recessed, faired over, or dispensed with in the interest of making movement and escape easier.'

The ejection seat issue proved more complex than merely a weight reduction exercise. Boeing had designed the canopy as an emergency egress method for ditching and crash landing, or for ejection *after* the canopy had been manually jettisoned. Again, the unreliability of the technology involved meant that explosive removal of the canopy might prove 'just as fatal to crewmembers'.

Replacing the ejections seats in the B-47 required considerable cost, both in terms of the seats, the airframe modifications, and the need to test their effectiveness. Boeing built a cockpit mockup sled for ejection tests at Edwards AFB. This sequence, taken on 22nd September 1953, shows a test of the copilot seat. *Photos BW90444 and 5139 (series) courtesy Boeing*

Boeing was not particularly supportive of the ejection seat, despite pilot enthusiasm, telling the Air Force on 25th October that 'specifications requiring ejection seats impose severe penalties' on high-speed bombers (Boeing test pilot Bob Robbins argued against this and reportedly kept the Air Force letter removing ejection seats in his files, saying, 'One day this will come back to haunt us'). Adding three seats, hatches, and actuators weighing 450 lb (204kg) each meant that, using a 6:1 ratio, the overall weight of the airplane would have to increase sixfold to meet the range requirement by 8,100 lb (3,674kg) in areas such as wings to support the added fuel needed and landing gear to support the heavier aircraft.

During 1951 a T-33 was modified to test ejection seats anticipated for use in the B-47. The first test, on 16th January, took place at 2,000ft (610m) and 525KIAS, and proved successful, as did subsequent tests. AMC requested a B-47 to repeat the tests in an operational airplane. Even if the ejection seats could function reliably, installing them in production aircraft was a logistic nightmare. AMC concluded in early 1951 that the seats could be installed no sooner than on the 240th airplane (B-47B 51-2197) due in March 1952, and earlier aircraft would require an expensive and time-consuming retrofit procedure. As an interim measure, AMC recommended installing ejection seats beginning with the 80th airplane (B-47B 50-0075) for the AC and copilot which would allow sufficient aircraft control for the navigator to bail out manually through the crew entry hatch. In fact, SAC was so desperate to get ejection seats that they asked for only one seat for the AC, who would maintain aircraft control for the copilot and navigator to bail out through the entry hatch. By 15th July 1953 the problem seemed to be resolved as the Ordnance Corps had delivered some 350 explosive actuators, although retrofit of previously delivered aircraft could not take place until September 1953. Plans were made to install the same seats as used in the B-47A in production B-47Bs.

In October 1953 Boeing delivered an ejection seat trainer to the Air Force that 'demonstrated the operation of the pilot's ejection seat, canopy, and control column functions in support of Air Force maintenance and air crew personnel training.' The seat had an upward travel of 32in (82cm) and a variable ejection force of up to 9g using high-pressure air. Eventually 21 were delivered, along with nine for the navigator's downward-firing seat.

Going Down?

In early 1949 the Air Force planned to award a contract for a downward-firing ejection seat. Both Stanley Aviation and Republic Aviation submitted bids although neither had any experience in manufacturing ejection seats. Stanley received a contract worth $119,576. The first ground test firing took place at Wright-Patterson AFB in 1951 using a horizontal track. A second contract was let to Stanley on 30th June 1952 for five additional seats, including two for flight tests. These were slated to take place at NAS El Centro, CA, with speed increments of 50mph (80kph) and altitudes between 8,000 and 10,000ft (2,438 and 3,048m). Seven initial drops using instrumented dummies verified that the seat separation equipment and

This track inside a hangar at Wright-Patterson AFB allowed testing of a downward-firing ejection seat prior to airborne evaluations. The seat proceeded down along the track and then moved horizontally to a braking pad. *USAF*

Above: The downward ejection test team poses in front of JB-47B 51-2052 at Eglin AFB. Each parachute landing was in the Gulf of Mexico and recovered by US Navy crews, hence the presence of sailors. *USAF via Bill Campbell*

Right: The live ejection tests were undertaken without the navigator's hatch in place. Imagine watching the world pass by beneath your feet from takeoff until ejection time! 44 indicates the test number, including dummy trials. Orange flight suit assisted in recovery, and yellow ejection seat in tracking. *USAF*

other components worked correctly prior to manned tests. An additional three to five drops took place at 'high speed [400 to 450mph (644-724kph)]'. Manned tests were scheduled for November 1952. First Lieutenant Edward G Sperry recommended several phases which would assess both manual and automatic as well as immediate and delayed seat separation and parachute opening. He also urged that the tests take place at Clinton County Airport near Wilmington, OH, close to Wright-Patterson AFB. The Air Force demurred, insisting that the tests take place at NAS El Centro and, given the cost of equipment (a seat was expected to be usable for only three tests), only 12 live and 12-36 dummy tests would take place.

In fact, the downward ejection tests were moved to the Air Force test facility at Eglin AFB, FL, rather than at the US Navy base in California. The first manned test took place on 7th October 1953 when Colonel Arthur M 'Chic' Henderson ejected from JB-47B 51-2052 flying at 203KIAS and 10,000ft (3,048m), followed by four additional live tests. During the sixth test on 20th October, First Lieutenant Henry P 'Hank' Nielsen broke his right shoulder and dislocated his right elbow, and during the next drop on 21st October First Lieutenant Sperry chipped a bone in his shoulder. Problems with the D-ring and leg restraints resulted in the immediate halt of the tests pending suitable improvements. Once resolved, tests resumed some nine months later in earnest with speeds increasing to 456KIAS and

Table 3-1. **B-47 Downward Ejection Seat Trials**

Test No	Date	Subject	Speed	Comments
1	07 Oct 53	Col Arthur M 'Chic' Henderson	203 KIAS	
2	Oct 53	MSgt George A Post	203 KIAS	
3	Oct 53	1LT Henry P 'Hank' Nielsen	260 KIAS	
4	13 Oct 53	1LT Edward G Sperry	260 KIAS	
5	16 Oct 53	1LT Edward G Sperry	325 KIAS	
6	20 Oct 53	1LT Henry P 'Hank' Nielsen	389 KIAS	injured
7	21 Oct 53	1LT Edward G Sperry	390 KIAS	injured
8	08 Jul 54	Col Arthur M 'Chic' Henderson	400 KIAS	
9	1954	MSgt George A Post	435 KIAS	
10	1954	1LT Edward G Sperry	399 KIAS	
11	1954	1LT Henry P 'Hank' Nielsen	424 KIAS	
12	1954	Col Arthur M 'Chic' Henderson	443 KIAS	
13	1954	1LT Edward G Sperry	460 KIAS	
14	1954	1LT Henry P 'Hank' Nielsen	476 KIAS	
15	1954	1LT Edward G Sperry	495 KIAS	
16	02 Aug 54	1LT Henry P 'Hank' Nielsen	426 KIAS	45,200ft
17	03 Aug 54	1LT Edward G Sperry	426 KIAS	45,200ft

JB-47B 51-2052 at Eglin AFB; 10,000ft/3,048m unless noted

Left: Major General Albert Boyd (l) presented the Distinguished Flying Cross to the four downward seat test personnel for 'extraordinary heroism'. From (l) to (r) after Boyd are Colonel Albert M Henderson, Captain Edward G Sperry, First Lieutenant Henry P Nielsen, and Master Sergeant George A Post. *USAF*

Below: The original Emerson A-2 turret proved ineffective, but with some modification it became the B-4 turret and was used pending fleetwide installation of the GE A-5 turret. This view shows the initial evaluation of the A-2 on B-47A 49-1906. *Photo courtesy Boeing*

altitudes reaching 45,000ft (13,716m). The downward seat proved effective and was installed in all B-47s. Despite their many development issues, both types of ejection seats raised crew morale, especially in light of the many structural fatigue problems that arose in the ensuing years.

The Fire Control System

By the end of the Second World War bombers were festooned with gun turrets. The B-17G and the B-24J, for example, had nose and tail turrets, belly and dorsal turrets, as well as side gunners. The Boeing B-29 had a manned tail turret and four remotely operated dorsal and ventral turrets. The Convair B-36 also had remotely controlled turrets. It would seem only natural that post-war bombers should be similarly equipped. Not everyone agreed with this perspective, however. During the war LeMay directed that all but the tail guns be removed from B-29s operating over Japan, an option which was later applied to the 'featherweight' B-36s. Consequently, there was considerable debate over the need for any type of defensive armament for the B-47. Boeing designed the airplane from the beginning equipped with a manned tail turret and many senior Air Force officials saw no reason to delete this. Others argued that the B-47's speed and high-altitude capability obviated the need for tail

guns which needlessly added weight, complexity, and cost to the design. Moreover, there was not an advanced and reliable turret available to equip the B-47. By the late 1940s, however, the Air Force and SAC compromised, deciding that the Stratojet would have only a tail turret.

The B-47's tail gun design went through several iterations. Early designs had a manned turret. Later, this was changed to a remote system, then replaced with a manned configuration, and finally back to a remote turret. No matter where the gunner was located – in front of the airplane or in a tail position – he was to have both optical and radar systems for aiming the guns using the new Draper disturbed reticle sight (named after its inventor Charles S Draper). In this configuration the guns and radar antenna were synchronized, resulting in faster movement, greater accuracy, and a larger field of search and fire.

Emerson Electric Manufacturing Company received a contract on 28th May 1945 to develop the A-1 turret for the B-45 and the A-2 for the B-47. The A-2 was equipped with twin 0.50 caliber machine guns. For almost six years the Air Force and Boeing waited for Emerson to manufacture a workable fire control system. Unfortunately, Emerson suffered from lack of engineering skill, quality control, production capability, and effective management. Military procurement sometimes works in strange ways but it is extremely difficult to understand why this situation was ever allowed to develop or dragged on for so long; political influence no doubt played a significant role. The Emerson program wasted millions of dollars and resulted in the delivery of the Air Force's new B-45 and B-47 without armament.

By the end of 1949 the Air Force began to pursue an alternate fire control system for the B-47 and asked General Electric to look at a system then under consideration for the proposed Boeing B-54. Although this did not prove viable, GE did come up with a workable solution for the B-47. On 18th January 1951 GE representatives met with Boeing officials to suggest that a derivative of the B-36 tail turret might be adapted to the B-47. Boeing and AMC concurred, and by 30th April a prototype turret had been installed on B-47A 49-1908. This used two 20mm cannons in lieu of the two 0.50 caliber machine guns. Flight tests began under Project EAGER BEAVER and revealed very few problems with the new A-5 turret. Throughout these tests B-47s were rolling off the production line without any tail armament, so Boeing installed a plain cone over the tail with 117 B-47Bs delivered in this configuration.

During August 1952 Brigadier General Horace A Shepherd, head of Air Force procurement and production engineering at the Pentagon, decided that some guns on the B-47 would be better than no guns at all. There were still quite a few Emerson A-2 turrets stored at Wichita. As the Air Force had already paid for them, Shepherd decided to install them in B-47s until the A-5 became a production line item, which did not happen until 1955. An N-6 optical sight and AN/APG-30 tail warning radar were added to the A-2 and the result became the B-4 remote control turret. The B-4 was eventually installed on 282 B-47Bs. The interim unit was relatively simple but resulted in an unanticipated problem. During high-speed flight, lateral turret displacement caused the aircraft to yaw to such a degree that it caused undue stress on the vertical stabilizer. To eliminate this impact of this adverse yaw Boeing prohibited rudder use during turret movement at speeds in excess of 330KIAS.

Installation of the GE A-5 system began on production line B-47s in early 1955, and plans were implemented to retrofit those aircraft already built. To meet this demand, GE subcontracted with the Crosley Company as a second A-5 source with Project CROSS BEAVER. Flight tests during EAGER BEAVER identified several weaknesses in the A-5, notably in responding to hostile ECM and shell ejection, leading to a series of improvements. In early July 1955 the Air Force awarded a $6 million contract to GE for an upgraded version of the A-5 making it more efficient and easier to maintain. Known as the MD-4, the new system was first installed on the 731st B-47 (52-0508) which became the standard SAC bomber (see below). The MD-4 included a range gate memory unit to reduce the effects of chaff, an AN/APS-54 tail warning radar, chaff dispenser, and an AN/ALT-6 jammer.

Despite these many improvements, the MD-4 was still an immature system. As one B-47 crewmember recalls, '…the fire control system was quite primitive and when we would go out on our yearly fire-out we would keep firing until all the rounds were gone or the guns jammed. I do remember one incident. We were trained to charge the guns only once. If the guns didn't fire we were to stow the guns and not attempt any further firing. That was good advice. When we got back from one mission I watched as the armorers came out to clear the guns and unused ammo. As it turned out, the gun charger had grabbed a misaligned round and broke it in half. The gun compartment was full of gunpowder from the broken round. Another charging action might have created a spark, and then what?'

Throughout 1953-1955 EB-47B 50-0052 was used to evaluate a T121/T182 30mm tail turret to replace the planned A-5 20mm system. In addition, two B-47s (51-17374 and an unidentified airplane) were used in 1954 to evaluate the T171 (later M61) 20mm Gatling gun. Tests were conducted at Eglin AFB and MacDill AFB, but this was deemed too expensive and too complex a modification for the B-47. Test data from the flights proved helpful, however, in installing the M61 in the Convair B-58 and the Boeing B-52H.

Tri-Company Production

Although Congressional purse strings were tight when the first B-47s were ordered, the abrupt start of the Korean War on 25th June 1950 loosened them dramatically. The Stratojet was never used in Korea and was never meant to be, but the war underscored the perceived Communist threat to the West. Suddenly Congress was willing to spend large amount of money to protect America and to counter Russia's newfound nuclear capability (the first Soviet atomic test – Operation 'First Lightning' – took place on 29th August 1949, 10 months before the onset of the Korean War).

SAC now began to think in terms of thousands of B-47s instead of just hundreds. It was obvious that Boeing alone could not meet this new production requirement so in December 1950 the Air Force considered other manufacturers. On 26th April 1951 the Air Force selected Douglas and Lockheed as the other production sources [the point was not lost on many that this represented the old BDV (Boeing-Douglas-Vega) B-17 Flying Fortress production pool of the Second World War]. Douglas activated the government's Tulsa, OK, plant (which manufactured B-24s Liberators in the 1940s). Lockheed used the former Bell B-29 facility at Marietta, GA. With Boeing's help both companies began to tool up and hire employees. So that both manufacturing and assembly groups could quickly gain experience in building the Stratojet, Boeing supplied Douglas-Tulsa with ten sets of B-47B assemblies and Lockheed-Marietta with nine. These aircraft carried both Boeing and Lockheed or Douglas construction numbers. Douglas also gained valuable experience by participating in the early B-47B modification program.

Table 3-2. **Tail Turret Programs**

Serial	Program	Serial	Program
49-1906	B-4 Fire Control System	51-2362	Crosley A-5 Evaluation
49-1908	A-5 Fire Control System	51-2363	A-5 Fire Control Suitability
50-0052	30mm Turret Evaluation	51-2400	A-3 (B-52) Evaluation
51-2359	GE A-5 Evaluation	51-2410	A-3 (B-52) Evaluation

Above: The GE A-5 turret replaced the middling B-4's twin 0.50 caliber machine guns with two 20mm cannon. This is the tail turret most commonly associated with the B-47. *General Electric*

Below: The upgraded GE A-5 turret became known as the MD-4, and included tail warning radar, a chaff dispenser, and a basic ECM jammer. These technicians are calibrating the radar tracker following a PDM visit to Douglas-Tulsa. *Photo T-2867PR McDonnell Douglas*

The 'Tri-Company Production Committee' sought to resolve the many problems of co-production by Boeing, Lockheed, and Douglas, and included some of the most prominent men in the B-47 program. Seated around the table are Major General Samuel R Brentnall, USAF head of the B-47 effort (l), Noah D Showalter, Boeing's Assistant Chief Engineer for the B-47 (right head of table, in light suit), and Wellwood Beall, Boeing's Vice President for Engineering (r). *Photo BW-45550 courtesy Boeing*

Air Force planners recognized the potential for problems from the start and set up a 'Tri-Company Production Committee'. Composed of representatives from the three manufacturers along with the AMC staff, the group was supposed to solve problems and insure that all B-47s would be essentially the same. Unfortunately the committee had an all but impossible job. Each manufacturer contracted with its own suppliers, leading to notable equipment differences. As B-47s entered maintenance centers it became essential to know the identity of their maker as Boeing modification kits did not always fit Lockheed airplanes, and so on. According to company lore, Douglas supposedly turned out an airplane that was a full six inches longer than standard dimensions! Long after Boeing shut down its Stratojet production and modification lines, Douglas and Lockheed maintained connections with the bomber. Indeed, Douglas maintained the last two EB-47Es in operational service right up to 20th December 1977 (see Chapter 7).

The 'Standard' Bomber

Over the first three years of B-47 production, 2,940 engineering changes were made to the Stratojet. At times, very few of the B-47s in service were similar, let alone identical. This resulted in substantial problems in operations and maintenance due to the lack of commonality. In fact, the Air Force decided that so many changes had been made to the B-47B that a new Mission-Design-Series (MDS) was necessary beginning with the 400th aircraft, and these became B-47Es (the C series was the abandoned B-47C and the D series were the two turboprop XB-47Ds – see Chapter 7). Despite this MDS change, early B-47Es were little different from the B-47B.

Initial efforts to upgrade the B-47B began in January 1952. This involved 309 out of 312 aircraft (51-2045 through 51-2356), with the remaining three (51-2052, 51-2103, 51-2137) slated for use by AMC. B-47B 51-2045 arrived on 31st January 1952 at Boeing-Wichita. While Boeing-Wichita was undertaking this Phase I upgrade, B-47s coming off its assembly lines without the relevant modifications were flown to Davis-Monthan AFB and then turned over to Grand Central Aircraft Company (GCAC) where they were fully configured under the GRAND CANYON program. As if the GCAC B-47 program did not have enough problems (it was already overwhelmed trying to convert B-47Bs into YRB-47Bs – see Chapter 6), the facility was located near the Tucson, AZ, airport. This meant that the airplanes had to be towed seven miles from Davis-Monthan AFB to the GCAC facility over steel planking (when completed, the airplanes flew out of Tucson AP; no explanation for this difference has been uncovered). Unfortunately, GCAC alone was unable to meet the demand for the GRAND CANYON modifications, so the upgrade of the 310 B-47Bs was

divided between Boeing-Wichita, Douglas-Tulsa, Lockheed-Marietta, and GCAC. Boeing completed 90 of these, beginning with a block of 40 starting with 51-2317, plus an additional 49 between 51-2193 and 51-2316 (AMC retained the remaining airplane). All 89 were delivered to SAC between November 1952 and February 1953, and were completed and delivered to SAC between May and August 1953. The remaining 203 B-47Bs were modified by Douglas-Tulsa (106 aircraft) and GCAC (88 aircraft), with nine assigned to unspecified test duties with Boeing and AMC.

During April 1953 SAC, AMC, and Boeing held a conference that established Boeing-Wichita Block 20 B-47s as the 'Strategic Air Command Standardization Bomber', beginning with the 731st airplane (52-0508). Douglas-Tulsa started with its 125th B-47 (52-0158) and Lockheed-Marietta with its 128th B-47 (52-0312) to meet these specifications. This Phase II standardization did not eliminate existing or planned changes, but instead meant that all B-47s would eventually receive the same modifications. Normalization included the return of ejection seats (raising the morale of at least the two 'upward firing' crewmembers!), an improved defensive armament with gun-laying radar and two M-39 20mm cannons, and enhanced electronic countermeasures (ECM). The B-47Es also now carried an approach chute that enabled the aircraft to keep the engines no lower than 55% rpm to allow for their slow spool-up time while still maintaining the necessary slow approach speeds. The brake chute was retained and an anti-skid braking device was added to the landing gear. In addition, Project RELIABLE allowed for better ground access to electronic components, and the J47-25 engines were configured for water/methanol injection. The internal ATO structure was deleted and replaced by a 33-bottle external rack, while a new liquid oxygen system, a high frequency (HF) liaison radio, and additional fuel capacity were incorporated.

HIGH NOON was the first program to rebuild 161 in-service B-47Bs. In order to deliver SAC airplanes first, Boeing decided to begin re-work with B-47Bs 51-2192 through 51-2356, including former YRB-47Bs within this serial range. The program was set up at Wichita, with the first airplane (51-2193) entering work in June 1954 and the last delivered in January 1956. These would be redesignated on paper as B-47B-IIs. This was not an official MDS change, but was instead a way to distinguish modified aircraft from those yet to be converted. A similar scheme was used for the B-47E.

The first 88 B-47Bs (49-2642 through 50-0082) created no end of logistics and operational issues given their many differences from the 89th B-47 (51-2045) onward. Consequently, during August 1952 AMC asked Boeing to standardize these early B-47Bs as TB-47Bs to 'reflect the true utilization of the aircraft.' Boeing agreed, and the

Table 3-3. **B-47 Modification Programs**

Date	Program	Contractor	A/c #	Purpose	Date	Program	Contractor	A/c #	Purpose
1952-53	GRAND CANYON	All	309	Fully configure B-47Bs	1958	MONTICELLO	LM	1	Electronic search and destroy
1952-53	BABY GRAND	GC	53	Install A-5 tail guns on Block 12	1958	TELL TWO	BW	3	Initial conversion
				B-47Es	1958-59	C NOTE	DT	99	Fuel cell check
1953	SUITCASE	GC, DT	91	Configure YRB-47Bs					(100 aircraft scheduled)
1953-54	FIELD GOAL	DT	64	Fully configure ATC TB-47Bs	1958-59	BIG RED	DT	138	FY59 IRAN
1953-54	TURN AROUND	BW	114	Fully configure B-47Es	1958-59	FIRST BASE	DT	42	IRAN
1953-57	EBB TIDE	BW	235	DB-47B, TB-47B, and B-47B-II	1958-59	AUNT FANNY	LM	199	FY59 IRAN
1954	DRAG ANGLE	LM	40	Wing strengthening	1958-59	TURN AROUND	OCAMA		Wing strengthening
1954-55	BLUE CRADLE	DT	45	ECM conversion	1958-59	TEE TOWN	DT	100	ECM pod modification
1954-55	DRAG ANGLE	DT	351	Wing strengthening	1959		DT	30	RB-47H modification
1954-56	HIGH NOON	BW	161	Fully configure B-47Bs to B-47B-II	1959-60	OPEN ROAD	DT	298	FY60 IRAN
1954-56	PEACH STATE	LM	270	Fully configure B-47Es	1959-60	TEA CUP	DT	88	FY60 IRAN
1954-56	OIL TOWN	DT	275	Fully configure B-47Es	1959-60	FUR COAT	LM	96	FY60 IRAN
1955	ROMAN I	LM	2	100" camera installation	1959-60	QB-47E	LM	14	Convert RB-47E to QB-47E
1955-56		LM	261	Nuclear weapons capability	1960-61	ARROW HEAD	DT	103	FY61 IRAN
1955-56		LM	827	Install reliable wing tanks	1960-61	SILVER BELL	DT	109	FY61 IRAN
1956		DT	28	RB-47H modification	1960-62	SILVER KING	DT	37	RB-47H modification
1956-57	BLACK BEAUTY	LM	204	FY57 IRAN	1961		LM	5	Emergency elevator power
1956-57		LM	279	Upgrade ECM	1961-62	CLEAR SKY	DT	171	FY62 IRAN
1956-57	BOX KITE	LM	214	FY57 IRAN	1961-62	RED BARN	DT	482	Wing strengthening
1956-57	BLUE BONNET	SAAMA	28	FY57 IRAN	1962-63		DT	437	FY63 IRAN
1957	PURPLE PALLET	DT	2	2 TB-47Bs for unknown purpose	1962-63	SLICK CHICK	DT	2	ECM modifications
1957		DT	34	RB-47H modification	1962-63	MIL RUN	DT	2	ECM modifications
1957	BUTCHER BOY	LM	92	FY57 IRAN	1962-63	DEEP RIVER	DT	2	ECM modifications
1957-58	BLACK GOLD	DT	278	FY58 IRAN	1963-64		DT	107	FY64 IRAN
1957-58	SOUTHERN BELLE	LM	253	FY58 IRAN	1963-64	TELL TWO	DT	3	Upgrade EB-47E(TT)
1957-58	BOW STRING	BW	105	FY58 IRAN	1963-65	BIG BLUE	LM	34	WB-47E conversion
1957-58	BLUE BONNET	SAAMA	36	FY58 IRAN	1964-65		DT	70	FY65 IRAN
1958	MILK BOTTLE	DT	196	Wing strengthening	1965-66		DT	70	FY66 IRAN
1958	MILK BOTTLE	LM	200	Wing strengthening	1965-66		DT	16	WB-47E IRAN
1958	MILK BOTTLE	SMAMA	291	Wing strengthening	1966-67		DT	10	WB-47E IRAN
1958	MILK BOTTLE	OCAMA	386	Wing strengthening	1967-68		DT	10	WB-47E IRAN
1958	MILK BOTTLE	BW	38	Wing strengthening	1969		DT	8	WB-47E IRAN

BW - Boeing-Wichita   DT - Douglas-Tulsa   LM - Lockheed-Marietta   SAAMA - San Antonio Air Materiel Area
OCAMA - Oklahoma City Air Materiel Area   SMAMA - Sacramento Air Materiel Area   IRAN - Inspect and Repair as Necessary

first 106 B-47Bs that had not been lost in accidents were converted to TB-47Bs by June 1953 as part of the EBB TIDE program. In addition to the 106 TB-47Bs for use by Air Training Command (ATC), EBB TIDE configured 30 B-47Bs as DB-47Bs (see Chapter 7). Finally EBB TIDE provided for the modification of the last batch of 98 B-47Bs (51-2092 through 51-2191) to the B-47B-II HIGH NOON standard. One additional airplane (51-2142) was designated as an RB-47B – see Chapter 6).

ATC requested further modifications to its TB-47Bs, leading Douglas-Tulsa to undertake Project FIELD GOAL beginning in January 1953. This included installation of a fourth crew position for the instructor pilot (IP) or instructor navigator (IN) – without an ejection seat – and removal of the tail gun (if installed). In addition, the TB-47Bs lacked any air refueling capability (the assumption was it would be taught to new aircraft commanders at their first duty station), ECM, and any atomic weapons delivery capability. FIELD GOAL ended in late 1954. The exact number of TB-47Bs modified by FIELD GOAL cannot be determined due to incomplete and conflicting records, but Douglas-Tulsa completed 48, with the Oklahoma City Air Materiel Area (OCAMA) accounting for 18 although three of the supposed OCAMA modifications remain suspect.

Early B-47Bs were once recognized by the large number of nose windows and internal ATO ports. During the upgrade programs to B-47B-II standards, however, new or modified noses with fewer windows were grafted on, the old ATO openings were covered over, and white 'anti-flash' paint was applied to the underside. This was

B-47s were delivered without tactical white anti-flash paint (sometimes ambiguously referred to as 'camouflage'), and were a mishmash of different colors based on the metal type or fiberglass.

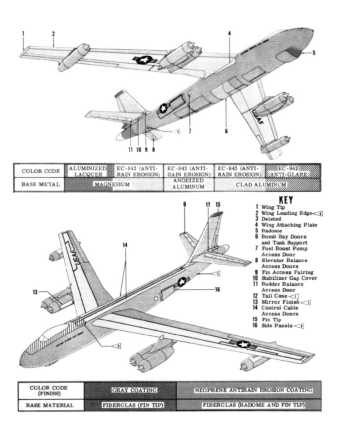

COLOR CODE	ALUMINIZED LACQUER	EC-843 (ANTI-RAIN EROSION)	EC-843 (ANTI-RAIN EROSION)	EC-843 (ANTI-RAIN EROSION)	EC-942 (ANTI-GLARE)
BASE METAL	MAGNESIUM		ANODIZED ALUMINUM	CLAD ALUMINUM	

KEY
1 Wing Tip
2 Wing Leading Edge
3 Deleted
4 Wing Attaching Plate
5 Radome
6 Bomb Bay Doors and Tank Support
7 Fuel Boost Pump Access Door
8 Elevator Balance Access Doors
9 Fin Access Fairing
10 Stabilizer Gap Cover
11 Rudder Balance Access Door
12 Tail Cone
13 Mirror Finish
14 Control Cable Access Doors
15 Fin Tip
16 Side Panels

COLOR CODE (FINISH)	GRAY COATING	NEOPRENE ANTIRAIN EROSION COATING
BASE MATERIAL	FIBERGLAS (FIN TIP)	FIBERGLAS (RADOME AND FIN TIP)

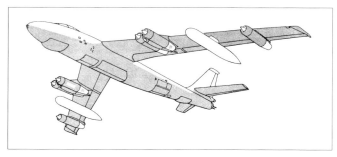

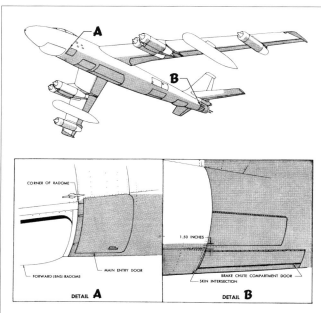

Left: The early anti-flash scheme extended from nose to tail and covered the engine pylons and nacelles. Drop tanks were typically unpainted, but have been noted with day-glo orange on the outer side as well as white.

Below: Nuclear tests in the Pacific determined that the white anti-flash paint was only needed on the undersides where flaps, ailerons, bomb bay doors, and similar structures were at risk from thermal damage. This reduced costs associated with the expensive paint which was prone to widespread peeling.

discontinuities within the B-47E fleet, including aircraft still in production as well as those already in service. The BABY GRAND program started in 1953 with the installation of the A-5 tail gun and fire control system in 53 Block 12 B-47Es 51-2357 through 51-2411 (51-2389 and 51-2392 were not modified as they were destroyed prior to delivery – see Appendix II). GCAC undertook this work over a period of 7-8 months per airplane. Beginning 27th April 1953 the Air Force approved the modification of 114 Wichita-built Block 17 through Block 19 B-47Es (52-0394 through 52-0507) by putting them through the TURN AROUND modification program before they left the plant. This saved an estimated $7.1 million by not having to return these for modification after delivery. The TURN AROUND revisions included ejection seats, 'power and range enhancements, bomb-bay modifications, and improvements to navigation, bombing, communication, and self defense equipment.' TURN AROUND was completed on 27th October 1954.

The Air Force contracted Lockheed-Marietta to modify the B-47Es they had built (51-15804 through 52-0311) along with some of Boeing-Wichita's early B-47Es (within the serial range 51-2357 through 51-17386), in a program known as PEACH STATE starting on 13th July 1954. During March 1955 Douglas-Tulsa began similar work on their unmodified B-47Es (52-0019 through 52-0127), the first 123 RB-47Es (51-5258 through 52-0755), and the balance of early Boeing-Wichita B-47Es (within the serial range 51-2357 through 51-17386) under the aptly named OIL TOWN.

The end of these multiple programs to upgrade older B-47s was by no means the end of ongoing improvements to the fleet. Beginning in 1953 the Air Force adopted a major change in the way it conducted major maintenance on its aircraft known as the Inspect and Repair As Necessary (IRAN) program. For the B-47 this meant each aircraft cycled through a major facility every two years. These facilities included Boeing-Wichita, Douglas-Tulsa, Lockheed-Marietta, OCAMA, and the San Antonio Air Materiel Area (SAAMA) at Kelly AFB (during 1957-58 only). An entire wing of aircraft would be brought to the facility and exchanged for a group that had already gone through IRAN. This ensured that all airplanes of any wing would be up to the same standards. It also played havoc with identifying aircraft unit assignments. Until the new unit repainted their new jets, the residual tail stripes and unit badges were very misleading.

It was not long, however, before the 'standard' B-47 became obsolete. This led to the 'heavyweight' B-47E beginning with the 862nd Boeing unit (53-2279) delivered in February 1955. This and subsequent aircraft would now be capable of a maximum unstick takeoff weight of 225,000 lb (102,058kg) allowing for a combat radius exceeding 2,000nm (3,704km) but still only half of SAC's desired 8,000nm (14,816km) combat range. The 'heavyweight' was quickly supplanted when the 1000th Boeing-built B-47E (53-2417) became the new 'ultimate'. Phase III improvements included upgraded ECM, technical changes to the bomb bay, and a third 40kVA alternator.

By 1962 the size of the B-47 fleet had been greatly reduced, structural inspections had become quite extensive, and there were still wide variations in airplane configurations. Douglas-Tulsa

designed to prevent the thermal heat from an atomic or thermonuclear detonation from burning or even melting critical structures (see Chapter 7). It was a very expensive paint but it would not adhere to the magnesium bomb bay doors, leaving them looking ratty. In the mid-1950s, according to one story, the SAC Inspector General (IG) was due to inspect the aircraft of a wing based in central Florida. In order to hide the peeling paint of his bombers, the wing commander sent his men to the local Sears & Roebuck department store with instructions to buy the required quantity of white house paint. The 'store-bought' paint adhered better than the special stuff and the IG personally congratulated the commander on the appearance of his airplanes!

With the 'standard' configuration and with the B-47B upgrade program underway, it was now possible to address similar

Table 3-4. **B-47 Roman Block Numerals**

B-47B-II	**B-47E-II**
200,000-pound gross weight capability	All B-47E-I modifications
33-bottle ATO racks	Phase XI modification
Aft auxiliary fuel tank (large ATO tank)	Phase III ECM
Phase III ECM	
Operable water injection	**B-47E-III**
Cycle I BNS modification	All B-47E-II modifications
Phase XI modification	Three-phase AC electrical power
	(constant speed alternators)
B-47E-I	
200,000-pound gross weight capability	**B-47E-IV**
33-bottle ATO rack	All B-47E-III modifications
Aft auxiliary fuel tank (large ATO tank)	230,000-pound gross weight capability
Phase II ECM	Cycle I CP BNS
Operable water injection	
Cycle I BNS modification	

became the sole modification depot, replacing the B-47 IRAN program with an individual aircraft modification initiative, and undertook all changes and upgrades to the B-47 fleet until the last two B-47s retired in 1977.

Contracts And Operation 'Stretchout'

By May 1953 the Air Force had issued contracts for 1,893 B-47Bs and B-47Es as well as 297 RB-47Es. Boeing had built 520 B-47s since March 1950, and was turning out approximately 25 per month. With the addition of the Lockheed-Marietta and Douglas-Tulsa airframes, B-47 production almost achieved a wartime pace. In September 1953, as part of a revised estimate by the Eisenhower administration for future requirements, the Air Force announced a reduction of 151 B-47s from current contracts. This also included the 'Stretchout' program, an attempt to spread B-47 production over multiple years, thereby keeping production teams together longer.

The revised B-47 delivery schedules were meant to dovetail into new airplane production programs that were just getting underway at all three manufacturers: Boeing with the B-52; Douglas-Tulsa with the B-66; and Lockheed-Marietta with the C-130. Although Douglas-Tulsa and Lockheed-Marietta suffered some adverse effects from the reduction in B-47 acquisitions, the assignment of a large share of B-47 IRAN efforts and special modification projects helped to offset much of the setback.

After all of the cut-backs and revisions had taken place, production ended during Fiscal Year 1957 at all three plants. Boeing delivered the last of its 1,373 B-47s (of all variants) on 24th October 1956. A month later, on 27th November, Douglas-Tulsa delivered the last of its 274 Stratojets. Lockheed-Marietta's last B-47 of 394 rolled out on 7th February 1957. In all 2,041 B-47s were built. Beginning with the B-47Bs, the cost per airplane was $2,249,456 ($18,373,590 in 2017 dollars), although this decreased to $1,869,667 ($15,207,508 in 2017 dollars) per airplane for the B-47E thanks to its greater production numbers.

Unanticipated Structural Fatigue

The B-47's wing was, without a doubt, its most innovative feature: swept back 36.5° (one degree less than the optimal 37.5°), highly flexible, designed with a high aspect ratio and thin cross section to reduce drag, minimal disruptions to the leading edge, optimized for high altitude flight, and provided the lift and maneuverability that gave the B-47 fighter-like performance. Aside from the obvious limit to internal fuel storage capacity, the wing was not well suited to sustained low-altitude operations. With the 1956 shift in SAC tactical doctrine from high- to low-altitude penetration flights, including the Low Altitude Bombing System (LABS), the B-47's wing revealed significant structural fatigue problems. There was considerable debate at the time if these were the result of SAC using the airplane in an operating regime other than that for which it was designed or an inherent design weakness. Ultimately it turned out to be both.

On 13th March 1958 B-47B 51-2104 splintered into four parts while making a shallow turn at 1,500ft (457m) after an ATO takeoff from Homestead AFB, FL. It had a total flight time of 2,077 hours. On the same day TB-47B 50-0013 broke up during unusual attitude training near Tulsa, OK, with 2,418 total hours. The surviving crew reported that 'the wing broke off' in flight. Boeing engineers were concerned that these were 'high time' airframes (greater than 2,000 hours) and focused their attention on similar aircraft to identify the problem and propose a solution. A week later, on 21st March 1958, B-47E 52-0244 experienced wing failure during an abrupt climb over the Avon Park Bombing Range in Florida, with only 1,129 total hours. Two weeks after that, on 10th April 1958, B-47E 52-0470 exploded in flight near Buffalo, NY, due to catastrophic structural

failure of the wing (1,265.5 hours), followed five days later on 15th April when B-47E 52-0235 experienced wing failure after takeoff into a thunderstorm (1,419.3 hours – see Appendix II). In little more than a month five B-47s were lost, and the last three could hardly be considered 'high time' jets.

The ensuing investigations shocked the Air Force and Boeing. The wings of the TB-47B had several small fatigue cracks around critical bolt holes. The remains of the Homestead AFB accident revealed a 9in (23cm) crack with fatigue origins. Although some investigators argued that the large crack could be attributed to pilot-induced excessive g-loading, the smaller ones present in all five crashes were almost certainly due to inherent fatigue. If the cracks were as widespread as investigators feared, it meant that B-47 would not last as long as Boeing had promised and as SAC required.

Boeing-Wichita had already solved two structural problems with the B-47. Less than two years into its service life the flexing wing had placed excessive stress on the fuselage-wing drag angles. Lockheed-Marietta and Douglas-Tulsa repaired 391 airplanes under the DRAG ANGLE modification project during 1954-55. During late 1957 a rash of cracked panels near the outboard engine made field repairs necessary. A few months later cracks were discovered on nine B-47s at MacDill AFB. Initial analysis showed that these were due to improper assembly techniques. Both of these problems came after the aircraft had started the new low-level bombing runs, but engineers were not prepared to link these cracks with low-altitude operations.

The five crashes added considerable urgency to Boeing-Wichita's ongoing Aircraft Structural Integrity Program (ASIP), especially as three had fewer than 2,000 hours of total flight time. Inspections of six TB-47Bs at McConnell AFB and six more B-47s at several SAC bases were made right away, and all 12 were found to have cracks. OCAMA – manager of the B-47 weapon system – issued flight restrictions on 3rd April 1958 limiting the airpseed to 360KIAS and acceleration to 1.5g [amended on 17th April to 310KIAS, 1.5g, and a maximum gross weight of 136,000 lb (61,689kg), a weight incapable of EWP operations – but SAC waived this for alert bombers; all restrictions were lifted on 19th August]. All abrupt maneuvers and flights through turbulence were to be avoided. Following the first three crashes, Boeing and the Air Force met on 9th April to initiate corrective action, beginning with a field-level inspection to look for fatigue cracks at wing station (WS) 354 and butt line (BL) 35 on 50 B-47s, and WS 254 on all B-47s. Inspections began at Lockheed-Marietta on 14th April but not at Douglas-Tulsa as only one boroscope was available, so Boeing placed a 'rush' order for additional scopes. Inspections at Douglas-Tulsa finally began on 17th April. In addition, TB-47B 50-0022 underwent a 'complete teardown' at Boeing-Wichita (it was eventually scrapped there on 16th December 1958), along with B-47Es 51-17368 and 52-0102, both of which returned to service.

After a week of inspections all three manufacturers – Boeing-Wichita, Lockheed-Marietta, and Douglas-Tulsa – discovered that the problem was far worse than anticipated. Inspecting only the areas associated with the known wing cracks failed to reveal the widespread extent of the fatigue. The original inspection plan was based on the faulty assumption that if cracks were not found in the critical wing area then the B-47 was assumed to be safe to fly. Of 25 inspected aircraft, six had cracks, but not all of them were on the outer wing splice. Four had significant cracks where the wing met the fuselage. The worst of these was on B-47E 52-0032 which had a 9in (23cm) crack at BL 35. Surprisingly, this was not a LABS-configured airplane and had logged below-average flight time (1,370 hours). In addition, B-47B 51-2207 had six cracks at WS 354 (with 1,545 hours) and B-47E 52-0147 had a 4in (10cm) crack at BL 35 (with 1,291 hours). Neither of these two were LABS aircraft and both

Above: McClellan AFB was eventually chosen as the fifth MILK BOTTLE repair facility, taking precedence over its F-86 and EC-121 PDM work. Hastily scrawled markings at the wing root on these B-47s are believed to be related to the repair program. *USAF*

Below: OCAMA served as the central coordinating point for the MILK BOTTLE program. Tinker AFB was a logical choice as it already supported B-47 repair programs. This view highlights the sliding canopy on the front B-47 and the clamshell canopy on the B-47 behind it. *USAF*

were low-time airframes. This lack of correlation was an early clue to the extent of B-47 problems. Moreover, the results of the New York loss showed the cause to be failure of one of the two critical bolts that linked the wing to the fuselage. One of these bolts, known by its shape as a 'milk bottle' pin and weighing 25 lb (11kg), plus a smaller bolt, were the primary means of attaching the wing to the fuselage. It was now apparent that no one had fully realized the extent of the B-47's structural problems. As of 5th May, 84 airplanes were grounded.

The Beginning Of A Solution

With the initial inspection underway, Boeing worked frantically to engineer an interim fix followed by a permanent repair. SAC needed a combat-ready bomber and was not happy with what it perceived as Boeing's haphazard approaches to resolve the fatigue problem. At a conference on 16th April Boeing decided to issue a technical order to fully address this serious situation, calling for a major inspection of all trouble areas, known and potential. It also provided for an interim repair that would give SAC usable airplanes until the final repair was available, which was not expected until June. Boeing issued Technical Order (TO) 1B-47-1020 on 21st April which provided for both interim inspection and repair, and on 29th May Boeing issued TO 1B-47-1019 for the permanent repair of all affected airplanes. Boeing also planned a 100-hour low-altitude flight test evaluation using TB-47B 50-0080 between 1st August and 1st November.

Given the large number of B-47s involved, the time and space required to inspect them, and the intensive labor requirements to do the work, AMC faced a daunting task. No single depot – known as an Air Materiel Area (AMA) – could handle the work without major changes. Each AMA normally had responsibility for only certain aircraft types. Some worked mainly on bombers, some on transports, and others on fighters. This simplified inventory requirements and allowed for the specialization of skills used by AMA workers. AMC hoped that OCAMA could be the sole source for the B-47 inspections and repairs but quickly realized this would be insufficient given its obligations to other aircraft such as the KC-97. AMC asked the three manufacturers to assist, but this risked delicate labor issues invoked by hiring large numbers of workers for a short period only to be followed by massive layoffs. Both Douglas-Tulsa and Lockheed-Marietta were given some work but only within their existing IRAN capabilities. Boeing would work on the B-47s based at McConnell AFB across the runway from its Wichita plant. Still, these efforts could not meet the expected demand. San Antonio AMA (SAAMA) was briefly considered but its heavy B-52 workload rendered this impossible. The Sacramento AMA (SMAMA) at McClellan AFB, CA, was primarily involved with fighters, and using their facilities would disrupt an extensive North American F-86D and F-86L program as well as a smaller Lockheed RC-121 contract. Other AMAs either lacked facilities or an adequate work force.

In the end AMC selected SMAMA at McClellan AFB. Their F-86D work was moved outdoors and other programs were suspended or deferred (a high priority Lockheed QF-80 program was not affected). Plans were made to shift workers over to the B-47 effort and retrain them. Public appeals were made for short-term workers over the summer months. All five sites began a 'war time' pace, and the program – now known as MILK BOTTLE – involved three daily shifts and six-day work weeks. By the end of the first week in May SAC had delivered 76 Stratojets to the depots, adding to the 194 B-47s already at the three manufacturers for various modifications. As could be expected, there were considerable problems. Transfer of skills from one aircraft type to another took more time than anticipated. While this had little affect on Douglas-Tulsa and

Lockheed-Marietta, OCAMA faced a steep re-education curve with the B-47. Labor strikes caused delays at Lockheed-Marietta from 7th through 21st May, and the first aircraft was not finished until 29th May. SMAMA faced a complete re-orientation from fighters to bombers. Its first TO 1B-47-1019 modification was to WB-47B 51-2115, which was returned to service on 17th June. During August SMAMA also repaired a B-47 at Eielson AFB, AK, which was deemed unfit to fly.

All five facilities had problems with supplies and tooling. MILK BOTTLE was given the highest priority logistics; parts were forthcoming but they often did not fit. Tooling developed as the program evolved, and much of it was engineered quickly and often did not do the job for which it was designed. The individual sites, particularly SMAMA and Douglas-Tulsa, modified the tools or made their own, leading to further reductions in commonality. Managing the program was a monumental task. OCAMA Commander Brigadier General Thomas P Gerrity and his staff proved to be amazingly resourceful in organizing the entire effort. The primary office was at Tinker AFB, but OCAMA had representatives at each site. In turn, each contractor and SMAMA had people at Tinker to represent their interests. Boeing placed men at each facility. The records of this period indicate an almost constant stream of telephone calls, teletype transmissions, conferences, and impromptu meetings with long hours and more than a few senior officials working seven days a week.

Interim and Permanent Repairs

For the interim TO 1B-47-1020, each of 457 B-47s had approximately 370 bolt holes reamed and filled with oversize bolts, and the milk bottle pins were inspected and replaced as needed. A boroscope and acidic dye penetrant were used to locate any undetected cracks. If any were found the holes were reamed again. If no other cracks appeared the aircraft was returned to service. All of this work required about 1,700 man-hours per airplane. Each B-47 presented its own unique set of problems, however, resulting in considerable variation in time needed to repair them. Douglas-Tulsa finished the first interim repair airplane on 12th May. Boeing estimated that this temporary fix would last about 400 hours, but this proved rather optimistic. At a later date these aircraft would then return for the final and ultimate repair.

The permanent repair effort was far more extensive and complicated. After each B-47 arrived at a MILK BOTTLE center it was disarmed and had its ejection seats secured. The bomb bay area was checked for radioactivity and if positive then it was decontaminated [the official OCAMA history is the first declassified reference to this radiation problem]. All fuel tanks were drained and purged. Early on this was done with nitrogen, but later JP-5 was used (JP-5 was less explosive than the regular JP-4 fuel). The water-alcohol tanks were also drained. Then all parts that would prevent access to those areas to be modified were removed. The most difficult of these involved the removal of three fuel cells and two water-alcohol tanks. All items were marked and placed in special crates so that they would be returned to the proper aircraft. Any part that needed repair was sent to the shop before reassembly. Roving defect crews went from aircraft to aircraft and corrected any safety-of-flight matters. The B-47s were then moved into the production lines with the exception of SMAMA and Boeing-Wichita, as Sacramento simply did not have the facilities and Boeing-Wichita was using Air Force hangars at McConnell AFB. Once 'on the line' the aircraft were positioned on jacks and the actual modification work began.

The repair work was concentrated in three areas. The first area was the one that gave the program its name, the milk bottle pin at body station (BS) 515. It was not so much the pin itself but the surrounding forging that was problematic. The second area of concern was WS

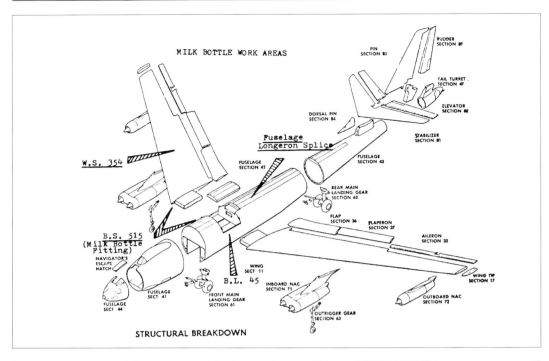

Top: The nature of the MILK BOTTLE repairs was extensive. Along with the subsequent longeron splice repairs associated with previously unidentified structural fatigue, proved both expensive and time consuming.
C Mike Habermehl

Center: Removing the 'milk bottle' required both muscle and skill for the small opening on top of the wing, as well as careful telephone coordination with personnel beneath the wing to ensure proper alignment. Additional work required smaller personnel to work inside the wing, hardly the place for the claustrophobic. After reinserting the pin teams used a theodolite to ensure the wing was correctly aligned before securing it in place. *USAF*

Bottom left: Some of the many tools used to remove and replace the 'milk bottle' bolt (r). Each facility used different tools and procedures, leading to a lack of commonality that would create problems for future depot-level maintenance. *USAF*

Bottom right: Drilling and reaming the wing bolt holes, seen here at WS354, required precise templates to ensure correct placement. Over time, each technician acquired the skills and finesse to do his own job, ensuring consistency and reducing errors. *USAF*

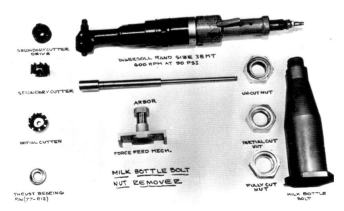

354 just outboard of the twin nacelle. This was actually the splice that joined outer and inner wing panels. The final area was BL 45 where the lower wing skin met the fuselage.

Removing the milk bottle pin was no small task given that access was only 24in x 18in x 8in (61cm x 46cm x 20cm). To insure that the pins, once out, would go back into the hole, the wings had to be kept in perfect alignment. Minor movement of the aircraft and changes in the aircraft structure due to temperature variations made this challenging. SMAMA devised a system of hydraulically actuated dial indicators, while OCAMA did the alignment using optical methods. Crews wore special clothing while working inside the wing. With the securing nut removed the pins were pulled, a process made even more difficult by corrosion. After trying other methods, a hydraulic puller was found to be the best tool for the job.

With the milk bottle pin removed specialists inspected the forging. Early in the program an etching compound was used to remove oxidized metal and other material that prevented a precise inspection. Later this was abandoned as the caustic substance proved to be dangerous to other parts of the aircraft structure. Repairing the forging involved three cuts with a special boring bar and was critical. The first two cuts were generally rough followed by a finishing cut. A bushing was inserted into the hole to bring the fitting back to original tolerances. Perfect wing alignment was absolutely necessary during this procedure. In addition, no one other than the men qualified to remove the pin was allowed near the aircraft at the time. Finally the milk bottle pin was reinserted using either a new or reconditioned item. About one-fourth of the pins showed evidence of corrosion early in the procedure, and at first these were discarded. However, due to a shortage of parts closer inspections were instituted and many of the condemned pins were cleaned up and returned to service.

The remaining two areas of concern were far less complicated. Repair of WS 354 involved removing the lower wing skin and adding doublers and reinforcers inside the wing. Approximately 850 bolt holes were reamed and new bolts inserted. The inner wing attachment at BL 45 required new splice plates, and the shear plate connecting the wing and fuselage was reworked and replaced. About 800 bolt holes were reamed and then filled with oversize bolts.

Dealing with the bolts in all three areas proved to be time consuming. Those that were stuck were either drilled out or cut and pulled. Each hole then had to be checked for defects by boroscope. The holes were then reamed at least 0.313in (0.08cm) and some required even more. The replacement bolts were an astonishing 135 different sizes, and getting the proper bolt to the right hole was a real problem. Each facility developed a system of stencils, jigs, and color-coding to insure proper mating. With the plates and bolts in place, a protective sealant was applied over all those areas receiving work. Some of the new bolts protruded into the airstream so they were coated with an aerodynamic putty to smooth the airflow.

Reassembling each airplane took some 350 man-hours. Hydraulic, fuel, and water-alcohol systems were checked before the tanks were filled. SAC crews conducted the flight testing. The crew that delivered one B-47 for work would pick up a completed one for testing and return it to service. With few exceptions the B-47s were accepted after the first flight. Some operational units complained about fuel leaks and a few other matters with the repaired airplanes, but considering the speed with which the project was done the work was quite acceptable.

As of early May, Boeing projected that each B-47 would require 1,700 man-hours for the full TO 1B-47-1020 repair. By the middle of May this increased to 2,700, but Boeing planners were hopeful that as a consequence of 'on-the-job-training' for engineers and mechanics alike this would drop to 1,300 man-hours by the 50th aircraft. Unfortunately, the figure rose substantially and by May 29th

peaked at 3,150 man-hours with 19 dedicated workers per airplane. Eventually this decreased by mid-July to 2,156 man-hours per airplane. These inaccurate estimates were understandable. For one thing, the so-called 'ultimate' repair took much more skill and precision than anyone had imagined. More wing skin needed to be replaced then originally planned. There were labor headaches caused by hiring new people and re-assigning others from different projects. The ultimate outcome of all of these problems was that SAC had to wait longer for its fleet to be ready. Input schedules were adjusted but it was many weeks before production met published schedules. At the end of June the program was 13 aircraft behind, and two weeks later this number had grown to 88. By the end of August, however, the facilities had caught up with the planned repair numbers, with OCAMA two airplanes ahead.

The MILK BOTTLE program ended at Douglas-Tulsa and Boeing-Wichita on 30th August, and by 16th September all the repairs were complete, with RB-47E 52-0812 the last airplane modified. Boeing had repaired 38 aircraft, Douglas-Tulsa had fixed 196, Lockheed-Marietta repaired 200, OCAMA modified 386, and SMAMA corrected 291. An additional 31 had been modified by field repair as they had cracks too large to allow flights to the facilities. This was not the end of the TO 1B-47-1019 modification, however. Project TURN AROUND at OCAMA completed work on those bombers that had received the temporary (TO 1B-47-1020) fix. Douglas-Tulsa and Lockheed-Marietta also accomplished this TO as they processed B-47s through IRAN. OCAMA completed the last aircraft on 11th February 1959.

One other major structural difficulty became a part of MILK BOTTLE program. The modification centers found 46 aircraft with forgings cracked beyond the limits of the TO 1B47-1019 repair. Of these seven were already scheduled for retirement. Boeing determined that the remaining 39 B-47s could be repaired by cutting out and replacing the entire suspect section. Because of its critical nature Boeing undertook this work, traveling to the facilities where the jets were located. By March 1959 all were returned to service.

Ongoing Research
The five MILK BOTTLE crashes and the subsequent high-priority repair program may give the misleading impression that both Boeing and the Air Force were unaware of (or at least ill prepared for) structural fatigue issues with the B-47. Initial efforts by AMC and ARDC to analyze the problem were hampered by guesswork and lack of any existing empirical data on fatigue in large swept-wing, high-speed jet aircraft. Some engineers at Boeing and AMC were not certain that the MILK BOTTLE repairs would last, or were even the correct option.

In early May 1958 Boeing-Wichita, Douglas-Tulsa, and NACA-Langley began a cyclic test program to investigate the relative life expectancy of the Stratojet and its repairs. Each agency received a B-47 airframe and subjected it to the rigors of simulated flight loads (Boeing-Wichita used TB-47B 50-0080, Douglas-Tulsa used RB-47E 52-0731, and NACA-Langley used RB-47E 52-0736). Beginning in July three B-47Es from the 305th BW (52-0114, 52-0288, and 52-0289) were equipped with oscilloscopes to measure low-altitude in-flight stresses. Eventually the number of instrumented B-47s grew to six for SAC, one for Boeing-Wichita, and one for WADC. The flights were suspended on 26th December after accumulating 333 hours of 'roller coaster' maneuvers. Tests resumed on 6th February 1959. Unfortunately, these long-term data and analyses were of little benefit to the MILK BOTTLE program as Boeing-Wichita had begun the prototype work on 23rd May, less than a week before TO 1B-47-1019 was issued. Not surprisingly, problems surfaced soon after the first airplanes returned to service. The interim TO 1B-47-1020 repair was designed to provide an additional 400 hours of safe flight prior to completion of the full modification. Tests revealed, however, that this was overly optimistic. Fortunately, most of the B-47s fixed early in the interim program were slated for the comprehensive repair before they reached the shorter limit.

On 8th August 1958, after 3,422 hours of actual and simulated flight time, the nose broke off of Boeing-Wichita's cyclic test TB-47B. The failure occurred in an upper longeron, one of the fuselage's longitudinal support beams. Little more than a month later, Douglas-Tulsa found a crack in the same area on their test RB-47E. That airplane had only 3,115 hours. Boeing-Wichita then mated the fuselage of TB-47B 51-2049 with wings of the original cyclic test B-47. Another longeron crack appeared on 16th September. Of even greater concern than the crack was the low time on the new airframe – just 2,251 hours. By 23rd September, inspections of high-time B-47s at McConnell AFB revealed two in-service B-47s with cracked longerons. Boeing-Wichita immediately disseminated time-critical inspection procedures to all modification centers. During a conference on 26th September, Boeing and the Air Force agreed that all B-47s with more than 2,000 hours would have an external plate

10in (25cm) wide x 160in (406cm) long added, as well as increasing the resilience of the existing longeron splice. Although not part of the MILK BOTTLE program, OCAMA repaired these defective B-47s. The rest of the B-47 fleet would receive these modifications as each passed 2,000 hours total time.

Unfortunately this was not the end of fuselage problems, and the longerons remained suspect. Analysis of previous crashes revealed that these parts were among 'the first fragments in the flight paths of crashed airplanes,' raising concern that these losses were due to previously unidentified structural fatigue. The AF Inspector General expressed concern about the lower longerons, especially in the area of the bomb bay, saying, 'The lower longerons are unrestrained on the lower side in the bomb bay for a length of over 26 feet [7.9m]. Under high gross weight, high-g conditions the lower longerons will deflect and twist. This deformation could increase at slightly increased loads under gust flight conditions so that failures would occur at a load factor less than the design value of 1.5 times the limit load factor of 2.0.' In short, the fuselage could break in half in the vicinity of the bomb bay under EWP conditions.

STRUCTURAL FATIGUE IN THE B-47: A PERSONAL OBSERVATION

Bob Robbins was a B-47 test pilot, engineer, and program manager. Few people acquired his understanding of the airplane and its underlying strengths and weaknesses. When asked for his assessment of the structural fatigue associated with the B-47 and the many initiatives to resolve it, Robbins shared his technical expertise with the author.

***

Before the B-47 military fleets became obsolete in relatively few years and were replaced before they accumulated very many flight hours. Consequently, while there were clearly defined requirements for structural strength, there were no military requirements for service life in either years or hours nor were there any defined usage requirements. Accordingly, usage, service life, structural fatigue and even stress corrosion problems prompted little concern at the time the B-47 was designed and put into production.

The B-47 fleet evolved over the years from the original plan for a small number of airplanes that would fly primarily normal high altitude missions in mostly smooth air to a huge fleet with increasingly severe demands on usage, especially at low altitude. Higher and

higher gross weights, aerial refueling to even higher weights [the B-47 gross weight grew from 125,000 lb (56,699kg) design gross weight and 162,500 lb (73,709kg) maximum gross weight on the XB-47 to 198,000 lb (89,811kg) for takeoff and 230,000 lb (104,326kg) with aerial refueling on B-47E-IVs], increased training requirements, low altitude (rough air) toss bombing and penetrating tactics, airborne alert and longer expected time in inventory all aggravated structural problems.

New materials such as the 7178 aluminum alloy were developed by the aluminum industry to help satisfy the aircraft designer's and the military's desire to keep structural weight to a minimum. Unfortunately, without serious emphasis on service life, these new materials were selected because of their high strength/weight ratio with little or no real consideration given to service life problems. Recognition of the more undesirable characteristics of these materials came slowly as did the more severe use to which they would be subjected. All these greatly increased manufacturing problems because of the increased care required to avoid nicks and scratches, and particularly because of the

possibility of damaging clamp up stresses in the manufacturing assembly of complex structural joints where heavy unyielding structural members come together. An almost perfect fit or very careful shimming of complex joints was required to avoid these problems. These more undesirable characteristics compared to previously used materials (such as 2024) include:

- Increased notch sensitivity and shorter critical crack lengths. This meant that nicks or imperfections more easily formed fatigue cracks under repeated loads, and short cracks that are hard to find on inspections more quickly grew to become large fractures under high loads;
- Shorter fatigue life under normal working stresses;
- Much shorter fatigue life under high level working stresses which occur at the high gross weights to which the B-47 was pushed;
- Increased brittleness; and
- Increased susceptibility to stress corrosion where the combination of applied or locked-in residual stresses and atmospheric corrosion caused cracks to develop. This was the primary problem with the milk bottle forgings.

Boeing conducted early structural tests with B-47B 49-2642 before handing it over to the Air Force. It was later used to evaluate the LABS capability of the Stratojet. *Photo courtesy Boeing*

As part of its cyclic test program, Boeing used the fuselage from TB-47B 51-2049 and the wings of TB-47B 50-0080 for the second set of cyclic tests. 51-2049 had just 2,251 flight hours, raising serious concerns about the longevity of the B-47 fleet. *Author's collection*

The MILK BOTTLE project had one immediate goal: return Stratojets to unlimited service with SAC. Hopefully, these B-47s would provide a reasonable number of years of service after these repairs. Defining 'reasonable', however, required both cyclic and flight tests. Cyclic tests were based on the assumption that aircraft fatigue could be simulated by applying alternate loads to the airframe. Stresses were applied by hydraulic actuators and measured by instruments in critical areas. The tests were divided into spectra representing 175 flight hours, with each spectrum comprising 28 cycles of takeoffs and landings, 202 cycles of high-gust loading, and 2,296 cycles of low-gust loading.

Using this cyclic data Boeing engineers calculated that the first significant failure (other than the longeron) would occur at 3,360 flight hours. Although this very conservative figure allowed for error, Boeing believed it was 'good enough to live with.' NACA-Langley, however, identified additional problems with its cyclic test aircraft.

When the longer and increasingly severe service life requirements began to evolve and the need to more adequately address fatigue and service life became evident, B-47 production well under way and the necessary data and engineering techniques were not adequate. For example, there was virtually no quantitative data available on the magnitude and frequency of atmospheric gusts (eg, turbulence) which was badly needed, particularly at low levels where the environment is severe. There were full-scale static tests articles but no full-scale cyclic test articles for fatigue tests. Up to this point fatigue testing was done primarily on a small specimen in the laboratory.

The B-47 structural problems alarmed the whole aviation technical community and forever changed the way airplanes were designed. Subsequent military airplanes such as the B-52, KC-135, FB-111 and the C-5A suffered problems similar to those of the B-47 before adequate corrective measures were firmly in hand. There were high-powered technical committees formed with representatives from leading technical universities, from the military, NASA, and industry to recommend long-range solutions to what was now recognized as a widespread problem. These recommendations included:

- Low-level flight test programs to record atmospheric gust magnitude and frequency data for engineering design analysis;
- Extensive fatigue testing of full-scale cyclic test articles, starting with complete B-47 airplanes and is now commonplace, as is full scale static testing;
- Establishment of service life design criteria for new aircraft;
- Development of new engineering approaches to the whole subject of aircraft fatigue and the design of damage tolerant aircraft structures; and
- Expenditure of a far higher percentage of the total engineering structures budget on fatigue considerations than was previously the case.

The B-47 not only set the design pattern for future generations of large military and civilian jet aircraft, it helped make those aircraft far safer by bringing sharp focus to the need for much greater attention to structural service life considerations.

Top left: **A single static test airframe was used to measure the B-47's stress loads during 1951. Engineers and technicians worked adjacent to the test rig, evacuating only during each test.** *Photo 45355-14 courtesy Boeing*

Top right: **Multiple clamps were attached to key surfaces during the stress tests, and hydraulic pressure was used to apply increasing loads to each component.** *Photo P10781 courtesy Boeing*

Bottom left: **Despite the use of a static test airframe, Boeing (and other manufacturers) had yet to understand the need for a cyclic test airframe. The B-47's ongoing fatigue problems led to the use of older B-47s to determine their structural life.** *Photo BW45325 courtesy Boeing*

Bottom right: **Pressurization tests, such as that seen here on an RB-47E, were designed to detect leaks in the pressurized crew compartment rather than assess cyclic stresses associated with multiple ascents and descents.** *Photo BW91032 courtesy Boeing*

At 5,000 hours of simulated flight, 52-0736 developed a 21in (53cm) crack at WS 170. Douglas-Tulsa found a 10in (25.4cm) crack in the same location on 52-0731 after 10,000 hours of cyclic testing. NACA was concerned that Boeing had not accounted for certain technical details in their lower 3,360-hour estimate. SAC, eager to keep its B-47s as long as possible, accepted Boeing's lower number. In fact, SAC really did not need that many hours anyway. The MILK BOTTLE history records that 'SAC had grown weary of the inspections' and that 'pilots had to have confidence in the B-47, even if the bomber command had to assume some risk after the months of MILK BOTTLE.' An ARDC official articulated this by saying, 'In order to do something we can live with, we have to accept risk. We will have to realize that one or two airplanes will get by and crack up. It's like sending 40 airplanes on a target and getting 25 back.' Clearly, the Air Force was willing to trade a few airplanes and crews to end the ongoing drama of MILK BOTTLE. At most, SAC estimated that no remaining B-47s would reach a total of 2,000 hours per aircraft *after* the TO 1B-47-1019 repair, believing that its B-47s would reach – at most – 3,500 to 4,000 total hours. By that time they would be replaced by B-52s, B-58s, and ICBMs, but this optimism failed to account for the RB-47Hs and WB-47Es that continued in service through 1967 and 1969, respectively.

Fatigue – An Ongoing Problem

NACA-Langley described fatigue as 'a disease. But knowing the symptoms, the signs, you have a chance to keep the patient going,' a view with which the Air Force readily agreed. This meant that the B-47 – and every other aircraft in the fleet – would receive regular extensive inspections. The greatest problems still occurred at joints and splices because of the discontinuities and stresses. This could be avoided if structures were made of single large pieces of material, but no one was proposing that new large aircraft be built this way. Instead, detailed inspections would be carried out at all joined pieces and bolt holes. Another part of the fatigue picture was even more difficult. Some cracks on B-47s were the result of stresses applied during manufacturing. While some of these were traceable to faulty technique others were of unknown origin.

The Stratojet suffered from subsequent fatigue problems, but each one was detected before it became serious. During 1961-1962, for example, Douglas-Tulsa cycled 481 B-47s through Project RED BARN, a modified MILK BOTTLE program. During inspections some corroded pins and forgings were found, but these were identified early enough to remedy the situation. One new area of concern was the 'pop bottle' pin. This was forward of the milk bottle and shared the same forging, but engineers decided these cracks and corrosion were not the result of fatigue. RED BARN also resolved problems at WS 203 between the inboard nacelle and fuselage much in the same manner that WS 354 had been during 1958. Longerons remained a concern after Boeing's cyclic airplane broke apart in 1959 due to structural deficiency in the longeron at BS 508 and at the water alcohol access door at WS 203, along with a later failure occurred at BS 497. Inspections were performed on 35 aircraft at Davis-Monthan AFB in 1960. No cracks were found and nothing further was done until FY63. At that time, OCAMA commenced longeron inspections on B-47s with more than 2,700 hours.

Early in the 1960s it appeared as though SAC might be using their B-47 bombers longer than anticipated, possibly even into 1969. OCAMA undertook two separate investigations to determine the long-term structural impact. In addition to a complete teardown of two aircraft every year, Boeing resumed cyclic tests. Three SAC B-47s (B-47Es 53-1870 and 53-1890 from the 380th BW and 53-1914 from the 98th BW) were selected for a 'Lead The Fleet' program. These would be flown intensively until they had accumulated 1,000 hours beyond the rest of the fleet. Special inspections would then be made at regular intervals to provide sufficient time to solve any newly discovered problems. Although these data would ultimately confirm the cyclic test loading and yield data for future production programs, they provided only modest help for the B-47. Reduction of the raw data proved to be a very complicated problem. As a Boeing spokesman acknowledged, explaining fatigue was difficult 'even if you are an expert.' Data collection was impressive, but the cracks followed no predictable pattern and 'varied widely from airplane to airplane.' Boeing could not explain 'why a fracture would occur in one area on a particular B-47, and at a different place on another.' The official MILK BOTTLE history notes that Boeing 'admitted that there were many facets of the bomber's structure that it did not yet fully understand. The Air Force was just as much in the dark.' In any event, all SAC B-47 bombers were retired by 1966. Even though some felt they were still of use (notably Power, who wanted them retained until he got more B-52s), many SAC and AMC officials simply would not trust them to last. They were happy to see them go and staunchly opposed using them any longer.

The final numbers from the B-47 structural fatigue fiasco are compelling: 31% (618 B-47s) of SAC's bomber fleet suffered from serious structural deficiencies. Of these 247 had cracks at BL 45, 143 had cracks at WS 354, 158 B-47s suffered from cracks at both BL 45 and WS 354, 53 had damaged BL 45 forgings, 17 experienced cracked BS 515 forgings, and 11 had longeron stress fractures. With the B-47 comprising more than half of SAC's deterrent force, the consequences for American national security were daunting. To their credit, Boeing, SAC, and AMC did a tremendous job in repairing these airplanes and mitigating the adverse impact on US security. The core of the MILK BOTTLE program lasted just over four months and cost $62,000,000 ($521,537,182 – half a billion – in 2017 dollars), yet it brought well over a thousand bombers back from an early grave. Indeed, many B-47 critics called the Stratojet 'a three year airplane', 'over the hill', and 'ready for the junkyard' but MILK BOTTLE attenuated these accusations. The Air Force and the aviation industry also learned a great deal more about fatigue, with close inspections becoming a part of the IRAN program and continuing today.

Voodoo Warfare

In the event of war between the USSR and the West, American and British bombers would be easily detected by Soviet early warning radars. As the Russian defensive arsenal grew in technical sophistication and spread in deployment, Western bombers faced radar-equipped Soviet interceptors as well as radar-guided air-to-air and surface-to-air missiles. Unable or unwilling to procure fleets of 10,000 or more bombers each armed with a single atom bomb to overwhelm Soviet defenses through sheer numbers, Western military planners appreciated the economic argument that electronic countermeasures (ECM) would allow a much smaller number of bombers to reach their targets by evading detection and destruction by radar-guided weapons. Although basic radar detection and interception of bombers began during the early years of the Second World War, throughout the Cold War radar and the means to jam it shifted from a mere component to the central feature of aerial warfare.

General Curtis LeMay and SAC were especially committed to the development and use of ECM for bombers, despite being considered little more than 'voodoo warfare' by non-believers. Critics argued in the late 1940s that unlike the B-36s and B-50s, the new B-47s would easily overcome Soviet defenses by virtue of their high speed and high altitude capability. Even if detected by Soviet early warning radar, B-47s could outrun the piston-powered Lavochkin La-9 *Fritz* and La-11 *Fang* or Yakovlev Yak-9 *Frank* fighters sent to intercept them, especially at night and in bad weather. Should one somehow manage to climb high enough for a firing pass the B-47's tail guns would make short work of the interceptor. The 1950 shock of the MiG-15 *Fagot* and its dominating performance against B-29s over Korea did little to dissuade the ECM supporters. Adding chaff would jam early warning radars, they argued, and installing a rudimentary radar-warning receiver would give the B-47 crew the necessary time to evade attack. SAC planners were keenly aware, however, that ongoing advances in Soviet military capabilities would negate any physical advantages temporarily held by the B-47. They also knew that any strike might have to take place in clear sunny weather and, given the B-47's suspect performance in instrument conditions, bad weather was just as detrimental to the bombers as to the interceptors. As a result, they insisted that the B-47 be designed from the start to carry a full complement of ECM gear, consisting of the 'black boxes' which generated or processed signals, components that powered the black boxes and provided the power to transmit jamming signals, structural mounting and wiring, and receiver and transmitter antennas. It was not a smooth evolution, however, and hundreds of B-47s were delivered and declared operational with ECM gear that worked only intermittently, never worked at all, or was not even connected.

There was some ambiguity at the time in the terminology associated with ECM, conflating the use of ECM for defensive purposes with the collection of electronic intelligence (ELINT) for use in compiling an electronic order of battle (EOB) and developing new ECM gear and tactics. Air Force and SAC records, for example, list the SILVER KING AN/ALD-4 ELINT receiver pod for the RB-47H as an 'ECM pod', when in fact it had nothing to do with jamming or countermeasures. To distinguish this difference more fully, B-47 ELINT capabilities are considered in Chapter 6.

Evolution

Beginning in early 1950 SAC's Deputy Commander, Major General Thomas S Power, called for an automated jamming system which would protect the newly delivered B-47 from enemy radars without the need for a specialized ECM operator. Because the copilot would operate this ECM gear by using little more than 'on' or 'off' switches when prompted by warning lights (not visible while he was turned around manning the tail guns), Power added, it had to be 'the ultimate in simplicity and reliability.' Automated and multi-frequency or 'sweep' ECM systems were then still under development, however, so Power settled for the more limited 'barrage' jammers which operated on a narrow frequency selected while the airplane was on the ground and were fairly unreliable.

During 1952 Lieutenant General Laurence C Craigie, the Air Force Deputy Chief of Staff for Development (and the first US military pilot to fly a jet airplane in October 1942) warned that, 'Attrition estimates for B-47 combat operations in 1955 and 1956 indicate that without effective countermeasures including ECM, B-47 losses to [anticipated] enemy air defense systems would be very high.' The situation was serious enough to prompt Air Force Vice Chief of Staff General Nathan F Twining to write to Bill Allen at Boeing to urge that ECM work be accomplished as quickly as possible.

None of the B-47As was delivered with an ECM capability as they were considered to be test and development airframes. With ECM technology still in its infancy – coupled with ongoing airframe production problems at Wichita – all B-47Bs and many B-47Es rolled off the assembly line with only ECM wiring and mounting frames in place. In many cases even this was inadequate, as wire bundles were often improperly secured or were of insufficient length to connect the components once they were installed. In the case of the AN/APS-54 warning radar, for example, the wiring ran adjacent to a hot air bleed duct, resulting in melted wires, short circuits, and an inoperable

Early intercept tests of a B-47A by F-94s and F-86s at Eglin AFB demonstrated that the B-47 was highly vulnerable to radar-guided intercepts, emphasizing the critical need for ECM. *Photo 43144AC USAF*

system. Still, it was better than nothing, as ECM historian Alfred Price optimistically recorded, 'Installing it now [would] reserve space in the [air]plane for better equipment, when it comes along.'

Moreover, Power wanted to determine the B-47's radar signature and how far away it could be reliably spotted and tracked by enemy radars. Knowing this information would influence SAC's tactical doctrine of when to turn on ECM as well route planning to avoid high concentrations of radar sites. Tests at Eglin AFB in March 1951, however, were alarming. Although a Lockheed F-94 was able to intercept a B-47 in only one out of seven attempts, a North American F-86D was successful in 36 out of 42 attempts, with all six failures occurring during the first mission, likely the result of ground controller inexperience. The F-86's speed and high-altitude capability effectively negated that of the B-47, eliminating its primary defensive ability. As the Air Proving Ground Command (APGC) history for the latter half of 1951 presciently warned, B-47 'ECM [should] be developed [as an urgent priority for] protection from air-to-air launched missiles and the gun-laying radar of all-weather fighters.'

B-47 ECM capability evolved through the mid 1950s in four major phases coinciding with other substantial operational improvements, beginning with rudimentary electronic jamming, followed by the installation of chaff dispensers and a radar-warning receiver, and then further improvements in subsequent phases, eventually culminating in two TEE TOWN ECM pods on 100 B-47Es. In addition to ECM equipment installed in individual bomber aircraft, beginning in 1953 SAC converted 51 B-47Es into dedicated, unarmed electronic warfare escorts as part of the BLUE CRADLE program using an unmanned pod in the bomb bay (they retained their tail guns). Finally, SAC acquired 50 B-47E ECM Phase V 'Capsule' escorts which carried a two-man pod in the bomb bay to provide an even more responsive strike force ECM escort.

In April 1953 SAC approved Project TURN AROUND for 114 B-47Es already off the assembly line and 'conditionally accepted' without installation of ECM gear, as well as all B-47Es from Blocks 55-75 from Boeing-Wichita, Blocks 1-25 from Douglas-Tulsa, and Blocks 10-40 from Lockheed-Marietta. These airplanes received a minimal Phase I ECM capability limited to the simultaneous jamming of two pre-set signals using the AN/APT-5A L-band radar jammer. Early plans to include the AN/ALT-3 communication jammer were abandoned after it was determined that Soviet interceptors were decreasingly using HF radio and were instead relying on VHF communications. As such, the AN/ALT-3 would be obsolete even before it became operational. B-47B 51-2200 served as the ECM

B-47B 51-2200 became the primary ECM test and evaluation aircraft at Eglin AFB, measuring power consumption, antenna interference, and internal structural requirements. The tail and wingtips were painted red. *Author's collection*

Installations Suitability platform, assessing everything from physical layout of the ECM equipment to its electrical demands to antenna interference.

By late 1953 Boeing began installing Phase II ECM gear in B-47Bs from Blocks 40-50 along with B-47Es that had not previously been equipped with Phase I gear (which were retrofitted with the AN/APT-5A jammer, first used during the Second World War). ECM gear new to Phase II included the AN/ALE-1 chaff dispenser and the AN/APS-54 wide-band (D through I) radar-warning indicator. The AN/ALE-1 was an improved version of the World War Two era A-6 dispenser, utilizing a more powerful motor and a better 'system of rollers to draw the chaff bundle tapes through the dispenser.' The dispenser was placed in the fuselage compartment originally used for the internal ATO. B-47 chaff normally dispensed at 10fpm (3mpm) with eight chaff bundles used every 1nm (1.9km). In addition, several new types of chaff were evaluated which not only masked the B-47 from ground radars but, SAC planners hoped, would offer a modicum of protection against radar-guided missiles.

'Project 27: B-47 Chaff Corridor' began on 9th April 1954 due to multiple problems with the chaff system, including strips hanging up on a fuselage-mounted UHF radio antenna, improper scattering and clumping when dispensed at the B-47's operational speeds, and inadequate radar blockage at 70Mc. The 376th BW from Barksdale AFB, LA, SAC's ECM test and evaluation unit (described below) had a low access priority at APGC at Eglin AFB, so tests with the radars there proved elusive. Further tests revealed that with higher release altitudes and speeds the chaff cloud was correspondingly less effective. Even under optimal conditions it lasted only 15 minutes, hardly enough time for multiple waves of bombers to penetrate

Soviet radars. Chaff guard radomes were manufactured locally at Barksdale AFB to cover the UHF antenna.

Additional test flights took place on 3rd and 11th March 1955 where the B-47E deployed chaff at random points and times, as well as over pre-planned areas. Continuous chaff-laying missions took place on 25th January and 9th March 1955, with the B-47 deploying a constant stream of chaff along its flight path. Tests on 13th April and 20th April 1955 were canceled due to weather and scheduling conflicts, respectively. The weather issue was troublesome, as SAC had long planned to rely on darkness and bad weather to evade Soviet interceptors. A mission on 27th April involved seven B-47s, and eight on 27th May. Despite these tests SAC had yet to resolve its chaff-laying strategy.

The AN/APS-54 display was little more than an arrangement of lights that indicated the quadrant of the threat radar, with an additional red light indicating a radar lock on. By March 1954 most of the AN/APS-54 units were 'completely unreliable' due to installation errors and excessive transmitter crystal burnout caused by other electronic equipment on the airplane, specifically the bombing K system and the A-5 tail gun radar. Testing continued, with four flights between 18th June and 23rd July 1954 totaling 22 hours. Beginning 9th February 1955 SAC evaluated the system under simulated combat conditions, involving a B-47 and up to four F-86Ds. The system worked only one out of six times, but no cause could be determined. Just as important as failing to warn of detection it gave false positive warnings. In May 1955 there were three missions involving two, three, and five B-47s, all of which resulted in total failure due to jamming, both by the 'hostile' radar and adjacent Stratojets.

Other critical weaknesses included wires melting or shorting as they passed next to the cabin heat spill valve, rendering the system useless across the fleet. As of 1st May 1955, for example, 42 out of 45 aircraft at one wing had inoperable AN/APS-54 systems. Failure of the AN/APS-54 due to improper installation was so widespread that it necessitated depot-level correction. SAC finally informed Boeing about the installation errors in November 1954 – some eight months after discovery – reflecting the poor level of coordination between SAC and Boeing regarding deliveries of new and modified aircraft. Moreover, it was utterly 'useless' when jammed. 'Auxiliary Project 35: Modification of AN/APS-54 for Automatic Self Protection Chaff Dispensing' began 1st December 1954. When the AN/APS-54 detected a gun-laying radar aimed at the B-47, the AN/APS-54 would turn on green lights at the copilot's station,

Table 3-5. **ECM Phase Development**

	Year	Capability	Aircraft Affected
Phase I	Early 1953	AN/APT-5A L-band jammer	B-47Es 51-2357 through 52-0176, 52-0202 through 52-0361, and 52-0508 through 52-0564
Phase II	Late 1953	AN/APT-5A L-band jammer, AN/ALE-1 chaff dispenser, and AN/APS-54 radar warning receiver	B-47Bs 51-2192 through 51-2356, B-47Es 52-0158 through 52-0201, and 52-0312 onward
Phase III	1954	AN/APT-9 and AN/APT-16 D/E/F-band jammer, AN/ALE-1 chaff dispenser, and AN/APS-54 radar warning receiver	B-47Bs 51-2092 through 52-2356, B-47Es 51-2357 through 52-0507, 52-0565 through 53-1924, 53-2028 through 53-2144, and 53-2261 through 53-4236
Phase IV	1955 - 1957	AN/ALT-6, -7, and -8 multi-band jammers, AN/APT-9 and AN/APT-16 D/E/F-band jammer, AN/ALE-1 chaff dispenser, and AN/APS-54 radar warning receiver	B-47Bs 51-2192 through 51-2356, B-47Es 52-0158 through 52-0201, 52-0312 through 52-0507, and 52-0565 onward
Phase IVa	1955 - 1957	AN/ALT-6, -7, and -8 multi-band jammers, AN/APT-9 and AN/APT-16 D/E/F-band jammer, AN/ALE-1 chaff dispenser, and AN/APS-54 radar warning receiver	B-47Bs and variants 51-2092 through 52-2356, B-47Es 51-2357 through 52-0507, and 52-0565 onward. All RB-47Es, RB-47Hs 53-4280 through 53-4309, 53-6247 and 53-6248, and all DB-47Bs
Phase V	Early 1956	See Table 3-8	50 B-47Es
Phase VI	Mid 1956	AN/ALT-6B multi-band jammer, AN/ALE-1 chaff dispenser, and AN/APS-54 radar warning receiver	RB-47Hs 53-4280 through 53-4309 and 53-6247 and 53-6248, and ERB-47Hs 53-6245, 53-6246, and 53-6249

alerting him to dispense chaff. This program was designed to automate this process. By April 1955 problems with the AN/APS-54 appeared to be resolved as a series of test flights with an F-86D demonstrated generally satisfactory results. However, this proved illusory. Indeed, SAC planners wondered if the system, even if it worked perfectly, would provide the crew with sufficient warning time of a radar lock.

Gradual improvements to automated 'sweep jamming' meant that ECM gear could cover multiple bands without the need for pre-set frequencies used by barrage jammers. Beginning in June 1954 Boeing Wichita began the HIGH NOON program (including upgrades other than ECM, described above), which lasted some two years and modified 161 B-47Bs. These B-47Bs received the Phase III ECM fit, distinguishable by the addition of external antennas on the aft fuselage for the AN/APT-9 and AN/APT-16 ECM gear. From June 1953 through October 1954 B-47E 51-2412 served as the ECM Phase III testbed. As part of Phase IV and Phase IVa modifications beginning in June 1953 (with B-47E 51-7043 as the prototype), Boeing implemented Engineering Change Proposal (ECP) 2760MK in 1955 to provide additional ECM equipment to some of the Phase III aircraft, as well as installation of side-looking AN/ALT-6, -7, and -8 antennas and a rearward-facing QRC-25 antenna on most of the remaining B-47 variants, including RB-47Es, RB-47Hs, and DB-47Bs. Deliveries of ECM equipment and supply stocks were notably inadequate. Some airplanes in a unit were equipped with only warning receivers and chaff while others had jammers as well. Fully configured airplanes tended to be placed on alert, leaving few available for training. This chronic shortage was finally alleviated by 1957.

Additional ECM improvements took place under Project DEEP RIVER beginning in 1962 to provide advanced ECM for 94 aircraft of the 301st BW and 376th BW. As part of Mod 1200, Douglas-Tulsa started work on two prototype aircraft in July 1962, with a projected fleet-wide cost of $14,820 per airplane, plus $659,426 for labor, technical data, ground equipment, and spares. Absence of equipment affected the planned rollout date of late August 1962, but SAC went ahead with its inspection of the first prototype on 29th-31st August despite the missing ECM gear. The second prototype was not ready until the first week in October. Plans to begin modification to the Lockbourne AFB aircraft slipped from October to November 1962 due to the lack of the new QRC-158 antennas, black boxes, and ground equipment, as well as the crisis in Cuba, considering that most of the B-47s slated for upgrade were instead on alert.

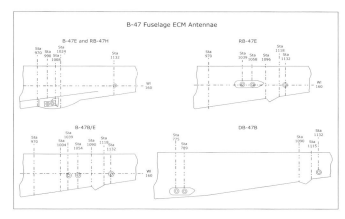

Deliveries of the various QRC-158 antennas (eg, -158-6, -158-7, and -158-10) were still not resolved in January 1963, and by mid February SAC's lack of optimism forced it to delay the operational date for the aircraft to 1st July 1963. 'Slippage beyond this date,' SAC officials warned, 'will result in slippage of the [North American Air Defense Command (NORAD)] SNOW TIME [penetration mission] schedule or operation [of the B-47s in wartime] with limited effectiveness.' Contracts for the antennas were finally awarded in July 1963 but deliveries would not begin for another 90 days (the exception was the -7 antenna, which required *25 weeks* to manufacture and deliver). Field teams completed the basic modifications by early March 1963 but the airplanes would be incomplete until all the antennas were delivered and installed.

Two concurrent ECM upgrade programs were Mod 1198 MIL RUN and Mod 1205 SLICK CHICK (not to be confused with the 1954 SLICK CHICK RF-100A overflight program). Both encountered problems similar to those in DEEP RIVER, adversely affecting not only those 94 B-47s but an additional 198 B-47Es. Reorganization of the procurement agencies meant that the November 1961 purchase request for the AN/ALR-18 transmitter was inadvertently combined with similar requirements for the B-52. In true bureaucratic fashion the B-47 component was then canceled by the B-52 agency. On 25th February 1962 OCAMA authorized the expenditure of $211,250 for a new contract. Technical disagreements between the Warner-Robins Air Materiel Area (WRAMA), which was responsible for the procurement of the AN/ALT-22 transmitter for Mod 1205, and Aeronautical Systems Division (ASD) led to further delays.

Above: ECM antenna placement on the aft fuselage of the B-47 differed by variant and time. As ECM technology evolved the transmitters changed from multispectrum 'barrage' jammers to transmitters that focused on specific threat bands.

Right: B-47E 51-7043 served as the Phase IV and IVa ECM prototype platform. Seen here in ARDC markings as a JB-47E, it was also the prototype for the Phase V manned ECM program, with the bomb bay bulge easily discernable. *Author's collection*

Initial plans called for the MIL RUN and SLICK CHICK modifications to be completed by field teams at each base. In October 1962, however, WRAMA directed that Douglas-Tulsa perform the installation, but Douglas demanded $1,881 per aircraft, double the contracted estimate. Already behind, SAC consented and work began 21st January 1963. Douglas-Tulsa would modify 98 aircraft and a Lear-Siegler Company field team would modify 286 airplanes, nearly 100 more airplanes than originally planned. A month later, on 25th February, the Air Force cut funding for the program from 384 aircraft to the original 292. Despite SAC's objections to this reduction, Douglas-Tulsa ultimately converted only 87 B-47s and Lear's field team modified only 205 airplanes. Interestingly, 38 airplanes assigned to the 100th BW required 'certain [unspecified] variations' from the basic kit design, necessitating additional engineering and delays. The final aircraft was not completed until July 1963 due to a wing crack.

The program delays for DEEP RIVER, MIL RUN, and SLICK CHICK had profound implications for SAC's readiness. SAC officials admonished OCAMA, WRAMA, and Douglas-Tulsa that 'the combat effectiveness of the B-47 fleet is at an unacceptable level until Mods 1198 and 1200 are complete.' Moreover, SAC warned that without DEEP RIVER the 'B-47 has a minimal penetration capability until Mods 1198 and 1205 are completed. Considering the number of B-47s involved, this [decreased] penetration capability has a significant impact on our EWO capability.'

ECM Escorts

In response to Power's February 1951 critique of the B-47's inadequate defensive capability, Boeing offered a manned capsule to be placed in the bomb bay of an escort B-47 much like the PORCUPINE or GUARDIAN ANGEL escort B-29s used against Japan. The capsule would hold four ECM operators and jamming equipment. SAC considered the Boeing proposal, but strongly preferred instead that each B-47 have autonomous ECM capability and carry an atomic weapon rather than four crewmen in the bomb bay. By February 1952 the Boeing proposal had gained serious traction, however, although SAC officials were concerned that it would take four years to reach operational units. In an effort to accelerate ECM escort deliveries, Boeing recommended an interim bomb bay pallet that was unmanned, carried additional jammers, and required less engineering and redesign efforts than a manned pod. An April 1952 meeting at Wright-Patterson AFB concluded by rejecting the four-man capsule, recommending instead a two-man capsule. By July ARDC called for the 'expeditious development' of the two-man pod with the 'utmost importance,' noting that the 'ECM pod enjoys the same overriding IA priority as the B-47 aircraft itself.' Despite this announced level of urgency, it would be two years before Boeing finally delivered the cost-analysis of the two-man pod. Historian Dan Kuehl called the manned pod program a 'technical nightmare' that 'required redesigning virtually the entire B-47 electrical system.' Foremost among these issues was the need for an emergency egress capability for the electronic warfare officers (EWOs), which was eventually resolved by the addition of downward-firing ejection seats. Pending the completion of the two-man pod initiative, SAC and Boeing moved ahead with an unmanned palletized ECM bomb bay pod known as BLUE CRADLE.

SAC originally envisaged one capsule-equipped escort B-47 for each bomb-carrying B-47 (totaling more than 1,000 capsule airplanes), but this number was eventually reduced to just 101 manned and unmanned ECM escorts. SAC tactical doctrine eventually settled on two BLUE CRADLE unmanned airplanes in each cell of 15 B-47s. In addition to their jamming capability, the escort airplanes were intended to carry decoys that mimicked the radar signature and operational characteristics of the B-47. Assuming that the decoys, including the planned McDonnell GAM-72 Green Quail

and the Fairchild XSM-73 Bull Goose, would overwhelm Soviet defenses and dupe radar operators and intercept controllers, SAC planners believed that 'if the defenses could be saturated by a factor of two, the kill probability against the [B-47] might be reduced by as much as half.'

By September 1953 the protean BLUE CRADLE pod was under development as part of 'Auxiliary Test Eight' undertaken by the 376th BW at Barksdale AFB (it was later redesignated as 'Project 25: ECM Bomb Bay Rack for B-47 Aircraft' in November 1953). This involved the local design and manufacture of a pod using 'parts on hand' to carry 24 full racks of ECM gear and 30 cartons of chaff (later 16 racks and 60 cartons) which could be loaded in less than two hours using standard bomb hoists. With the pod removed the airplane could once again carry atomic weapons. Total cost for the BLUE CRADLE program included $100,000 for preliminary engineering, $8,524 per airplane in parts and 500 man-hours of labor costing $2,630 for a total of $526,923. The BLUE CRADLE pod weighed 7,000 lb (3,175kg) and had two configurations based on chaff dispensing rates. The A configuration dumped chaff at a constant rate, while the B configuration – planned for September 1955 – used intervalometers to allow for variable dispensing rates. The BLUE CRADLE pod was equipped with removable wheels and a tow bar for ground handling. Bomb bay doors used for the YRB-47B photographic pod replaced the standard B-47 doors, substituting flush-mounted antenna and openings for the chaff chutes in lieu of camera openings. Flush-mounted plates covered these openings when the pod was not carried, and it could be installed in any B-47 once simple modifications were made to the doors. Plans for the ECM pod were delivered to ARDC on 6th January 1954 for validation, and handling tests undertaken using EB-47B 51-2300. Douglas-Tulsa was awarded the manufacturing contract to build the pods, and 376th BW aircraft were scheduled for conversion as pod carriers at Douglas-Tulsa. Tests of the pod's ECM equipment began in November 1953, with 14 AN/APT-5 and AN/APT-9 jammers in the cradle. During an early test against a radar site at Palermo, NJ, the pod provided effective jamming for two minutes until a number of the subsystems failed in sequence.

The BLUE CRADLE jets were operational with the 376th BW at Lockbourne AFB from July 1954 through 1965. Initial service proved challenging, as they experienced a substantial problem when six bomb hoist beams broke over a period of five months. 'Auxiliary Project 32: Suitability Test of Blue Cradle' was instituted on 1st September 1954 to determine the cause and corrective action. The problem was traced to improper installation technique by ground crews, and additional training alleviated the problem.

Table 3-6. BLUE CRADLE Aircraft

Converted 25 Mar-26 May 1954				
52-0394	52-0403	52-0413	52-0422	52-0431
52-0395	52-0405	52-0414	52-0423	52-0433
52-0396	52-0406	52-0415	52-0424	52-0434
52-0397*	52-0407	52-0416	52-0425	52-0435
52-0398	52-0408	52-0417	52-0426	52-0437
52-0399	52-0409	52-0418	52-0427	52-0439*
52-0400	52-0410	52-0419	52-0428	52-0440
52-0401	52-0411	52-0420	52-0429	52-0441
52-0402*	52-0412	52-0421*	52-0430	52-0454
Converted Nov-Dec 1955				
52-0467	52-0468	52-0469	52-0471	
Converted by Apr 1958				
52-0446	52-0447			
Total	51			

* Aircraft written off – for dates and further details see Appendix II

Ongoing BLUE CRADLE test flights in April and May 1955 showed that with four T-6 ECM units in the BLUE CRADLE pod, two T-8 units in the ATO compartments, and two QRC-27(T) jammers, ground radars could reliably skin-paint the BLUE CRADLE B-47Es from as far as 100nm (185km) away. Out of 10 test missions involving flights of up to six BLUE CRADLES there were only two confirmed 'kills', but these were by interceptors after making visual identification rather than those which relied exclusively on ground radar control. Again, at night or during bad weather the jamming capability proved highly effective, but in daylight against a numerically superior interceptor force the B-47 was highly vulnerable, even with ECM.

The BLUE CRADLE escorts were surprisingly effective once the technical bugs were resolved. During one exercise in 1957, 14 escorts created a corridor for a massive night penetration of B-47s from Canada against Boston, New York City, and other major East Coast cities. Flying at 25,000-30,000ft (7,620-9,144m), the BLUE CRADLE aircraft were interspersed among the bombers with all aircraft radiating ECM, creating a huge 'blob' on ground radar screens. This 'blob' proved to be an easy target for US and Canadian radars, and in the post-mission critique NORAD officials gloated that they 'killed everybody' by simply 'firing' SAMs in salvo mode at the 'blob', and by sending interceptors to 'attack' the massed formation. The reality was far different. Indeed, all 14 BLUE CRADLE jammers were 'shot down', but the bombers they escorted reached their targets unseen. One by one the bombers turned off their ECM, disappeared from the ground radar screens amid the strong BLUE CRADLE ECM signature, descended rapidly to 1,000ft (305m), and then proceeded undetected to their targets. For bomber crews the exercise was compelling proof of the value of ECM escorts and low-altitude tactics. For the BLUE CRADLE crews, the exercise demonstrated in no uncertain terms that they were truly expendable. Other missions using BLUE CRADLE aircraft, such as TEXAS LEAGUE and BIG WIND in late 1955 and early 1956, tested US and Canadian capabilities to detect and destroy hostile bombers.

Interestingly, on 21st September 1955 the Air Force approved the evaluation of an RB-47E converted into an escort ECM platform. The proposal called for hanging a pod 5ft (1.5m) below each wing between the inboard nacelle and fuselage. Each pod, measuring 30in (76cm) in diameter and 20ft (6m) in length, would carry either two chaff dispensers or three unspecified ECM transmitters and receivers 'providing ECM coverage in all directions.' They could also be adapted to carry forward firing chaff rockets when they became available. By the end of the year the external wing pod proposal had progressed sufficiently that it was designated as Phase VIII ECM, and B-47E 53-4238 – rather than an RB-47E – was modified between 31st May 1956 and 26th April 1957, although it is unclear if this was for just the TEE TOWN program or if it included evaluation of the wing pods. Boeing was reluctant to proceed, however, as the lack of test data on the chaff distribution pattern (especially close to engines), antenna radiation and reception patterns, weight and balance studies, and the structural integrity of the pod, strut, and wing presented significant unknown considerations. Considering that no B-47E appears to have been modified to carry these pods, the Phase VIII program presumably was canceled.

Douglas-Tulsa carried out another ECM modification of 100 B-47Es during 1958-1959. Known as TEE TOWN, this included the installation of long tubular ECM pods on each side of the rear fuselage (some aircraft were reported with the pod on only one side). These airplanes had ECM capability similar to the BLUE CRADLE jets while retaining the ability to carry weapons. The TEE TOWN aircraft were not given a new designation, and were operated by the 303rd BW, 43rd BW, 100th BW, and the 509th BW.

Table 3-7. TEE TOWN B-47Es

52-0149	52-0296	52-0461	52-0527	52-0592
52-0150	52-0310	52-0465	52-0528	52-0598
52-0160	52-0311	52-0473	52-0530	53-1820
52-0161	52-0313	52-0474	52-0531	53-1821
52-0162	52-0319	52-0479	52-0539	53-1825
52-0165	52-0325	52-0480	52-0540	53-2029
52-0167	52-0326	52-0481	52-0542	53-2030
52-0168	52-0332	52-0483	52-0545	53-2032
52-0169	52-0334	52-0484	52-0551	53-2033
52-0170	52-0337	52-0485	52-0553	53-2037
52-0171	52-0339	52-0486	52-0554	53-2279
52-0176	52-0351	52-0487	52-0566	53-2286
52-0192	52-0354	52-0491	52-0569	53-2293
52-0193	52-0360	52-0492	52-0577	53-2296
52-0195	52-0365	52-0498	52-0578	53-2298
52-0199	52-0374	52-0507	52-0582	53-2306
52-0201	52-0375	52-0519	52-0584	53-2308
52-0230	52-0376	52-0524	52-0588	53-2310
52-0293	52-0377	52-0525	52-0589	53-2312
52-0294	52-0404	52-0526	52-0591	53-2313

509th BW, TEE TOWN B-47E 52-0540 sits on alert in the UK. The pod, which reputedly provided ECM equivalent to the BLUE CRADLE B-47s, provided both additional ECM as well as a normal weapons load. *Author's collection*

Front quarter and frontal view of the TEE TOWN pod. White area is fiberglass antenna cover. Note small flat antenna on top in front of the pylon. *William T Y'Blood*

Phase V

Evaluation of the Phase V manned capsule ECM aircraft began in June 1953 using B-47E 51-7043 as the prototype (there are unofficial references to this capsule as 'Brown Cradle', which was a similar capability on the Douglas EB-66). Structural modifications included electrical power, pressurization, and temperature control, as well as the installation of two downward-firing ejection seats within a capsule contained in the bomb bay. Electrical connections from the ECM receivers and transmitters to displays and controls in the capsule were challenging to install. AN/APS-54 warning lights, normally at the copilot's station, were duplicated in the capsule, along with the controls to dispense chaff. Each EW had a Panoramic ECM indicator and controls for two of three ECM systems (AN/APT-6, -9, or -16). Antennas for equipment operating above 200Mc were flush mounted within the capsule fairing on the lower fuselage, while those below 200Mc were located at the wingtips or external stubs.

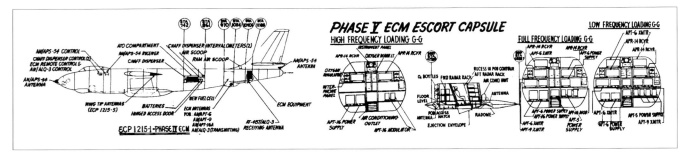

Each airplane 'carried up to eight slow-sweep jammers in a variety of configurations depending on the radar frequency coverage required,' as well as six additional barrage jammers and two more chaff dispensers. The 50 Phase V aircraft were initially assigned to multiple units, but by 1959 were all assigned to the 301st BW, also at Lockbourne AFB, through 1964.

Above: Official proposal drawing for the Phase V manned bomb bay pod ECM escort. Three cross sections ('G – G') show different configurations which could be installed prior to flight. *via Wai Yip*

Below: Phase V EB-47E 53-2412 on alert at RAF Brize Norton on a snowy day in 1962. Capsule bulge on bomb bay is clearly visible. Red tarpaulin over windscreen prevents ice and snow buildup. Thermal curtains are also in place, with the last curtains closed after takeoff. *Augustine Letto*

Table 3-8. **Phase V ECM**

Receivers	Two AN/APR-9 D/E/F/G/H/I band
	Two AN/ALR-18 threat detection
	One AN/APR-14 panoramic threat detection
	One AN/APS-54 threat detection
Chaff	AN/ALE-1
Jammers	Nine AN/ALT-6B E/F band
	One AN/ALT-6B G/H/I band
	One AN/ALT-6B D band
	One AN/ALT-7 20-310Mhz sweeping
	One AN/ALT-8B E/F band
	One AN/ALA-7 pulse generator
Later Generation Jammers	QRC-49 E/F band
	QRC-65 VHF communications
	QRC-95 E/F band
	QRC-96 D band
	QRC-139 used with AN/ALT-22
	(improved AN/ALT-6B) for use against SA-2
	AN/ALT-13 D/E/F/G/H/I band
	AN/ALT-15 A/B band (an improved AN/ALT-12)

Table 3-9. **E/B-47E Phase V Capsule Aircraft**

53-1881	53-1945	53-2131	53-2401	53-2413
53-1883	53-1963	53-2133	53-2402	53-4207
53-1886	53-1966	53-2135	53-2403	53-4210
53-1889	53-1968	53-2137	53-2404	53-4214
53-1900	53-1969	53-2138	53-2406	53-4215
53-1915	53-2121	53-2164	53-2407	53-4220
53-1929	53-2124	53-2168	53-2408	53-4221
53-1930	53-2126	53-2169	53-2410	53-4229
53-1940	53-2127	53-2383	53-2411	53-4242
53-1942	53-2128	53-2388	53-2412	53-6234

As one former Phase V pilot recalled, 'On tactics, we never had a racetrack EWO profile [between Leningrad and Moscow]. We were to fly from England at high altitude in a flight of five or six, maybe 20 miles apart, weaving and crossing flight paths so as to confuse the [Soviet] air defense controllers while the first wave strike force was going in at low altitude. Our path was going east while staying south of Moscow and recovering to Adana [Turkey. When launched from] Lockbourne we were to cover the second wave of bombers and soak up surface-to-air missiles for them. I don't think anybody ever thought we would complete the whole mission and, even if we did survive, we didn't really expect that there would be anywhere left to land. General nuclear war would have been truly nasty.'

Evaluation
This chronology of B-47 ECM acquisition and operations might easily suggest that it was largely the passive beneficiary of early advances in electronic warfare. In fact, SAC and the B-47 were crucial to the development and testing of both ECM equipment and the tactics necessary to use it effectively. With the increasing emphasis on electronic warfare during the formative years of the Cold War, SAC had committed an entire bomb wing to the development of ECM equipment and tactics. The 376th Bombardment Wing (BW) at Barksdale AFB served as SAC's primary ECM wing using B-29s in the standoff jamming role, and it routinely flew Unit Simulated Combat Missions (USCM) in conjunction with other SAC assets. From 24th to 27th July 1952, for example, the wing's B-29s flew to Kindley AB, Bermuda, then launched a 'diversionary ECM attack' on Washington DC along with other SAC bombers, including B-36s and B-47s. The ECM B-29s were successful in diverting a large number of interceptors away from the main bomber force, but were only marginally successful in accomplishing 'electronic jamming of GCI-fighter VHF communications.' During December 1952, 376th BW B-29s tested a new 'sweeping' jammer against an Eglin AFB-based F-94 equipped with a Russian RSI-6M-1 receiver acquired from a Yakovlev Yak-3. Results were encouraging on a technical level, with effective communication jamming up to 79nm (146km). Other initiatives included Project 20 GLOW WORM, where a pyrotechnic device or an 'electronic glow tube' could generate a light of sufficient intensity and brightness as to induce temporary blindness of a night-fighter pilot. The first test took place on 1st October 1953 using B-29 '290' (believed to be RB-29A 44-62290, later the prototype for the Airborne COMINT Reconnaissance Program – ACRP) and a Lockheed T-33. Results were encouraging. On a moonless night, interceptor pilot blindness lasted for 20 seconds at ranges up to 2,000 yards (1,828m), and with a full moon blindness faded after 10-12 seconds. On an operational level, however, the B-29s were clearly outdated and incapable of keeping up with the jet-powered B-47s, and temporarily blinding a fighter pilot was ineffective against radar-guided weapons. Consequently, SAC decided to upgrade its premier ECM unit to be on par with its new medium bomber.

On 9th September 1953 SAC's Second Air Force stipulated in a classified supplement to the 376th BW's organizational charter that

SEND OFF took place in October 1955. B-47s from the 2nd BW and thekck

in addition to maintaining its 'capability in normal strategic bombardment operations,' it would also fulfill a 'secret mission [to] develop and test both tactics and ECM techniques, and as a result of these tests recommend to Headquarters SAC, requirements for equipment, including that necessary to counter guided missiles, and the adoption of appropriate tactics and techniques by the Command.' The wing was also tasked to conduct 'ECM cover and diversions in support of strategic bombardment operations.' SAC also decreed that the B-29s would be phased out and scrapped, replaced by new B-47s. One squadron would convert to B-47s 'as soon as possible', with delivery of its first 10 B-47Es no later than 1st January 1954, just three months later. Additional squadrons would convert as aircraft became available. There were no slots available at the pilot and maintenance schools to meet this unexpected levy, however, so SAC directed that the first B-47 deliveries would begin in April or May 1954. The wing would be operationally ready by September 1954, although this was for its primary bombing mission rather than its secret ECM evaluation and escort missions.

The first use of an ECM B-47 in simulated wartime conditions took place on 9th April 1953 when 17 376th BW B-29s and a lone B-47 from WADC supported an attack by a force of 12 B-36s on Eglin AFB in Operation BLACKOUT. The B-47 and one B-29 laid chaff ahead of the B-29 ECM aircraft and the B-36 bombers flying at low level. The B-29 was unable to dispense 70% of its chaff, and the altitude and speed differential between the B-29 chaff laydown and the B-47 laydown meant that the chaff corridor was insufficiently dense and inadequately distributed to allow for a complete blinding of ground-based radar. Nonetheless, the B-47 chaff laydown effectively screened the first three B-36 waves from early warning and ground-controlled intercept (GCI) radars, allowing an uncontested attack on Eglin AFB. In addition to validating SAC's new low-level bombing tactics, BLACKOUT acknowledged the importance of the B-47 in ECM operations, and planners urged the assignment of additional chaff laying B-47s to the 376th BW to develop further tactics and to achieve operational readiness.

During July 1955, 376th BW B-47s took part in PICKET FENCE, an operational evaluation of the unit's bomber escort capability. Over a three-day period, 15 ECM escorts flew to Maine and back while jamming three ADC S-band radar sites. The B-47s were able to jam only two of the three sites, in part due to the 40nm (74km) distance between cells, which reduced their mutual jamming protection. Moreover, there were no standard B-47s in these gaps, which would have added additional ECM capability. Technical problems were equally rife. Some 10% of the AN/ALT-6 transmitters were accidentally turned off before takeoff rendering them useless, and an additional 25% failed before or during the flight. Over half of the AN/ALT-8 units failed completely. A follow-on mission known as

SEND OFF took place in October 1955. B-47s from the 2nd BW and the 306th BW joined the ECM escorts from the 376th BW as they returned from England. Results of the 12th October mission were impressive. The BLUE CRADLE airplanes and standard B-47 ECM gear created a corridor 250nm (463km) wide and 300nm (556km) deep, resulting in complete disruption of GCI radars and leaving them incapable of determining 'the type formation, tracks, or number of strike aircraft.' A mission on the following day dramatically emphasized the value of ECM escort. Bad weather precluded the use of ECM, and GCI radars and fighters 'effectively nullified the strike forces.'

Efforts to defeat hostile electronic warfare systems included far more than simply active jamming. Navigating a B-47 to its target required the observer to use the radar for ground mapping. Computing a position from a single sweep of the radar was not possible, so the radar had to function continuously as the observer plotted one point, did the math and calculated the position, and then repeated the process. The ongoing radar emission raised the likelihood of hostile detection of the B-47. To solve this problem SAC asked the 376th BW to find a way to allow the observer to operate the radar for a single sweep and then use the image to calculate the airplane's position. At the time, there was no mechanism for 'freezing' a radar scope image, so the 376th BW used the next best thing. 'Project 29: Use of Land Camera for Navigation with AN/APS-23' began 30th June 1954 and continued through May 1955. This used a Polaroid Land camera to photograph the scope and, one minute later, produced a print of the scope for the observer to use, eliminating the continuous radar transmission that could allow passive detection of the B-47.

'Project 30: Development of a Passive Station Keeping Capability' was meant to facilitate formation flying over long distances by alleviating pilot fatigue induced in manually maintaining precise formation for extended periods and in radio silence. Tests used infrared missile seekers in an attempt to determine if they could be linked to the autopilot, allowing for automatic and precise positioning in radio-silent conditions. Flight tests began in January 1955 using a 500-watt infrared quartz lamp and the GAR-1B Falcon infrared tracking head, but these proved unsatisfactory.

As the B-47E faced mass retirement in 1964 and 1965, efforts to resolve or upgrade their ECM capability became, at first glance, meaningless. The implications for the B-52 and any follow-on bomber, however, were profound. The missteps and errors and failures that plagued the evolution of B-47 ECM capability served to attenuate similar problems in developing the B-52 ECM capability. Indeed, the B-52 was originally designed without an electronic warfare officer, and LeMay's insistence in adding an ECM specialist was significantly influenced by the inadequacy of the strictly automated ECM capability of the B-47.

Table 3-10. **Phase V B-47E Distribution**

	1 Jul 56	1 Jan 57	1 Jul 57	1 Jan 58	1 Jul 58	1 Jan 59	1 Aug 59
2nd BW		9	9	9	4		
44th BW	13	10	10	10	2		
68th BW	1	3	3	3	3		
100th BW	1	1	5	5	5		
301st BW					17	36	50
307th BW	8	8	8	8	6	1	
308th BW	9	9	9	9	9	1	
376th BW		3	3	3	1		
509th BW	3	3	3	3	3		
Undelivered	15	4				12 (IRAN)	
Total	50	50	50	50	50	50	50

26th SRW had 4 but transitioned to 301st BW 15 Apr 58

Radio Relay

Throughout the late 1940s popular rhetoric warned of an 'atomic Pearl Harbor,' and US military leaders were keenly aware that it was only a matter of time before the continental US would be vulnerable to a 'bolt from the blue.' As Lieutenant General James H 'Jimmy' Doolittle opined, this threat would come from a robust Soviet nuclear weapons arsenal with airplanes configured for aerial refueling to deliver them, estimated to happen around 1955. Soviet bombers such as the Tupolev Tu-4 *Bull* (a reverse-engineered B-29) could reach targets in the northern United States from bases in the Chukotskii Peninsula only on one-way 'suicide' missions. The jet-powered Tupolev Tu-16 *Badger* and the turboprop Tupolev Tu-95 *Bear*, however, could reach virtually all SAC bases and civilian targets in the United States. Thanks to the radar warning sites that comprised the Distant Early Warning (DEW) line, running from locations in England, Greenland, Canada, and Alaska, US commanders would have several hours' advance warning of any impending Soviet bomber attack, and could act accordingly to launch SAC's own bombers on a retaliatory strike.

This luxury all but disappeared on 4th October 1957 when the Soviets orbited the *Sputnik* satellite. The R-7 *Semyorka* rocket which boosted the first satellite into space was the same SS-6 *Sapwood* intercontinental ballistic missile (ICBM) which could carry a thermonuclear warhead to targets in the United States. Even with the construction of the Ballistic Missile Early Warning System (BMEWS), American commanders would have at most only 30 minutes' advance warning of a Soviet ICBM attack. During this time, the US president and his advisors would have to understand that an attack was under way and reach a decision on what action to take. As the Soviets had already made the decision to plunge the world into nuclear winter by launching a nuclear first strike, it remained for the president to reach a simple decision – retaliate or not. Few doubted that President Dwight D Eisenhower would direct SAC to launch its bombers and tankers, hopeful they would get airborne before the first ICBM warheads reached SAC bases. After a variety of test programs associated with ground alert and rapid mass launches of aircraft, SAC determined that it needed 15 minutes from presidential notification to launch until the alert aircraft were airborne. That left the president and his advisors only 10-12 minutes to decide the fate of the world. The advent of submarine launched ballistic missiles (SLBMs) cut this time dramatically, leaving perhaps just 5 to 15 minutes total time from initial detection to first impact.

Suddenly the potential for an atomic Pearl Harbor seemed quite real. Aside from the vulnerability to Washington, DC, and the National Command Authorities (NCA – the president and his senior civilian and military advisors), SAC headquarters was at risk of pre-emptive destruction by land- and sea-based ballistic missiles. This meant SAC's commanders would be unable to launch a retaliatory strike. Moreover, as the US war plan evolved from a one-shot nuclear strike ('wargasm') to a more selective strategy based on changing requirements during and after the initial exchange of weapons, SAC would be unable to manage its nuclear strike force once its

underground headquarters at Offutt AFB, NE, was destroyed. Among other options, SAC established an airborne command post (ABNCP) fleet using five KC-135As configured with communications gear and a battle staff headed by a SAC general. Known as LOOKING GLASS, it began operations in 1960 and broadly 'mirrored' the capabilities of the underground command post at Offutt AFB. Beginning in April 1962 this was expanded to include three KC-135A auxiliary command post (AUXCP) units. The AUXCPs were assigned to tanker squadrons based at numbered air force (NAF) headquarters with the Eighth Air Force at Westover AFB, the Second Air Force at Barksdale AFB, and the Fifteenth Air Force at March AFB where they assumed ground alert and would launch upon declaration of Defense Condition (DEFCON) 2 (or higher) or as directed by the CINCSAC, providing a good measure of redundancy to the continuously airborne LOOKING GLASS orbiting somewhere over the Nebraska-Kansas border. Collectively these KC-135s were the aerial component of System 481L, the Post Attack Command and Control System (PACCS), providing SAC with the 'essential capability to exercise effective and flexible command, control, and direction of strategic operations following a sustained high-order thermonuclear attack.'

Once airborne, the East Auxiliary Command Post (EASTAUX – call sign *Grayson*) would orbit over Wilkes-Barre, PA. The Central Auxiliary Command Post (CENTAUX – call sign *Achieve*) would orbit over Arkansas, Oklahoma, and Texas. The West Auxiliary Command Post (WESTAUX – call sign *Stepmother*) orbited northeast of Las Vegas, NV, generally over the Grand Canyon to the Nevada-Utah border. These allowed the ABNCPs to communicate directly with SAC bomber (and later missile) units in their geographical regions, ensuring they would receive the launch message directed by the president even if SAC headquarters was a 'smoking, radiating ruin.'

Tests prior to operational deployment of the AUXCPs revealed a crucial weakness. The distance between *Stepmother* and the LOOKING GLASS and SAC Headquarters, for example, was nominally 947nm (1,753km), well beyond the range of existing ultra-high frequency (UHF) radios. Even with long-range high frequency (HF) radios it was not always possible to establish and maintain a connection between the AUXCPs, SAC's commanders at Offutt AFB, and SAC bases in remote geographical areas. This prompted SAC on 20th July 1962 to organize four EB-47L PIPECLEANER radio relay squadrons at Mountain Home AFB, ID, Lincoln AFB, NE, Lockbourne AFB, OH, and Plattsburgh AFB, NY. Each unit was slated to have nine airplanes (although the final strength varied), with nine EB-47Ls on 15-minute ground alert (two from each base except Lockbourne AFB, which had three). The EB-47Ls could then provide a UHF link between AUXCPs as well as relay messages to SAC bases in close proximity.

Originally intended to be known as Airborne Communication Relays (ACRES) assigned to Airborne Communication Relay Squadrons (ACRS), SAC commanders felt this revealed too much about its mission capabilities and decided instead on establishing EB-47L Support Squadron (SS), similar to the Douglas C-124 Globemaster units that hauled SAC personnel and equipment as well

Table 3-11. **EB-47L PACCS Squadrons**

Squadron	Air Division	Wing	Base	From	To
4362nd SS	818th SAD	307th BW	Lincoln AFB, NE	20 Jul 62	31 Dec 63
4362nd PACCS	818th SAD	307th BW	Lincoln AFB, NE	01 Jan 64	24 Dec 64
4363rd SS	801st SAD	376th BW	Lockbourne AFB, OH	20 Jul 62	31 Dec 63
4363rd PACCS	801st SAD	376th BW	Lockbourne AFB, OH	01 Jan 64	25 Mar 65
4364th SS	813th SAD	9th SAW	Mountain Home AFB, ID	20 Jul 62	31 Dec 63
4364th PACCS	813th SAD	9th SAW	Mountain Home AFB, ID	01 Jan 64	25 Mar 65
4365th SS	820th SAD	380th BW	Plattsburgh AFB, NY	20 Jul 62	31 Dec 63
4365th PACCS	820th SAD	380th BW	Plattsburgh AFB, NY	01 Jan 64	24 Dec 64

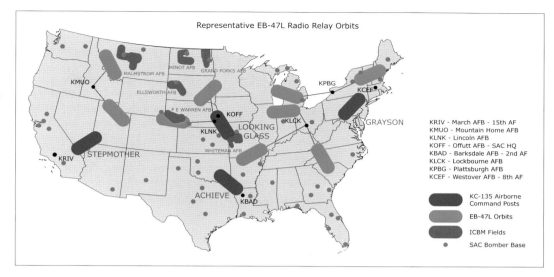

Right: PIPECLEANER EB-47Ls provided the radio link between the KC-135B airborne command posts to ensure secure connectivity between SAC's senior commanders and individual bomber and missile units.

Below: The primary radio gear for the EB-47L was installed in pressurized containers in the bomb bay. The PIPECLEANER jets did not have a combat mission *per se*, and instead would remain over the US in the event of general war, earning the units the nickname 'Doomsday Squadron'.

as nuclear weapons. The designation was changed on 1st January 1964 from Support Squadron to Post Attack Command Control Squadron (PACCS), leaving little doubt about their mission. The airplanes were assigned directly to SAC Strategic Aerospace Divisions (SAD), and the local B-47 wing provided only 'administrative, personnel, and maintenance support' for the EB-47L squadrons. Operationally the units reported directly to the SAC Headquarters Command Post. Their motto was *Vox Clarus Sum*, which liberally translates from the Latin to 'Message loud and clear.' The EB-47Ls were also reportedly (and unofficially) nicknamed 'Noah's Arc', a pun referring to a radio connection.

During late 1961 two B-47Es (52-0292 and 53-2329) were selected from the aircraft assigned to the 4347th CCTW to serve as proof-of concept aircraft. Texas Engineering and Manufacturing Company's (TEMCO) Aerosystems Division carried out the modification at its Greenville, TX, facility. Electronic Communications, Inc (ECI) manufactured the three (originally two) AN/ART-42 frequency modulated (FM) multiplex radio receivers, each installed in separate pressurized containers at the front end of the bomb bay, and three (originally two) AN/ARR-68 receivers located in the aft bomb bay. A small ram air scoop was located on the right bomb bay door, with an additional inlet and outlet

(positioned open or closed) adjacent to the door centerline. TEMCO removed the ECM transmitter systems, the AN/APS-54 radar warning system, the AN/ALE-1 chaff dispenser system, the tail guns and AN/APG-32 gun-laying radar (replaced by a simple tail cone), and the gun controls from the copilot's station, replacing them with the control heads for the three AN/ARC-89(V) UHF receivers. Two of these were used in normal operations with the third acting as a spare or in case of jamming. In addition to the radios and attendant equipment, the EB-47L carried a 5-minute tape recorder, which could record the Emergency Action Message (EAM) broadcast by the Emergency Rocket Communication System (ERCS) or an updated EAM broadcast by a SAC ground or airborne command post. Cost for the two development aircraft was some $2.6 million.

Flight tests were scheduled to begin on 17th August 1962, but 'development and bench-checks' of the redesigned equipment fell behind schedule. The first test flight finally took place on 4th September. While these tests were underway, contract difficulties arose over specifics of the air conditioning capability and who was responsible for costs. OCAMA recommended that until these were resolved, TEMCO should begin modifying aircraft with a final delivery date of May 1963 (later slipped to June). On 25th October, SAC concurred. By 1st January 1963 TEMCO had delivered only

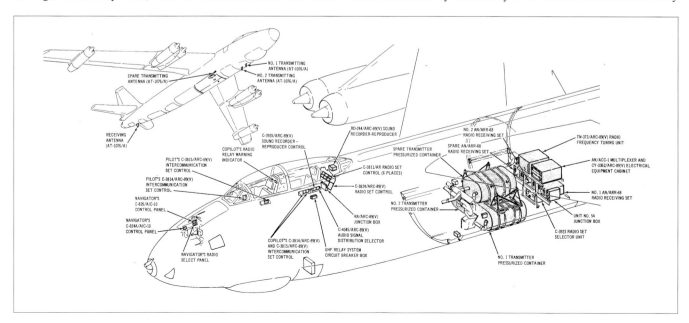

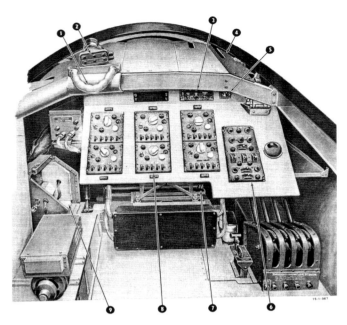

With the tail gun gear removed, the PIPECLEANER copilot controlled three AN/ARC-89(V) UHF receivers and a tape recorder which could transmit EAMs. The radio equipment was temperamental prompting maintenance personnel to fly along, hardly suitable in an EWP scenario.

three of the programmed four scheduled aircraft due to technical difficulties with the AN/ART-42 transmitter as well as mechanical problems on the aircraft. These unspecified issues were discovered on airplanes which had been sent to TEMCO for modification but had been in temporary storage for up to six months. The problem with the AN/ART-42 was the result of TEMCO's improper handling and installation of the unit rather than any inherent technical issue with the radio. ECI rebuffed TEMCO's claim of faulty manufacturing by pointing out, for example, that 21 radios returned to ECI 'bore TEMCO acceptance stickers indicating they apparently worked upon receipt.' Without further acrimony, ECI and TEMCO discreetly resolved the AN/ATR-42 issue, and TEMCO completed the final EB-47L in June and delivered it to SAC on 2nd August. Ironically, Secretary of Defense McNamara told Congress on 30th January 1963 that '…all of the [EB-47L] communications relay aircraft are already in operation.' In fact, this was not true as it reflected the original planned date rather than the actual delivery schedule.

During May 1963, SAC requested installation of an additional UHF system in response to jamming caused by other transmissions. OCAMA agreed, and on 1st July 1963 recommended installation of the third AN/ATR-42 radio. These were retrofitted to the entire fleet.

There is some contention over the number of EB-47Ls. According to TEMCO documents, the contract called for a total of 38 conversions,

EB-47L 52-0309 awaits the scrapper's torch at MASDC. The ram air intake on the bomb bay door is clearly visible. EC-135L radio relay jets replaced the EB-47Ls, resulting in their retirement after just barely two years in service. *Author's collection*

Table 3-12. **EB-47Ls**

52-0031	52-0066	52-0099	52-0220	52-0309
52-0033	52-0067	52-0105	52-0224	52-0510
52-0034	52-0069	52-0154	52-0291	52-0513
52-0035	52-0071	52-0204	52-0292	53-2329
52-0038	52-0078	52-0211	52-0298	
52-0041	52-0081	52-0212	52-0303	
52-0059	52-0082	52-0214	52-0305	
52-0061	52-0086	52-0217	52-0308	

including the two prototypes. In fact, only 36 were actually modified. B-47E 52-0057 was scheduled to be reconfigured to PIPECLEANER standards but apparently suffered from unspecified maintenance issues and instead was relegated directly to storage at Davis-Monthan AFB. The other unconverted EB-47L has not been identified.

The PIPECLEANER crew included the aircraft commander, copilot, and navigator, with the copilot assuming full responsibility for the radio relay duties as well as his own regular tasks. One advantage of being on an EB-47L crew was that whenever the klaxon blew on alert, chances were good that the decoded message would direct the PIPECLEANER aircraft to launch to practice establishing the link and exercise their PACCS functions. The rest of the alert force would shut down and head back into the alert facility and grumble that they were not flying. Occasionally a radio maintenance technician would fly along on training sorties to trouble-shoot the equipment which was prone to problems associated with water condensation inside the bomb-bay containers. Following a mission, according to former PIPECLEANER radio maintenance technician Master Sergeant Thomas E Bowman, the pods were opened and drained and the equipment 'removed to the field shop for drying out and operational testing before reinstalling on the airplane. A monumental task to say the least!' Another problem area was cooling and pressurizing the containers. A refrigeration unit cooled hot bleed air from the engines, ensuring the containers would remain below 155°F (68°C), with additional thermal regulation achieved by opening and closing the inlet and outlet doors. The radio containers were at ambient air pressure as the airplane climbed through 8,000ft (2,438m), at which point that pressure was maintained through 43,000ft (13,106m). Above 43,000ft, the system maintained a maximum differential of 8.8psi between the ambient air and the containers. By and large, however, the radio equipment 'either worked in flight or it didn't'.

In a rare opportunity to evaluate the EB-47Ls under simulated wartime conditions, the two PIPECLEANER prototypes using crews assigned to the newly activated 4362nd PACCS at Lincoln AFB were seconded to the DOMINIC US atmospheric nuclear test in the South Pacific. EB-47Ls 52-0292 and 53-2329, call signs *Baxter* and *Byron*, respectively, took part in the 9th July 1962 STARFISH-PRIME shot (see Chapter 7). Performance of the EB-47Ls was badly compromised by failure of the air conditioner unit to cool the radios, a harbinger of the maintenance nightmare to follow. The air conditioning failure prompted OCAMA to stop the modification process until TEMCO could resolve the issue.

The longevity of the PIPECLEANER program was brief. Plans to phase out the B-47 fleet coupled with the approval of additional KC-135 radio relay aircraft spelled the end of the 'Doomsday Squadron' EB-47Ls. During the FY65 budget planning cycle, Secretary of Defense McNamara told President Lyndon B Johnson that he 'concurred with the Air Force proposal to substitute 10 KC-135A aircraft for 36 EB-47Ls. It would significantly reduce O&M [operation and maintenance costs] and personnel expenditures while providing more effective and flexible capabilities.' The 4364th PACCS was the final unit to dispose of its aircraft, sending the three remaining EB-47Ls (52-0038, 52-0212, and 52-0298) to Davis-Monthan AFB on 26th March 1965.

CHAPTER FOUR

'By the Book'

When many former B-47 pilots recall their experiences with the airplane they share a common theme: '…when flown by the book.' 'It was a pleasure to fly, when flown by the book.' 'It was a safe airplane when flown by the book.' 'Those were my best days in SAC as long as we flew by the book.' The irony in these remembrances is that 'the book' – the B-47 Dash One flight manual – evolved along with the airplane. In some cases it was 'right on the money' but in others it was unhelpful or even dangerous. The Boeing engineers and test pilots who developed the Dash One could not account for every possible scenario that a crew might encounter while flying the world's first medium swept-wing multi-jet bomber. This meant that crews often improvised 'techniques' to achieve what the 'procedures' omitted. For example, some units developed and used nonstandard fuel burn sequences while on the ground prior to takeoff or during air refueling. Some units even published supplementary manuals that specified procedures not covered by the Dash One. While they may have seemed effective, they lacked the validation by rigorous testing to determine consequences that were not obvious to pilots but were ominous to engineers. Indeed, five B-47Es (51-7073, 51-15805, 52-0339, 52-0402, and 52-0562 – see Appendix II) were lost in cg-related accidents.

Why was cg management so critical? What was so different about the B-47 that managing its fuel burn sequence could prove disastrous if mismanaged? The answer lies in the B-47's design, as the B-47 stored nearly all its fuel in the fuselage. There were no internal wing fuel tanks as with previous SAC bombers. With too much fuel (and hence weight) in the forward section, the aircraft would be difficult to get off the ground or would pitch abruptly downward when landing. With excessive fuel concentrated toward the tail, the nose would rotate so steeply on takeoff the airplane would almost certainly stall, or would be uncontrollable during air refueling. Even the mere sloshing of fuel in partially filled tanks at light gross weight and aft cg could cause a startling abrupt pitch up! Relatively small errors in fuel loading or fuel system management could easily cause the cg to go outside controllable limits. SAC crews were cautioned to not trust their gauges while on the ground and to have the fuel tanks 'dip-sticked' before takeoff, as well as to carefully manage fuel in flight.

SAC's commitment to standardization led to everything about the B-47 being done 'by the book.' Ground mat specifies where each crewman's gear should be placed for pre-flight inspection, a tough procedure in the rain or snow. *USAF*

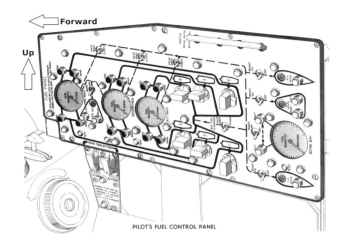

Crowded B-47 cockpit meant nonstandard layout for many instruments. In this case, the pilot's fuel panel was difficult to read precisely without the pilot craning his neck. After time, fliers learned to adjust.

This was particularly important when an inoperative engine necessitated a change from normal fuel management procedures. Even the fuel panel on the pilot's right side panel was problematic. It was vertical with the 'top' at the front of the side panel, requiring the pilot to tilt his head 90° for an accurate reading of the gauges. Consequently, any variation from 'the book' risked a catastrophic event that could claim both airplane and crew.

Other design problems presented similar challenges. The swept wing created handling issues for pilots. A yaw damper effectively limited the Dutch roll, but pilots still had to be aware of the powerful rolling moment that even relatively small amounts of yaw would cause with the swept wing, requiring prompt and effective control. The most common source of yaw was variation in engine thrust, especially from the loss of an outboard engine. This required the pilot to counter the asymmetrical thrust and resulting yaw by pushing on

Should SAC have to launch its bomber force without its crews adjusting to circadian rhythms, fliers often departed on training flights without adequate rest, a testament to crews that there were fewer accidents due to exhaustion. 330th BS crew from Castle AFB climb aboard (l) to (r) Captain Nick S Koss (N), Captain Eugene C Caughlan (CP), and Major Ben H Clements (AC). *USAF*

the appropriate rudder pedal. Too much corrective rudder – or a 'tap dance' on the rudder pedals – could result in a dangerous roll ending with total loss of control. Test pilot Bob Robbins worried that former B-17 and B-29 pilots had to get over 'rudder laziness' and master the delicate feel of the rudder, complicating their transition to the B-47.

These two examples reflect the many operational challenges faced by B-47 crews. Nearly everything about the airplane was new, and SAC did not always respond wisely to these unforeseen problems. SAC's rigid hierarchical crew structure placed the burden of control and authority solely on the aircraft commander (AC). The copilot, stuck in the back seat, could do little to assist in case of emergency other than read the checklist or offer suggestions that often fell on deaf ears. Crew resource management (CRM) techniques that would improve safety and reduce accidents in commercial airliners were still nearly a half-century in future. In addition, SAC ignored problems associated with circadian rhythm, leading to exhausted crews flying day and night sorties indiscriminately. To be fair, SAC commanders understood that should a wartime launch come its crews would not necessarily be well rested and would need to function under duress. It is hard to imagine, however, any more stressful situation than flying a thermonuclear strike mission, and as it often did SAC took matters to the extreme to simulate wartime conditions (or to excuse questionable command decisions).

SAC's reluctance to recognize this organizational dilemma was driven by traditional 'rank-has-its-privileges' beliefs, the demand for pilots – however competent – to fill seats in the B-47, and the pseudo-wartime mentality that its bombers would have to be ready to strike whether crews were rested or not. This is not an indictment of B-47 pilots in general; rather it is the recognition that some B-47 ACs were simply not fit to make the transition from B-29s or B-36s and the multiple crewmen who supported their flying to the B-47 where the AC was, in many ways, 'flying solo'. Former fighter pilots lacked the ability to work with the B-47's crew. SAC tended to overlook suggestions from copilots, and navigators were simply along for the ride in cases of loss of control due to poor airmanship by the AC. One need only to examine the many accidents in Appendix II to see how many were caused by the AC's poor judgment – taking off with flat tires, improper abort procedures, or confusing wing condensation with fire. On the whole, however, B-47 crews performed admirably under austere conditions, flying airplanes that were not fully ready for operations, and in a command where 'the book' often took precedence over common sense.

'SAC from the Bottom'

For many of SAC's future leaders flying the B-47 became a steppingstone toward promotion in rank or increased command responsibilities. A challenging airplane to fly well (and safely), a number of B-47 pilots and navigators progressed to other, more demanding aircraft. Not surprisingly, many were among the initial cadre of B-52 and B-58 crews, bringing their jet bomber experience to support the early operational deployment of SAC's two newest bombers. Two of the first SENIOR CROWN SR-71 crews were both B-47 alumni: Crew 10 was pilot Major Jerome 'Jerry' O'Malley and reconnaissance system operator (RSO) Captain Ed Payne, while Crew 11 was pilot Major Don Walbrecht and RSO Captain Phil Loignon (O'Malley would rise to four-star rank and become Commander, Tactical Air Command – COMTAC – before his tragic death in a North American T-39 crash in 1985).

This career enhancement for B-47 pilots was not, however, widely distributed. Indeed, a small number of B-47 crewmembers and maintenance personnel – especially copilots – disliked their assignment. Part of this antipathy was the result of their exposure to the B-47 and part derived from their assignment to SAC. For some pilots dragooned into SAC, either directly from pilot training where they dreamed of being fighter pilots or from jet fighter and interceptor units which were culled for high-time jet pilots to meet SAC's unending demand for experienced pilots to fly the nearly 2,000 B-47s which passed through its inventory, their time in B-47s was a bad memory. The problem was not limited to fliers. A SAC history from the early 1950s warned of the loss of experienced B-47 jet engine mechanics because *their wives* were unhappy with the quality of family life in SAC, which no doubt contributed directly to a dismal 24% retention rate.

For others, especially those with an established career in SAC flying B-29s, B-36s, or B-50s, a chance to fly the B-47 was a dream-come-true that finally put them on an equal footing with their peers in Tactical Air Command (TAC) and Air Defense Command (ADC) who flew jet-powered fighters and interceptors. The vast majority of B-47 crewmembers and 'wrench turners' who spent their time in SAC flying and maintaining the B-47 were satisfied with their assignment. Understanding the highly vocal battle between the two extremes is essential to appreciating the drain of experienced personnel in SAC and the consequences for US national security.

Then-Brigadier General Earl G Peck, writing in a June 1975 *Aerospace Historian* article, recalled, 'Looking back, although much of the flying I did in the B-47 was not particularly enjoyable – in fact it was tedious, demanding, and even grueling at times – [but] it was rewarding in terms of professional satisfaction.' Peck was assigned directly to the B-47 from pilot training in 1958. After three years in B-47s at Pease AFB he transitioned to the B-52 at Homestead AFB. Following a variety of staff assignments (but not including command of operational units) he was eventually promoted to Major General two years after his article was published. Peck's essay is certainly not an apologia for the B-47 as he covered many of the airplane's shortcomings. It did, however, provoke a variety of responses, most notably a detailed rebuttal in the same journal in March 1987 by former B-47 copilot Dennis K McDaniel entitled 'The B-47 From the Back Seat, SAC from the Bottom – One Pilot's Account'. [McDaniel says he was assigned to a different squadron than Peck at MacDill AFB 'at the same time in the late 1950s,' but Peck's official biography shows that he was not assigned to MacDill AFB at any time.]

McDaniel's critique begins with his 1958 graduation from 'advanced…training in the F-84F and F-100' when, he says, 'suddenly all [240] of my classmates…were *en bloc* transferred to B-47 school.' It is not surprising that they would have a 'chip' on their shoulders for this 'great injustice at the sudden demotion to bombers.' He adds that the 'six B-47 slots in [his] graduating class [at pilot training] had gone basically to the bottom students in the class.'

Aside from the disenchantment associated with the switch from a single-seat fighter to a multi-engine bomber, McDaniel derided SAC's absolute and monolithic obsession with rules, many of which made little sense in an evolving aviation world. For example, a copilot could not make a back-seat landing unless his aircraft commander had 350 hours in the airplane. As many new ACs lacked that much time, copilots simply watched from the back seat. Given that crews often flew only three times a month and that at the time touch-and-go landings were prohibited, most ACs chose to land in order to maintain their currency. For a brief time, copilots seldom – if ever – got to land. Ultimately, McDaniel's hostility toward the B-47 and SAC reached a crescendo in a spate of letters to *Aviation Week* written 27 years before his rebuttal to Peck.

Beginning on 30th May 1960 – in response to an unrelated letter critical of SAC's harsh lifestyle – B-47 aircraft commander First Lieutenant Thomas D Lambert wrote 'When SAC calls, there is a

For some new copilots and former jet fighter pilots, a B-47 assignment was undesirable. Most adjusted to their new careers, but more than a few found life as a SAC copilot to be an unsatisfying experience. Parachute inspection prior to a first flight in a TB-47B (l) to (r) Major Robert G McNary (IP), Captain Rondo R Pietscher (P), and Major Pierre A Tisdale (P). *USAF*

thing called DUTY to be attended to and one comes a-running.' McDaniel's reply, published auspiciously on 4th July 1960, was bitter. 'A few hours per month spent reading checklists from the back seat of a B-47 does not, in my humble century series-bred opinion, constitute satisfactory flying anyway.' The response was not surprising. McDaniel was grounded and chastised for 'publishing material without prior clearance'. He was invited to submit his resignation and on 23rd August, some six weeks after his letter was published, became a civilian (he later returned to flying with the Indiana Air National Guard as a Republic F-84F and RF-84F pilot). Subsequent letters were critical, if not downright hostile. First Lieutenant Ernest A Boehler, Jr, wrote on 18th July 1960 that 'today's professional aircrew has no place for any person unable to accept responsibility and the entire Air Force, especially SAC, can do better without this officer.' Conversely, First Lieutenant Robert O Boardman agreed with McDaniel. 'I can't help but think that my college degree, regular commission and two years of training [in F-100s] are being wasted on a job which could be done by any normally bright high school boy after two months.' SAC provided no opportunity for leadership or initiative, he added, '…with SAC I have generally found that rank below that of Lt. Colonel means very little except for pay, an occasional "sir" and a rather rare salute.' Not surprisingly, the letter-writing campaign ended as Lieutenant Colonel (!) William K Callam, a staff officer at Air Force Headquarters with seven years in SAC, did exactly what McDaniel described in his critical *Aerospace Historian* article – Callam blamed the squadron and wing commanders for not 'indoctrinating' (a term later known as 'SAC-umcising') the young lieutenant with the importance of undertaking his B-47 copilot duties blindly and without question.

Lest anyone conclude that this diatribe was just from one disgruntled fighter jock assigned to a SAC B-47, many of these issues were widely known over a number of years. In a 26th March 1956 letter to *Aviation Week*, for example, a SAC KB-29 copilot complained of the poor state of his aircraft and the misuse of his experience as an aeronautical engineer relegated to being a copilot that only read the emergency procedures checklists. SAC senior commanders appreciated this improper use of pilot resources, even if its rank-and-file officers did not. In the declassified *The B-52: Background and Early Development, 1946-1954*, writing about the 1951 requirement to build the B-52 with side-by-side cockpits, SAC officials noted that 'the tandem arrangement reduces the copilot to the role of flight engineer operating emergency flight controls' and reading checklists. In *Holding the Hand of Darkness*, former SAC B-47 copilot Arthur Hood recounts a story similar to that of McDaniel. 'I won't get much stick time in [the B-47], I thought. It was obvious that my job during flight was to operate the guns and the electronic countermeasures equipment, do all the paperwork, and worst of all perform the celestial navigation… During the last two flights my control yoke had been unlatched and stowed except for the takeoff, in-flight air refueling, and the landing; even then I didn't really get to use it.' Hood added, 'The only thing with a lower status than me is whale [expletive omitted].'

Hood said that his repeated inquiries about upgrading to aircraft commander were met with an icy glare: 'My chances of advancing

Left: A B-47 pilot adjusts his intercom wafer switch. LeMay understood that the tandem cockpit was ill-suited to crew coordination and copilot morale, as well as needlessly duplicated many instruments. He insisted that the B-52 have a standard 'airliner' cockpit instead. *Photo BW91437 courtesy Boeing*

Bottom left and center: B-47 copilots became proficient at 'shooting the sextant' to assist the observer in celestial navigation or using the gunnery simulator and firing the guns when loaded on training flights. For those who wanted to *fly* the B-47 this was never enough, but it taught skills that would enhance their crew coordination once they eventually became aircraft commanders. *USAF*

Bottom right: Back-seat landings were difficult but not impossible. The AC and his ejection seat blocked the view forward, plus the nose-high attitude during the final approach and flare further obscured the runway. *Author's collection*

to aircraft commander seemed faint. There still were majors riding in the copilot seat and they were far ahead of lieutenants in the line for advancement to the front seat.' At last, Hood was transferred to a KC-135 as an AC, but not without some consternation. 'More than four years in the back seat of that bomber, with only an occasional takeoff or landing, had eroded my sparse flying skills.' His predicament was not unique. The Castle AFB KC-135 instructor pilots 'were accustomed to B-47 copilots being short on most flying skills… They understood that these copilots might excel at gunnery, electronic countermeasures, and navigation but had little opportunity to actually fly an airplane during their stay in the B-47 program.'

In the superb collection of memoirs *Boeing B-47 Stratojet: True Stories of the Cold War in the Air* edited by Mark Natola, most of the stories include at least one, if not several, harrowing experiences. To be sure, there are plenty of great 'there I was' stories and suspicious tales of crew antics, but conspicuously absent are glowing testimonials to the airplane and SAC. For most B-47 personnel the airplane was the best available at the time to fulfill SAC's critical nuclear mission. They understood the gravitas of nuclear weapons and agreed that LeMay's 'by the book' approach was the best choice to ensure nuclear safety and prevent an inadvertent accident. There were several nuclear accidents with the B-47, but none of these was the result of failure to follow regulations, inherent flaws in the design of the B-47, or abysmal 'satisfaction level' of its crews. Indeed, LeMay wisely rejected the tandem seat arrangement of the XB- and YB-52 in favor of a side-by-side cockpit (first proposed in a variant of the YB-47C) that provided a far better learning and operational experience for SAC copilots.

During 1959 the author's father was a First Lieutenant flying North American F-86Ds in ADC with 1,000 hours in jets when he was

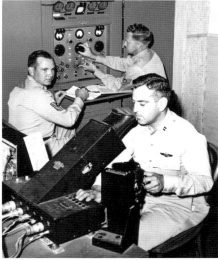

reassigned to SAC as a B-47 aircraft commander. When asked his favorite airplane to fly – ranging from Republic P-47s to de Havilland C-7s – he chose the B-47. 'It handled like a fighter, was a challenge to fly, and in the front seat you felt as if you were alone in a fighter. No, I would *not* have been happy sitting in the back seat.' Many readers with B-47 experience will agree that not everyone loved the airplane or SAC (and there were plenty who loved their time in the B-47 community), but all will agree that the mission was of grave national importance. Exactly how each person viewed their contribution to its fulfillment of that role remains equally contentious.

In all of these cases – good or bad – the critical component was local leadership. Aircraft commanders who understood that part of their job was to train their replacement worked hard to ensure that copilots acquired both the knowledge and the flying skills to make a smooth and efficient transition to the front seat. ACs also learned how to manage a crew to work together as a team to foster camaraderie and bolster crew morale. Squadron commanders who understood that a positive attitude was linked to an appreciation of the mission made sure to inculcate new crewmen with the seriousness of SAC's mission and that, to paraphrase LeMay, 'flying fighters is fun, flying bombers is important.' Wing commanders who understood that SAC was often working without the full resources it needed – especially during the transition to the B-47B in its early years – made sure to communicate that the wing's priority was America's priority, and cultivated subordinates who shared a vision that SAC was the 'A Team' which ensured US national security in a time of Cold War insecurity. To be sure, there were disgruntled fliers and maintenance personnel, and the levels of dissatisfaction varied over time. Ultimately a unit's morale was linked to the quality of leadership at all levels. For the vast majority of SAC B-47 personnel, that leadership was appropriate and made the best choices available under difficult circumstances.

SAC never did get its act together on B-47 personnel issues. By late 1963, as the B-47 was spending its final days in service, the Air Force projected that it needed 6,300 pilots in the 40-45 year age group (typically lieutenant colonels or higher) but there were 13,700 on duty. For senior pilots (aged 45 or greater) there were 6,300 in service with a requirement for only 450. Among the youngest pilots, ages 23-30 – mostly lieutenants and captains – there were 19,000 pilots against a requirement of only 9,500. Nearly all of these pilots were made redundant by the retirement *en masse* of the B-47. Secretary of Defense Robert McNamara declared even these requirements would decrease. Between FY64 and FY68, the 'overall pilot requirements will decrease from 41,000 to 18,000 – mainly because of the SAC [B-47] phasedown.' What McNamara failed to plan for was the future war in Southeast Asia. Many of the young B-47 pilots would soon find themselves in other airplanes over the jungles and rice paddies of Vietnam.

Flying the B-47

For SAC crews a B-47 flight began the day prior to the mission. In the absence of computerized flight plans, the navigator would complete the preflight plan with – among other tools – his Weems E6-B 'whiz wheel' circular slide rule, along with a bombing data sheet. The copilot would then plod through charts in the 11 Appendices in back of the Dash One to determine the airplane's weight and balance (Form F) and compute planned takeoff and landing data estimated for the next day's departure. Using the course data provided by the navigator, the copilot would then complete an aircraft performance sheet that listed optimal cruise altitudes, the amount of fuel burned for each leg, added during any air refueling, and the amount remaining after practice approaches and landings. He also prepared the pilot's flight progress chart to record the actual status of the mission.

Sequence of photos showing a typical preflight of a 67th BS B-47 from Lake Charles AFB. Aircraft commander Major Roy L Miller briefs navigator Captain D E Washmon (l) and copilot First Lieutenant R N Saye (r). Miller then conducts the walk-around inspection of the airplane with Crew Chief Airman First Class J R Barrette, checking, *inter alia*, that all panels are closed and sealed and that nothing is leaking. During engine start an unidentified assistant crew chief checks for ignition on engine #5. Although the fliers 'got the glory', the B-47 belonged to the crew chief and his team who often worked without recognition for their efforts to 'keep 'em flying'. *USAF*

On flight day the crew gathered their professional gear – helmets, parachutes, publications, and an inedible box lunch – and then attended weather briefings prior to heading to the airplane. They arrived at the jet some three hours prior to takeoff, more than enough time to complete the requisite checklists. Once again, SAC created inefficiency in B-47 operations. On-time takeoffs became a critical metric for SAC commanders to determine if its bombers and tankers

ATO departures were dramatic events designed to improve the B-47's marginal takeoff performance. They were fraught with potential danger of explosion or fire, and by the end of the B-47's operational life were rarely used in training. Note that this B-47E has an internal rack but is using the external 'horsecollar'. *Photo courtesy Boeing*

were ready to launch in case of an actual war order. Unfortunately, local units abused this in order to meet daily requirements. When the flight crew discovered a problem, the excessively early arrival at the jet easily allowed maintenance sufficient time to fix it before scheduled takeoff time. This masked the reality of what SAC's bomber force could actually do – there would be no time to fix broken jets during an EWP launch – and eventually during USCMs and ORIs alert airplanes that could not launch immediately were scored as aborts.

Takeoff in the B-47 created new challenges for the AC. Jet engine thrust was nearly constant throughout the takeoff roll, and the B-47 did not experience any propeller-related torque as power was increased on the jet engines. The bicycle landing gear placed the airplane in the proper pitch attitude for takeoff, obviating the need to rotate ('unstick' was used instead). The B-47 could use two different types of thrust augmentation – ATO and water injection – to shorten the takeoff distance and allow higher gross weights.

At the start of the takeoff roll, the AC held slight forward pressure on the control column and advanced the throttles to 100% rpm. Each takeoff roll included a decision speed (known as S_1) at which the AC would make the determination either to continue the takeoff or, due to any number of adverse factors, abort the takeoff. A number of pilots learned the hard way that any abort after decision speed would

'in all probability result in failure to stop on the runway,' causing the loss of airplanes and lives. At the calculated takeoff speed the AC released the forward pressure (unstick) and allowed the airplane to begin a natural climb and acceleration. This acceleration was not without its own subtle hazards. The J-8 attitude indicator was subject to deviations in pitch based upon acceleration or deceleration, and could indicate as much as 1.5 'bar widths' nose up as the B-47 became airborne 'during the takeoff run when using water injection and/or ATO.' Pilots 'chasing' the command bar ran the risk of improper climbout attitude or pilot-induced oscillation (PIO) during this critical phase of flight, especially at night or under instrument conditions without a visual horizon reference. Similarly, slight variations in AC or DC power or failure of key electrical components did not necessarily cause the red OFF flag to appear on the attitude indicator even though it had ceased to function properly. Again, failure to cross-check the J-8 with the other pilot could lead to significant unusual attitudes or even unrecoverable situations during takeoff and approach at night or bad weather.

For takeoffs with water injection, crews were encouraged to allow the engines to idle for 10 minutes prior to starting the water in order to minimize undesirable fluctuations in exhaust gas temperature (EGT), a procedure typically undertaken at the runway hammerhead

Above: The other method of augmenting takeoff thrust was water-alcohol injection. This required careful mixing of each, and three B-47s were lost due to improper proportions. *Photo P16669 courtesy Boeing*

Right: The two external ATO racks were jettisoned after use during takeoffs. The ATO bottles were more closely spaced on the horsecollar rack, and the split rack eliminated ATO heat on the bottom of the fuselage. If the rack could not be jettisoned after takeoff, the added weight and drag meant canceling the mission.

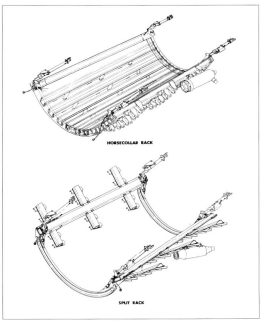

HORSECOLLAR RACK

SPLIT RACK

but unrealistic in wartime conditions. As with a normal takeoff, the AC pushed all six throttles to 100% rpm, after which he would start the water flow. Should any throttle subsequently be retarded to below 96% rpm the water injection for that engine would stop. The water was mixed with methanol at a specified proportion based on temperature and pressure altitude. Injecting this mixture into the engine's combustion chamber increased the mass flow of exhaust gases with a commensurate increase in thrust. The water injection system was designed to provide 80 seconds of additional thrust, but based on environmental and individual aircraft variations, takeoff planning assumed only 75 seconds of water. The system was divided into left and right side with a circuit fault that shut down the functioning side in the event of a failure of the other to prevent asymmetric thrust, but this did not cover all potential malfunctions. At least three accidents (B-47B 51-2139, B-47E 52-0179, and RB-47H 53-6248, see Appendix II) have been attributed to problems during a water-injected takeoff.

For ATO takeoffs the procedure was to 'fire the ATO approximately 10 seconds before takeoff'. To reduce ground roll the ATO could be started 15 seconds prior to takeoff. In either case the reduction in thrust at ATO runout was noticeable, and the AC had to be ready to lower the nose (if airborne) 'slightly before termination of ATO thrust to prevent excessive loss of airspeed.' The original checklist called for the copilot to call over the intercom at the appropriate time to 'Fire ATO.' On one occasion the intercom failed intermittently and all the AC heard was 'Fire!' prompting a near disaster. The checklist was changed to 'Start ATO'. B-47s that used either of the two external ATO racks – known as the 'horse collar' or 'split rack' – jettisoned the rack immediately after runout to avoid unnecessary drag. Doing so in populated areas occasionally resulted in property damage, although no injury or loss of life has been recorded. Many bases had designated jettison areas. Should it prove impossible to jettison the ATO rack the B-47 crew was required to terminate the mission as the added drag would prove too much for fuel burn and endurance.

In each of these cases it is clear that the AC bore the brunt of the takeoff process: forward pressure on the control column, correct throttle management, and starting the water injection or ATO when used, all while steering the airplane and maintaining control under adverse crosswinds or on wet or icy runways.

Once the airplane was airborne the AC directed the copilot to raise the landing gear and the airplane then accelerated to 20KIAS above takeoff speed. Flaps remained down until the airplane was at least 300ft (91m) above ground level (AGL), at which time the copilot raised the flaps while maintaining a 300ft per minute rate of climb. If the B-47 had not yet accelerated to 193-208KIAS, a ram air circuit switch interrupted flap retraction until the B-47 reached this minimum speed range. The airplane then accelerated to 310KIAS for climbout with the engines set at military rated thrust (MRT) of 98% rpm.

Takeoffs from high-pressure altitude, high-temperature airfields at maximum gross weight were exciting, to say the least. Missions were often delayed until night to take advantage of cooler air, hardly an option in an alert response to an attack on the US. ATO was often used, but brought its own set of problems. Many later B-47s crews had only one or two ATO takeoffs in their careers due to costs and losses of airplanes from malfunctioning ATO. In one case an ATO bottle came loose, swung around, and directed its blast at the fuselage. The skin soon burned through to a fuel cell and the whole airplane went up in flames. Three B-47s were lost in ATO-specific accidents (51-2391, 52-0321, and 53-4212 – see Appendix II). Over time SAC and Boeing determined that outside air temperature (OAT) had a significant effect on ATO performance. A 10°F differential between OAT and ATO bottle temperature resulted in a 180ft (55m)

Flaps on the B-47 were essential not only for takeoff and landing where they allowed for slower speeds, but for air refueling where they provided additional lift as the B-47 gained weight behind the slower KC-97. Major Vaun N Lininger (l) and First Lieutenant Prentice H Farris of the 320th BW at March AFB preflight the flaps. *USAF*

difference in takeoff roll. For example, following a chilly night with the bottles installed and a warm morning takeoff, the ATO bottles could not warm up sufficiently to equal the OAT, resulting in an increased takeoff distance.

Still, an ATO takeoff – especially at night – was something to be remembered as this anonymous anecdote from the Air Force Historical Research Agency (AFHRA) Oral History program recounts: 'So at midnight, one o'clock in the morning, the coolest part [of the day], we had six bottles of ATO to give us added thrust to get off the ground. I lined up as the first airplane… The other wing commander, a very good friend of mine, was in the tower that night… and all he saw as I went down the runway was the smoke and a little glitter and he knew the ATO hadn't fired properly because there wasn't the stream of fire coming out of it. I had a bunch of bad bottles. And he saw me disappear onto the overrun and he saw the dust coming off the end of the runway. He just shut his eyes, and then he opened them and he could still see the airplane flying out there about 15ft [4.6m] off the desert [floor]. I had gotten it into the air in the overrun [and then] out through the desert and gotten [high] enough to get the gear up. And when the desert rose, I was able to climb just about as much as the ground was rising… That was enough for him. He left the tower, went home, had three drinks and went to bed, and said, 'I'll never watch another night takeoff as long as I live.'

At altitude there were a few problems awaiting the crew, most notably one that the press found compelling for its nickname: 'coffin corner'. At high altitude the difference between the low-speed and high-speed stall (Mach buffet) was very close together (this is perhaps best associated with the Lockheed U-2's coffin corner). Should the B-47 slow a few knots it would experience a low-speed stall. Should it accelerate a few knots it would enter high-speed buffet and lose control, a problem exacerbated by swept-wing 'aileron reversal', especially as altitude increased. Moreover, SAC pilots were warned not to climb over thunderstorms and were told instead to fly around them. Any intentional penetration of severe weather or turbulence was to be made 3,000ft (914m) below recommended cruise altitude and at 0.74 Mach where there was a safer difference in low- and high-speed stalls.

The long thin wings that made the Stratojet fast also posed a dilemma of control at those speeds. Above 400KIAS the wing warped enough with aileron deflection to cause a noticeable problem. At 440KIAS this effect completely canceled out the ailerons, and above that a roll in the opposite direction could be expected caused by reversal or the 'anti-tab effect.' This aileron reversal occurred above the B-47E-IV structural placard speed limit of 425KIAS or 0.86 Mach and was never considered a significant problem by the Air Force, suggesting why the Air Force declined to install spoilers on the B-47 fleet (see Chapter 7).

To give the airplane good handling qualities, Boeing used a system of Q-springs and centering springs. A 'trim coordination' system was installed to provide the proper relationship between the powered controls and the power-off controls. This was adjusted when the plane left the factory or after maintenance on the controls. After adjustment, the servos that made the proper corrections were unhooked so that inadvertent inputs could not be made. When this small procedure was forgotten, it posed a grave potential for the pilot. If he lost the power controls, he could find himself with a very badly out-of-trim airplane. However, the system normally worked well with no serious problems.

Air Refueling

If there was a single issue that created problems in flight it was the mismatch in performance between the KC-97 tanker and the B-47 receiver during aerial refueling. The piston-powered KC-97 simply lacked the speed necessary to equal the B-47's jet speed, especially as the B-47 increased its airspeed as it took on more fuel (and hence weight). Until the advent of the jet-powered KC-135, B-47 crews followed a fairly routine – but not necessarily desirable – procedure for air refueling.

Normally the KC-97 would orbit 500ft (152m) above the B-47's route of flight and then descend to the planned refueling altitude as the Stratojet approached the rendezvous point. Using a complex formula based on altitude differential, rate of closure, rate of descent, and the time required to decelerate to the KC-97's speed, the B-47 would then descend to an altitude 500ft below the desired refueling altitude. This was hardly a trivial matter, as a premature descent by the B-47 would needlessly burn fuel at the lower altitude and a delayed descent would often result in an overrun of the slower KC-97. As a rule of thumb, the B-47 would descend at 2,500fpm (762mpm) at 330KIAS or 0.78 Mach, allowing for an expeditious (but not aggressive) closure. This decreased until the B-47 was 1nm (1.9km) behind the KC-97 at which point its speed was 'formation'

airspeed plus 25 knots, decreasing again at 0.5nm (0.9km) to formation speed plus 15 knots. Once below 295KIAS the B-47 would open the air refueling slipway door. The B-47 would finally decelerate to air refueling speed. In the case of KC-97E and KC-97F tankers, this speed was 5 knots greater than for the KC-97G. To avoid any overrun of the tanker the B-47 could use S-turns, deploy the flaps, or even lower the landing gear (although the inability to retract the gear after slowing would effectively cancel the mission). In any case, the B-47 would stabilize in the precontact position with a zero rate of closure prior to any contact.

Once contact was made the KC-97 began to transfer fuel at a rate of 3,500 lb/min (1,588kg/min). Should the scheduled offload exceed the 'deck fuel load' of the KC-97 (which carried JP-4 jet fuel in separate deck tanks), the first 70% of the offload would be at 3,500 lb/min, decreasing to 2,500 lb/min (1,134kg/min) for the remaining 30% from the KC-97's other tanks. The B-47 could lower the flaps to 20% to increase lift as it took on more weight; any greater flap extension would be counterproductive due to the creation of more drag than lift. Pilots were warned to maintain an airspeed no less than 20KIAS above stalling airspeed. At a gross weight of 160,000 lb (72,575kg) at 25,000ft (7,620m), for example, this was 186 + 20 = 206KIAS. Following a 44,000 lb (19,958kg) onload, however, this increased to 204 + 20 = 224KIAS (the maximum flaps 20% speed was 236KIAS, demonstrating the narrow airspeed margin at high gross weights). Optimal handling speed for a 200,000 lb (90,718kg) B-47 at 25,000ft was 275KIAS. Although the B-47 was capable of flying 50 knots less at 224KIAS, it was extremely sluggish and required considerable skill to handle it safely during the delicate air refueling process. This problem was not unique to the B-47, as any receiver during a heavy weight refueling becomes 'mushy' at high gross weights. What made it particularly challenging for the B-47 was the inability of the KC-97 to increase its speed sufficiently to obviate the need to refuel while on the extreme 'backside of the power curve.' In some cases the B-47 pilot could direct the tanker to begin a descent of 300fpm (91mpm) – later known as 'tobogganing' – to increase airspeed as the B-47 became increasingly sluggish.

Handling the B-47 was no easy matter, and pilots were instructed not to use the rudder to maintain contact in the receiver envelope. Doing so exacerbated the roll-due-to-yaw feature of the swept wing. Instead, pilots were told to 'drive' the B-47 using just the roll from the control column. Stalls during air refueling were not uncommon,

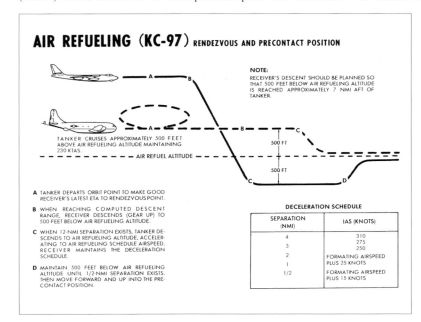

AIR REFUELING (KC-97) RENDEZVOUS AND PRECONTACT POSITION

NOTE:
RECEIVER'S DESCENT SHOULD BE PLANNED SO THAT 500 FEET BELOW AIR REFUELING ALTITUDE IS REACHED APPROXIMATELY 7 NMI AFT OF TANKER.

TANKER CRUISES APPROXIMATELY 500 FEET ABOVE AIR REFUELING ALTITUDE MAINTAINING 230 KTAS.

--- AIR REFUEL ALTITUDE ---

500 FT
500 FT

A TANKER DEPARTS ORBIT POINT TO MAKE GOOD RECEIVER'S LATEST ETA TO RENDEZVOUS POINT.

B WHEN REACHING COMPUTED DESCENT RANGE, RECEIVER DESCENDS (GEAR UP) TO 500 FEET BELOW AIR REFUELING ALTITUDE.

C WHEN 12-NMI SEPARATION EXISTS, TANKER DE-SCENDS TO AIR REFUELING ALTITUDE, ACCELER-ATING TO AIR REFUELING ALTITUDE AIRSPEED. RECEIVER MAINTAINS THE DECELERATION SCHEDULE.

D MAINTAIN 500 FEET BELOW AIR REFUELING ALTITUDE UNTIL 1/2-NMI SEPARATION EXISTS. THEN MOVE FORWARD AND UP INTO THE PRE-CONTACT POSITION.

DECELERATION SCHEDULE

SEPARATION (NMI)	IAS (KNOTS)
4	310
3	275
2	250
1	FORMATING AIRSPEED PLUS 25 KNOTS
1/2	FORMATING AIRSPEED PLUS 15 KNOTS

Left: The B-47 rendezvous with the KC-97 for air refueling was a precisely choreographed affair, both for procedural standardization as well as to manage the mismatch between jet bomber and piston tanker performance.

Above: Once contact was made it became a constant juggling act for the B-47 to stay in position behind the KC-97. Under some conditions there was just a 12KIAS window between recommended refueling speed and maximum flap speed, and the margin narrowed if the tanker could not maintain speed. *Howard Hendry*

TANKER AND RECEIVER FORMATIONS DURING FINAL CLOSURE

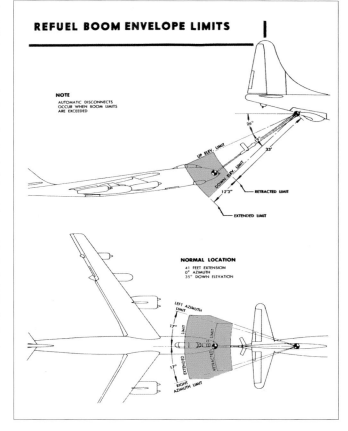

B-47s often took part in mass refuelings, sometimes involving entire squadrons or even wings. Careful positioning of both tanker and receiver was critical, as the B-47s frequently rotated between tankers to maximize onload, and midair collisions were always a danger.

and using any rudder could easily result in the conversion of the stall to a spin, which accounted for four B-47 losses (51-5252, 51-15805, 52-0566, and 52-0761 – see Appendix II). In addition, the copilot carefully monitored the engine rpm and EGT to avoid any compressor stalls. These were fairly common 'during or just after air refueling'. Interestingly enough, this occurred most often on the #4 engine, although Boeing was never able to determine why. Three B-47s (51-2274, 51-2440, and 51-7033) were lost during air refueling due to disintegration of the #4 turbine due to uncontained compressor stall.

It was possible to reverse-refuel from the B-47; that is, transfer fuel from the B-47 to the tanker. In addition, the KC-97 could also transfer its own 100 octane aviation gas (AvGas) to the B-47 in a fuel emergency, but this was a less efficient fuel for the B-47 and did little to extend its range by any significant amount. In one case, a B-47 over the North Atlantic burned more fuel while attempting to refuel from a KC-97 transferring AvGas at refueling altitude than if the B-47 had simply remained at higher cruise altitude.

Refueling from the KC-135 was far less troublesome. Air refueling speed was 275KIAS or 0.71 Mach, eliminating the hazardous speed disparity with the KC-97. In fact, the B-47 could, at higher altitudes and gross weights, actually become 'power limited' while refueling from the KC-135. In this case the tanker could decrease the rate of flow – normally 4,000lb/min (1,814kg/min) for the first 66% of the offload and 3,000lb/min (1,361kg/min) for the final 33% of the offload – or decrease power on the tanker's two inboard engines. In addition, the KC-135 could execute a toboggan maneuver.

Right: The small air refueling envelope became difficult to maintain as the B-47 gained weight from onloaded fuel. Pilot technique was critical to stay on the boom without stalling or entering a spin, both of which were occasional hazards.

REFUEL BOOM ENVELOPE LIMITS

Left: Ironically when the B-47 refueled behind a KC-135 there were conditions when the Stratojet was power limited, but pilots unequivocally preferred the Stratotanker. KC-135A 58-0004 became a KC-135R and was still in service in 2018, attesting to its longevity and the brevity of the B-47's career. *Author's collection*

Approach and Landing

The B-47 differed significantly from piston-powered bombers given its 'high speed, slow deceleration, and relatively flat gliding angle' during landing. The first warning of a stall during approach was 'considerably less' than earlier airplanes, and overreaction would lead to an 'excessive altitude loss'. Traditional stall speeds were 30% below approach speed, eg, 130KIAS approach and 100KIAS stall speed. With the B-47, however, this was reduced to a mere 6 knots, eg, 120KIAS 'touchdown' speed and 114KIAS first stall warning. The touchdown speed was based on the airplane's gross weight, measured in 5,000 lb (2,268kg) increments. The J47 engine required 12-20 seconds to accelerate from idle to 100% rpm, with very little thrust gained up to 55%, so Boeing recommended using 55% rpm throughout the approach and landing instead of idle when decelerating. A ribbon-type approach chute could be deployed throughout the approach to allow the airplane to fly at lower speeds while at high power settings. Limited to airspeeds below 195KIAS, the approach chute was 16ft (4.9m) in diameter and used either a 30in (76cm) or 36in (91cm) pilot chute.

When flown at the correct speed, the airplane was in an attitude that allowed both main gear to touch down simultaneously. Landings

Above: In order to maintain the slow-spooling engines at 55% rpm throughout the pattern without increasing airspeed, the B-47 used a small approach chute. After landing, a large brake chute helped slow the airplane. *Photo courtesy Boeing*

Below: The B-47 simulator was a small tent-like room (seen here with the top removed). Two instructors could oversee the pilot and copilot, while an operator programmed emergencies and monitored the ground track on the map to his left. The simulator had neither motion nor visual cues. *Author's collection*

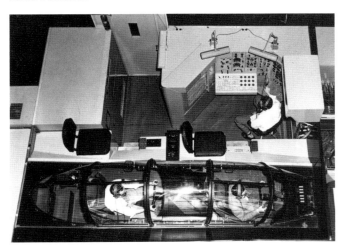

were made level or slightly rear gear first as touching down on the forward gear could cause some 'interesting' and potentially dangerous bounces. In gusty conditions, crews added 8 knots to the touchdown speed, allowing for 13-15KIAS above first stall warning. The airplane was successfully tested in 90° crosswinds at 25 knots (20 knots with the approach chute deployed) but could not use the traditional wing-low method. Instead the pilot had to 'crab' into the wind until just before touchdown and then eliminate the yaw using slight differential thrust along with judicious (sometimes 'considerable') amounts of rudder and up to 50% of available aileron deflection. Landing on the front gear during the transition from the crab could cause 'a bounce which may result in a stalled condition with the airplane out of control.' A Type D-1 32ft (9.8m) ring-slot brake chute was used during the landing roll at speeds less than 160KIAS.

Training

The original B-47 operational plan called for low-priority B-29 units to convert first, beginning with the 301st BW and the 43rd BW. Both were to have their full complement of 45 B-47s and combat-ready crews by January 1952. Boeing would train the initial cadre of SAC B-47 crews as part of Project WIBAC at Wichita Mid-Continent Airport. Instead, the 306th BW was chosen to be the B-47 Combat Crew Transition School (CCTS) because it had the most experienced pilots in SAC with an average age of 34. Once qualified in the B-47 after training with WIBAC at Wichita, these new crewmembers returned to the CCTS at Pinecastle AFB near Orlando, FL, where they trained the remaining 306th BW pilots and observers.

Initial training was fraught with miscues. The pilots' program called for 10 weeks of instruction including 150 hours of classroom work, 46 hours in the simulator (which was not yet available), and 40 hours in the B-47 (with the first airplane yet to arrive). Colonel Mike McCoy delivered the first Stratojet – B-47B 50-0008 – to the 306th BW on 23rd October, with 11 more in service by the end of the year. The observer course lasted for just 20 days and was not always at Wichita (other training sites included Mather AFB, CA, and Barksdale AFB, LA). This truncated observer's course did not include any flying. One observer claims that when he arrived in Florida he had never even been inside a B-47 and flew his first mission within four hours of reaching Pinecastle AFB! The initial cadre of observer training focused exclusively on K-system bombing-navigation system (BNS), comprising 40 major components made up of over 360 vacuum tubes and 15-20,000 separate parts. Despite the small space in the nose of the B-47 the observer had to be able to adjust the system, operate it, and repair it (usually limited to replacing vacuum tubes) in flight. On the ground it was at least possible for maintenance personnel to remove the navigator's downward hatch to reach some of the components!

By the end of 1951 the 306th BW had trained over 100 crews but had just 12 B-47s, none of which could be considered combat ready as they lacked tail guns and a fully operational BNS. LeMay lashed out at AMC's Armament Division for lagging behind, and his deputy, Major General Power, warned that unless AMC resolved these shortages, the situation would become 'the biggest scandal in Air Force history'. Despite these shortcomings McCoy's instructors ran an impressive program. They trained 191 jet aircraft mechanics and 511 jet engine mechanics, but they only needed 77 and 195, respectively, to meet the needs of the 306th BW. To keep the crews from losing their effectiveness some were assigned temporarily to B-29 crews. In order to slow down training output, the 306th BW was sidelined from training to operational engineering.

SAC commanders – disillusioned with the B-47's limited range – anticipated that there would only be four wings of its medium bomber pending delivery of the preferred B-52, so did not plan for a large output of newly qualified crews. SAC officials assumed that the 306th BW would train sufficient fliers and maintenance personnel for this modest number of crews. Moreover, as most of the newly built jets were assigned to test units or retained by Boeing for Phase testing there were very few B-47s to fly. In addition, the B-47 required far more 'concrete real estate' at SAC's B-29 and B-50 bases – at least 10,000ft (3,048m) of runway plus 1,000ft (305m) of overrun *at both ends*. Runways would have to be lengthened and parking aprons greatly expanded. Cost estimates soared to $24 million for the first six bases excluding support facilities and housing for the new crews and their families. Waiting for newly manufactured B-47s and bases to be built or upgraded would seriously undermine SAC's readiness, so SAC bizarrely insisted that each new unit would be combat ready in the B-47 *before they got any airplanes*. Suddenly SAC was confronted with a projection of almost triple the number of B-47 wings, a figure which the 306th BW could hardly support. To meet the demands of the 11-wing fleet and to prevent the 306th BW from losing its combat-ready capability, SAC asked Air Training Command (ATC) to take over all B-47 training.

Air Training Command

It made sense to continue B-47 crew instruction at Wichita where the airplanes were built and parts were assumed to be plentiful for training, so on 5th June 1951 the 3520th Combat Crew Training Wing (CCTW) was established at Wichita Mid-Continent Airport. Wichita AP became Wichita AFB on 15th May 1953, and was renamed on 15th April 1954 as McConnell AFB in honor of Fred and Thomas McConnell, former pilots and World War II veterans, and natives of Wichita.

Above: Ground school for the B-47 began haphazardly but slowly reached maturity once ATC became involved. Crews were expected to understand how each system worked in detail, especially in the absence of flight engineers. Captain David A Patterson (l), Captain Pershing G Zimmerman (c), and Major Robert L Litchfield (r) study the hydraulic system. *Photo BW 65184 courtesy Boeing*

Below: Having sufficient numbers of TB-47Bs at McConnell AFB was a start for ATC, but it still had to develop infrastructure such as hangars, classrooms, barracks, and fuel tanks. For nearly 18 months training and operations were badly out of phase. *Photo P15679 courtesy Boeing*

Under ATC classes of 25 SAC and two ATC instructor crews commenced every 10 training days, with the first class beginning 12th June 1951. During its first seven months of operation, 937 pilots, observers, mechanics, and technicians completed training. Cost per student hour ranged from $25.25 for flight crews ($237.72 in 2017 dollars) to $0.95 to $2.74 ($8.94 to $25.80 in 2017 dollars) for maintenance personnel.

The small flight crew represented a significant challenge. In the B-50, for example, there was a navigator, a bombardier, and a radar operator. In the B-47 all three of these positions were combined into the observer (later referred to as the navigator). A B-47 copilot served as copilot, flight engineer, gunner, radio operator, celestial navigator, and crew lackey. The B-47 aircraft commander had to master the complexities and subtleties of flying the new jet, memorize SAC operational procedures and combat tactical doctrine, and have a sufficiently deep understanding of the navigator's and copilot's duties to serve in a coordinating and advisory role. These combined positions effectively tripled the student curriculum, and meant that each crewmember was on the verge of task saturation throughout the flight. Indeed, for a brief period ATC trained pilots to fulfill the duties

Above: The availability of early airframes such as 50-0015 meant that they eventually could be converted under the EBB TIDE program to TB-47B trainers. They lacked weapons and air refueling capability, so were used to turn out pilots as quickly as possible with additional training at each gaining unit. *Photo courtesy Boeing*

Left: Apparently one commander of the 3520th CCTW elected to apply 'boss bird' markings to his TB-47B. Although only on the nose in this image – according to crew chief Claude 'Mike' Rish – the yellow, red, and black lightning bolt originally extended to the tail. *Photo HS5932C courtesy Boeing*

of all three positions known as 'three-headed monsters'. This proved both inefficient and highly unpopular. There were not enough airplanes available to allow for regular flights to remain proficient in all three positions, and pilots resented flying as navigators.

For the initial ATC cadre, pilots were expected to have 1,000 to 1,500 hours of four-engine flying time. Training began with six weeks of transition in the Lockheed T-33 to learn the techniques of flying jets (50-70 flight hours), followed by three weeks of basic flight operations in the B-47 (36-40 flight hours). Next came six weeks of combat crew training (approximately 100 flight hours) which included the observer, as they learned to 'work and think together through a series of simulated combat missions.'

As with the airplane's assembly process, the initial B-47 training program was 'completely out of phase' with the rest of the program. Despite press releases describing the Wichita air base as 'one of the finest in the world,' the lack of housing or barracks meant that instructors and students alike lived in tents amid a sea of mud in the rainy season and slush in the winter. Many of the airplanes on the ramp at WIBAC (including the TB-47Bs converted under the EBB TIDE program) were barely flyable, and certainly not of sufficient operational readiness to train crews in combat operations. Spare parts were in short supply, and variations among individual airplanes in

configuration made standardized training impossible. In addition to ongoing training at Pinecastle AFB, MacDill AFB, FL, acquired a local training role. All three bases were subject to the vagaries of weather. Cold weather and icing in Kansas, and thunderstorms and crosswind conditions at all three bases meant that training would be 'materially curtailed' during a substantial portion of the year as long as the B-47 remained a 'fair weather' airplane. Shortage of fuel storage areas, ramp space, and other infrastructure issues equally hindered training, especially at the Florida bases. The B-47 lacked an established supply chain. Only about 60% of the tools and parts needed to maintain operations – let alone provide training – were available, but ground-handling equipment and some types of government-furnished property (GFP) were in critically short supply. At one point some 1,800 aircrew and maintenance personnel sat idle at MacDill AFB awaiting the arrival of the B-47.

Training of specialists and maintenance personnel at Wichita proved to be 'impossible'. The K System simply did not work and the fire control system had yet to be selected, let alone built and integrated into the airplane. Flight simulators did not exist. SAC requested T-33s for *ab initio* jet training but these were delayed arriving in any meaningful quantity, and pilots with no experience in jet aircraft (nearly all of the initial cadre) had no means of

Table 4-1. **B-47 Main Differences**

Standard Feature	B-47A	TB-47B	DB-47B	B-47B/E	RB-47E/K	RB-47H
Long nose with camera window					X	
Solid nose with large radome						X
Solid nose with bomb site protuberance		X	X	X		
Transparent nose	X					
Air refueling			X	X	X	X
White thermal protective paint			X	X		
Long bomb bay doors	X					
Short bomb bay doors		X	X	X		
Provisions for right side missile			X			
Camera compartment with photo flash					X	
ECM compartment bulge						X*
Bomb bay tanks		X	X	X	X	X
Water injection and ATO provisions			X	X	X	X
External wing tanks			X	X	X	X
Single point ground refueling		X	X	X	X	X
Retractable aft radome			X			
Tail turret		X	X	X		X

* The ECM compartment bulge was retrofitted to the Phase V ECM B-47E/EB-47E and the TELL TWO EB-47E

Table 4-2. **B-47E Dimensions and Weights**

Wing span	
(some airplanes)	116ft / 35.3m
(other airplanes)	116ft 4in / 35.4m
Overall length	107ft 1.5in / 32.6m
Height	
(top of fin in taxi attitude)	28ft / 8.5m
Tread	
(between outriggers)	44ft 4in / 13.5m
Design Gross Weight	125,000 lb / 56,699kg
Maximum Takeoff Gross Weight	
(tire ply dependent – 24 ply & some 32 ply)	185,000 lb / 83,915kg
(B-47E-I with 32 ply tires)	200,000 lb / 90,718kg
(others with 32 ply tires and full external tanks)	221,000 lb / 100,244kg
(B-47E-IV with full external tanks)	230,000 lb / 104,326kg
Maximum Inflight Gross Weight	
(B-47E-I, -II, and -III with external wing tanks)	221,000 lb / 100,244kg
(B-47E-IV with full external tanks)	230,000 lb / 104,326kg

establishing and maintaining proficiency. As late as April 1953 pilots converting to B-47s received only half (35 hours) of the T-33 conversion training required due to lack of airplanes. Transition flights in the B-47 were limited to a fifth (25 hours) of those specified in the initial training syllabus. In many cases pilots were assigned to operational units barely qualified to fly the airplane – let along conduct an effective combat mission – requiring substantial local flight training. Many operational wings added 15-25 hours in the B-47 for new crews arriving from initial qualification. Copilots also received 24 hours (12 academic, 12 simulator – again, non-existent) in gunnery training.

There never seemed to be enough training slots available for new crews. Consequently, a few bases established local training programs for new copilots, allowing the 3520th CCTW to devote its slots exclusively to new aircraft commanders. This not only affected SAC's combat readiness, it led to the loss of airplanes and crew. Approximately half of all B-47 losses through 1953 were attributed directly to pilot error incidental to inadequate training. Efforts to promote safety were genuine but ineffective. As one official report pessimistically noted, 'It wasn't that the Forty-Seven was tough to fly, but it was more demanding of the pilot – he had to be right on his airspeeds, approach altitudes, and attitudes. Therefore, a crew, which had learned its lessons well during the training period could prevent serious or fatal accidents, *in most cases*' [emphasis added]. In its formative years, B-47 training was sadly insufficient.

ATC transferred B-47 training to SAC on 1st July 1958 with the closure of the 3520th CCTW and establishment of the 4347th CCTW, which was finally disbanded on 15th June 1963. By this time most of the training aircraft were B-47Es or RB-47Es that were no longer in service with SAC combat wings. In addition to the 4347th CCTW at McConnell AFB, the 70th SRW at Little Rock AFB, AR, undertook B-47 crew training.

Technical Description
Over 2,000 B-47s were manufactured over a span of 10 years, with XB-47 46-0065 effectively a different airplane than ERB-47H 53-4269, the final aircraft built. Variations in airframe, engines, and systems existed across every type of B-47 produced, whether early test platforms, initial bombers, reconnaissance versions, or the 'ultimate' bombers – the B-47E-IVa – which are covered in detail in this section. They also used a lot of materials. It was not only a challenge to manufacture and assemble these many parts it was a demanding process to understand how to use them correctly and maintain them properly.

AIRFRAME

The Wing
It was the wing that made the B-47 unique. The thin, laminar-flow wing had a span of 116ft (35.4m) and a sweepback of 36.5° at the 25% chordline. The airfoil was a proprietary Boeing design with a 12% thickness ratio and a 9.4 aspect ratio. Together these allowed the B-47 to operate at higher Mach numbers where jet engines offered improved range. The wing was highly flexible with a nominal upward deflection of 45in (114cm) and downward deflection of 16in (41cm). While at rest on the ramp the wing drooped naturally by as much as 5ft (1.5m). Static tests demonstrated a total deflection of 17.5ft (5.3m) prior to structural failure. This high degree of flexibility, coupled with the natural upward deflection of the swept wing, proved effective at alleviating gust loads by reducing the wing's angle of attack (AoA), thereby unloading the wing at the tip without sacrificing any structural integrity. The wings were shoulder mounted and fully cantilevered on the fuselage. In straight-wing airplanes the center of lift and the cg are closely aligned. However, in a swept-wing airplane the center of lift is forward of the cg causing high loading through the wing attachment and fuselage. Extremely large and strong forgings were used to attach each wing to the body with two oversize pins (the 'milk bottle' and 'pop bottle') at the attachment point.

The wing's stressed skin was made of the newly developed 75 ST aluminum alloy that required a two-stage heat treatment during manufacture. The skin tapered in thickness from 0.625in (1.58cm) at the wing root to 0.1875in (0.476cm) at the wing tip, with variations no greater than 0.005in (0.013cm). This close tolerance ushered in a new era of aircraft manufacturing requiring new methods, equipment, and skills which would be used on the B-52, KC-135, and eventually all of Boeing's jet airliners. The main component of the wing structure was a box beam consisting of spars at 17% and 58% of the chord with machine-tapered upper and lower skins longitudinally stiffened between spars. The rear spar was heavier than the front spar because it carried higher loads (B-47E wing loads could reach an excessively high 154 lb/ft² (752kg/m²). The wing ribs were of conventional design with a turned flange at the top and a riveted angle at the bottom. Special ribs distributed nacelle loads to the main wing structure. Flush-type countersunk rivets were machined flush with the skin after setting. Anti-icing ducts and electrical wiring were carried in the leading edge.

Several measures were used to control the stall characteristics of the swept wing, especially as the stall occurred on the outer portion of the wing much sooner than on inboard portions. Because the

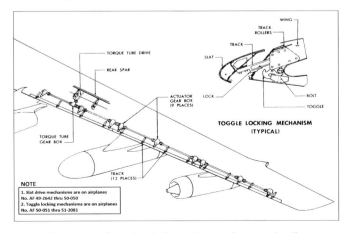

Early B-47s were configured with slats to improve low-speed stall performance. These proved cumbersome and were eventually eliminated.

inboard wing was farther forward, an outboard stall caused the nose to pitch upward due to the remaining lift from the inboard wing, leading to secondary stalls. Wing cambering – curving the leading edge downward – mitigated this tendency. The location of the jet engine pods also reduced stall problems by moving the onset of the stall inward, providing the pilot with better aerodynamic warning. This also contributed to a flutter-free wing. The earliest aircraft models had mechanical slats on the leading edge of the wing for improved slow speed control. The two XB-47s, the 10 B-47As, and B-47Bs 49-2642 through 50-0050 had a three-slat system with a mechanical drive. B-47Bs 50-0051 through 51-2081 (Block 25) used a toggle locking system which kept the slats closed until actuated, allowing them to extend commensurately with a reduction in airflow. The slats were eventually deactivated and bolted closed, and

Above left: Airflow separation over the outer wing allowed the inner wing to produce more lift, causing a pitch-up. Two rows of vortex generators minimized this separation and increased pitch stability. *Photo courtesy Boeing*

Above right: Boeing cleverly combined the outboard flap with the aileron, creating a 'flaperon' that served both functions. *Photo 92892 courtesy Boeing*

Below left: Five different companies – including the American Stove Company – built B-47 drop tanks. Each had slightly different aerodynamic qualities, leading to different limiting airspeeds at various altitudes. *Author's collection*

Below right: The external tanks could be jettisoned rather than dropped. This sequence shows how the drogue chute pulls the tank from behind, sliding it off the rails that attach it to the wing and struts.

eliminated altogether on Block 30 B-47s onward and all B-47Es and their variants.

Data from early fight tests showed that the B-47 exhibited a surprising tendency to pitch upward at the 'high' end of the performance envelope. At high speeds the airflow over the outer wing separated, resulting in buffeting and pitchup that rendered the aircraft unsuitable for its tactical mission of dropping bombs. Boeing solved this by placing small airfoils known as vortex generators – about the size of a playing card – on the top of the wing at an angle to the airflow in regions of separation. Theses were installed in two rows (at approximately 25% and 35% chord) beginning approximately above the external tank and continuing outward to the outboard engine. These caused a corkscrew motion in the air close to the wing and prevented it from separating from the wing.

Fowler wing flaps were mounted in two sections on each wing, and could be lowered to 22.5%, 50% or 100%. As the flaps were extended the outboard section augmented the ailerons and functioned as a 'flaperon.' The outboard flap was automatically moved 25° upward from the fully extended position as the adjacent aileron moved through the last two-thirds of its upward travel.

Several other changes were made to the wing as increasing demands were placed on the B-47. ECM antennas (AN/ALT-7) were added to the wingtip and lower outer wing of the RB-47H. Two water injection tanks, each holding 331gal (1,253 liters) were located in each wing root. The most noticeable change was the addition of external fuel tanks. Ryan and Goodyear built tanks under subcontract to Boeing, along with Beech and Fletcher (the American Stove Company also built spare tanks under contract to Boeing). Interestingly, each of the drop tank types had different maximum

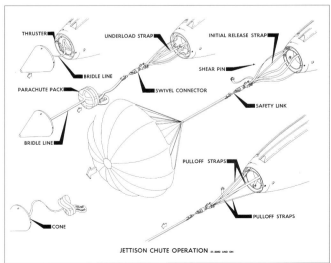

allowable airspeeds 'based on aerodynamic buffeting of the wing [resulting] from airflow disturbances caused by the tank installation.' At 10,000ft (3,048m), for example, B-47s equipped with the Beech tanks were limited to 387KIAS, those with Boeing tanks to 359KIAS, and finally airplane carrying Fletcher tanks to 339KIAS. The tanks also changed the wing flutter characteristics with commensurate limits to airplane performance. Each tank held 1,700gal (6,435 liters) of fuel that could be transferred to any engine or to any main tank, and could be jettisoned when empty. A small explosive charge blew off the rear cap on the tank, releasing a parachute. This would then slide the tank to the rear, off railings in the struts, allowing both the tank and struts to fall away. Spring-loaded cover plates rotated to cover fuel line openings in the bottom of the wing.

The Fuselage

The semi-monocoque fuselage had an oval cross-section and was covered with the same 75 ST stressed aluminum skin as the wing. The crew of three sat in tandem, with the pilot and copilot under a bubble canopy and the navigator in the nose. The bullet-resistant windscreen was heated by electric current. A single wiper was installed on the flat portion of the windscreen and was manually turned off and on. When disconnecting during air refueling, the wiper automatically started and operated at maximum speed to clear fuel spray off the windscreen and stopped when the air-refueling switch was reset to 'Before Contact.'

Immediately forward of the windshield was a yaw string, a simple piece of nylon cord to help pilots visually coordinate the use of the rudder in a turn. B-47B and early B-47E models had canopies that opened by sliding rearward approximately 14in (36cm). Later B-47Es had clamshell canopies that opened upward 14in for ventilation on the ground. Both styles could be jettisoned by explosive charges prior to emergency egress. Inside the canopy was the radio compass sensing antenna. Interestingly, the sliding canopy could be opened in flight at speeds below 215KIAS (say, for smoke and fumes elimination), although failure to depressurize the cabin before opening the canopy might release it entirely causing injury or damage to the airplane. The clamshell canopy could be opened only on the ground at speeds less than 100KIAS (eg, during landing rollout). Nuclear blast curtains for the pilot and copilot extended via rollers to cover the Plexiglas canopy to reduce flash blindness. An access hole was located above the copilot's station to permit the extension of the periscopic sextant used for celestial navigation.

Early Stratojets did not have ejection seats, but beginning with the 400th B-47B (51-2357) and retrofitted to the 135th through the 399th B-47B (51-2092 through 51-2356), all B-47s used seats made by Republic or Weber for the pilots and by Stanley for the navigator. The copilot seat was mounted on a swivel base that allowed him to operate the tail armament using the gunnery controls behind him. Ejection seat reliability was spotty, and a few crewmen perished when their seats either failed to fire or did so improperly (for example, B-47E 53-2134 – see Appendix II).

The pilot and copilot seats ejected upward after explosive charges had separated the canopy from the aircraft. If this automatic charge failed, the canopy could be jettisoned manually to allow ejection. Although the Republic and Weber seats were identical in function they had significant differences in design. In both cases the ejection sequence was the same – handgrips raised, triggers squeezed. Both seats used the 5in (12.7cm) back-style parachutes. The Weber seat had an all metal shelf which supported the lower end of the parachute pack whereas the Republic seat had two inches of foam rubber covering the forward part of the shelf. Each seat was designed for the occupant to sit on a MD-1 survival kit container (he could sit on a C-2A life raft kit if the MD-1 was not available). If there was no

Top: Compared to the B-52, forward visibility in the B-47 was limited even from the front seat. It was comparable to a fighter as seen in this view of a Phase V EB-47E taxiing during a Coco alert at RAF Brize Norton in the Spring of 1963. *Augustine Letto*

Above: Canopy view looking forward shows the sextant port over the copilot's position and the sunshade/blast curtain rollers above each position. *Photo courtesy Boeing*

survival kit or life raft, an MC-1 or A-5 cushion could be used. The cushions ensured that the head of the pilot or copilot would not slip beneath the headrest during ejection and cause serious injury. The seats had gas-operated automatic opening safety belts and the capability of automatically opening the parachute. Manufacturing flaws in the gas operating cylinders, among other technical issues, resulted in several fatalities when the seat did not function properly. Some seats were also modified with a man-seat separator. It was possible, but definitely not recommended, that the copilot could eject while facing aft. The seat could also eject in any position other than full forward or full aft, but this would likely result in seat failure and serious or fatal injury to the copilot. Minimum safe ejection altitude for the upward-firing seats was 125ft (38m) using the F-1B Timer opening at 1 second and 0ft with the parachute lanyard attached to the parachute D-ring opening immediately. These altitudes increased as the airplane deviated from level flight. Ejection was safe at all airspeeds.

Stanley Aviation Corporation produced the navigator's seat which catapulted downward. The minimum safe ejection altitude for the downward seat was 500ft (152m) using the F-1B Timer opening at 1 second and 400ft (122m) with the parachute lanyard attached to the parachute D-ring opening immediately. While the operation of the seat was similar to the pilot and copilot, this seat had an ejection 'D'

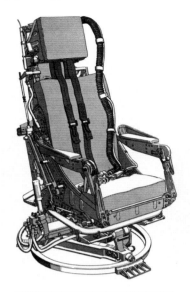

COPILOT'S SEAT—RIGHT FRONT VIEW
51-2357 THRU 52-507

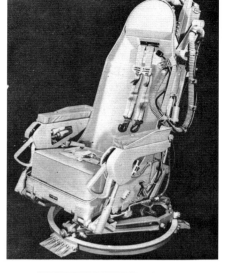

COPILOT'S SEAT—LEFT FRONT VIEW
51-2192 THRU 51-2356, 52-508 AND ON

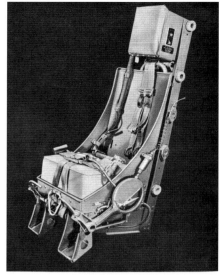

NAVIGATOR'S SEAT—LEFT FRONT VIEW
52-597

ring handle between the navigator's knees that initiated the ejection sequence. This began when leg brace handles on the side of the seat were raised to extend the footrests and leg retainers. The D-ring was then released for firing. The first pull jettisoned the hatch under the seat. The second pull ejected the seat. The navigator's cushions and survival kit options were similar to those of the pilots. Seats for ECM crewmen were identical to the navigator seat but the firing sequence was different. The first action of the sequence was to blow out the floor structure with knives attached through the frangible hatch under the seat. As the floor departed it pulled a static line that armed the seat catapult initiator. A second pull of the D-ring ejected the seat. There is no record of a successful ejection from the ECM compartment.

An extra folding seat was located in the forward walkway behind and the left of the navigator's seat. Another was sometimes added in the walkway by the copilot's station to accommodate an instructor. In aircraft equipped with the bomb bay capsule two webbed sling seats were added in the walkway for use during takeoff and landing. A conventional safety belt was provided and the seat could fold up against the left sidewall when not in use. Manual bailout was accomplished using the crew entry hatch, the navigator's hatch after he ejected, or the bomb bay (without capsule) or the EW's hatch after ejection (with capsule). Pulling the entrance door bailout handle released the entry door safety strap, jettisoned the entry door and then the ladder, unlatched the bailout spoiler, and finally fired the spoiler actuation air bottle that extended the spoiler. Once this spoiler was extended it was impossible to open the pressure door to the ECM compartment, so careful planning was required to avoid trapping the EWs should their ejection seats not be usable. A number of B-47s lacked the bailout spoiler, necessitating that bailout be attempted at slow speed, preferably below 195KIAS. This required that the AC slow the airplane by lowering the aft gear and flaps until the desired speed was achieved, then raising the landing gear to eliminate

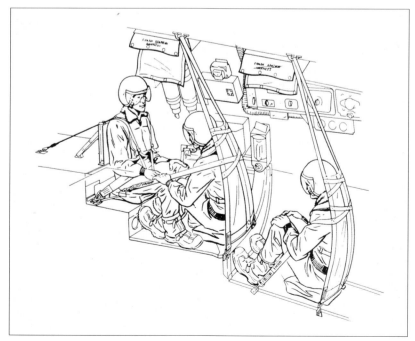

obstructions on bailout. In an uncontrolled bailout, however, crewmen exited the entry chute at any speed. Minimum bailout altitude with parachutes was the same as the downward ejection seat. Bailout over the side of the fuselage was recommended only under uncontrollable circumstances due to the potential for striking the wing or empennage.

Access to the crew compartment was via a door and extendable ladder on the lower starboard side of the fuselage. The entry way also served as an escape chute for crewmen not using ejection seats, including instructors, extra pilots, EWs, and crew chiefs. A large metal spoiler extended just forward of the door to provide protection from the wind blast.

The forward crew compartment was pressurized using high-pressure bleed air from the final compressor stage of the engines to pressurize and regulate the temperature of the crew compartment. Part of the air was cooled by a refrigeration unit, with the rest passing directly into a mixing chamber to be blended with the refrigerated air as required to maintain cabin air temperature as selected by the pilot. The air was discharged to each crewmember by an upper and a lower outlet at each station. The air was then removed from the cabin by pressure regulators or by the manual dump valve. [EB-47Ls also carried an air conditioning and pressurization system in the bomb bay for the AN/ARC-89(V) relay transmitters.] Cabin pressurization was supplied by air from the high-pressure supply duct of the thermal anti-icing system. This was regulated by master and slave regulators that maintained cabin pressure by releasing a sufficient amount of air. An emergency pressure release valve provided a means of quickly depressurizing the cabin.

Some models of the Stratojet (EB-47E, RB-47H, or ERB-47H) carried a pressurized, air conditioned manned capsule in the bomb bay that accommodated two, three, or four Electronic Warfare (EW) operators, depending on the variant. These crewmen sat in web seats along the port side of the main cabin for takeoff and landing. During climbout the EWs crawled through a narrow passageway along the port side of the fuselage between the pressure compartment and the outer skin prior to cabin pressurization. During descent the pilot would depressurize the main cabin and the EWs would return to the front for landing. The crawlway also provided access for bomber crews to check the weapons or the forward gear in the event of

This page, right: Crawlspace between the forward crew compartment and the bomb bay. During early EWP missions the copilot would use this to arm open-pit weapons. In addition, EWs would crawl through to reach the bomb bay pod. *Paul Swendrowski*

Below: With the exception of the external drop tanks, all fuel was carried in the fuselage. Although this contributed to the wing's efficiency it required considerable pilot attention to manage the cg properly.

malfunction. In the early days of 'open pit' nuclear bombs, the copilot or navigator carried the nuclear capsule through this passage for insertion into the weapon after the aircraft was launched.

The B-47 fuselage evolved over the years as additional fuel tanks, ECM equipment, changes to the ATO system, and other capabilities were added. Two of the most distinctive features were the Y-4 optical bombsight extending from the nose and a large radome on the bottom of the fuselage between the navigator's ejection hatch and the forward landing gear. Manufactured by Perkins-Elmer, the Y-4 optical bombsight was covered by a retractable aluminum cap when not in use (when the cover was open at speed between 160KIAS and 190KIAS the change in airflow caused the AC's airspeed indicator to read as much as 25 knots below that of the copilot). The sight was mounted slightly off-center below the AN/APS-54 antenna. Immediately below the sight was the AN/ARN-18 glideslope antenna. The large radome under the nose covered the AN/APS-64 or AN/APS-23 radar antenna for the bombing-navigation system. Pitot tubes were mounted on each side of the fuselage just forward of the crew entry door. The air refueling slipway door was located on the upper starboard quadrant of the nose, although this was relocated to the fuselage centerline on RB-47 and DB-47 variants. This door rotated forward from the front to expose the receptacle;

Opposite, top left and center: Republic ejection seats had a square headrest, while Weber seats had a rounded headrest. The seats were initially omitted as a weight- and cost-saving measure, but SAC finally relented and approved their installation.

Opposite , top right: Navigators and EWs seated in the bomb bay capsule used a downward-firing seat. A complicated ejection sequence restrained the occupant's feet and legs, then blew off (or shredded) the hatch, and finally ejected the seat.

Opposite, bottom : Depiction of the aisle folding seat and two webbed seats shows the cramped position of the EWs during takeoff and landing. Accompanying photo emphasizes the narrowness of the aisle and the crowded conditions experienced by extra crewmembers, in this case Major Jean Pierson (l), First Lieutenant John M Cyrocki (c), and Captain Reynolds S Watson (r) from the 44th BW. *USAF*

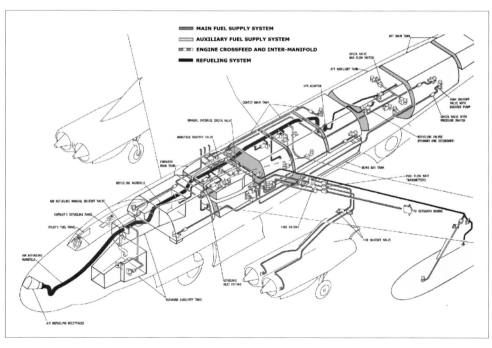

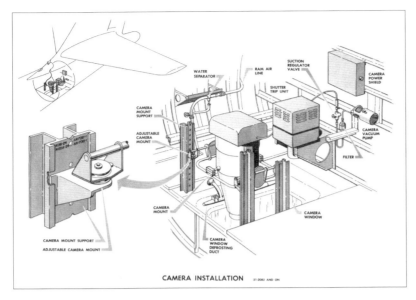

CAMERA INSTALLATION 51-2082 AND ON

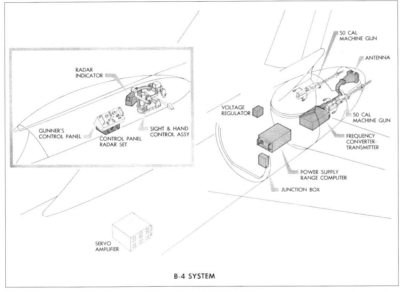

B-4 SYSTEM

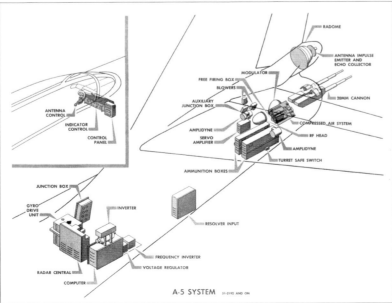

A-5 SYSTEM 51-2192 AND ON

Table 4-3. **B-47E Fuel Tank Capacity**

Forward Main	2,954gal / 11,182 liters
Forward Auxiliary	990gal / 3,748 liters
Center Main	2,874gal / 10,879 liters
Aft Main*	3,287gal / 12,443 liters
Aft Auxiliary	1,260gal / 4,770 liters
Bomb Bay	3,258gal / 12,333 liters
Left External Wing Tank	1,700gal / 6,435 liters
Right External Wing Tank	1,700gal / 6,435 liters
Total Volume/Capacity	18,023gal / 68,224 liters
Total Weight	115,347 lb / 52321kg

* Without aft lower ECM radome held an extra 158gal / 598 liters
Two water/methanol injection tanks each held 331gal / 1,253 liters,
totaling 5,296 lb / 2,402kg. Manufacturing tolerances allowed for ±
1.5% in tank capacity

whereas the centerline receptacle had two doors. Both styles were illuminated for night missions. The number of windows in the nose for the navigator gradually decreased as Stratojet models progressed. The reconnaissance models had noses that were quite different. The RB-47E nose was 33in (83cm) longer than the B-47E and had cameras mounted in the tip. The RB-47H had a large radome covering the AN/APD-4 and AN/APS-54 antennas on the nose.

The fuselage contained three main fuel tanks – forward, center, and aft – as well as forward and aft auxiliary tanks. All were self-sealing and vented. The rear portion of the bomb bay that was originally designed to carry the very large weapons of the late 1940s and early 1950s was later converted to accommodate an additional fuel tank. Under normal operating conditions, the forward tank fed engines #1 and #6, the center tank fed engines #2 and #5, and the aft tank fed engines #3 and #4 using boost pumps. A manifold connected the fuel tanks, allowing for fuel feed to any engine from any tank, balancing the fuel levels, and for single-point refueling. The single-point system allowed fuel flow rates between the limits of 600gpm (2,271 liters) at 40psi and 150gpm (568 liters) at 15psi. The air refueling system was connected to the fuel tanks through a 600gpm manifold. There was no fuel drain capability, which created problems for aircraft experiencing emergencies and that needed to land immediately at lighter weight. B-47E 52-0049 was lost following an in-flight fire while burning off fuel to land (see Appendix II).

A K-38 post-strike camera was mounted in the lower aft fuselage behind the aft fuel tank. Type K-17C, K-22A, or K-37 cameras could be carried as alternate equipment. To the rear of the camera were compartments for the approach chute (on the starboard side) and the brake chute (lower side). Many B-47s acquired a rear radome housing additional ECM antennas forward of the camera compartment, especially as the jets moved through PDM or upgrade modifications. The top of the fuselage between the canopy and empennage was covered by access panels that allowed access to the raceways containing the control cables to the rudder and elevators. These also provided wiring to the tail turret, approach and brake chutes, and other equipment in the rear fuselage. An emergency life raft was located beneath a hatch on the upper starboard fuselage at the trailing edge of the wing.

Early B-47s had no tail armament as the Air Force and Boeing subcontractors struggled to build and procure a suitable turret (see Chapter 3). These early jets carried a simple aluminum cone to cover the turret area and required pie-shaped weights or blocks as ballast. Early B-47Bs carried the Emerson A-2 turret with 0.50 caliber automatic weapons but no radar. These never proved satisfactory and were soon replaced with the General Electric A-5 (the same system as on the B-36) or the similar but improved MD-4. The turret could move through 45° of azimuth and 37° of elevation. The A-5 and MD-4 turrets used two M24A-1 20mm cannons with a normal rate of fire of 750 to 900 rounds per minute. The A-5 held 350 rounds and the MD-4 held 480 rounds per gun, not a lot for potential multiple engagements during an EWP encounter. Although the maximum range of the projectile was 5,750 yards (5,258m), the maximum effective range was a more modest 1,500 yards (1,372m). The copilot used the AN/APG-32 gun-laying radar to control the turret.

The wing of the B-47 did not allow for mounting the landing gear in a conventional fashion. Instead, the main gear was arranged in a tandem (bicycle) configuration. Each gear consisted of a two-wheel truck mounted on a conventional air-oil piston-type shock strut that retracted forward by an electrical motor-driven ball-bearing mechanism. There were six duplex expander tube-type brakes (two on each forward main gear wheel and one each on the inboard side of the rear wheels, operated by the pilot's rudder pedals. The front gear could be steered with the rudder pedals through a 120° arc while taxiing, 12° for takeoff, or could be disengaged to swivel for tight ground maneuvering during towing (there was some interest at Boeing in modifying the B-47's landing gear to caster like that on the later B-52 to facilitate crosswind landings, but this was not pursued despite tests on B-47A 49-1901 for the B-52). During gear retraction, springs centered the wheels and the unit was disconnected from the rudder pedals. The landing gear retracted in approximately 11 seconds and extended in just 4 seconds, although in extreme cold temperatures (or cold soaking following lengthy flights at high altitude) the extension time could reach as much as 90 seconds.

The main tires were 56in (142cm) x16in (41cm) and inflated with 150 to 230psi of air depending on the gross weight of the aircraft, and were either 24- or 32-ply. An antiskid device allowed optimum braking under all runway conditions. To balance the aircraft laterally on the ground, small single-tire outrigger gear were located in each inboard engine pod. These 14-ply tires were 26in (66cm) x 6.6in (16.8cm) with 150 to 225 psi of air (depending on aircraft gross weight and whether external wing tanks were used), and also retracted forward. The torque links on the outriggers could be disconnected to allow them to swivel through a full 360° rather than the normal 28° inboard and 93° outboard travel.

Shimmy damping was built into the steering metering and compensator assembly on the main wheels as well as the outriggers. The rear truck and outriggers could be lowered to function as a speed brake (known as the Drag Control System – DCS) when required to achieve a high rate of descent from altitude. A switch at the copilot's station actuated this feature. In the event of malfunction, an Emergency Landing Gear Extension (ELGE) system was located to the port rear of the copilot's station. Each gear could be winched down separately. An emergency retraction system provided for retraction of all gear should the normal system malfunction. The pilot could retract all the gear with a switch or the copilot could retract each gear individually.

Opposite page, top: The installation of a post-strike camera was a vestige of Second World War battle damage assessment. The need to escape a nuclear detonation meant that B-47s were typically not in a position to photograph their effectiveness.

Center and bottom: The B-4 twin 0.50 caliber tail gun was a modified Emerson A-2 system and saw limited operational use. The GE A-5 twin 20mm tail gun was upgraded into the MD-4 and proved more effective than the A-2, although both frequently jammed.

This page, top: Despite having bicycle landing gear, the B-47 was surprisingly nimble when taxiing. This Phase V EB-47E shows ability of the forward gear to turn up to 60° either side of center and the outriggers to caster commensurately. *Augustine Letto*

Bottom: B-47B 51-2355 demonstrates the Drag Control System used to slow the airplane. The DCS also helped increase the rate of descent during jet penetrations. *Photo courtesy Boeing*

Table 4-4. **AN/APG-32 Radar Parameters**

	Search Mode	Hand Control or Track Mode	Fire Mode
Azimuth	60°	57°	45°
Elevation	45°	37°	37°
Normal Range	8,000yd / 8,749m	8,000yd / 8,749m	1,500yd / 1,640m
Max Range	24,000yd / 26,247m	24,000yd / 26,247m	*
Min Lock-on Range	250yd / 273m	250yd / 273m	0

* Max range of 24,000yd was used only for equipment checks or momentary scans for targets. 'Lock on' was only possible when target was between 8,000yd and 300yd.

Above and below: The B-47 was originally designed to carry only conventional weapons such as this mockup using 500 lb HE bombs. It was eventually configured to carry a variety of atomic weapons that required a chain loading system, as seen in this drawing.
Photo courtesy Boeing

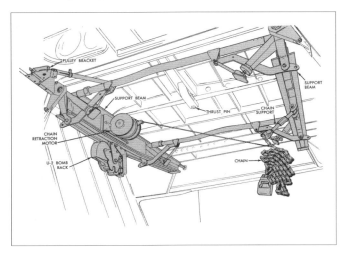

Early B-47s had a 26ft (7.9m) bomb bay. As weapons became smaller a fuel tank was installed in the aft portion and shorter 13ft 10in (4.2m) doors replaced the 26ft 5in (8.1m) 'long' doors, and the area beneath the bomb bay fuel tank was covered. The doors were fast opening (2 seconds) and closing (5 seconds), and were hydraulically operated but electrically controlled. The bomb bay doors could be selectively controlled to provide for bomb aiming, automatic selective, train, or salvo release. During early weapons testing, serious buffeting occurred each time the doors were opened. Eventually spoilers, powered by hydraulic actuators, were installed in front of the bomb bay and opened with the doors to eliminate the problem. Operating the bomb bay doors caused fluctuations in airspeed (5 knots low), altitude [150-200ft (46-61m) low], and vertical velocity indicator [1,500ft/min (457m/min) low] 'due to the wake of disturbed air' that adversely affected the pitot-static system.

The bomb bay could carry a variety of clip-in racks for different types of weapons and configurations. During the early 1960s there was some interest in developing the B-47 as a low-level tactical ground attack platform (see Chapter 7), and some aircraft were modified to carry a Hayes SUU-24/A dispenser to drop cluster weapons. This was a rectangular container with 24 cells able to accommodate one or more bomblets, and was mated to the MAU-6/A rack in the bomb bay. This combination never saw service, however, and the Dash One eventually warned that 'the SUU-24/A Dispenser will not be used operationally in the B-47E airplane.' The bomb bay also carried the flyaway box when the B-47 was headed for REFLEX or alert missions at remote bases. This carried a complete set of Technical Order manuals, covers for various parts of the airframe, remove-before-flight streamers, and various other equipment needed to maintain the B-47 on the ground.

The B-47's engines were underpowered at takeoff, necessitating some kind of augmentation to get the jet airborne with an EWP fuel and bomb load. This resulted in a rocket-assisted takeoff system (generally referred to simply as ATO) installed in the aft fuselage. Early B-47s had nine ports on each side of the fuselage for internally carried ATO rockets that produced a total of 18,000 lbf (80kN) of thrust for 14 seconds. Later B-47s had the internal system deleted and were equipped with jettisonable external racks, either of the 'horsecollar' or the 'split-rack' type. The horsecollar could carry up to 19 15KS1000 rockets or 33 16NS1000, and the split-rack was capable of up to 30 of either rocket. Aerojet-General Corporation manufactured the 15KS-1000 which came in three Mods varying in total weight from 143-145 lb (65-66kg). The Mod 0 and Mod I had 72 lb (33kg) of propellant and the Mod II carried an additional 5 lb (2.3kg) of propellant. Phillips Petroleum made the 16NS-1000, which weighed 195 lb (88kg) with 90 lb (40kg) of propellant. The space vacated by deleting the internal system was used for ECM gear, including chaff dispensers.

Exterior lighting provided guidance for night flying, visibility for collision avoidance, and light to inspect the airframe. Fixed landing lights were located in each inboard engine nacelle. Position and navigation lights consisted of a green light on the starboard wingtip, a red light on the port wingtip, a yellow light and a white light on the tip of the vertical fin, and two white fuselage position lights, one on top and one on the bottom. One red rotating beacon was located on the vertical fin and another was on the bottom of the fuselage forward of the front landing gear. A light installed on each side of the fuselage forward and above the wings illuminated the wings to check for icing.

The Empennage

The tail section was located above the fuselage to avoid jet wake and wing turbulence. The vertical and horizontal surfaces were of stressed skin construction, were swept 35°, and had a thinner section thickness than the wing. This ensured that the tail's critical Mach number would always be above the maximum diving speed of the airplane. The vertical tail, or fin, was the aft termination of the AN/ARC-65 liaison radio wire antenna, and it also provided the air source for the Q-spring. The fin spar was located at 47% chord with ribs spaced at 9in (23cm) normal to the spar. The rudder was connected to the aft edge. Atop the tail was a removable fiberglass tip that housed the AN/ARN-14 VOR and AN/APN-69 rendezvous radar antennas. A flux valve remote compass transmitter was located inside the base of the fin. The fixed horizontal tail was mounted low on the fin. Its single spar was located at 50% chord with ribs spaced 8in (20cm) normal to the spar. The elevators were attached to it.

Flight Controls

B-47 flight controls consisted of ailerons for roll, elevators for pitch, and a rudder for yaw. Powered flight controls were used because of the weight and speed of the Stratojet. Three separate and independent electrically driven hydraulic pumps were used to actuate the control surfaces, one in each wing and one near the tail. With the power units operating the full force of moving the controls was supplied by the hydraulics. This gave the pilots no aerodynamic feedback, however, so an artificial feel system was incorporated. The rudder and elevators provided this 'feel' through Q-springs, bellows that utilized ram air to apply restraint to the pilot's input. This was proportional to, but much lower than, the dynamic air loads on the control surfaces. Aileron control feel was provided by a centering spring that was not proportional to the air loads. Automatic cable tension regulation from the control column and rudder pedals eliminated any control sloppiness within the design temperature range.

Manual control was available with the power off. Control forces were considerably higher but augmentation was supplied through the use of servo tabs on the surfaces and internal balance seals. Trim tabs were located on each outboard aileron, elevator, and on the rudder, and were manually controlled. When the flaps were extended automatic trim compensation reduced the necessity for manual trimming.

Primary flight control surfaces were equipped with aerodynamically operated balances to aid the pilot in manually controlling the airplane. This was accomplished through the use of balance areas composed of balance panels, balance seals, and openings that permitted the change in air pressure to act directly on the balance panels. These were attached to and extended forward from the leading edge of the control surface. The balance seals were attached to the leading edge of the balance panel at a midpoint on the trailing edge of the surface spar, forming upper and lower bays (port and starboard bays in the rudder). Balance bays were arranged so that air pressure differentials in the bays caused by changing the attitude of the airplane or control surfaces reduced the pilot control forces. This made it necessary for the pilot to overcome only 20% of the undampened forces.

Trim tabs were located on all control surfaces and could be moved by wheels on the pilot and copilot control stands. These were only used during flight with the control system power off. The elevator had two tabs, although the port tab was permanently fixed. With the controls powered the trim tabs had no effect on control surfaces. Trimming during normal flight was actually accomplished by adjusting the trim controls to reposition the centering springs and Q-springs which moved the entire control surface. The trim tabs also moved to their appropriate positions so that if power was lost no violent trim change would result. A trim tab coordination panel at the pilot's station was used to coordinate the position of the tab and the neutral position of the aileron centering springs and the Q-spring. After any maintenance involving flight control adjustments, a 'trim check' flight was made.

A yaw damper was incorporated from the earliest days to control Dutch roll, the characteristic roll-yaw movement of swept-wing aircraft. The unit applied a damping correction to the rudder by controlling the length of the rudder push-pull rod. This action was not transmitted back to the pilot through his controls, but the feel was instead relayed by the rudder Q spring. In later years the damper was disconnected.

ENGINES

The six jet engines were mounted in four pods on pylons ahead of or beneath the wings. The inboard pylon contained two engines while the outboard pod held a single engine. These provided aerodynamic benefits to the wings, described above. The pods also protected each engine from the others in case of serious malfunction, as well as protecting the fuselage fuel tanks and bomb bay. Extreme engine failures, notably those with shorn turbine blades, still damaged adjacent engines or punctured the fuselage. Short inlet ducts and exhaust pipes reduced friction loss in engine airflow that would otherwise result in deterioration of both thrust and specific fuel consumption. The inboard pods carried the outrigger landing gear and the landing and taxi lights. Outboard pods also served as antenna mounts on the RB-47H. The use of these pylons and pods made ground maintenance fairly comfortable. Engine changes could be done easily and quickly; Boeing loved to show a sequence of photos showing an engine change with an inset image of a clock ticking away the minutes.

Fire extinguisher doors and burnout panels were located in the nacelles adjacent to each engine as a safety measure. The nacelle cowling had a series of hooks, pins, and quick release latches for ease of maintenance. Each engine was mounted to the airplane structure at two points. The forward mount consisted of a saddle attached to the engine midframe side-mounting pads by ball and socket joints, and the midframe top-mounting pad attached by a saddle brace. The rear mount was connected to the support structure by a single pin.

General Electric designed and manufactured the J47 engines, with the Allison Division of General Motors later producing additional engines. The engines were used to provide power for the hydraulic system, thermal anti-icing and air conditioning systems, and the electrical system. The General Electric J47 (first designed as the TG-190) had an absolute altitude limit of 50,000ft (15,240m). The J47-23 and J47-25 were limited to an operating ceiling of 45,000ft (13,716m), while the J47-11 was 50,000 ft. Each variant was limited to 30,000ft (9,144m) for a maximum starting altitude. The J47-23 was

The crew that flew B-47B 51-2076 for its 1,000th hour without an engine change prepares for flight. From (l) to (r) Major Robert L Wagner (N), Captain Dwight W Blanton (CP), Major Cleon W Greiffendorf (AC), and Major Jack W Dollahon, squadron operations officer. Note goggles in lieu of visors. *USAF*

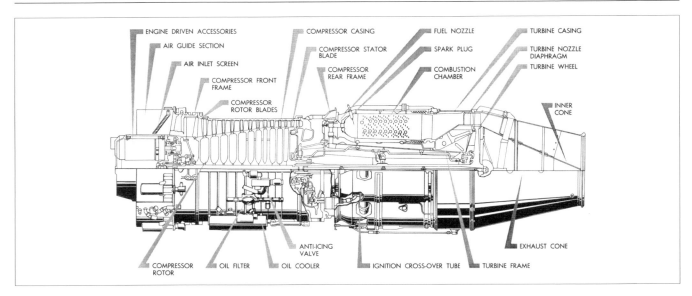

ENGINE DRIVEN ACCESSORIES
AIR GUIDE SECTION
AIR INLET SCREEN
COMPRESSOR FRONT FRAME
COMPRESSOR ROTOR BLADES
COMPRESSOR CASING
COMPRESSOR STATOR BLADE
COMPRESSOR REAR FRAME
FUEL NOZZLE
SPARK PLUG
COMBUSTION CHAMBER
TURBINE CASING
TURBINE NOZZLE DIAPHRAGM
TURBINE WHEEL
INNER CONE
EXHAUST CONE
COMPRESSOR ROTOR
OIL FILTER
OIL COOLER
ANTI-ICING VALVE
IGNITION CROSS-OVER TUBE
TURBINE FRAME

the first of the B-47E engines (pending delivery of the J47-25) that incorporated a high airflow compressor, retractable inlet screens (which were later made inoperable and eventually removed) and a thin disc turbine wheel. The engine became increasingly dependable over its service life. The first J47s in 1949 had an allowable time-between-overhaul of 150 hours. Six months later this was increased to 300 hours, reaching 400 hours in mid 1951. By the end of that year allowable time further improved to 600 hours and by 1955 finally reached 1,200 hours for the J47-23 and J47-25. The following year the J47-25 achieved an impressive 1,700 hours between overhauls. This was good news for SAC but bad news for GE, as an order for 1,500 additional J47-25s was canceled in early 1955. Still, GE was sufficiently proud of its engine's reliability that it took out a two-page advertisement in the 29th August 1955 issue of *Aviation Week* to boast that 19th BW B-47B 51-2076 had flown 1,000 hours [490,000nm (907,480km)] without any of its six J47s requiring overhaul.

All variants of the axial flow, 12-stage J47 shared common design features. The nose of the engine was made up of the airguide section and accessories drive section. This included the airguide sectors (which were anti-iced) and four island covers used as injection points

for fuel, oil, anti-icing air, throttle linkage, and electrical connections. Early models had retractable inlet screens for foreign object damage (FOD) protection, but this failure-prone feature was later eliminated. Accessory drive gears for the auxiliary components were installed in the compressor front-frame center-section. The components were mounted on frame pads and splined to reduction gears, which meshed with a common driveshaft coupled to the compressor rotor. The auxiliary components included the starter-generator, tachometer generator, fuel regulator, fuel pump, lubrication and scavenge pump, and stopcock.

The compressor rotor consisted of 12 stages on a steel shaft. The front nine of these stages were machined from 14S aluminum forgings, with the rear three made of heat-treated 410 chrome-steel forgings to withstand higher temperatures. Spacer rings between stages 1 and 10 were made of 14S aluminum and spacers between stages 10 and 12 were of 405 chrome steel. The compressor rotor was of a new type construction called curvic coupling and resulted in more efficient torque transmission while preventing circumferential shifting of the stages. The compressor wheels were geared on both sides, meshed together, and secured with axial tie-bolts.

Above: Cross section of the J47-23 engine reflects the limits of jet engine technology at the time. The mean time between failure of the engines slowly increased, but component failure was still a regular occurrence.

Left: The engine pods facilitated ground repairs, although the inner pod still required a small stand to reach the top of the engines. Overall the B-47 was fairly maintenance friendly, but some 'wrench turners' may have a different view after changing an engine in -20° weather. *USAF*

Table 4-5. **B-47 Engine Differences**

	J35-7 (TG180)	J47-11	J47-23	J47-25/-25A
B-47 Variant	XB-47	B-47A	B-47B	B-47B /B-47E
Pressure Ratio	04:01	5.05:1	5.35:1	5.45:1
Ignition Source	Vibrator Coil	Vibrator Coil	Opposite Polarity	Opposite Polarity
Airflow at Maximum Thrust	73 lb/sec	93.4 lb/sec	101.5 lb/sec	103.5 lb/sec
Limiting Mach Number	n/a	0.955	0.85	0.85
Maximum Rated Thrust (5 min)	4,125 lbf / 18.3kN	5,200 lbf / 23.1kN	5,880 lbf / 26.2kN	6,970 lbf / 31.0kN*
Normal Rated Thrust (continuous)	3,420 lbf / 15.2kN	4,730 lbf / 21.0kN	5,240 lbf / 23.3kN	5,320 lbf / 23.7kN
Specific Fuel Consumption at Normal Rated Thrust	1.026	1.071	1.037	1.028

* With water injection at 500 lb / 227kg per minute

The compressor casing (stator) was made of 355 aluminum, split horizontally, bolted together, and secured at the ends to the Dow-C magnesium front frame and the 355 aluminum compressor rear frame. The front and rear frames, forming the main mounting structure, were not split. The compressor rear frame supported the front end of the combustion chamber and served as a support for the #2 bearing. Four engine mounting pads, two on the horizontal and two on the vertical centerlines, were located on the compressor rear frame. The stator casing held multiple subassemblies. The electrical components included the main junction box, vibrator, ignition coils, emergency fuel regulator solenoid, and anti-icing valve. Fuel system components were the emergency fuel regulator, flow divider and drip valve, small slot manifold, large slot manifold, and fuel piping. Finally, the lubrication system provided for the oil cooler, oil filter, and related piping. The compressor section delivered bleed air to power the water injection system on airplanes so equipped.

The eight combustion chambers were supported by the compressor rear frame and the turbine frame front end. Each combustion chamber consisted of an outer shell and a removable inner liner with openings to permit compressed air to enter from the outer chamber. A fuel nozzle installed at the front end supplied atomized fuel. Some of the compressed air entered the nozzle at the cap while the balance was fed to the liner throughout its length via holes and louvers. Igniters were installed in two of the chambers. Cross-ignition tubes connected the forward ends of the chambers. Inside of each tube were inner crossover tubes which linked individual inner-liners permitting flame propagation from one chamber to the next. Iconel transition pieces at the aft end of each chamber delivered gas flow to the turbine nozzle diaphragm. Fabricated of 321 stainless steel, the aft frame was bolted to the compressor rear frame and supported the turbine and exhaust assemblies. It also embodied the support plates to which the combustion chambers were attached. For takeoff, a water-alcohol mixture could be injected through four nozzles located around the circumference of each combustion chamber. The nozzles were fed from individual manifolds located around each chamber which were fed from a single manifold surrounding the engine.

The J47 turbine was a single-stage unit. The turbine rotor and compressor rotor shafts were joined with a splined fit between the 12th stage compressor wheel and the front end of the turbine shaft. The turbine shaft was supported by two bearings, #3 at the mid-section of the shaft and #4 at the wheel end of the shaft. Turbine buckets were forged from heat-resistant S-816 alloy. The turbine wheel was made up of a ring of Timken 16-25-6 stainless steel welded to a 4340 steel hub. The front face of the turbine was cooled by air extracted from the 8th stage compressor. The rear face was cooled by air from the 12th stage. The nozzle diaphragm consisted of inner and outer rings of 321 stainless steel, between which 64 cast blades were welded. The exhaust cone was bolted to the turbine casing. Four rods secured to the outer cone supported the inner cone.

The engine electrical system had two circuits: starter-generator and ignition. The starter-generator was a directly coupled 24V DC unit that ran at engine speed. During ground starts it functioned as a motor to accelerate the J47 to about 550rpm (9%) for ignition. This unit then provided additional torque up to approximately 1,700rpm, assisting the engine to accelerate to its minimum idling speed of 2,200rpm (15% to 25%). As the engine reached 3,500rpm the unit supplied a continuous generator load of 300amp and 24V. A reverse-current relay switched from starter to generator and protected against a reversal of current from batteries to the starter-generator. The high-voltage ignition spark in combustion chambers #3 and #7 took place between the tips of two separate single-electrode igniters. Opposite polarity voltages were supplied to the igniters by two ignition coils operating back-to-back. This high-potential ignition system also made high altitude starts possible.

The engine oil supply system consisted of an oil tank, oil tank pressure regulator valve, oil tank filler cap, and oil shutoff valve for each engine. The pressurized tank was located between the wing spars inboard of each nacelle. Oil capacity for each tank depended on its shape. Cylindrical tanks held 9.1gal (34 liters) while hopper-type tanks held 8.75gal (33 liters). Specification MIL-O-6081 Grade 1010 oil was used at outside air temperatures (OAT) above -20.2°F (-29°C) or Grade 1005 for temperatures below -20.2°F. The oil lubrication system was a recirculating positive-displacement type composed of a three-element lubrication and scavenge pump, double element rear bearing scavenge pump, oil cooler, oil filter, check valve, and oil jet. Element #1 sent oil under pressure through the oil filter to the compressor rear frame. A separate jet was used to lubricate each bearing. A two-element pump scavenged oil from the rear of the engine and sent it through the lubrication oil cooler where it was cooled by fuel. Element #2 provided oil to the main gearcase passages and into five jets that lubricated the gears and front compressor bearing. Element #3 was the scavenge element of the system which passed oil back to the tank.

A fuel regulator governed the engine fuel control system. It managed the variable control oil pressure, which in turn controlled the main fuel pressure by means of a bypass valve. As the variable oil pressure increased, the fuel pressure also increased by reducing the fuel bypass flow. The regulator was dependent on the throttle setting, altitude conditions, airspeed, and general engine limits. The bypass fuel returned to the fuel pump inlet while the remaining fuel passed through a manually operated stopcock, the oil cooler, and finally a flow divider. This divider sent part of the fuel into the small-slot manifold for low fuel flow and the rest into the large-slot manifold. The large-slot manifold operated in parallel with the small-slot for required high fuel flow. It was operative until the fuel pressure in the flow divider reached its upper limit. A vent and drain system removed fuel and oil leaking from accessories after engine shutdown. Another vent system maintained required pressures on the three air-oil seals in the engine.

Engine anti-icing was supplied from the compressor to the rear frame and the bullet nose accessory cover and was controlled manually by the pilot. A manifold duct also carried some of this hot air to the fairings at the four island junction points. The inlet-guide vanes and front frame struts were continuously anti-iced by air bled from the 12th stage compressor at two points on opposite sides of the casing.

An engine compressor stall warning system used six sensing units, one for each engine, and relayed exhaust gas temperature (EGT) and rpm. Anytime engine rpm was between 60% and 80% and EGT was above 575°C, the warning light for the affected engine would illuminate following a 10-second delay. The warning lights were located on the copilot's instrument panel.

During 1954 GE developed a reverser for the J47 capable of 35% reverse thrust to aid in reducing the B-47's landing roll. SAC declined to purchase these due to cost, their complexity, and the added weight which would reduce the B-47's range. Another proposal in 1956 by Curtiss-Wright called for the replacement of all B-47 engines with the J65 engine. This engine produced 7,239lbf (32.2kN) thrust and was produced under license based on the Armstrong Siddeley Sapphire, and would be built at Studebaker-Packard plants. The proposal would lead to the production of some 20,000 jet engines just for the B-47 fleet. SAC planners felt that the increase in thrust of some 1,500lbf (6.7kN) per engine did not warrant the $1 billion cost with no 'gain in speed or altitude'. Moreover, SAC viewed the proposal as little more than a way to 'bail out the ailing car-maker,' which it was.

OTHER SYSTEMS

Electrical Systems
The B-47 utilized both AC and DC electrical systems, with circuit breakers and/or fuses protecting all electrical equipment. External power receptacles provided external power to the main AC or DC bus, fire control system, and BNS. As the demand for more capable electronics (especially ECM) increased over the years, modification programs updated the electrical system, especially in capacity.

The DC system used a single-wire ground return bus that received power from six engine-driven 400amp starter-generators. It also had two 12V high-rate discharge lead acid batteries linked in series or two nickel-cadmium batteries (one 9-cell and one 10-cell) comprising a 24V system connected to the bus. The batteries provided emergency starting power in case of generator failure as well as continuous partial voltage stabilization when the engines were running. Carbon-pile voltage regulators and generator control relays functioned automatically to maintain a 28V output from the generators and trip the generators in case of an under- or overvoltage or ground fault condition. Controls and indicators as well as voltmeter test jacks were provided at the copilot's station.

Three systems were used in different aircraft across the B-47 fleet to provide AC power. The first of these was a 20kVA Alternator Power System. This comprised three single-phase 2,500 volt-ampere inverters that supplied AC power regulated at 400cps, a three-phase inverter for the BNS, and main and spare three-phase instrument inverters. The single-phase inverters supplied 115V to the main, secondary, and fire control system buses. The three-phase inverter supplied 115V 400cps to the BNS A, B, and C gyros. On late model B-47s, a spare three-phase inverter was installed to power the BNS and/or flight instruments in case of failure. The emergency instrument inverter supplied enough power to the flight instruments to maintain limited flight if both alternators failed. The three-phase inverter output was 117V at 400cps. Two 20kVA alternators, one each on engine #1 and #6, furnished unregulated 115V AC at 380-800cps. The alternator outputs were connected to the aircraft buses by means of relays that were energized by a bus selector switch. Two switches on the unregulated AC power panel on the copilot's sidewall panel controlled the alternators.

The second AC power system utilized two 40kVA alternators located on engines #1 and #6. Governed drive units provided a sustained output speed of 6,000rpm when input speed were between 3,000 and 8,100 rpm. The units were normally operated in parallel but could be operated individually. The third AC system was identical to the previous one but with a third 40kVA alternator added to the #5 engine. Automatic paralleling control was required and was accomplished by synchronizing each alternator with the main AC bus.

Hydraulic Systems
The Stratojet had three hydraulic systems: main, emergency, and rudder surface/elevator power control system. The main and emergency systems normally operated at 3,000psi. These were interconnected by a series of shuttle valves so that the emergency system would take over should the main system pressure fall below that of the emergency system. All hydraulic systems were filled from a common main tank that held 7gal (26.5 liters) of hydraulic fluid (Specification MIL-O-5606). The warning and indicating system was located on the copilot's hydraulic panel.

The main hydraulic system powered the brakes and steering, the canopy (both sliding and clamshell), the air refueling system, and the bomb bay doors. Normal hydraulic pressure in the flight control system was 1,500 psi. The air refueling system consisted of the slipway door and latching toggles that secured the refueling boom nozzle in the receptacle. The flight control hydraulic systems positioned the primary flight control surfaces and the flaperons, and consisted of a surface power control panel, an aileron-flaperon hydraulic system, and a rudder-elevator hydraulic system (a back up elevator hydraulic system was installed on airplanes modified for LABS). The flight control hydraulic systems also prevented transmission of forces from the flight control surfaces to control cable systems, and prevented control surface flutter at high speeds.

Cockpit Systems
The AC and copilot had basic flight control and instruments duplicated at both positions. Each pilot had a control column for roll and pitch and rudder pedals for yaw. When not in use the control column could be disconnected and stowed in a cutout section of the instrument panel. The left handle of the column carried an autopilot/air refueling disconnect switch and a microphone switch. A 'Boeing B-47' emblem was mounted on the hub of the wheel (Douglas-Tulsa and Lockheed-Marietta had similar emblems bearing their company names). Both AC and copilot had adjustable rudder pedals (with the Boeing logo) that supported the entire foot. All controls were connected to their power units by cables, with manual backup via cables directly to the control surfaces. The navigator had a directional controller for guiding the airplane during bombing runs.

Six engine throttles were located on side stands to the right of the AC and copilot positions. These side panels also held the ATO switch, flap selector, trim wheels for all three flight axes, the emergency gear retraction switch, and the DCS switch to extend the rear main gear and outriggers for speed braking.

The pilots' instrument panel was very crowded with flight instruments, engine indicators, and various warning lights. Flight instruments included the B-1 attitude indicator, N-1 directional indicator, ID-249 ILS and TACAN indicator, ID-250 azimuth for the AN/ARN-6 radio compass, ID-310 distance indicator for TACAN, Machmeter, accelerometer, altimeter, vertical velocity indicator, turn-and-slip indicator, and AN/APN-22 radar altimeter. A magnetic compass was mounted on the right windshield frame. Engine instruments included tachometers, fuel flow meters, EGT gauges, and oil pressure gauges. There were lights for water injection, bombs away, compass inoperative, anti-skid, empennage overheating, and

1. Instrument Panel
2. Surface Power Control Panel
3. Brake Chute Deployment Handle
4. Pilot's Switch Panel
5. Fire Warning Test Panel
6. Ignition Switch Panel
7. Pilot's Control Stand
8. Bomb Salvo Switch
9. Canopy Lock Lever
10. Fuel Control Panel
11. Magnetic Compass Light Switch
    or TAC-VOR Selector Panel

pilot's station (typical)

1. Instrument Panel
2. Landing Gear Control Panel
3. Air Refueling Panel

copilot's station

air refueling. The landing gear selector handle was on the mid-right side.

On the pilot's left sidewall was the autopilot controller that was springloaded or used electrical power to fold away or extend when in use. The A12D automatic pilot maintained attitude, altitude, and heading, provided a stable bombing platform when connected to the bombing-navigation system, and provided an accurate flight path

when working with the automatic landing approach system. The autopilot used an internal vertical gyro for pitch and roll data, and inputs from the N-1 compass system directional gyro provided yaw data. Other items installed included the map case, a variety of emergency equipment, and a food warmer.

The copilot had virtually identical flight instruments on his smaller panel but with fewer warning lights. His engine indicators were

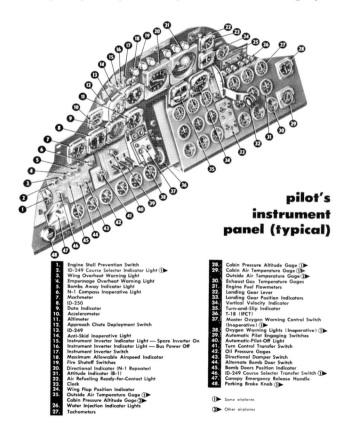

pilot's instrument panel (typical)

1. Engine Stall Prevention Switch
2. ID-249 Course Selector Indicator Light ①▸
3. Wing Overheat Warning Light
4. Empennage Overheat Warning Light
5. Bombs Away Indicator Light
6. N-1 Compass Inoperative Light
7. Machmeter
8. ID-250
9. Data Indicator
10. Accelerometer
11. Altimeter
12. Approach Chute Deployment Switch
13. ID-249
14. Anti-Skid Inoperative Light
15. Instrument Inverter Indicator Light — Spare Inverter On
16. Instrument Inverter Indicator Light — Bus Power Off
17. Instrument Inverter Switch
18. Maximum Allowable Airspeed Indicator
19. Fire Shutoff Switches
20. Directional Indicator (N-1 Repeater)
21. Attitude Indicator (B-1)
22. Air Refueling Ready-for-Contact Light
23. Clock
24. Wing Flap Position Indicator
25. Outside Air Temperature Gage ①▸ Cabin Pressure Altitude Gage ②▸
26. Water Injection Indicator Lights
27. Tachometers

28. Cabin Pressure Altitude Gage ①▸
29. Cabin Air Temperature Gage ①▸
30. Outside Air Temperature Gage ②▸
31. Exhaust Gas Temperature Gages
32. Engine Fuel Flowmeters
33. Landing Gear Lever
34. Landing Gear Position Indicators
35. Vertical Velocity Indicator
36. Turn-and-Slip Indicator
37. T-18 (IFCT)
38. Master Oxygen Warning Control Switch (Inoperative) ①▸
39. Oxygen Warning Lights (Inoperative) ①▸
40. Automatic Pilot Engaging Switches
41. Automatic-Pilot-Off Light
42. Turn Control Transfer Switch
43. Oil Pressure Gages
44. Directional Damper Switch
45. Alternate Bomb Door Switch
46. Bomb Doors Position Indicator
47. ID-249 Course Selector Transfer Switch ①▸
48. Canopy Emergency Release Handle
49. Parking Brake Knob ①▸

① Some airplanes
② Other airplanes

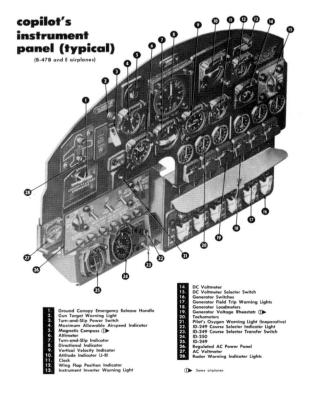

copilot's instrument panel (typical)
(B-47B and E airplanes)

1. Ground Canopy Emergency Release Handle
2. Gun Target Warning Light
3. Turn-and-Slip Power Switch
4. Maximum Allowable Airspeed Indicator
5. Magnetic Compass ①▸
6. Altimeter
7. Turn-and-Slip Indicator
8. Directional Indicator
9. Vertical Velocity Indicator
10. Attitude Indicator (J-8)
11. Clock
12. Wing Flap Position Indicator
13. Instrument Inverter Warning Light

14. DC Voltmeter
15. DC Voltmeter Selector Switch
16. Generator Switches
17. Generator Field Trip Warning Lights
18. Generator Loadmeters
19. Generator Voltage Rheostat
20. Tachometers
21. Pilot's Oxygen Warning Light (Inoperative)
22. ID-249 Course Selector Indicator Light ①▸
23. ID-249 Course Selector Transfer Switch ①▸
24. ID-250
25. ID-249
26. Regulated AC Power Panel
27. AC Voltmeter
28. Radar Warning Indicator Lights

① Some airplanes

limited to tachometers, although EGT gauges were installed on TB-47Bs. Electrical controls and indicators were a prominent feature of the copilot's panel. The air-refueling panel was located to the front of the copilot's throttle stand as were the engine compressor stall warning lights. The ATO rack could be released by pulling a handle on the side of the stand. On the floor behind the throttle stand was the handle that controlled the air-refueling valve. Circuit breakers were mounted on the sidewall behind the throttle stand.

The copilot could swivel his seat to the rear and gain access to the gunnery station. Although either A-5 or the MD-4 units could be installed they were much the same with a few differences in control boxes and the antenna control handle. Aircraft with the A-5 system had the radio compass loop antenna installed on the decking just inside the rear canopy.

While the gunnery system was designed to be somewhat automatic, the copilot was required to turn the unit on, set altitude, airspeed, and temperature, manually select a target, monitor tracking, and fire the guns when the target was in range. The automated features detected pursuing aircraft and warned the copilot, allowed the copilot to select the most dangerous pursuing target, tracked a selected target, corrected target position data to allow for parallax, ballistic, and lead errors, and continuously controlled the direction of the tail guns. The copilot fired the guns by pressing the 'Fire' button on the left side of the main panel. The tail guns would fire only if the safety switch was in the FIRE position, the turret and radar antenna were within 3° electrical alignment (accounting for computer corrections), the turret was not at an azimuth or elevation limit, and the system was in 'hand control' with the manual antenna control handle 'action switch' depressed or in automatic track mode with the radar range gate locked onto a target radar return. The copilot was required to differentiate between chaff and actual aircraft, eliminate ground return, recognize a pursuit curve attack and straight line attack, as well as perform emergency in-flight maintenance on a faulty unit or perform an emergency manual search.

The main features of the copilot's left sidewall were the radio and ECM control panels. Also featured were two thermos bottles and a cup dispenser. The ELGE handles were on the floor against the port rear wall. Relief cups were located alongside. All aircraft were provided with from one to two relief tubes (horns) although former crewmen will testify that the system seldom worked as intended. Two 1qt (0.95 liters) relief containers were located at each station. A chemical toilet was installed on some B-47s and was located under the pilot's floor when stowed and swung into the walkway for use.

A narrow and sloping walkway led downward into the nose to the navigator's station. The prominent features of this position were the periscopic bombsight, the bombsight stabilizer, the plan position indicator (PPI) scope, instrument panels, and a desk. The bombsight stabilizer was a large cylindrical unit located on the airplane centerline under the bombsight which contained slaved gyros that provided the stable vertical and true north references with which the computer resolved the bombing problem. On the left edge of the desk was the navigator's tracking control (with the 'dead man's' switch to engage the control). The bomb control panel was on the right sidewall above the desk. On the left sidewall were various control boxes for the rendezvous radar and radar camera. Between the navigator and pilot were several amplifier racks and spares for the electronics.

Bombing-Navigation System
The MA-7A bombing-navigation system (BNS) was composed of the ME-5 computer, AN/APS-64 radar, MA-4 optical bombsight group, OA-704/APS-23B interconnector group, and the AN/AWA-2 pulse generator. The MA-7A featured a 10in (25.4cm) plan position indicator (PPI) indicator and a pulse generator (for indirect bomb damage assessment), and a radar with tunable magnetron. The MA-7A was actually an improved version of the previous K-4A system which used an AN/APS-23 radar but had less range.

When the system was used for bombing, the target was sighted by radar or the optical sight. Wind correction and ballistics data were

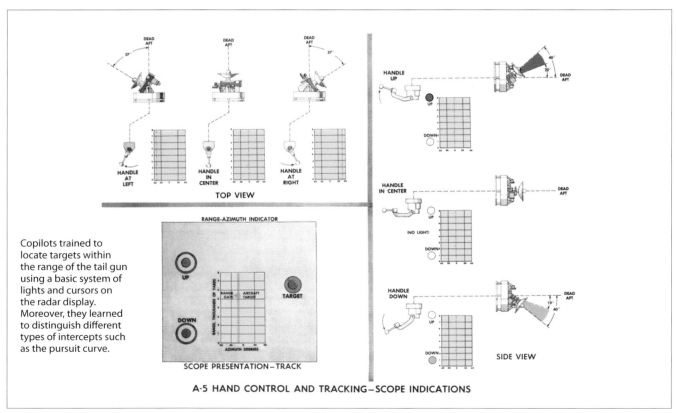

Copilots trained to locate targets within the range of the tail gun using a basic system of lights and cursors on the radar display. Moreover, they learned to distinguish different types of intercepts such as the pursuit curve.

A-5 HAND CONTROL AND TRACKING—SCOPE INDICATIONS

Table 4-6. Standard Communication Gear

Type	Equipment	Function	Primary Operator	Range
Interphone	AN/AIC-10A	Communication for Crew; Audio from other electronics	All Crew	Inside Aircraft
UHF Command Radio	AN/ARC-27	Short, 2-way voice	Pilot, Copilot	Line of sight
Liaison Radio	AN/ARC-65X	Long range 2-way voice and CW	Copilot	250-2,000nm / 463-3,704km) depending on operating frequency and time of day
Radio Compass	AN/ARN-6	Low freq. homing	Pilot	Up to 200nm / 370km
Direction Finder	AN/ARA-25	UHF homing	Pilot	Line of sight
Localizer/VOR	AN/ARN-14	Navigation/Inst. Approach	Pilot	45-100nm / 83-185km
Glide Slope	AN/ARN-18	Instrument Approach	Pilot	25nm / 46km
TACAN	AN/ARN-21	Distance and bearing to TACAN station	Pilot	200nm / 370km
Marker Beacon	AN/ARN-12	Location Marker Signal for Instrument Approach	Automatic	Low Altitude

entered and thereafter the system produced a continuous bombing solution displaying heading and time-to-go information to the pilot. The system could be coupled to the autopilot and intervalometer circuits to completely automate the bombing run, opening and closing the bomb bay doors and releasing the weapon. As a navigational aid the system would continuously compute and display dead reckoning latitude and longitude. Corrections could be entered when a known landmark was in optical or radar sighting distance. The system also permitted use of grid navigation methods for polar flights. True airspeed, true heading, and wind component information was provided to the crew continuously.

An automatic O-15 camera system was used in conjunction with the BNS to photograph the PPI radarscope, and was attached by a periscopic mount. Photos could be made every scan, every other scan, every four scans, or every 12 scans. The O-23 system operated in conjunction with the O-15 to make photographic records of radar and optical images appearing in the bombsight. The camera body and magazine were mounted on the bombsight. Photos could be made of radar or optical images, or both.

Communications and Navigation System

The bomber configuration carried standard communications and navigation equipment, many of which were legacy types from the Second World War while others were fairly new designs. The interphone system was notorious for failure or intermittent operation, and was not separate from radio transmissions. This meant that should a crewman actuate the interphone during a radio call he would block out the radio transmission.

Electronic Countermeasures Systems

B-47s were equipped to carry electronic countermeasures (ECM) transmitters to jam enemy radars and prevent detection (see Chapter 3 for the evolution of ECM equipment and dates of installation). Transmitters were located in pairs in the aft radar compartment, camera compartment, right and left ECM compartments, and/or the bomb bay. The particular transmitters used depended on the tactical situation and the radar frequencies expected to be encountered. Each installation required three components to be installed: the transmitter, the transmitter control box, and the power supply. Aircraft equipped with the TEE TOWN pod carried additional transmitters externally. All of the equipment was turned on and off with controls at the copilot's left sidewall.

Each B-47 was also equipped with two AN/ALE-1 chaff dispensers. These were installed in the left and right ECM compartments (the original internal ATO compartment). An AN/APS-54 radar warning system was installed on the nose and tail and provided indication if the aircraft was threatened by airborne interception or gun-laying radar. A light on the AC and copilot instrument panels warned of a threat, and this was accompanied by an audible tone. AN/APX-25 IFF equipment provided identification

to friendly surface or airborne radars. Dedicated Phase V or BLUE CRADLE B-47 jamming aircraft are described in Chapter 3.

Utility Systems

An anti-ice system was designed to prevent ice formation on aircraft surfaces. Hot bleed air from two ports on each engine compressor protected the wings, empennage, engines, air refueling slipway door, and the nacelles. Air from the lower port was used for the nacelle struts while air from the upper port was used for the wings, empennage, and the air-refueling door. The pitot heads, air-refueling slipway, windshield, and Q-spring air inlet were protected by the electrical system. Blowers provided air to defrost the pilot's windshield and canopy, and navigator's windows. An electric heater was also used for the windshield.

A 305psi high-pressure liquid oxygen system supplied breathing oxygen to the crew. The regulators automatically reduced the system pressure to approximate ambient regulator pressure regardless of the altitude. Liquid oxygen was stored in two A-2 8 liter (2gal) converters that automatically converted the liquid to the gaseous state on demand from the crew.

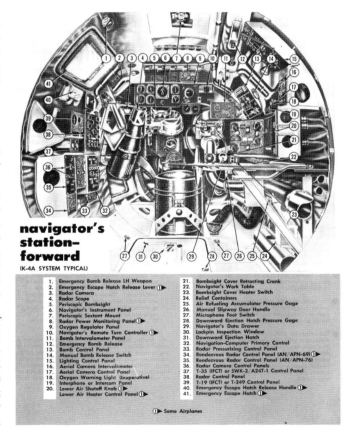

navigator's station— forward
(K-4A SYSTEM TYPICAL)

1. Emergency Bomb Release LH Weapon	21. Bombsight Cover Retracting Crank
2. Emergency Escape Hatch Release Lever ①	22. Navigator's Work Table
3. Radar Camera	23. Bombsight Cover Heater Switch
4. Radar Scope	24. Relief Containers
5. Periscopic Bombsight	25. Air Refueling Accumulator Pressure Gage
6. Navigator's Instrument Panel	26. Manual Slipway Door Handle
7. Periscopic Sextant Mount	27. Microphone Foot Switch
8. Radar Power Monitoring Panel ①	28. Downward Ejection Hatch Pressure Gage
9. Oxygen Regulator Panel	29. Navigator's Data Drawer
10. Navigator's Remote Turn Controller ①	30. Lockpin Inspection Window
11. Bomb Intervalometer Panel	31. Downward Ejection Hatch
12. Emergency Bomb Release	32. Navigation-Computer Primary Control
13. Bomb Control Panel	33. Radar Pressurizing Control Panel
14. Manual Bomb Release Switch	34. Rendezvous Radar Control Panel (AN/APN-69) ①
15. Lighting Control Panel	35. Rendezvous Radar Control Panel (AN/APN-76)
16. Aerial Camera Intervalometer	36. Radar Camera Control Panels
17. Aerial Camera Control Panel	37. T-35 (IFCT) or SWK-2/A24T-1 Control Panel
18. Oxygen Warning Light (Inoperative)	38. Radar Control Panel
19. Interphone or Intercom Panel	39. T-19 (IFCT) or T-249 Control Panel
20. Lower Air Shutoff Knob ①	40. Emergency Escape Hatch Release Handle ①
Lower Air Heater Control Panel ①	41. Emergency Escape Hatch ①

① ▶ Some Airplanes

CHAPTER FIVE

Ready for War

Many aviation and military historians tend to take for granted that the B-47 was designed *ab initio* with the capability of delivering an atomic weapon (then known as 'special weapons'), and that operational procedures changed little beyond the shift from high-altitude to low-altitude bombing induced by the evolving Soviet SAM threat. In fact, the B-47 was never originally intended to carry an atomic weapon. It was not until 10th September 1948 that AMC and Air Force Headquarters officially decreed that the B-47 would be a 'special weapons' airplane, nearly nine months after the first flight of XB-47 46-0065. Consequently, this meant that the 'definitive' B-47 weapons configuration evolved over time, placing excessive – and unrealistic – demands on the airframe design and development and undermining its operational readiness for SAC. Moreover, atomic planners enumerated three crucial axioms that defined the relationship of an atomic bomb to its delivery system: '(1) the magnitude of the explosion would have great bearing on the delivery system selected; (2) … the size of the explosion should be influenced by the means of delivery, the targets to be struck and the psychological factors as well as the scientific and technical aspects of the weapon; and (3) the weight and configuration of the bomb and

airborne equipment should be adjusted to the vehicle of delivery.' This created the ultimate 'chicken and egg' paradox for the B-47 and atomic weapons: which came first, the bomber or the bomb?

Know Your Nukes

Chuck Hansen's 1988 book *US Nuclear Weapons: The Secret History* remains the definitive starting point for anyone interested in the technical history of the atomic bomb. These weapons were closely linked to SAC given that its B-29s, B-36s, and B-50s were initially the only methods of delivering the bombs to targets in the USSR and its allies (sea- and ground-based weapons, plus tactical air-dropped bombs, would come later). As the B-47 evolved into a combat-ready bomber, so too did SAC's stewardship of and operational tactics with atomic weapons.

Early atomic bombs such as the Mark IV and Mark VI were the size of a Volkswagen Beetle, weighed 10,000 lb (4,536kg), required the insertion of a 'core' which initiated the nuclear reaction, and in peacetime were maintained by the Atomic Energy Commission (AEC). A B-47 could carry one of these early 'open pit' weapons. There is some ambiguity about which crewmember was responsible for the 'care and feeding' of an atomic weapon once it was loaded. Some former B-47 fliers recall that it was the copilot who monitored the weapons and inserted the pit from the 'birdcage' container needed to arm open pit atomic weapons. Others state unequivocally that this was the navigator's duty. Official sources have not been declassified to determine the truth, but it is likely that at different times both the

Above: Fully armed with a nuclear weapon, ATO racks, chaff, and 20mm cannon shells, B-47E 53-2164 basks in the English countryside on 18th August 1963. It was nearly a decade before the B-47 fleet was fully ready for war, only to be retired two years later. *via Stephen Miller*

Left: A single Mark VI atom bomb filled the B-47's bomb bay. This 'one-bomb, one-airplane' ratio meant that SAC required multiple B-47s for many of the more than 1,000 targets in the USSR to ensure their destruction. Ultimately this forced weapon size to decrease and bomber capacity to increase. *NMUSAF*

Table 5-1. **Known B-47 Nuclear Incidents** (see Appendix II for complete descriptions of losses)

Date	Aircraft	Serial	Unit	Incident Location	Summary
10 Mar 56	B-47E	52-0534	306th BW	Mediterranean Sea	During a deployment to Sidi Slimane AB, *Inkspot 59* descended through cloud cover for air refueling. Contact was lost and the airplane presumably crashed into the Mediterrean Sea. Its two nuclear capsules have not been located.
27 Jul 56	B-47E	53-4230	307th BW	RAF Lakenheath, UK	While practicing touch-and-go landings, B-47E 53-4230 crashed into a nuclear weapon storage igloo containing 3 MkVI nuclear weapons. There was no high explosive detonation, but the 'bomb disposal officer says [it was] a miracle that one mark six with exposed detonators sheared didn't go.'
11 Oct 57	B-47B	51-2139	379th BW	Homestead AFB, FL	The crew of *Derby 38* attempted takeoff with flat outrigger tire. The airplane failed to accelerate properly, and the crew further mishandled the situation leading to a stall and crash. The single nuclear weapon was damaged but recovered.
31 Jan 58	B-47E	52-0242	306th BW	Sidi Slimane AB, Morocco	During a Coco alert taxi the aft wheel casing failed and the rear fuselage struck the ground rupturing the aft fuel tank. Despite the ensuing fire the fully configured nuclear weapon did not detonate. Base residents were evacuated, and although contamination of the wreckage was high, there was limited radioactivity beyond the crash site.
05 Feb 58	B-47B	51-2349	19th BW	Savannah, GA	During a night training mission, F-86L *Gold 01* collided with B-47B *Ivory 02*. The B-47 crew was ordered to jettison the sole Mk15 Mod 0 nuclear weapon on board to prevent widespread contamination should they crash on landing. The weapon was jettisoned into the Wassau Sound off the coast near Savannah. The weapon was not located, and has been the subject of contentious search efforts, including a hoax claim that a honeymooning couple had found the bomb while scuba diving.
11 Mar 58	B-47E	53-1876	2nd BW	Mars Bluff, SC	Shortly after takeoff for an overseas deployment, the navigator of *Garfield 13* accidentally jettisoned the single unarmed nuclear weapon. The conventional explosive detonated on impact, creating a crater 70ft (21m) in diameter and 30ft (9m) deep on the property of Walter Gregg of Mars Bluff, SC, 6.5nm (12km) east of Florence, SC. Gregg and five members of his family sustained minor injuries; five other homes and a church were damaged.
04 Nov 58	B-47E	51-2391	341st BW	Dyess AFB, TX	During takeoff an ATO bottle exploded on ignition, rupturing fuel lines and leading to an uncontrollable fire. The B-47E crashed shortly after takeoff. The sole nuclear weapon on board was destroyed. Contamination was restricted to the immediate area of impact.
26 Nov 58	B-47E	53-4212	44th BW	Chennault AFB, LA	An ATO bottle exploded while the airplane was on the ramp, leading to complete destruction of the B-47E and the sole nuclear weapon on board. No explosion of the weapon occurred and contamination was limited to the immediate vicinity of the airplane.
01 Jan 60	B-47E	52-5243	380th BW	Plattsburgh AFB, NY	While on alert, ground power was applied leading to an unintentional gear retraction. The fuselage broke in two leading to a massive fuel spill. Fortunately, the fuel did not ignite.
Jan 63	B-47E	n/a	40th BW	Forbes AFB, KS	The aircraft commander of an alert B-47 inadvertently actuated the navigator's nuclear weapon control switch. In a futile effort to mask this serious but modest misbehavior, he actuated the pilot's nuclear weapon readiness switch, removed the nuclear weapon safety wiring, and broke the seals for the weapon. The AC then reported a SEVEN HIGH (suspected sabotage) to account for the event.
26 May 64	B-47E	52-0525	509th BW	RAF Upper Heyford, UK	This airplane was struck by B-47E 53-2296, which was destroyed. As 52-0525 was on REFLEX alert when it was damaged, it certainly carried a nuclear weapon. The airplane was eventually scrapped, but there is no reference to any adverse nuclear event.

Unverified B-47 Nuclear Incidents

Date	Aircraft	Serial	Unit	Incident Location	Summary
30 Nov 56	B-47E	52-3360	301th BW	Port Arthur, Canada	While on an Operational Readiness Inspection flight over Canada, the airplane suffered from aileron control failure. The crew bailed out and the plane crashed. There is no official confirmation that the plane carried a nuclear weapon, but the Canadian government had earlier in November approved overflight of B-47s carrying nuclear weapons while participating in an ORI, and some search-and-rescue crews claim they were told to look for the downed fliers and a 'nuclear weapon'.
28 Feb 58	B-47E	53-6204	310th BW	RAF Greenham Common, United Kingdom	B-47E 52-2154 jettisoned its drop tanks, one of which fell 65ft (20m) from B-47E 53-6204, which was being fueled. Anti-nuclear activists claim it had a 'B28' nuclear weapon on board, which experienced a conventional explosion, killing 2 and scattering radioactive contamination in an 8nm (15km) radius. Both the US and UK governments deny this event involved nuclear weapons or a fire. Claims of a nuclear incident remain unconvincing.

copilot and navigator performed this duty. Later atomic weapons such as the Mk15 and Mk28 thermonuclear bombs had the core built in and were known as 'sealed-pit' weapons.

Although SAC would use the bombs, the AEC was the custodian of the bombs. Through 1952 atomic bombs were stored at AEC facilities known as National Stockpile Sites, with 'launch timing under the [Emergency War Plan (EWP)]…measured in hours and days'. In the event of war, SAC Douglas C-124s would fly to these locations, collect the bombs, and deliver them to bomber bases. This incurred both a substantial time and operational penalty. In the event of surprise attack there was insufficient time to retrieve the bombs.

Even with advance warning it might take as long as 24-36 hours to deliver the first bomb to a SAC base for loading. In turn, bomb crews lacked the regular training needed to load the weapons correctly and expeditiously. Early no-notice inspections of weapons loading teams (including the vaunted 509th BW) revealed widespread errors in loading and lack of 'nuclear surety' knowledge. LeMay pushed to have the bombs and their capsules stored at SAC bases to facilitate their immediate use when needed and to ensure that crews were properly trained and current in loading them. In September 1952 President Harry S Truman approved the joint storage of bombs and capsules at SAC bases in the US and overseas. It ultimately fell to

newly elected President Dwight D Eisenhower to implement this transfer more fully. In April 1954 he authorized the storage of 183 atomic bombs at overseas locations, including the UK and French Morocco for the B-47s deployed there. In December he approved the storage of atomic weapons at 22 additional Air Force bases, and by 1956 bombs and capsules were stored at all SAC bases.

LeMay wanted more. His philosophy of 'train like you fight' required SAC crews to practice loading actual atomic weapons – rather than 'shapes' – into his bombers, and then fly actual profile missions. In June 1954 Eisenhower approved SAC's request to carry 'complete' bombs (both bomb and capsule) on SAC bombers during major exercises such as Unit Simulated Combat Missions (USCM) and operations such as IRON BAR. This also required extensive international diplomatic coordination, as the British Prime Minister insisted on being informed of any SAC flights over the UK which carried atomic weapons. By 1959 these proved exceptionally tedious as SAC had to provide the Air Ministry with possible 'deviation of flight plans, flight number and call signs, type of aircraft, time and day of flight, number of people aboard, and other data' for each flight. Canada approved SAC overflights (known as 'XYZ Missions') on a case-by-case basis. Whether or not this courtesy extended to the King of French Morocco remains debatable. At the end of 1954 the US had 2,063 atomic weapons of all types, and SAC controlled 167 of these. By 1957 SAC had 1,655 bombs under its control.

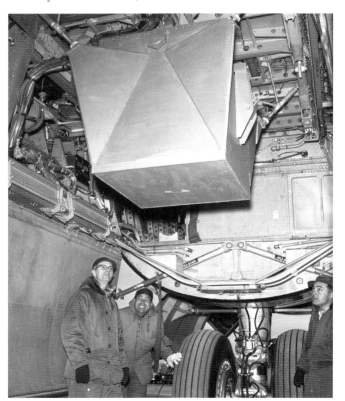

Once the SAC alert force was established, General Power (who had replaced LeMay as CINCSAC in October 1957) requested authority to launch a portion of the alert force under simulated wartime conditions. Air Force Chief of Staff General Thomas D White declined given the risk of inadvertent atomic explosion of open-pit bombs in the event of a crash. Estimates of such an explosion ranged from 1 in 500 to 1 in 10,000 based on the status of safety pins and other arming conditions. Aside from highly publicized incidents in French Morocco and Georgia, B-47E 52-3360 crashed in Canada on 30th November 1956 while on an XYZ mission and presumably carried an atomic weapon or at least the non-nuclear components, so crash concerns were not unreasonable (see Appendix II).

Power pushed for the accelerated delivery of sealed-pit bombs, which finally began to trickle into SAC's inventory. By 30th June 1958 B-47s at Pease AFB and Plattsburgh AFB received the Mk 39 Mod 1, while those at Mountain Home AFB received the Mk 15 Mod 2. 'To provide a realistic no-notice test of the alert force,' Power wrote in May 1958, 'weapons must be flown. During [USCMs] in order to generate and launch on an EWP schedule while exercising all phases of ground support it is mandatory to fly this [sealed-pit] weapon.' Not surprisingly, the AEC rejected this request, and by December 1958 SAC awaited President Eisenhower's final decision on the matter. Eventually the point was moot as in 1959 SAC began its airborne alert program using B-52s equipped with fully operational sealed-pit thermonuclear weapons.

An Atom Bomber

In August 1946 the Air Staff decreed that all 'future bombers capable of carrying bombs equivalent in weight to the A-bomb should be required to carry the A-bomb itself,' and two or more if space was available. This meant that if an atomic bomb weighed 10,000 lb (4,536kg) then any future bomber designed to carry a 10,000 lb non-nuclear weapon – such as the XB-47 – must be able to carry an atom bomb. This was far easier said than done. AMC representatives responsible for linking military capabilities to contractor designs lacked the necessary clearances to discuss weapons details with the bomb designers at the Sandia Laboratories in Albuquerque, NM. Moreover, even if they had access to this classified information they could not share it with aircraft designers who lacked the security clearances to work with atomic weapons-related programs. The time involved in granting new clearances was excessive, especially given the number of requests for new clearances. This not only made it difficult for engineers at Boeing trying to design the B-47 but hindered AMC liaison officers by excluding them from these secret data. At best the engineers were told only general dimensions (known as Type B information) of the 'Fat Man' atom bomb, for example, so they could design the length, height, and width of the bomb bay, and the general weight of the bomb so they could estimate the airframe needed to carry it and fuel on its strike mission. Other crucial details, such as the bomb's center of gravity (cg) and suspension point(s) were absurdly considered classified Type A information which could not be released to uncleared parties, complicating the placement of internal structures on which to hang the bomb as well as how the bomb was to be loaded into the aircraft. The dilemma was clear: the Army Air Force (and later the Air Force) was responsible for

Above: Pease AFB and Plattsburgh AFB were the first B-47 units to equip the Mk39, an improved Mk15 thermonuclear bomb. The massive explosion dictated a change in SAC's delivery tactics. *NMUSAF*

Left: The AEC and Sandia Labs refused to share technical details about early US atomic bombs, forcing Boeing to speculate on the actual weight, cg, and suspension when designing the B-47's bomb bay. Dead weight was used during structural and flight tests. *Photo Courtesy Boeing*

Table 5-2. **B-47 Special Weapons**

Weapon Type*	Weight (lb/kg)	Length (in/cm)	Diameter (in/cm)	Yield	Entry†	Exit†	Comments
Mark IV	10,900/4,536	128/325	60/152	1-31 kt	Mar 49	May 53	Not used operationally by B-47s
Mark V	3,175/1,440	128.5/326	43.75/111	11-47 kt	May 52	Jan 63	B-47 use canceled in 1954
Mark VI	8,500/3,856	128/325	61/155	8-160 kt	Jul 51	Jan 61	
Mk 15	7,600/3,447	139/353	34.7/88	1.7-3.75 Mt	Apr 55	Apr 65	
Mk 28 IN	1,980/898	96/243	29/74	70kt - 1.45 Mt	Aug 58	Apr 92	
Mk 28 RI	2,340/1,061	147/373	22/56	70kt - 1.45 Mt	1960	1964	
Mk 36	17,500/7,938	149.8/380	58.5/149	9-10 Mt	Apr 56	Jan 52	
Mk 39 ‡	9,500/4,309	139/353	42/107	1.7-3.75 Mt	Feb 57	Nov 66	
Mk 41	10,670/4,840	148/379	50/127	10 Mt	Sep 60	Jul 76	
Mk 43	2,100/953	150/381	18/46	< 1.0 Mt	Apr 61	Apr 91	

IN = free fall inertial; RI = parachute retarded inertial; kt = kiltons; Mt = megatons; * = includes all subvariants;
† = denotes entry and exit into Air Force service; ‡ = SAC histories show this as a B-47 weapon but other sources do not; variant of the Mk 15

delivering the atom bomb, but the Manhattan District and Sandia Laboratory were responsible for *designing* the bomb and were loath to share any physical details about it because of excess secrecy.

Solutions to the security issue were long in coming and generally inadequate. Many employees left Boeing for work elsewhere rather than sit idle while awaiting even a temporary clearance. Boeing engineers were forced to submit questions to only a handful of AMC or Sandia personnel who responded without explanation or clarification about their answers. In February 1948 the Atomic Energy Commission (AEC) established guidelines that illustrate these handicaps. The AEC would furnish dimensions to Boeing engineers for the construction of a mockup bomb bay. Boeing would then build and ship this to the Sandia Laboratory at Albuquerque where AEC designers with the requisite security clearances would make the necessary changes. This updated mockup would then be returned to Boeing but AEC would retain any special parts developed for the atomic bomb installation – essentially giving Boeing an empty box with missing components. For example, declassified documents from the 2nd July 1950 conference on the proposed TX-14 weapon indicate that the device should not exceed a weight of 50,000 lb (22,680kg), a diameter of 62.5in (159cm), and a length of 240in (610cm) but did not reveal how the device would be loaded into or mounted in the bomb bay or how it would be released. As far as the AEC was concerned, the 'carrier should be tailored to the bomb'.

AMC responded to this dysfunctional relationship by emphasizing the necessity of designing bombers and weapons cooperatively. During late 1948 AMC officials told AEC security managers that 'the atomic bomb has been considered as a weapon inflexible to diameter, weight, shape, and destructive capability. It is now known that atomic bombs can be designed to vary these factors. [On behalf of improving bomber design, AMC is] vitally interested in maintaining the concept that an atomic weapon is *an integration of the bomb or warhead, and the vehicle which carries it*' [emphasis added].

In theory this unlocked sealed doors for Boeing. The Air Force Mockup Board convened in December 1948 to determine a weapons configuration for the B-47B. This resulted in three variants: *normal* – to carry just an atomic bomb; *alternate* – to carry general purpose bombs; and *special* – a general purpose bomb bay with extended doors running the full length of the bomb bay. All B-47Bs were to be delivered in the normal configuration but kits would be supplied to permit changing from normal to special in 60 man-hours per airplane. The B-47 would carry the Mark IV, Mark V, and Mark VI atom bombs in use (or projected use) by the Air Force as well as the US Navy-developed Mark VIII.

Inspections of the Boeing mockup in early 1949, however, revealed that the planned bomb bay would not accommodate the Mark III and 'possibly not even the Mark VI' without additional changes. On 15th and 16th March 1949 AFSWC loaded a fully operational Mark IV bomb into the mockup, and affirmed that the

proposed changes would make the B-47B a 'suitable atomic bomb airplane.' These included eliminating the right-hand forward auxiliary bomb bay fuel tank, installation of guide rails, adjusting sway braces, extending the catwalk on the left side, relocating some of the lighting, modifying the left rear auxiliary fuel tank to carry 15gal (57 liters) less, providing 10° fall clearance at both ends of the bomb bay, incorporating a mechanical release to salvo the bombs, and including additional indicator lights on the copilot's panel. For all of AMC's efforts, however, there were still substantial problems to be resolved. In addition to these changes, Air Force Headquarters proposed a standardized 'universal' bomb suspension system consisting of 'bomb racks, moveable shackles, sway braces, and arming control.' The Air Force wanted one system for the B-29, B-36, B-47, and B-50 but eventually abandoned this due to technical delays and the unique nature of the B-47's bomb bay and fuselage integration.

What followed was a tedious and highly technical debate over the placement of the bombs in the bomb bay – the type of rack to be used, where the mounting point lugs should be placed (based on each bomb's cg), wiring bundle pathways, and even sensitivity of the equipment and bomb to ambient temperatures. This was not straightforward as all B-47 supporting structures and equipment for suspension and release of the atomic bombs were built directly into the fuel tank floor that formed the ceiling of the bomb bay. Once assembled, changes could not be made without extensive and costly rework of the fuel tank at the depot level. Most importantly, the central issue was not which atomic weapons the B-47 would carry when it was declared operational, but what weapons it *could* carry

A 'clip' of four Mk28 hydrogen bombs eventually became a standard load, allowing a single B-47 to hit up to four targets or deliver two bombs on one target. For a time B-52s were equipped with this configuration although with ADM-20 Quail drones, which the B-47 could not carry. *NMUSAF*

years into the future as new weapons were designed. Tests in February 1951 found that the sway braces worked well for the Mark IV, were incompatible with the Mark V, and required redesign to work with the Mark VI. These unsatisfactory results did not bode well for future weapon compatibility with the B-47 bomb bay.

The B-47 was designed for the mammoth early atomic weapons like the Mark IV and Mark VI. A hook suspension and sling suspension – both used with the U-2 rack – each could carry a single large bomb. As development continued, the yield increased while miniaturization of warheads allowed smaller casings, so a single 10,000 lb Mark IV could be replaced by four 1,980 lb (898kg) Mk28s. A bolt-in suspension system could carry two bombs, while a clip-in suspension based on the MAU-5/A rack could accommodate one, two, or four weapons. By 1960 all B-47s were configured with this latter clip system.

These varying systems proved satisfactory in dropping the Mark IV and Mark VI weapons, but were wholly inadequate in dropping the Mark V bomb. The Mark V was a low-density, low moment-of-inertia weapon. Each test drop at a speed of 550 knots true air speed (KTAS) resulted in violent pitch oscillations caused by airflow into the bomb bay with the doors open. Boeing devised a solution that lowered the bomb more than 10in (25.4cm) inside the bomb bay, reducing the time it was in disturbed airflow prior to exiting the bomb bay. In 1954, however, the Air Force washed its hands entirely of the B-47/Mark V combination and this modification was eliminated.

The bomb bay doors proved equally troublesome. The XB-47 was originally designed to carry high explosive (HE) bombs weighing

Above: B-47B 50-0003 displays the 'long' bomb bay door, designed to carry the Tallboy HE bomb. Interestingly, this image also shows an external ATO rack associated with tests at Edwards AFB. *Author's Collection*

Below: The B-47's bomb bay doors were opened to a horizontal position and the shrouded trailer holding the nuclear weapon maneuvered into place. This image is quite possibly the only one of this procedure, and shows Hosey's swivel hook proposal. *USAF via George Cully*

12,000 lb (5,443kg) or more and at least 21ft (6.4m) in length such as the T-10 'Tallboy' (redesignated as the M-121). This necessitated a large bomb bay with 'long' doors measuring 26ft 5in (8.1m) installed on the XB-47 and B-47A. These were required to open in 2 seconds and close in 5 seconds. A hydraulically operated emergency system could close the doors in 15 minutes. Following the September 1948 declaration that the B-47 would carry special weapons, XB-47 46-0066 took part in 10 air drops of Mark IV 'shapes' in late 1948 and early 1949 during Operation HANDBOOK. On 2nd February 1949, 46-0066 dropped two Mark IV shapes over the Salton Sea, CA, range from an altitude of 35,000ft (10,668m) and airspeed of 232KIAS. HANDBOOK revealed that only minor adjustments to the bomb bay would be needed to drop an atom bomb in lieu of a standard 10,000 lb HE bomb. At speeds greater than 250KIAS with the doors open, however, air turbulence in the bomb bay caused considerable instability. During February 1951 an unspecified B-47A (possibly 49-1907) was fitted with three fixed ground-adjustable spoilers just forward of the bomb bay and 'short' bomb bay doors measuring 13ft 10in (4.2m) in length. This arrangement eliminated this turbulence at speeds up to 450KIAS and was subsequently used on all of SAC's B-47s, with a removable panel covering the bomb bay fuel tank.

Loading atomic weapons into the B-47 was especially frustrating. The airplane's notorious range shortfall led to the installation of multiple fuel tanks in the bomb bay, complicating the loading procedure due to obstructions where armorers would need to stand. In addition, the larger Mark IV and Mark VI bombs had to be installed from a pit beneath the bomb bay as the doors did not open sufficiently to allow the bomb to be pivoted under the fuselage. This was not a problem for the B-50 or B-36 with their tricycle landing gear, but the B-47 could not be maneuvered over a traditional pit because of its unique bicycle landing gear. This necessitated a flat steel cover be placed over the pit as the B-47 was towed across, after which the cover was removed. As smaller 'light case' weapons were introduced they could be ramp loaded instead of pit loaded as the older heavier models had been. Moreover, the trailers which carried the bombs were horizontal while the B-47 rested in a nose high posture. Until suitable equipment was developed early bombs were simply propped up in a matching attitude. [In December 1953 Technical Sergeant Mark Hosey, Jr, developed a swivel hook to load atomic weapons more efficiently into the B-47. He revised this design in June 1954, reducing the weight by half and improving safety features. Tests with the 376th BW at Barksdale AFB resulted in a reduction of 6-10 manhours in loading a bomb and a reduction in personnel from eight to five. The swivel weighed 62 lb (28kg) and cost $60. It is not clear if Hosey's swivel saw widespread use, but its creation reflects the complexity of loading and unloading atomic weapons in the B-47.]

Equipment to monitor the status of the atomic weapon once loaded created additional problems for Boeing engineers. The 'inflight monitoring, inflight control, and flight circuit tester equipment' were all originally placed near the 'weaponeer', meaning the observer/navigator. Unfortunately, the navigator could not see these instruments without considerable effort, and AFSWC decided that they be duplicated at the copilot's station where he would see them as part of his routine visual crosscheck of instruments. This modification was completed by January 1951 but these instruments do not appear in the Dash One images of the cockpit, possibly out of security concerns or because they were not undertaken on a fleet-wide basis.

Plans Versus Reality

Once the Air Force had finally decided to have the B-47 carry atomic weapons, it remained to determine when they would be operationally ready. SAC planned for the 43rd Bombardment Group (BG) and 301st BW to be the first units to convert to the B-47, each equipped with 45 jets. This necessitated a massive production effort, with airplanes rolling off the production line incapable of combat operations. According to AMC the first 45 airplanes (10 B-47As and 35 B-47Bs) would be delivered between April 1950 and June 1951, with the next 45 by November 1951. SAC rejected this lengthy transition and instead suggested that five of the B-47As be assigned to AMC, Air Proving Ground Command (APGC), and Air Training Command (ATC) with the remaining five B-47As and the first 13 B-47Bs sent to the 306th BG to form a lead crew and transition school, facilitating subsequent unit conversions. Each following batch of 15 B-47Bs would be assigned to squadrons attached to the 43rd BW and 301st BW, with an expected conversion time of only 30 days.

The reality, however, was that none of the 10 B-47As and the first 20 B-47Bs would have any special weapons capability whatsoever. All subsequent B-47Bs would be configured to carry both the Mark IV and Mark VI by January 1952. Even this was an unrealistic estimate. In November 1949 AMC directed that Boeing configure the 10 B-47As with 'tactical equipment' allowing them to carry special weapons. Although this meant that all 10 B-47As could theoretically accommodate atomic bombs, only three were modified as actual carriers: 49-1903 and 49-1907 were assigned to the Air Force Special Weapons Command (AFSWC) with the 4925th Test Group (TG) at Kirtland AFB and 49-1900 was retained by AMC. This would allow the Air Force to use the B-47A as a prototype for B-47Bs configured with atomic weapons. All three B-47As were configured with short bomb doors and relevant equipment for the

Mark IV and Mark VI weapons. As for the B-47Bs, SAC – justifiably upset – complained bitterly that the first 250 would be unable to carry atomic weapons.

In February 1951 AFSWC initiated Project WICHITA to determine the compatibility of the Mark IV, Mark V, and Mark VI with the B-47B bomb bay. Results were disappointing. The B-47B was declared 'not operationally ready' because of 'insufficient clearance between the tail fins and the [fuel] tank which formed the rear bomb bay wall.' In April AMC authorized Boeing to modify all B-47Bs to accommodate atomic weapons. The ON TOP program made similar modifications to all Air Force bombers intended to carry atomic weapons such as the B-36 and B-50. Bomb bay changes would be incorporated beginning with the 88th B-47B (50-0083) while still on the production line and would be retrofitted into the 87 B-47Bs previously delivered. Phase I of the ON TOP program planned for the first 58 B-47Bs (through 50-0053) to carry the Mark IV and Mark VI by 1st January 1952, with Phase III enabling these 58 jets to carry the Mark V by 1st July 1952. Phase IV would provide Mark VIII capability in 16 of these 58 B-47Bs by 1st April 1952 (Phase II did not apply to B-47s). In fact Boeing was unable to meet even these modest conversion numbers. By the end of December 1951 only 19 B-47Bs had been modified and of these only nine delivered to SAC.

In February 1952 B-47B 50-0026 was assigned to the AFSWC for Mark IV and Mark VI compatibility tests, revealing 45 significant discrepancies 'in functional, flight, and climatic tests.' To complicate matters further, SAC and AMC decided that the first 87 B-47Bs (through 50-0082) – which were assigned to test, training, and research roles – would not be configured to carry atomic weapons. Boeing, however, had already installed much of the necessary gear in these airplanes, and AMC declared that unless SAC insisted they would remain so configured. SAC did not object.

Overall, ON TOP proved less effective than desired in delivering atomic-capable B-47s. By May 1952 AMC had decided that the first 87 B-47Bs would retain the ability to carry Mark IV and Mark VI weapons (even though they were not in tactical units capable of using them) and could be modified to carry the Mark V, which was canceled for the B-47 in 1954. AMC also decided that B-47Bs 50-0083 through 51-2126 would be fully configured to carry Mark IV, Mark V, and Mark VI weapons, but would require some final modifications to do so either in the field or at depot level. Finally, AMC decided that beginning with B-47B 50-0084 all aircraft would be capable of carrying Mark IV, Mark V, and Mark VI weapons. SAC directed that eight of 16 kits designed to carry the Mark VIII

AMC retained 49-1900 to evaluate the B-47's ability to carry Mark IV and Mark VI atomic weapons. SAC was furious that none of the first 250 B-47Bs were delivered with atomic weapons capability. *Photo BW45245 courtesy Boeing*

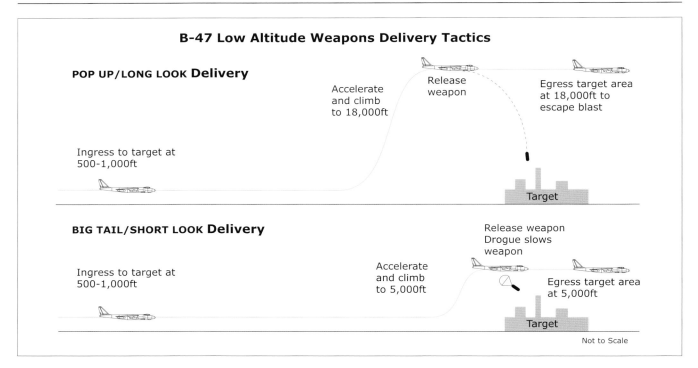

B-47 Low Altitude Weapons Delivery Tactics

POP UP/LONG LOOK Delivery

Accelerate and climb to 18,000ft

Release weapon

Egress target area at 18,000ft to escape blast

Ingress to target at 500-1,000ft

Target

BIG TAIL/SHORT LOOK Delivery

Release weapon
Drogue slows weapon

Ingress to target at 500-1,000ft

Accelerate and climb to 5,000ft

Egress target area at 5,000ft

Target

Not to Scale

penetrator weapon would be assigned to MacDill AFB with the remaining eight stored at OCAMA for future distribution at SAC's discretion, although the Mark VIII was not employed operationally.

A Change in Tactics

Throughout its early years SAC's bombing tactics were little different than those used over Germany during the Second World War. High altitude massed formations, now augmented by radar, would unleash conventional weapons against Soviet industrial and military targets located near population centers. Until 1950 there simply were not enough atomic weapons in the US inventory, and war plans such as OFFTACKLE relied extensively on conventional weapons delivered over several months to defeat the USSR. Piston-powered bombers would fall prey to the speedy MiG-15, a problem which the B-47 promised to eliminate. During the 1950s newly developed heat-seeking air-to-air missiles threatened high-flying B-47s, however, forcing SAC to consider low-altitude strikes to mask the B-47's heat signature against surrounding terrain. Increasingly capable Soviet

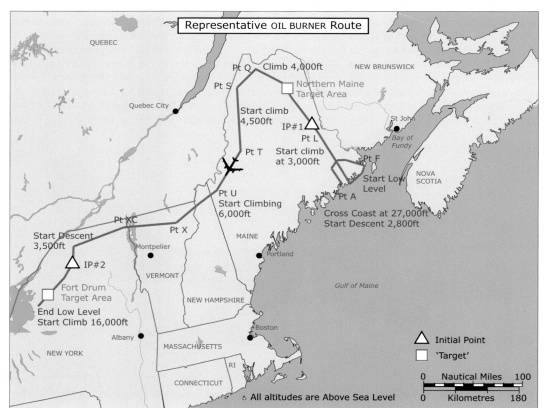

Above: SAC developed low-altitude bombing tactics based on the B-47's need to identify the target, necessitating a climb prior to release. Initial plans called for the B-47 to egress at high altitude to avoid the blast, but later changed to a dive back to low altitude.

Left: Low-level OIL BURNER routes trained SAC crews in navigation over long distances, similar to planned strikes of the USSR. Altitudes shown are absolute, with actual terrain height 500ft lower. After exiting the route the crew climbed to 16,000ft to resume its flight plan.

Opposite: Five small pins could be installed in the upper fuselage of the B-47 to provide the aircraft commander with the LAST RESORT bomb aiming system. Results were poor and the modification was not retained.

long-distance early warning radar and short-range air intercept radar further meant that B-47s could survive only by flying at extremely low altitudes beneath this radar coverage. Beginning 1 January 1956 SAC focused on low-altitude tactics for the B-47. Following the 1st May 1960 Soviet shootdown of Central Intelligence Agency (CIA) pilot Frank Powers and his U-2 by an SA-2 *Guideline* surface-to-air missile (SAM), the days of high-altitude, high-speed bombers were numbered.

Unfortunately, MILK BOTTLE limits imposed significant restrictions on low-altitude atomic weapons delivery tactics, most notably the aerobatic toss-bombing technique known as the Low Altitude Bombing System (LABS – see Chapter 7). This had the B-47 fly at low altitude and accelerate into a half Cuban-eight climb, 'tossing' its atomic bomb as the airplane passed through 45° of pitch, followed by rolling upright at the top and then accelerating away from the ensuing atomic blast (see Chapter 7). These low-altitude flights were known as HAIRCLIPPER missions. According to the 306th BW history for June 1957, the name derived from the 'whimsical' claim that the crews flew so low that they could 'clip the hair of a man standing on the ground.' The 22nd BW, 310th BW, and 306th BW each provided 20 crews for initial qualification. The stresses this placed on the B-47 during training flights, coupled with several fatal crashes, emphasized the need to replace this relatively aggressive maneuver with something more docile but equally effective.

One such procedure was POP UP, where the B-47 approached the target at an altitude of 500-1,000ft (152-305m), accelerated, and then climbed to an altitude of 18,000ft (5,486m) over the target. This allowed the B-47 to avoid the detonation blast wave. The development of a drogue parachute for thermonuclear weapons led to the replacement of POP UP with BIG TAIL, where the B-47 climbed to only 5,000ft (1,524m) above the target prior to weapon release. BIG TAIL was later renamed SHORT LOOK, and POP UP was renamed LONG LOOK. Training for both SHORT LOOK and LONG LOOK began in 1957 and continued through October 1959 using established low-level day visual flight rules (VFR) routes. This involved a low-level navigation leg at an altitude of 500-1,000ft over a 150nm (278km) course. Airspeed for the first half of the route was 280KIAS and 390KIAS for the last half, with the final 5 minutes at 400KIAS. In order to begin training for these missions, SAC required an aircraft commander to have 150 hours in the B-47, of which at least 50 were as an AC (this translated to an average of 8-10 flights prior to training). Four sorties were required for certification. The first was at 2,000ft (610m) over flat terrain (or open ocean), followed by a second over undulating terrain at 500-1,000ft with an instructor pilot in the back seat. The final mission, also at 500-1,000ft, was over mountainous terrain. From 4th-29th May 1959, 17 B-47 wings took part in the SPRING TONIC evaluation. The results of the 170 sorties showed that the SHORT LOOK tactics were less accurate than traditional high-altitude radar bomb runs although they achieved a 1nm (1.9km) Circular Error Probable (CEP). The following year during the TOP RUNG test these results improved to 2,650ft (808m) CEP.

War planners assumed that 6% of the B-47 strike force would be lost to ground impact in night and instrument meteorological conditions (IMC), and that an additional 3% would require a brief climb prior to the planned climb point to take a radar fix, subjecting them to hostile attack. Moreover, the increasing emphasis on low altitude flying resulted in a commensurate increase in fuel consumption, once again highlighting the need for more (and better) tanker support.

By September 1959 SAC dictated the need to expand training to meet all operational requirements, especially at night or under instrument flight rules (IFR). This led to six months of protracted negotiations with the newly constituted Federal Aviation Agency

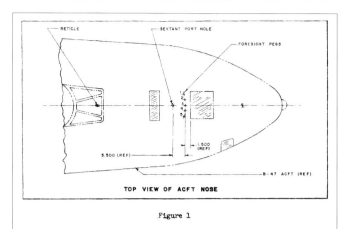

TOP VIEW OF ACFT NOSE

Figure 1

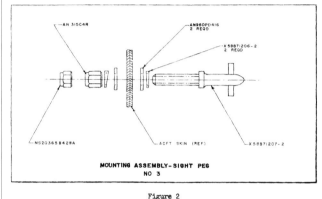

MOUNTING ASSEMBLY-SIGHT PEG
NO 3

Figure 2

(FAA) to approve seven (later nine) dedicated OIL BURNER routes, with the first established at Joplin, MO. These were typically 20nm (37km) wide by as much as 500nm (926km) long, and B-47s and B-52s would be restricted initially to altitudes no lower than 1,000ft (305m) and a maximum of 20,000ft (6,096m), with airspeeds no greater than 300KIAS 'to avert the possibility of disturbance from sonic booms.' The routes would be in use an average of 10 hours per day during two 5-hour blocks five days a week, and would avoid peak commercial and general aviation use. SAC and the FAA continued to quibble over OIL BURNER procedures as SAC sought to make its training more realistic at lower altitudes and higher airspeeds. Ultimately SAC established three primary bombing tactics for the B-47: SHORT LOOK, LONG LOOK, and high-altitude synchronous radar bombing.

The frequency of aborted training missions due to radar failure or other technical issues worried SAC planners. Under wartime conditions B-47 crews would not have the luxury of aborting their mission should any equipment fail, be damaged by enemy action, or be jammed by enemy countermeasures. Consequently, SAC established a fourth bombing category for B-47 crews known as LAST RESORT. This established 'the point of release by computing the release data and determining a start timing point utilizing the aircraft commander's or pilot's LAST RESORT bomb sight.' Results were expectedly poor, with a CEP of 8,183ft (2,494m) in the first quarter of 1963, although this improved to 6,356ft (1,937m) by the second quarter.

One tactic developed in late 1959 was known as LARGE CHARGE. This involved 'two radar synchronous direct or offset releases on a single run' against at least two (or more) different targets. Originally this was used only in high-altitude bomb runs, but was eventually applied to low-altitude runs as well, leading to a series of combined tactics such as SHORT LOOK LARGE CHARGE.

Conventional Weapons

The B-47 was originally designed to carry conventional bombs including 10,000 lb and 20,000 lb (9,072kg) high explosive (HE) weapons. The airplane was built with a 'long' bomb bay capable of holding the 21 ft (6.4m) T-10 'Tall Boy' 12,000 lb (5,443kg) HE bomb, but the bomb bay was eventually shortened and the airplane equipped with 'short' bomb bay. Three factors were responsible for this change: 1) the general elimination of the need to carry large Tall Boy type HE bombs due to the advent of atomic weapons; 2) the need for additional fuel to meet minimum range requirements led to the installation of fuel tanks in the bomb bay; and 3) the decreasing size of atomic weapons obviated the need for large bomb bays. When configured with the 'long' bomb bay doors the XB-47 and B-47A could carry a single Tall Boy type bomb or six 2,000 lb (907kg) or 12 x 1,000 lb (454kg) or 16 x 500 lb (227kg) HE bombs. With the 'short' bomb bay doors they could carry three 2,000 lb, four 1,000 lb, or four 500 lb HE bombs. The potential for reverting to the long bomb bay still existed, but this was an expensive and time-consuming process.

Having the capacity for HE bombs and having the ability to carry and drop them are two different things. During 1951 and early 1952 AMC looked for ways to increase the B-47's general purpose bomb capabilities. Each bomb size called for a different type of rack to carry it and each rack called for certain modifications to the aircraft in which it was installed. AMC expressed a desire for the B-47 to be able to carry anything from a single 12,000 lb bomb to 32 x 500 lb HE bombs, including undefined external stores. Boeing devised a plan that reduced the number of racks from seven to three and all B-47s could be modified to use them interchangeably. One rack was for the 500 lb and 1,000 lb bombs, another rack was for the 2,000 lb bombs, and the third rack would hold the 10,000 lb and 12,000 lb bombs.

From 1954 onward the B-47 had a dedicated conventional mission capability which SAC strenuously opposed. In large measure SAC planners simply hoped that its conventional mission in general would be ignored, and were adamant that the B-47 would not be misused in a non-atomic role. During the 1955 crisis between the People's Republic of China (PRC) and the Republic of China (RoC – Taiwan), the Joint Chiefs of Staff asked SAC if it could use its B-47s equipped with HE bombs to attack key PRC targets. SAC's reply was telling. 'Without modification,' the 31st March 1955 reply began, 'only four (4) 500 lb or 1,000 lb bombs can be carried by each B-47. With a fairly extensive modification program [from the short bomb bay to the long bomb bay], totaling some 1,100 man hours per aircraft, this

capability can be improved to permit loading of twenty-one (21) bombs per aircraft.' The JCS, SAC added, 'should not overlook the fact that once the [B-47s were] modified, it will take a depot modification in excess of the previously quoted 1,100 man hours [per aircraft] to convert each aircraft [back] to the atomic configuration.' Moreover, there were only 28 long bomb bay kits in existence, with a production capacity of just 10 per month.

With some 150 prospective targets in the PRC, SAC analysts noted that using only atomic weapons two B-47 wings (90 jets each) could permanently neutralize all 150 targets in a single night. Using HE explosives, however, with unmodified B-47s (given the shortage of conversion kits) would take 74,755 tons of bombs, or a total of 37,378 B-47 sorties. Over a period of one week, this would require 534 B-47s (with no attrition) operating on a 24-hour continuous basis. Many targets would require additional strikes to destroy them again after being repaired. Even if SAC had that many B-47s in 1955 there was nowhere to put them. 'There are but four (4) bomber bases in being in the Far East suitable to accept [B-47] operations.' The crisis resolved itself without SAC's intervention, nuclear or conventional, but this largely analytic exercise made it clear that atomic bombs were SAC's weapon of choice and that conventional B-47 operations were little different than B-17 or B-24 sorties during the Second World War.

In a 1st November 1957 Top Secret letter from CINCSAC General Power to Air Force Chief of Staff General Thomas D White, Power noted that he was 'increasingly disturbed over the requirement which directs me to maintain a conventional bombing capability in my B-47 force.' Assigning any B-47s to a conventional war would impair SAC's general war mission proportionately. He complained that 'over the past three years this headquarters has pointed out the combat sacrifices which must be accepted if the B-47 force is required to have a conventional weapons capability. To date no action has been taken to delete this requirement.' SAC was obligated to 'maintain weapons loading and servicing personnel in overseas areas to support the conventional' mission. Power added this requirement was 'far too expensive when compared with the tangible potential it represents, and could be eliminated by the deletion of the HE requirement.' The solution, Power suggested, was 'appropriate [low] yield atomic or thermonuclear weapons…to meet local…conditions.' After all, he concluded, 'recent Russian statements make it amply clear that future wars will not be fought with World War II weapons, and I believe our capability should be aligned accordingly.'

Left: Wind tunnel testing of conventional HE bombs used a net to catch the simulated bombs. Grid on the left side allowed engineers to study the trajectory of the bombs at varying speeds. *Photo Courtesy Boeing*

Opposite, left: Much to Power's dismay, SAC retained a conventional bombing mission in addition to its nuclear strike role. Power argued this siphoned money and men from its primary mission. B-47B 51-2068 drops 8 x 500 lb bombs. *USAF*

Opposite, right: B-47s from the 9th BW, 40th BW, 98th BW, and 100th BW took part in live weapon drops at Eglin AFB and elsewhere as part of the SHORT TRIP conventional weapon tests. There were no serious plans to use B-47s in SEA. *USAF*

Power's protest fell on deaf ears. White replied that the Air Force commitment to strategic bombing doctrine called for a full spectrum of weapons to combat limited aggression: 'It is the policy of the United States to place main, but not sole, reliance on nuclear weapons'. The 1958 crisis in Lebanon demonstrated just that, forcing SAC to implement its BLUE BAT conventional deployment (described below). From 1958 through 1961 SAC grudgingly trained its B-47 crews in dropping conventional weapons. Few crewmembers recall actually doing this, and most of the equipment sat idle. In Congressional testimony during 1963 McNamara claimed, 'At the time of the [1961] Berlin Crisis we purchased, if I remember correctly, 250 sets of bomb racks for conventional ordnance in B-47s, but it was just a one-time emergency use. There has never been any real intention to use that type of bomber for conventional ordnance carrying purposes.' No record of these purchases has yet been uncovered, and McNamara's dissembling over conventional missions for the B-47 reflects either ignorance of the existing requirements or intentional misrepresentation to Congress to sell his high-priority TFX program, which later became the F-111. This conventional requirement was eliminated in 1962 but Power ordered its resumption in 1963 due to pressure from the JCS to expand SAC's capability (and hence relevance) to the Kennedy administration's new emphasis on fighting 'brush wars' rather than Eisenhower's 'massive retaliation'.

By the early 1960s SAC had a conventional strike portfolio as part of its 52-series of operations plans (eg, OpPlan 52-63 from 1st March 1963 through 1st July 1964). This required war reserve materiel (WRM) to support 45 B-47s at Andersen AFB in the Pacific and Torrejón AB for the Middle East (RAF Brize Norton was the alternate for Torrejón AB), each supporting eight sorties. The 9th BW, 40th BW, 98th BW, and 100th BW were committed to these contingency operations. Increased tension in Southeast Asia, particularly the growing US military air combat operations in Laos and Vietnam, led SAC to expand its conventional mission planning. In March 1964 SAC recommended moving B-47s from Andersen AFB to Kadena AB, Okinawa, increasing their number from 45 to 60, and replacing them on Guam with additional B-52s.

By this point B-47 units had little experience in loading and dropping conventional weapons. Between March and June 1964 B-47s took part in the SHORT TRIP weapons tests at Eglin AFB, Edwards AFB, and ranges at Wendover, UT, and Matagorda, TX (concurrent with SOUTH BAY B-52 conventional drops). SHORT TRIP Phase I tests were conducted from 7th-10th March by the 9th BW, which flew four sorties carrying, with each airplane carrying 7 x

750 lb (340kg) M-117 high explosive (HE) bombs dropped from 2,000ft (610m) and 2,500ft (762m). Phase II tests resumed on 16th March and continued through 10th April. B-47s from the four contingency units (9th BW, 40th BW, 98th BW, and 100th BW) flew a total of 45 missions from their home stations and dropped live M-117 bombs. High-altitude daylight missions were flown at 20,000ft (6,096m), and 32,000ft (9,754m) over Wendover and Matagorda, with low-level night missions conducted over Edwards AFB. CEP for the high-altitude missions was 1,200ft (366m) and 675ft (206m) for the low-level missions. Some B-47s were equipped to carry the Hayes SUU-24/A dispenser system. This was a 24-compartment rectangular box attached to the special weapons clip-in bomb rack. Each compartment had a capacity for three ADU-253/B cluster bomb adapters (a total of 72), and the adapters were filled with W/BLU-3/B grenade bomblets. The dispenser could release one cell at a time at regular intervals or a salvo drop would empty all 24 cells in rapid succession.

Phase III tests took place at Eglin AFB from 14th through 25th April. A single B-47 from the 100th BW dropped an increasing mix of HE bombs from varying altitudes and release times. SHORT TRIP Phase IV continued at Eglin AFB with the 100th BW B-47 flying eight sorties against a revetted target, including drops from as low as 100ft (30m). SHORT TRIP concluded with practice sorties on 27th and 28th June, and a final Phase V demonstration flight on 30th June, when five B-47s dropped a variety of weapons from altitudes ranging from 100ft to 3,000ft (914m) with a CEP of 412ft (126m). Additional tests took place in October and November 1964. During June and July 1965, a B-47 jettisoned its drops tanks filled with water during six 'Reliability of Wing Tank Release' tests. Despite the innocent-sounding program name the crews were under the impression that the purpose of the tests was to determine the suitability of the B-47 to drop its tanks when filled with napalm.

Although these tests were reasonably successful there were no plans to use the B-47 in a conventional role in Southeast Asia. SAC's protests notwithstanding, the reason had little to do with any reduction in SAC's SIOP capability. The 1954 Geneva Accords which ended the French war there and divided Vietnam into North and South stipulated that any future combat aircraft used there would be limited to piston-powered airplanes such as the Douglas A-1 Skyraider and the North American T-28 Trojan. The US and North Vietnam both ignored this restriction, and Congress finally decided to abrogate this portion of the Accords. By 1964 Northrop F-5s, Martin B-57s, and the panoply of US Navy aircraft were in widespread use in Southeast Asia, and the B-47 was slated for imminent retirement. Moreover, according to Boeing engineer Don Sutcliffe, Boeing *did* complete an engineering study to use the B-47 in Vietnam, but discovered that all the 'long' bomb bay doors had been scrapped. Producing replacement doors to allow the B-47 to operate with a more capacious long bomb bay was an expensive proposition, but modifying the attachment points in B-52's bomb bay and adding external pylons would result in more bombs carried per airplane than on the B-47.

Table 5-3. **Maximum Loads of Conventional Weapons**

Munition	Load	Munition	Load
M117	7	Mk 83 Mod 1	4
AN-M59A1	7	M117/M21 Parapack	14
M124	7	Mk 35	7
M129E1	7	Mk 36	7
AN-M65A1	6	GBU-5/B	7
AN-65A1	6		

The Alert Force

In a three-page letter that began 'Dear Curt,' Second Air Force Commander Major General Frank A Armstrong put in no uncertain terms the B-47's absolute dependency on forward bases and air refueling. His 18th July 1955 letter concluded by saying 'If we lose our refueling bases we cannot strike… We "go" provided we can refuel. We "stay home" if we cannot.' Armstrong made a compelling case for the importance of tanker bases at Goose Bay, Labrador, in Africa, and in the UK. He lamented the inadequacy of deploying entire wings overseas, telegraphing the routes B-47s would take in the event of war. Armstrong added that LONG HAUL, which simulated an attack on the USSR from MacDill, was a 'hand to mouth operation' requiring three refuelings per bomber with a high likelihood of at least one tanker being lost. In short, he concluded, 'the tail is wagging the dog.' SAC's bombing capability was dependent on the tanker, not the bomber, an idea that seemed reasonable in 1954 but was 'not sound' in 1955.

Two weeks later Armstrong received a reply. 'Dear Frank,' LeMay wrote, 'your point on vulnerability of these bases is well taken.' Even if SAC were to lose its island bases, as well as those in North Africa, Spain, and the 'Mediterranean Area,' the 'late production models of the B-47 will still have the capability of taking off from or staging through Hunter AFB or several bases in the northeast area, and fly non-stop to such bases *as might be available* in Spain or North Africa' [emphasis added]. Clearly LeMay had no better answer, hoping that some bases *might* survive a Soviet pre-emptive attack designed to cripple SAC's strike force. LeMay also opposed the ongoing long-term deployment of entire wings overseas because of the degrade in their operational capability and the cost involved. Interestingly, he concluded by saying that he hoped that the United Nations would redefine 'aggression' and recognize that SAC was now operating in an 'age when it can no longer be considered an issue of morality that a nation must receive the first physical blow before it can respond with force; in fact, the first blow can signal the end of a conflict rather than a beginning.'

These two letters represent the intellectual foundations of what would become the SAC alert force. Prior to 1954 SAC's offensive doctrine was based on the mass forward deployment of its bombers

to staging bases for attacks on the USSR. Recognizing that these bases would be vulnerable to Soviet pre-emptive strikes, operations such as PAUL REVERE, HIGH GEAR, FULL HOUSE, and LEAP FROG evaluated the ability of B-47s to fly directly from Zone of the Interior (ZI – or bases in the continental United States – CONUS) to Soviet targets while utilizing air refueling and then recover to forward bases for post-strike regeneration. In 1955 LeMay approved a special 'quick strike' capability to allow a modest bomber force to launch within a few hours of notification. Given 12 hours of warning, SAC could launch 180 B-47s. That number jumped to 880 with 48 hours of warning. Acutely aware that a surprise Soviet attack on SAC bases – an atomic Pearl Harbor – would be the end of America's strike force, on 5th October 1955 LeMay requested to start a ground alert program which Air Force Chief of Staff General Nathan F Twining agreed to 'in principle' on 14th December. The Air Council endorsed this in March 1956 but final approval for a ground alert force was not given until December 1957. SAC's ultimate goal was to have one-third of its force on continuous alert with a 15-minute reaction time by 1st July 1960.

Initial desires to maintain 100% alert proved illusory. There was simply not enough money available to fund this kind of operation. Morale would suffer as crews lived with their airplanes and not their families. Tactical issues, especially the problem of air refueling, limited how many bombers could be on alert at any given time. Forward-based B-47s could reach their targets without refueling but B-47s in the CONUS required a single refueling if they were launched from bases north of 40° North latitude. B-47s south of this line required two refuelings. As there were not enough tankers

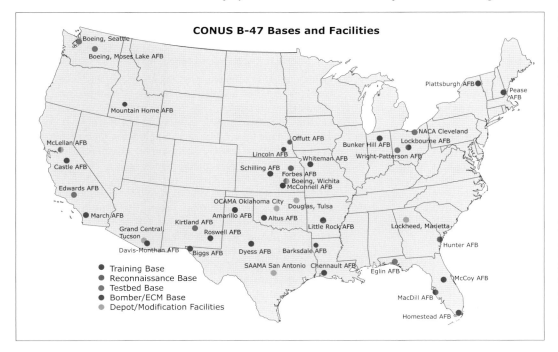

CONUS B-47 Bases and Facilities

Boeing, Seattle
Boeing, Moses Lake AFB
Mountain Home AFB
McLellan AFB
Castle AFB
Edwards AFB
March AFB
Grand Central Tucson
Davis-Monthan AFB
Biggs AFB
Offutt AFB
Lincoln AFB
Schilling AFB
OCAMA Oklahoma City
Amarillo AFB
Kirtland AFB
Roswell AFB
Dyess AFB
SAAMA San Antonio
Whiteman AFB
Forbes AFB
Boeing, Wichita
McConnell AFB
Douglas, Tulsa
Altus AFB
Little Rock AFB
Barksdale AFB
Chennault AFB
Bunker Hill AFB
Wright-Patterson AFB
NACA Cleveland
Lockbourne AFB
Plattsburgh AFB
Pease AFB
Lockheed, Marietta
Hunter AFB
Eglin AFB
McCoy AFB
MacDill AFB
Homestead AFB

- ● Training Base
- ● Reconnaissance Base
- ● Testbed Base
- ● Bomber/ECM Base
- ● Depot/Modification Facilities

Above: SAC's nascent B-47 strike force was utterly dependent upon KC-97s for air refueling, the 'tail wagging the dog.' SAC's ability to strike Soviet targets required a dedicated force – both bombers and tankers – ready to launch which became the alert force. *Tom Hildreth*

Left: Getting B-47s from their bases in the CONUS (or ZI) to targets in the USSR meant air refueling. ZI bases had the benefit of additional warning time of any impending Soviet bomber strike, but this advantage disappeared with the advent of Soviet ballistic missiles.

available (nor could any more be funded), the number of B-47s on alert was limited accordingly – Armstrong's 'tail wagging the dog'. Proposals to provide 'hardened' shelters at B-47 bases were equally cost prohibitive. To harden a single B-47 wing to 100psi overpressure (a standard measure of protection from atomic blasts) would cost $42 million, a figure which increased to $55 million for the 200psi needed for thermonuclear blasts. Extensive studies revealed that one-third alert was the minimum needed to have a deterrent effect. Any more would become prohibitively expensive. Using 1960 projected figures, this translated to a total of 585 bombers and 349 tankers of all types. Each wing would be responsible for 15 bombers and seven tankers.

Evaluation of the alert concept began on 1st November 1956 with the 2nd BW and on 15th November with the 308th BW. Over the following five months of Operation TRY OUT, both wings maintained 30% of their B-47s and KC-97 tankers on continuous alert (except for the 1956 Christmas holiday). The airplanes were fully configured for their Emergency War Plan (EWP) mission, including atomic weapons. By the time the exercise ended on 29th March 1957 this total had decreased to 12 B-47s per wing. Throughout the exercise the two wings underwent daily tests ranging from responding to the airplane to an actual launch on a Unit Simulated Combat Mission (USCM). Both flew a total of four BOW STRING I missions designed to determine how many B-47s they could launch within an hour's notification. They also flew three BOW STRING II missions to determine how long it would take to launch all 90 B-47s plus 34 KC-97s. Overall the units loaded 621 atomic weapons, 7,372 ATO bottles, and 1,216,000 rounds of 20mm ammunition.

Results were mixed. The wings could maintain 30% alert but only if fully manned, all non-emergency leaves were canceled for the duration, no off-base professional training was allowed, and one-third of personnel suffered from a serious drop in morale. On the positive side the test showed that the first B-47 could be airborne 15 minutes after alert notification, with subsequent aircraft following every minute. The goal, however, was every alert aircraft airborne within 15 minutes (a figure predicated on the remaining time following 30 minutes' warning of a Soviet ICBM launch minus 15 minutes of presidential decision-making to retaliate). SAC decided to add a fourth B-47 squadron and a flight-line maintenance squadron to each wing to address these and other shortcomings.

Operation WATCH TOWER took place at Little Rock AFB from September through November 1957 and involved RB-47Es from the 70th SRW, B-47Es from the 384th BW, and KC-97s from the 70th AREFS. The goal of WATCH TOWER was to determine the ability to launch the alert force within the allotted 15-minute window. Each wing had four B-47 squadrons and each tanker squadron had four flights with eight crews on alert every day, which later dropped to

Programs such as TRY OUT and BOW STRING demonstrated the limits of the planned alert force. Flight crew proficiency ebbed while sitting idle on alert, while maintenance personnel worked long hours every day. Readiness and morale dropped considerably. *USAF*

seven. Crews were on alert for 48 hours once every eight days. As with TRY OUT, participating units were still responsible for regular flying and training, as well as routine maintenance. During WATCH TOWER the units took part in four simulated alert responses, well known to anyone who has ever 'been there.'

'Alpha – Crews proceeded to their aircraft, completed the engine check list, called the wing control room [Command Post] and informed them they were ready to start engines. The control room logged the time and the crew recocked the aircraft. Goal for this alert was E [Execution time] plus 19 minutes.

'Bravo – Crew started engines, ground crews signaled clear to taxi, and the crews called the control room. The control room acknowledged the call and the aircraft was recocked. The goal was E plus 22 minutes.

'Cocoa – Aircraft assumed its proper position in the taxi order and proceeded to the takeoff runway. When the green light was received the lead aircraft simulated takeoff by applying full power then cutting back after reaching 50 knots. The lead aircraft then returned to the parking area and the other aircraft simulated takeoff at one-minute intervals. Goal for the lead aircraft to start its simulated takeoff was E plus 30 minutes [SAC documents refer to 'Cocoa', 'Coco', and even 'Coca'].

'Delta – This was an actual takeoff. Goal was E plus 30 minutes.'

On 1st October 1957 some 43 SAC bombers and tankers went on alert in the UK and French Morocco, with 87 more in the US. Those in the UK were most vulnerable to a preemptive Soviet strike or sabotage but had the highest priority targets. *via Stephen Miller*

At the time of TRY OUT and WATCH TOWER there were no alert facilities and no 'Christmas tree' alert ramp. Crews were billeted in facilities all around the base and aircraft were spread across the parking ramp. In addition, aircraft taxied to the active runway, which often meant the opposite end and a lengthy taxi time.

During WATCH TOWER there were 21 Alpha alerts, 18 Bravo alerts, and 35 Cocoa alerts. On 12th November there was a Delta alert. The 70th SRW launched five RB-47s (with two aborts) and the 384th BW launched three of four B-47s (one was unavailable due to maintenance). No tankers launched due to bad weather in the refueling area. To achieve the 15-minute goal, WATCH TOWER revealed that crews needed to live adjacent to their aircraft, located at both ends of the ramp to reduce taxi time. Concurrent with Operation WATCH TOWER at Little Rock AFB, Operation FRESH APPROACH took place with the 9th BW at Mountain Home AFB, ID. The goals and procedures were the same, with 10 B-47s and five KC-97s on alert. From 9th-13th September, the unit underwent a no-notice EWP evaluation. All B-47s took off at E plus 30 minutes followed by their tankers.

Both WATCH TOWER and FRESH APPROACH made clear the need for a dedicated alert facility and specific alert parking areas, each of which cost a considerable amount of money which was likely not to be forthcoming. Available funds reached $25 million in early 1957, well short of the $287 million SAC requested. Several studies followed, all of which showed the total cost of the new ground alert program would still be well of out budgetary limits. The launch of *Sputnik* on 4th October 1957 changed everything, resulting in 'drastic' increases to the alert budget with an incremental lump sum of $75 million by the end of 1957.

The first 130 SAC aircraft went on alert on 1st October 1957, with 87 of these in the CONUS and 43 at overseas bases. CONUS bases had a two-hour reaction time while those overseas had a 30-minute time. According to a top secret 25th October 1957 briefing paper written by Eisenhower National Security Advisor Robert Cutler, only 117 B-47s could be airborne within the 2-hour CONUS reaction time.

This number included both those on alert and those which could be generated in sufficient time. Cutler's briefing noted that for a single-wing base with 15 B-47s and seven KC-97s on alert, it would take 16 minutes to get them airborne with only tactical warning, but with 'strategic warning' – likely several days needed to generate them – it would take 31 minutes. For a 'superwing' base with two full wings with 30 B-47s and 14 KC-97s on alert, it would take 27 minutes to launch with only a single runway but 16 minutes with a double runway. With sufficient warning time to generate all in-commission airplanes with 104 on alert, it would take 57 minutes and 31 minutes, respectively. Cutler added that the large number of B-47s available to launch was misleading and assumed full manning at all positions. The limiting factor in SAC's readiness, Cutler warned, was the lack of maintenance personnel. Between January and August 1957 the re-enlistment rate for first-term SAC maintenance personnel was a paltry 22.1% and for jet mechanics at all ranks it was just 24.7%. By the end of 1957 SAC had 134 B-47s on alert worldwide, but without qualified people to fix and generate them, the number of B-47s ready for war was an illusion, especially as on 1st January 1958 the CONUS reaction time decreased from 2 hours to just 30 minutes.

One crucial and unresolved problem arose from the new alert program: fratricide. Prior to the implementation of the FULL HOUSE and LEAP FROG missions in 1954 SAC bombers were deployed to forward bases under controlled circumstances. If launched from an alert posture under combat conditions, however, they were unintentionally 'fair game' for North American Air Defense Command (NORAD) interceptors and surface-to-air missiles (SAMs) attacking incoming bombers. NORAD policy was, in the words of General LeMay, to 'shoot 'em down and sort 'em out on the ground.' Outbound B-47s were no different in the 'radar eye' than incoming Soviet bombers, especially over America's northeast corridor which would be heavily congested in both directions. SAC planners were especially concerned about US Army Nike-Hercules SAMs equipped with a 40kt warhead that could destroy multiple B-47s in a single shot. Deconfliction efforts remained a crucial problem for SAC and NORAD, with carefully planned outbound routes and Identification-Friend or Foe (IFF) electronic systems serving as initial solutions. Regardless, SAC acknowledged that 'some' of its B-47 force would never leave North America due to 'blue-on-blue' kills.

Construction of new alert facilities also began in earnest. On 25th October 1957 SAC decreed that alert aircraft no longer required earthen barricades between aircraft. This meant the alert aircraft could be parked in a 'herringbone' arrangement (popularly known as the 'Christmas tree') on a ramp at a 45° angle to the end of the runway. Alert billeting ranged from existing buildings to mobile trailers that could be moved from one end of the runway to the other as winds

Above: Whether in the CONUS or the UK, crew vehicles for the alert force were a ubiquitous sight. These are seen at RAF Brize Norton. The number on the bumper indicates crew and alert pad spot.

Left: Early alert programs failed to account for driving distances or taxi times to the active runway. These were eventually resolved, with the alert facility at RAF Brize Norton showing its close proximity to the alert aircraft. *Both photos: Augustine Letto*

HURRY HURRY sought to get more B-47s airborne within as brief a time as possible. 22nd BW (l) and 320th BW (r) B-47s tested the program at Edwards AFB, including formation takeoffs. Dense black smoke from water injection and ATO obscured visibility for subsequent waves. *via Larry D First*

changed (this 'rotational' idea was quickly dismissed, but trailers were used pending completion of the permanent alert facilities). Power wanted 'adequate and comfortable' accommodations for the alert crews, telling his wing commanders that 'substandard temporary quarters would not be tolerated.' He wanted each alert facility to have new 'furniture, radios, TV sets, games, etc...as well as maid and janitor service. Special messing was to be available to alert crews.' He even went so far as to ask for alert pay but was never able to get this approved. As of 30th June 1959, 67 new alert facilities were completed, under construction, or in design. Each had two floors, with operations, messing, and recreation on the first floor and sleeping accommodations in the basement, giving rise to the nickname 'Mole Hole.' The first new alert facility to become operational was at Westover AFB, MA, which operated B-52s.

HURRY HURRY

The 15-minute goal of getting the entire alert force airborne after receipt of warning proved elusive. By late 1959 the best SAC could achieve was 20 minutes. The problem was complex and ranged from the times needed for crews to reach their airplane, start, taxi to the optimum runway (a process that took considerable time when the wind favored the non-optimal runway), and become airborne. Moreover, the math simply did not add up: getting 15 B-47s and seven KC-97s airborne in 15 minutes or less was impossible with a one-minute interval between airplanes, especially given the time needed for the first airplane to be ready for takeoff. Indeed, SAC found that under its current alert launch procedures, 35% of its B-47 force and 67% of its KC-97s could not be airborne within 15 minutes.

Rather than focus exclusively on further dispersal of the alert force – an expensive proposition at best – on 30th June 1959 SAC requested that ARDC assess the ability to 'get more aircraft into the air consistent with the minimum warning condition.' This meant determining 'minimum takeoff intervals of B-47s at 220,000 lb (99,790 kg) unstick weight utilizing water injection and firing the maximum load of 16 NS 1,000 ATO units', as well as determining 'the feasibility of two-plane B-47 formation takeoffs on a 300ft (91m) [wide] runway' as configured above. ARDC agreed and the tests began at Edwards AFB to utilize the expansive runways there. Known as Project HURRY HURRY, B-47s from the 22nd BW and 320th BW at March AFB took part in the tests from 1st-22nd September 1959.

Results were excellent for both night and day takeoffs. B-47s could launch sequentially at a rate of four per minute on a 200ft (61m) wide runway. On a 300ft-wide runway six B-47s could launch at a rate of six per minute. In both cases, rolling takeoffs were the most effective technique because they 'eliminated the stop at the end of the runway before the [B-47] made its run,' maintaining its momentum from taxiing. ARDC was not inclined to advocate formation takeoffs for the B-47, especially at night, due to the lack of adequate visual

references for station keeping. SAC agreed, and by 5th January 1960 the Air Staff had approved the 'Free Flow' alert takeoff concept.

Training for individual units began later that month with the 306th BW at MacDill AFB and the 19th and 376th BWs at Homestead AFB, FL, under OPEN ROAD Phase I. The 306th BW flew missions on 18th and 21st January using 12 crews (four combat ready, four senior, and four select). To avoid accidents, special runway markings were used, including lines three feet wide painted across each runway and high-intensity flashing lights to identify the decision point ('go-no go') amid the smoke from preceding airplanes. Crews were asked to assess visibility, turbulence, and any nighttime flash blindness caused by the igniting ATO. On 18th January the 306th BW launched 12 B-47s in 2 minutes 20 seconds from start of takeoff of the first B-47 until the last B-47 was airborne. The test on 21st January cut this time by 19 seconds with an average interval of 6.7 seconds between B-47s.

Results at Homestead AFB were less than hoped for. During the first launch on 25th January the final four B-47s had to abort their takeoffs after the ninth B-47 ran off the runway while taxiing. The other eight were airborne in 2 minutes 52 seconds. During the second mission only 10 of the 11 airplanes were able to launch (with one abort) in 3 minutes and 2 seconds and an average interval of 15 seconds between each airplane. The aborts proved helpful, however, in determining what procedures crews should follow. Turbulence was not a factor, but the intense smoke from the alcohol-injected takeoff and the ATO made visibility problematic, especially at night.

Effective 8th April 1960 SAC incorporated the minimum interval takeoff (MITO) into its alert procedures, and by 30th June 375 B-47 crews were qualified in MITOs. This meant that SAC expected the first B-47 to be airborne no more than eight minutes after initial alert with the remaining B-47s and KC-97s airborne within the following seven minutes. This was critical as SAC prepared to increase the number of aircraft on alert while assuring they would all become airborne within 15 minutes. By February 1961 Air Force Chief of Staff General Thomas D White initiated studies that would increase the ground alert force to 50%. White argued that Soviet weapons would destroy the remaining 66% of non-alert aircraft, a waste of resources and unspent strike assets. Power agreed that SAC could support 50% alert, which was accomplished between 30th June and 31st July 1961. To support this, SAC instituted its Improved Maintenance Program (IMP). For the B-47, this meant a reduction in routine inspections by 59% and increased the inspection interval for J47 engines from 300 to 600 hours.

Alert crews were fair game for SAC's dreaded Operational Readiness Inspection (ORI). The stuff of legend, an ORI began unannounced when a staff transport without a flight plan appeared on final approach to a SAC base with an alert commitment. Careers hung in the balance as the SAC inspection team assessed the ability of the alert force to execute its EWP. For B-47 units the critical areas were

'alert mission effectiveness' and 'synchronous bombing percentage.' To be considered fully effective, a unit alert force required 'successful completion' of an alert launch of all aircraft within five minutes of the scheduled takeoff time, it had to fly a 'reliable' high-altitude navigation leg and accomplish a 'reliable' low-altitude bombing attack. The alert aircraft also had to complete all air refueling requirements, meet a controlled arrival time at the simulated H-hour control line (popularly known as the 'Fail Safe' point), and fly the entire simulated EWP route. For a unit with eight B-47s on alert, six had to be considered as 'effective' to pass the ORI. On 1st October 1963 SAC changed the low-altitude bombing requirement to successful completion of the 'most difficult' primary delivery tactic of the unit's alert force. These were, in descending order of difficulty, SHORT LOOK LARGE CHARGE, SHORT LOOK, LAYDOWN LARGE CHARGE, LAYDOWN, HIGH ALTITUDE LARGE CHARGE, and HIGH ALTITUDE SINGLE RELEASE. B-47 units remained surprisingly effective when compared with B-52 and B-58 units. Out of 155 required ORI sorties in October through December 1963 for example, B-47s completed 145 for a 93.5% effectiveness rate, with B-52s achieving 92.8% and B-58s at 84.6%.

Originally SAC ended an ORI with a Coco alert exercise. This changed on 1st October 1963 with the Coco exercise taking place at

the beginning of the ORI. This automatically excluded as ineffective any airplane that failed to meet the Coco reaction time. In addition, this allowed the unit to download the EWP weapons on the alert B-47s prior to flying the ORI. Prior to this SAC units undertook ORIs and USCMs with nuclear weapons on board, but accidents involving the airplanes and weapons demonstrated the risks inherent in peacetime launches with nuclear weapons. Moreover, SAC ORI and USCM routes frequently took the airplanes over Canada, creating a delicate diplomatic issue that had to be resolved prior to any such overflights. These were known as 'XYZ Procedures,' and included (for example) Operation ROADBLOCK on 29th and 30th November 1956 where 72 B-47s overflew Canada. Of these, 36 B-47s carried both nuclear and non-nuclear components. The airplanes retraced this route between 3rd and 5th December.

By late 1961 SAC added the BAR NONE exercise to its evaluation repertoire to 'realistically assess unit's total EWP capability to strike unfamiliar targets through evaluation of all assigned combat-ready crews and aircraft.' The principal differences between and ORI and a BAR NONE were that the latter only applied to bomber units, was a scheduled quarterly requirement, and evaluated all combat-ready crews (whereas an ORI only evaluate those crews on alert at the time of the ORI).

B-47s in the UK

The inherent shortfall in the range of the B-47 created significant problems for SAC's mission planners. B-47s simply could not reach targets in the USSR when launched from bases in the United States without at least one air refueling. Even then they lacked the range to reach post-strike bases for recovery and reconstitution. Problems with refueling – ranging from technical issues to incompatible speeds to lack of crew mastery – made in-flight refueling a risk that SAC planners wanted to mitigate. SAC chose to use the same solution for the B-47 as it had for its B-29 and B-50 force: forward basing in the United Kingdom and North Africa. Early plans called for 195 B-47s and 65 RB-47s at English bases during a pre-war buildup, reaching 390 B-47s and 130 RB-47s should war erupt. During January 1953 SAC sought to validate these plans by deploying the 306th BW B-47s to England in May 1953. LeMay rejected this proposal due to the lack of combat-ready crews and because the 306th BW had yet to execute a successful simulated EWP evaluation.

Efforts to evaluate the operational readiness of the B-47 had been underway since August 1952 but had been repeatedly deferred due to delivery delays, logistics issues, and lack of combat-ready crews. Eventually known as SKY TRY, this test would 'determine the suitability of the modified [Phase II] B-47B to support the Strategic Air Command War Plan; to determine the logistic support required to sustain one B-47 squadron at maximum operational capability under simulated combat conditions; and to test the adequacy of a tentative TO [technical order] (1178P) to support, maintain, and operate a B-47B squadron under simulated combat conditions.' The test would last 30 days. Most importantly, the test would reveal what, if any, modifications would be necessary in order for the B-47B to be declared 'mission ready.' The original plan was for the test to take place in November 1952, but bureaucratic wrangling among the four different commands – SAC, AMC, APGC, and Air Defense Command (ADC) – made this

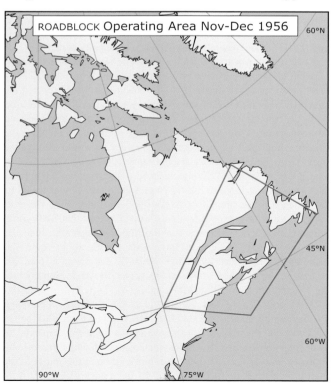

Above: IMP reduced inspection times for J47s from every 300 hours to every 600 hours. Replacing an engine was still a time-consuming process, as seen on this 19th BW B-47B. *USAF*

Left: ORIs and USCMs often overflew Canada while carrying nuclear weapons or their components. Via the US Department of State and NORAD, SAC garnered approval for these 'XYZ Missions.' B-47E 52-3360 crashed in Canada on 30th November 1956 during Operation ROADBLOCK.

B-47Bs from the 306th BW at MacDill AFB undertook Project SKY TRY in early 1953. Results were generally positive but identified key shortcomings, especially in the K system. Nonetheless, this paved the way for the first operational deployment to the UK. *USAF*

impracticable. Moreover, AMC and APGC argued that SAC's intent to conduct the test in the United Kingdom was a bad idea given the overseas logistics needed and the lack of prior B-47 operations in the UK, and instead insisted that the test take place at MacDill AFB.

Project SKY TRY finally took place from 22nd January through 19th February 1953 using 15 Phase II B-47Bs assigned to the 367th Bombardment Squadron (BS) of the 306th BW at MacDill AFB. The test included 'day and night penetrations of Air Defense Command areas, RBS [Radar Bomb Scoring], camera attacks, T-59 [simulated Mark VI atomic] bomb releases, day and night formation raids, day and night bomber stream missions, and pre- and post-target air-to-air refueling.'

Results were surprisingly good. The squadron flew 10 mission profiles made up of five day, two night, and three day-night RBS profiles over cities including Richmond, VA, and Denver, CO. Five missions included in-flight refueling, with one of these involving pre- and post-strike refueling, with 87 out of 88 successful air refuelings. Average time from 'start descent' to initial contact was 15.8 minutes, with an average of 3,093 lb (1,403kg) of fuel transferred per minute. Flight times ranged from 7+30 to 11+55 hours over distances between 3,095nm (5,732km) and 4,655nm (8,621km) and at speeds varying from optimum cruise speed of 0.74 Mach to the maximum speed of 0.83 Mach. Fighters intercepted seven of the 10 missions. Out of the total of 150 planned sorties, 126 (84%) were effective over the target, and 109 (72.7%) finished the mission completely. Of the aborts, 21 were due to pre-strike radar failure, with the remainder due to problems with in-flight refueling and systems failures. During the fourth mission on 31st January, bad weather forced 14 B-47s to divert to Hunter AFB, GA. Maintenance teams flew to Hunter AFB, allowing the B-47s to return to MacDill AFB the next day to maintain the required operational timing. None of the B-47s was ever out of commission due to lack of parts although the 'percentage rate of aircraft-not-fully-equipped ranged from 33 to 67%.'

Commanders were cautious about being overly optimistic about the B-47's performance during SKY TRY, summarized in the final report: '…certain important deficiency areas, principally in the bombing and defensive armament systems, presently impose serious limitation on the aircraft's combat effectiveness. Increased design complexity and the impact of the more severe operating requirements introduced by higher airplane performance have had their effects on the reliability of these systems and the training criteria for operators and maintenance personnel. Until the B-47 is equipped with an acceptable armament system with which to defend itself against the type of interceptor attack which will probably be used against it, the aircraft will be forced to operate under a serious tactical penalty.'

The K-system was the primary weakness, with 215 in-flight malfunctions reported with 26.7% of the aircraft reporting a failure prior to reaching the first target and 32.7% aborting prior to the second target. The B-4 gun turret with the AN/APG-30 tracking radar had a 60-64% failure rate which 'increased with cold soaking'. Moving the turret left or right caused the airplane to yaw significantly, and the tail section hindered visual sighting of targets. During daylight hours 51% of intercepts resulted in effective firing passes on the B-47s, although this dropped to 21% during darkness.

Despite the shortcomings identified during SKY TRY SAC was sufficiently encouraged by the B-47's performance to move ahead with the first overseas deployment. On 7th March 1953 SAC directed the 306th BW to prepare for the initial 90-day rotation to the UK. Should the 306th BW be unprepared to do so, the 93rd BW at Castle AFB would undertake the deployment using its B-50Ds.

England, At Last

After many delays, both in production and operational preparedness, SAC was finally ready to send its newest bomber to England. Colonel Michael N W McCoy, Commander of the 306th BW, led a pair of B-47Bs from MacDill AFB to RAF Fairford. Departing 6th April 1953, they stopped at Limestone AFB, ME, for refueling, and then proceeded to England, setting an unofficial speed record of 553.8mph (891kmh) en route (see Appendix IV). The two airplanes actually diverted to RAF Brize Norton on 7th April when their 'wet' anti-exposure suits caused hyperthermia (one source reports that McCoy was 'incapacitated' by his suit, but recovered prior to landing). The two visited other bases, including RAF Lakenheath on 14th April.

What McCoy found was problematic. The runway at RAF Fairford was indeed the requisite 10,000ft (3,048m) in length but had no overruns. Lines were hastily painted on the runway which reduced the overall length to 9,800ft (2,987m) with resulting penalties in fuel load and takeoff performance. Ultra-high frequency (UHF) radios were largely non-existent, and ground controlled approach (GCA) facilities were 'primitive' by SAC standards. McCoy returned on 21st April to oversee the final preparations for the deployment, which was accompanied by considerable press attention. On 22nd May, for example, Air Force Vice Chief of Staff General Nathan F Twining announced that the 306th BW would deploy to the UK 'as part of the Air Force's established program for maintaining the mobility of Strategic Air Command.'

McCoy led the full wing's deployment to RAF Fairford, with the 45 B-47Bs departing MacDill AFB in three waves on 2nd, 3rd, and 4th June 1953. Some 22 KC-97Es deployed to Harmon AFB, Newfoundland, where they could refuel any B-47 in case of emergency, but no air refueling was planned for the trip to England. Each B-47 routed through Limestone AFB with 15 reaching RAF Fairford on the 4th, 12 on the 5th, 16 on the 6th, and two stragglers on the 7th of June. Several set additional unofficial speed records along the way.

Once in the UK the B-47s flew frequently to familiarize crews with the UK environment and ground support personnel with the new

Far left: Brigadier General Henry K Mooney (l) welcomes Colonel Michael N W McCoy to Limestone AFB on 6th April 1953 during the first B-47 trip to the UK. Mooney was the 6th AD commander, and deployed to Limestone AFB ahead of McCoy's two B-47s. *Photo BW90061*

Left: Whether or not he flew to England in B-47B 50-0008 named *The Real McCoy!* in his honor, Colonel Mike McCoy was a flamboyant, popular commander. His 306th BW was the first B-47 unit to deploy to the UK, and what he found was not to his liking. *Photo HS5665*

Upper: B-47B 51-2323 about to land at Limestone AFB en route to England in June 1953. There were no plans to make the trip nonstop from MacDill AFB with air refueling, although KC-97s were on alert at Harmon AFB in the event of emergency.

Lower: One tranche of 306th BW B-47Bs lined up waiting for fuel at Limestone AFB. Crews launched immediately after servicing for RAF Fairford. Note special nacelle markings on the second B-47. *Photo BW90076*

Below: B-47B 51-2271 lands at RAF Fairford to join other 306th BW B-47s already in place. Facilities were hardly impressive and the runway and taxiways were rough, prompting fears of damage to the delicate K system. *Photo BW90190*
All photos courtesy Boeing

airplane. Weather was an unexpected problem, with unseasonal fog forcing the wing to lower the approach minima from 1,000ft (305m) ceiling and 2nm (3.7km) visibility in the daytime [1,500ft (457m) and 3nm (5.6km) at night] to 300ft (91m) and ¾nm (1.4km) in the daytime [300ft and 1nm (1.9km) at night]. The runway at RAF Fairford remained a source of concern. Given its rough finish and the presence of stiff crosswinds, crews worried about dragging an outboard engine pod or excessive bumps leading to damage to the airplane's sensitive electronics. Indeed, radar aborts were frequent, although how many were caused by the rough taxiways and runways was not specified in the post-mission critique. Crew accommodations were still rather 'austere' and overcrowding was commonplace. Stockpiles of JP-4 jet fuel were inadequate but quickly overcome. Unplanned 'bounces' by friendly fighters were forbidden, and the B-47s were prohibited from any flight operations closer than 300nm (556km) from the USSR or communist-bloc areas.

On 29th-30th June, the wing took part in Operation BIG LEAGUE, designed to test the wing's capability against continental retardation targets. Results were poor, largely due to weather, which resulted in additional training missions in July. These produced the desired results during a simulated EWP mission flown on 16th July. All 44 planned launches took place, and 40 sorties were 'effective' over the target. The following week the unit flew Exercise WORLD SERIES with similar results.

The deployment received the personal attention of CINCSAC General LeMay, who visited England from 13th May through 16th June, and of Vice CINCSAC Major General Power from 24th August through 7th September. Six B-47Bs relocated to Nouasseur AB in French Morocco on 12th August under Operation SAFARI to evaluate those facilities. The deployment was marred by the loss of B-47B 51-2267 on 2nd July at RAF Upper Heyford, which the official SAC history glaringly omits, saying instead that the rotation took place 'without serious mishap (see Appendix II). The 306th BW returned directly to MacDill AFB in three waves departing on 4th, 5th, and 6th September, with each refueled en route. B-47B 51-2273 suffered turbine failure of the #5 engine and diverted to Limestone AFB, returning to MacDill AFB on 13th September. The B-47's foreign debut was a general success, but there were still significant operational issues to resolve.

Addressing these problems fell to the 305th BW which replaced the 306th BW, although the 305th BW deployed to RAF Brize Norton rather than RAF Fairford. The problems were largely the same: inadequate UHF radio and GCA facilities, bad weather complicating the use of both visual RBS ranges and British bases in general. B-47Bs visited RAF Fairford, RAF Lakenheath, RAF Greenham Common, and RAF Upper Heyford to assess their suitability for future B-47 operations as well as to introduce base personnel to the Stratojet. The 305th BW also planned to send 15 B-47s and five KC-97s to Sidi Slimane AB, but only one B-47 made the trip. On 2nd November 1953, 41 B-47s finally managed to reach Sidi Slimane AB, returning to RAF Brize Norton over the next four days.

By the end of 1953 the 22nd BW had completed plans for the high-profile deployment of 10 its new B-47Es flying nonstop from March AFB to RAF Upper Heyford using in-flight refueling with the remaining 35 jets routing through Limestone AFB. Poor weather – both in Maine and in the UK – played havoc with the deployment. Following the initial departure from March AFB on 3rd December, severe fog in the UK prevented them from flying the next leg to RAF Upper Heyford. Additional B-47Es from March AFB continued to arrive at Limestone AFB, and attempts to move the airplanes onward failed due to a blizzard in Maine. By 22nd December only 13 B-47Es were in England, with the remaining 32 jets having diverted to Sidi Slimane AB in Morocco or were snowed in or broken at Limestone AFB. The final 22nd BW B-47E (52-0024) arrived on Christmas Day, ending what turned into a 23-day outbound deployment!

These lessons were not lost on SAC planners who had failed to account for more than one de-icer at Limestone AFB or the impact of bad weather not only on the mission aircraft but also on the C-54, C-97, and C-124 support airplanes. Weather minima in the UK of 1,500ft ceilings with 3nm visibility were often unobtainable, preventing arrivals from the US or local operations in general. In addition, the 22nd BW had just converted from B-47Bs to B-47Es, and many had been sitting idle for weeks in the warmer climate at Davis-Monthan AFB where they underwent the BABY GRAND update, as well as their home base in sunny southern California. Arriving in the cold, snow, and icy conditions at Limestone AFB seriously undermined their ability to operate in all weather conditions without degradation, an issue which significantly worried SAC planners.

Above: 306th BW operations from RAF Fairford were occasionally curtailed by wet weather which turned the ground into mud and overcast that hindered approaches and landing. *Harold Siegfried*

Below: CINCSAC General Curtis LeMay visited RAF Fairford to assess the initial B-47 deployment to the UK. Overseas bases were crucial to the EWP, with key targets such as Soviet bomber bases and command centers. *Photo BW90189 courtesy Boeing*

Left: Despite multiple logistics issues and the tragic loss of 51-2267, the initial B-47 deployment was a qualified success. Note red outer wings. *Harold Siegfried*

Upper: B-47B 51-2295 *Cheri-Lynn* departs RAF Fairford for the nonstop flight to MacDill AFB on 4th September 1953. *Photo HS920 courtesy Boeing*

Lower left: The first 305th BW crew to arrive at RAF Brize Norton on 4th September greet the Vice CINCSAC. From (l) to (r) are Lieutenant Colonel Paul Von Ins, Captain Philip H Beagle, Major General Thomas S Power, Major C E Christie, Brigadier General James C Selser, and Staff Sergeant James Hacks. *USAF*

Lower right: B-47Es from the 22nd BW at March AFB were caught in a blizzard during their stopover at Limestone AFB. Insufficient cold weather maintenance gear, seen here at Boeing-Wichita, hampered efforts for the 35 jets to continue to RAF Upper Heyford. *Photo BW92503 courtesy Boeing*

Below: B-47E 52-0327 lands at Lake Charles AFB. The 68th BW evaluated 45-day deployments rather than 90-day rotations, which resulted in improved morale and no loss in the unit's EWP readiness. *USAF*

On 17th February 1954 all 44 B-47Es deployed to Sidi Slimane AB and Wheelus AB to take part in a HIGH GEAR exercise along with 33 B-47s from the 301st BW already present at Sidi Slimane AB (22nd BW 52-0023 crashed in the UK on 8th February – see Appendix II). These rotations to North Africa were essential to maximize the exposure of B-47 crews and support personnel to all available overseas bases prior to the start of any conflict. They also had the effect of raising morale of the crews who had 'suffered' through a cold and foggy deployment to England and were 'rewarded' with the better weather in North Africa, although winter there could be notoriously fickle.

Nearly a year had elapsed since the first B-47 visit to the UK, but this had not been enough time to address all the deficiencies at every planned SAC deployment base. B-47Es from the 303rd BW at Davis-Monthan AFB departed for RAF Greenham Common beginning 3rd March 1954, with the relocation sullied by the loss of 51-2416 crashing on takeoff at Davis-Monthan AFB (see Appendix II). Once finally in place, the 303rd BW flew in the BROWN DERBY exercise on 19th March. The dismal state of the runway and taxiways at RAF Greenham Common resulted in the wing moving on 30th March to RAF Fairford, which was not a lot better and still lacked overruns.

An evaluation of a 45-day rather than the existing 90-day deployment to the UK fell to the 68th BW from Lake Charles AFB. The rotation took place between 14th June and 7th August 1954. Results of the shorter duration were not surprising: better morale associated with shorter deployment and a lower degradation of the unit's EWP preparedness. Unfortunately the wing lost two B-47s while in the UK which notably undermined the otherwise improved morale (51-17385 on 20th July and 51-2382 on 6th August – see Appendix II).

During 1955 SAC had altered overall strike planning sufficiently to change its priorities for UK basing, resulting in 'Main Bases' from which B-47s would launch EWP strikes, 'Post-Strike Bases' to which aircraft would return for reconstitution following an EWP strike, and 'War-Only Standby Bases' to be used in the event others were unusable. The main B-47 bases included RAF Brize Norton, RAF Greenham Common, RAF Upper Heyford, and RAF Lakenheath. Post-strike bases were RAF Fairford, RAF Mildenhall, and RAF Chelveston. The war-only bases were RAF Homewood Park (Heathrow), RAF Lindholme, and RAF Full Sutton. SAC's requirements for the main and post-strike bases meant that they would need to be visited at least twice a year by B-47 units and that the runways be at least 10,000ft in length plus 1,000ft overruns at each end. These requirements led to some problems with the UK's Air Ministry as it would fall to them to requisition private property or re-route local roads to lengthen runways or build overruns needed by the B-47.

Throughout 1955 B-47 wings deployed extensively to the UK at RAF Upper Heyford, RAF Fairford, and RAF Lakenheath. By this point most of the rotations were direct to the UK from their home bases. Notable among these were the OPEN MIND deployment from 1st through 8th February involving airplanes from the 22nd BW, 301st BW, 303rd BW, 320th BW and 376th BW, and 26th SRW, and SIGN BOARD from 1st through 7th March from the 93rd BW at Castle AFB. On both occasions the B-47s used the RAF bases for post-strike reconstitution and then flew promptly back to the US rather than remaining in the UK. The summer of 1955 saw the first deployment of the new BLUE CRADLE-equipped B-47Es from the 376th BW – then at Barksdale AFB – from 14th July through 14th October 1955. B-47E 52-0421 crashed on takeoff from Barskdale AFB on 14th July, and 52-0397 was lost at RAF Upper Heyford on 2nd August (see Appendix II). Despite these losses the 376th BW was able to complete its EWP training from RAF Upper Heyford.

At the end of the year the 98th BW conducted two unusual missions as part of its deployment to the UK. Beginning on 7th

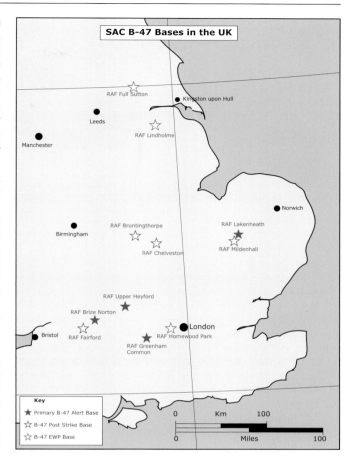

SAC B-47 bases in the UK evolved over time, shifting from primary strike to post-strike recovery bases, as well as emergency operations bases. In addition, transfers of bases from SAC to USAFE altered the EWP and forced B-47s to share already crowded locations.

November 43 B-47Es participated in Operation SADDLE ROCK which involved a 'special weapons exercise' at Lincoln AFB followed by a mass night air refueling in the North East Air Command (NEAC) area and finished with camera-scored bombings against UK targets before landing at RAF Lakenheath. This was the first 'cradle to grave' simulation of an EWP complete with weapons, mass refueling, and simulated strikes to deploy to the UK. In the second mission, on 5th December 10 of the wing's B-47Es flew back to the United States as part of the TEXAS LEAGUE test of ADC units in the US and Canada. The B-47s returned to RAF Lakenheath on 9th December.

By 1956 B-47 deployments to and from the UK had become fairly common, although there were the occasional glitches due to weather, mechanical failures, and accidents. There were only two simulated post-strike deployments in 1956, both through RAF Lakenheath. SWAN DIVE took place in late February and BIG WIND in mid-March. During their return from BIG WIND the 376th BW used its BLUE CRADLE B-47Es to jam US and Canadian air defenses.

The 1956 Soviet invasion of Hungary and the Suez Crisis involving the Franco-British and Israeli invasion of Egypt, beginning in late October (described below), affected B-47 operations from the UK. The 310th BW deployed 45 B-47Es, 11 KC-97Fs, and eight KC-97Gs on 3rd October 1956 from Smoky Hill AFB, KS, to RAF Greenham Common in Operation LUCKY BOY, the first such rotation here since March 1954 (the tankers went to RAF Upper Heyford). The 310th BW went on full alert as the Middle East crisis developed, with minimal local flight operations. This reduced flying pleased the local residents who had justifiably complained about the excessive

noise the B-47s produced. General LeMay visited the unit on 13th December, and the wing returned to Smoky Hill AFB on 9th January 1957 in Operation RED ROBIN.

Operational exercises in the UK benefitted from an occasional sense of humor. For example, on 13th August 1956 the 307th BW took part in Operation PINK LADY. Target 'Bravo' was the top of the bell tower at the Tower of London and Target 'Golf' was the 'center of the bridge [near] Windsor Castle.' One wonders if the new Queen was in residence at the time! In an incident on an unknown date involving a 98th BW B-47, the T-59 'shape' – a facsimile of the Mark VI atomic bomb – failed to drop over the oceanic bomb range. Instead it had 'plopped' unceremoniously onto the bomb doors, a situation which the crew finally understood as the B-47 neared RAF Lakenheath. The crew pulled the emergency bomb release handle and the 'shape' finally dropped onto a homeowner's garden leaving a 30ft x 15ft x 14ft (9m x 4.6m x 4.3m) crater which proved quite expensive to repair. A similar event took place on 3rd March 1958 in Ashton Keynes involving the accidental jettisoning of a wing tank from a 100th BW B-47E.

After years of extensive construction, protracted real estate deals, proposals and counter proposals, and testy exchanges between SAC and the Air Ministry, the B-47 EWP basing situation reached a fairly stable point in 1957. The main bases remained RAF Brize Norton, RAF Greenham Common, RAF Upper Heyford, and RAF Lakenheath. The four post-strike bases expanded to include RAF Chelveston, RAF Fairford, RAF Mildenhall, and RAF Bruntingthorpe. The EWP-only bases underwent multiple changes too extensive and of marginal consequence to detail here. A SAC-mandated reduction in flying hours affected operations from the UK, although B-47E 51-17381 from the 380th BW deployed to RAF Brize Norton did manage a static display at the Paris Air Show (along with a KC-97/B-47 aerial refueling demonstration). Three other 380th BW jets took part in the 'Three Capitols" air race between Paris, Rome, and Madrid (see Appendix IV).

North Africa

Given the limits in range of SAC's early B-29 and B-50 bomber force, planners elected to deploy the bombers to forward bases, eliminating their dependence upon tankers as well as reducing their time to target. In North Africa five bases in French Morocco were selected – Nouasseur, Sidi Slimane, Ben Guerir, El Djema Sahim, and Boulhaut. Construction of the first two was on a 'crash' basis, and the latter two were completed for fighters only. SAC was equally interested in Greek bases for the B-47 (Tymbaktion and Araxos) as well as facilities in Turkey (Izmir and Adana). By October 1953 the three Moroccan bases were each slated to accommodate 90 B-47s and 40 KC-97s. Between 12th and 20th August 1953, six 306th BW B-47s deployed to RAF Fairford visited Nouasseur AB for

Top: During 1955 B-47s were regular visitors to RAF Upper Heyford, Fairford, and Lakenheath. Local residents and town councils were not always eager to welcome the airplanes due to their noise and occasionally 'noisy' crews. *Author's collection*

Center: B-47s deployed to RAF Greenham Common during the 1956 Suez Crisis, notably the 310th BW from Smoky Hill AFB. Two decades later the base would be site of extensive protests associated with cruise missile deployment. *Author's collection*

Bottom: B-47s were eagerly welcomed at UK airshows, such as this one at RAF Gaydon. SAC security rules meant they were often parked away from the crowd or performed only flybys. *Author's collection*

familiarization and evaluation of the base's resources. The first mass deployment to North Africa took place on 2nd November 1953 when 41 B-47s from the 305th BW arrived at Sidi Slimane AB from RAF Brize Norton. B-47s routinely shuttled between bases in North Africa and England, usually in flights of three as plans to move entire squadrons proved impractical.

The first deployment to Morocco directly from the CONUS was 15 YRB-47Bs from the 91st SRW at Lockbourne AFB on 6th January 1954 to Sidi Slimane AB (see Chapter 6), followed by 45 B-47Es from the 301st BW at Barksdale AFB on 10th February, also to Sidi Slimane AB. The 301st BW jets flew a HIGH GEAR simulated strike mission en route to North Africa. During August and September 1954, the 2nd BW and 308th BW from Hunter AFB flew the first LEAP FROG mission designed as a simulated strike from the CONUS assisted by in-flight refueling with recovery at an overseas base. The 2nd BW flew 45 B-47Es in three waves and attacked targets in southern France before recovering at Wheelus AB, Libya. The 308th BW flew 44 B-47Es and a single B-47B on a similar profile and recovered at Sidi Slimane AB. Two 308th BW B-47Es returned directly to Hunter AFB, earning their crews the Mackay Trophy (see Appendix IV). LEAP FROG II followed in November 1954 with 80 B-47s from the 305th BW and 306th BW at MacDill AFB attacking targets in southern Europe and recovering at Sidi Slimane AB.

Not surprisingly, SAC's interest in overseas bases in North Africa ran afoul of US Air Forces – Europe (USAFE) organizational interests. SAC was unwilling to yield operational authority of its aircraft to USAFE when they deployed to southern Europe and North Africa, necessitating the establishment of SAC's 5th Air Division (AD). Plans to establish SAC bases in Spain were deferred in 1955, as were potential bases in Portugal and the Canary Islands. Dhahran, Saudi Arabia, was evaluated as an EWP base along with seven additional bases there. Between November 1955 and January 1956, 46 B-47Es from the 305th BW deployed to Sidi Slimane AB, during which time they also visited Wheelus AB, Dhahran AB, and Adana AB. The 305th BW B-47s, as well as those from the 2nd BW, flew a HOT POINT mission on 4th November 1955. The first wave of this simulated attack resulted in 66 B-47s arriving at Sidi Slimane AB at a rate of one B-47 every four minutes!

The 91st SRW sent 45 RB-47Es from Lockbourne AFB to Ben Guerir AB on 3rd August 1956, and the 308th BW deployed 46 B-47Es (of which nine were Phase V capsule ECM jets) on 21st August to Sidi Slimane AB as part of the response to the deepening Suez Crisis. The presumption was that if Egypt's President Gamal Nasser invited Soviet 'advisors' and forces to buttress the Egyptian military in the face of any impending Franco-British military action, SAC's presence in the 'soft underbelly' of the USSR would discourage Khrushchev from accepting the invitation. The 306th BW sent 46 B-47Es to replace the RB-47Es at Ben Guerir AB on 23rd October, and the 70th SRW deployed 44 RB-47Es to Sidi Slimane AB on 26th October, with the 308th BW returning to Hunter AFB. War erupted on 29th October when Israel, after prior coordination with France and Britain, dropped paratroopers into the Sinai Peninsula. French and British forces attacked Egypt two days later. All of this occurred as the Soviet Union sent its forces into Hungary to quash a popular anti-communist uprising. By the morning of 5th November President Eisenhower was deeply worried over Russian actions in the Middle East and the potential for direct confrontation with Soviet forces. Eisenhower noted that if the Soviets attacked 'the French and British directly, we would be in a war.' Of equal concern to Eisenhower and his advisors was the possibility that Soviet forces in Syria would attack Israeli forces or bases. Although Eisenhower was willing to risk direct military confrontation with the USSR – perhaps even general war – on behalf of long-time allies England and

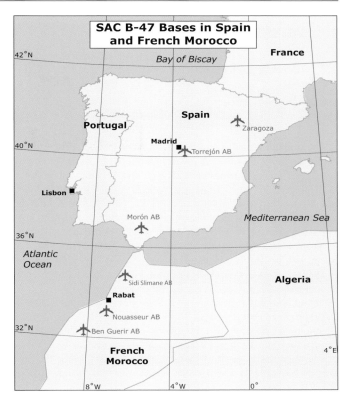

Above: In addition to SAC bases in French Morocco, B-47s operated from three bases in Spain. These tended to be more popular (warmer) destinations than wintertime England. EWP mission routes took the B-47s into the southern USSR with recovery in Iran, Saudi Arabia, and Turkey.

Below: Crews deployed to UK bases would frequently fly a profile mission en route to bases in North Africa. Here 22nd BW crew from RAF Upper Heyford visit Sidi Slimane, from (l) to (r) Major J W Cotton (AC), Lieutenant Gilbert E Bigdon (CP), and Captain Gayle C Miller (N). *USAF*

France, it is difficult to imagine that the United States would risk nuclear war over a conventional Russian attack on Israel. SAC went to an elevated state of readiness beginning 16th November. The units in North Africa presumably were on full alert during this time, although it is not clear if any of the 70th SRW RB-47Es flew regional photo missions given the extensive use of Central Intelligence Agency (CIA) U-2s operating from Det B at Adana AB. Fortunately superpower confrontation was avoided and SAC resumed its normal readiness level on 15th December.

The number of full-wing deployments to North African bases decreased in 1957 as REFLEX ACTION (commonly referred to simply as 'REFLEX') deployments began. The 305th BW relocated 46 B-47s to Ben Guerir AB on 7th January and the 379th BW sent 46 B-47s to Sidi Slimane AB from Homestead AFB, FL, on 10th March, with the final full-wing deployment involving 43 B-47Bs from the 19th BW, also from Homestead AFB, on 8th May 1957. Subsequent rotations to North Africa would only be REFLEX movements. Zaragosa AB, Spain, saw its first contingent of B-47s on 23rd July 1957, leading to an increase in operations from Spain with a concurrent reduction in operations from North Africa the following year.

Yet another crisis arose in the Middle East during July 1958 in Lebanon. Sectarian tensions between Lebanese President Camille Chamoun, a Christian, and the increasing majority of the Muslim population led to a national strike and efforts to overthrow Chamoun in an armed rebellion. On 14th July, a coup in Iraq killed the pro-Western King Faisal, a sign which Eisenhower took as indicative of pro-Nasser, Soviet-backed efforts to destabilize the Middle East. On the same day Chamoun appealed to the US to intervene under the Eisenhower Doctrine to maintain Lebanon's independence.

SAC went to an elevated state of alert beginning 15th July. Although no additional B-47 units deployed to North Africa in response to the crisis, beginning on 1st July B-47s went on alert at Zaragosa AB, Torrejón AB, and Morón AB in Spain, sufficiently augmenting forward forces in the region. SAC had 1,425 B-47s assigned, although 253 were undergoing the MILK BOTTLE modification. Some 17 hours after the alert began, 961 of 970 B-47s required were on alert and configured for their EWP mission. By 18th July SAC had 1,132 B-47s and 1,630 crews ready, including 405 B-47s already on alert in the CONUS and overseas. At 130 hours after notification, SAC was at its peak with 1,297 bombers of all types configured, with 396 B-47s and 10 Phase V ECM B-47s on alert. The entire alert was accorded high visibility to signal the Soviet Union not to act in either Lebanon or Iraq. Whether or not this was intended, the SAC 'show of force' proved successful and the alert ended on 30th July.

Interestingly, SAC had a lesser-known conventional role in the crisis. An undetermined number (almost certainly six) of 310th BW B-47s at RAF Mildenhall and 10 B-47s from the 68th BW at RAF Fairford were configured with conventional bomb racks. Although SAC strenuously opposed using its assets for conventional warfare, it was nevertheless prepared to fulfill this role. Operations Plan 1-58, known as BLUE BAT, began on 15th July and lasted through 25th October 1958. Further details are not known.

Little changed in terms of REFLEX rotations and basing in both North Africa and Spain between 1958 and October 1962 during the Cuban Missile Crisis. During October and November 1962, B-47s were dispersed in the CONUS and those abroad remained on alert with a cessation of flying throughout the crisis, including routine deployments to and from overseas bases (described below). REFLEX in North Africa ended on 30th June 1963 when SAC withdrew its forces from Morocco. Although unconfirmed, it is believed that the final B-47 REFLEX unit at Sidi Slimane AB was the 68th BW, the 306th BW at Ben Guerir AB, and the 384th BW at Nouasseur AB.

REFLEX

The ground alert program in the CONUS offered an important lesson for overseas bases. Rather than deploying entire wings of B-47s plus their tankers and support aircraft for 90 days at a time, SAC recognized the value in placing a smaller number of B-47s on alert and rotating them more frequently. Operation REFLEX ACTION began on 1st July 1957 at Sidi Slimane AB, French Morocco. Five B-47s each from the 305th BW, 306th BW, 308th BW, and 379th BW went on alert and were replaced approximately every 15 days with fresh B-47s and crews. Results were positive, with only 'irritating' rather than 'critical' problems encountered such as inadequate housing and messing, shortage of maintenance personnel, and even Jeeps in disrepair. Nonetheless, SAC was sufficiently impressed, and B-47s at Sidi Slimane AB went on 30-minute alert effective 1st October 1957 on a full-time basis, with most of the earlier problems resolved. B-47 crews were especially pleased. Fliers from the 306th BW called REFLEX ACTION 'the most effective, practical, best planned, and coordinated EWP Plan.' Others said it 'gave them the kind of readiness the American people had been led to expect of SAC.' Subsequent REFLEX deployments to Sidi Slimane AB were known as SHOTGUN ALPHA, to Ben Guerir AB as SHOTGUN BRAVO, and to Nouasseur AB as SHOTGUN CHARLIE.

As the declassified history of SAC's alert program recounts, overseas REFLEX operations were far more valuable than maintaining only CONUS alert. The benefits of REFLEX included 'the need to keep some aircraft [overseas] due to political considerations; the necessity

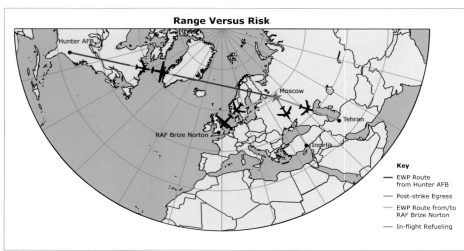

Range Versus Risk

Key
— EWP Route from Hunter AFB
— Post-strike Egress
— EWP Route from/to RAF Brize Norton
— In-flight Refueling

Above: 55th SRW RB-47Es deployed en masse to Ben Guerir AB in 1955 as part of CRISS CROSS and DEEP ROCK. The wing's RB-47Hs, ERB-47Hs, and TELL TWOS operated in small numbers overseas. *USAF*

Left: SAC understood the 'range vs risk' issue in B-47 basing. Those in the ZI were safer but needed air refueling and took longer to reach their targets, which were usually secondary. Overseas bases were at greater risk, needed post-strike refueling, but would hit critical targets.

Opposite: REFLEX action substantially reduced the cost of deploying a wing overseas. In the case of the 98th BW, seen here, sending 5-10 B-47s was more cost effective than sending 45 airplanes plus all their associated support equipment and personnel. *USAF*

of attacking Soviet targets as soon as possible after initial warning; the limited number of tankers available to the command did not permit launching the entire force from ZI bases; and because the very existence of these forces posed difficult targeting problems for an attacker who must hit them and ZI bases simultaneously to effect a surprise attack.'

REFLEX also resulted in a considerable savings. Deploying the 307th BW from Lincoln AFB, NE, for example, involved moving 45 airplanes, 1,600 personnel, and 190 tons of cargo at a cost of $2,774,000. Fixed costs once overseas raised the total by another $42,428,000. REFLEX reduced the deployment cost by nearly 40% and fixed costs dropped to $14,736,000. Improved safety was an added benefit of REFLEX. Deploying large numbers of B-47s meant an equal number of KC-97 tankers with little room for aborts or missed refueling, risking a B-47 divert or worse (B-47E 52-0534 was lost on 10th March 1956 with its nuclear capsules – see Appendix II). For REFLEX operations, however, only 5-10 B-47s deployed at a time in their peacetime configuration. Upon arrival they would undergo a thorough maintenance check (especially for fuel leaks), cameras would be loaded, and they would receive their EWP fuel load. Once moved to the alert ramp, they would be configured with ATO racks, chaff, 20mm ammunition, approach and drag chutes, water alcohol, liquid oxygen, and a Mk 39 weapon. The incoming crew would 'cock' the airplane on alert and were given the rest of the day off for rest. The following day they began their 22-day alert cycle – 14 days on alert and 7 days off alert, then return to their CONUS base. In 1962 this changed to a 28-day tour with three weeks on alert separated by two rest periods of three-and-one-half days each.

The return trip from any REFLEX deployment was always accompanied by mixed emotions. Husbands were eager to reunite with wives, fathers with families, and there was always something that needed to be done around the house. For some crewmembers there was little to do while deployed and not on alert, making for a boring trip. Conversely, there was a sense of happy detachment about being away from the daily grind of operations at SAC home bases, and returning to the routine oversight of squadron commanders and additional duties was not always a welcome prospect. Still, there was considerable enthusiasm for the flight home, not the least of which was how much swag could be carried back across the Pond.

The capacious bomb bay meant that large items could be hoisted inside, including small cars such as an MG! One of these was reportedly lost on 1st July 1959 when B-47E 51-15805 departed controlled flight during air refueling and crashed into the Atlantic Ocean near the Azores. The most common items were alcohol (carried inside the pressurized portion of the fuselage to avoid freezing) and electronic equipment, notably large and very heavy German hi-fidelity gear from Telefunken and Grundig. Other items included an organ and huge slabs of Spanish marble. RB-47 crews reportedly carried expensive Turkish carpets in the aft fuselage radome. Crews became very creative at hiding these items to avoid the unwanted attention of the Customs inspector, especially when forced to land at bases not accustomed to B-47s returning from abroad.

The success at Sidi Slimane AB led to an increase in the number of REFLEX deployments both overseas and, interestingly enough, within the CONUS. Five B-47s from the 509th BW at Walker AFB, NM, sat REFLEX alert at Pease AFB (WHITE OAK), five B-47s from the 97th BW at Biggs AFB, TX, were on REFLEX alert at Plattsburgh AFB, NY (NORTH CLIFF), and the 44th BW at Lake Charles AFB, LA, and the 321st BW at Pinecastle AFB, FL, each had three B-47s on REFLEX alert at Loring AFB, ME (SADDLE CREEK). B-47s from the 22nd BW and the 320th BW at March AFB, CA, deployed to Eielson AFB, AK. Subsequent Alaska deployments were split beginning 8th January 1959 when six B-47s from the 96th BW and six from the 341st BW, both at Dyess AFB, TX, went to Eielson AFB and Elmendorf AFB, respectively.

On 1st October 1957 nine B-47Es from the 68th BW at RAF Brize Norton were placed on full alert in preparation for the anticipated REFLEX ACTION alert to begin in January 1958. Original plans called for B-47s from SAC's 2nd Air Force (AF) and 8th AF to provide 15 B-47s apiece, with six wings responsible for five B-47s each to RAF Fairford (2nd AF) and RAF Greenham Common (8th AF). Each cadre of five would arrive on a Tuesday, Wednesday, or Thursday, sit alert for seven days, and then depart the following Wednesday, Thursday, or Friday. This proved cumbersome, especially following the addition of RAF Brize Norton as the third UK REFLEX base and the extensive modification work associated with the MILK BOTTLE program. In another major change, REFLEX B-47s no longer carried EWP nuclear weapons from their home base to their REFLEX base. Instead, the weapons were permanently based in the UK and uploaded during the alert cocking procedure once the B-47 arrived in England.

The last 90-day rotation to England ended in April 1958 as the 100th BW flew its B-47s back to Pease AFB. In the end REFLEX reduced the mass movements but resulted in constant movements. During each week in June 1958, for example, 81 alert aircraft overseas conducted 162 deployments and redeployments. At least 20 Lajes-based KC-97s provided en route air refueling for these B-47s as part of Operation SHORT PUNT. By 1st July there were 194 B-47s and four Phase V B-47 ECM jets on alert in both CONUS and overseas. SAC decreased the reaction time for all alert aircraft to 20 minutes for the first aircraft to launch with subsequent takeoffs at one-minute intervals. By March 1959 REFLEX reaction times had improved substantially, with an average Alpha alert time of '5.26 minutes, Bravo, 11 minutes, and Coco, 14.9 minutes.'

As of January 1959 seven UK bases supported REFLEX alert under the program name WILDCAT and hosted 42 B-47s, including six 301st BW Phase V Capsule ECM aircraft at RAF Brize Norton. The decision in 1959 by the French government to remove all NATO nuclear-capable aircraft from French bases meant that three tactical fighter

Table 5-4. **Spain and North Africa REFLEX Alert Bases**

Base	Code Name	Base	Code Name
Sidi Slimane AB	Shotgun - Alpha	Zaragosa AB	Shotgun - Delta
Ben Guerir AB	Shotgun - Bravo	Torrejon AB	Shotgun - Echo
Nouasseur AB	Shotgun - Charlie	Morón AB	Shotgun - Foxtrot

Phase V capsule EB-47Es were an integral part of the alert force, especially at overseas bases. By the early 1960s these deployed only to the UK. *Augustine Letto*

wings were forced to relocate to West Germany and the UK. Four of SAC's B-47 bases – RAF Bruntingthorpe, RAF Chelveston, RAF Lakenheath, and RAF Mildenhall – transferred to USAFE's 3rd AF. This resulted in shuffles among the remaining three B-47 REFLEX bases and the withdrawal of all Phase V ECM aircraft from the UK to Pease AFB [eight ECM aircraft returned in 1960, with four each to RAF Upper Heyford (BLUE CRADLE) and RAF Greenham Common (Phase V)]. By the end of 1959 there were only 24 B-47s on alert in the UK.

The 1961 Berlin Crisis resulted not only in a halt to planned B-47 unit deactivation but an increase during July in the number of B-47s on alert in the UK. Although each base typically saw three B-47s added to its alert force, and the total reached 39 B-47s. In addition, all 16 of the Phase V and BLUE CRADLE EB-47E ECM airplanes on overseas alert were in the UK. Total numbers increased further by August 1962 with 48 B-47Es and 20 EB-47Es on alert. The onset of the Cuban Missile Crisis in October 1962 saw the temporary cessation of deployments to the UK, with an augmented total of 56 B-47Es and 22 EB-47Es on alert. By the end of the year these had decreased to the previous levels of 48 and 20, respectively.

A top concern for President John F Kennedy's administration was the issue of 'gold flow', which referred to US payments to other countries in exchange for basing rights. By 1963 this affected SAC REFLEX operations in the UK, Spain, and North Africa, leading to the CLEARWATER initiative to reduce or eliminate these expenses, saving $21 million annually. CLEARWATER would remove all reflex B-47s from the UK and Spain (40 aircraft each) by 1st April 1965. Affected bases would be RAF Brize Norton (returned to the UK) and RAF Upper Heyford (retained as a dispersal base) in the UK, and Morón AB and Torrejón AB in Spain. By the end of 1963 there were 39 B-47Es and 20 EB-47Es remaining in the UK. By 1st July 1964 SAC had eliminated REFLEX at RAF Fairford and RAF Greenham Common, both of which reverted to the UK, and the 10 BLUE CRADLE EB-47Es returned to Lockbourne AFB. This reduced the total number of B-47s in the UK to 30. Further CLEARWATER reductions spelled the end of UK alert, despite the strongest protests from CINCSAC General Power who told Congress 'I cannot endorse a proposal which

eliminates a vital SIOP capability when adequate replacement is not available.' Nonetheless, REFLEX ended with the departure on 3rd April 1965 of 380th SAW B-47E 53-1884 from RAF Brize Norton back to Plattsburgh AFB.

AIR MAIL

The 5,000nm (9,260km) distance from the CONUS to Andersen AFB, Guam, made the frequent rotations used in REFLEX next to impossible for the Pacific theater, instead relying on entire wings to relocate for alert duty. In late 1957 General Power moved to change this to the deployment of 15 B-47s at a time from any given wing with 10 going on alert upon arrival. Should the need for more bombers arise under increased tensions, the remainder of the wing's B-47 would deploy accordingly. Five crews and maintenance personnel would rotate via Military Air Transport Service (MATS) flights every 10 days, with one third of the deployed personnel flying local training missions. Plans included a split alert force (such as the one in Alaska) beginning October 1958 with five B-47s at Andersen AFB and the other five at Kadena AB, Okinawa. The Joint Chiefs of Staff (JCS) approved the new Guam rotation on 1st February 1958.

The first AIR MAIL alert began on 1st July 1958 with B-47s from the 96th BW at Dyess AFB deploying under Operation GREEN FIRE, followed by the 43rd BW in October. Plans to use Kadena AB were postponed indefinitely. While REFLEX B-47s in North Africa and England dealt with the crisis in Lebanon, the newly established AIR MAIL B-47s found themselves embroiled in a crisis in Asia. Following a similar crisis in 1955 (described above), the People's Republic of China (PRC) declared its intention to 'liberate' the Republic of China (RoC – Taiwan). Rather than attack Taiwan directly, PRC forces began intense shelling of several islands held by the RoC, namely Quemoy and Matsu. Should the PRC expand this military action against Taiwan or establish a military blockade of the island, the US would be obligated under treaty with the RoC to intervene. For most senior planners in the Eisenhower administration this meant the use of small-yield nuclear weapons against PRC bases along the coast adjacent to Taiwan.

On 25th August 1958 the JCS informed the Commander-in-Chief, Pacific (CINCPAC) Admiral Harry D Felt, that the 15 B-47s on Guam could be made available with Mark VI weapons to strike 'communist airfields harboring MiG-17 fighters.' Should the crisis escalate further, additional B-47s could conduct nuclear strikes against PRC military and industrial targets further inland. Such action would almost certainly provoke Soviet assistance to the PRC, leading to general war with the US. CINCPAC preferred additional conventional weapons, and on 31st August requested a squadron of B-36s carrying HE bombs be deployed to Guam. The JCS rejected this, saying that any additional forces would come from CONUS as they were needed. The crisis resolved itself without US-PRC confrontation, but it did highlight the need for greater discretion in weapon selection. The JCS wanted more flexibility to choose either conventional or nuclear weapons, but SAC argued that small-yield nuclear bombs were more effective. Whether or not SAC wanted to admit it, the B-47's inability to carry conventional weapons without degrading SAC's EWP mission lay at the heart of this debate. It would resurface again in 1964 over the use of SAC bombers in Southeast Asia.

Beginning in January 1959 the AIR MAIL rotation changed from one wing providing 15 B-47s to four wings (22nd BW, 320th BW, 43rd BW, and 303rd BW) each providing four B-47s apiece. The hot and humid weather on Guam played havoc with the B-47's electronics, especially the radar, leading to frequent malfunctions. By the end of 1959 SAC had 275 B-47s on alert in the CONUS and overseas out of a total of 519 aircraft on alert. B-47 AIR MAIL ended on 1st April 1964 when they were replaced by B-52s.

Table 5-5. **UK REFLEX Alert Bases**

RAF Base	Code Name	RAF Base	Code Name
Fairford	Wildcat - Alpha	Chelveston	Wildcat - Echo
Greenham Common	Wildcat - Bravo	Bruntingthorpe	Wildcat - Foxtrot
Brize Norton	Wildcat - Charlie	Upper Heyford	Wildcat - Golf
Mildenhall	Wildcat - Delta		

Above: With considerable attention focused on the REFLEX missions to England, Spain, and North Africa, few people were aware of the AIR MAIL deployments to Andersen AFB on Guam. The 3rd AD there used 53-1918 as a 'hack', seen here landing at Yokota AB on 15th May 1965. *Toshio Tagaya*

Right: B-47s, B-52s, and KC-135s took part in the DUSTY BEARD and DUSTY BEARD II dispersal program, assessing their ability to operate from dry lakebeds. Surprisingly, these were incorporated into the SIOP as emergency recovery fields. *USAF via William T Y'Blood*

Dispersal

Prior to the establishment of the alert force, B-47s took part in a dispersal program. By 1954 SAC decided that there would be no more than 45 B-47s at a single base because it made for a lucrative target and it would be impossible to launch a generated force within the 8-10 hour warning window provided by the Distant Early Warning (DEW) system of an incoming Soviet bomber attack. This proved especially problematic for 90-aircraft 'superwing' bases. Consequently, the dispersal goals were twofold: to increase the targeting requirements for Soviet bombers and missiles, and to get more bombers in the air in the limited time (ie, avoid 'runway limitation'). CINCSAC General Power was supportive of the dispersal program, but warned Congress that 'there are disadvantages' for any dispersals longer than two weeks due to crew inactivity and loss of training. Moreover, the dispersal bases would require considerable capital outlay for 'strengthening pavement, additional communications, secure areas' and physical plant.

The problem of dispersal remained unresolved until 6th July 1960, when AF Vice Chief of Staff General LeMay told Power to 'exercise B-47 dispersal bases immediately.' The following day SAC executed OpOrd 38-60 Operation CLUTCH PEDAL, sending one or two B-47s to 52 non-SAC military and civilian airfields (14 for 2nd AF, 14 for 8th AF, and 24 for 15th AF. B-47s deployed on 11th June and returned to their home bases on 12th June. No weapons were taken, and each B-47 carried its crew of three, a crew chief, and just his tool box – if the B-47 needed more maintenance than he could provide it was counted as a 'lost sortie'. Only 46 bases ultimately took part, as venues such as Chicago's O'Hare IAP, Los Angeles IAP, and Baltimore's Friendship IAP were exempted to avoid disruption to civil air service at major locations. A total of 92 B-47s deployed with one air abort and one delayed for a starter change. Results were positive, as SAC reported 'excellent reception and good facilities at all bases.' Consequently, SAC would conduct dispersal training each quarter for aircrew and maintenance familiarization.

Perhaps the most unusual effort associated with the pre-strike dispersal and post-strike recovery of SAC assets was the September 1961 DRY STONE program. SAC identified 201 dry lakebeds for use as natural alternative landing sites (NALS). The initial operational feasibility test, known as DUSTY BEARD I, took place on 6th-7th March 1962 when a B-47 and KC-135 landed at Bicycle Lake near Edwards AFB. The crews spent the night while on simulated alert. A follow-on evaluation, DUSTY BEARD II, validated dry lakebed dispersal procedures, as well as determined their suitability for the forthcoming

North American RS-70 (B-70). Between 10-26th April 1962, bomber and tanker strike teams rotated every two days to one of four dry lakes (Hidden Hills, Silver Lake, and Three Sisters West in California, and Mudd Lake in Nevada). For the first week teams included B-47s and KC-135s, with B-52s and KC-135s for the second week. Takeoffs and landings were all conducted under day Visual Flight Rules (VFR) conditions, with only minor difficulties. Within an hour of landing, all airplanes were on simulated alert. Over the course of two weeks, crews responded to 26 Bravo alerts (reporting to the airplane, starting engines, and declaring ready). The maximum reaction time was just eight minutes. Overall DUSTY BEARD II demonstrated that EWO operations from dry lakes were feasible, but would 'probably be utilized as a "last resort" recovery area.' Beginning 1st July 1963, DRY STONE locations were included in the SIOP. Returning B-47s and B-52s would be directed to specific lakebeds, where 'sufficient KC-135 tankers would have a primary or secondary EWO assignment to support these bombers.'

Cuba and B-47 Dispersal Operations

At the height of the Cuban Missile Crisis, on 22nd October, US forces assumed Defense Condition (DEFCON) 3 posture, one step higher than SAC's normal day-to-day readiness level. Changes for SAC included regeneration of previously degraded bomber and missile sorties. With the DEFCON 3 announcement, the JCS directed that SAC's B-47 fleet be dispersed as needed and upgraded to full Emergency War Order (EWO) priority. At noon on 22nd October 183 B-47s from 17 medium wings at 15 bases were equipped with nuclear weapons in full EWO configuration and the airplanes prepared for EWO launch upon their arrival at 32 dispersal bases, including civilian airports. B-47s already on alert were not relocated. Moreover, 26 B-47Es from the 306th BW at MacDill AFB were evacuated to Hunter AFB as part of RIDERS UP, SAC's pre-established evacuation plan. This freed ramp space in the Florida Military Emergency Zone (MEZ) for potential tactical offensive operations against Cuba as well as ensuring the B-47's survivability in the event of a nuclear strike from Cuba against US bases in Florida. There were two evacuation options: GAY CROWD assumed an orderly departure (which in fact took place) and CRISP BACON, which presumed a fast reaction departure.

Most significantly, the newly dispersed B-47 sorties would be upgraded from 'second cycle' to 'first cycle' status. In the event of war, second cycle bombers normally would be refueled by tankers flying their second EWO mission, having already refueled another bomber en route to its target, then landed, refueled, and re-launched

Above: During the 1962 Cuban Missile Crisis many B-47s relocated to dispersal fields, in this case to Port Columbus, Ohio. The Air Force Reserve photographer intentionally cropped the serial number for security purposes. *Photo courtesy Boeing*

Below: Even after accounting for the Cuban Missile Crisis, the number of B-47s on alert peaked in 1962. As ICBMs went on alert the total number of bombers on alert dropped considerably, and by the end of 1965 there were no more B-47s on alert.

to refuel a second cycle bomber. Instead, SAC upgraded 41 of the dispersed B-47s to first cycle status by assigning 87 KC-97s to refuel them at Goose Bay AB, Labrador, Harmon AB, Newfoundland, and Lajes AP, the Azores. Despite being redesignated to first cycle status, the B-47s were not actually on alert, as they were 'not subject to immediate launch.' Instead, they were slated to takeoff if and when needed within an hour of notification.

At 8:00 AM on 24th October, US forces were placed in DEFCON 2 posture. B-52s and KC-135s began 1/8th airborne alert, meaning that 12% (75 B-52s) of SAC's strike force was airborne, fully loaded with EWO-configured weapons and ready to execute their strike mission. Not all DEFCON 2 actions were undertaken, however, as the KC-135A Post Attack Command and Control System (PACCS) aircraft were not launched or dispersed. Moreover, high-priority SAC reconnaissance missions remained in force, including RB-47H BOX TOP and COMMON CAUSE sorties, RB-47K BLUE INK sorties, and EB-47E(TT) IRON WORK sorties, as well as U-2 BRASS KNOB missions over Cuba or CROW FLIGHT worldwide sampling missions. Finally, DEFCON 2 required that all 'excess' REFLEX and AIR MAIL aircraft on overseas alert return to their stateside bases. Instead, Power directed that these airplanes (plus the local command support B-47s and RB-47Es) remain abroad, be configured for EWO missions with weapons, and be available to cover any aborted sortie. This augmentation/generation program brought command support aircraft at overseas bases, ie, those normally used by the Combat Support Groups (CSG) to EWO-capable status, and a handful of 'spare' US-based aircraft were ferried to overseas locations to increase local numbers. This meant, for example, a single 303rd BW aircraft

deployed to RAF Greenham Common where it sat alert with 96th and 307th aircraft.

The results of DEFCON 2 were impressive. Within 24 hours of the JCS directive, EWO-ready bombers rose from 912 to 1,436 and tankers from 402 to 916. Beginning 30th October, 30 excess B-47 REFLEX and AIR MAIL aircraft had assumed alert, including 11 in the United Kingdom, 14 in Spain and Morocco, three at Andersen AB, Guam, and two at Elmendorf AFB, Alaska. (The three excess sorties at Anderson AB, as well as the 17 alert AIR MAIL B-47s, deployed to Kadena AB, Okinawa, prior to the 11th November arrival of Typhoon Karen, which destroyed most of the base. These 20 B-47s returned to Guam on 13th November). Although small in terms of total numbers, the proximity of these additional bombers to the USSR and their assumption of full alert status meant that these B-47s were a significant addition to US strike capability. By 4th November, when SAC forces were at their highest, the number of EWO-ready bombers reached 1,479 with 1,003 tankers.

On 15th November SAC assumed a modified DEFCON 2 status, with 32 dispersed B-47s degraded and recalled to their home bases, leaving 151 B-47s at dispersal bases (37 first cycle and 114 second cycle). By 24th November the JCS authorized Power to end the B-47 dispersal. All airplanes (except the 306th BW jets at Hunter AFB) returned to their home stations, as did the additional KC-97s. Two days later SAC ended the alert requirement for additional B-47 REFLEX and AIR MAIL alert, command support B-47 alert, 'loaned B-47' alert, and B-47 generated alert. SAC returned to DEFCON 4, its normal posture, on 27th November, effectively ending SAC's elevated contribution to the Cuban Missile Crisis.

B-47s were clearly part of the 'second team' during the crisis. B-52s assumed the added role of airborne alert, and they carried more and larger nuclear weapons, including two GAM-77 (AGM-28) Hound Dog missiles. Although B-47s were still part of the extant ground alert force, it was the addition of B-47 dispersal aircraft to existing EWO-ready forces that, on the margin, proved crucial to SAC's ability to achieve full operational preparedness. The B-47 dispersal effort proved to be an effective way to redistribute the force, both as a protective means as well as to increase EWO readiness. Earlier practice programs such as CLUTCH PEDAL had given crews and support personnel experience in relocation (minus their nuclear weapons). Realistically, however, dispersal was a luxury that SAC had never considered as an option. In the event of a surprise attack (or even with limited advance warning), SAC's top priority was to launch the alert force rather than generate dispersal sorties. In the opinion of SAC planners, B-47 'sorties planned for dispersal were, in a sense, expendable.' The events of October allowed SAC the time needed to prepare for total-force generation, revealing the maximum first strike capability that SAC could achieve.

As with many other aspects of the B-47's history, its role in the SAC alert program, both at home and overseas, was crucial in identifying weaknesses and formulating operational tactics and plans. B-52 alert operations benefitted directly from the missteps and successes of the B-47 alert program, having worked out the 'kinks' in an evolving process that often seemed to make no sense. The B-52's range obviated the need for forward basing and REFLEX, although B-52s did occasionally deploy to the UK for orientation, along with the infrequent 'good will' flights – known in 1958 as ALARM BELL missions – intended to familiarize overseas CSGs and munitions units with the Stratofortress. B-52s continued AIR MAIL alert from Guam, however, which had the tactical benefit of putting Soviet targets in the Pacific Far East and in the People's Republic of China at further risk. The ultimate measure of the B-47's success on alert is not the legacy it left for the B-52 and other bombers, but that it was never used.

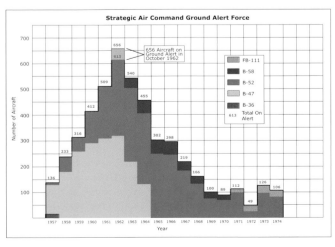

Strategic Air Command Ground Alert Force

CHAPTER SIX

The Unseen Mission

It was a beautiful day in the English Cotswolds, the kind fliers everywhere dream about. At 10:00 AM RB-47H 53-4281 became airborne from RAF Brize Norton. Copilot First Lieutenant F Bruce Olmstead raised the landing gear and monitored the airspeed to begin the flap retraction sequence. Navigator First Lieutenant John R McKone, hunched over his charts in the nose of the airplane, passed the departure heading to aircraft commander Captain Willard G 'Bill' Palm. Unstrapping from their webbed hammock seats in the narrow aisle adjacent to the pilots, the three electronic warfare officers (EWs) – better known as 'Ravens' or 'Crows' – began crawling aft to the tiny doorway leading to their capsule in what was the bomb bay in standard B-47s. A final glance up through the pilots' canopy was the last sunlight they would see. Even with the Arctic summer daylight, tonight's planned return time to RAF Brize Norton was well after dark. Once inside, Captain Eugene E 'Gene' Posa, First Lieutenant Oscar L Goforth, and First Lieutenant Dean B Phillips began the technical preparations for the multiple sensors and recording equipment crammed into the tiny compartment. It was still several hours before the jet would be 'on station', but the Ravens had to be inside their

Unknown to all but a very few, the secretive RB-47 missions were the B-47's only taste of combat. Despite three losses, the gains were tremendous for US intelligence agencies. 53-4301 lands at Yokota AB on 28th February 1966. *Toshio Tagaya*

capsule prior to main cabin pressurization as the RB-47H climbed to its cruise altitude. Moreover, their electronics were temperamental, often requiring in-flight repair or adjustment. Today, however, the airplane and its black boxes were in perfect condition. Unknown to the crew, they had each received their 'spot' promotion in rank.

They were not alone. Alongside the 'ferret' was a shiny new KC-135 filled with thousands of pounds of jet fuel that would allow the RB-47H, which did not carry external wing tanks, to complete its CASTLE GATE electronic intelligence (ELINT) mission along the east side of the Kola Peninsula, over the Barents Sea, and then back again to the UK. Refueling from the KC-135 was much easier than from the slower KC-97, and after filling the RB-47 west of Bødo, Norway, the KC-135 turned southwest and headed for England.

Exactly two months earlier a Soviet SA-2 *Guideline* surface-to-air-missile (SAM) had shot down Central Intelligence Agency (CIA) pilot Frank Powers in his U-2 over Sverdlovsk, deep within the USSR, prompting the termination of all US overflights of the Soviet Union and a moratorium on all peripheral missions. Palm's crew was the first from the 55th Strategic Reconnaissance Wing (SRW) based at Forbes AFB, KS, to resume reconnaissance flights along the European borders of the USSR. All 55th crews operating from RAF Brize Norton were highly experienced, having 'paid their dues' on less risky sorties from Turkey as well as weather reconnaissance

Top left: Duplicate scan of the crew of 53-4281 on its final flight on 1st July 1960. From (l) to (r) Captain Willard Palm (AC), Captain Eugene Posa (EW), First Lieutenant F Bruce Olmstead (CP), First Lieutenant Oscar Goforth (EW), First Lieutenant John McKone (N), and First Lieutenant Dean Philips (EW). *Author's collection*

Top right: MiG-19 pilot Captain Vasilii Ambrosievitch Polyakov shot down the RB-47H on 1st July 1960. What actually happened may never be known for certain, with two different people identified as Polyakov. *SOVFOTO*

Center: A MiG-19PM *Farmer-D* off the wing of an RB-47H, similar to the view which Olmstead likely had to the opposite side prior to the attack. *Colonel John Drost/USAF via Geoff Hays*

Bottom: Even though the RB-47H was unequivocally in international airspace, Khrushchev embraced its intentional destruction as a signal of Soviet power. In the wake of the U-2 Incident, few in the global community faulted the USSR for this blatant violation of international law.

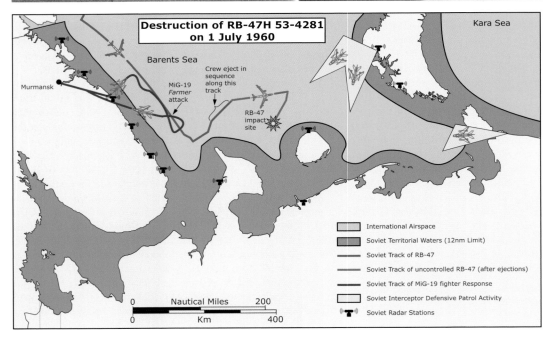

Destruction of RB-47H 53-4281 on 1 July 1960

Kara Sea

Barents Sea

Murmansk

MiG-19 *Farmer* attack

Crew eject in sequence along this track

RB-47 impact site

	International Airspace
	Soviet Territorial Waters (12nm Limit)
	Soviet Track of RB-47
	Soviet Track of uncontrolled RB-47 (after ejections)
	Soviet Track of MiG-19 fighter Response
	Soviet Interceptor Defensive Patrol Activity
	Soviet Radar Stations

Nautical Miles 0   200
Km 0   400

Opposite: President John F Kennedy and two happy wives were on hand at Andrews AFB, MD, to welcome home the two survivors of the July 1960 attack. (l) to (r) Gail Olmsted, Bruce Olmsted, John McKone, and Constance McKone. *Author's collection*

flights over Canada and Greenland. Palm's crew was no exception. For McKone and Olmstead, today's mission was their first time on this particular track. This was Goforth's first operational reconnaissance sortie. Historically these sorties flew as close as 25nm (46km) from the shoreline or border, although this was sometimes extended to 40nm (74km) or more as political circumstances might dictate. Russian radar tracking was notoriously inaccurate and many collections could be undertaken from farther out, both for the security of the airplane and crew as well as to minimize the chance of a confrontation. For added safety in the wake of the U-2 loss, the 'black line' mission track on McKone's navigation chart added another 10nm (19km) of lateral separation, so today's flight was 50nm (93km) from Soviet territory.

By mid afternoon the RB-47 passed Vardø, located at the northeastern tip of Norway and entered international airspace above the Barents Sea. Using his radar, McKone determined the airplane was 35nm (65km) from the Norwegian coast and directed Palm to turn southeast, maintaining their planned distance from the USSR. A subsequent radar fix told McKone the winds aloft had blown them slightly off course – 5nm (9km) – so they adjusted their track by three degrees left, taking them further away from the Soviet coast. Some 15 minutes later, halfway through their mission, they passed Murmansk. A third radar fix showed that the variable winds had again caused them to drift slightly to the west, so McKone directed a two degree turn to the east. They were now on track, heading 120° at 30,000ft (9,144m) and 50nm from the coast.

Once again, they were not alone. Olmstead spotted the contrail of an 'escort' paralleling their route, and turned his seat around for a better view. The unidentified interceptor made an abrupt left turn, crossed behind them, and moved to the RB-47's left side, but remained some 2-3nm (4-6km) behind them. Soon it turned back toward Murmansk and disappeared. It was late afternoon as McKone took his next radar fix at Holy Nose Cape to verify the crucial turn point which would take them away from the rapidly approaching Soviet coastline ahead to the south and instead point them northeast toward Novaya Zemlya.

Captain Vasilii Ambrosievitch Polyakov, Soviet MiG-19 pilot Second Class, was on alert at Kilp Yavr AB when the warning horn sounded around 5PM. His supersonic *Farmer* was airborne within 2 minutes, with a second airplane, variously recorded as another *Farmer* or a Sukhoi Su-9 *Fishpot*, due to launch some 10 minutes behind him. (There has been considerable argument over what type of MiG Polyakov flew. It has been reported as a MiG-19, a MiG-17 *Fresco*, and even a MiG-15 *Fagot*. In a September 1998 interview with the author, Olmstead stated unequivocally that Polyakov's interceptor was a MiG-19 *Farmer*.) Ground radar controllers directed Polyakov to the location of the unidentified intruder, which he had yet to spot visually due to wispy clouds above his MiG-19 at approximately 5,000m (16,404ft). After he leveled off at 30,000ft he could make out the profile of Palm's RB-47 ahead and to the left, away from the Soviet coastline. 'I transmitted to the ground control that it was an American plane, and the command…was to bring the plane down, *to make him land*' [ie, not to shoot it down but to force it to land – emphasis added] remembered Polyakov in an interview with BBC television producer Paul Lashmar. As Palm waited for the precise time for the RB-47 to begin its left turn, Olmstead was stunned to see Polyakov's MiG-19 approximately 40ft (12m) off the right wing, unclear where it came from or how long it had been there. In accordance with international flights rules, the *Farmer* was between the RB-47 and Soviet airspace, and Olmstead did not recall seeing any visual indication from the MiG-19 to follow it to land, but such a signal might have been given before Olmstead ever noticed the *Farmer*. McKone, unaware of the proximity of the MiG,

told Palm to start the planned slow turn away from the Kola Peninsula, and the RB-47 began its bank to the left.

Polyakov continued his narration: 'I transmitted back to the control that they [did not] follow the instructions. They said you can use or recharge the guns [ie, fire a warning shot] … I maneuvered to the other side underneath [the RB-47] and afterwards heard the command to shoot [it] down.' Polyakov opened fire, striking the RB-47's left wing and engines. On board the RB-47 Olmstead, who had started taking pictures of the MiG-19, dropped the camera and attempted to return fire using the A-5 tail gun, but Polyakov's *Farmer* was too close for a radar lock-on, so Olmstead fired visually, expending approximately 400 rounds of ammunition without success. Already in a turn to the left, the loss of thrust on those engines and damage to the left wing caused the RB-47 to enter a flat spin. Olmstead struggled to turn his seat around to help Palm regain control, and the airplane leveled briefly at 28,000ft (8,354m). According to *The Little Toy Dog*, the semi-official 1962 account of the loss (which some former 55th SRW crewmembers consider to have been written with artistic license), Olmstead reported that a second burst from the MiG-19 struck the RB-47 causing it to shudder violently and once again depart from controlled flight, but Polyakov only mentions a single burst: 'Fire started and when it disappeared into the clouds beneath I didn't see it anymore…' For 10 seconds Palm and Olmstead struggled to regain control, but to no avail, and Palm ordered the crew to bail out. Olmstead ejected first, breaking his back in the process. McKone ejected second, followed by Palm as the airplane continued to head northeast.

No one knows if the three Ravens tried to eject – there were no previous attempts to eject from the Raven capsule, and few Ravens believed that it would be survivable if attempted. McKone recalls seeing three parachutes in addition to his own, raising the possibility that at least one Raven did eject. Olmstead saw only two parachutes. The Soviets claimed to have recovered the body of Eugene Posa but refused to return it to the US, again suggesting that the Ravens may have attempted to eject. Miraculously, the RB-47 – now somewhat stable after the ejections, a not unheard of phenomenon – flew on for perhaps another 100nm (185km) before finally crashing in the Barents Sea. McKone and Olmstead were rescued by a Russian fishing trawler and subsequently transferred to a Soviet Navy *Riga-*

class frigate. They were then flown to Moscow and imprisoned in the notorious Lubyanka Prison (concurrent with Frank Powers), and eventually repatriated to the United States as heroes. According to Polyakov, Palm perished in the freezing waters. His body was recovered, returned to America, and on 5th August 1960 was interred in Arlington National Cemetery. The bodies of Goforth and Phillips were not recovered. Polyakov received the Order of the Red Banner.

Not surprisingly, accounts of the loss of 53-4281 differ in notable respects. For example, one version notes that Polyakov fired a warning shot which was ignored, prompting the second, lethal attack, but this does not comport with either Polyakov's BBC interview or *The Little Toy Dog*. Olmstead reportedly later told a colleague that he shot down the MiG-19 and saw a black parachute belonging to the Soviet pilot, supporting his claim. This may have been the third parachute which McKone mentions. In *The Little Toy Dog*, however, Olmstead does not mention shooting down the MiG-19, and says he only saw two parachutes – neither of which were black – and assumed they were McKone and Palm. The declassified 1965 History of the SAC Reconnaissance Center specifically cites the loss of a North Korean MiG-17 on 28th April 1965 as the first and only interceptor shot down by an RB-47 (see below). Assuming Olmstead would have told his SAC debriefers about his belief that he shot down Polyakov's *Farmer*, they either were able to dismiss his claim entirely or lacked sufficient evidence available through communications intelligence (COMINT) sources to verify the loss. In any case, SAC did not believe that Olmstead had shot down the attacking MiG-19, and he did not mention this claim to the author during his 1998 interview.

Olmstead also indicated that the 'Polyakov' seen in the Lashmar BBC documentary was not the 'Polyakov' who visited Olmstead in the Lubyanka. There is no way to verify the two different people Olmstead describes, but it is possible that the BBC interviewee was the pilot who shot down the RB-47 and the one in the Lubyanka was an imposter trying to get Olmstead to admit 'criminal negligence' for his 'violation' of Soviet airspace. Then again it might be Lashmar who was duped by an imposter Polyakov. Another source claims that the RB-47 was shot down in retaliation for a 1959 incident where Palm's crew shot down a Soviet interceptor. The evidence, however, for this extraordinary claim is simply nonexistent. In addition, purported transcripts of the 1st July 1960 intercept contained in the book which makes this assertion do not indicate that Polyakov's airplane was shot down.

Amid the international furor over the loss, including vitriolic arguments in the United Nations Security Council, the Soviets claimed that the RB-47 violated Soviet airspace and flew as close as 12nm (22km) to the USSR, a distance still considered to be in international airspace by all states except those in the communist bloc. In fact, the RB-47 was precisely on course but its fate had been preordained, and not because of an imagined 1959 incident. Declassified documents from Soviet archives show that Soviet First Secretary Nikita S Khrushchev – much like the purported plea by English King Henry II who asked, 'Will no one rid me of this turbulent priest?' which effectively ordered the murder of Thomas Becket, Archbishop of Canterbury on 29th December 1170 – implicitly ordered that Soviet interceptors shoot down the RB-47 in response to the U-2 incident, fully aware that it 'was not flying over Soviet territory; it was flying over neutral water.' Polyakov confirms this, saying when he first saw the RB-47 'it was yet beyond the territory of the Soviet Union.' Khrushchev later congratulated Soviet air defense forces, saying, 'Well done, boys, keep them from even flying close.' To his credit, in the contentious interview decades later Polyakov showed no personal animosity toward Palm's crew: 'I feel sympathy to the boys who found themselves in such a situation. They

were not guilty, they were just…fulfilling their duty. Each of us was doing his duty…it is impossible that all could have come out as winners.' Although he admitted that the RB-47 was in international airspace, he justified shooting it down because he believed it was headed toward a secret submarine base. Given the extreme compartmentalization of secrets within the Soviet military, it strains credibility to believe that a front-line MiG-19 pilot would have knowledge of a secret naval facility. Neither McKone nor Olmstead were aware of any such base, nor recall that it was part of their mission. Moreover, the decision to shoot down the RB-47 rested with ground commanders, not Polyakov, with Khrushchev's order deciding the fate of the RB-47 and its crew before it had even taken off from England.

Perhaps the greatest tragedy – and most controversial issue in the loss of Palm's RB-47 – is that it should not have happened at all. A declassified memorandum from the Eisenhower Library describes a 1st July 1960 White House meeting held at 12:00 noon. Written by Colonel John S D Eisenhower, the president's son, it notes that Chairman of the Joint Chiefs of Staff General Nathan F Twining and two aides met with the president, Undersecretary of State for Political Affairs Livingston T Merchant, and Major General Andrew J Goodpaster, Eisenhower's military aide. The purpose of the meeting was to gain President Dwight D Eisenhower's approval to resume peripheral reconnaissance missions following the moratorium established after the loss of the U-2 on 1st May 1960. According to the memorandum, 'Captain E R Hardin showed the President that the first mission, if resumption of the ELINT flight [was] authorized, would be almost totally nonprovocative in nature.' Following discussion about similar British flights and the generally benign nature of Soviet reactions to them, the president agreed that US ELINT flights could resume. The final paragraph of the memorandum merits quoting in full: '…the President granted permission to General Twining to resume these flights on the same basis as before [the U-2 loss on 1st May 1960]. He admonished General Twining to make his first missions extremely cautious. He commented that although these missions are legal, they do provide the Soviets plenty of reason to be annoyed in a worldwide psychological struggle. General Twining assured the President that the Soviet reaction to each flight would be carefully analyzed before proceeding to the next, and that great care would be taken to insure that the flights are no more provocative than necessary.'

As this noontime Oval Office meeting was underway, it was after 8 PM near Murmansk. McKone and Olmstead were already aboard a Russian fishing trawler in the Barents Sea and the remainder of the crew had perished in the frigid waters. When the meeting ended at 12:27 PM, no one at the White House was aware of the loss of the RB-47H. Moreover, when 53-4281 took off at 10:00 AM in England it was only 5:00 AM in Washington DC, *seven hours before President Eisenhower authorized the resumption of RB-47 peripheral ELINT missions*. The mission appears to have been scheduled with the expectation that the president would approve resumption of peripheral flights, but was launched on time unaware that the authorization had yet to be given. No one on the crew did anything inappropriate.

Following the loss of the RB-47H President Eisenhower directed the US to monitor reconnaissance operations more closely by establishing the Joint Reconnaissance Center (JRC) at the Pentagon. According to declassified SAC histories, RB-47 operations at RAF Brize Norton were 'curtailed' following the 1st July loss, and in November 1960 all reconnaissance operations at RAF Brize Norton were suspended and the RB-47s returned to Forbes AFB with plans to resume operations there on 11th January 1961. The moratorium on UK reconnaissance operations did not mean an end to these missions, however, as a temporary OL-6 was established in

November 1960 at Wheelus AB, Libya, using support personnel from RAF Brize Norton and Incirlik AB, Turkey, which was undergoing runway repairs. Sorties operated from OL-6 through 16th December 1960. In addition, the British imposed a prior approval requirement for all RB-47 (and later RC-135 and SR-71) missions from UK bases. A list of all proposed missions had to be submitted by the 15th of the preceding month for approval by the British Prime Minister, with each flight requiring final sign off 48 hours prior to departure. Delayed, canceled, or aborted missions were subject to a repeat of this process. (Missions which departed the UK and flew through the Adriatic Sea adjacent to Albania or over Greece adjacent to Bulgaria did not require British approval).

***

Throughout their operational lifetime, SAC's 1,400-plus B-47Bs and B-47Es were intended exclusively for one mission: to prevent war with the Soviet Union and its allies through the expectation of massive nuclear retaliation – Deterrence. Because the B-47 was never called upon to execute this mission, it acquired a public reputation similar to that of the Convair B-36 *Peacemaker* as never having seen combat. As the world found out on 1st July 1960, and as hundreds of little-publicized SAC RB-47 reconnaissance crewmembers knew from personnel experience, nothing could be farther from the truth.

It should not be surprising that B-47 variants would see operational service in a strictly reconnaissance role. Boeing first proposed the airplane in 1942 as a reconnaissance platform, and the Air Force and Boeing discussed a dedicated reconnaissance version of the B-47 as early as 11th March 1948. Boeing proposed an RB-47 which initially met all of the Air Force performance requirements except – not surprisingly – range and size, as the Air Force wanted a larger airplane that could perform a variety of reconnaissance missions. In early 1949 the Air Force issued a follow-on request for a study to determine if the RB-47 could perform low altitude photographic missions over Russian target areas. In response, Boeing submitted proposals to the Air Force in June 1949 for both a 'photographic reconnaissance' airplane and a 'tactical reconnaissance' version.

Throughout these formative discussions SAC insisted that the reconnaissance airplane provide both pre- and post-strike photography while operating at the same airspeeds and altitudes as the strike B-47s. This requirement revealed not only a critical weakness in SAC target planning – the absence of accurate pre-strike target data – but reflected a conventional warfare mentality that hampered SAC thinking about waging nuclear warfare in general. Assuming only one third of SAC's B-47s and remaining B-36s might successfully drop their first-wave weapons on targets in the Soviet Union, the amount of cloud cover, debris, and other detritus of war would make it very difficult (some might argue impossible) to determine real strike effectiveness. Whatever post-strike photo an RB-47 might take could well be little more than a giant black cloud covering thousands of square miles, especially as some targets (particularly those which had not yet been struck) might be obscured by the blow-off from upwind targets.

Traditional post-strike photos would also require a delay incommensurate with the new timeline of nuclear warfare. Even at jet speeds the amount of time necessary to get an RB-47 over the target, take a usable picture, and then fly to a dedicated recovery base in a post-nuclear environment was on the order of a day rather than hours. After landing, interpreters would have to develop the RB-47 camera film and then transmit it to SAC target planners at Offutt AFB, NE, (assuming it was still there). In the days before telecommunications satellites and in a hostile electromagnetic environment where short-wave radio transmission of photographs would be severely compromised, delivering strike photos would necessitate, for example,

TYPES OF INTELLIGENCE

Although there are many different types of intelligence, these are the primary 'INTs' associated with B-47 platforms.

COMINT (COMmunications INTelligence) – functional intelligence processed from voice, visual, and electronic communications, telephone, telegraph, television, facsimile, and satellite sources

ELINT (ELectronic INTelligence) – technical and intelligence information derived from foreign noncommunications electromagnetic radiations emanating from other than atomic detonations or radioactive sources

MASINT (Measurement And Signature INTelligence) – scientific and technical intelligence information obtained by quantitative and qualitative analysis of data (metric, angle, spatial, wavelength, time dependence, modulation, plasma, and hydromagnetic) derived from specific technical sensors for the purpose of identifying any distinctive features associate with the source, emitter, or sender and to facilitate subsequent identification and/or measurement of the same

NUDINT (NUclear Detonation INTelligence) – intelligence derived from the collection and analysis of radiation and other effects resulting from radioactive sources

PHOTINT (PHOTographic INTelligence) – processed information obtained from all forms of photography, film or electronic, including satellite (currently called **IMINT** for IMagery INTelligence)

SENSINT (SENSitive INTelligence) – early peripheral and overflight missions

SIGINT (SIGnals INTelligence) – intelligence combining COMINT and ELINT

TELINT (TELemetry INTelligence) – technical and intelligence information derived from intercept, processing, and analysis of foreign telemetry.

Definitions are from official US intelligence agency (NSA, CIA, JCS, etc) references, cited in Leo D Carl, *The International Dictionary of Intelligence* (McLean, VA: International Defense Consultant Services, 1990)

using a Douglas C-54 transport to carry the film from a recovery base in Iran back to Offutt AFB, a flight of 36 hours or more involving landing to refuel multiple times at bases that were subject to attack. After using this 2-3 day old photo to update their target tables, SAC planners would then forward new target data to another strike crew somewhere else in the world with another 24-36 hour delay prior to bombs landing on target. This also assumed that there were sufficient nuclear weapons left in the inventory and that they were accessible to second- and third-wave strike aircraft, most of which would operate from desolate recovery bases with little aircraft infrastructure let alone access to nuclear weapons. In a nuclear scenario, re-targeting is defined in hours, not days, and the requirement for the 'jet speed' of an RB-47 for post-strike reconnaissance proved ludicrous. Nonetheless, given that the B-47's speed and altitude were unmatched by all but supersonic fighters, it was natural to develop variants of the B-47 to gather photographic intelligence (PHOTINT), electronic intelligence (ELINT), atmospheric nuclear detonation intelligence (NUDINT), telemetry intelligence (TELINT) and even basic communications intelligence (COMINT) capabilities.

What has been surprising, however, is that until the 1990s the extent of these operations was a closely guarded (and well kept) secret. Former Raven Bruce Bailey's *We See All*, published in 1982, offered a glimpse into the shadowy reconnaissance world associated with reconnaissance missions along the periphery of the Soviet Union and other communist-bloc nations, as did Lindsay Peacock's 1987 study of the B-47. It was not until the publication of several magazine

Table 6-1 **Known Reconnaissance B-47s Attacked by the Communist Bloc**

Date	Aircraft	Crew	Reacting Nation	Type of Contact	Outcome	Remarks
15 Oct 52	B-47B 50-0073	Don Hillman (A/C) Lester Gunter (CP) Edward Timmins (N)	USSR	MiG-15	intercept	MiGs attempted to intercept the RB-47 during overflight of Chukostski region
08 May 54	RB-47E	Hal Austin (A/C) Carl Holt (CP) Vance Heavilin (N)	USSR	MiG-17	attacked	Overflight of Murmansk, attacked and damaged by multiple MiG-17s but returned to the UK
17 Apr 55	RB-47B-I 51-2054	Lacie Neighbors (A/C) Robert Brooks (CP) Richard Watkins (N)	USSR	MiG-15	destroyed	Near Petropavlovsk; all 3 crew perished
26 Jul 58	RB-47H	n/a	USSR	fighter	intercept	Claimed over the Caspian Sea and recovered in Iran
31 Oct 58	RB-47H	n/a	USSR	MiG-17	attacked	Claimed over the Black Sea
07 Nov 58	RB-47H	n/a	USSR	MiG-17	attacked	Claimed east of Gotland Island near Ventspils, Latvia, over the Baltic Sea. 2 MiG-17s from 20th VA
17 Nov 58	RB-47H	n/a	USSR	MiG-17	attacked	Claimed over Sea of Japan
27 Nov 58	RB-47H 53-4297?	n/a	USSR	fighter	attacked	Over the Baltic but avoided damage; returned to RAF Brize Norton, UK
27 Nov 58	RB-47H	n/a	USSR	fighter	attacked	Avoided damage and returned to Yokota AB, Japan
01 Jul 60	RB-47H 53-4281	Willard Palm (A/C) Bruce Olmstead (CP) John McKone (N) Eugene Posa (EWO) Oscar Goforth (EWO) Dean Phillips (EWO)	USSR	MiG-19 Vasilii Polyakov	destroyed	Over the Barents Sea; Olmstead and McKone survived
24 Sep 62	RB-47H 53-4287	Johnny Drost (A/C) Jim Reinhardt (CP) Clyde Duncan (Nav) Joe Cleary (EWO) Ray Ladnier (EWO) Bill Chambers (EWO)	USSR	MiG-19 Yak-25 MiG-17	intercept	Baltic Sea mission east of Gotland Island. (Drost took the photo on page 128 during this encounter)
1963	RB-47H	n/a	USSR	MiG-19	attacked	Claimed, no details
28 Apr 65	RB-47H 53-4290	Hobart Mattison (A/C) Hank Dubuy (CP) Robert Rogers (N) Robert Winters (EWO) George Back (EWO) Joel Lutkenhouse (EWO)	DPRK	MiG-17	attacked	Damaged but was able to land at Yokota AB, Japan, where it was scrapped. Copilot Hank Dubuy returned fire and according to COMINT intercepts shot down one MiG-17
1967	ERB-47H	n/a	USSR	fighter	destroyed	Journalist claim of 'ERB-47H' lost over Caspian Sea. No evidence of any loss of an ERB-47H or other variant

articles, extensive declassification of official US and British documents, and television documentaries in 1993 that the role of the B-47 in overflights of the USSR, beginning in October 1952 and continuing through 1956, became public knowledge. Indeed, revelations that the Lockheed U-2 made only 24 overflights of the Soviet Union on behalf of the CIA between 1956 and 1960 pale in comparison to the 156 B-47 overflights of the USSR from 27th March through 10th May 1956 during SAC's Operation HOME RUN. The Soviets shot down two RB-47s (one in 1955 and one in 1960, described above) on peripheral missions, and may have attacked a handful of others. In 1965 North Korean MiG-17s attacked an RB-47 that was able to land in Japan but was so badly damaged it never flew again. Soviet claims of attacks on other RB-47s have been reported but none verified.

RB-47H 53-4298 at Incirlik AB during December 1958. The tail number has been elided to '29' and the 55th SRW emblem removed from the SAC band for security purposes. *Courtesy of Angelo Romano*

RB-47 deployments were undertaken with a considerable amount of secrecy, or at least the effort to maintain secrecy. Although the airplanes usually retained the SAC emblem and 'Milky Way' band, unit markings were removed. A few enterprising crews managed to put names on their airplanes while deployed, but these were rare. RB-47s that deployed to RAF Mildenhall, RAF Brize Norton, Thule AB, Eielson AFB, or Yokota AB flew with the entire serial number clearly visible. Prior to late 1958, RB-47Hs and ERB-47Hs that deployed to Incirlik AB had their serial numbers truncated through different schemes that removed portions of their serial numbers (TELL TWO airplanes reportedly had their entire serial removed). These changes were typically undertaken during the en route stopover at RAF Brize Norton. In one scheme the first two digits and the last digit were removed. For example, 53-4280 became '28'. This process meant that the RB-47Hs at Incirlik AB would be '28', '29', or '30'. In other cases the first digit and the last two digits were removed (rendering '62') or the last three digits excised (resulting in '34'). However clever this intent, it was not always effective. Airplanes assigned to the 343rd SRS had red inlet cones in the engines while the 38th SRS had blue inlet cones. Consequently, Soviet interceptors might see a blue '30' one day from the 38th SRS and a red '30' the next day from the 343rd SRS! Even the designation of the airplanes varied. According to the declassified SAC 1961 history, SAC changed the Mission-Design-Series (MDS) of its reconnaissance B-47s to R-47s 'to clearly distinguish reconnaissance Stratojets from bombers' to lessen the propaganda potential should another one be

Table 6-2. **RB-47 MDS Changes, Aug 61**

Initial MDS	Subsequent MDS	Initial MDS	Subsequent MDS
RB-47H	R-47H	EB-47E(TT)	E-47E
RB-47K	R-47K	ERB-47H	ER-47H
RB-47E	E-47/R-47E*		

* Either MDS applied only to those still in service.
All returned to original MDS by 1965

Table 6-3. **55th SRW RB-47 Operating Locations**

Det 1	RAF Mildenhall, England (until 1 Feb 58)
OL-1	RAF Brize Norton, England (from 1 Feb 58)
OL-1	RAF Upper Heyford, England (from 21 Feb 65)
OL-2	Yokota AB, Japan
OL-3	Eielson AFB, Alaska
OL-4	Adana AB, Turkey (until 28 Feb 58)
OL-4	Incirlik AB, Turkey (from 28 Feb 58)
OL-5 (early)	Thule AB, Greenland
OL-5 (mid)	Hickam AFB, HI (1960)
OL-5 (later)	Wake Island
OL-6	Wheelus AB, Libya (Nov-Dec 60)
OL-6	MacDill AFB, FL (Oct 62)
OL-7	Clark AB, Philippines
OL-9	Hickam AFB, HI (later)
OL-36	Wheelus AB, Libya (later)

shot down by the Russians'. These changes to SAC documents and press releases – never used by the crews – fooled no one, although they were still in use as late as early 1965. In some cases, the changes duped SAC maintenance personnel, who inadvertently worked on the wrong airplane.

Photographers and 'spotters' duly recorded regular visits by 55th SRW RB-47Hs to English and Japanese bases, with deployment and redeployment flights eventually known as TEXAS STAR. Bailey's *We See All* chronicled the evolution of the 55th SRW from its early reconnaissance missions flying Boeing RB-50s to its heyday at Forbes AFB and its RB-47Hs to its subsequent move to Offutt AFB and acquisition of RC-135s. Press reports of incidents and the loss of Palm's crew in 1960 incorrectly echoed what was 'obvious' to all – in the shadowy world of strategic aerial reconnaissance, 55th SRW RB-47Hs were not just the most visible assets, they were the *only* assets. This *Videmus Omina* myopia ignores the 91 YRB-47Bs assigned to units like the 26th SRW and 91st SRW, and the 255 RB-47Es that replaced them. The first B-47 reconnaissance overflight of the USSR was undertaken in 1952 by a B-47B from the 306th BW at MacDill AFB, FL. The first RB-47 of any type to be shot down was one of two ROMAN I RB-47B-Is assigned to the 26th SRW at Lockbourne AFB, OH, lost in 1955. Of the 20 RB-47s that took part in the HOME RUN overflights, four were RB-47Hs from the 55th SRW and the remaining 16 were RB-47Es from the 26th SRW. Eight of these were specially configured RB-47Es that carried the AN/APQ-56 side-looking radar to acquire radar images of potential targets as part of the PETER PAN program. SAC's 55th SRW flew 15 RB-47K weather reconnaissance aircraft, and the Air Weather Service (AWS) assigned to the Military Air Transport Service (MATS) and later Military Airlift Command (MAC), operated 34 WB-47Es in the weather and atmospheric sampling role. Indeed, MAC's WB-47Es were the last US Air Force B-47s in operation before retiring in 1969. None of this detracts from the extraordinary effort and dedication of flight and maintenance crews from the 55th SRW. Rather, it acknowledges the same level of selfless achievement by fliers and 'wrench turners' from all of the B-47 aerial reconnaissance units throughout the Cold War. It also recognizes that reconnaissance B-47s supported a wide variety of missions, beginning with traditional PHOTINT and expanding to ELINT, TELINT, and NUDINT.

The Overflights

Aerial reconnaissance has always existed as a shade of grey in a black-and-white world. Although peripheral sorties were legal, during the decade between April 1950 and July 1960, the Soviet Union, the People's Republic of China (PRC), and the Democratic People's Republic of Korea (DPRK), attacked more than 200 Western aircraft – reconnaissance platform and civilian airliner alike – destroying 30, including two RB-47s. Overflights, however, were a different matter entirely. As American aerial reconnaissance expert Lieutenant Colonel Richard S Leghorn noted in 1946, 'whereas peacetime spying is considered a normal function between nation states, military aerial reconnaissance – which is simply another method of spying – is given more weight as an act of military aggression.' Although overflights clearly violated a state's sovereignty, under the United Nations Charter they did not constitute an 'act of war' or a *casus belli*, a justifiable reason to declare war.

Western military overflights of the USSR and PRC began under President Harry S Truman and continued under Eisenhower [as Sensitive Intelligence (SENSINT) missions], and included flights not only by the United States but Great Britain, Sweden, Iran, the Republic of China [Taiwan], and others. CIA U-2 overflights of the Soviet Union monopolized the historical record until the early 1990s when declassified records (from both sides of the Iron Curtain), showed that nearly 200 US military overflights took place between July 1946 and December 1956, far more than the 24 civilian U-2 missions between July 1956 and May 1960. With these revelations came specious claims that the military overflights were undertaken without authorization and were intended to provoke World War Three on terms favorable to hard-line General Curtis LeMay – a 'killer on the edge' – without presidential knowledge. Such assertions have been repudiated by compelling evidence of a clear link between the president and the military agencies responsible for carrying out the missions. These included North American HONEYBUCKET and ASH TRAY RF-86s and SLICK CHICK RF-100s under the command of the Far Eastern Air Forces (FEAF), SLICK CHICK RF-100s under US Air Forces Europe control (USAFE), and US Navy Lockheed P2Vs and McDonnell F2H-2Ps. Of all recorded US military overflights of the USSR, however, SAC B-47s were involved in nearly 80%, all of which were known to the president and senior civilian and military officials. The accounts that follow are derived from actual aircrew interviews. It has not been possible to verify some of the suspect altitudes and airspeeds listed below. For example, 40,000ft (12,192m) was barely attainable in a very lightweight airplane, and the maximum operational speed was 425KIAS. Nonetheless, the figures below are direct quotes from the pilots – *caveat lector*.

The First Mission

Few regions in the Soviet Union attracted as much early Cold War attention by US intelligence agencies as the Chukotskii Peninsula, just west of the Bering Strait. Were the USSR to launch an air strike against the United States it would likely originate from bases there. During the Second World War the United States provided the Soviets with thousands of Lend-Lease airplanes, nearly all of which reached the USSR via the Chukotskii Peninsula after passing through the Canada-Alaska-Siberia 'pipeline', although few American pilots flew the final leg into Russia where they would have gained valuable information about Soviet bases there. Conspicuously absent from the Lend Lease armada were Boeing B-29s, America's most advanced long-range bomber and the airplane that would eventually serve as the backbone of SAC's first strike force. During 1944, however, four US B-29s made emergency landings in the Soviet Union after bombing raids on Japan. Three of these were used for reverse engineering, flight testing, and production of a B-29 copy made by

the Tupolev design bureau known as the Tu-4, NATO code-name *Bull*. By the end of 1949 some 300 were in operational service with the *Dal'naya aviatsiya*, the Soviet long-range aviation force, and nearly 850 had entered service when serial production ended in 1952. Once configured for air refueling, US planners warned, the Tu-4s could easily reach SAC bases in the continental United States. These Tu-4s were based at Mys Shmidta and Anadyr in the Chukotskii

Peninsula in Siberia, at Balbasova AB in the Belorussian Soviet Socialist Republic, and at other locations from which they could strike American and Western European targets. The Siberian bases were the gravest concern for US intelligence analysts, prompting the need for, and presidential approval of, overflights missions.

Confirmed American military overflights of the Chukotskii Peninsula began with 'Project 23' in 1947 using RB-29s assigned to

Above: B-47B 49-2645 seen on 20th September 1951 at Eielson AFB just hours before it caught fire and burned, canceling the first planned B-47 overflight of the USSR. *Courtesy Boeing*

Center left: The crew of the first B-47 overflight of the USSR in B-47B 50-0073 (l) to (r) Major Edward A Timmins (N), Colonel Donald E Hillman (AC), and Major Lester E 'Ed' Gunter (CP). *Courtesy John Timmins*

Center right: The crew of the backup B-47 for the first overflight of the USSR in B-47B 50-0028 (l) to (r) Major Lloyd F Fields (CP), Major William J Reilly (N), and Colonel Patrick D Fleming (AC). *Courtesy John Timmins*

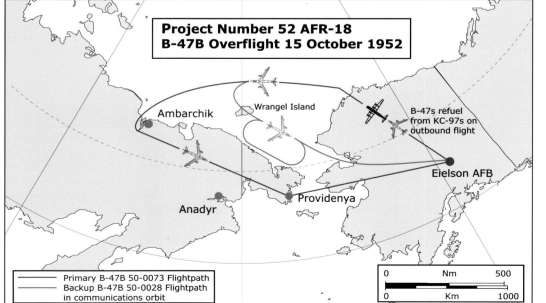

Project Number 52 AFR-18
B-47B Overflight 15 October 1952

Wrangel Island

Ambarchik

B-47s refuel from KC-97s on outbound flight

Eielson AFB

Providenya

Anadyr

———— Primary B-47B 50-0073 Flightpath
———— Backup B-47B 50-0028 Flightpath
 in communications orbit

0   Nm   500
0   Km   1000

Bottom: Hillman's crew completed the first B-47 overflight of the Soviet mainland from Ambarchik to the Chukotskii Peninsula. Fleming's crew served as backup, overflew Wrangel Island and provided communications relay.

the 46th Reconnaissance Squadron (RS) from Ladd Field, Alaska. This was a PHOTINT mission specifically looking for bomber bases (or those that could be quickly upgraded using slave labor from nearby Soviet prison camps) to accommodate Tu-4s. Occasional overflights continued through 1951 using RB-29s as well as US Navy P2V Neptunes. The speed and climb capability of the Soviet MiG-15 *Fagot* made overflights using piston-powered aircraft such as the RB-29 or RB-50 far too risky, so SAC was eager to benefit from the speed and altitude benefits that a reconnaissance B-47 offered. In mid-1951 that opportunity arose when President Harry S Truman approved an overflight of the Chukotskii Peninsula using B-47B 49-2645. The aircraft commander selected to fly the mission was Colonel Richard C Neely, with Colonel J G Foster as copilot and Captain D J Haney as navigator. The airplane was hastily equipped with an operational tail turret and had a camera pod similar to the one designed for the forthcoming YRB-47B installed in the bomb bay. Following a local orientation flight at Eielson AFB on 20th September, however, the airplane caught fire while being ground refueled and burned to destruction. It would be another year before a B-47 made its first overflight of the USSR.

On 13th August 1952 President Truman approved a replacement mission as part of Project Number 52 AFR-18 to 'obtain aerial photographs of specified targets in the [Chukotskii] area using two RB-47s.' This Top Secret mission was assigned to the 306th BW at MacDill AFB, which provided the flight crews, 'two photo-equipped B-47s,' and two KC-97 support aircraft from the 306th AREFS. Major General Frank A Armstrong was responsible for the execution of the mission, and 306th BW Deputy Wing Commander Colonel Don Hillman served as the task force commander and lead pilot. Both were briefed on the mission at SAC Headquarters by none other than General LeMay, underscoring the sensitivity of the operation. To maintain secrecy, the two B-47s would deploy from MacDill AFB to Rapid City AFB, SD, 'ostensibly to conduct photo [training] missions with the 28th Strat Recon Wg,' while Armstrong would proceed to Alaska under the guise of making 'preparations for a hunting and fishing trip' for a senior US Army general. Details of the overflight were withheld from the flight crews: 'no members of the Task Force other than Colonel Hillman will have knowledge of the purpose of this operation' until they were at Rapid City AFB, where they would fly three profile photo training missions to 'carry out the cover operations.' Mission crews were Colonel Hillman as aircraft commander of the primary aircraft, Major Lester E 'Ed' Gunter as copilot, and Major Edward A 'Shakey' Timmins as navigator, with Colonel Patrick D Fleming as aircraft commander of the backup aircraft, Major Lloyd F 'Shorty' Fields as copilot, and Major William J 'Red' Reilly as navigator.

By 10th July Hillman had selected B-47Bs 50-0028 and 50-0073 for the project, although 50-0028 first had to deploy to OCAMA for installation of the B-4 tail guns and the photo pod (the airplanes were chosen before Truman approved the mission so that it could be undertaken promptly once presidential authorization had been given). The entire mission nearly collapsed, however, when B-47B 50-0081 crashed on 22nd July 1952 on an unrelated training mission, grounding the entire B-47 fleet and briefly stranding 50-0028 at Tinker AFB. Waivers were quickly approved for the two mission aircraft, which resumed flying while the remainder of the fleet sat idle.

The two B-47s and two KC-97s departed for Rapid City AFB on 21st September for a six-day layover. While there Hillman conducted an orientation flight for the 28th SRW Wing Commander, Brigadier General Richard E Ellsworth, who sat in the copilot's seat while Gunter rode in the aisle. During the takeoff roll Hillman noticed the flaps were still retracted but managed to extend them in time for a safe takeoff, albeit after using the entire runway. Once again, the mission narrowly avoided a premature end. The B-47s finally headed to Eielson AFB on 28th September, but the weather remained overcast for the next two weeks. During this time the planners and crews debated a final issue: would there be two sequential missions each with one airplane on different days, or would both airplanes fly a single mission on the same day? SAC opted for a mission on two different days to ensure coverage over time, but in the end only a single flight was approved.

On 15th October the weather finally cooperated, and both B-47s took off with Hillman slated to conduct the overflight and Fleming as an airborne spare. They refueled near Point Barrow, AK, and flew together until just prior to entering Soviet airspace. With Hillman's airplane (50-0073) fully operational, Fleming (in 50-0028) returned to a communication-relay orbit. En route to their orbit area Fleming's B-47 overflew Wrangel Island, photographing the Soviet weather station there, catching a lone Li-2 *Cab* on the ground. Cruising at '40,000ft (12,192m) and 480KIAS', Hillman's B-47 entered Soviet airspace near Ambarchik and headed toward the Chukotskii Peninsula. Not surprisingly, Soviet radar detected the B-47 and MiG-15 *Fagots* were launched to intercept it. Fortunately, the B-47 was flying too high and too fast for the MiGs and the remainder of the overflight was 'uneventful'. In all, Hillman's 7¾-hour flight covered some 3,500nm (6,482km), of which 800nm (1,482km) were over the USSR. The photos 'proved valuable' despite the onset of some cloud cover during the flight. The Soviet regional commander, however, was sacked immediately, and a second regiment of MiG-15s deployed into the area. Tragically, Brigadier General Ellsworth later perished in the 18th March 1953 crash of RB-36H 51-13721, as did Colonel Fleming (a former US Navy ace) on 16th February 1956 in the first loss of a B-52 (53-0384).

Project GREEN GARTER
While assigned to Barksdale AFB, North American RB-45C Tornados from the 91st Strategic Reconnaissance Squadron (SRS), 91st Strategic Reconnaissance Wing (SRW) deployed to Yokota AB as part of the Far East Air Force (FEAF) during the Korean War. In addition to combat reconnaissance missions, they conducted multiple shallow overflights of the USSR and People's Republic of China (PRC). Most of these were related to the communist war effort rather than identifying strategic threats against the United States such as Chinese and Soviet industrial facilities, bomber bases, and, most importantly, atomic research and development sites. Following the wing's relocation from Barksdale AFB to Lockbourne AFB, OH, in November 1951, the RB-45 mission expanded to acquire photographic and radar scope imagery of these strategic targets, especially those in the Western USSR which threatened Europe the most. The Tornados were involved in a series of clandestine overflights of the USSR undertaken by Royal Air Force (RAF) crews flying the RB-45s in RAF markings. These were known as JU JITSU, and the first two missions took place on 21st March and 17th April 1952. Each utilized three airplanes refueled by USAF KB-29 tankers.

Despite the desirability of additional overflights, political tensions between the US and Britain over who would fly the missions – US or RAF crews – and British concerns that the flights might convince the Soviets that an attack was forthcoming resulted in the cancelation of another series of flights slated for December 1952. Known as PEPSIN, there would be three flights ('Red', 'Blue', and 'Yellow' routes) on 13th December, with a final flight of one airplane ('Black' route) on 15th December. This latter track was the northernmost of all RB-45 missions, reaching as far as Murmansk. Additional intelligence requirements and political approval led to one last RB-45 overflight mission on 28th April 1954, known as JU JITSU II. The three airplanes

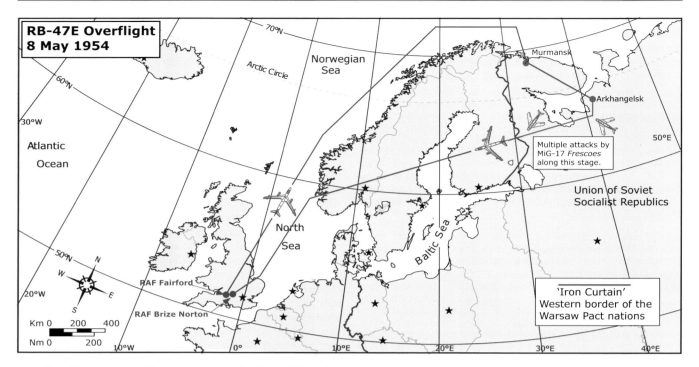

Austin's RB-47E overflight of the Murmansk region mirrored the route of the unflown 'Black' route from the canceled December 1952 PEPSIN RB-45C mission.

are believed to have covered the same routes as the planned December 1952 mission excluding the northern 'Black' route. They were refueled by KC-97Fs from the 91st ARS on temporary duty at RAF Mildenhall.

Concurrent with the April 1954 overflights, eight of SAC's new RB-47Es from the three squadrons of the 91st SRW at Lockbourne deployed to RAF Fairford, to support the ongoing Operation ROUNDOUT. This was a US effort to map all of Europe in the event of a successful Soviet invasion that required precision NATO bombing of occupied targets. The RB-47Es were, in fact, part of a classified, short-notice mission known as GREEN GARTER. On 6th May 1954, six of the GREEN GARTER RB-47Es flew a mass formation mission to photograph the Spitsbergen Islands north of Norway. Two days later, on 8th May, another six-ship mission launched from RAF Fairford. Three of the airplanes continued due east until they were approximately 100nm (185km) north of Murmansk and still in international airspace. Two of the aircraft then turned around and returned to RAF Fairford. The third RB-47E, commanded by Major Harold R 'Hal' Austin, continued into Soviet airspace. The second overflight had begun.

The flight started with a 7AM takeoff with Austin in the 'tail-end Charlie' position, followed by a radio-silent air refueling by the 91st AREFS KC-97Fs from RAF Mildenhall. The mission proceeded as planned, with the flight of three continuing toward Murmansk. At the critical moment as the other two airplanes began their return trip, Austin continued toward Russia. One of the other crews believed that he had 'lost his mind,' but avoided breaking radio silence to warn him in the off chance that he had a classified mission. Climbing to 40,000ft (12,192m) and flying at 420KTAS, the RB-47E coasted in around noon, allowing for the best visual photographic angle. Unfortunately, the RB-47 began producing contrails, making it easy to spot against the blue sky from the ground or by an interceptor pilot.

So far the flight was unremarkable as navigator Captain Vance Heavilin turned on the trimetrogon and K-38 cameras while the airplane overflew their target near Arkhangelsk. Copilot Captain Carl Holt spotted a flight of three MiGs, none of which was able to get close to the RB-47. Six more MiGs soon appeared, still below and behind Austin's airplane, but closer than the first three. After some 30 minutes over the USSR, a third group of six MiGs arrived, flying

in two groups of three. Again, they were behind the RB-47 but were nearly at the same altitude. Aware of the RB-47's track, the Soviets were now launching their MiGs in advance so they would have time to climb to 40,000ft to intercept the RB-47. After the fifth target, a fourth group of six MiGs, this time at 40,000ft, began to make firing passes at the RB-47. Although mission briefers had told Austin that the interceptors would be lesser MiG-15s and there were not 'significant numbers of [deployed] MiG-17s' – in either case both were 'highly unstable gun platforms at 40,000ft' – it was patently clear that the briefers were wrong. Holt turned his seat aft and began firing the two 20mm tail guns, although he was able to get off only a two- to three-second burst at the third MiG-17 before the guns jammed. The fourth MiG-17 made a firing pass as the RB-47 completed its run over the sixth target, at which point Austin recalls a 'whap' or bit of rough air. Unknown to the crew, they had been hit in the left wing flap 8ft (2.4m) from the fuselage, leaving a 4in (10.2cm) hole. The shell 'exploded into the fuselage [near] the forward main wheel well and #1 main fuel tank with many shrapnel holes, the largest being 9in x 6in [23cm x 15cm] in size.' A fifth flight of six MiGs began a series of firing passes, but none was able to hit the RB-47. Turning toward their eighth target, the RB-47 garnered the unwanted attention of a sixth flight of six MiGs, which began their efforts to down Austin's airplane as it completed its photo run and headed toward Finland, and even continued attacking the RB-47 once it had entered Finnish airspace. A final group of three MiGs intercepted the RB-47 over Finland, and was close enough to 'shake hands', apparently attempting to coerce Austin to return to Soviet airspace and land (or perhaps attempt an abortive ramming of the RB-47), but to no avail. Swedish and Finnish newspapers reported 'an air battle between jet planes of unknown nationality over northern Finland,' although a US spokesman reported that 'no American planes have been in the area.'

With the MiGs behind them, Austin's crew still faced the daunting challenge of getting home. Initial assessments indicated that they were 30 minutes behind schedule but had sufficient fuel to reach RAF Fairford without utilizing the stand-by KC-97 orbiting 50nm (93km) from Stavanger, Norway. Austin decided to climb to '43,000ft' (13,106m) and reduce power to maximum-range cruise. It would now take longer to get home but at least they would make it. Unable to contact the spare tanker due to what appeared to be a damaged UHF radio, the crew determined they were now falling farther behind schedule and no longer had sufficient fuel to reach RAF Fairford. Well over the North Sea Holt grew concerned that the fuel status was becoming so critical they might not reach any base in England and would be forced to bail out, losing not only the airplane but the valuable pictures they had just taken. About 150nm (278km) north of RAF Mildenhall, Austin began calling in the blind for the stand-by tanker there, and started a slow descent.

Aircraft commander Jim Rigley sat in his KC-97 near the departure end of the runway at RAF Mildenhall. Fully aware that only five RB-47s had returned from the mass flight earlier that day, he and his crew were listening to the radio and scanning the skies for any sign of the remaining RB-47. One crewmember thought he recognized Austin's badly garbled voice on the radio. That was enough for Rigley, who asked the tower for permission to launch. The tower declined, telling him to wait for traffic to clear. Rigley replied that he needed to refuel an emergency RB-47 and took off anyway [Rigley received an air traffic control (ATC) violation for this which LeMay later quashed]. Austin had descended to 10,000ft (3,048m) when he spotted Rigley's now airborne KC-97. In what Austin later recalled as the 'quickest and smoothest approach to refueling and boom contact I had ever made,' the RB-47 began taking fuel at only 3,000ft (914m). After taking on 10,000 lb (4,536kg) of fuel, Austin called for disconnect, saluted the boomer, and headed to RAF Fairford where he landed uneventfully.

British aviation researcher Colin Smith is the first to have concluded – almost certainly correctly – that Austin's mission was in fact the proposed 'Black' route from the December 1952 PEPSIN mission that was not undertaken during the April 1954 JU JITSU II missions by RAF RB-45s. Indeed, the Soviets were in a heightened state of readiness for Austin's flight, not because they expected it (LeMay's alleged provocation) but because of the JU JITSU II RB-45 overflights only 10 days before. These had no doubt agitated Soviet defenses to greater vigilance (indeed, former commanders were fired and their replacements were prone to react to any intrusion). Austin, it seems, had flown into a frenzied hornet's nest. His good luck in having a KC-97 tanker launch to refuel him as he neared flameout is likely also the result of the JU JITSU II missions. Although Austin was unaware of the 91st ARS role in refueling those RB-45s, the tanker crew which 'saved' him, in Smith's words, 'guessed (or knew) where he had been and that he might be in trouble.' Sadly for historians and 'spotters', the serial number of Austin's overflight RB-47E remains unrecorded. In an interview with the author, Austin confided that he simply did not recall which airplane he flew nor did he mark it in his logbook. No official records show post-flight repair work on any of

Table 6-4. GREEN GARTER RB-47Es

51-5270	51-5272	51-15822	51-15823
51-15826	51-15830	51-15839	51-15848

the eight GREEN GARTER RB-47Es that deployed to RAF Fairford.

Critics of Cold War era reconnaissance flights have cited this mission as proof that LeMay sought to provoke the Soviets into a war without presidential knowledge. One bit of evidence (among others) that disproves such claims is that immediately after his flight Austin's crew was treated to a meeting with US Ambassador to England Winthrop W Aldrich, whom they briefed in detail on all aspects of the mission. Aldrich informed Secretary of State John Foster Dulles, who would have relayed the results directly to President Eisenhower. Moreover, as Smith has clearly demonstrated in his research, planning for this mission (and the JU JITSU RB-45 missions), was extensive and involved both military and political officials from both sides of the Pond.

Austin's mission had an unplanned implication for SAC's B-47 fleet. Flying at 40,000ft, only one MiG was able to get a minor hit using guns. With air-to-air missiles still in their infancy and SAMs still in the future, SAC planners gained increasing confidence in the success potential for high-altitude B-47 strike missions. Flights at night and in bad weather, SAC officials believed, would have even greater chances for success as the fighters, which lacked on-board radar for final guidance to the target, would be unable to detect the bombers, allowing them to pass unchallenged. The comparative invulnerability of the B-47 fleet was further highlighted by the mass RB-47 overflights in 1956. (The acquisition of a DPRK MiG-15 in September 1953 gave the US a chance to test the B-47's ability to evade an attack, reportedly with poor results for the bomber. Claims that these tests used a Polish MiG-15 are inaccurate – the Polish defection took place in March 1953 and the MiG-15 was returned within weeks without ever reaching the United States.)

Operation HOME RUN

RB-47 overflights such as Hillman's in the Soviet Far East and Austin's over Murmansk (coupled with the JU JITSU RB-45 missions) provided considerable intelligence on Soviet offensive and defensive capabilities. In some cases, the results were negative – no heavy bomber bases filled with atom bomb laden Tu-4s were detected. In other cases, airfields full of MiGs as well as bustling industrial complexes were photographed, revealing both Soviet defenses along with prospective strategic targets. In neither case, however, were the areas that had been overflown helpful to the majority of SAC's Emergency War Plan (EWP). In the event of general war with the USSR, B-36s, B-47s, and the new B-52 would fly strike routes via Greenland 'over the top' of the world and enter Soviet airspace from the Arctic. In 1956 there was no intelligence on what defenses the Russians might have there, and the only means of acquiring this was by aerial reconnaissance. In addition, US planners had no knowledge

Table 6-5. **Operation HOME RUN Aircraft and Known Crews** (listed by Aircraft Commander)

26th SRW	26th SRW RB-47E	26th SRW PETER PAN	55th SRW	55th SRW RB-47H
LtCol Pete Moore	52-0688	52-0705		53-4285
Maj Larry Brown	52-0719	52-0706	**38th SRS**	53-4295
Maj Travis Koch	52-0720	52-0708	Capt Burton S Barrett	53-4296
Maj Floyd Robinson	52-0723	52-0711	Capt Robert S Hubbard	53-4303
Capt Ben Harris	52-0749	52-0712		
Capt Dan Guzowski	52-0788	52-0715	**343rd SRS**	
Capt John Lappo	52-0823	52-0721	Capt Richard A Cambell	
Charles 'Bud' Mundy*	52-3374	52-0725	Maj Donald A Grant	
Franklin Roll*				

[Others not identified]   * - rank not known

Rare photo taken at Thule AB during operation HOME RUN of RB-47H 53-4296 carrying the 55th SRW red lightning bolt on the tail. RB-47E 52-0719 is on the left. *Author's collection*

of what Soviet bomber bases might be operational (or under construction) in Siberia. What followed in April and May of 1956 was the most massive series of overflights of the USSR in history.

Operation HOME RUN began in earnest in January 1956 when SAC asked for 'volunteer' units to conduct the overflights under the guise of 'cold weather testing' at Thule AB, Greenland. The RB-47E photographic mission would be undertaken by the 10th SRS, 26th SRW from Lockbourne AFB, while the ELINT mission would be flown by four RB-47Hs, two each from the 343rd SRS and the 38th SRS, 55th SRW from Forbes AFB. Additional 26th SRW airplanes and crews from the 3rd SRS and 4th SRS would take part under the command of the 10th SRS, led by Major Lloyd Fields, copilot of the back-up B-47 during the 1952 overflight of the Chukotskii Peninsula. In February Fields led a small contingent to Thule AB as part of a survey to assess the base's suitability for the mission. Four weeks

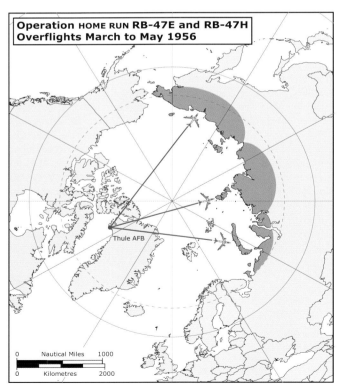

Operation HOME RUN RB-47E and RB-47H Overflights March to May 1956

Thule AFB

0   Nautical Miles   1000
0   Kilometres   2000

HOME RUN was the largest single overflight operation of the cold war. SAC RB-47Es and RB-47Hs flew 156 missions from Thule AB to collect PHOTINT and ELINT of Soviet bomber bases, radar facilities, and frozen tundra in Siberia.

later, on 21st March 1956, 15 RB-47Es (plus a 'training' RB-47E) and four RB-47Hs arrived at Thule AB. En route air refueling was provided by the 91st AREFS from Lockbourne AFB and the 55th AREFS from Forbes AFB. Official records show that tanker support for the operational missions came from the KC-97s assigned to the Thule Task Force, which at the time included KC-97s from the 71st AREFS and 341st AREFS from Dow AFB, ME, and the 96th AREFS from Altus AFB, OK, making for a crowded ramp. During some missions, more than one KC-97 would be needed for each RB-47 during the pre-strike refueling.

A typical sortie included four RB-47Es to take photographs of the region and a single RB-47H to record ELINT data produced by Soviet defenses in response to the overflight aircraft. Despite all the planning, HOME RUN began with a 'strike out.' During the first mission on 5th April, the four RB-47Es and lone RB-47H arrived at the air refueling point, but only two of the nine planned KC-97s were there, so the day's mission was aborted. Selected missions, all of which were radio silent, included one on 6th April over Novaya Zemlya, another on 11th April over the Laptev Sea to the bomber base at Dikson and back to Novaya Zemlya, and one on 25th April covering the bomber base at Tiksi thence to Wrangel Island, recovering at Eielson AFB. A mission on 27th April involved a PETER PAN RB-47E and two RB-47Hs over Tiksi, where unspecified MiGs attempted to intercept the flight.

On one momentous flight as part of a three-ship mission on 14th April to locate the never-before-seen-by-Westerners city of Norilsk, a critical source of nickel, an RB-47E flown by Captain John Lappo was late in returning to Thule AB. Landing with almost no fuel remaining, Lappo said that his target was initially covered by clouds, so he broke the cardinal rule of aerial reconnaissance ('one pass then haul ass') by circling back to take pictures of the target as it cleared. His dedication earned LeMay a reprimand from Air Force Vice Chief of Staff General Thomas D White. The letter admonished LeMay that SAC was not authorized to deviate from the approved plan and that such variation could jeopardize future missions. LeMay should instruct his crews accordingly. The letter also mentioned potential disciplinary action. True to form, LeMay was the consummate commander who recognized that in spite of operating outside the specified guidelines that the pilot in question had achieved the objective thereby eliminating the need for a second mission, a valuable lesson LeMay learned as a bomber commander. He replied simply, 'I have looked into this matter and I support my aircrews.'

(Lappo would later earn a degree of notoriety for flying a B-47 under the Mackinac Bridge in Michigan on 24th April 1959. Published reports claim this was in an RB-47E, but the 26th SRW had disbanded by then and was replaced with the 301st BW. Lappo was assigned to the 352nd BS which was fully equipped by then with the Phase V B-47E ECM aircraft, and was almost certainly the type he flew under the bridge. It suited SAC to keep the Phase V mission under wraps and the fiction of the RB-47E fulfilled that purpose.)

The RB-47Hs departed for Forbes AFB on 4th May, leaving just the 26th SRW RB-47Es at Thule AB. The final HOME RUN mission took place on 6th-7th May, when six RB-47Es, flying parallel tracks, overflew the entire Chukotskii Peninsula from Ambarchik to Providenya, including much of the same area covered by Hillman four years earlier. The RB-47Es landed at Eielson AFB, refueled and then returned to Thule AB. Operation HOME RUN ended with the return of the 26th SRW RB-47Es on 10th May 1956. Aside from the intelligence gleaned, HOME RUN reaffirmed the lesson from Austin's May 1954 overflight: B-47s could fly at high altitude with virtual impunity over the Soviet Union.

Despite Eisenhower's December 1956 prohibition on any further US military overflights of communist-bloc countries a few isolated incidents continued, compelling US Secretary of Defense Neil McElroy to issue an unequivocal directive on 31st July 1958. 'Existing instructions are explicit on limitations of all reconnaissance flights operating on the periphery of the Sino-Soviet boundaries. Recent violation…by an RB-47 aircraft has placed US in [a] serious position with respect to the USSR. This violation is being investigated. Responsible commanders down to and including aircraft commanders will review the specific limitations on all types of reconnaissance flights and adhere strictly thereto.'

PHOTINT Aircraft and Operations
During the late 1940s and early 1950s SAC planners were eager to acquire a photoreconnaissance airplane to match the anticipated performance of the *Stratojet*, and were especially interested in a B-47 modified for pre- and post-strike photographic work. Indeed, of the first eight wings slated for conversion to the B-47, two of them – the 26th SRW and the 91st SRW – would operate this yet-to-be specified reconnaissance model. AMC and Boeing met on 11th March 1948 to discuss the potential to modify the XB-47 for use in a strategic reconnaissance role. Boeing said the XB-47 could be redesigned to produce an ultimate design for strategic reconnaissance, and that AMC would be sent a preliminary design study to determine configuration and size of the airplane to meet strategic reconnaissance military characteristics. As with the strategic bomber variant, inadequate range remained the critical issue. One study suggested, for example, that a B-47 equipped with six Westinghouse J40 engines (then under development for the US Navy) and configured for aerial refueling could perform reconnaissance missions provided (1) the fuselage was extended to allow for additional fuel tanks, cameras, and an internal reconnaissance pod to accommodate the additional four crewmembers, (2) no defensive armament was carried, (3) jet fuel density of 6.9 lb/gal (0.83 kg/l) was used (4) aerial refueling at rate of 400gal/min (1,514l/min) was accomplished, and (5) the takeoff weight was no more than 192,800 lb (87,453kg). This yielded only a modest 400nm (741km) increase in unrefueled range resulting from conversion of bombs and ammunition to fuel and the deletion of self-sealing tanks in favor of lightweight tanks. Not surprisingly, SAC rejected this proposal, along with another that specified a 280,000 lb (127,006kg) airplane powered by turboprops.

Early in 1949 AMC and Boeing undertook further studies of XB-47's ability to accomplish 'low-altitude, photographic missions over major Russian target areas.' On 16th May 1949 AMC requested range estimates without aerial refueling, as well as the combat radius with aerial refueling at distances of 500nm (926km), 750nm (1,389km), and 1,000nm (1,852km) from the departure base. The airplane would carry of 'crew of three, four cameras and one scanner,

AN/APS-23 radar with scope recording camera, tail armament similar to the B-47, and maximum internal and external fuel including air-refueling provisions.' All other equipment not required for the mission would be deleted. In June 1949 Boeing responded with a proposal for Phase I development of an RB-47, including associated program costs of $170,600 for photographic reconnaissance and $111,400 for tactical reconnaissance. With the entire B-47 program in flux, however, Boeing could not estimate when the first RB-47 could be built, let alone delivered. Given SAC's priority on delivery of mission-ready B-47Bs, work on RB-47 development slowed to a trickle.

During early 1950 Boeing proposed that the planned B-47C be modified for reconnaissance as the Model 450-24-26 (see Chapter 7). In an act of budgetary sleight-of-hand, in mid-April this variant was briefly designated as an RB-56A to prevent funding competition. The Air Force was not persuaded by this change in MDS and it reverted to RB-47C on 15th May 1950 after less than a month. By 1951 SAC reluctantly agreed to acquire a number of RB-47Cs, but growing problems with the B-47C program meant that it would be at least two years (and likely more) before the first reconnaissance variant could be delivered, hardly an improvement over the projected delivery of a basic RB-47B. Boeing's interest in any variant of RB-47 was, to say the least, tepid. The company was very nearly overwhelmed trying to resolve the many development and production issues associated with the standard B-47B, and argued that any resources devoted to a reconnaissance variant would be ill spent. Nonetheless, Boeing continued to produce proposals for a variety of reconnaissance B-47s, including the eight-man 450-3-8.

After additional wrangling SAC elected to acquire 278 RB-47Bs, but again, manufacturing delays of the stock B-47B precluded the addition of any RB-47Bs to the production line with an expected delivery any sooner than at least 1953. AMC proposed that Douglas

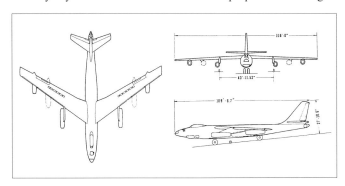

The ill-fated RB-47C reached the mockup stage based on the proposed B-47C/EB-47B. It was canceled for a variety of reasons, not least of which was its potential to siphon funds and resources away from B-47 bomber production. *Courtesy Boeing*

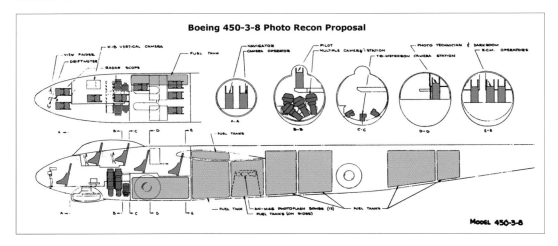

Boeing 450-3-8 Photo Recon Proposal

The Model 450-3-8 was clearly designed for long-range overflights, with photographers, a darkroom, and 3 ECM operators to provide jamming as well as ELINT collection.

The Model 450-11-17 was similarly configured but with a smaller crew and the 3 ECM/ELINT operators seated behind the aft main gear. It also used the abandoned liquid-fueled ATO system.

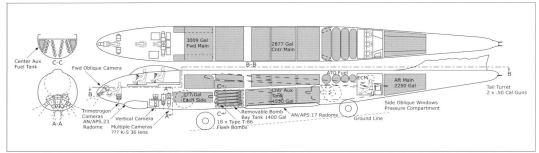

SAC considered the use of a removable camera bay in the proposed RB-47B. Although not taken up, these led directly to Project SUITCASE and the YRB-47B.
All images courtesy Boeing

and Lockheed build the RB-47Bs to allow Boeing to focus on the B-47B and its problems. This led to considerable bureaucratic and corporate 'see-sawing' over production schemes with all three manufacturers. In fact, Boeing recommended that 'serious consideration be given to eliminating the "RB" configuration until 1954,' and in the interim SAC should acquire an RC-97 version of Boeing's tanker/transport, which SAC rejected out-of-hand. Frustrated with Boeing's disinterest and inability to build an RB-47B for early deliveries, on 26th April 1951 SAC chose instead to fit a reconnaissance pod in the bomb bay of a number of newly built B-47Bs, resulting in a dual-purpose bomber-reconnaissance airplane would could be converted as needed to meet mission requirements. This option – based on a 1950 Boeing proposal known as Project SUITCASE – was not altogether unreasonable as these B-47Bs were certainly not mission ready as bombers. AMC, SAC, Boeing, and ARDC personnel met in May 1951 to establish the B-47 photo pod configuration. SAC expected that these pod-equipped airplanes would be available by January 1952, at least a year before Boeing expected the first RB-47B to roll off the assembly line, giving SAC a minimal strategic jet reconnaissance capability until the RB-47B design could be fully articulated and delivered. Configured with this pod, the airplanes would be designated as YRB-47Bs.

YRB-47B

The choice of the YRB-47B Mission-Design-Series (MDS) is not altogether clear. The 'Y' prefix indicated a 'prototype – service test', which makes sense only if one considers that the YRB-47Bs might have been considered 'prototypes' for the requested but delayed RB-47B, but they were not – certainly not in the numbers built. Although the YRB-47Bs had the same aircraft performance characteristics as the RB-47B, they differed substantially in mission capability from the proposed RB-47B, so were hardly prototypes for what would follow. One possible explanation is that the original intent was to acquire enough of these 'service test prototypes' to meet SAC's requirements without competing for funding with the RB-47B (and following cancelation of the RB-47B the subsequent RB-47E program). Naming the pod-equipped airplanes as YRB-47Bs emphasized to Congress their interim status pending delivery of the fully configured RB-47B (and later the RB-47E), allowing each of these programs to move forward without compromising the other.

AMC selected the Grand Central Aircraft Corporation (GCAC) in Tucson, AZ, to undertake the SUITCASE modification. GCAC was also involved in the post-assembly upgrade of standard B-47Bs known as GRAND CANYON, straining the company's ability to fulfill both this work and the YRB-47B conversion. Consequently, much of the

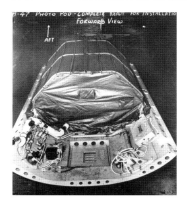

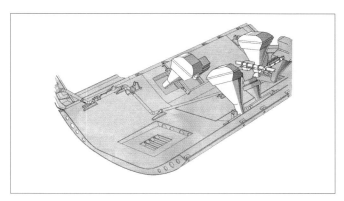

B-47B work was meted out to Douglas-Tulsa and Lockheed-Marietta, and half of the YRB-47B work similarly doled out to Douglas-Tulsa. YRB-47B conversion involved minimal changes as the pod attached directly to standard B-47 fittings. Specific modifications included removing the B-47B's bomb bay doors to make room for a camera pod, built by Aeronca. GCAC installed connectors for electricity, camera controls, and heating. The Universal Camera Control System (UCCS) was employed for single-point control of all cameras. The pod had a conformal metal bottom that mimicked the bomb bay doors, metal-ribbed fabric top, was equipped with electrical power, heat, and camera controls, and was removable, with the entire installation or removal process requiring approximately 12 hours. The camera suite included four K-38 cameras with a 36in (91cm) lens and three K-17 cameras with a 6in (15cm) lens in a tri-camera arrangement. A forward oblique camera position was filled with three K-22 cameras with 6in lenses. For high altitude night work three K-22 cameras and either a K-36 with a 24in (61cm) lens or a K-37 with a 12in (30cm) lens could be carried, although this capability had effectively no operational success.

There has been considerable confusion over the actual number of YRB-47B conversions, with as many as 132 serial numbers and as few as 24 associated with the program. SAC documents are contradictory. SAC logistics records show 85 YRB-47Bs but the SAC historian's records list 88. Similarly, the SAC aircraft record cards indicate that of the 85 B-47Bs redesignated as YRB-47Bs, only 30 actually were modified. This is almost certainly wrong, as the same record cards show 39 YRB-47Bs were *returned* to bomber configuration, suggesting sloppy record keeping. Even more confusing are the GCAC records which show that 49 airplanes passed through the GCAC facility, and 26th SRW histories which indicate that 41 YRB-47Bs were assigned to the wing, a figure that fails to account for YRB-47Bs assigned to the 91st SRW and other units. Aeronca records show 97 pods delivered, including two prototypes, but SAC documents show the procurement of only 90 pods. *The Development Plan for the B-47 (RB-47) (DB-47/B-63) Weapon Systems*, published 25th August 1953, states that 90 YRB-47Bs were produced [they are not individually listed here to save space].

Careful research by Colin Smith has shown that 91 aircraft were converted to YRB-47Bs. Of these, 45 were modified by GCAC and 46 were modified by Douglas-Tulsa, with deliveries to the 26th SRW and 91st SRW between April and September 1953, in some cases concurrent with deliveries of the RB-47E. Colonel Joseph J Preston delivered the first YRB-47B (51-2194) to the 91st SRW on 25th April 1953, while the first the RB-47E flew only two months later on 3rd July 1953 and was delivered to an operational unit in November 1953, quickly rendering the YRB-47B redundant. The 320th BW at March AFB received some of the newly converted airplanes but did not use them in a reconnaissance role. After the arrival of the RB-47E at Lockbourne AFB, the YRB-47Bs based there were reassigned

Top left: The camera pod in the YRB-47B included a thermal blanket to keep the cameras and film from freezing. *USAF*

Top center: The YRB-47B camera pod had multiple cameras which covered a wide arc of territory in front of and to either side of the airplane. *USAF*

Top right: Angles and placement of cameras in the YRB-47B pod.

Below: Posed photo using YRB-47B 51-2167 reflects the bittersweet moment when husbands left wives and families behind for lengthy TDY trips abroad. *USAF*

en masse to the 320th BW at March AFB and the 340th BW at Sedalia AFB, MO.

Two of the aircraft – 51-2054 and 51-2142, both former 26th SRW jets – were further modified into ROMAN I RB-47B-Is, described below. Two YRB-47Bs – 51-2253 and 51-2226 – were lost in accidents, both at Lockbourne AFB (see Section II). All of the surviving YRB-47Bs were converted back into standard B-47Bs as part of the HIGH NOON and EBB TIDE modification programs, with 11 YRB-47Bs converted into DB-47s.

Images of YRB-47Bs are relatively rare given their short service life. They were also indistinguishable from standard B-47Bs by other than their serial numbers – in this case 51-2292 – further limiting their appeal to photographers. *Author's collection*

Table 6-6. **YRB-47B Conversions**

GCAC Conversions				
51-2050	51-2063	51-2149	51-2173	51-2205
51-2054	51-2064	51-2152	51-2174	51-2208
51-2055	51-2065	51-2154	51-2179	51-2209
51-2056	51-2066	51-2157	51-2184	51-2214
51-2057	51-2132	51-2159	51-2187	51-2216
51-2058	51-2139	51-2162	51-2189	51-2219
51-2060	51-2142	51-2164	51-2195	51-2241
51-2061	51-2144	51-2167	51-2201	51-2242
51-2062	51-2147	51-2169	51-2203	51-2244

Douglas-Tulsa Conversions				
51-2194	51-2235	51-2252	51-2266	51-2288
51-2207	51-2236	51-2253	51-2268	51-2292
51-2213	51-2238	51-2255	51-2270	51-2293
51-2218	51-2239	51-2256	51-2274	51-2297
51-2221	51-2245	51-2258	51-2275	51-2301
51-2223	51-2247	51-2259	51-2280	51-2304
51-2225	51-2248	51-2261	51-2281	51-2311
51-2228	51-2249	51-2262	51-2285	51-2312
51-2229	51-2250	51-2264	51-2286	51-2313
51-2233				

The wartime mission for the YRB-47Bs would have been pre-strike and post-strike photoreconnaissance. 'Post-strike' missions were fairly obvious: the YRB-47Bs would take photographs to determine if targets had been destroyed or if they required additional bombing sorties, as well as locate targets previously unknown to SAC planners. Defining 'pre-strike' is more complicated. Under the assumption that SAC would only be called upon in a retaliatory strike against the USSR (rather than a pre-emptive or preventive strike), pre-strike reconnaissance would almost certainly have to be from

peripheral and overflight missions. No evidence of overflights of the USSR has yet been uncovered involving YRB-47Bs. Given that the YRB-47Bs were new to the 26th SRW and 91st SRW and throughout 1953 crews were in the process of checking out in the airplane and developing new tactical doctrine, it is reasonable to assume that the YRB-47Bs probably did not undertake overflight missions. In July 1953 five YRB-47Bs from the 91st SRW deployed to Eielson AFB as part of Project GREENHORN to 'determine the photographic capabilities of the aircraft,' raising the possibility of peripheral sorties along the Chukotskii Peninsula, but this is purely speculative. During January 1954, 15 91st SRW YRB-47Bs deployed to Sidi Slimane, French Morocco, as part of Project EBONY. While there they flew a 'maximum effort' mission on 18th January to photograph 44 targets, and in late February took part in HIGH GEAR (this included the relocation of the 301st BW and 305th BW to Sidi Slimane and the return of the 22nd BW from England) to 'test a new concept of reducing the time between deployment and bombs on target.' The YRB-47B role in this operation was likely pre-strike USCM photography to support the B-47Bs. In June 1954, 45 YRB-47Bs from the 320th BW deployed to RAF Brize Norton, where they are believed to have participated in Operation DIVIDEND, the 'annual UK air defense exercise' during the latter part of July. The airplanes also reportedly took part in 'highly classified' survey flights to Crete and Turkey, perhaps to evaluate possible candidates for post-strike recovery bases. An additional 31 YRB-47Bs from the 340th BW deployed to RAF Lakenheath in mid September 1955, but these were not configured with the photo pod.

For all the work and expense associated with the YRB-47B program, SAC gained a marginal daylight-only camera platform and a few months of time. In general the YRB-47B photo equipment was never very successful, however, and the YRB-47's greatest contribution was probably in preparing SAC's reconnaissance wings for the soon-to-follow RB-47Es.

RB-47B-I

Although there was never officially an RB-47B in service, during late 1954 Lockheed-Marietta began conversion of two former YRB-47Bs (51-2054 and 51-2142) into RB-47B-Is, known as the ROMAN I airplanes. The airplanes carried a 100in (254cm) lens camera in the forward left side of the bomb bay. The camera faced left and was gyro-stabilized at 15-20° below the horizon, and pointed out of the fuselage just ahead of the wing root. The copilot used a .50-caliber machine gun ring-and-post sight to frame the photo. Reports

Almost certainly a censored image of one of the two RB-47B-II ROMAN I jets (51-2054 or 51-2142) taken during tests at Lockheed-Marietta. The 100-inch camera faces the opposite side of the aircraft. *Lockheed*

suggest that when everything worked, the results were spectacular. The airplanes were assigned to the 26th SRW at Lockbourne AFB.

Both of these aircraft, along with RB-47Es 52-0687 and 52-0698, deployed to Eielson AFB on 1st April 1955 as part of Operation SEASHORE. On 18th April 1955 RB-47B-I 51-2054 was on a peripheral mission from Eielson AFB along the Kamchatka Peninsula when Soviet MiG-15s shot it down (see Appendix II). At the time, US officials were unaware that it had been attacked, assuming that it had crashed for technical reasons. Soviet officials intentionally misled US search and rescue efforts to mask their complicity, and it was not until Russian President Boris Yeltsin acknowledged the loss in 1992 that full details were known. After the disappearance of 51-2054, Operation SEASHORE came to an end and the three remaining airplanes returned to Lockbourne AFB on 7th May. The ROMAN I program was quietly dismantled and much of the documentation destroyed. The second ROMAN I aircraft (51-2142) later served with the 91st SRW (as a B-47B) and the 55th SRW (as an 'RB-47B') until it was sent to storage at Davis-Monthan AFB in November of 1957. Interestingly, the final version of the B-47 Dash One in 1969 still noted it as a 'YRB-47B modified to the Roman One classified configuration' but also listed it as an 'RB-47B-I.'

RB-47B-I INDIVIDUAL AIRCRAFT
51-2054 Lockheed-Marietta converted this YRB-47B into an RB-47B-I from 10th December 1954 through 11th February 1955. Shot down on 18th April 1955 (see Appendix II).
51-2142 Lockheed-Marietta converted this YRB-47B into an RB-47B-I from 16th December 1954 through 18th February 1955. Boeing demodified it into a 'B-47B' from 3rd November 1955 through 29th May 1956, when it returned to the 91st SRW. It was transferred on 19th July 1956 to the 55th SRW – listed as an 'RB-47B' – where it remained until its retirement to Davis-Monthan AFB on 6th November 1957.

RB-47E

The lack of Boeing's commitment to produce an RB-47B for early delivery to SAC coupled with the Air Force's ongoing indecisiveness about the B-47B in general and a proposed reconnaissance version in particular meant that Boeing never built or delivered an RB-47B. The first reconnaissance B-47 was the YRB-47B which was little more than a B-47B modified by GCAC or Douglas-Tulsa to carry a photo pod in the bomb bay. The two RB-47B-Is were former YRB-47Bs modified by Lockheed-Marietta to carry 100in cameras. By the time Boeing and SAC finally reached an understanding about how an RB-47 would be configured and produced, the newer B-47E was the logical (if not only) choice for conversion. Consequently, the first of three reconnaissance variants built by Boeing was the RB-47E.

The initial contract called for 297 RB-47Es. This was amended in 1953 with the addition of 52 RB-47Es, but when the new contract was finalized in June 1953 this number had increased to 77 at a cost of $1,506,317.80 per RB-47E, for a total of 374 airplanes. This latter figure was reduced from 77 to 65 under Project STRETCHOUT in an effort to reduce budgetary expenditures under newly inaugurated President Eisenhower. After additional contract gymnastics, the final breakdown was an initial order of 168 as part of AF33(600)-5148, an additional 52 under AF33(038)-21407, and 35 more with AF33(600)-22284, for a total of 255. This latter contract also stipulated the purchase of an additional 15 RB-47Es to be converted into RB-47Ks for weather reconnaissance (described below), but in the end SAC demurred to save money and directed that these 15 RB-47K conversion would come from the original 255, resulting in 240 RB-47Es [they are not individually listed here to save space, but are indicated in Appendix I]. Fourteen RB-47Es were lost in accidents (see Appendix II).

As with the bomber, the RB-47E went through multiple upgrades throughout its brief operational life as the RB-47E, RB-47E-I, and

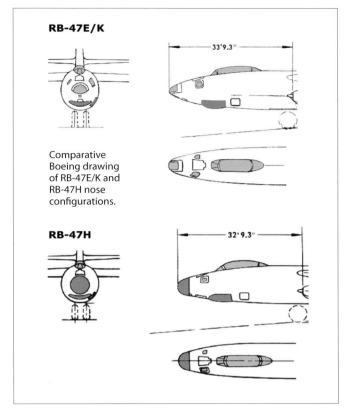

RB-47E/K

Comparative Boeing drawing of RB-47E/K and RB-47H nose configurations.

33'9.3"

RB-47H

32'9.3"

RB-47E-II. These referred to specific configurations rather than a unique MDS change. The new RB-47E – Boeing model 450-158-36 – reflected the same concurrent airframe, beefier landing gear, and J47-GE-25 engine changes as the B-47E. Range on the RB-47E improved to 1,915nm (3,547km), marginally better than the 1,760nm (3,260km) for the YRB-47B. The most obvious alteration was to the nose, which was 33in (84cm) longer with a centerline (versus offset to the right) air refueling receptacle.

The first 123 basic RB-47Es were configured with internal ATO, a limited ECM capability, and the Interim Camera Control System (ICCS) which was manually operated, severely limiting the airplane's high-altitude daylight photography capability as it did not 'allow the operation of multi-station and trimetrogon station simultaneously.' Plans to resolve this were hampered by lack of repair kits. As with the standard B-47, the RB-47E suffered from considerable production delays. The Hudson Motor Car Company, which made fuselage section 49, was unable to meet delivery schedules forcing Boeing to undertake the work in-house, commencing with 52-0699. Beginning with 52-0756, the 124th RB-47E produced, the airplanes were designated as RB-47E-Is and delivered with Phase II ECM, an external ATO rack, Cycle I bomb-navigation system, and a 200,000 lb (90,718kg) maximum gross takeoff weight (GTOW). The first 12 RB-47E-Is had the ICCS. With the delivery of the 136th RB-47E (52-0768) the ICCS was replaced with the UCCS which provided for the simultaneous automatic operation of all cameras, controlling shutter speeds, aperture, and image compensation based on preset data for ground speed, light, and altitude. The UCCS also incorporated an intervalometer so that large areas of territory could be recorded at regularly spaced intervals, as well photocell shutters activated by the flash lighting for night photography. Production shortages hampered the delivery of UCCS-equipped RB-47E-Is. Units 136-141 (52-0768 – 52-0773) received the UCCS, but units 142-176 (52-0774 – 52-0808) were delivered without the UCCS. Eventually the UCCS was retrofitted to all SAC RB-47Es. The serial

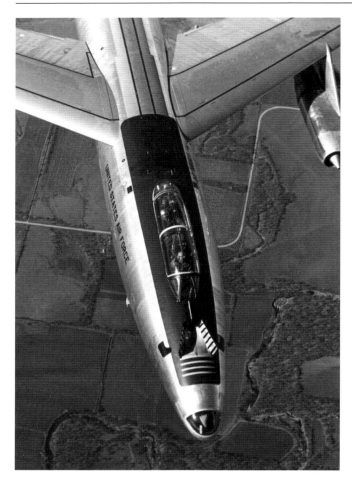

number of the first RB-47E-II has not been identified. This version incorporated the UCCS and had a 230,000 lb (104,326kg) maximum GTOW. Joint Boeing-Air Force flight tests from Wichita starting on 25th January 1955 certified the RB-47E-II for this higher gross weight. Earlier versions were upgraded (eg, RB-47E-I to RB-47E-II) as they passed through IRAN.

The RB-47E carried a variety of cameras. The oblique nose station held either a 24in or 36in (61cm or 91cm) focal length K-38. Three 6in (15cm) KA-3s were in the lower mid-fuselage trimetrogon station, although 6in T-11s could be carried in lieu of KA-3s, but these did not work with the image motion compensation (IMC) mechanism. For low altitude night photography three 7in (18cm) K-46s could be carried at the trimetrogon station. At the split vertical and vertical stations, 24in or 36in K-38s were used. The vertical position could also accommodate a 6in, 12in, or 24in K-17C, a 6in T-11, or a 12in K-37 for day charting, day mapping, or high altitude night reconnaissance, respectively. The vertical and split-vertical cameras could be operated together in a multiplex mode for day reconnaissance. Each camera station utilized optical quality windows. When the cameras or viewfinder were not in use, the windows were covered by hydraulically actuated doors that were flush with the exterior surface of the airplane. Defrosting and anti-icing systems were incorporated to insure the doors did not freeze shut or windows frosted over.

Each camera station had a dedicated function. The forward oblique camera produced a 36in x 12in photograph 60° ahead of the flight path centerline. These photos were used in target dossiers to give the bomber crew a visual presentation of physical features at the bomb run initial point (IP), as well as of the target itself. The split-vertical cameras were pointed inward 10° to produce an overlap of the covered area. The trimetrogon cameras provided horizon-to-horizon coverage with overlap, giving photo interpreters a stereographic image.

RB-47Es carried flash bombs and cartridges for night photography. Up to 10 M-120 flash bombs could be carried on B-11 shackles in a small bay forward of the camera compartment. The camera bay doors were controlled either by the camera system or the airplane's BNS if the target was acquired by radar. Each bomb utilized burning magnesium to produce 1.2 million candlepower of light. They were high-drag so as not to go off in the camera's field of view and were primed to detonate at one-half the aircraft altitude. Flash cartridges were used at altitudes of approximately 3,000ft (914m). Two A-5 cartridge ejectors were located on each side of the lower aft fuselage. Each ejector held 50 M-112 flash cartridges covered by a fairing with holes for each cartridge. If the cartridges were not to be used on a particular flight a solid cover replaced the fairing. Overall the cartridges were not very reliable (SAC called them the 'principle limiting factor' [*sic*] in the poor performance of the RB-47E's low-altitude night photography capability), and the whole system was in close proximity to fuel tanks. Consequently the cartridge system was seldom used, although one crewmember recalled that it was widely utilized in his unit, but this seems to be the exception rather than the rule.

The navigator operated the camera equipment although the pilot had an exposure indicator light on his panel and a camera operation switch on the control column. To see ahead of or below the airplane, the navigator used one of two optical viewfinder systems. One incorporated a wide-angle view forward, and delimited the coverage of the 6in and 12in cameras. The other system covered the area below the aircraft, provided manual drift information, and delimited the coverage of the 24in and 36in cameras.

Five units flew the RB-47E. The first two of these were the 26th SRW and the 91st SRW, both at Lockbourne AFB, OH. The 26th SRW operated the RB-47E from September 1953 through April 1958, while the 91st SRW was the first unit to equip with the type from April 1953 through November 1957. Both wings had YRB-47Bs at the same time as their newly delivered RB-47Es. The 70th SRW at Little Rock AFB, AR, flew RB-47Es from September 1955 (the first arrived on 10th September) through October 1961. As with Lockbourne AFB, Forbes, AFB, KS, also had a double wing of RB-47Es, comprising the 55th SRW and the 90th SRW. The 90th SRW received its first RB-47E on 25th June 1954, when Brigadier General David Wade and Lieutenant Colonel Vincent Crane delivered 52-0726. The unit became operationally ready in November 1954 and lasted through June 1960.

The 55th SRW received its first RB-47E on 27th September 1954 when Wing Commander Colonel Adam K Breckinridge landed RB-47E 52-0776 at 1815L. When fully operational and combat ready on 31st March 1955, the 55th SRW had three squadrons – 38th SRS, 338th SRS, and 343rd SRS – each equipped with 15 RB-47Es. A handful of RB-47Es remained with the wing after its transition to RB-47Hs and RB-47Ks. For example, according to the 1961 SAC History, the 55th SRW had five 'R-47Es' on hand (citing the temporary MDS revision), ostensibly for developmental work on behalf of AMC projects as well as HQ SAC staff proficiency flights.

The RB-47E's operational debut was not without problems. Following initial deliveries to the 91st SRW, wing personnel conducted a series of tests in December 1953 and 'determined that due to poor design the [RB-47E] was not capable of producing the photography required by the wing.' The 91st SRW complained of further 'inadequacies' in the 'night photoflash system, camera stabilization systems, electrical power distribution to cameras system, fuselage structural inadequacies, camera system controls, inadequacy of supplies of certain camera equipment and inadequacies in periscope sextant navigation equipment.' The multi-camera system achieved only a 74.5% acceptability rate for daylight photography, and 80% for the forward oblique. The airplanes had only UHF radios, limiting their ability to report their observations. Navigation was appalling, with a daytime celestial error of 15.1nm (28km). The RB-47Es had 'poor radar capability due to electrical interference and erratic sweep on the radar scope.' Wing cracks were discovered in

Although best known for operating E/RB-47Hs, RB-47Ks, and the TELL TWO EB-47Es, the 55th SRW also flew RB-47Es, including 52-0735 seen with the rare early (and conspicuous) tail marking. *C Nelson*

nearly half of the 52 airplanes assigned to the 90th SRW at Forbes AFB. Aft fuselage fuel cell leaks were widespread across the fleet and proved difficult to track down and correct. On 11th March 1954 LeMay railed about the deficiencies in the RB-47E's capabilities, especially night photography, uncovered by the 91st SRW tests. The majority of these would not be resolved until delivery of the 136th airplane (52-0768) equipped with the UCCS in October 1954. Even this system, which would correct many of the night photography shortcomings, was problematic. As of August 1954 only 19 UCCS assemblies had been delivered to Boeing, and of these 14 were rejected. It was well into 1955 before these and similar 'teething problems' were sufficiently remedied. At best, the RB-47E worked well for daylight PHOTINT missions, but was severely hampered in night operations.

As with the YRB-47B, the RB-47E mission was primarily pre- and post-strike photoreconnaissance, although it had an 'interesting' peacetime role in two of the most notable SAC overflights of the USSR. The first of these was the 7th April 1954 91st SRW deployment to RAF Fairford for an Operation ROUNDOUT mission designed to acquire imagery of 'strategic western European targets which might fall under hostile control in the event of war,' in this case over the Iberian peninsula. Eight RB-47Es took part in this GREEN GARTER deployment, and on 8th May one of these, under the command of Major 'Hal' Austin, undertook an overflight of Murmansk and the Kola Peninsula (described above).

The RB-47E was a satisfactory day and clear-weather photoreconnaissance platform, but suffered considerable limits at night and in bad weather. *Courtesy Boeing*

Other missions continued. During October 1954 the 26th SRW RB-47Es deployed to RAF Upper Heyford on Operational Order (OpOrd) 140-54 as part of the ROUNDUP series of missions designed to acquire imagery of Norway. The RB-47Es were prohibited from operating any closer than 225nm (417km) from the Soviet border or that of its satellites. While there, the RB-47Es also provided targets for interceptor practice by Norwegian fighters. This level of comity did not extend to international candor should one be forced to land in Norway for any reason: 'crews will be briefed to refer to their mission as a "routine navigational training mission" *being particularly cautious not to mention the fact that reconnaissance work is being done*' [emphasis in original]. In addition to the flights over Norway, the 26th SRW undertook concurrent overflights of Iceland as part of OpOrd 143-54. This also provided information 'on

the Soviet fishing fleet'. SAC intelligence officers noted that these ships, which averaged 250 in number, carried a variety of shipborne early warning (EW) radars typically found on Soviet naval vessels. Photographs of these 'fishing trawlers' would reveal their military capability in the vital Greenland-Iceland-United Kingdom (GIUK) 'gap', placing a portion of SAC bombers at risk during any strike mission. US interceptors based in Iceland, however, were not authorized to conduct practice intercepts on the RB-47Es. Landing in Iceland was strongly discouraged, as SAC feared genuine attempts to sabotage the aircraft or subvert the crew.

Additional mass deployments – usually the entire wing of 45 RB-47Es – continued in earnest in May 1955 when the 90th SRW deployed to Eielson AFB for a three-month stint, where they were joined in June 1955 by the 26th SRW. The following year 15 RB-47Es from the 26th SRW joined four RB-47Hs from the 55th SRW for the March 1956 mass overflights of the USSR in Operation HOME RUN (described above). Of these 16 RB-47Es, eight were configured with the PETER PAN AN/APQ-56 high-resolution radar (described below). The 91st SRW was similarly busy with a deployment of nine RB-47Es to Ben Guerir AB from 17th April to 16th May. As the Suez Crisis lurched toward possible war, the 91st SRW again deployed 45 RB-47Es to Ben Guerir AB from 3rd August to 4th October 1956. These were replaced by 44 RB-47Es from the 70th SRW from 26th October through 17th December. The 26th SRW deployed from Lockbourne AFB to RAF Fairford on 26th November 1957, practicing reconnaissance strike missions as well as serving as the occasional weather scout. They returned to Lockbourne AFB at the beginning of December.

This page, top to bottom: Although Boeing built RB-47E 52-0750, it visited Douglas-Tulsa for the MILK BOTTLE modification as indicated by the MB 190-167 sequence number on the nose. *T-3242 McDonnell-Douglas*

55th SRW RB-47Es photographed much of North Africa during Operation CRISS CROSS as well as visited Adana AB, valuable experience prior to their regular deployment there in E/RB-47Hs and TELL TWOS. *Howard Hendry*

A crew from the 55th SRW (note helmets) collected 52-4263, the final RB-47E, on 12th August 1955. From (l) to (r) are Captain Robert L Mayer (N), First Lieutenant Austin B Hogan, Jr (CP), Captain William A McCarty (AC), T E Gamlem (Boeing chief project engineer), Colonel Robert E Lee (AF plant representative), and Glenn Hull (assistant factory general superintendent). *Photo BW93291 courtesy Boeing*

Many RB-47Es ended their flying careers as training aircraft, including these examples at Little Rock AFB. They were arguably more useful in this role than as reconnaissance platforms. *Author's collection*

Opposite page: Although the AN/APQ-56 antenna was only 7 x 7 inches it was contained within a larger fairing on the aft fuselage approximately 18 inches high and 10 inches deep. *Augustine Letto*

Unlike the Lockbourne AFB RB-47E wings, the 55th SRW did not have an extensive operational history with the airplane. The entire wing deployed on 17th May 1955 in Operation CRISS CROSS to Ben Guerir AB, French Morocco, where they photographed much of North Africa. While there 10 RB-47Es also flew to Adana AB under Exercise BEAGLE HOUND to test the ability of the base to accommodate a considerable number of large aircraft. Between 20th-25th May, 35 RB-47Es flew a mass reconnaissance mission known as DEEP ROCK, and in June took part in AIR BLAST, an assessment of Ben Gueir's ability to handle large numbers of aircraft, in this case up to 77 RB-47Es and B-47s, plus 34 KC-97s. The deployment lasted until August 1955, by which time the first RB-47H had arrived back at Forbes AFB, signaling the start of the Wing's conversion from RB-47E to RB-47Hs, ERB-47Hs, and RB-47Ks.

In addition to photoreconnaissance, RB-47E units occasionally served as 'weather scouts.' Although not configured for weather data collection like the RB-47K or WB-47E, the airplanes flew in advance of USCMs or mass deployments. For example, RB-47Es from the 26th SRW conducted weather scout missions from Goose Bay, Newfoundland, Thule AB, and RAF Fairford during the November and December 1957 IRON BAR exercise. The airplanes flew to the planned air refueling areas and relayed cloud and wind conditions back to mission planners. RB-47Es were also assigned to various test support missions. The 26th SRW, for example, flew Operation GRAINFIELD sorties in October 1955 to support ARDC and Lincoln Laboratory projects associated with 'airborne electronic detection equipment.' The RB-47Es from the 91st SRW participated in multiple DEVIL FISH missions for ECM testing by the Lincoln Laboratory.

The first RB-47E to be retired was 51-5272 from the 91st SRW at Lockbourne AFB, departing for Davis-Monthan AFB on 14th October 1957. By 1960 when the 90th SRW retired its last RB-47E, the fleet had become fully redundant. U-2s were better able to collect higher quality aerial photography, including four years' worth over the Soviet Union, the People's Republic of China, and elsewhere. Satellites further weakened the case for retaining RB-47Es. Most were relegated to Davis-Monthan AFB for storage (see Appendix I), although 11 found their way into use as 'hacks' at Air Division or higher-headquarters bases for use in maintaining flight proficiency (and hence pay) of staff officers. Other RB-47Es were transferred to testbed duties, and 14 were converted into QB-47Es. Interestingly, a number of RB-47Es were used as trainers. The 4347th Combat Crew Training Wing (CCTW) at McConnell AFB received 32 RB-47Es, and similar numbers were transferred to the 70th SRW and 90th SRW, both of which had acquired a training mission by 1958. Of the 14 PETER PAN RB-47Es, 11 went to the 90th SRW as trainers.

SLAR-equipped RB-47s

Early in 1954 Curtis LeMay saw radar images taken by an RAF English Electric Canberra (believed to be Canberra B Mk 2 WH702 under the 'Red Setter' program) and demanded that the RB-47 have a similar capability within 90 days. In February teams from WADC and SAC visited Britain to examine the equipment in more detail, and on 25th March 1954 SAC requested that ARDC begin a program to develop a side-looking radar 'capable of detecting runways of a certain width from an altitude of 40,000ft' (12,192m). By 11th April ARDC launched this program with the 'highest priority'. This initiative began one of SAC's most important – and least known – strategic reconnaissance programs that would lead directly to the largest American overflight of the Soviet Union.

Throughout the early 1950s, the 'highest priority' of the Joint Chiefs of Staff (JCS) was the BRAVO counter air offensive program, designed to strike Soviet bomber bases before they could be used to launch atomic attacks against the United States and its allies. To fulfill this BRAVO tasking, SAC would be required to use radar bombing for accurate weapons delivery at night and in bad weather. This in turn meant that SAC needed radarscope images to identify Soviet bomber bases and to allow B-47 navigators to study each target as it would appear during an actual strike mission regardless of season, time of day, or weather. The extremely limited availability of target photos taken by traditional optical cameras could not provide the necessary radarscope images of bomber bases, particularly their snow- and ice-covered runways. This led to two critical components of SAC's intelligence and targeting strategy: overflight reconnaissance missions to gather the target images, and a suitable radar mapping system to generate the image. As a declassified 1954 Requirements Document explained, given that 'adverse weather obviously limits photographic detection of [BRAVO] targets, some means must be provided whereby this type of data may be obtained.' On 7th May 1954 SAC and ARDC issued a directive for the modification of 'in service RB-47 aircraft' to provide 'an immediate high resolution radar [HRR] reconnaissance capability' with the first installation completed by January 1955. Westinghouse was selected to develop a 'high resolution ground mapping radar' for use in both low- and high-altitude radar reconnaissance to be mounted on ten RB-47s assigned to the 91st SRW at Lockbourne AFB as part of the PETER PAN program. Due to excessive commitments of the 91st SRW, PETER PAN was reassigned on 29th June 1954 to the 26th SRW, also at Lockbourne AFB, with Lieutenant Colonel Lawson C Horner, Jr, in charge of the program. This new tasking was not officially approved until 14th July, and eventually resulted in the delivery of two prototypes, 14 operational PETER PAN RB-47Es, and a single MONTICELLO RB-47E used for advanced system testing.

PETER PAN

Despite its impression on LeMay, SAC argued that the British radar could not simply be transferred to an RB-47 as it was not optimized for high altitude operation, nor could it be easily configured to fit in a Stratojet. Consequently SAC initially directed ARDC and Westinghouse to develop a system that would detect runways from 40,000ft and a distance of 10nm (19km) along either side of the airplane's route of flight. If Westinghouse could meet these requirements then SAC would issue a request for an operational version to include a recording mechanism and other features.

Heart of the imaging system was the Westinghouse AN/APQ-56 side-looking airborne radar (SLAR) developed under Operation SIDE LOOK. The prototype AN/APQ-56 (XA-1) included a recorder with camera, receiver-transmitter, power supply, pressurizing unit and control box, and a single antenna, all of which added 323 lb (147kg) of weight to the airplane. The antenna was 7in (18cm) x 7in x 124in (315cm) and was mounted on the fuselage above the aft main gear.

PETER PAN RB-47E 52-0704 took part in the 1956 'Bomb Comp' at the 26th SRW's home base of Lockbourne AFB, but RB-36s swept both the reconnaissance and bombing categories. The AN/APQ-56 antenna is barely discernable below the #4 engine intake. *Augustine Letto*

The radar operated in the K_a-band with a pulse rate of 4,000pps at aircraft speeds ranging from 200-800KIAS and altitudes from 0-45,000ft (0-13,716m), and could map 10nm (19km) abeam the airplane. The radar return was displayed on a cathode ray tube which was then 'photographed and recorded on 70mm strip film moving at a rate proportional to the aircraft's ground speed.' Cost of the system was $370,000.

The XA-1 prototype was installed on one side of 4th SRS, 26th SRW RB-47E 52-0700 loaned to the WADC in July 1954 under contract AF33(616)-2248 (a Boeing B-17 was similarly modified for low-altitude tests). The airplane was flown to the Westinghouse Air Arm Division in Baltimore, MD, on 18th May 1954, where the entire side of a building was removed to allow the RB-47 to be enclosed for modification and testing. First flight was 59 days after program launch, and although the antenna pattern 'was not satisfactory,' the flight demonstrated the general feasibility of the program while 'easily' detecting the runways. High-altitude evaluation missions were flown at 26,000ft (7,925m) and accrued 600 hours of flight time while mapping 2,400,000 square miles (6,215,971km²). Subsequent test results were impressive, showing details such as major street intersections, locks of the Erie Canal, and power plant structures.

A follow-on contract – AF33(600)-27852 – was awarded in June 1954, a month *before* initial flight tests were completed, underscoring the extreme urgency accorded the program. This provided for 13 AN/APQ-56 (XA-2) systems, 11 of which were slated for installation on RB-47Es along with two bench test sets. The XA-2 included a second receiver-transmitter and antenna for bilateral radar imaging, increasing the total system weight to 506 lb (230kg). First delivery would be made on 1st December 1954 with additional sets delivered

Table 6-7. **SLAR-equipped RB-47Es**

Serial	Modified	Mission	Attrition	MASDC
52-0701	09 May 54	PETER PAN		05 Apr 60
52-0702	06 May 54	PETER PAN	21 Oct 59	
52-0703	11 May 54	PETER PAN		28 Apr 60
52-0704	16 May 54	PETER PAN		21 Apr 60
52-0705	09 Aug 56	PETER PAN		20 Apr 60
52-0706	06 May 54	PETER PAN		12 Apr 60
52-0708	11 Oct 56	PETER PAN		08 Apr 60
52-0711	15 Oct 56	PETER PAN		27 Apr 60
52-0712	29 Oct 56	PETER PAN		26 Jun 58
52-0714	10 Jun 54	PETER PAN		13 Apr 60
52-0715	22 Nov 56	PETER PAN		27 Jun 58
52-0716	13 Mar 56	PETER PAN	13 Apr 60	
52-0721	19 Sep 56	PETER PAN		12 May 60
52-0725	26 Mar 56	PETER PAN		30 Jun 58
53-4260		Prototype		
53-4262		Monticello		

every three weeks. Westinghouse would install them on 10 RB-47Es from the 4th SRS, 26th SRW at Lockbourne AFB (the 11th set was installed on RB-36H 51-13736 for operational testing). Four additional RB-47Es received the necessary mounting brackets for the system, which could be transferred with some difficulty among the 14 airplanes. The added weight and drag resulted in a 4% range degrade. The RB-47s flew 1,700 hours with the XA-2 variant, mapping 17,000,000 square miles (44,029,788km²). Westinghouse civilian technicians routinely flew on the proving sorties to evaluate the system and provide whatever in-flight repairs or adjustments might be possible. Other versions of the XA-2 were installed in Martin RB-57Ds, Douglas A3D Skywarriors, and Lockheed RB-69As.

As with many programs, the original plans changed over the course of testing and deployment. On 30th June 1954, the *day after* the PETER PAN program was reassigned to the 26th SRW, SAC directed the immediate discontinuance of the name PETER PAN to 'preclude possible security breaches', which explains why crewmembers don't recall this name. (Another name mentioned in this directive is MARATHORN RACE [*sic*], which may have been the planned operational order.) It is not clear if PETER PAN was subsequently used only in classified records or if it was dropped altogether, although SAC records continue to use the name through at least 1956. In declassified 26th SRW histories the program is referred to as 'WADC Project Q-56-700 (XQ-56 Radar)' or simply 'HRR'.

Efforts to improve the scanning range of the radar resulted in the replacement of existing power units beginning in March 1956. The range of the newer AN/APQ-56 (XH-1) improved somewhat to 15nm (28km), raising the system weight to 665 lb (302kg). This variant was short-lived, however, with the development of the XH-3 version in August 1956, which increased the range to 18nm (33km). As it was impractical to test the XH-3 on one of the existing PETER PAN RB-47Es due to operational commitments, Westinghouse modified RB-47E 53-4260 from the 55th SRW as the XH-3 prototype. It served with the 26th SRW from 23rd October 1956 through 14th May 1958 (see below for a more precise history) although apparently not in a fully operational capacity as SAC records show it was never designated as a PETER PAN aircraft.

Initial training and operational qualification were well under way by late 1954, with crews flying a modest 10+10, 16+00, and 22+35 hours September, October, and November, respectively. Although original plans called for the airplanes to be assigned only to the 10th SRS, they were distributed throughout the entire 26th SRW, with the 3rd SRS and the 4th SRS also operating them. Monthly operational total flight time increased in 1955 to an average of 40 hours, although in August and September 1955 this jumped to 103+40 and 78+30, respectively, as all Select and Lead crews undertook qualification training as aircraft were available. Paradoxically, this hampered traditional training requirements as the necessary 5nm (9.3km) offset needed meant that navigators were an equal distance 'off course' in their monthly SAC proficiencies, obligating 26th SRW commanders to seek waivers from SAC Headquarters for the crews!

The first real test of the AN/APQ-56 took place as part of OpOrd 510-55 Operation SNEAKERS, also referred to as SAFE CRACKER. Two airplanes (10th SRS RB-47E 52-0701 and 3rd SRS RB-47E 52-0705) were placed on 24-hour ground alert on 29th November. The following day two more RB-47Es (52-0704 from the 10th SRS and 52-0703 from the 4th SRS) replaced the earlier two, repeating this cycle until 5th December. The pair of airplanes would launch when directed by SAC Headquarters based on desirable weather and lighting conditions, and were intended to test the AN/APQ-56 radar by imaging bases in Canada, including Saguenay, Trinity Bay, Knob Lake, Ft Chimo, Frobisher, Coral Harbour, Churchill, and

Kapuskasing. The airplanes would turn on the AN/APQ-56 radar, the O-15 optical cameras, and the trimetrogon cameras 20nm (37km) prior to the 'target' and turn them off 10nm (19km) after passing the 'target'. Subsequent operational evaluations took place by mid December 1955 when AN/APQ-56-equipped aircraft from the 4th SRS overflew Eglin AFB, FL, and the Gulf of Mexico to calibrate the system against a maritime target. The 10th SRS flew a similar mission in January 1956.

By January 1956 six of the airplanes had been fully modified, with 52-0716 and 52-0725 fully configured by the middle and end of March. For SAC this was sufficient for the ultimate operational evaluation, the massive overflight of the USSR known as Operation HOME RUN. Ostensibly intended to 'conduct cold weather exercises with RB-47 aircraft and to test photo reconnaissance equipment under arctic conditions,' HOME RUN was in fact a joint PHOTINT and ELINT operation designed to locate Soviet bomber bases in the Siberian north as well as Soviet defenses there which SAC's bombers would face in the event of general war (described above). The 10th SRS was tasked to deploy 15 RB-47Es (ten departed on 21st March, with the other five departing on 22nd March) eight of which were configured with the AN/APQ-56 radar, to Thule AB for up to 60 days. Although the airplanes were at the time all assigned to the 10th SRS, some AN/APQ-56 qualified flight crews from the 3rd SRS and 4th SRS participated as well. A total of 313 26th SRW personnel took part, including 10 Westinghouse civilians responsible for maintenance of the AN/APQ-56 systems. Over the course of the operation, the RB-47Es and four 55th SRW RB-47Hs flew a total of 156 sorties over the USSR. The 26th SRW airplanes returned on 10th

May, accruing a total of 971+30 hours. Some researchers have uncovered evidence suggesting that the PETER PAN airplanes flew shallow incursion missions of the USSR in the vicinity of the Black Sea. Given that President Eisenhower suspended all military overflights of the USSR in December 1956, it is unlikely that such flights took place, although there are rare documented reports of inadvertent RB-47 'border violations' as late as 1958.

Subsequent missions were used to verify improved systems and image interpretation techniques, especially given the persistent shortage of spare parts and the need for more skilled maintenance technicians (the 26th SRW even sought to train its own personnel in AN/APQ-56 maintenance due to the limited number of Westinghouse contractors available). Operation SILVER CLOUD, for example, took place from 30th September through 11th October 1956 at Thule AB and imaged much of Greenland. In November 1956 PETER PAN aircraft began monthly overflights of the Cape Canaveral, FL, area, ostensibly to establish aerial radar images of rocket launch facilities to compare with prospective Soviet sites. In an interesting side story, AN/APQ-56 imagery resulted in the disciplining of a very famous aviator. Brigadier General Robert L Scott, former Flying Tiger ace, author, and subject of the movie *God is My Copilot*, was assigned to the Air Staff at the Pentagon. A vocal champion of Air Force priority in budgets, from 5th-7th October 1956 he was invited aboard the USS *Forrestal* in the Gulf of Mexico, along with Colonel William J Meng, commander of the 26th SRW. While there, Scott surreptitiously coordinated with the 26th SRW to take AN/APQ-56 images of the aircraft carrier through a hefty cloud deck. Amid a concurrent public imbroglio over roles and missions, someone leaked the images and

Above: RB-47E 52-0725 (seen during the 1958 SNOWFLURRY mission) took part in the 1956 HOME RUN overflights of the Soviet Union. Crews from all three squadrons in the 26th SRW flew these missions. The APQ-56 antenna is just below and forward of the national insignia.

Right: 52-0712 at Goose AB, Labrador, during the SNOWFLURRY operation. Black nose gear door matches the black tail band for the 4th SRS, 26th SRW. *Both: Augustine Letto*

The 'barren nothingness' of Thule AB hosts 26th SRW RB-47Es (including two PETER PAN jets in the center) during Operation SILVER CLOUD in late 1956. *Augustine Letto*

framed Scott for their release, and he was promptly invited to find another assignment outside of the Pentagon!

Operation LAST STAND took place on 13th March 1957 when the wing participated in an attack on a simulated BRAVO target near Cowley, WY, using target intelligence at least 13 years old, mimicking a photoreconnaissance 'strike' on a Soviet bomber base for which recent intelligence was unavailable. The first ten B-47s launched (at 15-minute intervals) were AN/APQ-56 jets from the 4th SRS. Results were disappointing. ECM operations were 'average', but the photo results were 'unsatisfactory' due to 'gross errors in navigation'. Although this poor outcome did not reflect directly on the readiness or effectiveness of the AN/APQ-56 system, the equipment clearly did not help. Initiatives to check out additional crews in the AN/APQ-56 continued in the following months, as did improvement efforts for the system itself. In mid-1957 the 26th SRW evaluated a '100KW' upgrade, intended to increase the range of the HRR scan, and in August alone logged in excess of 30 hours of test flights for this. Additional missions included HRR coverage of Dayton, OH, in September 1957 on behalf of the Aerial Reconnaissance Laboratory at WADC.

Ongoing operations of the HRR system proved troublesome. By December 1957, for example, reliability of the AN/APQ-56 had

plummeted to a dismal 16%, with the blame placed squarely on insufficient ground support from Westinghouse technical representatives and the inability of PETER PAN crews to repair the equipment in flight. The IRON BAR deployment to Thule AB and RAF Fairford that month had HRR effectiveness rates of 50% and 33%. HRR charting reliability for all of 1957 was a mere 21.3%. Despite this poor showing, mission tasking continued. Beginning 10th March 1958 the 4th SRS flew mission 58-26-Q1 against 11 targets in the US, including three in the east, three in the south, and five in the west. A single PETER PAN airplane was deployed to Davis-Monthan AFB, AZ, to provide coverage of the latter five targets.

The life expectancy of the PETER PAN airplanes was never intended to be lengthy. The onset of CIA U-2 overflights of the USSR beginning on 4th July 1956 and the potential for satellite reconnaissance coupled with the suspension of any military overflights portended the program's demise. The end for the PETER PAN program came abruptly. In a message dated 6th March 1958 SAC terminated the AN/APQ-56 program and directed the prompt removal of all equipment from the airplanes. This was particularly ironic given that the 26th SRW was then actively involved in a project utilizing the HRR. With the cessation of Project 58-26-Q1 in early April 1958,

Far left: Despite the promise of the HRR system, it proved less than satisfactory during major operations such as LAST STAND during 1957. In many ways it reflected the limits of the RB-47E as a PHOTINT collector.

Left: By the end of 1957, the AN/APQ-56 reliability had dropped to an appalling 16%, with an overall effectiveness rate of just 23%. The technology was simply too much, too soon for long-term success.

Bottom: Three PETER PAN jets (including 52-0725) were promptly retired to Davis-Monthan AFB in 1958, with the remainder serving as trainers with the 90th SRW. *All three photographs: Augustine Letto*

the AN/APQ-56 program finally came to an end. Three of the PETER PAN airplanes (52-0712, 52-0715, and 52-0725) were relegated directly to storage at Davis-Monthan AFB, and the remaining 11 were transferred to the 90th SRW where they functioned in a training role. Perhaps had the technology been more reliable and weighed less, the AN/APQ-56 might have found its way onto operational bombers to be used to locate targets during actual strike missions. As it was, it proved barely satisfactory for a niche reconnaissance unit, although its influence in prompting, if not justifying, Operation HOME RUN was far more considerable and should not be minimized.

MONTICELLO

The AN/APQ-56 SLAR had significant implications for target analysis and planning. Beginning in early 1957 the Deputy Director for Targets in the Air Force Directorate of Intelligence established Project MONTICELLO. Phase I of this program was designed to validate the 'value of area radar reconnaissance, …high speed and accurate data reduction, and …[the] possibility of an approximate 1,500ft (457m) positional accuracy reconnaissance capability.' To do this, MONTICELLO would gather basic intelligence acquired by conventional daylight cameras as well as standard- and high-resolution radar cameras. These data would then be combined through ground reduction and formulated into target folders.

Ultimately this would result in 'better and more timely intelligence for required target materials support.' The ultimate goal was to provide 'inertial and ground position indicator (GPI) type bombing systems' – in short, an actual map display of the bomber's ground course, the precursor of today's modern instrumentation.

By January 1957 Lockheed-Marietta had installed an AN/APQ-56 (XH-3) in JRB-47E 53-4262 for the MONTICELLO program (the airplane was previously an RB-47E with the 26th SRW until transferred to the 55th SRW on 1st September 1955, before being reassigned to Lockheed-Marietta and redesignated as a JRB-47E on 6th September 1956). The initial test crew from the 26th SRW included aircraft commander Captain John Lappo, copilot Captain Bob Giblin, and navigator Captain Harry Wolfe. Ground coverage of the radar extended to 36nm (67km). Moreover, the antennas were installed on the forward fuselage rather than in the back as with the PETER PAN RB-47s, and were modified to provide roll stability. The film was enlarged to 9.5in (24cm) which could be processed in flight. In addition to the external SLAR antennae on the forward fuselage, the airplane had a 'deepened' radome in place of the standard BNS radome under the nose. Jim May, who worked on the MONTICELLO program, said it reminded him of 'a B-17 ball turret.' Flight tests showed this new radome caused a significant compressibility buffet at normal B-47 cruise speed, forcing a

Above: RB-47E 53-4262 was the only MONTICELLO aircraft, and retained the tail marking from its duties with the 55th SRW. This image shows the test pitot system, the pylon-mounted roll-stabilized AN/APQ-56 radar on the forward fuselage, the deeper chin radome, and the star tracker at the fuselage-wing junction. *Ronald D Neal via William T Y'Blood*

Right: Close-up of the MONTICELLO jet showing modified BNS radome, test pitot arrangement, and starboard AN/APQ-56 antenna. *Author's collection*

reduction in cruise to 0.68-0.70 Mach to eliminate the buffet. Photographs of the airplane in retirement show the normal radome, so it was almost certainly not developed any further. The airplane flew 680 operational hours over an eight-month period ending in December 1957, mapping 9,792,000 square miles (25,361,164km²). Flights ranged in duration from 1+10 to 5+40 hours. System overheating led to frequent aborts early in the program, but these were eventually rectified.

A crucial test took place in November 1957 when 53-4262 deployed to Eielson AFB for 'an extensive operational trial.' This revealed 'a promising capability in all aspects with the possible exception of ground processing of the data.' The MONTICELLO test missions from Alaska looked at the many islands (both ice and terrestrial) north of the Chukotskii Peninsula, searching for airfields to which Soviet bombers could deploy prior to launching an attack on the United States. Standard film cameras could not detect the frozen, snow-covered runways, but AN/APQ-56 radar images could sufficiently discern the outline of the runway to allow for accurate targeting. Results using 'two prime points in the Siberia area [provided] an accuracy of 1,500ft (457m) or less.' The 'ability to locate specific points' still required further refinements using data acquired from 75 airfields in the US for calibration purposes known as 'MONTICELLO I½' which ended by early 1958.

Beginning in late 1957 ARDC expanded the MONTICELLO program to include the addition of 'infrared (IR) sensing equipment to reconnaissance and bombing systems' leading to the 'inclusion of an IR sensor' installed in the vicinity of the lower radome. This prompted the 1958 assessment of the MONTICELLO aircraft in a 'search and destroy' role known as MONTICELLO II using its SLAR and IR gear to detect targets during a combat mission. This may have been related to identifying prospective nuclear power or weapons development sites. On 23rd January 1958, RB-47Es from the 26th SRW flew Project 58-26-V1 to acquire 'large scale photography… of the Nuclear Research Site at Dawsonville, Georgia.' As with the PETER PAN photography of Cape Canaveral, perhaps this was to facilitate MONTICELLO detection of Soviet atomic sites.

The AN/APQ-56 equipment on 52-0711 was removed prior to its transfer from the 26th SRW, but the fairing remained. The airplane was scavenged for other parts after being placed in storage. *Author's collection*

Two of the PETER PAN jets were lost in accidents – including 52-0716 on 13th April 1960 – after they were reassigned to training units. The remainder were all stored at Davis-Monthan AFB. *Augustine Letto*

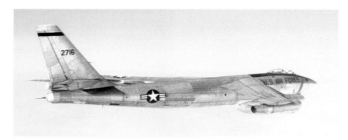

By early 1959 the program had been transferred *in toto* to the Rome Air Development Center (RADC). Results of this phase have not been declassified, but given the absence of any operational deployment of this capability they were likely not sufficiently favorable to merit further development.

AN/APQ-56 RB-47E INDIVIDUAL AIRCRAFT

52-0700 This 26th SRW RB-47E was the initial development aircraft delivered to Westinghouse Electric Corporation. It was located there between 18th May and 12th July 1954.

52-0701 Modified to carry the AN/APQ-56 radar on 9th May 1954. Transferred to 90th SRW by August 1958 for training. Retired to the 2704th Air Force Storage and Disposition Group (AFSDG) on 5th April 1960.

52-0702 Modified to carry the AN/APQ-56 radar on 6th May 1954. Transferred to 90th SRW on 3rd April 1958 for training. It crashed on 21st October 1959 (see Appendix II).

52-0703 Modified to carry the AN/APQ-56 radar on 11th May 1954. Transferred to 90th SRW on 20th March 1958 for training. Retired to 2704th AFSDG on 28th April 1960.

52-0704 Modified to carry the AN/APQ-56 radar on 16th May 1954. Transferred to 90th SRW on 24th June 1958 for training. Retired to 2704th AFSDG on 21st April 1960.

52-0705 Initially modified to carry the AN/APQ-56 radar during 1954, and received subsequent upgrade on 9th August 1956. Took part in the HOME RUN overflights. Transferred to 90th SRW on 30th June 1958 for training. Retired to 2704th AFSDG on 20th April 1960.

52-0706 Modified to carry the AN/APQ-56 radar on 6th May 1954. Took part in the HOME RUN overflights. Transferred to the 301st BW on 1st May 1958, and to the 90th SRW on 12th September 1958 for training. Retired to 2704th AFSDG on 12th April 1960.

52-0708 Initially modified to carry the AN/APQ-56 radar during 1954, and received subsequent upgrade on 11th October 1956. Took part in the HOME RUN overflights. Transferred to the 301st BW on 1st May 1958 and to the 90th SRW on 17th September 1958 for training. Retired to 2704th AFSDG on 8th April 1960.

52-0711 Initially modified to carry the AN/APQ-56 radar during 1954, and received subsequent upgrade on 15th October 1956. Took part in the HOME RUN overflights. Transferred to the 301st BW on 1st May 1958 and to the 90th SRW on 15th October 1958 for training. Retired to 2704th AFSDG on 27th April 1960.

52-0712 Initially modified to carry the AN/APQ-56 radar during 1954, and received subsequent upgrade on 29th October 1956. Took part in the HOME RUN overflights. Transferred to the 301st BW on 1st May 1958. Retired to the Arizona Aircraft Storage Branch (AASB) on 26th June 1958.

52-0714 Modified to carry the AN/APQ-56 radar on 10th June 1954. Transferred to 90th SRW on 27th March 1958 for training. Retired to 2704th AFSDG on 13th April 1960.

52-0715 Initially modified to carry the AN/APQ-56 radar during 1954, and received subsequent upgrade on 22nd November 1956. Took part in the HOME RUN overflights. Transferred to the 301st BW on 1st May 1958. Retired to AASB on 27th June 1958.

52-0716 Initially modified to carry the AN/APQ-56 radar during 1954, and received subsequent upgrade on 13th March 1956. Transferred to 90th SRW on 31st July 1958 for training. It crashed on 13th April 1960 (see Appendix II).

52-0721 Initially modified to carry the AN/APQ-56 radar during 1954, and received subsequent upgrade on 19th September 1956. Took part in the HOME RUN overflights. Transferred to the 301st BW on 1st May 1958 and to the 90th SRW on 2nd October 1958 for training. Retired to 2704th AFSDG on 12th May 1960.

52-0725 Initially modified to carry the AN/APQ-56 radar during 1954, and received subsequent upgrade on 26th March 1956. Took part in the HOME RUN overflights. Transferred to the 301st BW on 1st May 1958. Retired to AASB on 30th June 1958.

53-4260 Westinghouse modified RB-47E 53-4260 from the 55th SRW as the XH-3 prototype. It served with the 26th SRW from 23rd October 1956 through 11th March 1958 when it was assigned to the 376th BW until 9th April 1958 when it returned to the 26th SRW. It was reassigned to the 301st BW on 1st May 1958, and on 14th May was transferred to ARDC. It was subsequently designated as a JRB-47E and later an NRB-47E. It was retired to the 2704th AFSDG on 28th April 1961.

53-4262 By January 1957 Lockheed-Marietta had installed an AN/APQ-56 (XH-3) in JRB-47E 53-4262 for the MONTICELLO program. It was retired to 2704th AFSDG on 4th February 1960 (see Appendix III).

ELINT Aircraft and Operations

For years the Boeing RB-50G served as SAC's primary ELINT collection platform, along with even older RB-29s and RB-36s. Their limited flight performance made them especially vulnerable to attack by hostile jet fighters, notably the MiG-15 and MiG-17. Two RB-50Gs were shot down, one in 1953 and one in 1956, not to mention multiple incidents that did not result in aircraft losses. Given their speed, altitude, and range, it made sense to transition from the B-50 to the B-47 as an ELINT collection platform. This offered global range with aerial refueling, higher altitudes and hence greater sensor detection range, and greater speed so crews spent more time on station while covering greater distances instead of droning from the deployment base to the area of interest.

Conspicuously marked on the nose as 'RBH1', 53-4280 rolls out at Boeing-Wichita on 2nd February 1955. It functioned as a Boeing test aircraft until delivered to the 55th SRW on 24th July 56. *BW92747 courtesy Boeing*

RB-47H

SAC was keenly aware that the B-47 was highly vulnerable to Soviet electronic defenses, especially early warning and fire control radar systems. As early as June 1951 SAC articulated five 'phases' of electronic countermeasures for the B-47, with each phase increasingly sophisticated. Phases I-IV provided ECM systems for each aircraft. Phase V was a B-47 configured with a two-man ECM capsule in the bomb bay for 'escort protection' (see Chapter 3). In order to jam Soviet radars and other electronic defenses, SAC needed detailed technical data on their capabilities, intelligence which had been collected by RB-50s and RB-36s. On 25th June 1953, SAC's Vice Commander Major General Thomas S Power articulated the 'urgent requirement for a permanently installed electronic reconnaissance capability (Phase VII) in a limited number of B-47s in lieu of the two-man pod' (later expanded to a three-man pod). This would 'ferret out enemy radar defenses and return with the information on frequencies being used.' White wrote to LeMay on 22nd September 1953 saying, 'I have directed the Air Staff to see what can be done to find out more about the Russian capabilities and particularly to extend the frequency coverage of your ferrets... I will call on you to assist in the reconnaissance operations which will probably be required to help obtain the additional intelligence needed.' In response, on 30th October 1953 AMC directed the procurement of 30 RB-47Fs (this MDS changed to RB-47H on 9th March 1954) at a cost of $21.8 million for 30 Boeing Model 450-171-51 airframes. Some SAC and Air Force sources refer to these as 'ECM aircraft', but they were not true ECM 'jammers' in the sense of the Phase V or BLUE CRADLE ECM aircraft. Instead, the 'ECM' in this context refers to their mission to collect intelligence related to ECM. By 1960 these 'ECM' missions were known as BIG BLAST, ROYAL LARK, and TIGER HUNT. Details of each have not been declassified to link them to specific aircraft or mission, but BIG BLAST may have been a major RB-47 NORAD penetration exercise.

Production problems appeared almost immediately, most notably pressurization of the bomb bay capsule, delaying the projected delivery date from February to July 1955. SAC told Boeing, in no uncertain terms, that all airplanes must be delivered by 30th November 1955. Boeing responded, according to one AMC history, with a 'crash program' to build the airplanes (the last of the initial order barely made this deadline, with 53-4308 arriving at Forbes AFB on 23rd November 1955). The final contract was approved on 18th

April 1955 for a total cost of $44,754,720 plus $50,496,670 for spare parts, special tools, and ground equipment. Three months later, on 5th July, SAC requested five more RB-47Hs. To save money, AMC told Boeing that B-47E Units 1,091 through 1,095 would be cut, and substituted three ERB-47Hs (described below) and two RB-47Hs, resulting in a modest bill of $4,385,000 for five additional airplanes. A subsequent block of 12 RB-47Hs was canceled. Ultimately, Boeing built 32 RB-47Hs. The first RB-47H (53-4280) flew on 21st June 1955. The first delivery to the 55th SRW at Forbes AFB on 5th August 1955. Six RB-47Hs were lost, two of these to hostile fire. As with other RB-47 variants, the airplanes were redesignated as R-47Hs in the early 1960s, but reverted to RB-47H by 1965.

Externally the RB-47H was distinguished by multiple antennas and its rather bulbous nose, as well as the presence of a distended bomb bay area to accommodate both the Raven's pod and antennas. The nose was painted black, but has been photographed in grey because it had not yet been painted. White was tried operationally but proved too easy to spot from the ground and caused glare problems for the crew.

The heart of the RB-47H was the AN/APD-4, an automated 'high probability of intercept' D/E/F-band direction finding (DF) collection

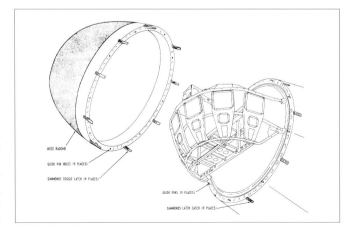

The frame inside the RB-47H radome held multiple receivers to collect ELINT. Despite some claims to the contrary, the E/RB-47Hs were all passive ELINT collectors and did not function as dedicated ECM jamming aircraft like the Phase V or BLUE CRADLE B-47Es. *USAF TO 1B-47(R)H-2-2*

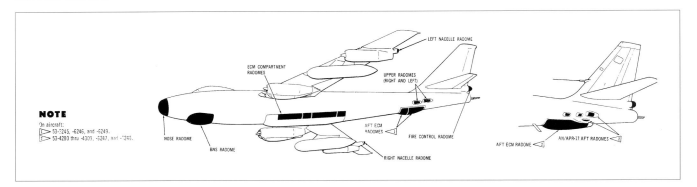

and analysis system. Rather than manually tuning the receivers through a range of frequencies to find and then record any signals of interest (SOI), the AN/APD-4 automatically scanned multiple frequencies and recorded them. The Ravens could then devote their attention to unique or unusual SOIs for further analysis. Critical to the success of the AN/APD-4 was the extensive number of antennas on the RB-47H. The nose radome housed an array of eighteen AN/APD-4 antennas with six sectors, as well as antenna for the AN/APS-54 warning detection system. Other antennas were in the wingtips (initially for the AN/ALT-7, but later converted to AN/APR-9 low-band receiver), the aft end of the outboard engine nacelles (AN/APD-4), in special slim pods later installed under the wing between the outboard engines and the wingtip (AN/APR-17), on the belly (AN/APR-17), on the vertical stabilizer (AN/APR-17), and in one large 'bathtub' on the aft ventral fuselage [AN/APR-17 RS-1 and 2, AN/ALD-4, AN/ALA-6 DF (direction finding), and QRC-91] and several small radomes (AN/APR-17 RL-1, AN/APD-4, AN/APR-17 RC-1 and RX-1) on the lower aft fuselage. The AN/ALA-6 DF units were actually of two types, one for high/medium frequencies and the other for low frequencies. There were also antennas for the AN/ASQ-32 and AN/ALT-6B.

The ultimate upgrade to the RB-47H and its ELINT collection capability came as part of the SILVER KING program. Boeing produced the prototype in 1960 using 53-4280, which, among other modifications, included the external AN/ALD-4 pod on the starboard fuselage with a total cost of $92,000,000. The AN/ALD-4 was originally intended for used by the Convair B-58 on its centerline pylon, but this proved unrealistic and was not taken up. Of the original 30 RB-47Hs, 15 were programmed to receive the SILVER KING modification (known as Mod 44), although some sources suggest that 18 were converted between April and November 1961 at Douglas-Tulsa, beginning with 53-4299. It is not clear if the AN/ALD-4 pod was permanently installed on all the airplanes, as some images show just the pylon. Tests with the pod initially evaluated a strut with a right angle, but this led to airplane control issues. These were solved by using a straight strut mounted at a 45° angle to the fuselage. The first operational SILVER KING ELINT sortie was flown from Forbes AFB in March 1962, with overseas sorties beginning in July 1962.

The RB-47H airplanes carried a different BNS than did other B-47s, utilizing the AN/ASQ-51 system with the AN/APS-64 radar and AN/AJQ-3 computer. An AN/APN-102 Doppler radar was installed to provide precise ground speed and drift data, and an AN/AVN-1 astro-navigational set provided updated position information to the BNS. The AN/ALH-2 system was used to record

crew and radio transmissions. Navigation data was annotated on the O-15 camera, ALD-4 video, digital and analog recorders, APD-4 films, and other systems in the EW compartment.

A declassified report from a 1957 Commander's Conference at Offutt AFB refers to SAC's 'strong opposition' to the Air Force's cancelation of an 'external weapon carriage modification of the RB-47.' This was distinct from the Crossbow anti-radiation missile to be carried by B-47s, which was also canceled (see Chapter 7). Additional details of this proposed external weapon are not known.

The RB-47H carried a crew of six, including the standard flight crew of three plus three electronic warfare officers (EWs) or 'Ravens'. The three Ravens occupied web seats in the aisle during takeoff and landing, and moved through a narrow tunnel into their bomb bay compartment prior to the airplane climbing past 10,000ft (3,048m) when it was necessary to pressurize the cabin. To facilitate entry into their seats, the Raven 2 went first followed by the Raven 3. The Raven 1 moved last, closing the pressure door behind him. Crews were assigned to two squadrons – the 38th SRS and the 343rd SRS. Many of the senior crewmembers were 'old heads' with years of experience in aerial reconnaissance flights; some were even Second World War and Korean War veterans with combat decorations. The 55th SRW received RB-47Es in 1954, and these were ultimately used these to familiarize flight crews with the B-47 and prepare for the arrival of the RB-47H. The 338th SRS served as the training squadron using the remaining RB-47Es (it later regained an operational mission with the arrival of the RB-47K).

During the initial years of RB-47H operations, only the most experienced aircraft commanders and navigators were assigned to the 38th SRS and 343rd SRS. Newly assigned copilots underwent a brief orientation program (typically a half-dozen six-hour missions) and were then assigned to a crew. When ready to upgrade, they were transferred to the 338th SRS where they qualified as aircraft commanders and gained experience flying RB-47K weather missions. After only a few months they had accrued sufficient hours and returned to their prior squadrons as RB-47H aircraft commanders. As the 'old heads' retired, all new aircraft commanders, navigators, and copilots went directly to the 338th SRS for training and qualification and typically flew RB-47K missions before being assigned to either the 38th SRS or the 343rd SRS.

Ravens were assigned directly to these two squadrons, where they gradually progressed in experience and responsibility. As might be expected, initial readiness was less than anticipated. One January 1956 report summarizing the conversion process from RB-47E to RB-47H lamented that training was 'greatly restricted due to ECM crews being grounded most of the month because of excessive noise in the ECM compartment.' This was resolved by modifying the air conditioning and pressurization system, and by providing each Raven with a custom-molded sound-suppressing helmet insert. The ELINT stations were equally problematic. Of the 27 RB-47Hs on hand, the report noted, all were configured with the Raven 2 position, 24 had

Table 6-8. SILVER KING RB-47Hs

53-4280	53-4287	53-4295	53-4299	53-4303
53-4282	53-4292	53-4296	53-4300	53-4304
53-4284	53-4293	53-4297	53-4301	53-4307
53-4285	53-4294	53-4298	53-4302	

Opposite page: RB-47Hs
(flagged as '2') had a
different aft ELINT radome
array than the three
ERB-47Hs (flagged as '1'),
although the remaining
radomes were the same.
USAF TO 1B-47(R)H-2-2

This page: Original canted
pylon for the AN/ALD-4
pod for the prototype SILVER
KING 53-4280 shows the
angle and placement on
20th July 1960. Final pylon
was effectively straight, as
seen on 53-4302 during
approach to Yokota AB on
6th April 1967. *BWA21377,
BWA21391courtesy Boeing,
and Toshio Tagaya*

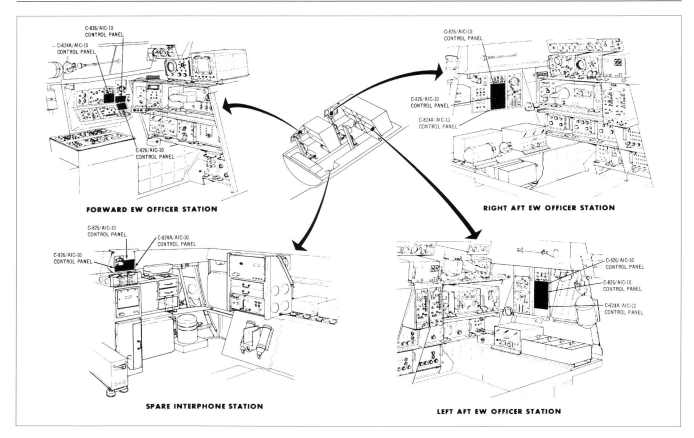

FORWARD EW OFFICER STATION

RIGHT AFT EW OFFICER STATION

SPARE INTERPHONE STATION

LEFT AFT EW OFFICER STATION

the Raven 1 position 'at least partially equipped,' and only two had the Raven 3 position 'partially equipped.'

The RB-47Hs routinely deployed to five main Operating Locations (OL): OL-1 at RAF Brize Norton (until 1st February 1958 this was Detachment 1 at RAF Mildenhall), OL-2 at Yokota AB, OL-3 at Eielson AFB, OL-4 at Adana AB, Turkey (renamed on 28th February 1958 as Incirlik AB), and OL-5 at Thule AB. There were other OLs as well, and the OL numbers changed over time. Crews would often 'cut their teeth' on missions from Turkey before flying more complicated (and dangerous) sorties from England or Japan. Surprisingly, there were often far more RB-47Hs [plus an occasional ERB-47H and two EB-47E(TT) TELL TWOS] at Incirlik AB than at any of the other OLs. In August 1963, for example, three RB-47Hs flew 22 sorties and two EB-47E(TT)s flew 18 sorties from Incirlik AB whereas one ERB-47H and one RB-47H flew only nine sorties from RAF Brize Norton.

RB-47Hs carried standard SAC markings but not the reflective white paint on the undersides. When deployed overseas the tail numbers were sometimes removed and/or changed for some flights. A few of the aircraft acquired nicknames that were for the most part applied only while the aircraft were overseas.

Although the RB-47Hs had yet to be declared fully mission capable in early 1956, they were nonetheless sufficiently ready to participate in Operation HOME RUN, beginning in March 1956 (described above). Crews were told only that they would participate in 'a cold weather exercise involving RB-47H aircraft and to test photo reconnaissance equipment under arctic conditions.' Four airplanes and crews (two each from the 38th SRS and the 343rd SRS) deployed from Forbes AFB to Thule AB on 21st March 1956. While there, they flew a total of 156 coordinated missions with 26th SRW RB-47Es over Siberia. The RB-47Hs departed Thule AB for Forbes AFB on 4th May.

Initial overseas deployments usually involved two RB-47Hs under a program known as SAM SPADE, which became TROJAN HORSE on 16th

January 1957, and peripheral ELINT missions were known as CASTLE GATE, which later changed to BOX TOP. Tracking these proved to be especially challenging, as official records frequently show the airplanes to be at Adana AB or even Chambley in France (through 1961) when in fact they were at RAF Mildenhall or RAF Brize Norton. The RB-47Hs often transited UK bases en route to Turkey, so this ambiguity is not entirely surprising.

The first RB-47H deployment following the HOME RUN missions took place at Det 1 at RAF Mildenhall beginning 1st July 1956, with the airplanes replaced in October and November. The deployment to Yokota AB began on 3rd July 1956 with three RB-47Hs. This was reduced to two airplanes in October 1959. Between September 1956 and May 1959 two RB-47Hs were deployed to Thule AB. A single RB-47H was located at Eielson AFB from June 1956 until October 1957, after which the number fluctuated. Two RB-47Hs at a time were deployed at Det 1 at RAF Mildenhall throughout 1957, averaging some 22-24 missions per quarter. The detachment at RAF Mildenhall closed on 1st February 1958 and the two RB-47Hs relocated to RAF Brize Norton. By early 1959 RB-47 operations at RAF Brize Norton were reduced given the increase in sorties from Incirlik AB and even Sidi Slimane AB, French Morocco, in February and March 1959. Indeed, from March through June 1959 there were no RB-47s deployed to RAF Brize Norton, although by July there were two RB-47Hs or one ERB-47H and one RB-47H on hand.

During January 1959 three RB-57D-2s (53-3964, -3965, and -3968) from the 4080th SW deployed to RAF Brize Norton for BORDERTOWN peripheral ELINT missions. Records suggest that 55th SRW RB-47Hs conducted sorties in conjunction with these missions to validate the System 320 SAFE (semi-automatic ferret equipment) under evaluation on the RB-57Ds. BORDERTOWN's success led to a repeat mission in January-February 1960, this time from Incirlik AB using the same three RB-57D-2s to collect ELINT on Black Sea defenses. After several aborted attempts, five missions were flown

in February. The largest of these was on 24th February and involved RB-57D-2s 53-3964 and -3968, RB-47H 53-4304, and ERB-47H 53-6245. The RB-57D-2s then returned to RAF Brize Norton, where an additional series of missions were flown in March in conjunction with ERB-47H 53-6245. Notable among the successful collections were 'signals in the X-band frequency range from a Soviet picket ship.'

The loss of RB-47H 53-4281 on 1st July 1960 brought considerable (and unwanted) public attention to SAC reconnaissance operations from the UK, with only a single RB-47H at RAF Brize Norton through October 1960, and none through the end of the year (although there may have been transits via England to Incirlik AB). This paucity of aircraft changed dramatically in late August 1961

with an influx of RB-47Hs and an ERB-47H, perhaps related to prospective Soviet nuclear tests at Novaya Zemlya. Activity remained modest through most of 1962, but decreased to almost nil with the onset of the October Cuban Missile Crisis as the 55th SRW's assets were otherwise involved with missions around Cuba. By 1963 lengthy RB-47H deployments resumed, along with reconnaissance GARLIC SALT KC-135As from the 34th Air Refueling Squadron (AREFS) monitoring Soviet nuclear tests, and the operational evaluation of the future ELINT system for the BIG TEAM RC-135C as part of GOLDEN PHEASANT missions. OL-1 relocated to RAF Upper Heyford on 21st February 1965, and RB-47Hs once again mixed with GARLIC SALT KC-135s. The 55th SRW relocated from Forbes AFB to Offutt AFB, NE, on 16th August 1966.

Opposite: Layout of the Raven compartment in the E/RB-47H shows the seating arrangement for each of the three Ravens. *USAF TO 1B-47(R)H-2-1*

Top: Forbes AFB was home to the RB-47H fleet until 16th August 1966 when the 55th SRW relocated to Offutt AFB. For many crews, England, Japan, and Turkey were the most common deployments, but there were other destinations as well. *USAF via William T Y'Blood*

Center: Although seen here in the UK well after 1960, RB-47H 53-4303 was one of the four 55th SRW jets that took part in Operation HOME RUN in 1956. *Author's collection*

Bottom: RB-47H 53-4301 undergoes an engine run at Yokota AB on 12th May 1966. The deployment of RB-47s there proved contentious, especially as some Japanese officials falsely claimed they only stopped there 'briefly' for fuel or crew rest. *Toshio Tagaya*

The RB-47Hs were the final B-47 variant in SAC's inventory, and were retired in two tranches – the first in 1965 and the last in 1967. Throughout 1967 the RB-47s assigned to the 55th SRW took part in their final operational deployments. Crew numbers in the 338th SRS dropped from 16 to 10 by 1st April, with most crewmembers transferred to the BIG TEAM RC-135Cs or the RIVET STAND KC-135R. At the same time, all eight of the squadron's RB-47Hs were deployed. On 8th May, 55th SRW Wing Commander Colonel William E Riggs undertook a final inspection tour of Torrejón AB, Spain, Wheelus AB, Libya, Incirlik AB, and RAF Upper Heyford using ERB-47H 53-6245. By mid-May, RB-47Hs 53-4280 and 53-4303 returned to

Offutt AFB following their final temporary duty (TDY) to RAF Upper Heyford. Both left Offutt AFB on 25th May for storage in MASDC at Davis-Monthan AFB, AZ. With the onset of the 5th June Arab-Israeli Six Day War, all RB-47/EB-47E(TT) operations at Wheelus AB were terminated and the airplanes relocated to Torrejón AB. EB-47E(TT) 53-2316 returned to Offutt AFB on 19th June concurrent with the termination of the HAVE TELL program (described below). Two RB-47Hs – 53-4302 and 53-4284 – returned from Incirlik AB on 26th June, and four days later were flown to MASDC. The final RB-47H – 53-4296 – left Offutt AFB for MASDC on 29th December 1967, under the command of Major Aaron C Cummins.

Above: 53-4280 was one of the last two RB-47Hs to deploy to RAF Upper Heyford in May 1967, with its mission taken over by BIG TEAM RC-135Cs. A decade of Ops sorties from the UK had come to an end. *Author's collection*

Left and below: A passing of the torch from the BOX TOP RB-47H to the BIG TEAM RC-135C at Offutt AFB on 29th December 1967. Major Aaron Cummins makes final preparations for the last SAC flight of RB-47H 53-4296 to Davis-Monthan AFB, where it is seen after arrival in a warmer climate. Note the mounting locations for the AN/ALD-4 pylon adjacent to the bomb bay. *USAF*

'Visitors'

RB-47Hs were routinely intercepted while on their missions, both by friendly forces and Soviet fighters, as illustrated by a BOX TOP sortie on 24th September 1962. During a six-hour mission to the Baltic Sea, 53-4287 was intercepted by a Swedish Saab J35 Draken. As the RB-47H continued its orbit east of Gotland Island, it was intercepted by a MiG-19 *Farmer*, a Yak-25 *Flashlight*, and a MiG-17 *Fresco*, along with a third unidentified aircraft. The MiG-19 switched its radar from 'search' to 'lock on', prompting the Raven 1 to jam its radar. The *Farmer* then moved to the left wingtip, where it was photographed in a very tight formation, and very nearly caused an international incident by forcing the RB-47H to enter Finnish airspace. The RB-47H crewmembers received the Distinguished Flying Cross for this mission.

Other encounters with hostile aircraft did not end so well. A Soviet MiG-19 shot down RB-47H 53-4281 on 1st July 1960 (described in the chapter opening) with the loss of four crewmembers and considerable international attention. The last verified attack on an RB-47 took place on 28th April 1965, almost exactly a decade after the loss of the first RB-47 on 17th April 1955. Lieutenant Colonel Hobart Mattison was in command of crew E-96 flying RB-47H 53-4290 on Mission #2304 from Yokota AB over the Sea of Japan along the Korean Peninsula. The flight, which took place during the first operational deployment for Raven 2 First Lieutenant George V Back, was normal until 11:10L (all times are South Korean local), at which point Raven 1 Captain Robert 'Red' Winters detected a weak signal of a *Scan Odd* airborne intercept (AI) radar from a DPRK MiG-17PF *Fresco-D*. Winters reported this to Mattison, but the signal was too weak for further analysis. Three minutes after this the signal reappeared, and Winters was able to locate it at the RB-47's 2 o'clock position, which

an unspecified ground radar ('GCI') confirmed was at a distance of 25nm (46km) and pacing the RB-47. Some 5 minutes later the MiG-17 was in the 5 o'clock position, again confirmed by GCI but then it suddenly disappeared. High cirrus clouds prevented any visual identification of the MiGs by the crew. The RB-47 reached its turn point at 39°30'N 129°05'E and an altitude of 33,000ft (10,058m). As the airplane turned toward its new heading of 044°, copilot First Lieutenant Hank Dubuy spotted two MiG-17s over his right shoulder in a trail position. Dubuy turned his seat around, switched the A-5 gunnery system to operation mode, and took two pictures of the interceptors.

At 11:25L the MiG-17 directly behind the RB-47 opened fire, and Dubuy asked for Mattison's permission to return fire. The reply was concise: 'Shoot the bastards'. The MiG's tracers whizzed past the RB-47's canopy and a number struck the tail section. Mattison pulled the power and began a diving 90° right turn to depart the 'Sensitive

Table 6-9. **RB-47H Distances to the USSR (Baltic Region, Jan-Sep 64)**

Closest Approach (in nautical miles)

Month	20-24	25-29	30-34	35-39	40+
January	3			1	1
February	1	3	1		1
March		1			2
April			1		4
May				2	3
June			3	1	
July		1	2		2
August	3				2
September	1		3		2

Source – USAF Ferret Flights, Secretary of State for Air, PRO, Kew

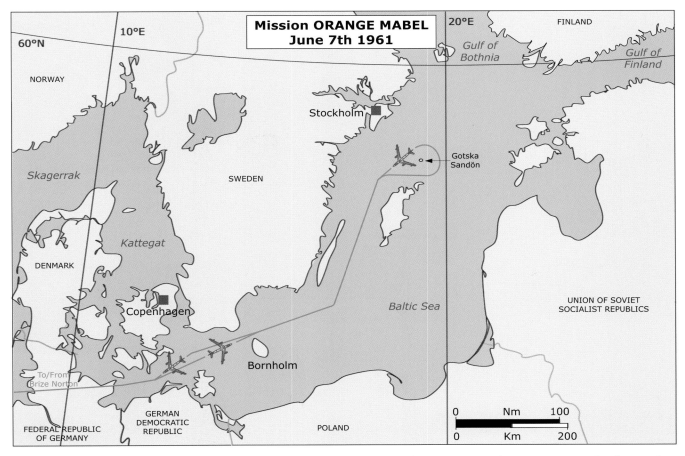

The ORANGE MABEL RB-47H Baltic mission was flown at 32,000ft and was in the 'sensitive area' between 2230Z and 0031Z. Its nearest point of approach to the DDR was 11nm and 63nm from Soviet territory.

Area' and to pick up speed, now flying on a heading of approximately 130°. Navigator Captain Robert 'Bob' Rogers confirmed a new heading of 140° to reach the nearest friendly airspace. The MiGs continued to make firing passes on the RB-47, even as it descended. The MiGs were close enough to the RB-47 to prevent Dubuy from getting a radar lock-on to fire the guns, so he did so manually, scoring

hits on the second MiG-17, which almost immediately entered a nose-down dive from which it did not recover, impacting the Sea of Japan. During one pass Winters dispensed a 5-second load of chaff which immersed the MiG-17 in chaff and the cardboard residue of the boxes, apparently confusing the pilot. This also may have contributed to Dubuy's inability to get a radar lock on, so Winters

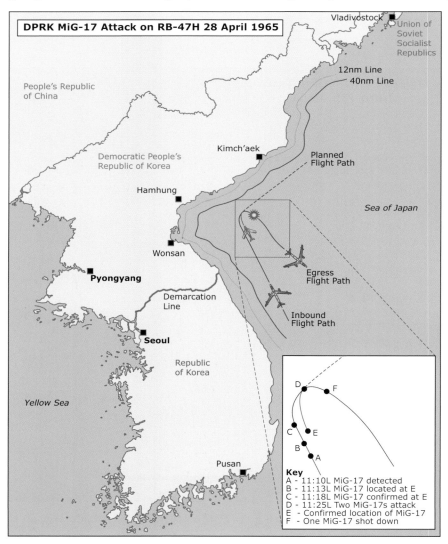

DPRK MiG-17 Attack on RB-47H 28 April 1965

Key
A - 11:10L MiG-17 detected
B - 11:13L MiG-17 located at E
C - 11:18L MiG-17 confirmed at E
D - 11:25L Two MiG-17s attack
E - Confirmed location of MiG-17
F - One MiG-17 shot down

did not dispense any additional chaff. The remaining MiG-17 made additional firing passes, and Dubuy reported seeing contrails from two more unidentified aircraft high and west of the RB-47.

By this time the RB-47 had entered a high-speed buffet, so Mattison decreased the rate of descent. In doing so he realized that the RB-47 had lost both normal and emergency elevator controls, as well as normal hydraulic systems. Throughout the descent Mattison broadcast a May Day report confirming they were being fired upon. The RB-47 was now level at an altitude of 16,000ft (4,877m), but Mattison chose to climb to 18,000ft (5,486m) to enter a cloud deck to 'hide' from the MiGs. This proved effective, and the attacks stopped. Rogers updated the heading to 120°, and the RB-47 benefitted from a 75-knot tail wind to reach Yokota AB.

The RB-47 and its crew were still not 'home free.' All the crewmembers, including Raven 3 First Lieutenant Joel Lutkenhouse, were shaken but not injured. Indeed, for the Ravens – without a window of any sort – the previous several minutes were like 'going over Niagara Falls in a wooden barrel'. The airplane was not so lucky. What appeared to be a fuselage fire originating in the aft main body tank left a trail of black smoke behind the RB-47, although this abated after a few minutes, likely because the fuel had drained out of the bullet holes. Moreover, Mattison had shut down engines #3 and #4 to prevent further fuel drainage from feeding a fire. The airplane had lost all normal hydraulic system quantity and pressure, leaving only the emergency system. Mattison called for a tanker to provide additional fuel and to serve as an on-site monitor should the crew be forced to bail out. He then climbed the airplane to 28,000ft (8,534m) for the optimal cruise back to Yokota AB.

The descent was uneventful, with the three Ravens coming forward as the airplane passed through 15,000ft (4,572m). Winters manually extended the landing gear and the airplane began its approach. Unable to slow the RB-47 sufficiently, Mattison performed a go-around. Best flare speed was calculated to be 133KIAS, but with the flaps at 60% (to flatten the approach angle) and to keep the nose from dropping (the center of gravity was significantly forward due to the empty aft fuel tank), the airplane could only slow to 153KIAS. During the landing from the second approach the airplane hit nose wheel first, ballooning 40ft (12m). With both pilots holding the control column full aft, they deployed the approach and brake chutes timed to blossom with the second bounce, which prevented gaining any significant height. Mattison slowed the airplane to a stop on the runway. Although supposedly confirmed by ground-based listening posts, the Air Force has yet to credit Dubuy with a confirmed 'kill' for shooting down the North Korean MiG-17, the only such kill for the B-47 fleet. The RB-47 was written off.

RB-47Hs found themselves embroiled in an election crisis in Japan. Following the loss of Frank Powers' U-2 on 1st May 1960, the Japanese government sought to distance itself from US aerial intelligence gathering operations that originated from bases in Japan. Acting out of total ignorance, the US Ambassador reassured the Japanese government that no RB-47s operated from Japan. In quintessential 'spin,' US officials subsequently tried to claim they were not 'based' there, and only landed there 'occasionally for fuel and crew rest'. Socialist ministers in the Diet correctly called this bluff, forcing the government to acknowledge these regular deployments. Fortunately there were no calls to eliminate these visits and the November 1960 Lower House elections proceeded amid greater interests in the new US-Japan Peace Treaty, the resignation of Prime Minister Nobosuke Kishi and cancelation of President Eisenhower's planned visit, student riots, and the dramatic assassination of Socialist leader Inejiro Asanuma.

RB-47s and Drones

In April 1964 the 4080th SW began operating Ryan drones under the HIGH BAR OpOrd in addition to its U-2s as part of its reconnaissance mission. Known as Project LIGHTNING BUG, these were designed to collect both ELINT and PHOTINT. After launch from a DC-130A the drone would fly its mission over denied territory and, upon arriving over a safe recovery area, shut down its engine and descend under a parachute. A locator beacon helped with final recovery by helicopter. Eventually, a Mid Air Retrieval System (MARS) was utilized to 'grab' the drone in flight with a recovery helicopter.

Project LONG ARM began in October 1963 when SAC assigned two RB-47Hs (53-4295 and 53-4296) and two Ryan 147E drones to a test program designed to assess the ability of a drone to collect ELINT in a high-threat area and relay that information to an RB-47 operating nearby in relative safety. Most of the normal reconnaissance equipment was stripped from the RB-47Hs for these missions and they were specially configured for the drone telemetry intercept and relay. After the program ended the aircraft were returned to normal configurations.

Key to the success for each drone mission was electronically 'mating' the drone to the RB-47H prior to each mission, so both aircraft had to be at the same location at least a day before the scheduled flight. The JCS directed that all work on LONG ARM be suspended on 8th January 1964, and it remained idle until March 1965 when resurrected by CINCSAC General John D Ryan to complement SAC's RB-47 and U-2 ELINT capabilities, notably the onset of BOX TOP ELINT sorties in Southeast Asia. On 17th March, the two RB-47s linked to two 147Es suspended beneath the DC-130.

Opposite: RB-47H 53-4290 shows the residual smoke trails on the aft fuselage beginning in the national insignia and extending aft with additional bullet holes on both sides. Damage on the right side is immediately aft of the AN/ALD-4 pylon. *Author's collection*

Right: RB-47Hs played a modest role in the war in Southeast Asia, mostly conducting peripheral BOX TOP ELINT sorties but also LEFT HOOK and UNITED EFFORT missions to record the telemetry acquired by drones. *Author's collection*

Another captive mission was undertaken in early April at McClellan AFB and again was successful. Free-flight operational profiles followed on 8th and 13th April at Eglin AFB. Both failed due to telemetry and recording problems. A repeat mission on 20th April failed, as did flights on 29th April and 11th May. Again, the issue was technical and contractor TEMCO made the required modifications to the telemetry equipment. Several flight tests took place from 8-10th and 22nd-23rd June and were finally successful. Full collection took place and the telemetry link functioned properly at distances up to 120nm (222km).

In expectation of imminent operational service in Southeast Asia, SAC prepared to deploy the drones, RB-47Hs, DC-130As, and necessary support personnel within 72 hours, but the issue of basing delayed the move. SAC recommended Yokota AB (55th SRW OL-2) given the common maintenance for the RB-47s with the BOX TOP RB-47s routinely visiting there. The JCS disagreed, however, and instead selected Clark AB, Philippines (55th SRW OL-7) or Kadena AB. The initial deployment began in August 1965. In addition to its ELINT missions, SAC also conducted BLUE SPRINGS PHOTINT missions using Ryan 147B and 147Gs, but these did not involve any RB-47s.

The ELINT drones were a practical solution to the problem of acquiring critical data regarding North Vietnamese SA-2 *Guideline* SAM sites, eliminating the risk to US reconnaissance crews. The drone would fly into a high-threat area to collect ELINT signals (acquisition, tracking, fire control, etc), and relay them in real-time to an RB-47H orbiting over the Gulf of Tonkin in relative safety. Even if the drone was shot down, the crucial ELINT was already transmitted and recorded for processing and analysis. This led to two different ELINT missions as part of Project LONG ARM, both involving RB-47Hs: LEFT HOOK and UNITED EFFORT.

LEFT HOOK was a 'Wild Weasel' decoy operation involving two 147Ds, and was designed as a 'search and destroy' effort for North Vietnamese SAM sites and radar controllers. The two drones emitted signals similar to TAC aircraft in hopes that the radar sites would target them, allowing TAC fighters in turn to attack and destroy the site. An RB-47H flying over the Gulf of Tonkin accompanied each mission to record any ELINT signals the drone might collect. The first flight took place on 20th August 1965 and the last on 31st August. Radio failure on the RB-47 during one sortie rendered the mission 'ineffective.' Overall, no sites were destroyed, and, with both available drones ultimately lost to hostile fire, LEFT HOOK was terminated.

The UNITED EFFORT mission gathered ELINT using four Ryan 147E drones that relayed the data to an RB-47H. Missions began from OL-7 in late 1965, with the first operational mission occurring on 16th October as the drone flew a perfect profile but the ELINT payload 'quit operating 20 seconds after launch.' The second mission, planned for 18th October, was canceled and rescheduled. The next two missions, on 20th October and 5th November, were marginally effective. Both drones were shot down and, although they collected some ELINT, were unsuccessful in acquiring any SA-2 fuzing data,

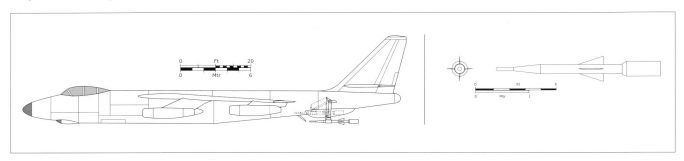

a top priority for the development of suitable ECM. The final mission took place on 13th February 1966 and ultimately collected the necessary SA-2 fuzing signal. Although it was lost to ground fire, the crucial data had already been relayed to the RB-47H, completing what Assistant Secretary of the Air Force Eugene Fubini called 'the most significant contribution to electronic reconnaissance in the last 20 years,' saying that this single 'mission had paid for the entire drone program up to that date.'

NEW BREED

By 1962 the CIA placed 'special emphasis' on gathering specialized ELINT related to the 'the Soviet early warning net, the SA-2 sites, and the MiG-21 capabilities.' This subcategory of ELINT included 'precision parameter measurements (PPM),' which assessed 'radar signal characteristics to a very high order of accuracy' as well as a radar's operating mechanisms that 'reveal its detection and tracking capabilities.' Precision measurements could then be combined to determine the radar's vulnerability to electronic countermeasures. These measurements include 'precise data on the maximum beam power, the total radiated power, the antenna gain, and variation in gain (side and back lobe distribution) around the antenna.'

Following tests in 1958 using an unidentified Fairchild C-119 with rudimentary PPM gear for flights through the Berlin Corridor linking Berlin with West Germany, initial CIA PPM operations began in early 1963 with FIELD DAY C-97G 53-0106 missions around Cuba and East Germany. In April 1963 Lockheed Air Services modified RB-47H 53-4291 into the 'Zot I' platform with a 'blivet' that was trailed behind the airplane to ensure that signal acquisition was not impaired by the RB-47's own electronic emissions. Major Johnny Drost's crew flew the airplane to Yokota AB on 21st June 1963, where they conducted nine NEW BREED missions near Sakhalin Island and throughout the Sea of Japan. To be clear, these were SAC aircraft flown by SAC crews – they were *not* CIA assets – the mission tasking came from the CIA. Not all SAC personnel were informed of the mission details, creating some problems for Drost which required CIA 'intervention' among the detachment staff! Collection tactics developed where the airplane would fly 'a radial path from the horizon to directly over the radar site,' turning away from denied airspace at the last possible moment, typically at a point tangent to the 12nm boundary. This provided optimum signal coverage, and the provocative flight path usually ensured that the radar would be turned on, however briefly. The system was not immune to problems, most notably on 21st August 1963 when the cable snapped, losing the 'blivet' entirely.

Between July and October 1963, the NEW BREED RB-47H flew missions in three different geographic areas, with emphasis on the *Tall King*, *Spoon Rest*, and *Knife Rest* early warning radars. In

Opposite page, top: Drawing shows placement of sensor support in both retracted and extended position.

Upper left: View of the 'Zot 1' sensor with the mount in the extended position. The 'blivet' would be released from the sway brace and trail in the airstream. Note Playboy bunny. *via Colonel Johnny Drost*

Bottom left: Aerial view of 'Zot 1' RB-47H 53-4291 with the 'blivet' support extended downward. Large object on the bottom of the fuselage in front of the sensor is the periscope used to monitor the blivet during extension and retraction. *via Colonel Johnny Drost*

Bottom right: NEW BREED and IRON LUNG crew photo in front of the support structure seen in the retracted position. It pivoted in the back while lowering the 'blivet' into position. Front row (l to r) Captain Clyde E Duncan (N), Captain James A 'Jimmy' Reinhard (CP), Major John Drost (AC); back row (l to r) Captain Stanley D Rock (R3), Captain William F Henderson (R1), and First Lieutenant Russell Lewis (R2). *via Colonel Johnny Drost*

Table 6-10. **Special ELINT Missions for RB-47H** 53-4291

Operation	Dates	Radar Type	Location
NEW BREED I	Jul-Sep 63	*Tall King*	Sakhalin Island
NEW BREED II	Jul-Sep 63	*Spoon Rest A*	
		Knife Rest B	Sea of Japan (SoJ)
NEW BREED III	Sep-Oct 63	*Tall King*	
		Spoon Rest A	Arctic above USSR
IRON LUNG	Oct 63	*Spoon Rest A*	Cuba
NEW BREED IV	Jan 64	*Spoon Rest A*	
		Knife Rest B	Arctic above USSR
IRON LUNG I	Jan-Sep 64		Yellow and East China Sea
IRON LUNG II	Feb-May 65		Yellow and East China Sea
LEAD OFF	Aug-Sep 65		Black Sea
HIGH PITCH	Jan-Mar 66		Yellow and East China Sea, SoJ
LOW PITCH	Sep 66		Cuba

October it added a new mission – IRON LUNG – and began operations around the periphery of Cuba. Additional missions over the next three years included LEAD OFF, HIGH PITCH, and LOW PITCH near the People's Republic of China and North Korea, as well as the Black Sea. During the last six months of 1965 it flew 12 sorties configured with a special dipole antenna. By 1966 the limits of the RB-47H had become apparent. Although it had the requisite range and duration aloft, it could not carry any additional equipment or crewmembers. In May 1967 the more capacious former RIVET STAND KC-135A 59-1465 replaced RB-47H 53-4291 and the mission was renamed BRIAR PATCH.

BONUS BABY

Of all the major intelligence missions associated with strategic reconnaissance, RB-47s were least involved in COMINT collection. They lacked the necessary room to carry the many linguists needed to monitor foreign-language radio broadcasts and operate the requisite equipment. Nonetheless, RB-47s were an important first step in the chain leading to platforms that served for 60 years during the Cold War and beyond.

Cold War COMINT programs trace their operational lineage to the Air Force Security Service (AFSS) and a lone RB-29A prototype (44-62290). By 1955 this led to DREAM BOAT RB-50Es converted under the HAYSTACK program and by 1957 to SUN VALLEY C-130A-IIs as part of the Airborne COMINT Reconnaissance Program (ACRP). These airplanes operated throughout Europe and in the Pacific theater along the coast of the Soviet Union (for the RB-50s) and in Europe (for the C-130s). Neither platform had the range, however, to fly 'over the top' from Alaska to England to collect intelligence from regions through which SAC's bombers would be expected to penetrate Soviet defenses, as well as monitor ongoing developments at the Soviet nuclear test sites on Novaya Zemlya Island. Moreover, the RB-50s and C-130s were slow, rendering them vulnerable to interception and attack by MiGs. These shortcomings necessitated the use of high-speed jets capable of air refueling.

The first known use of COMINT linguists on RB-47H missions took place in January 1959 from Thule AB as part of COOL STOOL. This successful initial evaluation led to the 1960 BONUS BABY program to carry COMINT equipment and two AFSS personnel in lieu of a full Raven complement. BONUS BABY missions flew throughout the Siberian Arctic between Eielson AFB and RAF Brize Norton, and along the Kamchatka Peninsula between Eielson AFB and Yokota AB. SAC assigned linguists to RB-47H missions on an *ad hoc* basis, and the program ended on 15th December 1962 when the RB-47Hs received the QRC-135A(T) automated recording system carried on BOX TOP sorties. All three of these RB-47H efforts demonstrated the value of COMINT collection on Arctic operations as well as self protection for the 'ferret', and led to the KC-135A-II OFFICE BOY COMINT platform.

Other Special Missions

In addition to ongoing reconnaissance missions, RB-47Hs flew a variety of special 'one off' missions. During August 1960, for example, RB-47Hs used their DF capabilities to track 'UHF SARAH', a UHF radio transmitter that simulated a search and rescue effort for a Mercury space capsule adrift at sea. The RB-47H was able to locate the radio accurately at 22nm (41km) while at 38,000ft (11,582m). On 21st September an ERB-47H (see below) was able to locate the transmitter accurately at 85nm (157km) and intermittently up to 115nm (213). In June 1964 two RB-47Hs helped find Soviet stations on ice islands floating in the Arctic Ocean as part of CAP PISTOL II. Once located, B-58s flew photographic missions over the ice stations. As part of the US commitment to the Central Treaty Organization (CENTO) which included Iran, Iraq, Pakistan, Turkey, and Great Britain, SAC participated in Shahbaz IX, the ninth annual CENTO exercise. From 2nd-4th December 1963, 55th SRW RB-47Hs

simulated attacking aircraft against targets in Iran and Turkey, flying nine sorties. Additional RB-47H missions took place during 1964 in Shahbaz X. On 14th and 15th July 1965, two RB-47Hs took part in ARTESIAN WELL to track a Soviet Tu-114 *Cleat* en route to New York City with a delegation to the United Nations (UN). No special signals were detected, just routine radio transmissions.

RB-47H INDIVIDUAL AIRCRAFT

53-4280 This was the Boeing prototype for the RB-47H. It served briefly with AMC and was not delivered to the 55th SRW until 24th July 1956. It was retired to MASDC on 27th May 1967. Noted with the name *Blue Nose Dog*.

53-4281 This airplane served as a reconnaissance testbed prior to its delivery to the 55th SRW. On 2nd August 1955 it was delivered to ARDC at Wright-Patterson AFB. After several modifications it was redesignated as a JRB-47H on 1st December 1955. It was finally transferred to the 55th SRW on 19th April 1956, although it retained the JRB-47H MDS until 30th November 1956 when it reverted to RB-47H. It was shot down on 1st July 1960 (see Appendix II).

53-4282 Delivered to the 55th SRW on 11th August 1955, and relegated to MASDC on 29th March 1967.

53-4283 Delivered to the 55th SRW on 5th August 1955 and crashed on 10th February 1956 (see Appendix II).

Left: This view of the underside of RB-47H 53-4280 shows the coloration of the many antennae covers. The aft ventral 'canoe' fairing was also black, as were the antennas just outboard of the #1 and #6 engines. *Author's collection*

Below: Radio-silent, fixed-time RB-47H launches were often unintentionally compromised by other aircraft waiting their turn, such as this PACAF F-105F at Yokota AB: 'Hey Tower, when is this RB-47 going to depart?' *Toshio Tagaya*

Bottom: This image shows the placement of the AN/APR-17 antenna outboard of the #6 engine. The E/RB-47Hs did not carry drop tanks and relied instead on air refueling to achieve the necessary range for their missions. *Author's collection*

53-4284 Delivered to the 55th SRW on 5th August 1955, and relegated to MASDC on 30th June 1967.
53-4285 Delivered to the 55th SRW on 5th August 1955. It participated in the HOME RUN overflights in 1956, and was relegated to MASDC on 14th July 1965.
53-4286 Delivered to the 55th SRW on 5th August 1955, and relegated to MASDC on 25th October 1965. Noted with the name *Goofy*.
53-4287 Delivered to the 55th SRW on 15th September 1955, and relegated to MASDC on 15th March 1967.
53-4288 Delivered to the 55th SRW on 8th September 1955, and relegated to MASDC on 21st July 1965. Noted with the name *Sweet Lips*.
53-4289 Delivered to the 55th SRW on 8th September 1955, and relegated to MASDC on 20th October 1965.
53-4290 Delivered to the 55th SRW on 2nd September 1955. It crashed on 27th April 1965 (see Appendix II).

Top: Two crews each from the 38th SRS and 343rd SRS flew missions in 53-4296 plus three other RB-47Hs during the HOME RUN overflights. *Author's collection*

Above: RB-47H 53-4296 left MASDC to serve as a testbed with Rockwell International, and was eventually placed on display at Eglin AFB, making it the most historically significant preserved B-47. *R L Lawson via William Y'Blood*

Below: This view of RB-47H 53-4301 landing at Yokota AB on 28th February 1966 shows the AN/APD-4 antennas in the aft end of the outboard engine pylons. The absence of the approach chute is notable. *Toshio Tagaya*

53-4291 Delivered to the 55th SRW on 7th September 1955, and relegated to MASDC on 5th January 1967. This was the NEW BREED 'Zot 1' aircraft for CIA missions.

53-4292 Delivered to the 55th SRW on 9th September 1955, and relegated to MASDC on 20th October 1965.

53-4293 Delivered to the 55th SRW on 6th September 1955, and relegated to MASDC on 6th October 1965.

53-4294 Delivered to the 55th SRW on 13th September 1955, and relegated to MASDC on 31st March 1967.

53-4295 Delivered to the 55th SRW on 15th November 1955. It participated in the HOME RUN overflights in 1956, and was relegated to MASDC on 5th January 1967.

53-4296 Delivered to the 55th SRW on 15th September 1955. It participated in the HOME RUN overflights in 1956, and was relegated to MASDC on 29th December 1967. It was later used for flight testing by Rockwell International. On display at the Air Force Armament Museum, Eglin AFB, Valparaiso, FL.

53-4297 Delivered to the 55th SRW on 12th October 1955. It crashed on 11th November 1962 (see Appendix II).

53-4298 Delivered to the 55th SRW on 16th November 1955, and relegated to MASDC on 11th August 1965.

53-4299 Delivered to the 55th SRW on 5th October 1955, and retired on 27th June 1966 for display at Salina, KS. Transferred in 1998 to the National Museum of the US Air Force, where it was restored and placed on display on 20th June 2005. Noted with the names *Dennis the Menace* and *Silver King*.

53-4300 Delivered to the 55th SRW on 5th October 1955, and relegated to MASDC on 8th December 1965. Noted with the name *Honorable Susie*.

53-4301 Delivered to the 55th SRW on 11th October 1955, and relegated to MASDC on 23rd March 1967.

53-4302 Delivered to the 55th SRW on 5th October 1955, and relegated to MASDC on 30th June 1967. Noted with the name *Playboys Playmate*.

53-4303 Delivered to the 55th SRW on 21st October 1955 It participated in the HOME RUN overflights in 1956, and was relegated to MASDC on 25th May 1967. Noted with the name *Queenie*.

53-4304 Delivered to the 55th SRW on 2nd November 1955, and relegated to MASDC on 17th November 1965.

53-4305 Delivered to the 55th SRW on 7th October 1955, and relegated to MASDC on 13th October 1965.

53-4306 Delivered to the 55th SRW on 5th October 1955, and relegated to MASDC on 25th August 1965.

53-4307 Delivered to the 55th SRW on 11th October 1955, and relegated to MASDC on 6th July 1965.

53-4308 Delivered to the 55th SRW on 23rd November 1955, and relegated to MASDC on 4th February 1966.

53-4309 Delivered to the 55th SRW on 15th November 1955. It crashed on 29th April 1960 (see Appendix II)

53-6247 Delivered to the 55th SRW on 18th January 1957, and relegated to MASDC on 27th October 1965.

53-6248 Delivered to the 55th SRW on 17th January 1957. It crashed on 27th October 1962 (see Appendix II).

Other named RB-47Hs included *Foot's Follies*, *The Joy Boys*, and *The Donkey Barbecue*

Top: On final approach to Yokota AB on 6th April 1967, RB-47H 53-4302 shows the proximity of the approach chute to the airplane. *Toshio Tagaya*

Above left: 53-4302 suffered a landing mishap at Andersen AFB, but was returned to service. *Author's collection*

Above right: Two unidentified RB-47Hs sport nose art and a shark's mouth at Eielson AFB during 1960. Crew for *The Donkey Barbecue* was under the command of Lieutenant Colonel Hobart Mattison, who later flew the RB-47H attacked by North Korea. *Ken Celander, author's collection*

ERB-47H

On 5th July 1955 SAC requested five additional RB-47Hs, three of which would be specially configured as ERB-47Hs. The mission of this new variant was 'a flying laboratory type ECM ferret to be used for electronic search for new and unusual types and uses of signals, and investigation and confirmation of electronic intelligence obtained from normal ferret operations.' These provided more detailed on-site analysis of SOIs. In many ways these airplanes were the precursor to the RC-135U COMBAT SENT.

Three ERB-47Hs (53-6245, -6246, and -6249), drawn from the 1955 RB-47H acquisition, were modified in 1956 under Project MISSING LINK, and delivered in 1957. Externally the ERB-47H was initially indistinguishable from the RB-47H. Eventually a small antenna for the AN/APS-54 detection system was added on the bottom of the nose radome, as were two additional small tail-mounted radomes. The ERB-47H used the same AN/APD-4 D/E/F-band DF collection gear as the RB-47H. Additional high-gain search antennas were included and provisions made for a special DF antenna. The ERB-47Hs did not carry the external AN/ALD-4 pod. They utilized the MB-1A bomb/nav system with AN/APS-64 radar. In addition to the standard flight crew, the ERB-47Hs carried only two Ravens. During the early 1960s they were redesignated as ER-47Hs or E-47Hs, which reverted to ERB-47H by 1965.

The first known deployment of an ERB-47H was on 23rd January 1958 when 53-6245 arrived at RAF Mildenhall. It was joined by 53-6246 on 1st February, and they both went to Adana AB in an effort to collect ICBM telemetry. This proved unsatisfactory, leading to the

rapid conversion of the EB-47E(TT) TELL TWOs. ERB-47H 53-6246 returned to Incirlik AB in early 1966 for temporary use as a proficiency trainer for the TELL TWO crews following the loss of 53-2320 in 1965. It was not configured to record telemetry. The ERB-47Hs often operated in conjunction with RB-47Hs (described above), and deployed for missions to each of the four main 55th SRW OLs.

An example of the unique laboratory nature of the ERB-47Hs was the installation of the QRC-185 Data Link Interceptor Receiver, which was 'designed specifically to intercept, analyze, and record Soviet Union Type "A" Data Link transmissions as part of the Soviet Semi-Automatic Air Defense System (SSADS).' This operated in the 90-160 megacycle range and was installed on ERB-47H 53-6249.

ERB-47H INDIVIDUAL AIRCRAFT
53-6245 Delivered to the 55th SRW on 23rd December 1957, and relegated to MASDC on 7th September 1967.
53-6246 Delivered to the 55th SRW on 19th December 1957, and relegated to MASDC on 9th January 1967.
53-6249 Delivered to the 55th SRW on 23rd December 1957, and relegated to MASDC on 11th January 1967.

Above: ERB-47H 53-6246 briefly served in an unsuccessful attempt to collect TELINT, a mission eventually undertaken by the TELL TWO. It also acted as a trainer for the TELL TWO crews at Incirlik AB. It is seen here during a mission preflight. *Author's collection*

Bottom: The ERB-47H was intended as a 'flying laboratory' designed to collect fine-grain ELINT rather than the more generalized 'vacuum cleaner' mission of the RB-47H, and was a precursor to the RC-135U COMBAT SENT. *Author's collection*

The TELL TWO Program

The 4th October 1957 launch of *Sputnik* from the Baikonur Cosmodrome in the Soviet Union led to US fears and Soviet boasts that Russian intercontinental ballistic missiles (ICBMs) could hurl atom bombs at New York and London, shocking the American public and leaders alike and spawning the fictitious 'Missile Gap.' Hard-line congressional Democrats, led by the likes of Texas Senator Lyndon B Johnson, claimed that the United States was not only behind the Soviets in developing a ballistic missile program (which was true) but that the Soviets were significantly ahead of the United States in missile technology and capability (which was false) and, most importantly, the United States was dangerously under-spending on strategic weapons and defense (which was equally false). In making these histrionic claims, Johnson and his colleagues were unaware of CIA U-2 photos of Soviet missile facilities, as well as other reliable intelligence sources, which showed that Soviet missile technology was clearly not ahead of the West. Nonetheless, this fictitious 'gap' created an urgent demand for accurate intelligence about the state of Soviet rocket and missile technology, and in turn a need for a dedicated TELINT platform designed to meet the needs of the CIA IRON WORK program to collect boost-phase telemetry sent by the rocket to Soviet scientists. The challenge, however, was not necessarily in converting a suitable airplane, but for the chosen airplane to be in the right place at the right time. SAC responded initially by assigning two specially configured ERB-47Hs delivered during late 1957 to the 55th SRW at Forbes AFB for interim IRON WORK TELINT needs. Almost immediately SAC recognized that the two ERB-47Hs could not adequately fulfill the TELINT mission, and started a replacement program in earnest.

Beginning in March 1958 Boeing converted three B-47Es (53-2315, 53-2316, and 53-2320) into EB-47E TELINT platforms at the company's Wichita facility. These three aircraft then replaced the two ERB-47Hs, prompting repeated and inaccurate reports that there were five TELINT EB-47Es. In September 1961 the three EB-47Es were redesignated as EB-47E(TT)s. The 'TT' suffix reflected their TELL TWO mission and should not be confused with the TEE TOWN ECM pods installed on 100 B-47E bombers, nor did it stand for 'TyuraTam', the name erroneously given by Western analysts to the Baikonur Cosmodrome where Soviet ballistic missiles were launched. The EB-47E(TT)s were assigned to the 55th SRW at Forbes AFB until 16th August 1966, at which time they moved with the wing to Offutt AFB, NE. They routinely operated from the 55th SRW's OL-4 at Incirlik AB. One was lost in a 1965 landing accident there, and the other two were retired in November 1967 to MASDC. In January 1969 they were 'reclaimed and dropped from the USAF inventory', a polite way of saying they were scrapped.

Operational History

TELL TWO operations from Incirlik AB exploited the base's close proximity to the major Soviet launch and test sites, ensuring a quick response time for the EB-47E(TT) to take off and arrive on station to observe the missile test under way. There were two main orbit areas, one over the Black Sea and the other over Iran, each optimized for collection for launches from Kapustin Yar and Tyuratam (Baikonur), respectively. To do this, one airplane was maintained on alert at all times, with both a primary and a back-up flight crew ready to fly and a third crew in reserve. A TELL TWO could be airborne within 15 minutes with the crew responding from anywhere on base such as the tennis courts, the Officer's Club, or the barracks (popularly known among the crews as the 'Middle East Holiday Inn'). For security purposes until 1959 the TELL TWOs reportedly had their full serial number removed upon arrival, which sometime led to maintenance being done on the wrong airplane!

On multiple occasions both deployed TELL TWOs were airborne at the same time. Once airborne, the TELL TWO orbited at its maximum altitude to improve its line-of-sight collection of TELINT sent by the missile (or relayed by Soviet ground stations) to the Soviet mission control. The primary SOIs included pre-burnout second-stage launch data, which revealed the range and payload capability of Soviet ICBMs.

Most historical accounts exclusively credit PHOTINT from CIA U-2 overflights of the USSR with identifying the weaknesses in Soviet ballistic missile capability, thereby ending the Missile Gap. This parochial view ignores, however, the role of other assets such as the TELL TWO and the intelligence derived from TELINT. In conjunction with a ground-based radar in Turkey, a clandestine US Navy aerial program operating in Pakistan, a US Navy program using Douglas A3Ds at Incirlik AB, and U-2 TELINT missions, TELL TWO airplanes collected intelligence demonstrating the foibles of Soviet missiles. Whereas the vaunted U-2 photos showed how *few* missiles the Soviets had and the extensive time needed to prepare and launch them, TELINT revealed just how *ineffective* those few missiles were,

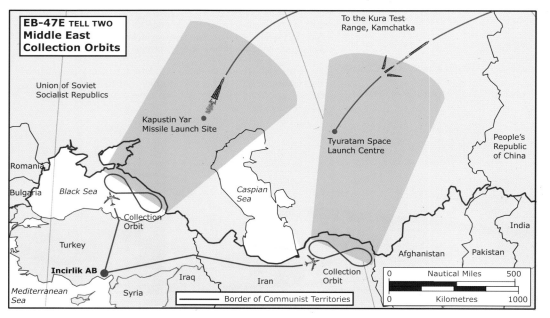

EB-47E TELL TWO Middle East Collection Orbits

To the Kura Test Range, Kamchatka

Union of Soviet Socialist Republics

Kapustin Yar Missile Launch Site

Tyuratam Space Launch Centre

People's Republic of China

Romania

Bulgaria

Black Sea

Caspian Sea

Collection Orbit

Turkey

India

Incirlik AB

Afghanistan   Pakistan

Iraq

Iran

Collection Orbit

Mediterranean Sea

Syria

| 0 | Nautical Miles | 500 |
| 0 | Kilometres | 1000 |

Border of Communist Territories

Left: The TELL TWO jets normally launched from Incirlik AB and operated in two different orbit areas depending on the expected Soviet launch site.

Opposite page, top: TELL TWO had a crew of five, with just two Ravens. This crew photo was taken at Incirlik AB with the early forward radome configuration. On the right is 55th SRW 'legend' Reggie Urschler, who retired as a Brigadier General. *Author's collection*

disarming critics such as Johnson who charged that the Soviets needed only the limited number of missiles shown in U-2 photographs because they were so accurate and powerful. The first ICBM TELINT collection took place in December 1958, with the first joint SAC-CIA collection on 9th June 1959 during a coordinated mission using both a CIA U-2 and a SAC EB-47E(TT) for the launch of an R-7 from Baikonur (a CIA history incorrectly records the launch site as Kapustin Yar). CIA pilot Jim Barnes flew his U-2 at high altitude over the Iranian and the Afghan borders with the USSR. The U-2's automated System VII collected 30 seconds of L-band TELINT prior to first stage burn, while the TELL TWO, flying at a lower altitude, was able to collect TELINT from the second stage using 'manned equipment'. The R-7 test proved to be a failure, as it landed 'far from its aim point.'

Not all SOIs were associated with ballistic missile launches. Beginning with the 2nd January 1959 launch of *Luna 1*, the first flyby of the moon, CIA U-2s and SAC TELL TWOs monitored Soviet space operations. On 18th March 1965, for example, an EB-47E(TT) crew detected the first Soviet space walk. In fact, TELL TWO TELINT contributed to the US technical understanding of how the Soviet spacecraft would actually work during the space walk. A TELL TWO crew tracked the launch of *Cosmos* 57 on 12th February 1965, an automated prototype of the *Voskhod* 2 spacecraft which cosmonaut Alexeii Leonov would use five weeks later, and was designed to test the operation of its airlock, a critical component of the planned space walk mission. *Cosmos* 57 was launched at 0730Z, with TELINT collection beginning 17 minutes later. By comparing this telemetry with that from previous *Cosmos* and *Voskhod* missions, CIA analysts were able to determine how the airlock worked. In addition to initial launch tracking of manned missions and satellites, the TELL TWO would often remain in its orbit for several hours after the Soviets launched a satellite from Baikonur. The TELL TWO was then able to collect the initial telemetry downlink from the satellite completing *its* initial orbit, a considerable intelligence coup.

TELL TWO operations were subject to political sensitivities. In late 1959 an RAF Canberra photographed an airborne TELL TWO while on an operational mission in its normal orbit over Iran, and these photographs were subsequently published in an Iranian newspaper. The flights had been previously known only to the Shah, the Iranian Defense Minister, and a senior air force general, and quickly became the focus of considerable Iranian criticism and indignation. Operational sorties were halted for about a month, although crew proficiency and training flights continued during this period. Operational reconnaissance flights resumed from Incirlik AB in early 1960 as the public clamor had run its course and died away.

A 1965 plan to base the two remaining TELL TWO aircraft and six crews permanently at Incirlik AB beginning in 1966 was canceled as US-Turkish relations soured due to pressure from the Soviet Union on the Turkish government to stop the flights in a 'show of fraternal amity'. In response to the loss of an RB-57F on 14th December 1965 (see below), the JCS suspended all aerial reconnaissance operations from Incirlik AB on 27th December. It is not clear from where the missions originated during 1966 – aircraft records show that 53-2315 and 53-2316 both deployed to Incirlik AB from January through April and September through November 1966, so perhaps the December 1965 JCS suspension was only temporary. The TELL TWO program officially relocated to OL-36 at Wheelus AB by 8th February 1967 and operated as part of the BURNING SAND Operational Order (OpOrd). Missions from OL-36 in the first half of 1967 were far fewer in number. TELL TWO 53-2315 deployed there from 6th January through 14th March 1967, and was replaced by 53-3216 from 11th March through 19th June 1967. Only two operational missions took place in April and two more in May. Flights from Wheelus AB

HALL   FORTIN   BIRMINGHAM   BROCKEL   URSCHLER

exclusively monitored the re-entry of the Soviet manned space flights. Political tensions in the Middle East made the continued presence of OL-36 untenable, and 53-2316 relocated to Torrejón AB, Spain, on 5th June 1967 due to the onset of the Arab-Israeli Six Day War. These missions now required air refueling because of the greater distances from the TELL TWO base to the orbit area. Given the short-notice launch warnings, this increased distance also adversely affected the aircraft's ability to be on station for the missile's launch. These flights also demanded sensitive political arrangements to allow the TELL TWO to overfly friendly nations, approval for which was by no means guaranteed. The long-distance missions were not as effective as their predecessors flown from Incirlik AB, and consequently Mediterranean TELL TWO operations ceased with the return of 53-2316 to Offutt AFB on 19th June 1967.

Other EB-47E(TT) operations included missions throughout the early 1960s from Hickam AFB, HI, in response to Soviet ballistic missiles fired into the Pacific Ocean. One such operation, known as PEGGY ANN, took place in June and July 1960. During the flights from Hickam AFB, the TELL TWO copilot used a large spectrographic camera to photograph the re-entry of ballistic objects. Other missions from Hickam AFB took place in September and October 1960. At the same time, 53-2315 deployed to Thule AB, Greenland – an unlikely location – for an unknown mission from 14th September through 19th October 1960, possibly for a sea-launched ballistic missile or a ground launch from Plesetsk in the USSR. Project BIG ARM, conducted in 1961, may have involved TELL TWOs, but this remains unconfirmed. Sorties were also flown from May through September 1966 from OL-5 at Wake Island (efforts to operate from Midway Island were compromised by the hazard posed by the numerous albatrosses which lived near the runway).

The EB-47E(TT) is reported to have operated in conjunction with the RC-135S. The TELL TWO, flying from Incirlik AB, collected launch data while the WANDA BELLE, flying from Shemya AFB, AK, collected re-entry data for the same event. Beginning in late 1965 the WANDA BELLE RC-135S underwent system upgrades and modifications, leaving a critical gap in reentry coverage over the Kura Test Range at Klyuchi, Kamchatka. From September through November 1966 both of the two remaining TELL TWOs relocated to Shemya AFB, and that program was renamed HAVE TELL. Fliers familiar with the weather at Shemya AFB and the B-47's poor abilities to handle significant crosswinds were adamantly opposed to this deployment, but it went ahead anyway. As predicted, a TELL TWO was nearly lost during landing at Shemya AFB but safely made it back to Eielson AFB. Crews for the EB-47E(TT)s were assigned to the 338th SRS, 55th SRW which was activated on 25th March 1967

Top and center: The early TELL TWO configuration by Boeing had two flat panel arrays mounted on the nose using two struts. Because they were modified from B-47Es, the TELL TWOs had the normal offset air refueling receptacle. Once at Incirlik AB crews often applied officially unapproved nose markings, in this case the ubiquitous Playboy Bunny with the name *The Playmate* on the flat panel array and a small crow above the crew entry door. Major Johnny Drost flew the 'Zot 1' NEW BREED missions. *John Kovacs, Author's collection*

Bottom: This crew photo shows the Douglas-Tulsa dipole on the nose (and the covered aft strut from the earlier version) as well as the flat panel array on the aft fuselage of another TELL TWO. Behind AC Major George E Baltes (l) is one of the A3Ds also used to collect TELINT. *Author's collection*

at Offutt AFB. With the return of the RC-135S, the HAVE TELL program was terminated, the 338th SRS was inactivated on 25th December 1967 and the two EB-47E(TT)s were relegated to MASDC.

The EB-47E(TT) carried a normal crew of five: pilot, copilot, navigator, and two electronic warfare officers (EWs – 'Ravens'). Pilots and navigators new to the squadron (or newly upgraded) would typically make their first operational deployment – or 'project' as they were then called – in a TELL TWO, gaining overseas operational experience in a comparatively 'safe' environment prior to deploying in an RB-47H on more demanding peripheral missions. Ravens, however, required mission certification in the RB-47H prior to a TELL TWO deployment. For any experienced crewmember a TELL TWO deployment was neither desirable nor bearable, as the attractions of 45-90 days in Turkey paled in comparison with a similar period spent by crews deployed in England or Japan. Due to the hazardous nature of the 'projects,' crews often received 'spot' promotions following their first mission, a benefit which certainly attenuated some of the disadvantages of deploying to Turkey.

Configurations varied between the three airplanes and throughout the lifetime of each TELL TWO. In the initial configuration delivered by Boeing, the aircraft had a large aerodynamically shaped rectangular box structure mounted on both sides of the forward fuselage. In later configurations undertaken by Douglas-Tulsa, this structure was replaced with large dipole antennas, one mounted on either side of the nose, although a box-shaped fairing appeared on each side of the aft fuselage in this later configuration. These functioned just like the forward antennas but for signals of different wavelengths. Similar, if not identical, antennas appeared on early COBRA BALL RC-135S configurations. The TELL TWO also had receivers mounted in the wingtips. All three aircraft had the bomb-bay crew pod similar to the Phase V capsule carried in EB-47Es and in the RB-47H. This pod contained a portion of the electronic mission equipment, as well as the Ravens who operated the reconnaissance gear, and was equipped with downward-firing ejection seats. During takeoff and landing the two Ravens sat in webbed sling seats mounted below and to the left of the pilot and copilot. The reconnaissance system was a series of fixed-frequency receivers connected to recording devices. The system had a limited ability to evaluate other pre-programmed frequencies and in these cases was controlled directly by one or both of the Ravens. In addition to monitoring the reconnaissance gear, the Ravens spent a great deal of time changing reels of recording tape, a routine if not boring job.

Operational Pressures

TELL TWO mission pacing was hectic, averaging 15-25 operational flights per month. Both 53-2315 and -2316 were airborne on 16th September 1963, for example, in anticipation of a planned Soviet launch from Tyuratam, but no launch took place. On 17th September 53-2316 was again airborne and monitored the launch of an SS-8 *Sasin* ICBM, which was reported to President Kennedy the following morning in his Top Secret 'President's Daily Brief' (PDB), emphasizing the importance of the flights. Another mission using both TELL TWOs took place on 18th October 1963, and tracked the launch of the *Cosmos* 20 PHOTINT satellite. TELL TWO 53-2315 landed after flying 6+55 hours, but 53-2316 received 35,000 lb (15,876kg) of fuel and remained on station to monitor the first orbital downlinks from the satellite, and landed 10 hours after takeoff. During the last six months of 1964 the EB-47E(TT)s flew 111 missions from OL-4. This dropped to 86 missions and 582+35 hours for the first half of 1965, then surged to 121 missions for the latter half of 1965. The TELL TWOs also flew 16 search and rescue missions for the lost RB-57F in December 1965.

These heavy demands proved disastrous as TELL TWO 53-2320 crashed while attempting to land on 3rd April 1965 at Incirlik AB following an operational mission. Crosswinds were gusting at 31-32 knots, substantially above the B-47's crosswind limit of 25 knots. Given the particularly sensitive nature of the equipment on board and TELL TWO mission there were no authorized divert bases. Further, there were no tankers available to refuel the TELL TWO as it orbited waiting for the crosswinds to subside. With its fuel nearly exhausted, just before noon ground commanders decided to attempt a landing despite the out-of-limit crosswinds. Following a smooth approach, the aircraft bounced slightly upon touchdown, at which time a gust of wind caught the upwind wing and caused the other wing to dip, dragging the #6 engine pod. The pilot applied the appropriate recovery procedures, but the J47 engines' slow spool-up time and asymmetric thrust due to the loss of the #6 engine doomed the airplane. About 100ft (30m) in the air and now well to the right of the runway (in fact, approaching the alert fighter hangars), it stalled and crashed. The navigator was killed in the crash, and the Raven 2 died of his injuries some 30 hours later. Another TELL TWO suffered a nearly identical fate while landing at Shemya AFB in high crosswinds (mentioned above). It was damaged but the pilot was able to recover and fly the airplane back to Eielson AFB where it landed safely. It underwent repair and returned to service. Although there is a natural tendency to blame the pilots for these landing accidents, it must be remembered that existing operational procedures forced the pilot, crew, and airplane into an unrealistic situation beyond their capabilities. Operational pressure to land the TELL TWO at its primary base overrode sound flying judgment to divert to a suitable alternate, a situation similar to one in March 1981 which claimed COBRA BALL II and six lives at Shemya AFB.

Despite its success in collecting TELINT the TELL TWO had several significant weaknesses: inadequate expandability, limits on operations in crosswinds, and the lack of any real optical collection ability. The EB-47E(TT) had no room for any additional crewmembers or gear, especially the desired (and bulky) optical sensors. Most importantly, the TELL TWO had no measurement and signature intelligence (MASINT) capability beyond basic telemetry. A copilot wielding a hand-held camera offered little of intelligence value trying to photograph the missile only briefly and at an unacceptable distance. Few crews ever saw a launch. Advanced spectral, infrared, and ultraviolet cameras that were in use in the burgeoning American space program, however, could observe a missile's exhaust plume and could determine the chemical makeup of the fuel. High-speed optical film could allow for careful study of stage separation or other mechanical functions, as well as ascertain precise external dimensions that would reveal internal structures. In addition, the EB-47E(TT)s were optimized for boost-phase collection only, and could do little to provide intelligence on the re-entry phase which could reveal missile accuracy and warhead capability. Consequently, a variety of optical platforms were developed and tested to alleviate this shortcoming, although none of these were

Table 6-11. **EB-47E(TT) IRON WORK Missions, September 1963**

Date	Crew	Aircraft	Hours	Collection
04 Sep 63	Legard	53-2315	6+55	
05 Sep 63	Legard	53-2315	6+30	
10 Sep 63	Chambers	53-2316	6+20	
13 Sep 63	Smiley	53-2315	7+30	
13 Sep 63	Chambers	53-2316	7+20	
14 Sep 63	Smiley	53-2316	6+30	
16 Sep 63	Legard	53-2316	5+45	
16 Sep 63	Smiley	53-2315	6+45	
17 Sep 63	Legard	53-2316	7+15	SS-8 *Sasin* (R-9A) Baikonur - PDB*
18 Sep 63	Smiley	53-2315	7+05	
24 Sep 63	Gray	53-2316	7+35	
25 Sep 63	Smiley	53-2315	8+50	
26 Sep 63	Gray	53-2316	8+55	SS-7 *Sadler* (R-16U) Baikonur
28 Sep 63	Smiley	53-2315	8+00	SS-9 *Scarp* (R-36 8K67) Baikonur - PDB
30 Sep 63	Gray	53-2316	6+05	

* PDB (President's Daily Brief) indicates collection reported to US President John F Kennedy

applied to the TELL TWO. Most of these new systems were employed operationally on Air Force Systems Command (AFSC) JKC-135As in their support of American missile launches, including Project SKYSCRAPER, the Radiation Monitoring Program (RAMP), and the Terminal Radiation Program (TRAP).

In the early 1960s SAC decided to replace the 30-plus RB-47Hs with 10 BIG TEAM RC-135Bs for peripheral ELINT missions. The goal was to retire all the RB-47s by 1965, but delays in the BIG TEAM program caused this date to slip until 1967. While this ultimately resulted in a quantum improvement in SAC's ELINT collection capability, BIG TEAM was hardly suitable to replace the EB-47E(TT) for TELINT. Consequently, SAC planned to retain the TELL TWO through 1970. Finding a suitable replacement was a convoluted process.

In addition to TELL TWO operations from Turkey and NANCY RAE missions from Alaska, the US Navy conducted ICBM TELINT missions from Peshawar, Pakistan. Little is known about these missions, which collected mid-phase telemetry, other than that they earned the wrath of the Pakistani government following repeated violations of restricted airspace over Pakistan and India, as well as reports of unacceptable crew behavior while on the ground. Following their eviction, Pakistan agreed to undertake the flights provided they were made in airplanes owned by the Pakistan Air Force (PAF) and flown by Pakistani crews. This led to the conversion by BIG SAFARI of two B-57Bs known as PEE WEE I (52-1536) and PEE WEE II (52-1573). In addition to a longer nose, the all-black B-57Bs had a large dipole antenna on either side of the forward fuselage. These were in operation throughout 1963 and early 1964 as part of the LITTLE CLOUD program. At the same time, USAF began conversion of the first two RB-57Fs from B-57Bs (52-1559 became 63-13286 and 53-3864 became 63-13287). These were both PEE WEE III aircraft and were designed eventually to replace the two PAF PEE WEE B-57Bs, and became operational in early 1964.

During 1963 SAC evaluated the PEE WEE 1 RB-57B to replace the TELL TWO but determined that it was unsatisfactory. The following year the Air Force recommended that SAC replace the TELL TWO with three PEE WEE III RB-57Fs. The SAC airplanes were part of the LITTLE DUKE program, distinguishing them from the PAF LITTLE CLOUD aircraft. SAC agreed enthusiastically, noting that the planned maximum altitude of 82,000ft (24,994m) for the RB-57F would significantly improve boost-phase collection for the IRON WORK program. The 3rd April 1965 crash of EB-47E(TT) 53-2320 added urgency to the replacement effort, as SAC argued that it could not meet its TELINT requirements with only two aircraft, assuming one was operational and the other was used for mandatory training and

proficiency flights, local maintenance, or at Douglas-Tulsa for programmed depot maintenance (PDM) and upgrades. (In October 1965 SAC directed that ERB-47H 53-6246 be reassigned to OL-4 at Incirlik AB for use in local training and pilot proficiency flights. It was not modified to fulfill the IRON WORK mission, and in any case did not arrive at OL-4 until early 1966.)

SAC had two choices: replace the destroyed TELL TWO with another modified B-47 from storage at Davis-Monthan AFB or opt to replace the two remaining EB-47E(TT)s with the LITTLE DUKE RB-57F. Either way, the soonest any new airplane would be available was late 1966 or early 1967. As an interim solution, SAC requested that four Military Air Transport Service (MATS) C-135Bs – soon to be replaced by Lockheed C-141s – be converted to TELL TWO follow-on aircraft, but nothing came of this request. SAC briefly considered replacing the TELL TWO with a Ryan 147E drone controlled by a GC-130, but this was rejected as too unreliable for a no-notice operation such as IRON WORK.

In September 1965 Air Force Logistics Command (AFLC) directed the conversion of three B-57s into the LITTLE DUKE RB-57Fs containing the BLACK FORCE sensor equipment. The airplanes were

scheduled for delivery in April, May, and June 1967. Despite official approval to proceed, funding was suspended pending completion of additional testing of the BLACK FORCE sensor suite. PEE WEE III RB-57F 63-13287 had returned to BIG SAFARI for PDM, and was equipped with the BLACK FORCE sensor for evaluation and operational flight tests. On 14th December 1965 this airplane and its US crew of two were lost over the Black Sea on its first evaluation flight, perhaps shot down by a Soviet SAM, almost certainly accidentally. It is not clear if this tragic event spelled the end for the LITTLE DUKE replacement of the TELL TWO, but no further efforts were made to acquire RB-57Fs, leaving SAC without an IRON WORK program to collect boost-phase TELINT until this was incorporated in the RC-135S COBRA BALL in the late 1990s.

EB-47E(TT) INDIVIDUAL AIRCRAFT

53-2315 Delivered to Boeing-Wichita for conversion to an EB-47E in May 1958, and officially redesignated as an EB-47E(TT) in September 1961. Relegated to MASDC on 30th November 1967.

53-2316 Delivered to Boeing-Wichita for conversion to an EB-47E in March 1958, and officially redesignated as an EB-47E(TT) in September 1961. Relegated to MASDC on 29th November 1967.

53-2320 Delivered to Boeing-Wichita for conversion to an EB-47E in May 1958, and officially redesignated as an EB-47E(TT) in September 1961. Crashed on 3rd April 1965 (see Appendix II).

Top: As with the RB-47s, the TELL TWOs did not carry external wing tanks. An unpainted flat panel radome is barely discernable on the side of the bomb bay. *Author's collection*

Center: Many of the airplanes which were once essential to gathering the intelligence upon which Western leaders made critical decisions found their way to storage – and eventual scrapping – at Davis Monthan AFB, including 53-2316. *USAF*

Bottom: 53-2320 shows the forward dipole antenna and aft flat panel array, as well as the extended bomb bay for the Raven compartment. Operational pressures contributed to its loss on 3rd April 1965 at Incirlik AB. *Author's collection*

Fact or Fiction?

There are persistent reports of two (perhaps three) B-47s converted by Lockheed-Marietta during the late 1950s for CIA overflights. Known as 'Black Beauties' for their all-black paint scheme, the airplanes were ostensibly part of a 1950s and 1960s CIA program. These unverified RB-47s reportedly had their wings lengthened considerably and their six General Electric J47 engines replaced with four Pratt & Whitney J57s or TF33s similar to the proposed YB-47C. Range of the airplane was said to be on a par with the U-2, and the CIA RB-47s could reach altitudes well above 60,000ft (18,288m). One supposedly crashed while on a training mission over Tennessee, and another was allegedly shot down over the USSR.

No credible aviation researchers believe in the existence of Black Beauty RB-47s, especially seconded to the CIA. However, some enthusiasts continue to argue that an 'ERB-47H' supposedly lost over the Caspian Sea in 1967 was in fact a CIA Black Beauty RB-47 operating from Iran. Others argue that the Tennessee accident was actually a cover story using the crash of an unspecified cargo plane. At least three KC-135 boom operators have independently sworn to the author they refueled such an airplane. One claimed that his tanker was ordered to orbit at a point just outside the USSR and refuel 'whatever showed up,' which happened to be an all-black B-47. Another asserted that he refueled an all-black B-47 near Alaska (when pressed he claimed he could distinguish an all-black B-47 from an RC-135 with a black wing). A third said the B-47 was used for missions against Cuba in 1958, but this makes little operational sense. In 1958 Cuba was still an 'American playground' under the absolute control of President Fulgencio Batista. There was no need for such a sophisticated aerial asset to collect what could easily have been gathered by wandering unimpeded around the island with cameras.

The name 'Black Beauty' was indeed associated with the B-47, but only as part of a $37 million subcontract to Douglas-Tulsa Aircraft Division to perform routine Inspect and Repair as Necessary (IRAN) maintenance on 204 standard B-47 bombers, and certainly not as part of some ultra-clandestine overflight program.

The Iran 'ERB-47H' loss is based on a visual report by an Iranian writer who claims to have seen the airframe in a junk pile near Teheran, Iran, and extracted a 20mm bullet without the shell from the wreckage. There has been no independent corroboration of this claim, and a published photo of the 20mm bullet proves nothing about its source. No loss of any of the three ERB-47Hs is known to have occurred; all three were retired and scrapped. All of the RB-47Hs have been similarly accounted for. Moreover, 55th SRW veterans have no knowledge whatsoever of any E/RB-47H operations from Iran or the loss of any E/RB-47Hs other than the ones previously discussed (although the Shabaz exercises cannot be overlooked entirely). As with the alleged ROBIN Canberra and the SLICK CHICK RF-100A Kapustin Yar overflight missions, claims of CIA RB-47s are almost certainly apocryphal.

Weather and Atmospheric Sampling Aircraft

Under the command of General LeMay SAC effectively became an autonomous, self-sufficient air force. It had its own fighters, bombers, transports, and supporting infrastructure. LeMay argued that SAC's mission was too vital and too complicated to be vulnerable to the shortcomings and different priorities of multiple commands. This singular vision contributed, in part, to SAC's desire to provide its own weather gathering capability tailored to supporting the command's primary mission of flying nuclear strike missions from bases in the United States, the United Kingdom, and the periphery of Asia. The most important operational requirement was to ascertain the weather over Canada, where the majority of US-based B-47s would air refuel. The weather data gathered by lower-flying Boeing

WB-50Ds proved wholly inadequate, especially at the higher altitudes where the B-47s would cruise (but this was in fact the altitudes where they would refuel, although LeMay discounted this argument). Consequently, SAC asked Boeing in 1953 for a dedicated weather version of the B-47. Development of this new platform proved challenging, so SAC settled on an interim weather collection system for delivery in mid-1954 with the ultimate version available for SAC operations in 1955. In addition, the Air Force's Air Weather Service had the primary aerial sampling mission to detect foreign atmospheric nuclear detonations. Given that they operated the same basic WB-50Ds as did SAC for its weather mission, it was not unreasonable to develop a sampling variant of the B-47.

RB-47K

SAC's requirements for its ultimate weather ship were demanding: the ability to determine (1) the airplane's absolute altitude within 50ft (15m); (2) the temperature, pressure, and humidity below the aircraft; (3) the height and bases of clouds; (4) the wind speed and direction below the aircraft; (5) improved flight level temperature measuring; (6) a camera with the ability to control the number of frames exposed over a given period; (7) a monitoring system to record the many observations; (8) an improved aerograph to maintain a continuous record of the atmosphere; and (9) radios to transmit weather data to the ground. The technological state of the art for this equipment was still in flux, and technical delays in each of these areas contributed to overall delays in the definition and procurement of SAC's ultimate weather ship.

As mid-1954 approached SAC still did not have its new weather platform nor was it likely to get one in the immediate future, so SAC requested that 15 RB-47Es be modified for the task. AMC and ARDC did not believe the weather equipment was sufficiently mature and recommended against the modification. They suggested deferring the modification work until 1957-58. SAC insisted, however, and on 5th November 1954 the Air Force ordered the 15 weather aircraft for SAC, designated as RB-47Ks. These rolled off the assembly lines as RB-47E-45-BW airplanes built to Boeing model 450-158-36 standards. Once modified for the weather mission they were redesignated as RB-47K-1-BWs.

Externally the RB-47K was no different than the RB-47E except that the flash ejector cartridge system was deleted and provisions made for the dropsonde dispenser. The weather reconnaissance system consisted of weather cameras and measurement devices. The optical equipment included a DR2A-M cloud study camera to photograph the clouds (or absence of clouds) along the airplane's route of flight. The cloud study camera moved through an arc of 71° and took photographs at the extreme left, center, and extreme right positions. With each exposure a strobotron in the recording chamber flashed, supplying the necessary light to record pertinent data (film frame, time, and a data card) from the recording chamber on each film exposure. In lieu of sophisticated devices to record multiple weather observations made repeatedly over the course of a multi-hour flight, SAC settled on simply taking a picture of the instrument displays. These instruments were located near the navigator's station, and at regular intervals a DR2A-M weather data monitoring camera snapped a picture of the actual instrument readout – crude but effective. Both cameras had a wide-angle 35mm focal length f/2 lens, and a magazine capacity of 200ft (61m) of 35mm film. Overall the RB-47K was equipped with five cameras (forward, left and right oblique, and two vertical cameras), allowing it to function in a PHOTINT capacity as well, although its primary mission remained weather reconnaissance.

The RB-47K also incorporated a radio system composed of a dropsonde and an SCR-718-E radio altimeter. The AN/AMT-6

At first glance the RB-47K could be easily mistaken for an RB-47E. In fact the airplanes were nearly identical as the 'K model' was modified from the earlier 'E model.' *Courtesy Boeing*

dropsonde used the AN/AME-1 dispenser mounted in the strike camera compartment and an AN/AMR-1 receiver installed in the navigator's compartment. The dispenser carried eight dropsondes that were ejected at predetermined points throughout the mission. A parachute slowed the dropsonde's descent to 1500fpm (7.62mps). It recorded pressure, temperature, and humidity at various levels, all relayed back to the RB-47K and recorded on a moving strip chart.

All of the RB-47Ks were operated by the 338th SRS, 55th SRW at Forbes AFB, with the first airplane – 53-4265 – arriving on 13th December 1955. The same airplane was also the first to be retired to the 2704th AFSDG at Davis-Monthan AFB on 6th June 1963, with 53-4278 bringing the operational life of the RB-47K to a close when it flew to the 2704th AFSDG on 13th May 1964. As with the remaining RB-47s, they were known on paper as R-47Ks from 1960 through 1963, but to flight crews they remained RB-47Ks. Two airplanes – 53-4270 and 53-4272 – served as GRB-47K ground instructional trainers. A single RB-47K was lost on 27th September 1962 (see Appendix II).

The RB-47Ks were certainly less well known than the RB-47Hs which appeared routinely at overseas bases. Nonetheless, they were extremely busy, flying weather missions every day of the year. Crewmembers new to the reconnaissance world typically gained operational experience by flying these missions prior to moving on to the more demanding and dangerous RB-47H peripheral sorties. Flights departed early in the morning, flew north over Canada and then returned to Forbes AFB. Weather over Canada was extremely vital, as this was where SAC's bombers had their first air refueling

In addition to their weather collection mission, the RB-47Ks facilitated pilot transition to the RB-47H, including gaining proficiency in aerial refueling. Day-glo markings on the RB-47K and KC-135 show telltale fading. *Howard Hendry*

on their strike sorties, and the weather data was used each day to brief SAC alert crews on conditions to expect should their mission be launched. The WHOOPER CRANE – ALPHA weather sortie flew over Hudson Bay (8.5 hours unrefueled). Another sortie was WHOOPER CRANE – BRAVO, which reached Goose Bay (11.5 hours with refueling). Observations were taken every 20 minutes and transmitted to ground stations hourly, conditions permitting. The outbound altitude was 16,000ft (4,877m) – the altitude where the bomb-laden B-47s would refuel – and the return leg flown at 36,000ft (10,973m).

Perhaps the most important RB-47K missions were those that took place during the 1962 Cuban Missile Crisis (described below), where they provided both weather reconnaissance and surveillance of Russian shipping. There were also special missions flown to support various SAC exercises and other 'higher headquarters directed' requirements. Under a program known as GOLDEN JET (renamed PLANNED PARTY in October 1963), RB-47Ks provided weather data for SAC operational evaluations of its combat wings such as Unit Simulated Combat Missions (USCM) and Operational Readiness Inspections (ORI), as well as NORAD SNOW TIME penetration exercises. RB-47Ks provided photographic reconnaissance to locate suitable sites for future RBS Express (mobile radar bomb scoring unit) as part of GYPSY FIDDLE. Other missions included support for US government agencies. On 16th October 1963, for example, an RB-47K overflew the Aransas Wildlife Area to photograph national wildlife reservations along the Texas coastline on behalf of the Department of the Interior. In other cases, RB-47Ks assisted in emergency damage assessments (such as hurricanes or earthquakes). Following the 19th August 1963 mid-air collision of two B-47s over Irwin, IA, Captain Regis F Urschler's crew flew a short-notice photography mission on 22nd August in an effort to locate a missing crewmember.

RB-47Ks did not routinely deploy to overseas locations and instead operated from Forbes AFB. Exceptions included the September 1961 resumption of Soviet nuclear testing at the Novaya Zemlya site, prompting the shotgun arrival of four RB-47Ks at RAF Brize Norton (53-4266, 53-4267, 53-4270, and 53-4276), along with two additional RB-47Ks (53-4272 and 53-4274) passing through RAF Brize Norton en route to Incirlik AB. These movements suggest that the RB-47Ks were capable of atmospheric sampling, much like the WB-47Es used in the CONSTANT PHOENIX program (described below), although some former RB-47K crewmembers clearly reject this claim. Nonetheless, the declassified 1961 SAC History notes that 55th SRW RB-47s 'gathered stratospheric fallout samples during Soviet nuclear tests.' Perhaps the RB-47Ks simply monitored the weather patterns near the blast site to determine the spread of any fallout, leading to misidentification of its mission as 'sampling'.

Table 6-12. **RB-47Ks**

Serial	MDS 2	MDS 3	MDS 4	Date
53-4265	R-47K	RB-47K		
53-4266	R-47K	RB-47K		
53-4267	R-47K	RB-47K		
53-4268	R-47K	RB-47K		
53-4269	R-47K	RB-47K		
53-4270	R-47K	RB-47K	GRB-47K	18 Jun 63
53-4271	R-47K	RB-47K		
53-4272	R-47K	RB-47K	GRB-47K	18 Jun 63
53-4273	R-47K	RB-47K		
53-4274	R-47K	RB-47K		
53-4275	R-47K	RB-47K		
53-4276	R-47K	RB-47K		
53-4277	R-47K	RB-47K		
53-4278	R-47K	RB-47K		
53-4279	R-47K			27 Sep 62

Table 6-13. **RB-47K GREASED LIGHTNING Crews**

A/C	Crew #	Squadron	Date	Aircraft
Gmitter	E-69TT	343rd SRS	14 Oct 63	53-4275
Hicks	E-37TT	38th SRS	14 Oct 63	53-4278
McCoid	E-58	38th SRS	15 Oct 63	53-4278
Jones	S-49	38th SRS	15 Oct 63	53-4277
Creel	E-20TT	343rd SRS	*	

* This crew is believed to have flown missions from Shemya AFB

Additional deployments include those to Eielson AFB. On 10th October 1963, for example, 338th SRS Crew E-36 flew RB-47K 53-4276 to photograph 'certain areas of Alaska' as part of Operation NATIVE SKIES. A week later, three RB-47Ks (53-4275, 53-4277, and 53-4278) provided advance weather information for the record-setting flight from Tokyo to London of B-58A 61-2059 *Greased Lightning* on 16th October 1963. The RB-47Ks each flew two missions from Eielson AFB on 14th and 15th October, and one from Shemya AFB. Crews returned to Forbes AFB on 16th and 17th October. Diverting the airplanes and crews for this mission had the undesirable consequence of delaying ongoing photo training efforts!

Despite the paucity of overseas deployments, plans to send RB-47Ks to overseas locations to conduct 'fast reaction ... search and surveillance' operations were developed as part of OpOrd 264-64, known as BLUE FIN. Based on lessons learned from the Cuban Missile Crisis, BLUE FIN comprised three RB-47Ks 'with a complete camera configuration' and six mission crews (plus a mission-planning crew). BLUE FIN involved 'detection, identification, and surveillance of a specific surface vessel. Once the specific target is identified, constant surveillance will be maintained until release by Headquarters SAC.' The airplanes would fly standard search patterns until a ship was sighted, and then execute a series of photo passes beginning at 5,000ft (1,524m) then descending to 1,000ft (305m) while flying parallel to, then over, then abeam the vessel to obtain positive identification. Throughout this process the copilot would

take photographs using a hand-held camera. Special procedures were in place to refuel the RB-47K from a KC-135 'as needed' to maintain surveillance of the ship until relieved. A similar program known as WHITE LIGHTNING (OpOrd 100-64) provided for the deployment of six RB-47s 'of any available type' to Harmon AFB, Newfoundland, Kindley AB, Bermuda, and (if needed) Ramey AFB, PR. This mission would perform 'reconnaissance tasks' under periods of heightened international tensions, and included dedicated KC-135 tanker support from the 96th AREFS at Altus AFB, OK, and the 900th AREFS at Sheppard AFB, TX.

RB-47K INDIVIDUAL AIRCRAFT

53-4265 Rolled out as an RB-47E on 3rd June 1955, began conversion to RB-47K on 16th June 1955. Delivered to the 338th SRS on 13th December 1955. Relegated to the 2704th AFSDG on 6th June 1963, and scrapped by 3rd October 1969.

53-4266 Rolled out as an RB-47E on 9th June 1955, began conversion to RB-47K on 17th June 1955. Delivered to the 338th SRS on 21st December 1955. Relegated to the 2704th AFSDG on 11th June 1963, and scrapped by 3rd October 1969.

53-4267 Rolled out as an RB-47E on 14th June 1955, began conversion to RB-47K on 17th June 1955. Delivered to the 338th SRS on 25th January 1956. Relegated to the 2704th AFSDG on 11th June 1963, and scrapped by 3rd October 1969.

53-4268 Rolled out as an RB-47E on 16th June 1955, began conversion to RB-47K on 20th June 1955. Delivered to the 338th SRS on 7th January 1956. Relegated to the 2704th AFSDG on 13th June 1963, and scrapped by 3rd October 1969.

53-4269 Rolled out as an RB-47E on 21st June 1955, began conversion to RB-47K on 24th June 1955. Delivered to the 338th SRS on 26th January 1956. Relegated to the 2704th AFSDG on 13th June 1963, and scrapped by 3rd October 1969.

53-4270 Rolled out as an RB-47E on 24th June 1955, began conversion to RB-47K on 5th July 1955. Delivered to the 338th SRS on 13th January 1956. Relegated to GRB-47K on 18th June 1963 at Amarillo AFB, TX.

53-4271 Rolled out as an RB-47E on 27th June 1955, began conversion to RB-47K on 5th July 1955. Delivered to the 338th SRS on 13th February 1956. Relegated to the 2704th AFSDG on 6th May 1963, and scrapped by 3rd October 1969.

53-4272 Rolled out as an RB-47E on 1st July 1955, began conversion to RB-47K on 6th July 1955. Delivered to the 338th SRS on 13th February 1956. Relegated to GRB-47K on 18th June 1963 at Amarillo AFB, TX.

53-4273 Rolled out as an RB-47E on 5th July 1955, began conversion to RB-47K on 8th July 1955. Delivered to the 338th SRS on 26th March 1956. Relegated to the 2704th AFSDG on 6th May 1963, and scrapped by 3rd October 1969.

53-4274 Rolled out as an RB-47E on 8th July 1955, began conversion to RB-47K on 12th July 1955. Delivered to the 338th SRS on 26th March 1956. Relegated to the 2704th AFSDG on 12th May 1963, and scrapped by 3rd October 1969.

53-4275 Rolled out as an RB-47E on 12th July 1955, began conversion to RB-47K on 15th July 1955. Delivered to the 338th SRS on 29th February 1956. Relegated to the 2704th AFSDG on 6th May 1963, and scrapped by 3rd October 1969.

53-4276 Rolled out as an RB-47E on 15th July 1955, began conversion to RB-47K on 20th July 1955. Delivered to the 338th SRS on 28th February 1956. Relegated to the 2704th AFSDG on 12th May 1963, and scrapped by 3rd October 1969.

53-4277 Rolled out as an RB-47E on 19th July 1955, began conversion to RB-47K on 1st August 1955. Delivered to the 338th SRS on 28th February 1956. Noted with the nickname *Roadrunner*. Relegated to the 2704th AFSDG on 13th May 1963, and scrapped by 3rd October 1969.

53-4278 Rolled out as an RB-47E on 22nd July 1955, began conversion to RB-47K on 1st August 1955. Delivered to the 338th SRS on 23rd March 1956. Noted with the nickname *San Fernando Red*. Relegated to the 2704th AFSDG on 13th May 1963, and scrapped by 3rd October 1969.

53-4279 Rolled out as an RB-47E on 27th July 1955, began conversion to RB-47K on 3rd August 1955. Delivered to the 338th SRS on 29th February 1956. Crashed on takeoff from Forbes AFB on 27th September 1962, killing the three crewmen (see Appendix II).

55th SRW flight crews acquired flying time and experience on RB-47K WHOOPER CRANE weather missions over Canada. They would then transition back to RB-47H ELINT missions. 53-4278 seen at Davis-Monthan AFB on 5th October 1967. *Stephen Miller*

WB-47B/E

The RB-47Ks provided a dedicated source to meet SAC's weather requirements, but – not surprisingly – SAC was loath to make them available for the aerial weather missions of other military and civil agencies. Moreover, the promise of weather satellites under development in the late 1950s and early 1960s spelled a decreased demand for an expensive dedicated aerial weather reconnaissance fleet. Satellites could photograph large swaths of the Earth's surface, revealing cloud cover and, using multiple images over time, actually show movement of large weather patterns. Similarly, the proliferation of ground weather stations, especially in remote areas, increased the number of reporting sites for data such as barometric pressure and local winds. Until these satellites reached maturity, however, the USAF's Air Weather Service (AWS) and its aerial component under the Military Air Transport Service [MATS, redesignated Military Airlift Command (MAC) on 1st January 1966] relied on a variety of weather airplanes such as the Boeing WB-50 and WC-135, Lockheed WC-130, Martin/General Dynamics WB-57, and two variants of the WB-47.

The 'Hurricane Hunter'

During 1954 three Category Four Hurricanes – Carol, Edna, and Hazel – hammered the east coast of the United States in quick succession, with Hazel passing directly over Washington, DC. Hazel's 110mph (177kph) winds reached as far inland as Ontario, Canada, and carved a path of destruction that left over 600 dead with damages exceeding $350 million. In August 1955 two more powerful hurricanes – Connie and Diane – again pummeled the east coast, with Diane earning the notoriety of being the first hurricane to cause over a billion dollars in damage. In the wake of Diane, President Eisenhower created the Presidential Commission on Storm Modification, an initiative that led in 1956 to Congress authorizing the US Weather Bureau to create the National Hurricane Research Project (NHRP) to improve understanding of the meteorology of hurricanes and thereby enhance forecasting and early warning.

The sole WB-47B initially carried just the logo of the National Hurricane Research Project (NHRP) on its nose, but later acquired more distinctive paint schemes.
Howard Hendry

Hurricane experts Robert Simpson (l) and Cecil Gentry (r) stand beneath the emblem of the NHRP. The center of the stylized hurricane is part of the building and not part of the emblem.
Author's collection

In 1956 the Air Force loaned the Weather Bureau three airplanes – two Douglas DC-6Bs N6539C and N6540C and B-47B 51-2115. Tracing the history of the B-47 is confusing at best. Records show it was assigned to MATS on 16th March 1956. From 20th March until 21st September 1956, it was transferred from the 19th BW to General Precision Laboratories (GPL) in Pleasantville, NY. Curiously, it returned to SAC on 10th December 1956 with the 321st BW and then back to GPL on 5th March 1957 through 4th May 1957. The airplane was then assigned to the 321st BW from 4th May to 4th June 1957, followed by another stint with the 19th BW until 22nd August 1957 when it was assigned to the 55th WRS at McClellan AFB, CA, suggesting inaccurate record keeping as NHRP records show the airplane flew its first mission into Hurricane Audrey sometime between 25th and 29th June 1957! Records indicate the earliest reference to 'WB-47B' was 5th March 1957 but official documents show the MDS change to WB-47B took place on 30th April 1958. This 'merry-go-round' assignment history and the conflicting operational dates can be attributed to SAC crews flying the weather missions in 1956 and SAC's expertise in maintaining the B-47, as well as AWS crew training pending 51-2115's final transfer to the AWS. Although it was assigned on paper to the 55th WRS, it operated as part of the 59th Weather Reconnaissance Squadron (WRS) at Kindley AB, along with two WB-50s (46-0007 and 46-0032). The unit, known as the 'Hurricane Hunters', was under the scientific leadership of noted hurricane expert Robert Simpson. The WB-47B operated using the static call sign *Gull 2115*.

GPL modifications included installation of AN/APN-81 navigation equipment. While flying above the outflow layer, the airplane was instrumented to take temperature, humidity, and pressure measurements, later to be punched onto computer cards for analysis. It also carried an on-board radarscope which was photographed at regular intervals.

Researchers sought to describe the three-dimensional structure of hurricanes, as well as monitor the middle- and upper-level winds which were thought to steer the storm, and hence better predict the hurricane's path. To do this the WB-47B penetrated multiple storms – it was the only WB-47 of any variant authorized to do so – accruing 126.5 flying hours *inside* hurricanes. AWS records indicate that it penetrated Hurricanes Betsy, Dora, Ethel, Flosie, and Greta in 1956. In June 1957 the WB-47 flew into Hurricane Audrey, which formed so quickly that only 51-2115 was able to get airborne in time to make a single flight before Audrey made landfall in Louisiana. Subsequent flights included 17th September 1957 into Hurricane Carrie, followed five days later into Hurricane Frieda. The 1958 season included flights on 18th August into Hurricane Cleo, a week later three flights into Hurricane Daisy, and finally Hurricane Helene on 26th September. The flights provided important scientific data on subjects such as mean atmospheric soundings, hurricane rainfall distributions, storm surge surveys, and radar descriptions of hurricane structure.

The NHRP operated the two WB-50s and the WB-47 on loan from the Air Force, which raised complications about maintenance, safety, and compliance with regulations. During 1958 these two organizations agreed that NHRP would only operate civilian aircraft (such as the DC-6s) and that the WB-50s and WB-47 would return to Air Force duties. The Air Force replaced 51-2115 by donating JB-57A 52-1419 (N1005) to the NHRP as a civilian 'WB-57A'.

Beginning in November 1958, 51-2115 was relocated to the 55th WRS at McClellan AFB and continued general weather collection duties. Among these was calibrating the accuracy of newly introduced weather satellites, in particular TIROS II, launched 23rd December 1960. Flying at 40,000ft (12,192m), the WB-47B overflew the same location as the satellite which orbited at an altitude of 400nm (741km). Simultaneous photographs were compared to evaluate the precision

and clarity of the satellite images. The airplane was quietly retired from operational use on 15th August 1963 and it became a GB-47B training airframe for the student mechanics at Amarillo AFB, TX.

This airplane is often attributed to Project STORMFURY, but this association is suspect and unlikely. The US Weather Bureau created STORMFURY in 1962 as part of a radical scientific program aimed at altering the weather. This involved artificial stimulation of convection outside the hurricane eye wall through seeding with silver iodide. The artificially invigorated convection, it was believed, would compete with the convection in the original eye wall, lead to reformation of the eye wall at a larger radius, and thus produce a decrease in the maximum wind. The original results appeared to be promising, but later were discounted due to flaws in the basic science and understanding of hurricanes. STORMFURY became operational in 1963, with the first flights between 17th-20th August, two days after WB-47B 51-2115 was retired from flight duties and permanently grounded in Texas. No STORMFURY missions were flown between 1964 and 1968. On 7th August 1968 WB-47E 51-2427 flew a

Top left: WB-47B 51-2115 appears in its first 'colorful' scheme. Curiously, both SAC and AWS crews operated the airplane and it was assigned to a variety of units throughout its brief career. *John Bessette*

Top right: During later 1958 JB-57A 52-1419 (N1005) replaced the WB-47B in an effort to eliminate 'military' aircraft from the NHRP fleet. *George Letzer via Stephen Miller*

STORMFURY monitoring sortie from Ramey AFB, PR. During 1969 another unspecified WB-47E took part in a STORMFURY mission as a weather monitor using the static call sign *Stormfury Juliett*.

Above: Final paint scheme on 51-2115 seen at Andrews AFB in December 1962, when it was assigned to traditional weather-gathering duties at McClellan AFB. *Robert Mikesh via Stephen Miller*

Above right: Despite claims to the contrary, 51-2115 did not participate in the STORMFURY program, which began two days after the WB-47B was retired. *Author's collection*

Right: WB-47Es did take part in the STORMFURY program, as depicted in these drawings of two experiments conducted during the 1969 hurricane season. Unlike the WB-47B, they did not penetrate the hurricane.

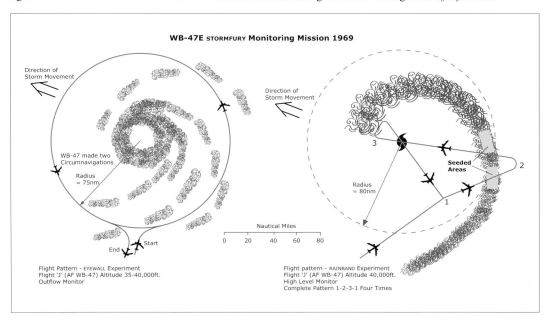

An Improved Platform

By 1960 the AWS WB-50s suffered from airframe fatigue – fuel leaks grounded the fleet at one point – and the inability to fly at high altitudes and for extended durations. Plans in early 1960 to reduce the AWS even further garnered the immediate attention of CINCSAC General Thomas S Power, who not only opposed this reduction but suggested that the WB-50s be replaced by retiring SAC B-47s. LeMay, now Air Force Vice Chief of Staff, endorsed this idea, as did MATS commander Lieutenant General William 'Bill' Tunner and even the commander-in-chief of Pacific Command, Admiral Harry D Felt. In May 1960 the Air Staff reversed its decision to make further cuts in the AWS fleet and approved the conversion from WB-50D to WB-47Es.

SAC's success with the RB-47K made the B-47 an attractive choice. First of all, it was readily available, as B-47Es were being withdrawn from bomber duties and could be quickly converted. Secondly, its higher performance meant it would more nearly match the operating environment of the majority of USAF aircraft, gathering data at altitudes up to 40,000ft (12,192m) frequented by the ever-increasing jet community. Finally, the B-47 offered significant operational savings compared to its predecessor. A WB-47E took 50% less time to do the same job as the WB-50, for example, with projected savings of some $88,000 per month per airplane. Despite these obvious advantages AWS was reluctant to accept the WB-47 given the B-47's history of structural problems. Indeed, AWS agreed to take the WB-47s provided they did not conduct hurricane penetrations, leaving this riskier mission to its fleet of WC-130s.

In 1961 Lockheed Marietta was awarded contract AF34(601)13150 to modify 34 B-47Es into WB-47Es as part of the BIG BLUE program. Of these, 13 were from the 4347th CCTW and 11 were from the 306th BW, reflecting the decreased importance of the B-47 versus the B-52 and ballistic missiles. The first airplane – 51-2373 – began modification on 28th May 1962 and was completed ten months later on 15th March 1963, although it was not delivered to McClellan AFB until 20th March. Subsequent conversions took far less time, ranging from three to four months, although the shortage of assembly line slots meant that airplanes were frequently stored at Lockheed-Marietta's plant for several months prior to modification. In May 1963, for example, 11 B-47Es were stored pending conversion.

As late as March 1964 several Lockheed documents relating to the WB-47E refer to the airplane as the W-47E, in line with the 1960 DoD directive that the 'B for bomber' mission be removed from airplanes associated with reconnaissance (e.g., R-47H, R-47K, etc.). Notable among these was the 'W-47E Partial Flight Document,' which served as the basis for the WB-47E Dash One. No other DoD or MATS documents (including the WB-47E Dash One) have been located to corroborate this, so operational use of 'W-47E' should be undertaken with healthy skepticism.

In 1963 the Air Weather Service became the DoD's 'single manager for atmospheric sampling and daily airborne [weather] operations,' although SAC retained its RB-47Ks for 'strategic weather reconnaissance'. AWS planners believed that the WB-47E would achieve a large measure of success through automation, so the WB-47 carried a crew of three compared to 10 on the WB-50. Computers, which were still large and temperamental, formed the basis of the WB-47E's airborne data systems. Lockheed installed four computerized subsystems: horizontal measurement, vertical measurement, data handling, and communications. The core of this automated capability was the Bendix-Friez AN/AMQ-19 Meteorological (MET) System, developed initially by the Systems Engineering Group and the Aeronautical Systems Division (ASD) of the Air Force Systems Command (AFSC).

The horizontal component incorporated a new AN/APN-102 Doppler navigation system and an AN/ASN-6 computer to provide accurate wind data and aircraft position. A Rosemount Total Temperature Probe, accurate to ±1°C, was installed on the left forward fuselage. Additional instruments, including an MA-1 Pressure Altimeter, collected pressure and dew point information. The existing AN/APS-64 search radar was modified by removing the BNS components and configured for routine navigation and storm detection, while the AN/APN-42A radar altimeter relayed absolute height data to the MET system. The vertical component utilized an AN/AME-3 dispenser installed where the tail guns were previously located. This carried nine AN/AMT-13 dropsondes. When ejected at 30,000ft (9,144m), each dropsonde would descend via parachute to the surface in approximately seven to nine minutes while relaying temperature, pressure, and humidity data back to the WB-47. The AN/AMQ-19 receiver in the aircraft locked onto the instrument less than one second after ejection and maintained contact throughout the drop.

The data handling and communication subsystems were the most crucial components of the new equipment. The copilot served as the 'Meteorological Officer' (MO), making cloud observations, controlling the release of the dropsondes, and transmitting the weather data to ground stations. The gunnery panel was replaced with the appropriate weather system controls. All raw data went on magnetic tape where it was placed in buffer storage, although the MO would manually enter cloud observations. It was then transmitted via the AN/ARC-65 single side-band (SSB) radio to a ground station, which accomplished the final data reduction. The intent of this new communications system was to eliminate the errors which accrued due to manual transmission via Morse code from WB-50s to ground stations; however, the MET system was never trouble free. In spite of extensive reliability testing, the 55th WRS devoted much of its training time exclusively to troubleshooting the equipment. By the latter half of 1964 the horizontal system was so unpredictable that the MO had to make and record all observations manually. Some former crewmembers report that the MET system never worked. In 1968 most of the vertical system was removed and afterward, the WB-47E could only complete its weather mission in the horizontal plane, one factor contributing to its retirement the following year.

Other WB-47E modifications included deletion of the tail armament (replaced by the dropsonde dispenser), wing tanks and associated plumbing, and the in-flight refueling capability. Air sampling scoops (U-1 and I-2 foil systems) and related equipment were added inside and outside the bomb bay. These modifications reduced the overall weight of the airplane by nearly 60,000 lb (27,216kg), allowing for better range despite the absence of drop tanks. Navigation systems were improved with the addition of the AN/APN-70 LORAN.

AWS received the prototype WB-47E on 20th March 1963 when 51-2373 arrived at the 55th WRS at McClellan AFB. The first operational WB-47E – 51-2360 – was delivered to the 55th WRS on 24th May 1963, and the final WB-47E – 51-7066 – was delivered on 15th November. The 55th WRS provided all initial and recurrent training for AWS WB-47 crewmembers. The airplanes were originally assigned to four squadrons and a detachment, although this evolved over time.

The WB-47E was quickly pressed into service, with its first operational mission accomplished on 6th June 1963. On 27th October 1963 a WB-47E flew its first typhoon reconnaissance. The first hurricane mission for the WB-47E took place on 28th August 1964 for Hurricane Cleo. The WB-47E, unlike the earlier WB-47B, was not intended to penetrate the hurricane to collect weather data. Instead, the WB-47E mission was to pinpoint the location of the hurricane by flying above it and reporting on the location of the eye.

Right: Pacific theater commanders strongly supported acquiring the WB-47E to meet regional weather collection and sampling requirements, leading to a regular presence at Hickam AFB. *Nick Williams*

Below: The WB-47Es were stripped of all unnecessary weight, including wing tanks, tail guns, air refueling gear, and other bomber-specific items. This gave it the range and altitude which SAC wanted in its bombers. *USAF via William Y'Blood*

Above left: Much of the computerized meteorological gear was placed in the unused ATO compartments. ECM antennas remained but the equipment was removed. *Author's collection*

Above : Removing the BNS not only reduced weight but allowed many WB-47 flights – such as Alaska to California – to take place without a navigator. This image shows the open radome to good effect. *Author's collection*

Left: Even at lighter operating weight the WB-47E used water injection for takeoff, especially at hot locales such as Hickam AFB or Andersen AFB. *N E Williams*

Top: Basing the WB-47Es at McClellan AFB not only offered the advantage of easy access to the Pacific theater, but the base housed part of the Air Force Technical Applications Center (AFTAC), responsible for CONSTANT PHOENIX sampling, a WB-47 mission that is often overlooked. *USAF*

Below: Captain Robert Bailey, Major Dale Sutherland, and Captain David McGrath from the 53rd WRS prepare to monitor Hurricane Dora in September 1964. Bailey and McGrath wear Senior Pilot wings, and Sutherland has Command Pilot wings, attesting to the high accrual of flight time and the experience of WB-47 fliers. *Author's collection*

Consequently, WB-47Es flew through weaker portions of the hurricane, but not to the extent of missions flown by WC-130s. The 53rd WRS flew coordinated storm missions out of Hunter AFB, GA, with WB-50s flying at 10,000ft (3,048m) and the WB-47Es operating at 30-40,000ft (9,144-12,192m). The 54th WRS flew typhoon missions out of Andersen AFB, Guam, in a similar manner.

WB-47Es flew a total of approximately 18,000nm (33,336km) on daily missions at 18,000ft (5,486m). The crews took observations at 150nm (278km) intervals and released dropsondes every 450nm (833km). Flights were made along standard routes (or tracks) with pre-determined weather observation points. The tracks were named for native birds, although some names were replaced to meet air traffic control requirements that names be five or fewer letters.

In addition to these regular duties, the airplanes assisted with overseas fighter and troop deployments. The first such use of WB-47Es took place in October 1963 in support of Exercise BIG LIFT, a North Atlantic Treaty Organization (NATO) strategic mobility test. Later that year WB-47Es provided weather advisories for Operation SHIKSHA, a joint India-US-UK-Australian air defense training exercise. Fighter 'drags' to Southeast Asia prompted WB-47E missions to the planned refueling areas. A 'pathfinder' sortie made a weather observation 12 hours prior to the planned fighter takeoff, with a 'scout' sortie repeating this at 3.5 hours before takeoff.

WB-47E missions were an integral but unheralded part of the air war in Southeast Asia. The first such mission took place on 7th August 1965 from Clark AB, Philippines, to gather weather data for ARC LIGHT B-52 refueling tracks. Beginning in July 1966 the newly established Det 2, 57th WRS at Clark AB provided twice daily weather surveys of SAC ARC LIGHT B-52 and YOUNG TIGER KC-135 refueling tracks. The 53rd WRS at Hunter AFB had conducted these weather missions while on temporary duty (TDY), so it made sense to relocate the unit entirely and seven WB-47Es were reassigned to Clark AB. Missions – using the static call sign *Loon 99* – were flown at 26,000ft (7,925m), the standard air refueling altitude for B-52s. These sorties were not insignificant, with the WB-47s logging 3,800 hours in FY68 and 4,296 hours in FY69.

Thousands of hours were flown in support of satellite and missile recovery programs. During the first six months of 1961, for example,

Det. 2, 55th WRS flew 73 missions as part of Project DISCOVERER. Later operations included COLD MISS sorties to verify weather conditions in the recovery area for the Fairchild JC-119 recovery aircraft that collected the photo package ejected by CORONA satellites. During the days of the early manned spacecraft flights WB-47Es scouted the weather in the capsule recovery areas. Other unusual WB-47 missions included 54th WRS aircraft participating in fog dispersal experiments at Elmendorf AFB, AK, during the winter of 1967-68. WB-47Es of the 53rd WRS flew sampling missions during 1968 to gather ash from an erupting volcano in Costa Rica.

CONSTANT PHOENIX

Although direct detection and monitoring – spies, photographs, and the like – of the Soviet atomic weapons programs was the most desirable evidence of Soviet progress, the only easily accessible information came from indirect detection and monitoring by long-range aerial weather reconnaissance. These efforts date to September 1947 when US Secretary of War Kenneth C Royal announced that

Above: The black U-1 sampling scoop is visible on WB-47E 51-2417. This collected atmospheric particulate matter released following a nuclear explosion, but it was primarily used to establish a baseline level to compare with any possible detonation. *USAF*

Below: WB-47s typically flew an aggregate total of 18,000nm (33,336km) per day over established tracks. These flights provided daily weather and sampling updates, but were eventually supplemented by weather satellites. *Author's collection*

Table 6-14. **WB-47E Units**

Squadron	Wing	Base	From	To	Route Names/Comments
53rd WRS	9th WRG	Kindley AB, Bermuda	08 Jan 62	01 Jul 63	Gull Gull Sierra - Cuba Weather Easy Aces - replaced Gull Sierra
53rd WRS	9th WRG	Hunter AFB, GA	31 Aug 63	08 Jul 65	Gull Easy Aces
53rd WRS	9th WRW	Hunter AFB, GA	09 Jul 65	14 Jun 66	Gull Easy Aces
53rd WRS	9th WRW	Ramey AFB, Puerto Rico	15 Jun 66		Gull
54th WRS	9th WRG	Andersen AFB, Guam	18 Apr 62	30 Jun 65	Vulture (later Swan)
54th WRS	9th WRW	Andersen AFB, Guam	09 Jul 65	Sep 65	WB-47Es to Hickam AFB Sep 65
55th WRS	9th WRG	McClellan AFB, CA	08 Jan 62	08 Jul 65	Lark Lark Victor - McClellan AFB to Hawai'i
55th WRS	9th WRW	McClellan AFB, CA	09 Jul 65	01 Nov 69	
Det 1		Eielson AFB, AK			Ptarmigan (later Stork) - Alaska to North Pole Loon - Bering Sea to Japan Loon Alpha - Alaska to Hawai'i
Det 2		Hickam AFB, HI		Sep 65	
Det 3		Kindley AB, Bermuda			
56th WRS	9th WRG	Yokota AB, Japan		08 Jul 65	Buzzard (later Robin)
56th WRS	9th WRW	Yokota AB, Japan	09 Jul 65	66	
57th WRS	9th WRW	Hickam AFB, HI	15 Sep 65	10 Nov 69	Petrel - Hawai'i to Equator North to Alaska
Det 2		Clark AB, Philippines	08 Jul 66	68	

overall responsibility for the Long Range Detection Program (LRDP) would be assigned to the Army Air Force, and on 16th September 1947 the newly constituted US Air Force was charged 'with responsibility for detecting atomic bomb explosions,' creating the CONSTANT PHOENIX aerial sampling program.

By July 1948 AWS WB-29s carried special filters to collect radioactive materials from the atmosphere. The first Soviet atomic test – Operation FIRST LIGHTNING – on 29th August 1949 was detected five days later by WB-29 44-62214 from the 375th Weather Squadron (WS) flying over the Northern Pacific Ocean. Sampling included the 'retrieval of microscopic pieces of the bomb itself, which [were] subjected to radiochemistry to analyze the materials used,' and has since become an essential ingredient in nuclear test ban agreements. These missions proved extremely effective and demonstrated 'outstanding success in collecting good early [atomic] debris samples.' The WB-29s were supplanted by WB-50s for the daily flights along fixed routes selected because of their likelihood to detect radioactive particles released into the atmosphere after an atomic test. Other missions covered high-altitude sampling [such as SAC's High Altitude Sampling Program (HASP) U-2 missions as part of the

CROWFLIGHT program] and low-altitude sampling (beginning with Convair B-36 SEA FISH missions that were eventually replaced by GIANT FISH B-52s) flown over the Pacific Ocean and in the Arctic region at altitudes near 2,500ft (762m).

On 31st August 1961 LeMay – now Air Force Chief of Staff – declared that the AWS would be the DoD single manager for all sampling operations effective 1st April 1962, excluding SAC's U-2 HASP mission. WB-47Es undertook air sampling missions on behalf of the Atomic Energy Commission (AEC), Defense Atomic Support Agency (DASA), Public Health Service (PHS), Air Force Technical Applications Center (AFTAC) and other agencies. The atmospheric research equipment (ARE) included the U-1 and I-2B foil system, a B-400 rate meter, and a gaseous collection system. A Special Equipment Operator (SEO) from AFTAC operated the system which was located at the instructor navigator's position.

A typical sampling mission from Eielson AFB departed north at 18,000ft (5,486m) at the 500mb level, then climbing to 30,000ft (9,144m) at the 300mb level, and finally reaching 39,000ft (11,887m) at the 200mb level. If the crew detected any indications of possible nuclear residue they were authorized to follow it across Canada,

Top left: Eielson AFB was a crucial WB-47 base, with standard tracks to McClellan AFB, Hickam AFB, and Yokota AB. They provided both weather data and were the first to reveal Soviet or Red Chinese nuclear tests. *Author's collection*

Top right: Majors Richard L 'Dick' Purdum and Don 'Tiny' Malm deliver 51-2362 to MASDC on 24th October 1969. It had just completed IRAN. *Author's collection*

Center: 51-7066 seen less than a month after its final flight on 30th October 1969 to the Seattle Museum of Flight, where it remains on display. *Jim Morrow via Stephen Miller*

Bottom: According to MASDC records, 51-2414 made the final WB-47E flight on 31st October 1969 from Hickam AFB to Davis-Monthan AFB, eclipsing the Museum of Flight's WB-47E by one day. *N E Williams*

landing at Goose Bay. In later years this sampling capability was deleted from the aircraft and the mission taken over by WC-135Bs.

The WB-47Es had a rather long life considering they were near the end of their operational careers when they began their new role. One airplane (51-2402) flown by Det 1, 55th WRS logged well over 6,000 hours. When converted to a WB-47E it had already accrued over 3,100 hours of SAC bomber flying, and passed the 4,000-, 5,000-, and 6,000-hour marks while flying weather tracks out of Eielson AFB. At that point it was the high time airplane for all B-47s. Indeed, the WB-47s were among the highest of all B-47s in terms of total flight hours.

Reductions in the WB-47E fleet began in 1965 with the arrival of the WC-135B. Five were retired in 1965 (replaced by an equal number of WC-130Es), and one each in 1966 and in 1967. Four WB-47Es were lost in accidents. On 25th August 1969 Air Weather Service Commander Major General Russell K Pierce, Jr, directed the immediate retirement of the remaining WB-47E fleet as part of the AWS contribution to a $1 billion reduction in the USAF budget for FY70. Pierce's action may have been in response to Air Force Chief of Staff General John D 'Jack' Ryan's well-known dislike for the AWS mission – a contempt echoed decades later when another Chief of Staff, General Merrill A 'Tony' McPeak, abruptly cut funding for the WC-135 mission. The final ARC LIGHT support mission took place on 5th September 1969. This placed considerable strain on AWS operations, especially in SEA, compelling the WC-130 and WC-135B fleets to work harder. The B-47 had always been cramped, and the WC-135s that replaced them had larger crews and much more room in which they could work. The newer airplanes obviously had fewer flying hours so offered improved maintenance reliability, an important consideration given the global operations and daily demand on the airplanes and crew.

The WB-47Es were the last B-47 of any Air Force variant to see operational service, so competing claims of the 'final flight' should not be surprising. On 24th October 1969 Majors Richard L 'Dick' Purdum and Don 'Tiny' Malm flew 51-2362 from Douglas-Tulsa AP, where it had just completed IRAN, to MASDC, retiring a completely refurbished airplane! Lieutenant Colonels Raymond Hamilton and William Payton flew 51-7066 from Hickam AFB to McClellan AFB on 29th October 1969. The following day they flew it to Renton, WA, where it was handed over to the Museum of Flight. According to the MASDC records, however, the final flight of a WB-47E took place on 31st October 1969 when 51-2414 arrived at Davis-Monthan AFB, AZ, after a non-stop flight from Hickam AFB.

WB-47B/E INDIVIDUAL AIRCRAFT

51-2115 Transferred from the 19th BW on 16th March 1956 for conversion into the sole WB-47B. Assigned to the 59th WRS at Kindley AB, Bermuda, through November 1958 when it was transferred to the 55th WRS at McClellan AFB. It was retired in August 1963 and used as a ground instructional trainer.

51-2358 Transferred from the 306th BW for conversion into a WB-47E on 1st March 1963. Delivered to the 55th WRS Detachment at Eielson AFB on 29th July 1963. Retired to MASDC on 9th September 1969.

51-2360 Transferred from the 96th BW for conversion into a WB-47E on 7th January 1963, and delivered to the 55th WRS at McClellan AFB on 24th May 1963. Retired to static display at New England Air Museum, Windsor Locks, CT, in June 1967, and in October 2002 was moved to the Heritage Museum at Hill AFB, UT (see Appendix III).

51-2362 Transferred from the 306th BW for conversion into a WB-47E on 28th February 1963. Delivered to the 55th WRS Detachment at Eielson AFB on 19th July 1963. Retired to MASDC on 24th October 1969.

51-2363 Transferred from the 4347th CCTW for conversion into a WB-47E on 6th May 1963. Delivered to the 56th WRS at Yokota AB on 27th September 1963. Retired to MASDC on 13th September 1969.

51-2366 Transferred from the 4347th CCTW for conversion into a WB-47E on 9th April 1963. Delivered to the 53rd WRS at Hunter AFB on 30th August 1963. Scrapped in place after nose gear collapsed upon landing at Clark AB, Philippines, on 20th June 1967 (see Appendix II).

51-2369 Transferred from the 4347th CCTW for conversion into a WB-47E on 25th March 1963. Delivered to 54th WRS at Andersen AFB on 23rd August 1963. Retired to MASDC on 1st July 1965.

51-2373 This former AFLC B-47 was the prototype WB-47E. It entered modification on 28th May 1962, which was completed on 15th March 1963. It flew to the 55th WRS at McClellan AFB on 20th March. Retired to MASDC on 15th October 1969.

51-2375 Transferred from the 4347th CCTW for conversion into a WB-47E on 15th April 1963. Delivered to the 53rd WRS at Hunter AFB on 6th September 1963. Retired to MASDC on 15th October 1969 (it was flown to MASDC on 14th October but was not accessioned until the following day).

51-2380 Transferred from the 4347th CCTW for conversion into a WB-47E on 25th April 1963. Delivered to the 53rd WRS at Hunter AFB on 13th September 1963. Retired to MASDC on 9th September 1969.

51-2383 Transferred from the 306th BW for conversion into a WB-47E on 1st February 1963. Delivered to the 55th WRS at McClellan AFB on 7th June 1963. Retired to MASDC on 3rd May 1965.

51-2385 Transferred from the 4347th CCTW for conversion into a WB-47E on 14th May 1963. Delivered to the 53rd WRS at Hunter AFB on 4th October 1963. Retired to MASDC on 30th June 1966.

51-2387 Transferred from the 4347th CCTW for conversion into a WB-47E on 29th April 1963. Delivered to the 56th WRS at Yokota AB on 20th September 1963. Retired to static display at Oklahoma City State Fairgrounds, Oklahoma City, OK, on 6th October 1969, but relocated on 29th June 2005 to the Kansas Aviation Museum in Wichita, KS (see Appendix III).

51-2390 Transferred from the 306th BW for conversion into a WB-47E on 19th February 1963. Delivered to the 55th WRS at McClellan AFB on 5th July 1963. Retired to MASDC on 13th September 1969.

51-2396 Transferred from the 306th BW for conversion into a WB-47E on 12th March 1963. Delivered to the 55th WRS at McClellan AFB on 9th August 1963. Retired to MASDC on 2nd July 1965.

51-2397 Transferred from the 4347th CCTW for conversion into a WB-47E on 16th May 1963. Delivered to AWS 53rd WRS at Hunter AFB on 11th October 1963. Crashed at Ramey AFB, PR, on 5th December 1966 (see Appendix II)

51-2402 Transferred from the 306th BW for conversion into a WB-47E on 26th February 1963. Delivered to the 55th WRS at McClellan AFB on 12th July 1963. Retired to MASDC on 12th September 1969.

51-2406 Transferred from the 306th BW for conversion into a WB-47E on 6th February 1963. Delivered to the 55th WRS at McClellan AFB on 14th June 1963. Retired to MASDC on 10th September 1969.

51-2408 Transferred from the 306th BW for conversion into a WB-47E on 7th March 1963. Delivered to the 54th WRS at Andersen AFB on 31st July 1963. It was reassigned to the APGC at Eglin AFB on 30th June 1965.

Starboard rear quarter view of WB-47B 51-2115 shows the stylized paint scheme. Curiously, the airplane has the approach and brake chutes still attached after shutting down. *Author's collection*

Above: 55th WRS WB-47E 51-2373 clears the active runway at Hickam AFB on 23rd April 1969, just six months before the fleet would be retired. *Stephen Miller*

Left: Several WB-47s have been preserved, including 51-2387 which resided first in Oklahoma City and then in Wichita. *Gordon Macadie*

Below left: 51-2397 lands at Yokota AB on 13th August 1965. It crashed at Ramey AFB on 5th December 1966. *Toshio Tagaya*

Bottom left: By mid 1969 senior Air Force leadership had little interest in a weather fleet made up of WB-47s, WB-57s, WC-130s, and WC-135s, and hastily retired the WB-47 fleet as a cost saving measure. *Author's collection*

Bottom right: For many SAC B-47 pilots accustomed to cold Northern Tier bases, an assignment to WB-47s offered a warm respite at locations such as Hickam AFB. *Author's collection*

Opposite: WB-47Es were in service from 1963 until 1966, when they were supplanted by WC-135Bs. 51-7063 sits next to its replacement at McClellan AFB on 17th October 1967. *Stephen Miller*

51-2412 Transferred from the 4347th CCTW for conversion into a WB-47E on 21st May 1963. Delivered to the 53rd WRS at Hunter AFB on 18th October 1963. Retired to MASDC on 8th September 1969.

51-2413 Transferred from the 4347th CCTW for conversion into a WB-47E on 9th May 1963. Delivered to the 56th WRS at Yokota AB on 27th September 1963. Retired to MASDC on 9th September 1969.

51-2414 Transferred from the 4347th CCTW for conversion into a WB-47E on 4th April 1963. Delivered to the 54th WRS at Andersen AFB on 23rd August 1963. Retired to MASDC on 31st October 1969.

51-2415 Transferred from the 68th BW for conversion into a WB-47E on 17th January 1963. Delivered to the 55th WRS at McClellan AFB on 31st May 1963. Retired to MASDC on 8th September 1969.

51-2417 Transferred from the 68th BW for conversion into a WB-47E on 28th January 1963. Delivered to the 55th WRS at McClellan AFB on 31st May 1963. Retired to MASDC on 12th September 1969.

51-2420 Transferred from the 68th BW for conversion into a WB-47E on 4th February 1963. Delivered to the 55th WRS at McClellan AFB on 14th June 1963. Ran out of fuel and crash-landed at Lajes Field, Azores, on 10th November 1963 (see Appendix II).

51-2427 Transferred from the 4347th CCTW for conversion into a WB-47E on 23rd May 1963. Delivered to the 53rd WRS at Hunter AFB on 25th October 1963. Retired to MASDC on 7th September 1969.

51-2435 Transferred from the 306th BW for conversion into a WB-47E on 12th February 1963. Delivered to the 55th WRS at McClellan AFB on 21st June 1963. Retired to MASDC on 8th September 1969.

51-5218 Transferred from the 4347th CCTW for conversion into a WB-47E on 27th May 1963. Delivered to the 53rd WRS at Hunter AFB on 26th October 1963. Retired to MASDC on 10th September 1969.

51-5257 Transferred from the 68th BW for conversion into a WB-47E on 14th February 1963. Delivered to the 55th WRS on 28th June 1963. Retired to MASDC on 10th September 1969.

51-7021 Transferred from the 68th BW for conversion into a WB-47E on 25th February 1963. Delivered to the 55th WRS at McClellan AFB on 5th July 1963. Retired to MASDC on 7th September 1969.

51-7046 Transferred from the 301st BW for conversion into a WB-47E on 5th June 1963. Delivered to the 53rd WRS at Hunter AFB on 31st October 1963. Retired to MASDC on 8th September 1969.

51-7049 Transferred from the 301st BW for conversion into a WB-47E on 5th March 1963. Delivered to the 55th WRS Detachment at Eielson AFB on 26th July 1963. Stalled during takeoff at Eielson AFB, AK, on 21st April 1964 (see Appendix II).

51-7058 Transferred from the 306th BW for conversion into a WB-47E on 14th March 1963. Delivered to the 54th WRS at Andersen AFB on 16th August 1963. Transferred from the 53rd WRS at Ramey AFB on 30th June 1969 to Douglas-Tulsa for PDM, but was relocated to OCAMA at Tinker AFB on 11th October, and marked for reclamation there on 12th October 1969.

51-7063 Transferred from the 301st BW for conversion into a WB-47E on 25th June 1963. Delivered to the 55th WRS at McClellan AFB on 15th November 1963. Retired to MASDC on 13th September 1969.

51-7066 Transferred from the 376th BW for conversion into a WB-47E on 17th June 1963. Delivered to the 54th WRS at Andersen AFB on 8th November 1963. On 30th October 1969 it flew to Renton, WA, where it was put on display at the Museum of Flight.

The Missiles of October

Of the October 1962 Cuban missile crisis Ray Cline, the head of the CIA's Directorate of Intelligence at the time, wrote, 'I cannot imagine a more intimate linking of [aerial] intelligence in all functional categories with the highest level of decision making.' It has become almost cliché to think of the crisis as the exclusive domain of the U-2 which gathered the majority of the photographs that informed presidential decisions and made front-page headlines. Excellent histories such as William Ecker's *Blue Moon Over Cuba* and Michael Dobbs' *One Minute to Midnight* have shown both the important role of US Navy Vought RF-8s in gathering low-altitude photographs as

well as the previously unknown presence and threat of Soviet nuclear weapons in Cuba. Both have hinted at the contributions of RB-47s to peaceful resolution of the crisis, but a full story remains untold.

SAC's participation in Cuban reconnaissance began as early as 1960 to develop a baseline electronic order of battle. An RB-47H flew sorties on 14th and 17th November to determine if the Cubans had received MiG-17PF *Fresco-Ds*. Results of the missions were negative. Increasing concerns over the transfer of Soviet military gear to Cuba prompted two RB-47H ELINT missions on 1st May 1962 'in the Caribbean area'. These identified significant electronic emissions from Soviet-built radars and weapons tracking and guidance gear. One of these sorties, flying 40nm (74km) south of the westernmost tip of Cuba, detected a *Scan Odd* radar, the first time this signal had been noted in Cuba, confirming the presence of radar-equipped MiG-17 *Frescos* or MiG-19 *Farmers*. That same month SAC's Ryan 147 drones and GC-130 motherships began QUICK FOX overflights of the island out of MacDill AFB, FL (SAC transferred this mission to TAC on 4th November 1962). These drone operations may have been the source of rumors erroneously suggesting that QB-47s took part in overflights of Cuba.

SAC's COMMON CAUSE RB-47H ELINT missions began on 14th September 1962. During the nine-hour flight, an RB-47H was refueled once by a KC-135 from the 96th Air Refueling Squadron (AREFS) at Altus AFB, OK. Known pejoratively as 'Lost Cause' missions, these were initially completely overt, with an unclassified flight plan filed with Air Traffic Control (ATC) for a round-trip flight between Forbes AFB and Key West, FL. Upon reaching Key West, however, the RB-47H would request ATC to approve a 'local clearance', where it would then fly peripherally near or around Cuba, exercising caution to avoid Cuban airspace or triggering an aerial response by Cuban interceptors. Should it be necessary, US fighter coverage was available from aircraft on 5-minute alert from NAS Leeward Point at Guantánamo Bay, Cuba, or Homestead AFB, FL. Moreover, the RB-47H was authorized to 'fire to destroy' any hostile interceptor should it attack. All RB-47s flying COMMON CAUSE missions were required to have a fully operational gunnery system or else they were to abort the flight (typical of the global BOX TOP sorties as well). Once the peripheral portion of the mission was complete the RB-47H would update its flight plan with ATC and begin the homeward leg of the flight back to Forbes AFB.

Four additional COMMON CAUSE missions took place prior to 14th October when tasking changed to two missions per day, including flights from MacDill AFB. Double missions were flown over the next week, although there were no missions on 16th October. After a brief

Although CIA and SAC U-2s have received the lion's share of credit for reconnaissance during the Cuban Missile Crisis, US Navy RF-8 Crusaders and 55th SRW RB-47s were an integral part of safely resolving the crisis. *Toshio Tagaya*

stand-down, a single mission was flown each day from 23rd through 25th October. Beginning on 26th October COMMON CAUSE missions increased to three a day, which continued until 22nd November, when they were reduced to a single sortie. Between September and November, RB-47Hs flew 116 COMMON CAUSE sorties totaling 1,065+20 hours.

Weather reconnaissance RB-47Ks were equally busy during the Cuban Missile Crisis. Tropical Storm Ella had formed southeast of Cuba on 14th October, the same day that RB-47Ks started one or two daily six-hour BLUE INK missions from MacDill AFB, gathering weather data for use in planning SAC U-2 BRASS KNOB overflights as well as tactical low-level missions. During each mission the RB-47K circumnavigated Cuba. Weather data were relayed in real time via HF radio to SAC headquarters. Ella reached hurricane strength on 17th October as it moved northward along the US coast. Through 26th October, 18 BLUE INK missions took place. After a pause in U-2 sorties following the loss of Major Rudolf Anderson, Jr, in U-2F 56-6676 to an SA-2 on 27th October, missions resumed on 1st November. By the end of the month 54 additional missions were flown. On 11th November, however, RB-47H 53-4297 crashed on a BLUE INK mission while departing MacDill AFB in place of an RB-47K that had returned to Forbes AFB for a camera modification (see Appendix II). In addition to weather reconnaissance missions in the vicinity of Cuba, three RB-47Ks flew WHOOPER CRANE-BRAVO sorties from Plattsburgh AFB, NY, beginning 30th October, to assess the weather in the northeast refueling areas.

COMMON CAUSE and BLUE INK missions were not without risk from interception. Surprisingly, however, the greatest threat was not to the RB-47s but to US fighters that tracked or 'locked on' to the airplanes while on patrol. In one night incident an RB-47H very nearly fired on a US interceptor engaged in a 'tail chase,' unaware that it was a friendly aircraft. Authorized to 'shoot to kill' in the event his airplane was under attack, the copilot was able to determine at the last moment that the interceptor was American. Subsequently, all aircraft (other than overflights) were required to use normal IFF procedures. Moreover, all USAF and Navy tactical aircraft were warned 'to stay clear of the RB-47 tail area.' On 28th October Second Air Force planners at Barksdale AFB recommended that fighters escort all COMMON CAUSE missions, but SAC Headquarters rejected this proposal.

The loss of Major Anderson and his U-2 on 27th October raised serious concerns about the tracking of the U-2s, both by US and hostile radars. US radar could reach an altitude of 100,000ft (30,480m) and as far as 218nm (404km) from Key West, easily tracking a U-2. Unfortunately, this radar could not provide 'flight following', which included both tracking and 'surveillance of the vicinity so friendly aircraft could be warned of [an impending] hostile act.' Moreover, the radar offered no warning capability of a SAM launch. Given the short time between SAM launch and impact, any warning would have to come from pre-launch ELINT or COMINT from the launch crews and their command node. Consequently, RB-47Hs were tasked to fly a route parallel to the U-2 track but no closer than 50nm (93km) from the Cuban coastline. In addition to its ELINT role, the USS *Oxford* provided COMINT warning advisory support.

In fact, a COMMON CAUSE RB-47H sortie detected the launch preparations for the SA-2 which shot down Major Anderson. Under the command of Captain Stan Willson, the crew detected a variety of Soviet radar signals including the *Spoon Rest* SA-2 target acquisition radar. Shortly thereafter they detected signals from a *Fruit Set* fire-control radar, indicating that an SA-2 was being prepared to launch against a target. The Ravens determined that it originated from a known SAM site near Banes – precisely where Major Anderson's U-2 was flying – although the Ravens were unaware of this. The RB-47H copilot broadcast the code words 'Big Cigar' to SAC headquarters, warning of a prospective launch. Unfortunately, there was no mechanism in place to warn Major Anderson directly.

RB-47s also took part in BLUE BANNER missions, a sea surveillance initiative designed to identify and track all merchant shipping in the central Atlantic in an effort to spot any Soviet ships (or those of its allies) that might be carrying offensive weapons to Cuba. Five RB-47s departed Forbes AFB before dawn on 25th October. Mission routing was from Forbes AFB to Bermuda for air refueling, additional sea search followed by another air refueling, and then back to Forbes AFB. Each airplane carried a second navigator to act as an observer. When an airplane spotted a ship, it descended to 5,000ft (1,524m) to take photographs and record the name of the vessel, after which it climbed and resumed its search pattern. Following the 15-hour mission, four of the five RB-47s returned to Forbes AFB, with the fifth airplane landing at Kindley AB due to a radio malfunction. Another five RB-47s repeated the mission on 26th October, but with far less success. Three airplanes suffered air aborts due to equipment malfunction and a fourth missed its air refueling. All four landed at Kindley AB, but returned to Forbes AFB the following day.

A different sea surveillance mission on 26th October was far more specific and had serious implications for escalating the crisis into all-out war. Once President Kennedy had issued the quarantine (rather than an embargo) around Cuba, US officials were suddenly in a position of having to enforce the quarantine, and his team of senior advisors known as the Executive Committee (ExComm) 'wanted to show it had the resolve to stop and board a Soviet ship.' This turned out to be the Soviet tanker *Grozny*, last seen headed toward Cuba and closest to the quarantine line. It had 'suspicious-looking deck cargo' and had 'hesitated' following imposition of the quarantine. Intelligence officials debated whether the *Grozny* carried rocket fuel or ammonia for a nickel plant (which it had on several earlier trips to Cuba). Irrespective of what she was carrying, the ExComm wanted to stop the *Grozny* to send a message to Soviet First Secretary Khrushchev as well as pull off a public relations coup. Should the *Grozny* reach Cuba unchallenged it would reveal American naval weakness and a lack of political resolve, both of which would play into Khrushchev's and Cuban leader Fidel Castro's hands.

Five RB-47 BABY BONNET sorties were flown on 26th October to locate the ship, which had escaped surveillance by US Navy ships and patrol aircraft. Four RB-47s departed Forbes AFB at three-hour intervals, completed an air refueling and search pattern, then landed at Kindley AB. The fifth airplane was the RB-47 which landed previously at Kindley AB. The first day of BABY BONNET sorties proved unsuccessful, so additional flights were planned for 27th October. Two of these departed Kindley AB without incident, but the third – RB-47H 53-6248 – crashed on takeoff due to improper water injection mixture, killing all four on board (see Appendix II). A fourth RB-47H then aborted its takeoff – fortuitously as it too had the same incorrect water-alcohol mixture and would almost certainly have suffered a similar fate. Less than two hours later – at 06:45 – an RB-47 commanded by Captain Joseph E Carney located the *Grozny*. The ship attempted to evade observation by maneuvering into a rain shower, and – surprisingly for a 'commercial tanker' – actively jammed the RB-47's radar following its initial identification pass. Carney remained with the *Grozny*, which was 350nm (648km) from the quarantine line, until the US Navy destroyer USS *MacDonough* (DDG-39) could reach and then shadow it. As it turned out, the *Grozny* stopped short of the quarantine line on 28th October, and the ExComm breathed a sigh of relief.

All of the RB-47s at Kindley AB returned home on 29th October, although two remained on ground alert at Forbes AFB should they be needed for future BLUE BANNER sea surveillance sorties. These were officially terminated on 29th November.

By the end of November the Cuban Missile Crisis was considered 'over', but RB-47s continued COMMON CAUSE peripheral ELINT missions, although the actual number of sorties varied. During August 1963, for example, there were 32 sorties totaling 281+50 hours. Each sortie recorded a variety of electronic signals. Flying in RB-47H 53-4284 on 12th August, Captain Regis F Urschler's crew collected 19 manual intercepts, six acquisition radars, nine early warning radars, and one fire control radar. The flight on 30th August, Mission Number FG-228 under the command of Captain Joseph J Gyulavics in RB-47H 53-4290, recorded 25 'manual intercepts', six early warning radar signals, one IFF signal, four HF radio signals, four acquisition radars, four fire control radars, and a previously unidentified signal. During the last six months of 1964 there were 71 flights, but this dropped to 35 by early 1965 and rose to 50 by the end of 1965, largely due to the changes in frequency of GOLDEN TREE SAC U-2 sorties (renamed from BRASS KNOB after the mission name was compromised). COMMON CAUSE sorties increased to 103 during the first six months of 1966.

The Cuban Missile Crisis neatly summarizes the scope and importance of the RB-47 fleet. The airplanes provided weather and photoreconnaissance, search-and-identification, and ELINT monitoring and collection. With the retirement of the RB-47H in 1967, Cuban peripheral ELINT missions were undertaken by several RC-135 variants under BURNING CIGAR and COMINT missions under CUBAN CANDY. The same changes applied to other SAC reconnaissance missions as they shifted from the RB-47 to multiple versions of the RC-135 as well as satellites. For 15 years RB-47s served as the crucial components in transitioning from the limits of unsophisticated piston-powered converted bombers to dedicated jet-powered aircraft crammed with the most technologically advanced sensors and skilled operators.

Above: Multiple 55th SRW RB-47 BABY BONNET missions were flown to locate the *Grozny*, and on 27th October Captain Joseph E Carney's crew found the Soviet ship, averting needless escalation. *Author's collection*

Right: Long after the end of the Cuban Missile Crisis, RB-47Hs flew almost daily COMMON CAUSE missions to collect ELINT on Cuban and Soviet systems. Captain Reggie Urschler's crew flew 53-4284 on 12th August 1963. *Toshio Tagaya*

CHAPTER SEVEN

A Bridge to the Future

There has never been a time in the history of aviation more alive with creativity and more imbued with a sense of urgency than the first two decades after the end of World War II. The appeal of airpower as a panacea for projecting American power around the world, the 'proof' of the value of strategic bombing as the tool that 'won' the war, especially against Japan, the onset of the cold war and its attendant demands for new weapons to wage a new kind of war, the role of the jet engine and the swept wing in building new airplanes, and the engineering challenges that beset Western manufacturing in general and aviation in particular all set the stage for ideas that would radically transform the world of aviation.

Not all of these ideas were sensible, realistic, achievable, or even possible. Project PLUTO, conceived in 1956, was an unmanned, nuclear-powered and nuclear-armed Mach 3 cruise missile that would streak across the surface of the Soviet Union at only hundreds of feet above the ground, evading surface and aerial defenses while spewing radioactive waste everywhere. Piggyback operations of bombers and fighters – whether attached at the wingtip as in the B-36 and F-84 Project TOM TOM or the Fighter Conveyor (FICON) project or carried in the bomb bay as in the McDonnell XF-85 Goblin – would not only protect US bombers but would eliminate the need for carrier aviation (and the associated budget threat from the US Navy) or the need for fighter bases adjacent to distant lands. No matter what the problem, there was some kind of aviation solution, however bizarre, that was just a few years and a few millions of dollars in the future.

The B-47 was not immune to these unrealistic visions. A nuclear-powered B-47, a turboprop-powered variant (which seems a giant leap backward), a supersonic Stratojet, remote-controlled flying bomb versions, B-47s carried on the wingtips of a B-36, and even a gunship for use in Vietnam all made it not only to the drawing board, but, in some cases, underwent extensive test flights. B-47s were

important testbeds for two reasons: they represented the latest iteration in airplane technology and design, making them well suited for advanced aerodynamic testing; and they were increasingly available as early B-47As and B-47Bs plus the retirement of B-47Es and RB-47Es meant that excess airplanes could be put to good use for one-off test projects or permanent conversion. In addition, B-47s were used for a variety of development tests for both the B-47 and B-52.

The post-war years included a variety of prefixes associated with test aircraft. Among these was 'E' for 'Exempt', prompting confusion over 'EB-47Bs' as electronic warfare or airborne command post aircraft. Similarly, 'T' referred to 'Training', not test, and was applied to numerous TB-47s configured for basic qualification training. Several of these were subsequently used for testing, however, and

Top: A number of B-47s served as testbeds at Wright-Patterson AFB, including these three NRB-47Es and JB-47E (lower left). The two NRB-47Es on the right were painted white on all upper surfaces with back theodolite markings, possibly in support of a program related to the SR-71.

Above: A dozen B-47s became ground instructional trainers for new maintenance personnel and were designated as UB-47s and later GB-47s. 50-0020 is seen here at Lowry AFB minus its tail section and outer wings. *Both: Author's collection*

Table 7-1. **Early B-47 Development & Test Aircraft**

Serial	MDS	Test	Dates	Serial	MDS	Test	Dates
46-0065	XB-47	Split Aileron (B-52)	Oct 53 - Jun 54	51-2047	B-47B	Long Bomb Bay Capacity	Jun 53 - Jan 54
46-0066	XB-47	Special Weapons	n/a	51-2052	B-47B	Downward Ejection Seats	Jun 53 - Mar 54
49-1900	B-47A	Aeroelasticity Research	Jun 53 - May 55	51-2071	B-47B	Special Weapons Carriage and Release	n/a
49-1901	B-47A	Crosswind Gear (B-52)	Jun 53 - Jun 54	51-2078	B-47B	Release Vehicle - Special Weapons	n/a
49-1905	B-47A	Crew Escape Investigation/Atomic Power	Jun 53 - Jun 54	51-2080	B-47B	Cluster Bomb Suitability	n/a
49-1906	B-47A	B-4 Fire Control	n/a	51-2103	B-47B	XB-47D Turboprop	n/a
49-1908	B-47A	A-5 Fire Control	Jun 53 - Dec 54	51-2198	B-47B	J47 Engine Stall Characteristics	Jun 53 - Jun 54
49-1909	B-47A	Contamination Test	Jun 53 - Oct 53	51-2200	B-47B	ECM Installations Suitability	n/a
49-2642	B-47B	Structural Integrity	Jun 53 - Jan 54	51-2222	B-47B	Release Vehicle - Special Weapons	Jun 53 - Jun 54
49-2643	B-47B	J57 Engine	Jun 53 - Jul 54	51-2232	B-47B	Release Vehicle - Special Weapons	Jun 53 - Jun 54
49-2644	B-47B	Liquid ATO	Sep 53 - Jan 54	51-2279	B-47B	Anti-icing Improvement	Jun 53 - Jun 54
50-0001	B-47B	Bomb and Fuse Development	n/a	51-2357	B-47E	Bomb Bay Airflow	Jun 53 - Mar 54
50-0003	B-47B	Bomb Ballistics	n/a	51-2359	B-47E	A-5 General Electric	Jun 53 - Jan 54
50-0005	B-47B	Camera and Reconnaissance Systems	n/a	51-2362	B-47E	A-5 Crosley	Jun 53 - Oct 54
50-0009	B-47B	Probe and Drogue (YB-47F receiver)	Jun 53 - Nov 53	51-2363	B-47E	A-5 Fire Control Suitability	Jun 53 - Sep 53
50-0017	B-47B	AN/ARC-21, Phase VII	Jun 53 - Oct 53	51-2400	B-47E	A-3 Fire Control (B-52)	Jun 53 - Dec 54
50-0018	B-47B	A-12D Autopilot	Jun 53 - Sep 55	51-2410	B-47E	A-3 Fire Control (B-52)	Jun 53 - Dec 54
50-0019	B-47B	HIRAN TAC Bombing	n/a	51-2412	B-47E	ECM Phase III	Jun 53 - Oct 54
50-0027	B-47B	WADC Repair	n/a	51-5219	B-47E	YDB-47E Prototype	Jun 53 - Jan 55
50-0028	B-47B	APGC	n/a	51-5220	B-47E	YDB-47E Prototype	Jun 53 - Jan 55
50-0037	B-47B	AEC Research	n/a	51-5244	B-47E	A-12 Autopilot	Jun 53 - Feb 54
50-0040	B-47B	Probe and Drogue (KB-47G tanker)	Aug 53 - Nov 53	51-5257	B-47E	Heavyweight Takeoff Tests	Jun 53 - Nov 54
50-0052	B-47B	30mm Turret Evaluation	Jun 53 - Oct 53	51-5258	RB-47E	Engine Test, RB-47 Configuration	Aug 53 - Feb 54
50-0053	B-47B	HSBD Bombing System	Jun 53 - Jun 55	51-5259	RB-47E	Camera Control System	Aug 54 - Nov 54
50-0054	B-47B	K-4A Suitability / J57 engines	Jun 53 - Nov 53	51-5260	RB-47E	Limited Performance Test	Aug 53 - Jan 54
50-0056	B-47B	Bomb Ballistics	n/a	51-5261	RB-47E	RB-47 Instrument Suitability	Nov 53 - Mar 54
50-0080	B-47B	K-5 System	Jun 53 - Jan 55	51-7043	B-47E	ECM Phase IV and Phase V	n/a
50-0082	B-47B	YB-47C (ground mockup only)	n/a	51-7045	B-47E	Range Augmentation Changes	n/a
51-2045	B-47B	K System Deficiencies	Jun 53 - Jun 54	51-7069	B-47E	Range Augmentation Changes Suitability	n/a
51-2046	B-47B	Special Weapons Carriage and Release / XB-47D Turboprop					

Table 7-1a. **USAF B-47A/B Testbeds**

EB-47A		51-2071	Sep 52 - Dec 55	50-0018	n/a	51-2222	Jan 56 - Feb 61	50-0052	Dec 55 - Nov 56
49-1903	Sep 51 - Sep 52	51-2078	Nov 52 - Dec 55	50-0027	n/a	51-2279	Feb 56 - Jan 58	50-0053	Dec 55 - Feb 58
49-1905	Nov 54 - Sep 56	51-2103	Apr 52 - Dec 54	50-0037	n/a	51-2328	Dec 57 - Mar 60	50-0054	Dec 55 - Dec 56
49-1907	Feb 52 - Dec 54	51-2155	Sep 54 - Oct 54	50-0040	Jan 55 - Dec 55	51-2350	Jun 56 - Jan 61	50-0062	Sep 57 - Aug 59
49-1909	Apr 52 - Dec 54	51-2160	Oct 54 - Feb 56	50-0053	n/a			50-0064	Mar 60 - Oct 64
		51-2198	Feb 53 - Jan 56	50-0054	n/a	**JRB-47B**		50-0066	Dec 56 - May 61
EB-47B		51-2222	Mar 53 - Jan 56	50-0052	Apr 55 - Dec 55	50-0005	Dec 55 - Nov 56	50-0067	Dec 56 - Sep 58
49-2644	Jun 52 - Jun 53	51-2232	Apr 53 - Apr 54	50-0077	n/a			50-0077	Dec 55 - Sep 58
50-0002	May 52 - May 53	51-2279	Feb 53 - Feb 56			**JTB-47B**		50-0080	Dec 55 - Nov 56
50-0003	Jun 52 - Jun 53	51-2300	Feb 53 - Apr 53	**JB-47B**		49-2643	Dec 55 - Nov 56	51-2075	Mar 56 - Mar 60
50-0004	Jan 53 - Apr 53			51-2047	Dec 55 - Feb 57	50-0002	Dec 55 - Oct 56	51-2078	Dec 55 - Dec 56
50-0017	Apr 53 - Jun 53	**ERB-47B**		51-2052	Dec 55 - Feb 57	50-0003	Dec 55 - Nov 56	51-2090	Jul 57 - May 61
50-0018	Jan 52 - Jun 53	50-0005	Oct 52 - Dec 55	51-2071	Dec 55 - May 56	50-0009	Dec 55 - Aug 58		
50-0020	Jan 52 - Apr 53			51-2075	Jan 56 - Feb 56	50-0014	Dec 55 - Dec 56	**NB-47B**	
50-0027	Feb 52 - Jun 53	**ETB-47B**		51-2080	Jan 56 - Dec 56	50-0017	Dec 55 - Oct 56	51-2328	Mar 60 - Apr 61
50-0037	May 52 - Jun 53	49-2643	Sep 54 - Dec 55	51-2155	Feb 56 - Jun 57	50-0018	Dec 55 - Jan 57		
50-0052	Feb 52	49-2644	n/a	51-2159	Sep 56 - Aug 57	50-0019	Jan 56 - Feb 56	**NTB-47B**	
50-0054	May 53 - Jun 53	50-0003	n/a	51-2160	Feb 56 - Jun 57	50-0027	Dec 55 - Nov 56	50-0040	Mar 60 - Jan 61
50-0077	Jun 52 - Jun 53	50-0009	Jan 55 - Dec 55	51-2198	Feb 56	50-0037	Dec 55 - Mar 58	50-0062	Aug 61 - Apr 67
51-2046	Jun 52 - Dec 54	50-0017	n/a	51-2200	Mar 56 - Jun 58	50-0040	Dec 55 - Mar 60		

Table 7-1b. **USAF R/B-47E Testbeds**

EB-47E		51-2410	Nov 56 - Apr 59	53-4238	May 56 - Feb 58	52-0389	Aug 60 - Jan 61	**NRB-47E**	
51-2357	May 53 - Mar 56	51-7043	Dec 55 - Mar 60	53-6210	Sep 58 - Mar 62	53-2104	Mar 60 - Sep 69	51-5258	Mar 60 - Apr 67
52-0389	Apr 55 - Dec 55	52-0221	Dec 55 - Feb 64	53-6218	Feb 57 - Mar 58			53-4257	Mar 60 - Jun 68
		52-0370	Jan 56 - Jul 67			**JRB-47E**		53-4260	Mar 60 - Oct 61
JB-47E		52-0389	Dec 55 - Jun 60	**JDB-47E**		51-5258	Dec 55 - Mar 60	53-4261	Mar 60 - Dec 65
51-2357	Mar 56 - Jul 63	52-0514	Feb 56 - Sep 66	53-2346	Feb 57 - Oct 59	51-5261	May 56 - Sep 59		
51-2359	Mar 56 - Mar 60	53-2104	Jan 57 - Mar 60			53-4257	Dec 55 - Mar 60		
51-2363	Jan 56 - Jun 58	53-2108	Dec 55 - May 65	**NB-47E**		53-4260	May 58 - Mar 60		
51-2368	Jun 56 - May 61	53-2276	Jan 58 - Oct 67	51-2359	Mar 60 - Feb 61	53-4261	Jun 58 - Mar 60		
51-2394	Jun 56 - Mar 60	53-2280	Dec 55 - Oct 67	51-2394	Mar 60 - Apr 61	53-4262	Feb 57 - Nov 60		
51-2400	Nov 55 - Dec 58	53-2281	Nov 55 - Nov 59	51-7043	Mar 60 - Jun 60				

Table 7-2. **Ground Test and Training B-47s**

UB-47B		GB-47B		UB-47E		GB-47E		GEB-47E	
50-0020	Jun 62 - Oct 62	50-0020	Oct 62 - Oct 63	52-0180	Jun 62 - Oct 62	51-2357	Jul 63 - May 65	51-7044	Feb 65 - n/a
50-0037	Jun 62 - Nov 62	50-0037	Nov 62 - Sep 65			51-7048	Jan 65 - Nov 65		
50-0046	Sep 62 - Nov 62	50-0046	Nov 62 - Jun 64	**TB-47B**		51-7081	Jan 65 - Nov 65	**GRB-47K**	
51-2098	Jun 62 - Oct 62	51-2098	Oct 62 - May 64	50-0011	Jun 53 -Aug 57	52-0180	Oct 62 - May 64	53-4270	Jun 63 - n/a
51-2152	Jun 62 - Oct 62	51-2115	Aug 63 - Oct 63			52-0200	Jan 65 - Nov 65	53-4272	Jun 63 - n/a
51-2198	Jun 62 - Oct 62	51-2152	Oct 62 - May 64			52-0227	Jan 65 - Nov 65		
		51-2198	Oct 62 - May 64						

were designated as ETB-47Bs. By the 1950s the prefix 'J' entered use for 'Temporary Test', and was later replaced by 'N' for 'Permanent Test.' Other B-47s which acquired a ground training role used the 'U' for 'Utility' and 'G' for 'Ground', leading to UB-, GB-47Bs, and UB-, GEB-, and GB-47Es.

The paucity of historical records, the excessive secrecy associated with many research projects in the late 1950s and early 1960s, and the lack of independently verifiable memoirs all limit the depth of analysis of B-47 test and research programs. Some airplanes are associated only with a program name, often without a specific serial number. Official histories sometimes refer to a program but note that it was 'too classified' to be discussed in the existing document. Many of the participants suffer from the limits of memory, confusing years, serial numbers, colleagues, and even the nature of the program. It remains for future researchers to uncover more details about these topics.

POWERPLANTS

Aside from the basic awareness that the J47 engine was essentially underpowered and unreliable for sustained jet-bomber operations, B-47 testbeds served to evaluate powerplants for both the B-47 and other airframes. Of these, only the B-47C was a realistic option for full-scale production. The remainder were (mostly) hypothetical tests of other engine types to determine their suitability for other bombers and fighters. For example, during early 1971 NB-47E 53-2104 was loaned to General Electric as a testbed for TF34 engine tests prior to installation on the Lockheed S-3A Viking. The test engine was mounted on the left wing tank pylon, with the first flight on 21st January 1971 lasting 1+52 hours. Following the tests 53-2104 was relegated to MASDC on 7th November 1974, and was ultimately moved to the Pueblo Air Museum, CO (see Appendix III). Other tests included the 1960 project by Cornell Aeronautical Laboratory which installed a contrail suppression system on the #1 engine of an unidentified B-47 in an effort to make it harder to spot high-altitude bombers by looking for their contrails.

The B-47C and Derivatives

Continuing improvements in jet engine development meant that efforts to mate the sleek B-47 airframe to better engines with greater thrust and reliability were sure to find favor among engineers, designers, SAC planners, and hopefully, congressmen with budgetary authority. By placing the engines in pods beneath the wing, Boeing designers made it relatively easy to install newer, larger-diameter engines on the B-47 without the expensive structural redesigns required for the Tupolev Tu-16 *Badger* and the de Havilland Comet which had their engines buried within the tight confines of the wing root, or the English Electric Canberra with the engines integral to the wing (but which many thought was superior to the B-47). Moreover, by early 1949 the B-47 had already undergone one major engine change (from the J35 used in the XB-47 to the J47 used in the B-47B), proving that the re-engining concept was fundamentally sound. The engine replacement project also seemed to make economic sense, as with more powerful thrust the B-47 could go from six to four engines, saving money over the cost of the entire fleet.

With these thoughts in mind Boeing proposed the B-47C, a major improvement not only in powerplants but in structural design as well. In addition to the YB-47C/YB-56 reconnaissance version described in Chapter 6, Boeing considered a number of variants which were all labeled as 'B-47Cs'. Early development work began on the Model 450-24-26 with contract AF33(038)-12883 on 17th May 1950. This B-47C would have a new wing, a modified fuselage to accommodate side-by-side pilot seating strongly favored by LeMay, and the outrigger landing gear would be relocated to a fairing between the inboard and outboard pylons. The planned first flight would be in July 1951, and the B-47C would enter production in 1952 beginning with the 88th airplane (50-0092) on the assembly line.

Boeing recommended the Allison J35-A-23 engine based upon its availability and cost, resulting in the Boeing Model 450-19-10, but this variant retained the tandem cockpit of the standard B-47, reflecting the many iterations of B-47C versions. Four of these engines (versus six J47s) would give the B-47C nearly 3,000 lbf (13.3kN) of additional thrust, increase combat radius by 603nm (1,117km), service ceiling by 2,900ft (884m), and cruising speed by

GE used former US Navy NB-47E 53-2104 as a testbed for the TF34 engine which was installed on the Lockheed S-3, and later on the Fairchild Republic A-10. *Both photos Robert Ferguson/Lockheed*

Right and below left: At first glance this could be mistaken for a B-52, but it is in fact the EB-47B/B-47C proposed by Boeing. This mockup, seen in 1952, surely influenced Boeing designers when they modified the B-52A at LeMay's insistence to include side-by-side seating. The B-47C was not procured. *Photos A47625 and A47573 courtesy Boeing*

Below right: Boeing offered an innovative maintenance feature on the EB-47B/ B-47C in the form of extendable cowlings on the Allison J35 engines. This added weight and complexity, both of which further compromised the airplane's range. *Photo 113593 courtesy Boeing*

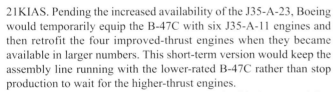

21KIAS. Pending the increased availability of the J35-A-23, Boeing would temporarily equip the B-47C with six J35-A-11 engines and then retrofit the four improved-thrust engines when they became available in larger numbers. This short-term version would keep the assembly line running with the lower-rated B-47C rather than stop production to wait for the higher-thrust engines.

The Air Force was sufficiently impressed with the re-engining proposal that it signed multiple contracts with Boeing. The first of these was dated 14th August 1950 and called for 175 B-47Cs and 35 RB-47Cs. The following day this was amended to 21 B-47Cs and 86 RB-47Cs. By September 1950 AMC had allocated $4,122,427 for the project. Boeing was clearly ready for this, and within six weeks – on 23rd October – Air Force officials examined the mockup in Seattle. What the new version would be designated, however, was not so quickly or easily resolved. In early correspondence the Air Force referred to the airplane as the YB-47C, whereas Boeing inexplicably chose the designation EB-47B. The Air Force then changed its mind, arguing that it was a sufficiently modified airplane as to warrant a new MDS, and in April 1956 the airplane was designated the B-56 (including the RB-56 reconnaissance variant). Less than two months later, however, the Air Force recanted, indicating that there were insufficient differences between the B-56 and the B-47 to merit the new MDS. Difficult as this was to believe – new engines, new wing, and possibly even a new fuselage made

the B-56 substantially different from the B-47 in multiple ways – the Air Force officially designated the airplane as the B-47C.

All of this bureaucratic wrangling proved for naught as the operational data for the J47 began to suggest that its teething problems were abating. The thrust and reliability improvements possible with the J35, coupled with the added expense of installing and then replacing the lower thrust J35-A-11 now seemed marginal compared with the number of J47s already in production and service. By 27th December the contract had dwindled to no B-47Cs and just 19 RB-47Cs. The J35-equipped B-47C now seemed to be too little, too late. Eager to salvage something from its efforts, Boeing was quick to suggest that J57 engines (planned for the B-52) would make the B-47C even more effective. By 12th April 1951, however, the Air Force elected to 'freeze' acquisition of new bombers, leaving the B-47C in limbo with orders for only the 19 RB-47Cs remaining.

The Air Force then decided in late 1951 to procure only one B-47C, equipped now with J71 engines each with 10,090 lbf (44.8kN) of thrust, although this was soon changed to J57s with 11,100 lbf (49.4kN) of thrust. The sole B-47C ended up as little more than a box of blueprints and a single airframe (50-0082 – the 87th airframe on the production line). Mockup engine struts and pods were used on 50-0082. LeMay was openly opposed to the B-47C, rightly seeing it as just another competitor that might interfere with the acquisition and production of additional B-52s. The final contract on 3rd July 1953 eliminated all

The J71 engines on the B-47C were offset from the pylon centerline. For the inboard pylons this allowed placement of the outrigger landing gear strut. The J71 engines did not have the extendable cowlings found on the J35-equipped proposal. *Photo A44777 courtesy Boeing*

Among the many different turboprop designs for the B-47 were a four-engine pusher (Model 450-24-26), a twin-engine pusher (Model 450-32-10), a standard twin-engine configuration (Model 450-33-10), and a four-engine twin-jet variant (Model 450-113-28). Boeing settled on the standard twin version which became the XB-47D (Model 450-162-28).

orders for both the B-47C and RB-47C, effectively ending the program. After cancelation the airframe was broken up, although the aft fuselage was used to repair a B-47 that suffered a hard landing at McConnell AFB, and much of the remaining fuselage transferred to Kirtland AFB, NM, for use as a ground instructional trainer.

Boeing and AMC considered at least two additional B-47C derivatives. One of these was the B-47X (Program II), also known as the B-47-II (Model 450-166-38). This was similar in configuration and capability to the B-47C but configured with the GAM-63 Rascal. The other was the B-47Z, equipped with four Pratt & Whitney J57-P-1

engines. It incorporated new wing leading and trailing edges and a new tail. It had a 33.5% chord-wise increase in wing area and 45% increase in the area of the horizontal stabilizer. A stronger landing gear permitted heavier gross weights, and provisions were made to carry the GAM-63 Rascal missile. The B-47Z offered 'appreciable' improvements in takeoff run, maximum cruise speed, bombing speed, bombing altitude, and an 800nm (1,482km) increase in the unrefueled range of the B-47E, but with its crew increased to four (pilot, copilot, navigator-gunner, and bombardier). As with the B-47C, LeMay was simply not interested and these projects never reached the prototype stage.

The XB-47D

During the 1940s the turboprop seemed to be a very attractive powerplant for military aircraft. It offered better projected performance in terms of takeoff and climb, and its fuel consumption was significantly lower than the turbojet. Boeing had in fact developed a turboprop variant alongside the XB-47 (as they did with the B-52). At least 39 different powerplant combinations were studied for the B-47, and 15 of them were turboprops. Most of these were mounted in a normal tractor position, but a few used a pusher-type arrangement found on the B-36. In the end, however, Boeing finally decided the turbojet offered more potential.

A 1949 study 'Strategic Bombing Systems Analysis' by Edward Paxson claimed that bombers with a small cross section and powered by turboprops would be the only airplanes capable of successfully penetrating Soviet airspace. In response to this study and given the high fuel consumption of turbojet engines, the Air Force asked Boeing to convert two B-47Bs (51-2046 and 51-2103) into XB-47D turboprops (Boeing Model 450-162-28) to assess the viability of large high-speed, swept-wing bombers. By February 1951 Boeing had completed the basic design work. AMC issued a contract in April, and a mockup was completed by January 1952.

The modification work was done at the Seattle plant with a Curtiss Wright YT49-W-1 turboprop replacing the two J47s in each inboard nacelle. The T49 was a derivative of the British Sapphire engine. These large powerplants drove 15ft (4.6m) diameter four-bladed Curtiss turbo-electric propellers that each produced 9,710 equivalent shaft horsepower (ESHP). The first flight was planned for early 1953,

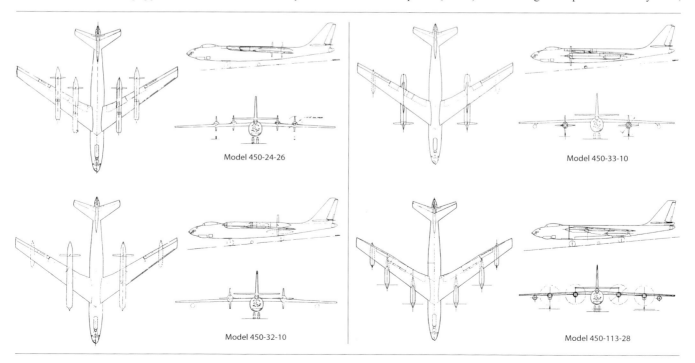

Model 450-24-26

Model 450-33-10

Model 450-32-10

Model 450-113-28

Above: During the post-war years turboprops appeared to offer greater fuel efficiency and range, so the Air Force asked Boeing to develop a turboprop version of the B-47 to evaluate these claims. *Boeing via Jay Miller*

Right: Massive cowling housed the Curtiss Wright T49 engine as well as the outrigger landing gear. The propeller radius was 15ft, and the outrigger gear was essential to prevent blade contact during landing, especially in crosswinds. *Photo A71131 courtesy Boeing*

but as of 9th May 1955 the airplane had yet to fly. Taxi tests kept the aircraft grounded with prop trouble. Difficulties with engine development further delayed the first flight until 26th August 1955, with test pilots Raymond L McPhearson and Lew Wallick flying 51-2103 from Boeing Field in Seattle to Moses Lake (renamed Larson AFB in 1950). The second XB-47D (51-2046) made its first flight on 15th February 1956.

Above: The XB-47D was plagued with development troubles that delayed its first flight, and these issues never abated. What appears to be a suture on the forward fuselage of 51-2103 are in fact instrument cables from the engine taped to the fuselage and wing. *USAF*

Below: After protracted ground tests the first XB-47D finally flew in August 1955, with the second airplane (51-2046) making its first flight on 15th February 1956. *Photo courtesy Boeing*

Top left: The XB-47D was unstable during air refueling, and tended to 'porpoise' in the pitch axis. Note the nonstandard 'U.S. Air Force' marking on the starboard wing. *Photo courtesy Boeing*

Top right: In the event of an engine failure the huge prop blades created a sudden and enormous amount of drag prior to the pilot feathering the prop. This led to severe yaw which Boeing solved with an automatic feathering system. *Photo A71130 courtesy Boeing*

Left: Despite the many technical problems which beset the XB-47D, it offered performance similar to the turbojet B-47 and nearly double the range. Upper wing surface is tufted for airflow separation studies and fairing on top of the vertical stabilizer housed a camera. *Boeing via Jay Miller*

Above: B-47B 49-2643 served as the J57 testbed at Boeing-Wichita, and used modified B-52 cowlings on the outboard engines.

Right: J57 tests at Wright-Patterson AFB used B-47B 50-0054 and modified KC-135 cowlings. The goal was to garner test data in preparation for the introduction of the B-52 and KC-135 into fleet service. *Both: courtesy Boeing*

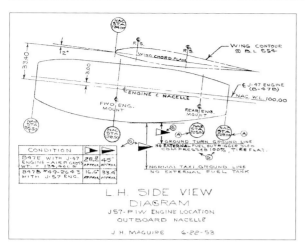

Top left: Technical drawing of the J57 outboard engine pod on B-47B 49-2643. Under normal conditions the pod was 12in closer to the ground than the J47 pod. During extreme turns the J57 was just 16in off the ground.

Top right: Comparative front view of 49-2643 (l) with the J57 engine and a standard B-47 with the J47 engine (r). Test flights also supported NACA noise reduction research. *Photo courtesy Boeing*

The whole program was fraught with problems. Although the J65 turbojet version of the engine had proven itself, the addition of reduction gears and propeller simply did not work well. The two airplanes achieved a grand total of only 51 hours of flight testing, with the dismal average of only 1.8 hours between the need for an engine or propeller replacement. During aerial refueling trials behind a KC-97 the XB-47D had a pronounced porpoising tendency as it entered the refueling envelope. There was also some difficulty in controlling the airplane with an engine out. The drag of the propeller was very high and caused severe yawing and rolling at the moment of failure and before it was feathered, leading to an automatic feathering system.

As flight test engineer for the XB-47D Robert 'Bob' Larson told the author, the program was more than just a testbed for turboprops. The project was 'aimed at a new airplane development, one that would significantly improve the payload and range capability of the B-47'. Had the powerplant proved reliable there might have been a serious attempt to produce B-47s with turboprops. Actual flight performance was not much below that of the standard B-47 and the range was much better. The XB-47D had a maximum speed in level flight of 597mph (961kph) at 13,500ft (4,115m) and could climb at 2,910ft/min (887m/m) with a service ceiling of 33,750ft (10,287m). It could fly as far at sea level as the standard B-47 could at optimum cruise, almost doubling its range which was obviously attractive to SAC. The last flight was made on 26th June 1956 and both airplanes were scrapped at Seattle.

J57 Engine Testbed
There was little doubt that one of the B-47's greatest weaknesses was its J47 engine. Poor reliability, inadequate thrust, lengthy spool-up time, high fuel consumption, and low time between overhaul all contributed to its undesirable reputation. With a maximum thrust of 5,800 lbf (25.8kN), the J47 was unsuited for the planned B-52 even with eight engines. The J57 engine that Pratt & Whitney had been developing was in the 10,000 lbf (44.5kN) range, which made it a better match for the B-52 and the proposed YB-47C and B-47Z. Test flights of the J57 had been undertaken on a B-50, but this lacked the altitude and speed to assess the engine under all conditions. Using the YB-52 and XB-52 for these tests would detract from the overall B-52 program schedule, so Boeing and Pratt & Whitney chose to install a J57 engine on each outboard position (#1 and #6) of B-47B 49-2643 at Wichita, with B-47B 50-0054 from WADC at Wright-Patterson AFB similarly configured with J57s in support of the KC-135 and Boeing 707 program.

Modification of each B-47 was extensive but straightforward. After removing the J47 and attaching the J57 to new engine mounts,

a B-52 cowling (or KC-135 cowling in the case of 50-0054) was reworked to fit the B-47. Each J57 engine required changes to the fuel and oil systems, hydraulics, water injection, electrics, bleed air ducting, and wing structure, notably reinforcing the outboard aileron for 60in (152cm) on either side of the outboard pylon and adding two rows of vortex generators to the upper wing surface. Only partial thrust from the J57s could be used on takeoff due to the tendency of the wing to twist.

In addition to flight testing the J57, the modified B-47s were used on behalf of NACA research into jet noise causes and mitigation at the Lewis Flight Propulsion Laboratory in Cleveland. Researchers determined that jet noise originated from the intake, the body of the engine (compressor whine caused by the rapidly spinning compressor blades), and exhaust noise caused by the turbulent mixing of internally generated airflow (thrust) and external airflow around the nacelle. The exhaust noise was the most significant, and NACA researchers assessed different exhaust shapes to compare noise reduction with loss of thrust and increased drag. Three configurations were evaluated: a corrugated nozzle with multiple lobes and open in the center, a corrugated nozzle with multiple lobes with a centerbody, and a tubular nozzle. Tests were conducted with a 12-lobe corrugated nozzle. In addition, further evaluations were made with and without a cylindrical ejector aft of the nozzle which allowed ambient airflow to mix with the exhaust.

Test results showed that the multi-lobe exhaust with a centerbody and no ejector had the lowest drag increase and lowest thrust loss, incrementally better than the multi-lobe exhaust with the open center. This was implemented on a variety of early airliner jet engines as 'pipe organ' exhausts. In its concluding report NACA noted the advantages of the bypass turbofan as optimal for future airliner designs.

Canadair's CL-52
During early 1953 Canada's Avro Gas Turbine Division (which would become Orenda Engines) undertook a private venture to develop a next-generation jet engine resulting in Project Study (PS) 13. Eventually known as the Iroquois, the PS 13 could produce 19,250 lbf (85.6kN) of thrust and 26,000 lbf (115.7kN) of thrust with

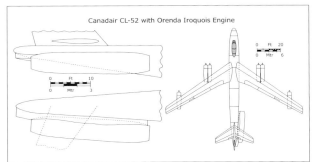

Top: Orenda considered using a B-52 or a Vulcan for its testbed, but it settled on TB-47B 51-2059. After its delivery to Canada the airplane was further modified. *Canadair via Terry Panopalis*

Center left: The Iroquois engine was aligned with the B-47's pitch axis but was offset outward some 5°, contributing to a noticeable yaw while in flight.

Center right: Controls for the Iroquois were located at the copilot's station, with the throttle to the left of the main quadrant. *Canadair via Terry Panopalis*

Bottom: Old meets new as the CL-52 sits opposite an Avro Canada CF-100. This view illustrates the anhedral of the engine mount as well as the placement of the RCAF emblem on the right wing. *Canadair via Terry Panopalis*

afterburner. This made it a good candidate for the Avro Canada CF-105 Arrow interceptor which was then under development. Ground tests of the PS 13 began on 15th December 1954 but the engine's weight and size made flight testing problematic. Orenda considered using a B-50, a B-52, and an Avro Vulcan, eventually settling on a B-47. The US Air Force agreed to loan TB-47B 51-2059 to the Royal Canadian Air Force (RCAF) which in turn bailed it to Canadair Ltd under contract to Orenda. Canadair assigned it the designation CL-52 and it operated in Canada with the registration X059. Interestingly, the Canadair flight notes and some official documents incorrectly list 51-2059 as a 'TB-47E'.

On 19th February 1956 Canadair started detailed technical discussions with Boeing engineers about airframe modifications. After considering locations under the wing, in the bomb bay, and even embedded in the fuselage, engineers elected to place the engine in a 29.4ft (9m) x 6ft (1.8m) nacelle located on a stub pylon attached to the starboard side of the aft fuselage. This required considerable

internal structural stiffening of the airframe to support the additional weight. The Iroquois weighed 4,680 lb (2,123kg), and the 10 cowling subcomponents added 1,179 lb (535kg) for a total of 5,859 lb (2,658kg). Effects of the pod and pylon were determined by a series of wind tunnel tests done at Boeing Wichita, the University of Wichita's low-speed wind tunnel, and Convair at San Diego. The front of the nacelle was angled outward 5° leading to a slight yaw during flight, and the large nacelle created considerable ground-effect lift during takeoff and landing. The strut installation and structural reinforcement were completed at Wichita.

Other modifications to the TB-47B included installation of an additional throttle at the copilot's station to control the Iroquois, removal of bomb bay and forward auxiliary fuel tanks, installation of a removable test rack in the bomb bay, and placement of multiple test instruments at the copilot's station and the observer's position. To counterbalance the Iroquois engine and its pylon, 10,000 lb (4,536kg) of ballast was added to the front of the TB-47. Ballast in the former fuel cell cavities comprised two layers of canvas bags filled with lead shot and held in place with wooden planks. Lead plates were bolted into place in the nose, with brass plates similarly secured in the nose radar compartment. A 3in (7.6cm) diameter fuel line was added from the refueling manifold to the test engine. Two methyl bromide fire extinguishing systems were installed, one for the main engine and one for the accessory gear. A dorsal fin extension accommodated some of the 100,000ft (30,480m) of additional test wiring, and surface plating was added to protect the fuselage in case of engine destruction.

US Air Force Colonel Robert E Lee and Major Jay Brown delivered 51-2059 to Cartierville, Quebec, on 16th February 1956. Over the following 14 months the nacelle and a dummy Iroquois engine were installed. During this time the Canadair flight crew – Michael Cooper-Slipper (pilot), Leonard 'Len' Hobbs (copilot), and John McLachlin (flight engineer) – flew to Wichita for 10 weeks of B-47 training (other than the courses related to nuclear weapons and air refueling). While there they earned the admiration of their SAC counterparts at the Officer's Club bar: 'Do you mean that you little old Canadians have got the biggest engine in the world? And you're going to put it in the tail of a B-47? Man, you're crazier than we are.' [The Iroquois acquired a reputation as the loudest engine in the world, with one claim suggesting that while running at full power the noise could kill a man 100ft (30.5m) away.]

After fourteen months of conversion work, the first flight of the completed nacelle took place at Cartierville on 15th April 1957 when Cooper-Slipper and Hobbs flew X059 from the Canadair plant to Orenda's facility at Malton, Ontario. Flight tests there were carried out at first with a dummy engine. Finally, on 13th November 1957, a real Iroquois was taken aloft and started for the first time. Overall the test program proceeded well. When the Iroquois was operating at high power settings it was necessary for the three J47s on the starboard side to be reduced to idle thrust and the #1 J47 operated at full thrust to countermand the yaw induced by the Iroquois. On

several occasions all six of the J47s were shut down and the airplane flew using only the power from the Iroquois. During the only flight where the Iroquois was operated at full afterburner it threw turbine blades and caused extensive damage to the nacelle and horizontal stabilizer. This resulted in a general beefing up of the structure with 'chain mail' sheeting placed inside the nacelle.

The CF-105 Arrow project, and with it the Iroquois, was canceled on 29th February 1959 in the midst of a huge political controversy (Cooper-Slipper suggested that Canadian Prime Minister John G Diefenbaker be dragged behind a CF-105 at Mach 2 for this decision!). The Iroquois logged a total of 31 hours of flight time on the Stratojet. Cooper-Slipper and Hobbs returned the TB-47B to Tinker AFB on 28th May 1959, still configured with the test nacelle and a mock-up engine. The following day it was flown to AASB at Davis-Monthan AFB, where it was scrapped by 12th August 1959.

Top: The Iroquois took up the center portion of the nacelle, with its afterburner extending to the rear. Addition of the engine and nacelle necessitated some 10,000 lb of ballast be added to the front of the CL-52.

Center: First flight with an Iroquois took place on 13th November 1957 (a Wednesday!). By the time the Avro CF-105 project was canceled on 29th February 1959 the engine had accrued just 31 hours of operational time on the CL-52.

Bottom: The CL-52 could easily fly using just the Iroquois engine with all six J47s shut down. The Iroquois was flight tested just once at full afterburner; it shelled turbine blades and damaged the aft fuselage and empennage. Despite appearance of this photo, the CL-52 was natural metal, not white. *All: Canadair via Terry Panopalis*

The Atomic B-47

During the late 1940s and early 1950s, multiple plans were proposed for atomic-powered airplanes. The Atomic Energy Commission (AEC) issued a report on 18th August 1950 which called for the evaluation of both a subsonic and supersonic atomic airplane. The subsonic airplane would be an atomic-powered B-47C, and was intended to be an interim testbed to obtain flight experience with atomic reactor powerplants. The ultimate development would be a yet-to-be-defined supersonic aircraft based on experience gleaned from the atomic B-47C. The AEC asked United Aircraft Corporation to explore the feasibility of these airplanes, leading to a contract for an atomic powerplant produced by Pratt & Whitney.

The AEC asked Fairchild Aircraft to undertake a similar study of the adaptability of existing airframes to use atomic power for propulsion, with the intent of having a nuclear airplane flying by 1954. These included the Convair XC-99 and B-36, as well as the B-52 and the B-47. For each airplane Fairchild considered using just atomic power and atomic power in combination with 'chemical' augmentation, essentially a ATO system.

The Fairchild report examined two basic variants of an atomic B-47, but noted that while such an airplane was 'technically possible…characteristics of the engine installation may be intolerable from an operational or service standpoint.' Indeed, the report went on to say, 'the aircraft does not look desirable, and a general arrangement of the aircraft was not included' in the report, and that 'a new airplane could be designed to give better performance than the modified B-47.'

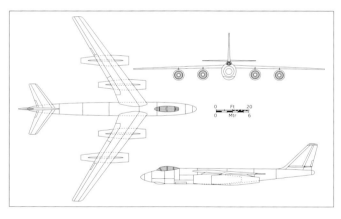

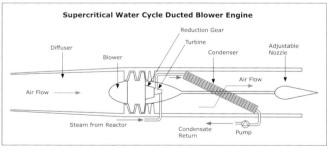

Supercritical Water Cycle Ducted Blower Engine

Assuming a maximum gross weight of 227,000 lb (102,965kg) and using four XJ53 engines, projected performance using the smaller L-14-4 reactor alone was pitiful. Rate of climb at sea level was reportedly just *37ft/min* (11m/min)! With the chemical augmentation this increased to a more impressive 8,000ft/min (2,438m/min). The larger L-17-4 reactor, which raised the overall gross weight to 250,000 lb (113,398kg) improved the rate of climb to 2,000ft/min (610m/min), and reached the airframe structural limit of 6,420ft/min (1,957m/min) when augmented. Overall, the reactor offered few advantages beyond a 10-knot improvement in top speed, with the only real performance benefit being essentially unlimited range. Given the cost, complexity, and other undesirable factors, it should not be surprising that an atomic B-47 failed to get off the drawing board, especially with the termination of the B-47C program.

B-47B 50-0037 was assigned to 'AEC research' during the 1950s, but details of its actual MDS (it changed several times) and its role remains undetermined. Convair had three B-47s on bailment contract during this same period, but which of these was assigned to atomic airplane testing is not altogether clear. B-47A 49-1905 was delivered to Convair on 2nd September 1956 following use as a ground instructional trainer at Lowry AFB, CO, with the 3514th Technical Training Wing (TTW). One document (which has not been independently verified) suggests that it was used for ground tests of an experimental nuclear powerplant. The unit was reportedly fitted in the bomb bay to assess the effects of radiation on aircraft structures. Records show that 49-1905 was 'tested to destruction' by 20th December 1957. Whether or not this was due to radiation or some other cause is unknown. JB-47Es 51-2400 and 51-2410 were both bailed from Boeing-Seattle to Convair in December 1955 and November 1956, respectively. Their role at Convair has not been determined, but may have been either associated with the 'atomic' airplane or as test aircraft for the GE T171 (later M61) tail gun for the B-58.

WEAPONS SYSTEM TESTING

B-47s were involved in three broad categories of weapons testing: those to be used by the B-47 such as conventional or atomic weapons, those to be used by other aircraft, or for an aircraft under development. For example, the B-47 functioned variously as a target (eg, the QB-47E) or as an operational testbed (eg, for the ADM-20 Quail decoy). Five B-47Es (52-0158, 52-0166, 52-0185, 52-0536, and 53-2275) served as ground targets at NAWS China Lake, CA. During August 1961 JTB-47B 50-0064 took part in B-58 ejection capsule tests at NAS El Centro on behalf of the 6511th Test Group (Parachute). B-47E 51-7043 was involved in an experimental program that installed forward-firing chaff rockets in wing pods in lieu of drop tanks. An unidentified B-47 carried a lead sulfide infrared warning receiver on top of the vertical stabilizer. In a program known only as 'Dirty Bird', a B-47 was used in a study to determine how camouflage might make low-flying aircraft less visible. Some former B-47 personnel claim they saw a camouflaged B-47 at Eglin AFB, which might be related to the SLEEPING BEAUTY I and II tests conducted in 1959. These involved possibly two B-47s – one painted all white and the other painted olive drab on the top and white on the bottom – in tests to determine the ability of interceptors to locate and identify low-flying aircraft by radar and visual means. Not surprisingly, the all white airplane was easily detected visually whereas the olive drab B-47 was not. B-47A 49-1901 was configured with crosswind landing gear for use during 1952-53 in evaluating the system on the B-52. Interestingly, the B-47 was even considered for use as an unmanned weapon, as with the BRASS RING and SOD BUSTER programs.

Opposite page

Top: Notional design of a B-47C converted for use as a subsonic atomic-powered testbed. Once sufficient test data were obtained the next step would be a supersonic testbed, but this would not have been a B-47 derivative.

Center: An atomic-powered engine works in theory by using a reactor embedded in the aircraft fuselage to heat water into steam to turn the turbine, producing thrust. Superheated steam would then be condensed and reused. A practical application remains thankfully elusive.

Bottom: JB-47E 51-2410 originally served as a testbed for the B-52 fire control system and was later bailed to Convair, possibly for tests associated with the B-58 tail gun. *Author's collection*

This page

Top: JTB-47B 50-0064 served as the testbed for the escape capsules on the B-58. At least two capsules were carried in the bomb bay (with the doors removed, seen here) and then dropped to assess their mechanics and ballistics. *USAF via Robert L Lawson*

Center and bottom: Frontal view of B-47A 49-1901 demonstrating the crosswind landing gear under evaluation for the B-52. Barely discernable are the alignment wheels between each set of main tires. During landing the alignment wheels touched first, ensuring that the main gear were pointed down the runway instead of angled to one side. *Photos courtesy Boeing*

A handful of B-47s were used in several weapons programs that have yet to be fully identified. In the last half of 1963, for example, NRB-47E 51-5258 was used in Project BLACKBIRD, 'a high priority, classified project directed by the Secretary of the Air Force on an on-call basis.' Whether or not this was related to the development of the Lockheed SR-71 has not been determined, but cannot be excluded. This same airplane was later used in 'V/H Sensor Research' in the first half of 1964, certainly suggesting a correlation with the SR-71 program. By 1965 it took part in 'Spectral Filtration' along with RB-47E 53-4257. NB-47E 53-2104 was used in Aeronautical

Systems Division (ASD) tests of 'Reefing Line Cutters' in the first half of 1964 along with JB-47E 53-2108. Later that year it was associated with 'Human Performance in Advanced Systems,' and finished 1965 in 'Development of Chaff Units.' Throughout 1964 NRB-47E 53-4257 was part of the 'Hi Acuity' program, and in the first half of 1964 was the lead aircraft in 'Spectral Filtration' program. It was replaced in this role by NRB-47E 53-4261 through the end of 1964, when it resumed these duties along with RB-47E 51-5258, and in 1965 took part in QRC-228 testing. It crashed on 29th December 1965 (see Appendix II).

TROPIC MOON IV

As the war in Southeast Asia progressed it became clear to American combat planners that military supply routes for insurgent forces in South Vietnam were active at night and under jungle cover. Beginning in early 1966 the US Air Force started a program known as SHED LIGHT with the intention of modifying an existing airframe to incorporate new technologies such as low-light level television (LLLTV), infrared (IR) scanners, and laser designators capable of penetrating the dense jungle foliage. Among these were four Douglas A-1E Skyraiders equipped with LLLTV that deployed to Nakhon Phanom RTAFB under TROPIC MOON I, and three Martin B-57Bs, also with LLLTV plus laser sensors as part of TROPIC MOON II. Neither of these programs was particularly successful, and the Air Force sought additional solutions as part of the Self-Contained Night Attack (SCNA) aircraft study. Two other aircraft received considerable attention for their part in this program – the General Dynamics F-111A and the B-57G, the latter known as TROPIC MOON III. During 1967, as these were undergoing initial development, the Limited

Warfare Office at Wright-Patterson AFB invited Boeing to participate in the SCNA program. This called for modifying 30-40 aircraft, with a maximum of 72 converted airplanes.

Boeing and Emerson Electric Company jointly proposed the B-47 as the TROPIC MOON IV (this name may have been used only by Boeing in its proposal). The existing BNS was supplanted by a new radar operated by the weapons officer who replaced the navigator. Sensors included an LLLTV system, an IR scanner, and a laser designator. The bomb bay carried a Hayes dispenser for dropping bomblets, as well as two twin-turrets each with a 20mm M61A1 Gatling gun mounted in the belly. In one version of the proposal, Boeing recommended replacing the six J47 engines with four J57s. With approximately 700 B-47s in storage at MASDC, Boeing argued they could take their pick of the best low-time airframes for conversion. By early 1969 it was clear that the Air Force was not interested in the Boeing proposal. Pacific Air Forces (PACAF) commander General John D 'Jack' Ryan was hostile to these 'special ops' programs in general, complaining that PACAF was being forced to use whatever 'junk' Wright-Patterson could dream up. Moreover, the B-57G TROPIC MOON III program seemed to be paying operational dividends, and reclamation at MASDC was randomly destroying B-47s without regard for their potential conversion.

Other proposals for using the B-47 in Southeast Asia ran the spectrum from conventionally armed tactical bomber to a drone similar to the BRASS RING variant. In 1965 Boeing received a small contract to research an external stores capability on the B-47 in combination with a return to the original 'long' bomb bay. OCAMA studied a high-density bomb bay configuration so the airplane could carry more conventional weapons. A June 1965 study for the Air Command and Staff College (ACSC), Air University, Maxwell AFB, examined the use of the B-47 in the role of reconnaissance and interdiction in limited and counterinsurgency warfare. The author compared the B-47 with the RF-101 and F-105D, and found that the bomber could perform both tasks assigned to these two fighter types. He proposed that the B-47 be modified with a new strike camera for reconnaissance, the long bomb bay, an external bomb pylon where the drop tanks were mounted, and a B-3A bomb release intervalometer control to be used with the MA-7A in order to release from 1 to 50 bombs at pre-set intervals. The B-47's MA-7A bombing/navigation system allowed radar or optical sighting of targets with dual offset capability. This allowed the system to drop bombs on a target even though the target was not on the radar scope.

Three different mission profiles were envisioned for this modified Stratojet. As a pure reconnaissance aircraft, it would have had a range of 3,300nm (6,112km). As an armed reconnaissance bomber carrying 18 x 1,000 lb (454kg) bombs, the range dropped to 2,900nm (5,371km). The final profile replaced the wing tanks with bomb pylons. This configuration resulted in a range of 2,400nm (4,445km) with 34 x 1,000 lb bombs. At the time the study was written there were some 300 B-47s still in the active inventory. These could be modified as they were retired from SAC units and, if the program proved successful, there were many more stored in the desert for more conversions or as a source of parts. Not surprisingly, this 'ivory tower' idea did not result in any modifications.

One additional program calling for B-47 combat operations in Southeast Asia was a derivative of the earlier MB-47 BRASS RING project. This later initiative, purportedly known as SOD BUSTER, incorporated a TV camera in the nose of a QB-47 'to transmit video to a DF-100F drone director whose back-seater was flying the Stratojet.' Distances between the drone and controller of as much as 50nm (93km) were achieved, but the plan was for the DF-100 to fly 10-15nm (19-28km) behind the QB-47. The bomber would carry 35,000 lb (15,876kg) of explosive slurry in its fuel tanks and would

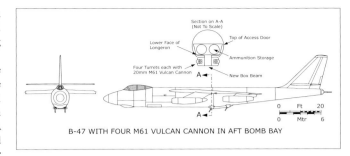
B-47 WITH FOUR M61 VULCAN CANNON IN AFT BOMB BAY

dive directly into the target. According to one estimate, a single QB-47 sortie (total cost of $664,000) could achieve what 73 Republic F-105 sorties (total cost of $9,610,280) could do under the same wartime assumptions.

Atomic Testing

The first use of a B-47 in a live atomic test took place during Operation GREENHOUSE in April and May 1951. XB-47 46-0066 was part of the blast effects research during each of the three detonations. The XB-47 did not carry or drop a weapon, but instead received basic instrumentation to assess the blast's overpressure, gust loads, and heat on the airframe while tracking its exact position relative to ground zero. The Air Force transferred 46-0066 to Boeing on 8th June 1950 for a variety of modifications, including a bomb bay fuel tank and 'special bomb bay configurations' to increase range and reliability. In addition, Boeing replaced the K-2 bombing system with the AN/APQ-24 system. The airplane was returned to the Air Force on 1st October 1950.

Crew for each of the three atomic flights included pilot Major Robert W 'Bob' Halliday, copilot Major James E 'Jim' Bauer, and observer Lieutenant John T 'Ted' Jurcyk. For the DOG test on 7th April, *Elaine 24* flew at 24,800ft (7,559m) and was 6,800ft (2,073m) from ground zero. On 20th April, *Elaine 33* (the call sign changed with each test) increased its altitude during the EASY test to 33,000ft (10,058m) and its lateral separation to 18,810ft (5,733m). It reached the farthest point on 8th May for the GEORGE test, when it was slated to be at an altitude of 35,000ft (10,668m) and 45,500ft (13,868m) from ground zero. Unfortunately, a rapidly developing rainstorm engulfed *Elaine 35* and its participation in GEORGE was canceled. Test results confirmed that the XB-47 could tolerate a relatively low-yield atomic blast when the bomb was dropped from high altitudes. The question remained, however, how well the B-47 would fare if it were to drop higher yield weapons, including the yet-to-be-tested hydrogen bomb.

The Hydrogen Bomb

The first detonation of a fusion hydrogen bomb was planned for the IVY series of tests in late 1952. IVY-MIKE was not an actual bomb but a structure containing a fission atomic bomb that would ignite the 54-ton thermonuclear (TN) assembly. A successful detonation took place on 1st November 1952, with a yield of 10 megatons (Mt). IVY-KING followed on 16th November and utilized a Mk 18 bomb dropped from a B-36H, with a yield of 500 kilotons (kt). SAC lacked test data on the blast radius of a hydrogen bomb and was justifiably concerned about the effect of the blast on the delivery aircraft. Four SAC bombers were assigned to evaluate this effect: B-36D 49-2653 (*Easy 01*), B-47B 50-0037 (*Easy 02*), and B-29As 45-21863 (*Easy 03*) and 44-84035 (*Easy 04*). The two B-29s dropped instrumented canisters that transmitted altitude, temperature, and pressure as they descended through the blast area. The B-36 and B-47 were configured with thermocouples, strain gauges, accelerometers of various types with recording meters and oscilloscopes, and flew at varying altitudes and lateral positions from the blast. These data would suggest the maximum yield which could be used without damaging or destroying the delivery aircraft.

According to the declassified Defense Nuclear Agency (DNA) Project IVY test report, B-47B 50-0037 was assigned to the 2nd BW at Barksdale AFB (which is odd considering the 2nd BW did not receive its first B-47 until February 1954!) and its flight crew of three and some 30 maintenance personnel were seconded for the tests. In fact the airplane was assigned to the Air Proving Ground at Eglin AFB through 31st March 1952, when it was reassigned to WADC at Wright-Patterson AFB. On 25th May 1952 it was redesignated as an EB-47B (at the time 'E' denoted 'exempt' use). Sensors were installed during June and July for Project C.1.3.610 'Free Air Pressure as a Function of Time,' and it arrived on Kwajalein on 28th September. Crew for the test flights included Major James E 'Jim' Bauer (copilot), Captain Eugene 'Gene' Deatrick (aircraft commander), and Captain Charles J 'Charlie' Gilmore (observer). During one rehearsal flight on 18th October, a severe rainstorm, lack of a suitable ground-controlled approach (GCA) system, and minimum fuel forced it to land on the emergency divert strip at Roi Island. The runway was only 4,100ft (1,250m) in length, but ATO and a nearly empty fuel load made the subsequent departure scary but successful.

For each test the B-36 and EB-47 were positioned 'at the very threshold of damage [so that] the actual structural distortion and skin temperature rise under realistic conditions [could] be determined.' Each airplane had a 5-second tolerance to be in position, otherwise any error would either 'endanger the aircraft and crew or tend to

make the data less meaningful.' For the MIKE test, the EB-47 was at 35,000ft (10,668m) and 11nm (20km) from ground zero. For the KING test, it was at 35,000ft and 9,800ft (2,987m) lateral distance from ground zero. In both cases the EB-47 was on a heading of 180° from ground zero, and in neither test did the EB-47 experience any contamination.

Additional tests continued with the CASTLE series during March through April 1954 using the same WADC airplane from the IVY test, although on 10th June 1953 50-0037 was redesignated as an ETB-47B. It operated in conjunction with B-36D 49-2653 (*Elaine 01*) for Project 6.2b 'Thermal Effects on B-47B Aircraft in Flight' using the call sign *Elaine 02*. Thermal increases were no more than 200°F (93°C) on the thin-skinned ailerons and elevators, with minimal resulting deformation. SAC planners wanted more information, however, specifically the blast effects on the airframe, wings, and a more detailed assessments of the thermal effects with and without anti-flash paint, tests which would be an integral part of the REDWING tests.

Nevada Test Operations

Atmospheric tests in March and April 1953 as part of UPSHOT-KNOTHOLE took place at the Nevada test site and involved B-47s both in blast measurement and Indirect Bomb Damage Assessment (IBDA) roles to determine if a 'radar return from a nuclear explosion could determine ground zero, yield, and height of burst.' For the DIXIE test on 6th April 1953 a B-47 from the 4925th Test Group (TG) flew above 40,000ft (12,192m) and – approximately eight minutes after the detonation – released five canisters containing sensors and telemetry equipment. A canister was dropped every 650ft (198m) and passed through the ascending cloud. Reports also indicate that '11 or 12' B-47s from MacDill AFB orbited the blast site at 37,000ft (11,278m) for 50 minutes after the blast. They were configured for IBDA Project 6.3 'Interim IBDA Capabilities of Strategic Air Command'. For the SIMON test on 25th April seven B-47s from the 305th BW at MacDill AFB flew a mass formation IBDA mission at 37,000ft. They flew over the shot site and tested the 'IBDA equipment and familiarized themselves with operations pertaining to nuclear warfare.'

Additional Nevada tests included the TEAPOT series from 18th February to 15th May 1955. An RB-47E from Lockbourne AFB and one from Forbes AFB photographed the TURK detonation on 7th March from directly above ground zero at altitudes above 40,000ft. Two RB-47s conducted IBDA assessments for the APPLE-2 test on 5th May, both from high altitudes. The 'HA' (high altitude) test on 6th April involved dropping a 3.2kt device from a B-36 at 36,620ft (11,162m). Just prior to release seven F-86s and an unidentified B-47 'laid a smoke trail' to assist in blast photography. In addition, two RB-47Es from the 55th SRW took photographs of the test, while four B-47s from Davis-Monthan AFB flew over ground zero some three minutes before the blast at altitudes from 34,000ft to 39,000ft, much like the UPSHOT-KNOTHOLE SIMON test. A final test on 15th May – ZUCCHINI – once again had three B-47s from Davis-Monthan AFB conduct IBDA flights.

REDWING

B-47s were involved in additional atmospheric nuclear tests in the following years. During the REDWING series of tests between May and July 1956, four B-47Es took part in two distinct scientific studies. The first of these was essentially a rehash of the 1952 IVY and CASTLE series. B-47E 52-0389 – nicknamed *Bubba Boy* – from WADC was assigned to the 4930th Support Group (SG) at Eniwetok for Project 5.1 'Thermal and Blast Effects on a B-47E Aircraft in Flight' from 1st April through 23rd July 1956. The crew included Captain Thomas M Sumner (aircraft commander), Claude Brown (copilot, rank not

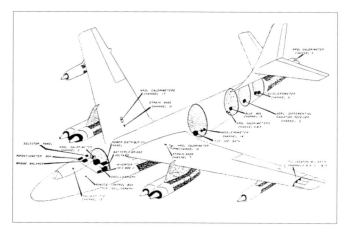

B-47B 50-0037 was configured with a variety of sensors to measure thermal and physical stresses associated with a nuclear blast.

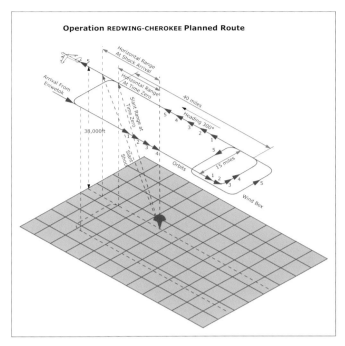

Operation REDWING-CHEROKEE Planned Route

known), and Joe Dean (navigator, rank not known). This assessed overpressure, gust, irradiance, radiant effects, and structural bending, shearing, and torsion in the wings and stabilizers, engine performance, as well as thermal effects on the airplane in an effort to update the *B-47E Weapons Delivery Manual* prepared by OCAMA. The B-47E was positioned abeam ground zero for the MOHAWK and HURON shots, and was heading away from ground zero for the remainder of the detonations. Precise positioning was accomplished by a ground signal utilizing the pilot's instrument landing system (ILS) needle (the main transmitter failed during the 20th May CHEROKEE test, forcing all the test aircraft to utilize their own navigation). In each of the later tests, 52-0389 was markedly closer to ground zero than in the IVY tests. The altitude was comparable at 35,000ft (10,668m) but the distance was 5.4nm (10km). Unfortunately, the B-52B drop aircraft (52-0013) released the weapon early, with the WADC B-47E effectively above ground zero when it exploded. The only choice was to accelerate to Mach 0.81 and hope to survive – they did.

Results were daunting. The highest airframe temperatures recorded were during the DAKOTA shot on 25th June, reaching 547°F (286°C), sufficient to distort the elevators and ailerons but not enough to render them ineffective (they nearly melted during the botched CHEROKEE shot). During the DAKOTA test the wing flexed to 89% of its maximum design limit, with the highest stress at Wing Station 615 near the inboard edge of the aileron. Several portions of the airframe, such as the bomb bay doors, showed significant buckling

Above: During the REDWING-CHEROKEE test the B-52 dropped the bomb early, which meant that B-47E 52-0389 was not *ahead* of the blast as planned (seen here), but almost directly *above* it. The airplane and crew barely escaped.

Right: The two prototype EB-47L PIPECLEANER radio relay jets took part in the FISHBOWL series of the 1962 DOMINIC atmospheric nuclear tests. Results showed considerable disruption of radio communication.

and distortion from the overpressure and blast effects. The white anti-flash paint reduced the surface temperature gains by a consistent 50%.

In addition to the blast effects B-47, three B-47Es (52-1416, 52-3354, and 52-3369) from the 301st BW took part in the REDWING tests as IBDA aircraft. These took 'long range radar scope photos of the burst to ascertain if such a technique would be valuable to measure burst yield.' A memoir by Lieutenant Colonel Robert H Ottman, who flew one of these missions, suggests that the ultimate goal was to 'assess the damage from the detonation on the ground.' Considering that the REDWING tests were effectively over water and very small islands, this seems less plausible than the intent to use the on-board radar to determine blast size (and hence yield). During the CHEROKEE test when the B-52 drop aircraft released the weapon early, the resulting 3.8Mt blast accidentally damaged many of the research aircraft, including at least one of the IBDA B-47Es. Test results showed, among other things, that the thermal curtains were so insufficient as to merit immediate replacement. The ability of the onboard radar to measure blast effects was inconclusive, and the three IBDA airplanes returned to operational use.

Overall REDWING produced the desired results for the B-47. It validated prior test data on survivability, verified the need and benefit of using white anti-flash paint on the undersurfaces (corroborated by a similar test using a Douglas JB-66), and reaffirmed the existing B-47 weapons delivery procedures for high-altitude bomb delivery. Indeed, the final report concluded that the 'B-47E not participate in any future nuclear tests for the purposes of determining its weapons delivery capabilities.'

B-47 operations in support of atmospheric nuclear testing continued with the 1957 series known as PLUMBOB. On 19th July 1957 two RB-47Es photographed the Douglas MB-1 (AIR-2) Genie nuclear rocket fired from F-89J 53-2547 during the JOHN test. IBDA sorties resumed with the SMOKY test on 31st August involving two unidentified B-47s operating from Indian Springs AFB, NV, as did NEWTON on 16th September and WHITNEY on 23rd September.

Operation DOMINIC

Two PIPECLEANER radio relay EB-47Ls (52-0292 and 53-2329, call signs *Baxter* and *Byron*, respectively) provided the communications link between Hickam AFB and airborne command post (ABNCP)

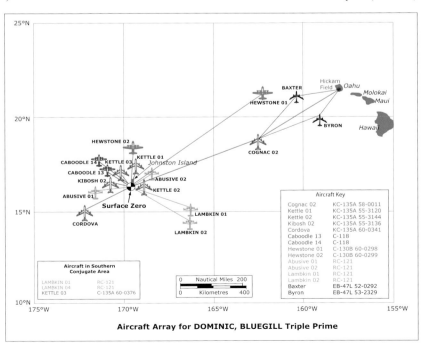

Aircraft Array for DOMINIC, BLUEGILL Triple Prime

Aircraft Key	
Cognac 02	KC-135A 58-0011
Kettle 01	KC-135A 55-3120
Kettle 02	KC-135A 55-3144
Kibosh 02	KC-135A 55-3136
Cordova	KC-135A 60-0341
Caboodle 13	C-118
Caboodle 14	C-118
Hewstone 01	C-130B 60-0298
Hewstone 02	C-130B 60-0299
Abusive 01	RC-121
Abusive 02	RC-121
Lambkin 01	RC-121
Lambkin 02	RC-121
Baxter	EB-47L 52-0292
Byron	EB-47L 53-2329

Aircraft in Southern Conjugate Area	
LAMBKIN 01	RC-121
LAMBKIN 04	RC-121
KETTLE 03	C-135A 60-0376

KC-135A 58-0011 for the 9th July 1962 DOMINIC STARFISH BLUEGILL TRIPLE PRIME test. SAC Project number 7.4 'Communications Propagation Investigation Equipment' assessed 'high-altitude nuclear blast effects on a KC-135 ABNCP and UHF, HF, and LF propagation and communication systems performance.' This measured 'nuclear effects on (1) Ground/air/ground operation of 15-channel UHF FM multiplex system; (2) Ground and airborne operation of high-powered LF system; and (3) SAC HF command communications system.' KC-135A 58-0011 functioned in the ABNCP configuration and served as an air-to-air-to-ground relay between Hickam AFB and the task force's surface ships. KC-135A 60-0341 (call sign *Cordova*) from Larson AFB, WA, served as an 'airborne transmitting platform for LF propagation tests and as an airborne receiving platform for HF and UHF tests…' Boeing installed a special 'high power' LF transmitter and trailing wire antenna (TWA) in this standard KC-135A tanker, and provided technicians to operate them during the nuclear detonation. Test results were ominous. Although UHF communications were restored fairly rapidly, they were limited by line-of-sight and had a marginal radius of 250nm (400km). Effects on HF and LF were far more serious. HF transmissions returned to normal after two hours, but LF communications – intended for use with underground and submarine launch facilities – were still not usable after 20 hours.

JB-47E 51-2279 was originally assigned to the WADC until 1955 when it transferred to the AFSWC. It remained there until 1958 when it reverted to a standard B-47E. *USAF*

B-47E 53-2276 parked next to B-52B 52-0013 which dropped the ill-timed CHEROKEE bomb. 53-2276 was reportedly associated with EMP testing while assigned to the AFSWC. *USAF*

Other Test Support

B-47s were also used in support of the development of special weapons for other aircraft. One B-47 was used in tests of the McDonnell Model 96, a combination fuel tank/bomb case that was to be carried by the F-101. The first test drop was made on 16th March 1954 but the weapon combination was never successful. From 1957 to 1959 a B-47 was used for drop tests of the TX-41 – a proposed weapon for the North American XB-70 – from altitudes up to 40,000ft (12,192m). Some drops were free-fall while others were parachute-retarded. In late 1959 and early 1960 the Stratojet was used in drop tests for the TX-53, a weapon designed for use in the Convair B-58's pod. Four drops were made at Edwards AFB but some difficulty was encountered in separating the weapon from the bomb bay, reminiscent of earlier B-47 drop problems. Several modifications were attempted including additional spoilers for the B-47.

ATOMIC AND NUCLEAR TESTING INDIVIDUAL AIRCRAFT
In addition to the three testbed B-47s listed above, 13 more were associated with atomic testing while assigned to the 4925th Test Group (TG) of the AFSWC at Kirtland AFB. Specific tasks or missions for each of these have not been declassified in sufficient detail to make accurate tie-ups possible.
50-0002 This EB-47B was assigned from 6th November 1952 through 27th January 1953.
50-0026 This B-47B was assigned to the 4925th TG for only five days beginning on 21st March 1953. It crashed on takeoff on 26th March 1953 (see Appendix II).
50-0077 This B-47B arrived at AFSWC on 9th May 1952 and was redesignated as an EB-47B on 24th June 1952, and as an ETB-47B on 6th June 1953. It was transferred to the 6510th Air Base Group (ABG) at Edwards AFB, CA, on 19th October 1954.
51-2046 The airplane served as a 'special weapons carriage and release vehicle.'
51-2071 This B-47B was delivered from Douglas-Tulsa to the AFSWC on 20th September 1952. Three days later (23rd September) it was redesignated as an EB-47B, and on 1st December 1955 became a JB-47B. The airplane served as a 'special weapons carriage and release vehicle.' It was transferred to the 3520th CCTW on 14th June 1956 as a B-47B for use as a trainer.

51-2078 This B-47B was delivered from Douglas-Tulsa to the AFSWC on 1st November 1952, and it was redesignated as an EB-47B on 18th November. It became a JB-47B on 1st December 1955. The airplane served as a 'special weapons carriage and release vehicle.' It was transferred to the 3520th CCTW on 9th August 1956 as a B-47B for use as a trainer.

51-2155 Transferred from the 3520th FTW to the AFSWC on 17th September 1954 and redesignated as an EB-47B on the same day. It became a JB-47B on 27th February 1956. Redesignated as a B-47B on 31st October 1967. Relegated to MASDC on 28 August 1968 (see Appendix I).

51-2160 Transferred from the 3520th FTW to the AFSWC on 9th October 1954 and redesignated as an EB-47B on the same day. It became a JB-47B on 27th February 1956. Redesignated as a B-47B on 16th October 1956 and then transferred to the 321st BW on 1st November 1956 as a DB-47B.

51-2222 This former B-47B was assigned to the AFSWC on 25th March 1953 from Boeing-Wichita as an EB-47B. It was redesignated as a JB-47B on 12th January 1956. The airplane served as a 'special weapons carriage and release vehicle.' It was relegated to the 2704th ADGP on 29th June 1960 (see Appendix I).

51-2232 This former B-47B was assigned to the AFSWC on 21st April 1953 from Boeing-Wichita as an EB-47B. The airplane served as a 'special weapons carriage and release vehicle.' It crashed on 30th April 1954 (see Appendix II).

51-2279 This EB-47B was transferred from WRDC to the AFSWC on 23rd August 1955. It was redesignated as a JB-47B on 27th February 1956. It was reassigned to the 379th BW on 28th January 1958.

53-2276 This B-47E was transferred from the 303rd BW to the AFSWC on 18th December 1957. It was redesignated as a JB-47E on 16th January 1958, and became a B-47E on 31st October 1967. It was reportedly associated with electromagnetic pulse (EMP) testing. The final date of its association with the AFSWC is 2nd April 1968. It was subsequently transferred to the Eighth Air Force Museum at Barksdale AFB, LA (see Appendix III).

53-2347 Transferred from APG to the AFSWC on 26th January 1956, and was redesignated as a JB-47E on 27th February 1956. It was eventually returned to operational service with the 509th BW.

Toss-Bombing Modifications (LABS)

A 1954 demonstration of the Hughes GAR-2 (later AIM-4) Falcon air-to-air heat-seeking missile at the White Sands Missile Range for a group of senior SAC officials left them stunned. The Falcon, fired from 30° off-angle, easily tracked the Lockheed QF-80 drone and handily destroyed it. If an infrared (IR) missile could do that to a single-engine aircraft, SAC's observers worried, it would certainly be easier to shoot down a B-47 with six engines as heat sources. In an unrelated problem, existing plans to use ribbon parachutes to slow the fall of atomic weapons relied on the bomber flying at high altitude and high speed. Concerns over the potential of Soviet interceptors – such as the MiG-19 *Farmer* and MiG-21 *Fishbed* – capable of reaching high altitudes while operating at supersonic speed, especially if equipped with IR missiles, meant that SAC tactical doctrine would have to shift to low-level penetration. Low altitude would provide a modest defense against IR missiles as the ground would help mask the bomber's IR signature, but it also meant that bombers would be unable to evade the blast effects of thermonuclear bombs no matter how much drag a parachute might induce.

One solution to both of these problems was to use the 'toss-bombing' technique (later known as Low Altitude Bombing System – LABS), where the low-flying bomber would release its weapon during the upward arc of a climbing maneuver and then reverse course to avoid the blast from a high slant range. This was not unreasonable in a fighter, but for a medium bomber this kind of flying was radically different from the 'straight-and-level' bomb runs so deeply inculcated into the bomber crew force. SAC's Lieutenant Colonel Doug Nelson (later the SAC program manager for the Lockheed SR-71) put numbers to this proposal by suggesting that the B-47 fly at 500ft (152m) above ground level (AGL) and at 425 KIAS.

From September through December 1954 Boeing test pilots Richard W 'Dick' Taylor, Jack Funk, and Lew Wallick conducted 14 test flights in B-47B 49-2642. Prior to the B-47 flights they flew similar profiles in a Lockheed T-33, which Taylor said handled similarly to the B-47. Before flying the half-loop, Taylor, Funk, and Wallick flew a series of barrel rolls in the B-47 (one wonders if these didn't influence fellow Boeing test pilot A M 'Tex' Johnston's famous 'Gold Cup Roll' of the Boeing 367-80 on 6th August 1955). The first

over-the-top trial was made using 16 ATO bottles fired at the onset of the climb 'for added thrust to permit the most conservative maneuver.' Taylor recalled that the B-47 gained about 10,000ft (3,048m) during each maneuver, as did the lofted bomb, and took less than a minute to complete. As long as the airplane carried at least 100KIAS at the top of the half-loop Taylor believed it could complete the maneuver safely. Testing was not without incident however. On one flight the forward landing gear doors ripped off. During a negative-g test, Taylor lost the hydraulic boost system and was only able to recover 1,000ft (305m) above the ground. Although Boeing described the results as 'very satisfactory' it recommended further tests at a variety of gross weights, different cgs, and with the bomb doors open. Calculations based on using a Mark VI weapon with a burst heights ranging from ground level to 2,000ft (610m) with yields up to 676kt showed no risk of damage or irradiation to the aircraft or crew. Detonations of larger yield weapons, especially thermonuclear bombs, would almost certainly affect the B-47 as shown in the IVY and subsequent IBDA tests.

The actual bomb-tossing procedure was fairly straightforward. When the B-47 was 5nm (9.3km) from the target, a light and needle on the LABS gyro directed the pilot to pull up as he advanced the throttles to full power. The pilot then applied and maintained 2.5g until the airplane entered the initial stall buffet. At 45-55° of pitch the weapon was released. The B-47 continued inverted over the top and then began its 20° nose-low descent while rolling back to a normal upright position. Early Boeing documents incorrectly describe this as an 'Immelmann' maneuver, when in fact it was a half Cuban eight maneuver.

Additional tests by APGC followed at Eglin AFB using B-47Es 51-7069, 52-0370, and 53-2277. Low-altitude tests were conducted by Major Barnett B Young, SAC's B-47 program manager as aircraft commander, Captain Eugene Murphy as co-pilot, and Major George Gradel as navigator. Test flights began over Florida in daylight and

Table 7-3. **LABS B-47s**

Test and Development				
49-2642	51-7069	52-0370	53-2277	
HAIRCLIPPER B-47Es				
51-2358	52-0020	52-0251	52-3356	53-6201
51-2362	52-0021	52-0252	52-3357	53-6202
51-2390	52-0058	52-0255	52-3358	53-6203
51-2396	52-0096	52-0256	53-2145	53-6204
51-2398	52-0101	52-0379	53-2146	53-6205
51-2402	52-0102	52-0380	53-2147	53-6206
51-2406	52-0152	52-0381	53-2148	53-6207
51-2408	52-0153	52-0383	53-2149	53-6208
51-2415	52-0155	52-0384	53-2150	53-6209
51-2419	52-0194	52-0385	53-2151	53-6211
51-2422	52-0202	52-0388	53-2152	52-6213
51-2431	52-0203	52-0393	53-2153	52-6214
51-2433	52-0205	52-0453	53-2154	52-6215
51-2438	52-0228	52-0455	53-2155	52-6216
51-2444	52-0231	52-0462	53-2156	52-6217
51-5236	52-0232	52-0463	53-2157	52-6218
51-5255	52-0233	52-0464	53-2262	52-6219
51-7025	52-0234	52-0475	53-2263	52-6220
51-7026	52-0235	52-0476	53-2264	52-6221
51-7034	52-0236	52-0610	53-2268	52-6222
51-7039	52-0238	52-0611	53-2269	52-6223
51-7041	52-0241	52-0612	53-2271	52-6224
51-7051	52-0242	52-0614	53-2272	52-6225
51-7053	52-0243	52-0615	53-2274	52-6226
51-7066	52-0244	52-1409	53-2275	52-6227
51-7068	52-0245	52-1411	53-2276	52-6228
51-7072	52-0246	52-3343	53-2354	52-6229
51-17373	52-0247	52-3344	53-4239	52-6230
51-17376	52-0248	52-3345	53-6199	52-6231
51-17379	52-0250	52-3354	53-6200	52-6239

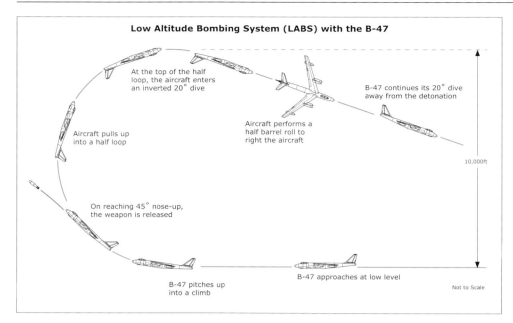

Low Altitude Bombing System (LABS) with the B-47

At the top of the half loop, the aircraft enters an inverted 20° dive

Aircraft pulls up into a half loop

B-47 continues its 20° dive away from the detonation

Aircraft performs a half barrel roll to right the aircraft

On reaching 45° nose-up, the weapon is released

10,000ft

B-47 pitches up into a climb

B-47 approaches at low level

Not to Scale

Left: The LABS profile was a half Cuban eight during which the B-47 gained approximately 10,000ft of altitude. The maneuver was not inherently dangerous when flown properly.

Below left: Boeing test pilots Jack Funk (l) and Dick Taylor (r) prepare for a flight in B-47E 51-7069 from Eglin AFB as part of the LABS evaluation program. Taylor had a long career with Boeing and became known as the 'father' of ETOPS – Extended-range Twin-engine Operational Performance Standards for commercial airliners.

Below center and right: B-47B 49-2642 was used for the initial LABS flight tests undertaken by Taylor, Funk, and Wallick. The initial tests were not without mishaps, including the near loss of the airplane following hydraulic boost pump failure. *Photos courtesy Boeing*

good weather, and eventually progressed to night, all-weather sorties over mountains in Idaho and Maine. Phase II testing involved both Young's crew and a SAC crew to verify the low-level training regimen, culminating in a flight on 15th April 1955 from Kindley AB, Bermuda, to 'attack' the Sandy Hook, NJ, ECM and radio complex. Although Young's crew completed the mission without being intercepted, the other B-47E (53-2277) crashed on takeoff. Phase III testing began with Boeing test pilots verifying that the bomb would clear the bomb bay. Over the next 90 days APGC crews dropped approximately 80 simulated bombs on Eglin AFB ranges 52 and 54A, with the final drops using 'shapes' of actual nuclear weapons. Accuracy of the drops was 'acceptable'.

In 1956 the Air Force moved to make LABS operational in SAC bomb wings. The first issue to resolve was identifying potential LABS aircraft. To ensure roll stability, Boeing recommended choosing any B-47s that were capable of operating with 4 units of aileron trim at 425KIAS – essentially most of the fleet – but preferred sorting through the fleet to find those B-47s that could perform the maneuver with only 2 units of aileron trim at 425KIAS. SAC chose the latter approach, and selected 150 B-47s for the HAIRCLIPPER LABS configuration. Lockheed did the modification work at its Marietta facility, including installation of the AN/AJB-4 LABS system, a roll gyro, and a very accurate tube-type Lear accelerometer. A 'pull up' and 'roll out' light was added to the pilot's instrument panel. A backup elevator power unit was installed as a back up to the primary one.

The second problem SAC faced in making LABS an operational reality was crew training. Boeing recommended a four-stage program over 22 sorties. These began with ground instruction followed by four low-level navigation sorties. The pilots then made two flights in a T-33 for aerobatic familiarization. The third stage included six flights for basic aerobatics in the B-47, notably barrel roll training. The final phase involved eight full crew training flights, including the half-loop, with 24 total releases of a 'shape'. Training the SAC force, however, proved to be far more difficult. At least four B-47Es were lost during LABS training: 53-6229 on 29th October 1957, 52-0241 on 4th December 1957, 52-0388 on 5th February 1958, and 52-0244 on 21st March 1958. Not surprisingly, former fighter pilots who had been forced into SAC found the procedure much easier to master than many of the 'old head' bomber pilots with little or no recent aerobatic experience.

Deep structural weaknesses leading to the MILK BOTTLE repair program, however, effectively killed LABS. Low-altitude penetration tactics remained, however, with the B-47 using a 'pop-up' maneuver with the bombs equipped with a ribbon parachute for delay as the B-47 made an aggressive 150° turn. Ultimately LABS was a costly – and fatal – failure. There were never plans to use LABS for the B-52, so it was essentially a stopgap measure for the B-47 which was seen as an interim bomber pending delivery of the B-52. If there was a bright spot for LABS, according to one SAC alumnus, it derived from forcing the Soviet Union to spend enormous sums of money on

low-altitude defenses while the US focused additional resources on its own ICBM strike force. This claim may be difficult to prove, however, as LABS ended in 1958, well before the Kennedy administration emphasized ICBMs over bombers beginning in 1961.

The Bomber/Missile MB-47

Much to the dismay of SAC's Commanding General Curtis LeMay, having atomic weapons and being able to deliver them were two disparate propositions. After assuming command of SAC in October 1948 LeMay recognized that there were insufficient atom bombs in the inventory and not all of SAC's B-29s were configured to carry what few bombs there were. LeMay was not alone in his concern over the immature state of America's atomic arsenal. On 8th December 1949 Air Force Headquarters directed AMC to identify new initiatives related to atomic 'weapon characteristics, weapon effects, logistics, and defensive methods.' The Deputy Chief of Materiel, Lieutenant General Kenneth B Wolfe, specified that AMC should seek new delivery methods, 'taking advantage of nuclear powerplants, rocket developments, and guided missile techniques.' He also emphasized the need to 'optimize each weapons system employing new atomic weapons and new methods of delivery.' Almost immediately the AMC study was pre-empted by a highly classified and extremely urgent tasking to identify within two and half years a vehicle to do a 'very special job.' This was the delivery of a 10,000 lb (4,536kg) 'package' over a distance of 4,000nm (7,408km) with an accuracy of no more than 2nm (3.7km) from a target's center. Moreover, the weapon carrier was not expected to survive the weapon's effects. This 'very special' weapon was, of course, the thermonuclear hydrogen bomb, then in development.

This seemed to be an ideal role for a guided missile, but the two-year deadline eliminated this option given the nascent level of Air Force missile technology. This led to the consideration of an existing Air Force bomber modified into a drone or guided missile. Any such airplane had to be 'inexpensive, dependable, reasonably invulnerable to enemy counteractions, scheduled as a production item, easily stabilized for automatic control, and available for flight test in the near future.' Major Gwayne S Curtis from the office of Director of Research and Development took charge of the study responsive to these guidelines. Only three bombers met these criteria: the B-36, the B-47, and the Northrop B-49. Curtis rejected the B-36 as too expensive and too vulnerable to enemy fighters. He considered the B-49 to be 'most invulnerable' to enemy actions but was far more expensive than the other two candidates. By default, Curtis recommended that the B-47 become the guided missile/drone of choice.

Several barriers remained to moving ahead with this new Project EAGLE. At least three B-47s, preferably from the B-47A production batch, would be needed, but these would compete with other testing

Above: B-47A 49-1905 was the BRASS RING director aircraft, seen here making its first flight in October 1952. *via Jay Miller*

Below: There were two BRASS RING drone/carrier aircraft – B-47B 49-2646 and 50-0001. Overall the project saw mixed results. The flight tests were generally satisfactory but defining the mission proved elusive. *Photo courtesy Boeing*

and research and development demands on a limited number of B-47s. More importantly, there was as yet no suitable guidance system available to 'fly' the unmanned B-47 to the target. Curtis believed, however, that by 1951 there would be sufficient maturity in this technology to resolve the guidance issue. Project EAGLE quickly earned the support of Major General St Clair Streett, formerly SAC's deputy commander and now AMC's deputy commander. He considered the project 'wholly justified in view of the total expense and destructive capability of the package carried.' Despite this endorsement, Air Force Headquarters disagreed, however, as Major General Donald L Putt believed that the jet-powered B-47 could escape the hydrogen bomb's blast effects if the crew took appropriate evasive action and the bomb was slowed by a parachute. Ultimately, Putt created Project CAUCASIAN to assess all aspects of delivery of thermonuclear (TN) weapons. Project EAGLE would be a subprogram under CAUCASIAN and was renamed BRASS RING.

By March 1950 AMC had approved the use of one B-47A (49-1905) as the director aircraft and two B-47Bs (49-2646 and 50-0001) as the carrier drones (had the program progressed to operational status, the carriers would have been designated MB-47s). Boeing was responsible for aircraft modification under contract AF33(038)-12883 dated 13th September 1950, with the innocuous Boeing project name MX-1457. North American Aviation was awarded the contract for development of a guidance system for the carriers. Sperry provided the automatic flight controls. Budget planning estimates for the entire program reached $4,900,000 over the next three years. The director B-47A 49-1905 was delivered on 1st May 1951 and it made its first flight in October 1952, eventually logging 23 hours. On 10th March 1953 a carrier B-47 flew a successful flight under remote control. Ultimately the airplanes logged a total of 119 flight hours out of the programmed 147 hours.

Table 7-4. BRASS RING Flight Data

MDS	Serial	Role	Total Hours	Total Flights
B-47A	49-1905	Director	23+09	14
B-47B	49-2646	Carrier	41+46	22
B-47B	50-0001	Carrier	54+15	44
			119+10	**80**

Technical problems arose immediately. The drone would need to operate in all weather conditions, day or night. Cloud cover would impede the necessary stellar navigation used to correct gyroscopic drift, allowing the airplane to stay under clouds for no more than an hour. Above 28,000ft (8,534m), however, clouds were fewer and thinner so would not adversely affect the navigation system. Equally troublesome was the ineffective level of stellar monitoring during daylight. In both cases, Boeing engineers used an equal measure of 'hope' with technical acumen to resolve these issues.

Concurrent with these technical problems the BRASS RING program suffered from operational indecision. In 1950 no one knew the size or weight of a hydrogen bomb. Boeing engineers estimated it could range from 20-25ft (6-7m) in length, be 5-9ft (1.5-2.7m) in diameter, and weigh anywhere from 10,000-80,000lb (4,536-36,287kg). Moreover, no one knew if it would actually work and if so what the blast effect might be. Again, Boeing engineers assumed a 40Mt blast detonated at a height of 10,000ft (3,048m) would produce a fireball capable of 'charring wood' within a 20nm (37km) and a hurricane-force wind beyond that. Ultimately, they decided, survival of a B-47 under these conditions would depend on pure dumb luck. Lack of technical data from an actual thermonuclear blast (which would have to wait until the 1952 IVY tests) meant that the operational procedures for BRASS RING would remain unknown, adversely affecting the development of the airplane and its systems.

Early plans called for each carrier B-47 to take off under the control of a director aircraft, climb to altitude, and establish cruise conditions. The director crew would then verify the carrier's systems and set its instrumentation to automatically accomplish the remainder of the mission. The carrier would then proceed on a Great Circle route to the target [for purposes of avoiding intercept the North American system allowed for a deviation of 350nm (648km) and the Sperry system 180nm (333km)]. How the carrier would deliver the weapon remained to be determined. In one scenario the bomb would be dropped following an automated – but otherwise normal – bombing run. What to do with the carrier after bomb release was not fully considered. In another scenario, the carrier simply dove into the target, eliminating it and the problem of what to do with the carrier. Target planners determined that 60.5% of all Soviet targets were within 4,000nm of Limestone AFB – which would be the east coast base for the carriers – and the remaining targets covered by carriers launched from Eielson AFB.

Target date for the completion of the first aircraft was July 1952. Ongoing delays by all three contractors reflected the extreme complexities of satisfying this fully autonomous carrier scenario. Nonetheless, the contractors remained extremely optimistic about meeting this deadline despite the many difficulties that ensued. North American's autonavigator was a constant source of trouble. The company had decided to use the unit being designed for the Navajo missile as the basis for its work. Not only did it not work correctly but weighed three times more than projected. With problems mounting, especially those with the guidance system, it became apparent that the aircraft could not be ready by the mid-1952 date. This led to a new mission profile which saw the director escorting the carrier aircraft until it was within 40-50nm (74-93km) of the target. The carrier would then proceed using a pre-set dead-reckoning

technique. For this method to be adopted, however, longer range B-47Es would be needed for directors and each carrier would require two directors for redundancy (or two directors for three carriers). This new profile would provide a means to deliver the bomb by December 1953, some 18 months late.

As if this modified scenario did not eviscerate the need for a fully autonomous carrier, AMC completely obviated the need for a complicated technological solution by suggesting that the carrier B-47 have a flight crew. The original BRASS RING proposal called for a 4,000nm range, but this was unachievable in either of the autonomous scenarios without some means of air refueling. The final AMC protocol used a standard crew of three to navigate the airplane during its cruise to the target while accomplishing two air refuelings to achieve the desired range. At some unspecified point following the second refueling (typically over the Arctic Ocean), the crew would bail out and the carrier would continue to its target. This prompted a series of tests for a safe method of egress for the crew, many of which were done in conjunction with work on the bomber version since the B-47Bs had no ejection seats. Although some of the engineers felt that the crew eliminated the need for the director B-47, the majority felt that role was still very much needed. In short, there would still need to be a director and each carrier crew was considered expendable.

Technical delays, bureaucratic wrangling over responsibility for test venues, substandard performance, and other 'paperwork' slowed development progress to a near halt. Infighting between Sperry and North American over whose equipment would be ready first quickly became irrelevant when both were well behind schedule and overweight (in May 1952 North American simply withdrew from the program).Boeing was subject to unanticipated changes as the AFSWC continually changed its mind about what a hydrogen bomb would look like or even weigh, forcing multiple design changes to the B-47 carrier airframe. Even after the first successful IVY test (which was in fact a device rather than a bomb) AFSWC could not determine the actual specifications of the first hydrogen bomb. At this point no BRASS RING carrier could be expected to be operational before July 1954.

By this time CAUCASIAN planners had increasingly favored the use of 'ribbon' chutes to retard the fall of nuclear weapons, allowing the bomber to avoid the blast effects which were better known following the IVY tests. Surprisingly there were doubters who felt that this method would subject the bombs to interception by Soviet warplanes and/or anti-aircraft fire from the ground! The success of the drogue chute effort and the technical problems faced by Boeing and Sperry raised doubts about the potential success of the carrier program. By 4th February 1953 the BRASS RING program, according to its declassified official history, 'hung by a thread.' If the 4,000nm range was an absolute requirement for the hydrogen bomb carrier, then BRASS RING 'warranted continuation.' If not, then the manned B-36 or manned B-47 would suffice pending the operational delivery of the B-52. In the absence of any immediate threat in early 1953, the Air Force waived the 4,000nm requirement. B-47s operating from forward bases in Africa, Asia, and Europe could deliver hydrogen bombs without the need for the director-carrier drone combination. The BRASS RING program was officially terminated on 1st April 1953 just as Boeing was close to finishing its test program. The B-47A director aircraft remained at Edwards AFB as part of the test inventory. The two B-47B carriers were subsequently redesignated as TB-47Bs and eventually removed from the inventory on 27th July 1954. The BRASS RING staff at AMC proposed other uses for the carrier B-47s such as collectors of atmospheric samples in nuclear testing and target drones (see QB-47Es). No requirements were found to exist, however, and the program was quietly put to sleep. The program had cost $2,300,000.

The GAM-63 Rascal was originally tested on DB-50D 48-0075 with the intention to declare it operational on DB-47s based at RAF Greenham Common. *Author's collection*

THE STRATOJET AND AIR-LAUNCHED MISSILES

Ongoing improvements to the Soviet air defense system meant that SAC's bombers would be intercepted much further away from their targets than desired. Long-range fighters, more precise early warning radars, SAMs, and greater defense in depth resulted in SAC planners figuring that fewer gravity bombs would ever reach their targets. Ultimately this led to a variety of air-launched missiles that could penetrate (or deceive) Soviet defenses, adding 'Hound Dog', 'Quail', 'ALCM', and 'cruise missile' to the nuclear lexicon. Not surprisingly, these had their origin in multiple test programs undertaken by B-47s.

Rascal

AMC planned an elaborate deployment scheme for the Bell Aircraft GAM-63 Rascal (Project MX776B), an outgrowth of the postwar Shrike program. The GAM-63 was 32ft (9.8m) long and 4ft (1.2m) in diameter. It carried a 3,000 lb (1,361kg) atomic warhead (initially a Mark 5 but this changed to a Mk 27) at Mach 2.95 for a range of 75-90nm (139-167km). After being launched from an altitude of 35,000ft (10,668m) the missile would climb to 65,000ft (19,812m) and then dive to the target at a 35° angle. Early tests were carried out with the DB-50D and DB-36H, but it was the B-47 that contributed most to its development and also its demise.

In late 1951 AMC declared that the B-47 would carry the Rascal, and its first overseas deployment would be to RAF Greenham Common in early 1956. On 22nd May 1952 AMC issued contract (AF33)600-22108 authorizing the procurement of a mockup 'director bomber' (DB). This was ready by December 1952, and work subsequently began on two YDB-47Es (51-5219 and 51-5220) at a cost of $7,376,566. The first flight was from Seattle in December 1953. During 1955 and 1956 two other B-47Es (53-2345 and 53-2346) were converted to the DB-47E configuration. Tests were flown out of Holloman AFB, NM, including actual launches. After fifteen months of testing, the Air Force approved a definitive contract (AF34)601-1506 on 10th March 1955, calling for 32 B-47Bs to be modified as director aircraft with 30 earmarked for modification as part of the EBB TIDE B-47B update.

The DB-47B modification inactivated the starboard bomb bay door and installed the strut for missile attachment. A retractable guidance antenna was installed in the lower aft fuselage, and the air refueling doors were relocated to the centerline of the nose similar to the RB-47. Additional electronic components were added in the bomb bay and observer's station. In order to incorporate the missile guidance equipment the bombing-navigation system was changed to the MA-8.

The first two DB-47Bs (51-2180 and 51-2190) were delivered on 14th November 1956 to the 445th BS, 321st BW at Pinecastle AFB, FL. The last arrivals included the YDB-47B prototype (51-2186), coming from Wichita on 13th July 1957, with the final DB-47B (51-2165) arriving on 24th July. [SAC records erroneously show 51-2175 as a 'GAM-63 capable DB-47B', but it was a B-47B with 3520th CCTW when it was lost 28th March 1956 (see Appendix II).] Target date for the 445th BS to become operational was December 1958. Until then, the DB-47Bs served as standard gravity bombers.

During late 1957 and early 1958 the 445th BS made numerous captive flight tests, and the first production GAM-63 arrived at Pinecastle AFB on 30th October 1957. Finally on 17th February 1958 a 445th BS crew fired a Rascal for the first time. It was released about 72nm (133km) from the target and impacted 1,100ft (335m) left of the target area. By the middle of May 1958 only three crews had qualified, largely due to the inadequate number of Rascals on hand, not to mention their poor reliability. On 13th and 16th May 1958, for example, the Rascals simply failed to launch. Another test on 23rd May successfully launched, but managed to fly only 30nm (56km) from the launch point, landing 45nm (83km) short of the target. On 9th June a fourth crew qualified with a live firing that missed its target by 1nm (1.9km). No more launches occurred until 16th September when the Rascal crashed only 4nm (7.4km) from launch. A subsequent shot on 24th September was better, but still missed the target by 3nm (5.6km).

This poor operational record was not surprising. General LeMay never favored the B-47/GAM-63 combination. As early as 1952

Table 7-5. **DB-47 Conversions**

DB-47Bs				YDB-47Es	
51-2160	51-2169	51-2178	51-2186	51-5219	51-5220
51-2162	51-2170	51-2179	51-2187		
51-2163	51-2171	51-2180	51-2188	**DB-47Es**	
51-2164	51-2172	51-2181	51-2189	53-2345	53-2346
51-2165	51-2173	51-2182	51-2190		
51-2166	51-2174	51-2183	51-2191	**JDB-47Es**	
51-2167	51-2176	51-2184		53-2345	53-2346
51-2168	51-2177	51-2185			

Top and center: During 1953 Boeing converted two YDB-47Es as the Rascal prototypes. 51-5219 was primarily used for captive carry tests and structural assessment. 51-5220 functioned as the systems integration testbed, including flights from Holloman AFB. *Boeing photos via Jay Miller*

Bottom: By 1956 B-47E 53-2346 had been converted into a DB-47E. Although the four Rascal testbeds were B-47Es, the planned fleet of 30 operational jets were all DB-47Bs. *USAF*

Below: The DB-47 carried missile guidance systems and computers in the bomb bay, with the retractable guidance antenna located in the aft fuselage.

Right: The navigator's compartment shows the additional equipment and modified radar unit required to launch and control the Rascal. This view looks forward through the narrow aisle, with the seat visible to the right. *USAF*

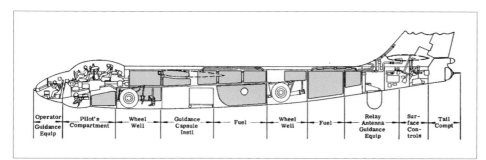

Below: DB-47B 51-2165 departs Pinecastle AFB on a training sortie. Crew qualification was a lengthy process due to the shortage of GAM-63s and fully configured DB-47s, as well as the Rascal's poor performance record. *USAF*

Above: The mount for the Rascal obstructed the starboard bomb bay door, so these were inactivated. Loading the GAM-63 required a pit adjacent to the Stratojet, seen here during loading tests on a DB-47E at Holloman AFB. Delays in constructing these facilities at Pinecastle AFB contributed to the eventual cancelation of the program. The DB-47 carried the Rascal at an angle, and the GAM-63's lower tail fin retracted while on the ground.
Left photo USAF, center and right photos USAF via Dennis Jenkins

LeMay preferred the Northrop SM-62 Snark over the Rascal, but even the SM-62 proved unsatisfactory. As disappointing operational evaluation data poured in from the 445th BS, LeMay objected to the Rascal program because it imposed substantial weight and drag performance penalties on the B-47, it needlessly complicated B-47 maintenance, it added $300,000 to the unit cost of modified aircraft, and it induced additional costs and problems in overseas logistics.

Second Air Force Headquarters asked that conversion be stopped after the delivery of just one airplane out of concern that the modification and training associated with the Rascal program would undermine the wing's Emergency War Plan. In addition, the new facilities required to maintain the Rascal were incomplete and behind schedule.

The Air Force Council rebuffed LeMay by claiming that the penalties on B-47 performance were 'not severe' and that the missile enabled the aircraft to deliver a nuclear warhead at supersonic speed. Besides, they added, this may someday be the only way to deliver any warhead from any airplane. SAC was unconvinced, but urged that if they were going to get the Rascal – which they clearly did not want – that it be the best weapon possible. Unfortunately, this was an utterly unrealistic goal. Without SAC's fullest support, the Rascal suffered from funding problems throughout its lifetime, and was almost canceled several times. Moreover, the Rascal underwent multiple (and, as some argued, needless) design changes. Initially the Rascal was to be controlled by signals from the DB-47 (vulnerable to detection and jamming), then it was to utilize an autonomous inertial guidance system, and then finally it only needed to be 'compatible' with the B-47's K System. Overall, the missile went through some 70 design changes, none of which resolved its many technical problems. In late 1958 SAC again recommended that the program be canceled and this time Air Force Headquarters agreed (sources differ on the date – 29th September or 29th November 1958). All parts of the Rascal project were rapidly disbanded. The storage and loading facility was still only 77% complete, and only 19 of the planned 30 DB-47Bs had either been fully or partially converted to carry the missile. All aircraft reverted to the gravity bomber configuration.

Crossbow

Two JB-47Bs (51-2328 and 51-2350) were equipped with four underwing pylons to carry a quartet of Radioplane GAM-67 Crossbows. These air-to-surface missiles were designed to home in on enemy radar transmitters, much like the anti-radiation missiles carried by 'Wild Weasels.' A manned capsule similar to that on B-47 ECM versions was installed in the bomb bay.

Flight tests at Holloman AFB, NM, began in December 1955 with the first successful powered flight on 2nd July 1956. The Crossbow's performance was less than hoped for. The cruise speed was 50KIAS less than predicted and its range was less than the average Soviet radar, rendering it ineffective as a long-distance homing weapon. The program was canceled in June 1957.

BOLD ORION

Improvements in Soviet early warning radar, interceptors, and SAMs meant that manned bombers were increasingly unlikely to reach their targets within the USSR. Programs like the Rascal for the B-47 and the GAM-77 Hound Dog for the B-52 were intended to overcome these threats. In both cases, however, these were fairly short-ranged weapons. By 1957 the Air Force was interested in an air-launched ballistic missile (ALBM) and the Martin Company received a contract for Weapons System 199B (WS-199B). Known as BOLD ORION, the missile was not intended as a viable weapon but as a technology demonstrator for potential ALBMs, including WS-138A which became the GAM-87 Skybolt.

The first six test launches used the Thiokol TX-20 single-stage solid-fueled rocket launched from YDB-47E 51-5220 during a 'zoom climb' profile. Former Rascal testbed JDB-47E 53-2346 also participated in the BOLD ORION tests. The second test launch ended in failure, but the other five achieved desired goals. Nonetheless, overall performance was less than optimal, and an Allegany Ballistics Laboratory (ABL) Altair rocket was added as a second stage, increasing the range to over 1,100nm (2,037km). All 12 launches were conducted from the Air Force Eastern Test Range (AFETR) at Patrick AFB, FL.

The final launch was an evaluation of the BOLD ORION as an anti-satellite weapon. During late September 1959 a B-58 launched an

Opposite page, top: Crossbow tests were undertaken on two JB-47Bs, each configured with four GAM-67s. The EWs sat in a bomb-bay pod, visible here. Despite its potential, the Crossbow never met expectations and was canceled. *USAF via Jay Miller*

Opposite page, bottom: The proliferation of Soviet early warning radars put SAC's bombers at risk even before entering Soviet airspace. The GAM-67 Crossbow-equipped B-47 'wild weasel' was an attempt to eliminate these radars. *Photo courtesy Boeing*

This page, right: Like Rascal, BOLD ORION was a large missile carried externally. The first airborne launch was from YDB-47E 51-5220. *Martin Aerospace*

Previous sources incorrectly list 51-5220 as a 'YDB-47B' and the sole BOLD ORION carrier. In fact, 51-5220 was a YDB-47E and JDB-47E 53-2346 was the second BOLD ORION testbed. *Martin Aerospace*

ALBM toward the Discoverer V satellite prior to its re-entry, but this test failed due to telemetry problems. A subsequent planned launch in early October of a BOLD ORION from the YDB-47E toward the Explorer VI satellite (which had suffered multiple system failures and was last heard from on 6th October) was canceled two seconds prior to launch due to 'technical problems.' The BOLD ORION launch finally took place on 13th October. Released from 35,000ft (10,668m), the BOLD ORION came within 3.5nm (6.5km) of Explorer VI at an altitude of 136nm (252km). The test was deemed successful under the assumption that the BOLD ORION carried a nuclear warhead that would have obliterated the satellite. President Eisenhower was opposed to any militarization of space, however, and the American anti-satellite program was terminated.

Table 7-6. BOLD ORION **Launches**

Date	Stages	Mission	Results
26 May 58	Single	ALBM	Success
27 Jun 58	Single	ALBM	Failure
18 Jul 58	Single	ALBM	Success
25 Sep 58	Single	ALBM	Success
10 Oct 58	Single	ALBM	Success
17 Nov 58	Single	ALBM	Success
08 Dec 58	Double	ALBM	Success
16 Dec 58	Double	ALBM	Success
04 Apr 59	Double	ALBM	Success
08 Jun 59	Single	ALBM	Success
19 Jun 59	Single	ALBM	Success
13 Oct 59	Double	ASAT	Success

A trapeze-like structure lowered the Quail from the bomb bay into the slipstream prior to launch, reducing problems associated with turbulence in the bomb bay. *Photo courtesy Boeing*

The size of the Quail as it is finally released from the bomb bay trapeze (barely discernable) shows why it was never adopted for the B-47. Even with smaller nuclear weapons the Quail took up too much space in the bomb bay. *Photo courtesy Boeing*

Quail

Plans in the mid 1950s to equip SAC's bomber force with decoys designed to flood Soviet radars with spurious targets began with the Convair XGAM-71 Buck Duck for the B-36. Development ended as the B-36 approached retirement, but efforts to produce a successor decoy for the B-47 and B-52 resulted in the McDonnell GAM-72 Green Quail (in 1963 this was redesignated as ADM-20 and simply referred to as the 'Quail'). The GAM-72 simulated the cross-section/radar signature of the B-52. Captive tests began in July 1957 at Holloman AFB using B-52s. During 1958-1960 B-47E 52-0538 and JB-47E 53-2104 joined the B-52s in the 27 live launches.

Given that the Quail would take up valuable bomb bay 'territory', plans to carry it in the B-47 were shelved. B-47E 52-0538 was relegated to the 2704th ADGP at Davis-Monthan AFB on 23rd March 1960 where it was scrapped by 2nd February 1961. JB-47E 53-2104 was redesignated as an NB-47E on 18th March 1960 and used in additional test programs.

QB-47E

American concerns about Soviet strategic bombers led to the requirement for a long-range surface-to-air missile (SAM) capable of high speeds, with the ability to evade airborne electronic countermeasures (ECM), and carry a nuclear warhead. Beginning in the early 1950s Boeing and the Michigan Aerospace Research Center (MARC) collaborated on a design called the BOMARC, combining the two company's names. By 1955 this was designated the IM-99, and flight tests were well under way by 1957. The BOMARC worked in conjunction with the Semi Automatic Ground Equipment (SAGE) then under development for the North American Air Defense Command (NORAD). Operators at centralized SAGE sites would detect, track, and launch the BOMARC at an incoming target. The missile would then accelerate to speeds of Mach 2.5-2.8 and climb to 66,000ft (20,117m) and fly toward its target. Once the BOMARC was within 10nm (18km) of the bomber it would use its internal guidance system for final tracking until detonation. Moreover, Air Defense Command (ADC) needed a more suitable target for its McDonnell F-101 Voodoo and Convair F-106 Delta Dart tests. The Army also required a bomber-sized target for its Homing All the Way Killer (HAWK) and Nike SAMs. Early tests were undertaken using Lockheed QF-80 drones as target aircraft but these did not mimic the size of the bomber or its potential ECM capabilities. BOMARC needed a target that could test its fullest capabilities. Excess RB-47Es proved an excellent choice as they could carry extensive ECM, chaff, and infrared (IR) countermeasures, and had approximately the same radar signature as a Tupolev Tu-16 *Badger*.

In December 1958 WADC awarded contract AF34(601)-4852 to Lockheed-Marietta for the development and Category I tests of a drone variant of the RB-47E. Two airplanes (53-4250 and 53-4264) served as prototypes, which Lockheed designated as XQB-47Es (although listed only as a QB-47E and later a JQB-47E on their individual aircraft record card), and TB-47B 51-2061 served as a support aircraft. Flight tests began with 53-4264 in April 1959 at Marietta, and relocated to Eglin AFB in May to determine the characteristics of the altered pitot-static sensing system (a long test probe was added to the nose) used in the drone stabilization and control equipment (DSCE) and A-12D autopilot altitude control. An F-100F served as the calibration aircraft. Results showed 'no appreciable change in pitot-static system accuracy.' Category II testing began on 4th January 1960 at the APGC facilities at Eglin AFB, FL. The two XQB-47Es flew a total of 44 test missions, all of which were manned by safety pilots. Lockheed received a further contract in April 1959 to modify a total of 14 RB-47Es (including the two prototypes), which were designated as QB-47Es on 25th November 1959. What followed is confusing and not fully understood. According to a newly declassified 1959 ARDC history, the Air Staff canceled the QB-47 entirely (Program Number 912A-

53-4250 (c) was the prototype QB-47E, and Lockheed designated it as an XQB-47E. Oddly enough, the entire program was canceled but 14 were eventually converted. *Lockheed Martin*

2128) but authorized completion of 'two prototypes and 12 production articles' with all further testing to be undertaken by APGC.

On 25th January 1960 all 14 airplanes were redesignated as JQB-47Es, but this was only reflected on the AFHRA record cards as other official records, press releases, and memoirs used QB-47E exclusively. Once converted the airplanes were assigned to the 3205th Drone Squadron at Eglin AFB. Category II tests ended in June 1960 after a total of 116 flight hours. Training and check out for ground and air crews, including indoctrination flights over the Gulf of Mexico, took place from April to May 1960 at Eglin AFB as part of Category III testing. Only sufficient QB-47Es to meet daily mission requirements were at Eglin AFB at any one time, with the remainder in temporary storage, likely at Marietta. If a QB-47 was lost or destroyed, a replacement would be flown to Eglin AFB, reducing its logistics 'footprint'.

Modifications to the airplanes cost $1.9 million each and included the installation of the Sperry DSCE which used an AN/ARW-64 UHF Guidance Radio providing control inputs, and an AN/APW-11 Radar Guidance Receiver-Transponder for ground-based radar tracking. Basic flight information used by the remote pilots included airspeed, altitude, heading, and RPM of engine #4 relayed by an AN/AKT-7 telemetry relay unit. The QB-47 carried two missile scoring systems, one electronic and one optical. Aerojet-General Company built the AN/USQ-7(XI-1) which could record miss distances of up to 4,000ft (1,219m). Four electronic 'firing error indicator receiving antennas' were mounted on the nose, top of the trailing edge of the vertical

Table 7-7. **Known QB-47E Dispositions**

Serial	Entered Modification	Out of Service	Location	Comments
52-0816	28 Mar 60	20 Jun 64	Eglin AFB	Scrapped
52-0817	28 Mar 60	08 Mar 62	EGTR	Lost control and was too low for attempted recovery.
52-0820	31 May 60	31 Aug 62	EGTR	Scrapped
52-0822	15 Jun 60	21 Jun 62	EGTR	Scrapped
52-0823	20 Jun 60	19 Aug 63	Eglin AFB	Ran off the runway and into traffic on a nearby road, killing two civilians.
53-4248	n/a	18 Aug 60	EGTR	Destroyed by BOMARC
53-4250	n/a	12 Jan 61	EGTR	Prototype #2 XQB-47E for Category II and III tests.
53-4253	n/a	07 Feb 62	Eglin AFB	Scrapped final QB-47 converted
53-4255	n/a	28 Sep 61	EGTR	Scrapped
53-4256	n/a	10 Aug 68	MASDC	MCGS
53-4258	n/a	17 Aug 61	EGTR	Scrapped
53-4259	n/a	23 May 61	Eglin AFB	Damaged in a landing accident at Field #3.
53-4263	n/a	22 Aug 68	MASDC	MCGS
53-4264	28 May 58	22 Mar 62	EGTR	Prototype #1 XQB-47E for Category I tests. Failed to respond to controller and was destroyed in flight.

Each QB-47 carried two underwing pods configured with cameras for optical measurement of miss distances. Fuselage-mounted camera can be seen above aft gear door. *Norm Crocker*

The QB-47 was the only B-47 variant equipped with a tail hook, but not for carrier operations! There are no records that show how many times the hook was used for operational landings. *Norm Crocker*

stabilizer, and on each wingtip. Bell & Howell manufactured the 6290A optical system, consisting of 14 x 16mm movie cameras programmed at 200 frames per second. Twelve cameras were contained in pods mounted in place of the external fuel tanks, providing full spherical coverage. The remaining two cameras were mounted in the fuselage ahead of the tail section to calibrate the position of the wing pods. Numeric data from the film was extrapolated to punch cards and entered into an IBM 704 computer for precise determination of the missile as it passed the QB-47, accurate to approximately 1,500ft (457m).

The QB-47 ECM suite was extensive using both internally and externally mounted transmitters and chaff dispensers. Some 15 units, including two AN/ALT-7s and a combination of 13 interchangeable AN/ALT-6, AN/ALT-7, AN/ALT-8, and QRC-49 sets could be carried internally. External ECM gear included multiple flush-mounted

antennas located on the aft fuselage by the empennage for eight sets of AN/ALT-6 and AN/ALT-8 transmitters and two AN/ALQ-31 wing pods with four sets of the same transmitters. Both AN/ALE-1 and AN/ALE-2 chaff dispensers were contained in the aft fuselage, along with AN/ALE-14 flare ejectors mounted externally over the ATO compartment. Two AN/ALE-9 forward-firing chaff dispenser pods could be attached to the wing pylons.

Structural changes to the QB-47Es included removal of the tail guns, ATO, and in-flight refueling gear, as well as installation of an arresting hook for use whenever the brakes failed or were inadequate to stop the airplane after landing. A 1in (2.54cm) steel arresting cable was suspended 6in (15cm) above the runway some 1,100ft (335m) prior to the overrun. The cable was attached to two rails parallel to the runway. When pulled by the arresting hook hydraulic pistons slowed the QB-47 to a stop (All-American Engineering, which

Should the QB-47 be unable to stop using brakes there was an arresting cable at the departure end of the runway. This would ensure the airplane would not run off into the grass following a 'hot' approach and landing. *USAF*

manufactured the system, also proposed this capability to stop B-52s and KC-135s, but SAC was, not surprisingly, unenthusiastic). The barrier was declared operational on 6th July 1960 following trials first using a truck and then a QB-47. During 1960 a hurricane forced the temporary evacuation of the QB-47Es to an unidentified SAC base in Texas. Tired of answering questions about the unusual appearance of the airplane – and especially about the tail hook – one crew chief told curious onlookers that the QB-47s were part of a test to deploy B-47s on aircraft carriers. Whether or not this tale prompted SAC B-47 crew transfer requests *en masse* remains part of the lore of B-47 history.

The airplanes were also configured with a destruct package consisting of 150-grain Primacord installed around the inside the aft fuselage at the aft main fuel tank bulkhead as well as the upper and lower longerons. If connectivity and control were lost, the QB-47 was programmed to enter a shallow left orbit and fly until its fuel was exhausted or a destruct command was received, blowing off the aft fuselage and empennage. A 'shotgun' aircraft – a fighter armed with live weapons – accompanied the QB-47 over land and provided a final backup should the internal destruct system fail. QB-47E 53-4264 was destroyed on 22nd March 1962 after it went into a left bank, control could not be reacquired, and the internal destruct system was activated.

Category I-III tests verified the remote control equipment would work properly, but the challenge of unmanned flight remained. Known as 'Nullo' flights, an abbreviation for Null Operator (and should not be confused with NOLO for No Live Operator), the QB-47E was under the control of ground-based MRW-5 operator for takeoff and landing, safety pilots flying in one of two Lockheed DT-33 companion airplanes until reaching the Eglin Gulf Test Range (EGTR) over the Gulf of Mexico (as well as while returning to land), and finally a ground-based radar site for the profile portion of the mission. Flight operations took place at Field #3 at Eglin AFB to minimize risk should control be lost. To assist the ground and airborne controllers, seven special external lights were added to the QB-47.

Following two simulated Nullo missions in July 1960, the first actual Nullo flight was scheduled for 21st July. This was canceled at the last minute due to conflicting Civil Aeronautics Authority (CAA) regulations over minimum safety altitudes. This was lowered from 20,000ft (6,096m) to 4,000ft (1,219m), and all QB-47s were grounded pending the installation of the parts required to incorporate this change. Following this upgrade, which began on 23rd July, the launch was planned for 26th July, but this was canceled due to bad weather, as were planned launches on 27th July and 4th August. The first Nullo flight finally took place on 5th August. Major Malcolm G Nichols (AC) and Captain Charles C Nunnery (CP) started QB-47E 53-4248 and taxied it into place at the end of the runway. As they exited the airplane an explosive ordnance disposal (EOD) team primed the destruct system (which was fully activated when the flaps were retracted, and inactivated when the flaps were extended). Now completely unmanned, the QB-47E took off at 8:21 AM and flew for four hours and two minutes over the EGTR. A single BOMARC-A was fired at the QB-47E flying at maximum range and 500KIAS on an in-bound course. The AN/USQ-7 cameras showed that the BOMARC passed within lethal range of its warhead, completing a successful test. Just prior to landing at Field #3, a wind gust caused the airplane to balloon, prompting a go-around. The next approach and landing were uneventful, stopping 3,300ft (1,006m) down the runway. The second Nullo flight on 11th August also suffered from landing issues. After bouncing three times, QB-47E 53-4250 departed the runway at Field #3. Damage was minimal, and, following a one-time flight authorization to Eglin AFB, it was repaired and returned to operational status within two months.

Table 7-8. **QB-47E External Indicator Lights**

Purpose	Color	Location
Anti-skid Inoperative	Yellow	Top of vertical stabilizer
100% Throttle Light	Clear	Both sides of vertical stabilizer
Low Fuel Warning	Red	Top and bottom of fuselage
Airspeed On	Red	Behind canopy
ILS Lock-on Light	Yellow	Both sides of the nose
Gear Down and Locked	Red	Under nose
ARW Carrier Light On	Clear	Behind canopy

Nullo missions were carefully choreographed both for mission safety and effectiveness, beginning five days before the flight when all personnel were alerted of an impending mission. Two days prior to the scheduled mission, crews flew a primary and backup QB-47 and the two DT-33s to Field #3 where they were serviced and given a thorough pre-flight maintenance check. On mission day the MRW-5 ground-control unit was moved to the approach end of the runway (based on surface winds) some five hours prior to takeoff. The MRW-5 was a modified Chevrolet 1½-ton panel truck with a roof platform where the two operators stood. The ECHO controller was responsible for the elevator (pitch) and throttles, and the ROMEO controller was in charge of the rudder (heading). An hour prior to departure the arresting barrier was installed and a flight crew started the QB-47 engines and then taxied to the end of the runway. The first DT-33 (YANKEE) would depart 20 minutes prior to the drone launch as the MRW-5 ground crew ensured full control of the QB-47. The EOD team installed the initiators for the destruct system, and the 'shotgun' airplane was orbiting in place to fly formation with the QB-47E once it was airborne.

The MRW-5 team was responsible for the takeoff, usually with water injection due to the short 8,000ft (2,438m) runway, and the

The first Nullo flight took place on 5th August 1960 with 53-4248. After taxiing the airplane into position the crew got out and waited until its return. This image has not been verified as the first flight, but it certainly represents how it would have appeared. *USAF*

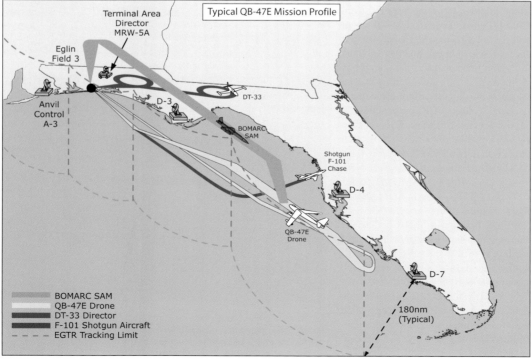

The ground controller (seated atop the truck) had duplicate flights controls for takeoff and landing. During METAL STICK missions, a flight crew remained in the QB-47 to facilitate ground controller training and proficiency. *USAF*

A representative QB-47 mission included multiple collateral airplanes, including one ready to shoot down the drone should connectivity be lost. QB-47 53-4264 did lose contact but was destroyed by the on-board system.

DT-33 crew assumed control of the QB-47 during climbout and cruise. The airborne pilot controlling the QB-47 from the back seat of the YANKEE DT-33 was known as the ALPHA pilot. A back up DT-33 – ZULU – carried the BRAVO pilot. When the QB-47 was within range of the EGTR Site A-3 on Santa Rosa Island, ALPHA would transfer control to OSCAR, the ground-based range controller, who would then 'fly' the QB-47 during the intercept profile. Altitudes ranged from 500ft (152m) to 44,000ft (13,411m). Speed was limited to Mach 0.81, and maneuvering limits were defined by the aircraft's maximum weight of 180,000lb (81,647kg). The local SAGE unit, known as ANVIL CONTROL, was responsible for directing the missile launch and intercept. Under optimal conditions, test engineers preferred to shoot two BOMARCs during each Nullo mission, although this often proved impossible given ongoing technical problems with the BOMARC.

Duration of the profile portion of the mission – planned for three hours – exceeded the endurance of the DT-33s, so they landed, were refueled, and were prepared for a 'scramble' launch should the QB-47 not have been shot down by the BOMARC (or other missile being tested). As the QB-47 was returning to land, ANVIL CONTROL would scramble the DT-33s to control it as it exited the EGTR and headed over land. After entering traffic pattern altitude the DT-33 transferred control to the MRW-5 operators for landing. An instrument landing system (ILS) was installed for use on Runway 18, but lack of funds limited Runway 36 to only a localizer approach. Once the drone was stopped on the runway the EOD disarmed the destruct system and removed the initiators, ground crews installed the landing gear downlocks, and the safety crew taxied the airplane back to the ramp. In addition to actual Nullo flights, QB-47s flew METAL STICK missions. These incorporated a safety crew in the QB-47 and were used for MRW-5 and DT-33 controller training.

Just as US bomber tactical doctrine increasingly relied on low-level penetration missions, US planners were concerned that Soviet bombers would use similar tactics. Efforts to test the BOMARC against targets flying at extreme low levels were limited by the line-of-sight range from the SAGE ground stations and range safety requirements. Using the DT-33s was considered too risky, as the distance between the DT-33 and the QB-47 was small enough that the BOMARC might inadvertently target the DT-33. Consequently, on 30th September 1960 the Air Force awarded the Sperry Corporation contract AF 33(600) 37918 to install the AN/APW-22 Microwave Command Guidance System (MCGS) in two QB-47s and QF-80C 45-8592 (already modified into a drone under Project BAD BOY) for flights as low as 50ft (15m) above the water. The DFCS was removed from QB-47E 53-4256 and the MCGS installed beginning 24th February 1961, followed by 53-4263 on 17th March. The controller aircraft was Lockheed GC-130A 57-0497 equipped with the AN/APW-23 Airborne Director system. Flight tests were undertaken over the White Sands Missile Range (WSMR) in New Mexico while deployed to Holloman AFB. QB-47E 53-4263 flew with manned backup on 18th May and 12th June 1961, with 53-4256 also flying a manned test sortie on 12th June. The first Nullo MCGS mission was on 28th June in 53-4263, which flew again on 29th June and reached a minimum altitude of 500ft (152m) for approximately one minute. The third Nullo MCGS mission was in 53-4256, also on 29th June. By January 1963 APGC determined that the costs for using the MCGS had become prohibitive and the system was removed from both airplanes, restricting them to a minimum of 500ft. Previous DFCS Nullo flights were limited to 1,500ft (457m). The first low-altitude post-MCGS Nullo flight was on 2nd January 1963 in 53-4263, which was successfully repeated on 14th February. The remaining four QB-47 missions in 1963 were all at 500ft.

There was a total of 54 Nullo missions from Eglin AFB from 1960 through 1964. Of these, 51 were considered 'effective' and 42 were

53-4250 performs a Nullo landing. Despite considerable practice these carried genuine risk. On 20th June 1960 52-0823 ran off the main runway at Eglin AFB and killed two civilians. *Photo 119410 courtesy Boeing*

Two QB-47s were assigned to the Microwave Command Guidance System program in 1960 to enable flights as low as 50ft above the Gulf of Mexico. Tests reached 500ft before they proved to be too expensive and were canceled. *Author's collection*

'recovered' after the test was over, but this did not mean they necessarily landed safely. Two of the 42 recovered flights crashed over the EGTR due to loss of control, and two more were lost in landing accidents, including one at Eglin AFB's main runway (rather than Field #3), resulting in the deaths of two civilians in a nearby car (see Appendix II). Eight QB-47s were shot down. The first of these was 53-4248 during the third mission on 18th August 1960 when it was struck by a direct hit from a BOMARC. QB-47s were designed as service drones, rather than target drones, and engineers projected that 1 out of 7 BOMARC launches would physically hit the QB-47 but the actual loss rate was much higher, and air-to-air missiles proved far more deadly in destroying the drones. Each QB-47 that survived a mission received a missile symbol painted on its nose. At one point 53-4258 reportedly carried 26 BOMARC symbols, although Air Force records note that the highest number of 'misses' was 16, but this unidentified QB-47 was shot down on its next mission. QB-47E 53-4256 was seen at MASDC with three silhouettes of a Lockheed YF-12 on its nose, suggesting that it survived three tests of the AIM-47 missile. According to Air Force records, there were only seven live AIM-47 firings at Eglin AFB, with five of these against Ryan Q-2Cs and two against QB-47s. On 25th April 1966, YF-12A 60-6936 piloted by Jim Eastham fired an AIM-47 at 53-4256 flying at 1,500ft (457m). The missile apparently hit the QB-47 empennage, taking off 3ft (0.9m) of the left horizontal stabilizer, but

Table 7-9. **QB-47E Low Level Nullo Missions**

Date	Serial	Location	Comments
28 Jun 61	53-4263	Holloman AFB	1st MCGS test flight
29 Jun 61	53-4263	Holloman AFB	2nd MCGS test flight @ 500ft AGL for 1 minute
02 Jan 63	53-4263	EGTR	1st Low Nullo at 500ft AGL
14 Feb 63	53-4263	EGTR	2nd Low Nullo at 500ft AGL
27 Jun 63	50-0823	EGTR	Low Nullo 2+35 at 500ft AGL
10 Jul 63	50-0823	EGTR	Low Nullo 1+45 at 500ft AGL
26 Jul 63	50-0823	EGTR	Low Nullo 2+30 at 500ft AGL
19 Aug 63	50-0823	EGTR	Low Nullo 3+20 at 500ft AGL, fatal crash on landing

controllers managed to bring it back to land. It survived a second test shot by the same YF-12 on 21st September 1966, this time while flying at 'sea level'. Where the third YF-12 silhouette on 53-4256 came from remains unknown.

By 1967 the two remaining QB-47s (53-4256 and 53-4263) began deploying to Holloman AFB for tests in other programs. In August 1968 they were retired to MASDC, where they were listed as 'QB-47Es' rather than 'JQB-47Es.'

There was some discussion in SAC during 1959 about the conversion of an unspecified number of RB-47Es into SQB-47s, similar to the earlier BRASS RING MB-47 program. On 5th July 1959 General Power asked SAC's Office of Operations Analysis to determine the availability of remotely piloted nuclear-armed airplanes used in the first-wave, low-level penetration attacks and establish a requirement for their use. Planners estimated that the first airplane would be available by 12th January 1962, with 600 converted by 1st July 1965. Each SQB-47 would cost $200,000, and keeping them on alert would cost only $100,000 per annum versus $1.2 million for the manned alert force. They naively estimated that 90% could survive a launch under alert conditions, and 90% of these would reach their targets using inertial guidance. Aside from needing

an extensive airborne control force made up of other B-47s, KC-135s, or C-130s, actual QB-47 test operations at Eglin AFB revealed the prohibitively extensive equipment and procedures needed for drone operations, and the project was dropped.

Claims that QB-47s participated in the US overflight operations during the Cuban Missile Crisis in October 1962 are untrue. The airplanes were not configured to carry any type of reconnaissance gear, and their speed, altitude, and limited maneuverability made them completely vulnerable to interception and destruction, especially by SAMs. US Navy Vought RF-8 Crusaders and CIA (later SAC) U-2s fulfilled all overflight missions. These erroneous claims may have derived from the QUICK FOX drone overflight missions.

BIG MOMMA

Arguably the most spectacular test involving B-47 was Armaments Division Project 1957 'Protection Shelter for Tactical Aircraft,' otherwise known as BIG MOMMA. The goal was to determine the protective benefits of different type of 'steel bin type revetments' for parked B-52s in case one exploded. The original plan called for six B-52s to be parked at varying distances and in different types of protective shelters at White Sands, NM. All would be fully fueled, some fully armed. One of these would then be blown up to determine the effects on the other five. Even using retired B-52s this proved excessive, so the plan was altered to use two B-52s and three B-47s, although this was eventually increased to four B-47s.

The two B-52Bs (52-0007 and 52-0010) were each fully fueled, carried 66 x 750 lb (340kg) high explosive bombs, and a full load of 0.50 caliber machine gun rounds in the tail gun. The four B-47Es (53-1825, 53-2367, 53-2391, and 53-6237 – all transferred from storage at MASDC) had only full fuel loads. The airplanes were placed around the 'donor' B-52. The first test took place on 19th May 1966 with a follow-on test on 7th June 1966 using the remnants of the first test. Results were not surprising. The two B-47s parked opposite the donor B-52 were utterly destroyed, while those parked in revetments – even adjacent to the donor B-52 – suffered significantly less damage.

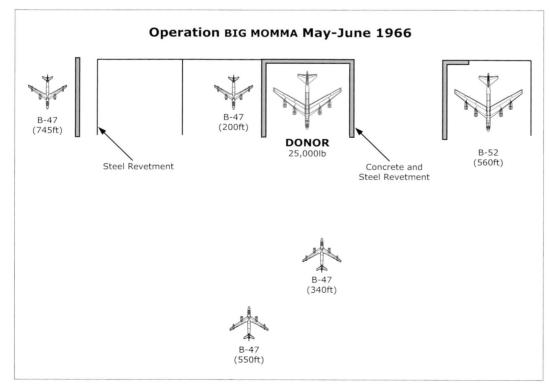

Operation BIG MOMMA May-June 1966

B-47 (745ft)

Steel Revetment

B-47 (200ft)

DONOR 25,000lb

Concrete and Steel Revetment

B-52 (560ft)

B-47 (340ft)

B-47 (550ft)

Above: Nose markings on 53-4256 remain a mystery. AF records show that there were only two missiles fired at QB-47s during YF-12 tests. Reason for the third silhouette is unknown. *Author's collection*

Left: The BIG MOMMA test resulted in the loss of two B-52s and four B-47s while assessing various methods of protection from ground explosions. A poor quality video exists on the World Wide Web showing the ultimate outcome.

Opposite: Identity of the second YB-47J prototype remained elusive given the absence of any MDS change. The image shows the MA-2 nose bulge, confirming that 53-2282 was the missing airplane. *USAF*

ADVANCED AERODYNAMICS AND AVIONICS

The B-47 was essentially an interim solution between the generation of aircraft that had flew in the Second World War and the generation of airplanes that would fly throughout the Cold War. As such it served as a testbed for new bombing and navigation systems – as well as the landing gear – for the B-52, improvements in aerodynamic handling of large swept-wing jets, and even improved designs for the next generation of air refueling tankers. Long missions strapped into ejection seats proved to be the source of considerable crew fatigue, and Boeing and ARDC undertook several tests to evaluate more comfortable seats, including an 80-hour flight on 30th November 1959 (see Appendix IV). Another test flight took place with the canopy removed entirely to determine if proposed cockpit modifications would help pilots assume the proper position for ejection.

Spoilers

The B-47's wings were perhaps its most important and innovative feature, allowing it to fly at high speeds normally associated with jet fighters. Conversely, the B-47's wings equally represented much of the airplane's weaknesses such as aileron reversal at high speed and the inability to slow down in flight, especially during approach and landing. The prototype XB-47s 46-0065 and 46-0066 was equipped with leading-edge slats to help with landing, but these were installed only on B-47As and early B-47Bs. The addition of vortex generators helped control boundary layer separation at high speeds, but otherwise the wings were kept 'clean' for both high-speed operations and to reduce drag and hence increase range. Spoilers were briefly considered for use on the B-47, but Boeing engineers decided that there was too little aerodynamic knowledge about their effects, positive or otherwise, and decided against installing them.

Boeing later proposed that SAC consider adding 'dual purpose spoilers' to the wings. These would 'increase safety during landing operations and remove the restriction to high-speed flight imposed by lateral control [reversal].' Boeing's engineers found that 35% of all B-47 accidents were the result of improper approach and landing procedures. By installing an upper-wing spoiler made up of six hydraulically actuated sections, the spoilers allowed the removal of the outboard half of each aileron, the 'culprit' in lateral control reversal. Boeing noted that the spoilers would also allow the B-47's placard airspeed to increase from 425KIAS to 500KIAS thanks to better lateral control. Moreover, the spoiler eliminated the need for the approach chute and its associated weight, but necessitated strengthening the wing trailing edge due to the aerodynamic forces generated by the spoilers when raised. During approach and landing the B-47 could be flown at higher speeds with a greater stall margin, as well as a steeper glide slope with less floating during the flare. Tests with 14 Air Force pilots using 46-0065 and 51-2052 validated these calculations with high marks of pilot satisfaction. The spoilers increased the B-47's weight by 235 lb (kg) and induced a 0.5% drag penalty to range which would be offset by the removal of the approach chute and its associated structures. Based on 1,000 conversions, the spoilers would cost $17,310.00 and require 2,481 man-hours per airplane to install.

SAC was not willing to spend the money on the conversion, nor was it willing to have a substantial portion of the B-47 fleet in modification to install the spoilers. Boeing test pilot Robert L 'Bob' McPherson told the author that there was 'no plan' to solve the B-47's aileron reversal problem with the spoilers. The spoilers did have a certain appeal to SAC planners, however, who agreed that they should be used on the B-52G and B-52H in lieu of ailerons.

The YB-47J

Given the poor reliability of the B-47's K bomb/nav system, SAC decided not to use it in the B-52, proposing instead to incorporate the MA-2 radar bombing system. Built by IBM, the MA-2 was optimized for high-altitude bombing. Plans called for testing the MA-2 in two production B-47Es to provide quantitative data on its 'reliability and utility'. B-47E 53-2281 was redesignated as a YB-47J, although the identity of the second MA-2 airplane is unclear. B-47E 53-2282 was at Seattle for unspecified modification work at the same time as 53-2281, but its records do not show that its MDS changed to YB-47J, nor do any other aircraft bear this MDS. A photograph does show the fairing on the nose, indicating that 52-2282 was the other prototype but did not have an MDS change.

SAC planners believed that the two prototypes were insufficient to demonstrate the effectiveness of the MA-2, and sought to procure an entire squadron of B-47s configured with the MA-2 to provide 'real world' operational data as well as identify areas requiring correction. Moreover, they believed that the MA-2 could reduce the B-47 bombing system's abort rate and would offer a bombing system with equal or greater accuracy. AMC Procurement Directive 53-153, issued in April 1954, directed that the MA-2 system would be installed in 15 additional B-47s for service tests on a squadron basis. AMC solicited bids for these extra aircraft from Boeing, Douglas-Tulsa, and Lockheed-Marietta, ranging from $3,975,000 to $918,677 (plus 5.5% fee) to $567,067, respectively. Boeing's higher bid included all the prior and 'sustaining' engineering work accomplished or projected through 15th March 1959. Money was not the only issue,

Fairing on the starboard nose of the YB-47J prototype shows the extra space required for the MA-2 system. SAC argued that two test aircraft would not be sufficient, and the MA-2 was installed on 15 newly built Lockheed-Marietta B-47Es. *USAF*

MA-2 B-47E 53-1913 (I) from the 44th BW while at Tinker AFB for MILK BOTTLE in 1958. *USAF*

TB-47B 51-2061 lands at Dobbins AFB during the microwave landing tests in 1958. *Department of Defense*

Table 7-10. **MA-2 B-47E Conversions**

53-1913	53-1920	53-1927	53-1934	53-1937
53-1914	53-1921	53-1928	53-1935	53-1938
53-1919	53-1926	53-1933*	53-1936	53-1939

* Crashed 25th October 1956

as both Douglas-Tulsa and Lockheed-Marietta promised the 15 additional B-47s would be ready with only 2-4 weeks' delay beyond 'presently scheduled deliveries.' Conversely, Boeing planned to fly the 15 B-47s from Wichita to Seattle for modification, a process which would add some nine months to their expected delivery date. After some bureaucratic manipulations, Lockheed's final bid was $671,800, and the contract was approved on 27th May 1954 and awarded to Marietta.

The converted B-47Es were the final 15 Lockheed-Marietta B-47Es delivered to the 44th BW at Lake Charles AFB in October 1956. None were redesignated as YB-47Js or B-47Js and all retained the B-47E MDS. One airplane 53-1933 was lost on 25th October 1956 (see Appendix II), and 53-1914 was the first of the MA-2 jets to revert to the MA-7 in use with standard B-47Es.

Fly By Wire

Long before airplanes such as the General Dynamics F-16 and the Lockheed F-117 began using digital fly by wire (FBW) systems instead of mechanical linkages to the control surfaces, NB-47E 53-2280 served as the testbed for the first FBW system (during 1965 this airplane was part of the 'Terrain Signal' research). Under program head Colonel William Giesler, the Flight Dynamics Laboratory (FDL) at Wright-Patterson AFB conducted three phases of tests, all in the pitch axis. A total of 100 flight tests took place between 14th December 1967 and November 1969. During Phase I a redundant electronic system ran parallel to the existing hydromechanical elevator controls, duplicating the pitch commands from the control column. A side-stick controller was incorporated in Phase II. A separate elevator actuator was installed for Phase III. Giesler reported the aircraft handled well.

Although not technically a true FBW proposal, AMC, Bell Aircraft, and Lockheed-Marietta assessed the viability of a microwave landing system using TB-47B 51-2061. The tests, which took place in 1958, utilized a radar van adjacent to the runway. Once airborne, the crew of 51-2061 monitored the automatic landings, which were reportedly successful (ie, it did not crash!).

'Needlenose'

Rockwell International acquired RB-47H 53-4296 on 15th July 1968 on behalf of the Air Force Avionics Laboratory (AFAL) 'to obtain flight test data for advanced avionics with a primary effort of testing a forward looking all-weather high and low altitude radar in a high performance aircraft.' Rockwell removed the aft bomb bay fuel tank and replaced it with avionics racks, and reconfigured the former Raven station in the bomb bay to accommodate test gear and stations for four crewmen. The wing tanks were replaced by a variety of electronic pods. For precise navigation the airplane acquired a Litton LTN-51 inertial navigation system (INS). Most visibly, Rockwell transplanted the nose radome from a General Dynamics F-111, leading to the airplane's nickname of 'Needlenose.' Over the next eight years 53-4296 tested a variety of avionics equipment including a synthetic aperture radar prior to the airplane's retirement on 30th April 1976 as a static display at the Air Force Armament Museum at Eglin AFB (see Appendix III). By 4th September 1979 the nose from B-47E 51-5251 had been grafted onto 53-4296, replacing the former F-111 radome.

Former RB-47H 53-4296 served Rockwell Autonetics on behalf of the AFAL. It was based at Los Angeles IAP and acquired its distinctive 'needle nose'. *Author's collection*

During the mid 1970s 53-4296 tested a synthetic aperture radar, seen here with the 'needle nose' removed. *Rockwell International via Jay Miller*

Air Defense Programs

Throughout the 1950s and 1960s B-47s supported a variety of tests associated with the evolving US and Canadian air defense network. Operational units were tasked with many of the routine evaluations. The 26th SRW, for example, flew Operation GRAINFIELD sorties in October 1955 to support ARDC and Lincoln Laboratory projects associated with 'airborne electronic detection equipment.' RB-47Es from the 91st SRW (and other units) took part in multiple DEVIL FISH missions for ECM testing by the Lincoln Laboratory. Between 14th-23rd January 1959, JTB-47B 50-0053 participated in Operation SWORDFISH. It flew four flights a day to assist in the ARDC calibration of the new SAGE defense system. Following a divert to Westover AFB, MA, on 7th February for an engine failure, the crew attempted a 5-engine takeoff to return to Wright-Patterson AFB, but the airplane crashed, killing the crew (see Appendix II).

The Tankers

During the early years of the Cold War the issue of range became the principal limiting factor in strategic operations. The B-47 needed aerial refueling to fly from bases in the United States to targets in the Soviet Union. Fighters needed aerial refueling to deploy overseas to support conventional commitments in Europe and Asia. Developments in refueling hardware in the US and England resulted in two competing air refueling systems: Boeing produced the 'flying boom' and Flight Refuelling, Ltd, focused on probe-and-drogue refueling. By 1951 competition between the two systems had reached an impasse. Bomber pilots preferred the flying boom as it provided high fuel flow rates and was easier to use during long-duration missions. Fighter pilots, including those from the US Navy and US Marine Corps, preferred the probe-and-drogue as it was simpler to

Left: EB-47B 50-0040 became the Boeing hose-reel tanker testbed, carrying the unofficial MDS of KB-47G. It made its debut at the Dayton Air Show a year after this image was taken. *USAF via Jay Miller*

Below: YB-47F 50-0009 refuels from the KB-47G. In daylight and calm skies the drogue was fairly stable, but at night or in turbulence the receiver had a difficult time finding, connecting, and remaining in contact with the basket. *Photo P12420 courtesy Boeing*

Left: Air refueling with fighters offered the possibility of Boeing replacing TAC's KB-50s with RB-47Es converted into tankers. The final proposal utilized two drogues from the wing tanks, but TAC demurred. *Photo P12422 courtesy Boeing*

Below: The proposed Thieblot 'flying pipe' was similar to the Boeing KB-47E proposal but utilized a rigid drogue lowered from each wing pylon. Again, TAC rejected the design, holding out instead for KC-135s which never materialized.

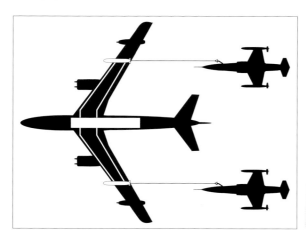

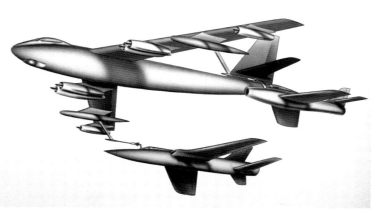

use and its lower flow rate was more than adequate for the smaller offloads associated with fighter refueling. Moreover, the probe-and-drogue had become the *de facto* system for British aircraft, with potential sales to other NATO countries making it the standard system.

Boeing intended the B-47 to be refueled using its proprietary flying boom, which enjoyed the strongest possible support of CINCSAC General Curtis LeMay. However, given the indecision within the US Air Force over which system – or both – would be used, Boeing decided to hedge its bets by evaluating the B-47 as a probe-equipped receiver. Piston-powered tankers of the day, such as the KB-29P and the newly developed KC-97, were too slow for the B-47. Consequently, Boeing elected to evaluate a drogue-equipped tanker variant of the Stratojet, which raised the possibility of Boeing producing both a bomber and a tanker version of the B-47. Interestingly, this was a Boeing-sponsored project but it was flown by Air Force crews.

Two airplanes were modified to test the concept. EB-47B 50-0040 became the KB-47G tanker and B-47B 50-0009 became the YB-47F receiver. The KB-47G was modified with a hose and reel in the bomb bay. Flight tests in 1952 at Eglin AFB proved disappointing. Flying at jet speeds higher than existing piston-powered probe-and-drogue tankers such as the KB-50, the long distance from the KB-47G's fuselage opening to the extended drogue caused significant vertical and horizontal oscillation of the drogue, making for a difficult hook up. Even if Boeing managed to solve this problem, the probe-and-drogue still had a significantly lower transfer rate than its flying boom. Most importantly, Boeing simply could not produce the number of KB-47Gs SAC required in addition to the disappointing production rate of the standard B-47 bomber. Any delays in fixing the probe-and-drogue oscillation issue or in producing bombers were simply unacceptable.

Surprisingly, on 13th August 1952 the Air Force opted for the probe-and-drogue system as the standard for all new aircraft acquisitions. LeMay, unwilling to forego the bomber-friendly flying boom, successfully argued that this decision not be retroactive to existing aircraft. Both the B-47 and the planned B-52 would use the flying boom, justifying the production of the KC-97 and KC-135 and eliminating the need for the KB-47G.

Nonetheless, plans to display the 'KB-47B' at the September 1953 National Aviation Show at Dayton, OH, went ahead, shortly after the first KB-47G/YB-47F jet-to-jet air refueling on 1st September 1953. Press reports noted that the 'KB-47B' tanker could be converted into a bomber in 'just a few hours,' and speculated that air refueling could be conducted at the absurd speed of 600mph (966kmh) and altitude of 40,000ft (12,192m). Perhaps the most prescient comment about the new tanker was the potential for the planned Boeing 707 tanker. Whatever success the B-47 tanker might achieve represented the increased likelihood that Boeing would proceed with the Boeing 367-80 as a prototype for a military jet tanker.

The KB-47G was still carrying its refueling equipment in August 1956 during its subsequent PDM at Wichita. Since no manuals existed for the installation, sequential photos were taken of its removal. The hose and reel were re-installed before it departed, reflecting the importance that Boeing placed on any potential tanker contract.

On 23rd July 1956 the Air Force had authorized a study to convert B-47Es into tankers, using a refueling pod in place of each wing tank. This 'KB-47E' would replace Tactical Air Command's (TAC) piston-powered KB-50s to permit refueling at 'jet speeds and altitudes.' Conversion costs proved excessive, and the installation of jet engines on the KB-50s increased their speed sufficiently to merit cancelation of the 'KB-47E' on 11th July 1957.

On 14th July 1958 the Air Force reversed itself and declared the flying boom as its standard refueling system. TAC, whose fighters were dependent upon the probe-and-drogue system, was unwilling to let the issue die quietly. In 1959 Boeing proposed modifying retired RB-47Es into drogue-equipped tankers for TAC. The RB-47Es would be stripped of non-essential equipment and the fuel system would be modified for transferring fuel to the receivers. A 'buddy type' refueling store would be located at the former wing tank position. Rendezvous lighting and electronics would be added. The proposal estimated that 12,000 lb (5,443kg) of fuel could be transferred to each of four North American F-100Ds with a refueling time of 15 minutes per receiver. The tanker would be able to fly its missions above 30,000ft (9,144m). The projected timeline called for the prototype to be ready by 4th August 1960, and the first modification to be complete by 18th August. Cost of the 101-airplane proposal was $6,660,000.

Another proposal for using former B-47s was submitted concurrently to the one from Boeing by the AJ Thieblot Aircraft Engineering Corporation, founded by former Fairchild Aviation engineer Armand J Thieblot. The proposal was similar to Boeing's but used an articulated arm – known by the proprietary name 'Flying Pipe' – to lower the drogue into the slipstream from the wingtank refueling pod. The receiver then connected to the drogue but in much closer proximity to the tanker than Boeing's hose which trailed farther behind, raising concerns over turbulence and the potential for collision. Despite the potential for 100 new jet tankers TAC was unwilling to pay for either program. TAC officials argued that its KB-50s could still perform the refueling mission, there was no requirement to refuel at the extreme altitudes the new tanker offered, and TAC still hoped to get its own fleet of new KC-135s. Any RB-47 tanker conversion would undermine this goal, and the RB-47E tanker conversion proposal came to a justifiable end.

OTHER AGENCIES

Aside from the bombers, ECM, and reconnaissance variants used by SAC and the weather variants operated by MAC, most of the testbed B-47s served with Air Force commands such as APGC, AMC, and ARDC. Surprisingly, B-47 variants also flew with both the US Army and Navy in test and operational evaluation roles, and with US civilian agencies as well.

Army Support

Two B-47s were seconded to Douglas-Tulsa in support of US Army tests related to the Nike surface-to-air missile (SAM). In an amazingly circuitous paper trail, in 1959 the Air Force leased TB-47B 51-2077 for the Nike-Hercules system to the Western Electric Company which loaned the airplane to Bell Telephone Laboratory and then contracted Douglas-Tulsa to perform maintenance and conduct flight operations. Bell Labs had the US Army contract to develop the Nike missile radar. Initial testing was conducted from McGuire AFB, NJ, located in close proximity to the Bell Labs in Whippany, NJ. Additional flight tests took place at the White Sands Missile Range in New Mexico, from Ascension Island in the Atlantic Ocean, and from Kwajalein Island in the Pacific Ocean. DB-47B 51-2181 joined the program on 9th May 1960 for the Nike-Zeus missile.

For the tests 51-2077 was painted with a red vertical stabilizer (the large serial '2077' remained on natural metal, as did a smaller '12077' below the large numbers) and the outer two-thirds of the bottom of the horizontal stabilizers were also painted red. A wide red band was painted on the top and bottom of the wing inboard of the outer engine

nacelles. The word 'NIKE' was painted in black on the nose. The color scheme for 51-2181 was the same but had 'NIKE 2' on the nose.

Tests at White Sands were conducted at the limits of the B-47's altitude capability. The airplanes would depart Tulsa, OK, and fly to White Sands, burning off fuel to allow them to reach 41,000ft (12,497m). The crews would use the autopilot for the tests as the B-47 was very difficult to hand fly at this altitude. Occasionally the B-47s would operate from Biggs AFB, TX, to allow more time on station.

The B-47s were equipped with tracking antennas, high intensity lighting, and a system that dropped a 12in (30cm) diameter aluminum ball through a chute at the rear of the aircraft. This ball would simulate an enemy ICBM disbursing multiple re-entry vehicles, forcing the Nike radar to acquire and track them. A US Navy Douglas A4D Skyhawk was used in a similar way, flying close to the B-47 then diving away rapidly. DB-47B 51-2181 performed similar operations from Ascension Island. The Douglas crew of Grant Younger (pilot), Chuck Hammet (co-pilot), Travis Blount (navigator), and Bill Updike (pilot inspector) flew 51-2181 to Ramey AFB, PR, then to Recife, Brazil, and then onward to Ascension Island. Test ICBMs were launched from Cape Canaveral, FL, and the B-47B helped calibrate the Nike radar which would then track the missiles. Following operations from Ascension Island 51-2181 returned to Tulsa on 18th May 1962 where it was moved to the dump and used for fire crew training. It was scrapped on 8th May 1963. 51-2077 was subsequently used for US Navy electronic countermeasures training (described below).

In the Navy
To the surprise of many SAC veterans, the last B-47s in operational service were those assigned to the US Navy. During early 1964 Alex P Whitmore and Travis Blount of the Douglas-Tulsa Special Flight Department visited the Johns Hopkins University's Applied Physics Laboratory (APL) in Baltimore, MD, which was contracted to assess missile operations in an ECM-heavy environment. Whitmore convinced the APL that they needed to use idle TB-47B 51-2077 as an airborne ECM test platform. APL agreed to a trial and the airplane flew to NAS Point Mugu for an evaluation against some US Navy

ships. Results of the test were positive enough to secure a one-year contract for the TB-47B, and the airplane was assigned to the 'Surface Missile System' evaluation program and given the call sign *SMS-1*.

The initial Douglas flight team was made up of pilots Alex Whitmore, Dean Abrams, and Bob Allison, and navigator Travis Blount. Others were added as mission demands increased, but this was often complicated by the shortage of experienced B-47 pilots (usually retired) who were willing to travel extensively. Whitmore had more Stratojet time than anyone else at the time. He completed his B-47 training at Wichita in May 1952, became chief of flight test at Douglas-Tulsa in 1954 when they were contracted to build B-47s, and was associated with the B-47 for the rest of his life. Unfortunately, 'Whit' did not live to see the end of the Stratojet era. He was killed in a tractor accident on his farm on 6th September 1976.

The first ECM deployment began on 23rd March 1964 to NAS North Island, CA, with subsequent domestic operations from NAS Miramar, CA, NAS Lemoore, CA, MCAS El Toro, CA, NAS Barber's Point, HI, NAS Oceana, VA, MCAS Cherry Point, SC, NAS Key West, FL, and NAS Roosevelt Roads, PR. NAS Barber's Point and NAS North Island were eventually removed from the rotations due to inadequate runway length. Overseas operations took place from Naval Station (NS) Rota, Spain, and Souda AB, Crete. Although operated by civilian contract crews based out of Tulsa AP, the Navy B-47s were assigned to the Fleet Electronic Warfare Support Group (FEWSG) at NAS Norfolk, VA.

The primary mission involved jamming the fire control radar of US Navy fighters and surface ships. Interestingly, the US Army heard

Table 7-11. **Initial US Navy FEWSG Aircraft**

MDS	Serial / BuNO	SMS No	Call Sign*
TB-47B	51-2077	SMS-1	
A3B	138968		*Nucar 01*
A3B	138922		*Nucar 02*
EB-47E	524100	SMS-2	*Nucar 03*
EB-47E	524120	SMS-3	*Nucar 04*

* Initially *Newcar* but changed to *Nucar* for FAA

about the 'resurrection' of 51-2077 and tasked the airplane with additional test flights on behalf of the Nike program. These dual demands meant that the airplane often flew two four-hour missions a day. On 29th October 1965, however, 51-2077 aborted a landing in heavy fog at NAS Point Mugu, striking the #1 engine which caught fire. The airplane was able to stop on the runway and the crew egressed safely. However, the fire department sprayed foam from the left side of the airplane pushing the flames from the burning engine toward the fuselage. The TB-47B was consumed by fire, but much of the ECM gear was saved and trucked back to Tulsa. It appeared that the US Navy's B-47 operations were at an end.

In fact, the Navy was quite pleased with the FEWSG B-47 capabilities, and in August 1965 arranged for former BLUE CRADLE EB-47E 52-0412 to be removed from storage at MASDC and restored for FEWSG operations. The loss of 51-2077 prompted the need for a replacement, with 52-0410 withdrawn from MASDC at the end of December (it is not entirely clear if 52-0410 was a true replacement for 51-2077 or was intended as a third FEWSG B-47). Modifications to 52-0410 and 52-0412 included installation of the latest ECM gear, additional racks in the bomb bay for more jammers, removal of the air

Below: EB-47E 52-0410 was the third B-47 assigned to FEWSG. The Navy assigned it BuNO 524100 instead of the more logical 520410, and it initially acquired the call sign *SMS-2* despite being the third B-47. *Thomas Waller via Stephen Miller*

Above left: Checkerboard applied to EB-47E 524120 was reportedly an early operational scheme, but it has not been previously seen. *Author's collection*

Above: Each EB-47E carried at least one ECM pod on the outer pylon, and could carry another pod or a drone on the other outer pylon. *Author's collection*

Left: SMS-3 launches a Beechcraft AQM-37 drone, simulating an incoming cruise or ballistic missile threatening a carrier task group. In other cases, aircraft have simulated the threat. *Author's collection*

Below: 524120 suffered its share of mishaps, including a gear up landing and being hit by an inert AIM-9. This hangar view shows the inner wing pylon for the AQM-37 and its control fairing, as well as 'Sooner Pride' for winning both the 1974 and 1975 college football national championship. *McDonnell Douglas*

Opposite, top: Ironically it was the US Navy that flew the last B-47s in operational service. Both of the EB-47Es were replaced in 1977 by two NKC-135As and eventually an EC-24A. Whitmore would have been proud. *McDonnell Douglas*

refueling gear and aft fuel cell #1 to make room for extra parts for deployments, ATO racks were also removed and additional chaff dispensers installed, while the tail gun was eliminated and replaced with an active jamming antenna. An ECM pod or a forward-firing chaff rocket pod replaced the wing tanks. A smaller pylon for the drone and another for its control fairing were installed under each wing between the fuselage and inboard engine nacelles. The copilot launched the drone, and the navigator handled the ECM operation using numerous active and two passive systems. To comport with the Navy's serial numbering system at the time, an extra zero was added to the end of each Air Force serial resulting in 524100 and 524120, with these two aircraft given the static call signs *SMS-2* and *SMS-3*, respectively (why the Navy failed to use 520410 and 520412 is unclear). With the addition of two A3B Skywarriors to the fleet, FEWSG changed the call signs to *Newcar*, which was truncated to *Nucar* to meet Federal Aviation Administration (FAA) computer requirements.

Deployments lasted up to three weeks, and each aircraft carried enough supplies to maintain itself for that period. (It is worth noting that this is exactly what General LeMay wanted the B-47 to do as it was entering the SAC fleet using a 'fly-away' kit.) The EB-47Es accumulated approximately 600 flying hours per year with a nearly 90% readiness rate. In addition to routine jamming exercises, the EB-47Es took part in several 'special' evaluation missions. During January 1966, for example, one EB-47E deployed to Goose Bay, Labrador, for cold-weather tests of the US Navy's Talos missile system. The Talos was to be fired at a Firebee launched from the EB-47E at 30,000ft (10,058m). The weather did not cooperate – it was too warm – so the Navy sprayed icy water on the ship's radar and completed the test. In another evaluation undertaken in March 1966 from NS Rota, the EB-47E acted as an aggressor force attacking a carrier task force as it approached the Straits of Gibraltar. To simulate supersonic anti-ship missiles, two F-4 Phantoms flew in close formation with the EB-47E. When 'launched' the F-4 would dive at supersonic speed and 'buzz' the carrier to complete the strike. When the task force attempted to use 'home on jamming' (HOJ) to track the EB-47E in order to 'shoot it down,' the EB-47E stopped jamming as soon as the task force began tracking it. During June 1967 an EB-47E contacted a US Navy submarine at a predetermined point between Bermuda and the Azores and launched a Firebee on a heading specified by the submarine to determine if it could shoot down the drone. As with most of the EB-47E operations, the flight crews did not learn the results of their efforts. During a flight to NAS Cecil Field, FL, EB-47E 524120 was unable to extend the forward landing gear, so pilot Bob Stevens managed a textbook belly landing. The airplane was repaired within a month and back in service.

The EB-47Es were certainly among the most 'shot at' airplanes in the US Navy, but on one occasion the attack was not simulated but real. While practicing air-to-air intercepts at 35,000ft (10,668m) some 100nm (185km) northwest of Guadalupe Island, something hit EB-47E 524120, forcing it into a diving right turn from which the crew

recovered at 20,000ft (6,096m). The #4 engine was missing and the #5 engine was on fire. After diverting to NAS Miramar the plane landed safely. Inspection revealed residue from an inert AIM-9 Sidewinder that had been fired by a US Marine Corps F-4 Phantom. After a portion of the right wing, the right inboard nacelle, and the outrigger gear had been replaced the airplane resumed normal operations. Legend has it that the Navy agreed to extend the contract for the FEWSG EB-47Es for five more years if they kept the episode 'quiet'.

By October 1970 the EB-47Es were also flying penetration missions against NORAD, much like the earlier SNOW TIME missions of the 1950s. The airplanes operated from Minot AFB and Grand Forks AFB, both in North Dakota, flew north to near Hudson Bay in Canada, then reversed course while jamming ground based radars and interceptors. According to one official, '…they scared the hell out of NORAD.'

During late 1977 NKC-135As 553134 and 563596 replaced the EB-47Es, acquiring the *Nucar 01* and *Nucar 02* call signs from the withdrawn A-3Bs. Both EB-47Es were retired to static displays.

TB-47B/EB-47E INDIVIDUAL AIRCRAFT

51-2077 Beginning in March 1963 this TB-47B served as the first Douglas ECM platform for the US Navy. It crashed at NAS Point Mugu on 29th October 1965 (see Appendix II).

52-0410 Beginning 3rd December 1965 this former BLUE CRADLE EB-47E was converted into an ECM platform for the US Navy. It was assigned to the FEWSG and given the BuNO 524100. On 20th December 1977 a McDonnell Douglas crew ferried her to Pease AFB, NH with the intent to display the airplane in 509th BW markings as soon as the weather permitted. With the anticipated closure of Pease AFB, during 1990 the EB-47E was prepared to move to Ellsworth AFB, SD. The wings and tail were cut off, however, leaving the airplane in such bad shape that it could never be reassembled. Components of the airframe eventually found their way to the National Museum of the US Air Force at Wright-Patterson AFB where they were used in the restoration of RB-47H 53-4299 and the rest auctioned as scrap (see Appendix III).

52-0412 Beginning 19th August 1965 this former BLUE CRADLE EB-47E was converted into an ECM platform for the US Navy. It was assigned to the FEWSG and given the BuNO 524120. On 1st October 1977, SAC's Vice Commander Lieutenant General Edgar S Harris, Jr, flew 524120 to Dyess AFB, TX. Wearing 'fresh' US Air Force markings as the *City of Abilene*, it arrived during the base's open house. It was subsequently placed on static display in June 1978. Curiously, even though it has 96th BW markings, the serial number on the tail still has the extra zero.

Right: Aerial view of 524100 showing the major modifications including replacing the tail turret with a Rope chaff dispenser, installation of ECM antenna on the bomb bay doors, wing pylons, and ECM fairings on the ventral fuselage aft of the main radome.
McDonnell Douglas

Evaluating High Altitude Airways

In the early 1950s there was little air traffic above 25,000ft (7,620m) except for military aircraft. This meant that there was no high-altitude route structure because no one had determined the space pattern and accuracy of navigation aids (NAVAIDs) at these higher altitudes. Consequently, in the mid 1950s the Airways and Air Communications Service (AACS – later Air Force Communications Service, AFCS) and the APGC began a joint project using a B-47 to study the radiation patterns and accuracy of ground-based navigation aids. This project would determine the radiation pattern and accuracy at high altitudes of existing NAVAIDs in plains, mountainous, and coastal geographic areas. CAA head Charles J Lowen negotiated with SAC to loan two B-47s to test operational problems facing the CAA in the 'anticipated certification process and air traffic control environment that loomed ahead with the advent of high-speed, high-altitude jet aircraft.' Known as the 'High Speed, High Altitude Evaluation of Ground Navigational Aids' program, the CAA (later the FAA), which had no jet aircraft of its own, was extremely interested in the project and cooperated fully. CAA provided specialty aircrew training and assisted in both data analysis and in presenting the research results to officials in Washington, DC.

Above: B-47B 51-2120 replaced ETB-47B 50-0017 as the AACS platform in 1956. When seen here on 15th May 1959 it had a relatively austere color scheme. *Robert Burgess via Stephen Miller*

Below: 51-2120 acquired several variations in color scheme, ranging from orange over silver to a more vibrant red over white. In any case the high visibility was intended to make other, slower moving aircraft aware of the jet's presence in terminal areas. *USAF, author's collection*

The original project was supposed to last for about one year or some 100 flying hours utilizing former APGC ETB-47B 50-0017 beginning 31st May 1955. On 8th June it was assigned to the 1800th Airways and Air Communications Wing (AACW) at Tinker AFB. In early 1956 it was redesignated as a JTB-47B. SAC provided maintenance and support for 50-0017, but it became increasingly difficult to keep in flying condition, curtailing its use considerably. Subsequently on 21st June 1956 it was transferred to Boeing-Wichita for conversion into a TB-47B and on 25th October it was assigned to the 3520th CCTW at Wichita.

On 15th June 1956 AACS received B-47B 51-2120 as a replacement for 50-0017, and it was assigned to the 1800th AACW Following a command-wide contest, it was named *Navaider*, but this was later changed to *Sweet Marie*. Subsequent unit changes include the 1865th Airways and Communications Flight on 18th December 1958, and the 1865th Facilities Checking Flight on 1st July 1961. Based at Tinker AFB, OK, 51-2120 remained in service until 9th October 1962 when it was transferred to the 340th BW at Whiteman AFB. It was retired on 20th March 1963 and placed on static display at Whiteman AFB (see Appendix III). The entire program lasted nearly eight years and accrued 984 flight hours.

The airplanes were extensively modified to carry the electronic flight check equipment. The tail guns were deleted and the bombing equipment removed from the bomb bay. The MA-7 BNS equipment was left intact because the AACS needed extremely accurate positioning. Impressively, from 40,000ft (12,192m) the airplane's position could be determined to within a few feet using gyro-stabilized optics with high-power magnification. A modified flight check panel was designed and installed behind the co-pilot's seat, replacing the gunnery system. New components included a variety of meters and microammeters to measure signal strengths, which were converted to hard copy using two Esterline Angus recorders which could be patched to any of the instruments on board. The airplane was configured with TACAN, VOR, ILS, LORAN, 75mc marker receivers, VHF, and UHF radios.

One example of the benefits of these flights was in determining the amount of airspace required for a holding pattern. Initial assessments provided for a holding pattern using 2-3nm (3.7-5.6km) lateral displacement. The AACS B-47 determined that this was too small for jet-powered aircraft and instead showed that they needed 6-8nm (11-15km) depending on the type of jet. The CAA revised their holding patterns accordingly.

Because the airplane operated in dense traffic areas and often at low altitudes in the vicinity of uncontrolled or VFR traffic, it was painted with a variety of high-visibility conspicuity markings. Colors ranged from day-glow red to Arctic international orange to insignia red to determine a color not likely to fade over time. These were used in combination with the existing silver and white B-47 color scheme.

NACA B-47A 49-1900 seen prior to being marked as NACA 150. Camera fairing on top of the fuselage at the wing root filmed wing flexure compared to pitch and roll. *NASA*

NACA's B-47

The National Advisory Committee for Aeronautics (NACA), the precursor to NASA, used B-47A 49-1900 (marked as NACA 150) for structural and loads research in the late 1950s. The B-47's thin swept wings and fighter-like performance made it an ideal platform for theoretical aerodynamic research. NACA 150 was transferred from the Langley Memorial Aeronautical Laboratory to the High-Speed Flight Research Station at Edwards AFB on 17th March 1953 where it was used for a wide range of research, including handling qualities, dynamic stability, gust loads, noise level measurements, aeroelasticity (the bending of the wings in flight), and a survey of the X-15 High Range tracking system. It was then reassigned to NACA's Lewis Flight Propulsion Laboratory at Cleveland, OH.

Between May 1953 and its 78th and final research flight on 22nd November 1957, NACA 150 undertook a variety of research activities, some of which were unrelated to the B-47 *per se* and instead focused on future aircraft designs. NACA also conducted a variety of ground-based research tasks on behalf of the B-47

program. Among the pilots who flew the NACA B-47 were later X-15 pilots Joe Walker, A Scott Crossfield, John B McKay, Neil A Armstrong, and Fitzhugh 'Fitz' Fulton.

In terms of pure aerodynamic research, one NACA study involved multiple tests at altitudes ranging from 15,000-35,000ft (4,572-10,668m) and at speeds from Mach 0.44-0.80. These showed that on a large swept-wing airplane the wing load did not move spanwise down the wing, but did show some forward movement. This validated the notion that future large bombers could have swept wings without concerns that they would break during flight. A similar test involved NACA 150 and a B-29 to evaluate the effects of wing flexibility due to turbulence on structural bending of the wing. Both airplanes flew at 2,000ft (610m), with the B-29 at 250mph (402kph) and the B-47 at 478mph (769kph). Results showed that the stiffer straight wing of the B-29 suffered detrimental stress, but thanks to the aeroelasticity of the B-47 wing it simply 'flexed' back into position with no discernable structural damage. The study did suggest that there was a limit to this, as an airplane with a 'huge' wingspan,

Right: Many notable NACA pilots flew 49-1900, including Joe Vensel (l), Joe Walker (c), and Stan Butchart (r). Butchart safely landed KC-135A 55-3125 following a collision with an NT-33 in 1957. Sadly, Walker perished in the collision of his F-104 with an XB-70 in 1966. *NACA E-1380*

Far right: Camera calibration on 49-1900 shows the relative size of the camera fairing. The B-47 was an excellent platform to study wing aeroelasticity compared to previous large aircraft with rigid wing structures. Note yellow and black warning stripe on long bomb bay door. *NACA via Boeing*

no matter how flexible, would reach a point where it would break the spar due to turbulence.

NACA ground tests on behalf of the B-47 included a study that analyzed simulator 'feel' of the elevators. Unlike earlier airplanes where control surfaces were directly connected to the pilot, the B-47 used artificial means to move the controls at high speeds (and hence high aerodynamic pressures that were beyond the pilot's physical strength to control precisely). These induced a slight lag due, for example, to 'servovalve friction' or thermal distortions in the Q-spring. The NACA study found that it was possible to replicate these variations and that they were within tolerances, contributing to improved designs for autopilots. NACA also completed a ditching study of the B-47 using a 1/24th scale model. Test results showed that the B-47 could safely ditch if the airplane flew as slow as possible, at the highest pitch attitude, and at 35° (100%) flaps. The inboard engine pylons would shear off, but the airplane was projected to stop within '6 fuselage lengths' or approximately 566ft (173m). Fortunately there is no record of a B-47 ever ditching, successfully or otherwise.

NACA also conducted at least one series of flight tests of interest to the 'sleeping public' with WADC EB-47B 51-2075. Jet engines and undesirable noise quickly became synonymous, and NACA's Lewis Flight Propulsion Laboratory was charged with exploring ways to reduce jet noise. The #6 engine nacelle was redesigned to evaluate different methods of attenuating the B-47's audible footprint. Although some of the lessons learned were applied to the Boeing 707 and other modern jets, they were not adapted for use on the B-47, B-52, or KC-135, and jet noise quickly became associated with the 'sound of freedom.'

A Cornell Aeronautical Laboratory study 'The Noise Field Around A B-47 Airplane,' dated 25th March 1954, believed to have been undertaken on behalf of NACA, assessed the 'results when a B-47 aircraft flies in the vicinity of [a] ground installation.' Calculations were based on measurements of noise levels near a J47 engine and 'concluded that little noise interference with normal voice communications will occur on the ground if the B-47 airplane remains outside a two-mile radius.' This was hardly consolation to the many ground personnel who suffered hearing loss due to working in close proximity to the B-47's noisy, high-pitched jet engine whine.

NASA Test Operations
During 1962-1963 one of APGC's B-47s was modified to electronically resemble NASA's Mercury space capsule. Flying at low altitudes and high speeds, it permitted US tracking stations to train for the early manned spaceflight missions. A similar program involved RB-47Hs and ERB-47Hs to detect the Mercury capsule should it be adrift at sea (see Chapter 6). During the Apollo lunar landing program, a B-47 was used to test the three re-entry parachutes used for the command module. Lieutenant Colonel Terry Scanlon recalls flying tests at 50ft (15m) above the golf course at Wright-Patterson AFB at approach speed plus 10KIAS. A single parachute was deployed to determine its survivability. During the first practice run, however, the copilot prematurely popped the chute causing the B-47 to lose nearly 30KIAS – well below stall speed – before it was successfully jettisoned. Subsequent tests were less dramatic and more successful. In a similar project from March through December 1958, a B-47 participated in the HOT HAND parachute recovery testing

Top: In an effort to reduce the noise footprint of the J47 and jet airliners in general, NACA used EB-47B 51-2075 with a modified exhaust on the #6 engine. Results were applied to future airliners, but not to SAC's bomber or tanker fleet. *NASA photo GRC-1957-C-46143*

Right: As airliners grew in size the FAA used two B-47Es, including 52-0554, to assess various improvements to fire control for large aircraft. *FAA*

intended for Fairchild JC-119s that would 'snatch' a descending film capsule jettisoned from early US spy satellites.

NAFEC
B-47Es 52-0542 and 52-0554 took part in tests sponsored by the FAA's National Aviation Facilities Experimental Center (NAFEC) to assess firefighting techniques. Purpose of the tests was twofold – to assess firefighting methods for large jet aircraft and to determine optimal methods to protect large aircraft from encroaching fires. Held between August 1967 and July 1971, the B-47s were evaluated in several different configurations. The tests measured rates of application and quantities of firefighting agents needed to 'prevent the aluminum skin…from melting under severe fire conditions.' Once the tests had ended the two airplanes were used for fire and crash routine training.

Basic Science
A 1956 initiative to map the earth's magnetic field involved a specially modified KC-97. Known as TAN GLOVE, the project began with an unidentified RB-47E equipped with a cosmic ray monitor sponsored by the Air Force Cambridge Research Laboratory (AFCRL) and ARDC. The RB-47 flew over the US taking intensity readings to calibrate the equipment that would be carried on the KC-97. Aside from the scientific research to locate the earth's geomagnetic equator and its relation to the geographic equator, the research was intended to aid in understanding satellite launches and orbits for the planned International Geophysical Year (IGY), not to mention ballistic missile operations. In 1963 JKC-135A 55-3120 took part in a similar program. TB-47B 50-0062 was associated with a program to acquire quantitative infrared (IR) data on rockets and ballistic missiles. The airplane operated from Ramey AFB, PR, and each wing tank carried an AN/APG-64 tracking radar to acquire the target, as well as an unspecified IR detection system.

DRAWING BOARD DISASTERS

Anyone who has watched science-fiction movies has almost certainly moaned or guffawed at some bizarre space ship or airplane depicted on the 'big screen.' Aside from the technical limitations associated with movie making, many of the designs were simply not realistic.

Goodyear proposed a 'piggyback' carrier for the B-47 which had its landing gear removed. Perhaps they assumed the crew would ditch or belly land after their strike mission. *Author's collection*

Some of the many B-47 designs which never left the drawing board. The Model 450-36-10 had a huge wing extension and massive fixed fuel tanks with wingtip gear. The Model 450-139-10 used six J57s in separate nacelles, but these could later accommodate larger engines as they were developed. Models 450-151-31 and 450-152-27 were both equipped with J57s with afterburner for supersonic flight. The -31 had retractable canards for added pitch stability.

The B-47 had its share of 'you gotta be kidding me' designs and proposals, some of which actually made it beyond the drawing board into a mockup that was, thankfully, canceled or scrapped.

During November 1955, for example, the Goodyear Aircraft Corporation (GAC) offered a plan to extend the range of the B-47 by removing the airplane's 'weighty landing gear'. The B-47 would use a 'piggyback' aircraft for takeoff and landing, which would be powered to provide additional thrust. It was never entirely clear how the piggyback would actually work, especially for landing. GAC also planned to use the B-47 as a 'high speed tow target'. This was an all metal, 1,400 lb (635kg) target for use at speeds in excess of 500mph (805kph). It was towed offset to one side of the B-47, which approximated a 'close simulation of a jet fighter.'

Boeing proposed a number of B-47 variants using different engines and wings. Typically these were J57s, but in some cases had afterburners for supersonic flight. The wings were either a modified

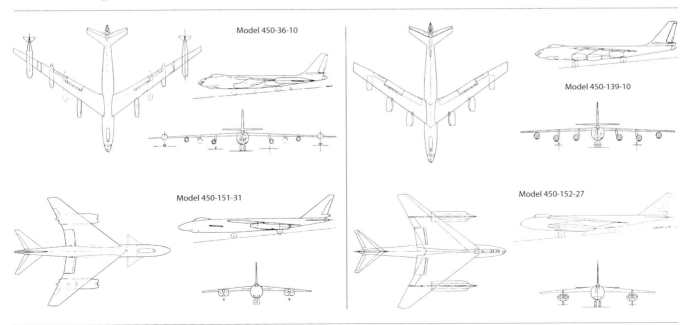

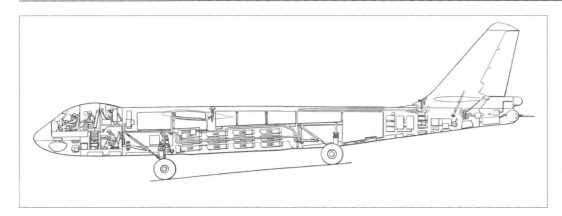

Left: Boeing even proposed a mine laying variant of the B-47, although it was unclear if it would be operated by SAC or the US Navy.

Below: In arguably the most bizarre design two B-47s could be attached at the wingtips of a B-36 in the TIP TOW configuration. A similar study put two F-86s on the wings of a B-47. Surprisingly, aerodynamic studies suggested these were both feasible.

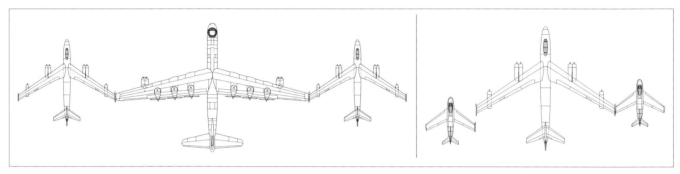

delta or other thick chord type. In one version the engines were buried in the wing root, but most of the designs retained some type of podded nacelle arrangement. In another version the fuselage was radically altered to appear like one of the early B-58 design studies. Another variant had a retractable canard on the forward fuselage. During late 1951 Boeing proposed a mine layer B-47 for the US Navy. It carried a crew of three or five in different cockpit arrangements. The first design used two turbojets and two turboprops, although a later study used four turbojets with afterburners. In August 1953 Boeing proposed a long-range interceptor version of the B-47. The Air Force was suitably impressed with the idea, but eventually this proposal lost out to the more reasonable plan to design an interceptor from scratch.

Arguably one of the most ludicrous ideas for the B-47 was to use it in the TIP TOW configuration with a B-36. After an airborne hookup, this would theoretically allow the B-36 to haul two B-47s with their engines shut down to a point closer to their targets, eliminating the problem of the B-47's inadequate range. The B-47s would then restart

their engines, decouple from the B-36, and then proceed on their strike routes. Another variation of a B-47 TIP TOW proposal included an F-86 coupled to the B-47's wing to provide fighter coverage near the target area. Interestingly, aerodynamic studies were undertaken that showed the feasibility of both TIP TOW projects.

Although B-47 testbeds never achieved the same widespread use and fame as Lockheed C-130 or Boeing KC-135 derivatives, they did serve as the first large jet testbeds. The B-47's speed, altitude, and endurance offered considerable improvements over existing B-29s, B-50s, and Lockheed C-121s that undertook early Cold War flight testing. Perhaps the B-47's greatest experimental legacy is not the number of programs it supported or any of the unusual configurations it saw, but rather the radical change in perspective it offered to scientists, engineers, and designers. Testbed B-47s and their successors created the opportunity to ask new questions about aerospace science and weapons development that were previously inconceivable to researchers and military planners.

Perhaps the greatest legacy of the testbed B-47s was their contribution to the establishment of a dedicated large aircraft fleet of testbeds, including C-135, C-141, and C-130 variants. *Author's collection*

CHAPTER EIGHT

Fast Fly

The 1960 US presidential election was characterized by its emphasis on change. Republican candidate Vice President Richard M Nixon represented continuity of policy established over the previous eight years of the Dwight D Eisenhower administration. Democratic candidate Senator John F Kennedy offered a different – and younger – vision of an evolving America. Surprisingly, Kennedy was more hawkish than Nixon, coining the phrase 'Missile Gap' and using it throughout his campaign to emphasize how Eisenhower's Republican administration was 'soft on defense,' with a finger pointed directly at Nixon.

Despite having been briefed during the campaign with U-2 photos and related intelligence – including TELL TWO sorties out of Turkey – that showed otherwise, Kennedy publicly lamented the 'gap' between the Soviet missile program and that of the United States, assailing Soviet successes with *Sputnik* and repeating Soviet First Secretary Nikita S Khrushchev's canard that the Russians were pumping out R-7 ICBMs 'like sausages', indicating both a robust development

program and a mature production capability. Kennedy decried the fledgling American missile and space program led by former Nazi scientist Werner von Braun, fraught with failures and lack of meaningful support by the Eisenhower administration. Kennedy's 'Missile Gap' preyed on the same fears and mentality that had yet to abate from the 1954 'Bomber Gap,' based on a misperception of Soviet Myasishchev Mya-4 *Bison* production that led to spurious claims of inadequacies in B-52 procurement.

Ultimately, Top Secret CORONA satellite imagery drove the final nail into the 'Missile Gap' coffin, but not until after Kennedy had been elected and inaugurated as president. Indeed, one of the first official pronouncements by Robert S McNamara, Kennedy's newly appointed Secretary of Defense, was to declare that the 'Missile Gap'

The XB-47 flew exactly 44 years after the historic flight of the Wright Brothers at Kill Devil Hills. Both proved to be seminal events in aviation history with long-standing legacies. *Photo 151340AC USAF*

Above left: Secretary of Defense Robert S McNamara saw the future of strategic airpower defined by ICBMs rather than manned bombers. Under his leadership SAC became a missile command that also had bombers. *JFKWHP-ST-A5-20-61, Cecil Stoughton, White House Photographs, John F Kennedy Presidential Library and Museum, Boston*

Above right: CINCSAC General Thomas S Power (c) wanted both ICBMs and new bombers. ARDC Commander General Bernard A Schriever (r) wanted more ICBMs as well. With limited funds McNamara sided with Schriever. *Author's collection*

was actually in favor of the United States. In the post-election fawning over the new 'Camelot', this early example of 'fake news' was easily ignored.

Equally overlooked was McNamara's economist vision of defense, one where the success of a weapon was measured by its cost effectiveness rather than its combat effectiveness. The 'Missile Gap' equally influenced the new defense secretary, who argued that hundreds of less expensive unmanned ICBMs were 'better' than thousands of manned bombers, their tankers, and their sundry training and operational expenses. Despite the vocal opposition of new Air Force Chief of Staff General Curtis LeMay, McNamara publicly declared the manned bomber to be too costly, if not obsolete. He told Congress in 1961, 'The introduction of the ballistic missile is already exerting a major impact on the size, composition, and deployment of the manned bomber force and this impact will become greater in the years ahead. As the number of ballistic missiles increases, requirements for strategic aircraft will be reduced.' Two years later he told the Senate Defense Appropriations Subcommittee, 'I do not know any responsible civilian or military leaders…who believe we can use [nuclear] free-fall bombs as a means of delivering warheads on Soviet targets in the decade of the 70s,' arguing instead for sea- and land-based missiles and a small contingent of air-launched missiles (nuclear free-fall bombs remain in use in 2018, revealing McNamara's myopia).

To LeMay and many other of McNamara's 'irresponsible' military leaders the as-yet-unproven liquid-fueled Atlas and Titan, and the

new solid-fueled Minuteman I ICBMs were little more than '[expletive deleted] firecrackers.' LeMay told the same Senate subcommittee in 1963 that the Air Force's basic philosophy affirmed that 'there will be a requirement for a manned system' beyond the B-52 bomber, 'and we should get on with it.' McNamara found an unexpected ally in CINCSAC General Thomas Power who wanted ICBMs added to SAC's alert force. Power, aided by the commander of the newly established Air Force Systems Command (AFSC) General Bernard A Schriever, became a vocal proponent of ICBMs while echoing LeMay's pro-bomber arguments. Power boasted that 'the B-47 in the hands of professionals could deliver weapons in the year 2000.' This dual-track approach to counter McNamara's accounting rationale, however, failed to give Power what he really wanted: a numerically larger strike force combined of *both* bombers – the B-47, B-52, and B-58, and the planned North American B-70 (all part of a 50% ground alert force plus an unspecified number of bombers on airborne alert) – *as well as* ICBMs.

With McNamara focusing on budget cuts and the shift from Eisenhower's 'Massive Retaliation' airpower strategic nuclear deterrent force to Kennedy's strategy showcasing Army Green Beret and tactical operations championed by General Maxwell D Taylor, there was only so much money in the budget. For the Air Force this meant buying just the F-110 (which became the F-4C) and the TFX (which became the F-111) in both the nuclear and non-nuclear role, but as McNamara was forced to admit, neither would have a 'strategic' mission. Interestingly, a 12th November 1963 *Washington Post* article alleged that McNamara, while president of the Ford Motor Company when it was contracted to make parts for the B-47 (see Chapter 2) may not have honored obligations to return government overpayments for failing to meet production requirements, and in so doing made Boeing look bad. This generated a conflict of interest with now-Secretary McNamara, creating a 'pattern of prejudice' against Boeing which cost it the TFX contract after repeated tries, instead selecting the General Dynamics F-111 to be built in Vice President Lyndon B Johnson's home state of Texas.

To McNamara the solution was obvious – cut the number of manned bombers, beginning with the B-47. With more than a thousand in service in 1961 the B-47 was an easy budgetary target. When Air Force and SAC officials agreed in 1959 to begin retiring the B-47 as 'obsolete', there was an unspoken agreement that it would be replaced by other manned systems, including additional B-52s (carrying the GAM-87 Skybolt missile) and B-58s, as well as the B-70. Following the 1960 election, however, all bomber production was halted and Skybolt eventually canceled. Power was furious, but McNamara deftly refuted his protestations in Congressional testimony. B-47s were too costly to maintain and

53-6244 from the 307th BW was the last B-47E built. It was delivered to SAC on 24th October 1956 and retired as a display at Wright-Patterson AFB on 22nd January 1965, flown by Captain Eugene T Hickman (AC), Captain Harold W Todd (CP), Captain Alfred F Ottaviano (N), and Airman First Class James R Sine (CC). McNamara was eager to be rid of the B-47 and scrapped them as quickly as possible. *Stephen Miller*

operate, and required forward bases that were expensive to reach and contributed to the 'gold flow' problem of US balance of payments abroad. Deterrence, McNamara argued, could be achieved with less expensive ICBMs. As a declassified 1965 USAFE history recounts, 'the development of an ICBM force in the continental US as well as missile-launching submarines resulted in the phaseout of a large portion of SAC's bomber force, particularly the B-47. While such factors as vulnerability of the REFLEX bases and the foreign exchange costs of keeping SAC bombers [on] alert overseas weighed heavily, [McNamara's] declining emphasis on the strategic bomber as the primary [US] deterrent was the reason' for the B-47's hasty retirement. McNamara wielded his budgetary axe in a program known as FAST FLY, designed to retire as many older aircraft as possible in a minimum amount of time (as well as expeditiously scrap those already in retirement). Although FAST FLY affected other aircraft, it has become synonymous with the sweeping retirement of the B-47. Excess B-47 crews were retrained to meet the projected 50% B-52 ground alert requirement or sent to ICBM units. Many of the Phase V EWs were assigned to RB-66s, where they received approximately 60 hours of flight time plus a basic reconnaissance course. A large number of these ended up flying combat missions in Southeast Asia.

End Game

A modest number of early B-47As, B-47Bs, and TB-47Bs were retired throughout the mid-1950s, largely because they had indeed become obsolete with the evolution of later versions of the B-47E. Fears in early 1956 that the Soviets would field an operational ballistic missile with a range of 1,500nm (2,778km) reflected the belief they this would 'nullify the effectiveness' of the B-47. Democratic Senator Henry 'Scoop' Jackson of Washington told the Senate that such a missile 'would cancel out our one vital advantage over Russian air-atomic power – our system of overseas air bases,' leveling 'these bases in a matter of minutes.' Without these bases, Jackson added, 'the effectiveness of the B-47 bomber...would be drastically reduced,' forcing SAC to rely upon 'the now obsolete B-36 and the ... B-52 – only now beginning to trickle off production lines.'

By 1957 withdrawals expanded to include small numbers of RB-47Es with the first retirement (51-5272) taking place on 14th October. Less than a year had passed between this little-noticed event and the delivery of the last production B-47E (53-6244) on 24th October 1956. Indeed, Boeing would not hand over the last B-47s (three ERB-47Hs) to SAC until late December 1957. The reduction of operational RB-47Es (rather than those used for initial crew training) began with the inactivation of the 91st SRW at Lockbourne AFB on 8th November 1957, followed the next year by the 26th SRW. During 1959 the 97th BW, 308th BW, and the 340th BW were the first tranche of B-47E wings deactivated, although its airplanes were reassigned to the 2nd BW and 380th BW, creating two new 'super wings' with 70 B-47s each. B-47 numbers dropped again in 1960 with the inactivation of the 43rd BW, 44th BW and 320th BW and the 90th SRW. Nonetheless, there were still 1,178 B-47Bs and B-47Es and 100 RB-47Es and RB-47Hs in the active inventory by the time of the 1960 presidential election.

A Soviet ultimatum to sign a unilateral peace treaty with the German Democratic Republic (GDR – East Germany) by the end of 1961 coupled with Kennedy's perceived weakness at the June 1961 summit conference with Khrushchev in Vienna led to an escalation in Soviet-American tensions. Kennedy responded in July by, among other actions, calling for $3.3 billion in additional defense spending and tripling conscription to increase the overall number of military personnel. In his televised speech on 25th July 1961 Kennedy announced that a dozen B-47 wings slated for retirement 'would be

By 1961 Davis-Monthan AFB was overflowing with B-47s destined for the scrapper's torch. Kennedy's tough stance on Berlin provided a respite for six bomb wings, but this would be short lived. *Author's collection*

retained to bolster America's strategic striking power'. Eventually this decreased to six B-47 wings (the 70th SRW, the 310th BW, 2nd BW, 68th BW, 306th BW, and the 22nd BW) and six squadrons of KC-97s (the 301st AREFS, 98th AREFS, 90th AREFS, 2nd AREFS, 340th AREFS, and the 306th AREFS) maintained on active duty. The total of B-47s of all variants dropped by 251 to 1,027 airplanes assigned to 19 bomb wings and one strategic reconnaissance wing.

Yet another crisis in late 1962, this time in Cuba, led to the unplanned retention of B-47s, but by 1963 nearly half of all B-47 units had been deactivated and their airplanes retired. Overseas operations declined with the cessation of REFLEX deployments to Morocco. The following year REFLEX ended at bases in the United Kingdom and all but two bases in Spain, while B-52s replaced the AIR MAIL B-47s on Guam. A 21st October 1963 article in *US News and World Report* titled 'The Death of the B-47' quoted 'officers' as saying the B-47 was 'the most dependable nuclear-weapon carrier in the US arsenal,' and were 'confident it could penetrate Soviet antiaircraft defenses,' a 'doubtful capability of the B-52' alleged during Congressional testimony seeking more bombers, better ECM, and standoff weapons such as the AGM-28C Hound Dog II. The B-47, officials claimed, added a 'measure of flexibility to the US deterrent at a time when the reliability and accuracy of missiles is still in question.' Not surprisingly, civilian opinions were substantially different. 'The B-47 as a strategic weapons system does not measure up well against Polaris [SLBM] or Minuteman missiles. It is costly to maintain, and has other [unspecified] drawbacks. With a money squeeze on, officials say, something has to go.' This was not an insignificant amount, as the cost of keeping the B-47 fleet operational from FY63 to FY65 totaled $797.5 million. By 31st December 1963 there were only 391 B-47Es, 46 EB-47E ECM jets, 22 PIPECLEANER radio relay EB-47Ls (two squadrons had been retired), and 27 reconnaissance B-47s of all variants.

Sunday 15th March 1964 was like most other days that year. 'I Want to Hold Your Hand' by The Beatles was tops on the radio, and moviegoers delighted to the Blake Edwards comedy *The Pink Panther*. Unknown to all but a very few Americans, however, a profound change took place in Strategic Air Command. Some 620 Atlas, Titan, and Minuteman I ICBMs were now on SIOP alert, compared with just 619 B-47s, B-52s, and B-58s. After 18 years, SAC had changed from a bomber command that also had ballistic

The PIPECLEANER EB-47Ls, including 52-0305, were rapidly retired and replaced with EC-135Ls for the PACCS radio relay mission. Only the E/RB-47Hs and WB-47Es remained in Air Force service past 1966. *Stephen Miller*

missiles to a missile command that also had bombers. By the end of 1964 there were 701 ICBMs and 464 bombers on alert. For the remainder of its history, there would always be more ICBMs than bombers in SAC.

As McNamara had envisaged, the primacy of the manned strategic bomber was nearing its end and not soon enough. In April 1964, just a month after SAC had become a 'missile command,' LeMay requested that the planned phase-out of the last remaining B-47 units be extended, retaining eight wings in 1965, three wings in 1966, and two wings in 1967. Doing so, LeMay argued, would address the shortfall in SAC's capability caused by the unplanned extended structural modification of B-52s. Air Force Secretary Eugene M Zuckert concurred, although he recommended keeping only six wings in 1965. McNamara, however, was not persuaded and the B-47 phase-out in 1965 was completed as scheduled.

The final REFLEX deployments to Morón AB and Torrejón AB ended on 31st March 1965, and by the end of 1965 there were no B-47s on alert anywhere in the world. In-service B-47s dropped to just 56 with the 9th SAW at Mountain Home AFB, 56 with the 100th BW at Pease AFB, two command support aircraft with the 3rd Air Division (AD) at Andersen AFB on Guam, and 18 reconnaissance variants with the 55th SRW at Forbes AFB, raising SAC's total to a mere 132 jets. The last two operational SAC B-47 bombers retired on 11th February 1966 when B-47E 53-2286 left Pease AFB and B-47E 53-6235 departed Mountain Home AFB for storage at Davis-Monthan AFB. The reconnaissance variants assigned to the 55th SRW lasted for another year, with RB-47H 53-4296 making its final flight from Offutt AFB to Davis-Monthan AFB on 29th December 1967. Over a period of some 15 years, the B-47 had gone from SAC's most numerous bomber, with more than 1,800 serving in some capacity to zero, with a total production cost – excluding general maintenance of bases, crews, and airplanes – of $3.5 billion.

A Last Gasp

Well before FAST FLY and McNamara, the Air Force planned the transfer of excess (read 'obsolete') B-47s to Tactical Air Command (TAC) rather than retire and scrap them. On 25th November 1956 the Pentagon announced that this would 'provide greater mobility in dealing with "brush fire" wars,' and the B-47s would be transferred 'gradually' to TAC as 'new long-range [bombers] were developed.' Most importantly, this would provide TAC with 'a global striking force which it does not now possess.' Little came of this proposal, as TAC had no interest whatsoever in second-hand B-47s.

The issue resurfaced early in the Kennedy administration. As senior Air Force officials realized that McNamara's resolve to retire the Stratojet as a strategic bomber could not be circumvented, they again proposed transferring the B-47 to TAC. This would theoretically provide TAC with a ready fleet of aircraft with a range and bomb-carrying capacity greater than existing TAC fighter bombers. More importantly, SAC planners quietly argued that in the event of impending general war with the USSR, SAC could repossess the B-47s and use them to support the SIOP, circumventing McNamara's plan to scrap them. On 17th July 1962, for example, the Air Force Estimates Board met at the Pentagon for an 'informational' discussion of 'B-47's in TAC.' Despite these exploratory initiatives (coupled with the proposed KB-47 tanker), TAC successfully rejected all efforts to assign the Stratojet to a tactical role.

'Royal' Stratojets Abroad

At first glance SAC's bomber force has always been a strictly American affair with no public effort to sell B-36s or B-52s to allied air forces. US planners successfully argued that there were insufficient bombers for SAC's needs let alone those of a friendly nation. Foreign planners were rightly concerned that owning US-built bombers then in use by SAC might well lead to their operational control by the CINCSAC, limiting their use to meet other regional needs. The Royal Air Force (RAF) did operate 87 B-29s as Washington B.1s in both the bomber and reconnaissance role as well as RB-45s in an overflight capacity (pedants may argue that the Soviet Air Force flew Tupolev Tu-4 *Bulls* in the form of reverse-engineered B-29s). The RAF was not particularly pleased with the performance of the Washingtons, the Tornados were merely 'loaners', and the Soviet Tu-4s were hardly the result of an overseas sales pitch. It is surprising, then, that the US tried to sell the B-47 abroad on three separate occasions, each of which resulted in a rather decisive 'thanks, but no thanks.'

British efforts to develop an indigenous atomic strike force proved troublesome as the twin problems of insufficient bombs and small initial numbers of Vickers Valiant bombers delayed any real RAF operational capability. Discussions between the British and Americans over the transfer of US nuclear weapons to the RAF had been underway since 1953, but they were not immediately compatible with the Valiant or its successor 'V-Bombers' the Avro Vulcan and the Handley Page Victor. British scholar Ken Young has admirably traced this issue in *The American Bomb in Britain*, and notes that by 1955 the British would have but 10 atom bombs and the first Valiant would be just beginning trials. Recognizing these limits, USAF Vice Chief of Staff General Thomas D White proposed on 14th May 1954 that the RAF accept 90 newly built B-47s for the 'generous' sum of only $400 million, with the USAF providing aircrew and maintenance training along with logistics support. As White argued, they 'were playing on the same team and if the RAF was equipped with one or two wings of B-47s it would be welcome strengthening to the side.'

The British responded by dissembling, claiming that the B-47s were simply excess production aircraft that the US wanted the RAF to pay for, wouldn't be available any sooner than the Valiant, and suffered from multiple technical weaknesses when compared to the RAF's own English Electric Canberra. These were essentially red herrings, as the B-47 was comparable in performance to the Canberra in speed, suffered only slightly in maximum altitude, could carry 20,000 lb (9,072kg) of weapons versus 8,000 lb (3,629kg) in the Canberra, had far greater range (plus aerial refueling) than the Canberra, and – perhaps most importantly – had an effective radar bombing system. Air Marshal Sir Hugh Lloyd, Commander of the RAF's Bomber Command, 'appreciated' these advantages. In reality, the 'deal killers' were the shifting of personnel in training from RAF aircraft to the B-47, the need for 10,000ft (3,048m) runways plus overruns, prior 'unhappy experience' with the Washington, Lockheed P2V Neptune, and North American F-86 Sabre in British service, and the 'loss of prestige that would result from accepting the offer.' Equally problematic was the British fear that the RAF B-47s would be 'placed under control of SACEUR [Supreme Allied Commander, Europe – an American]' meaning that British 'freedom to select targets of national importance would be impaired.' Consequently, on 11th June 1954 British Chief of Air Staff Air Marshal Sir William Dickson thanked American Air Force Chief of Staff General Nathan F Twining 'for the generosity and magnificence of the offer,' which the RAF regrettably had to decline.

B-47s Down Under

Australia's controversial acquisition of 24 General Dynamics F-111Cs in 1963 for the Royal Australian Air Force (RAAF) as the replacement for its fleet of 48 Canberras created a five-year gap between the Canberra's planned retirement and the introduction of the F-111 into service. To mitigate this, according to Melbourne's newspaper *The Age* on 24th October 1963, the US offered to loan '24 Boeing B-47E and RB-47E Stratojets' 'in the best condition' to the RAAF (other sources report 30 airplanes, all B-47Es). The B-47s would be loaned free of charge, although the RAAF would be responsible for 'operating expenses, spares, and reconditioning before return,' with a maximum cost of $US24.8 million. Training on the B-47 would commence no later than June 1964. The US insisted that the Australian government approve the entire proposal (both the F-111 and the B-47) within just 30 days. The Australian Cabinet met during the evening of 23rd October 1963, and in a three-hour marathon session approved the acquisition of the F-111s and – only 'if necessary' – the loan of the B-47s. To cement the loaner deal, Secretary of Defense McNamara ordered three B-47Es based at Andersen AFB, Guam, to undertake 'a demonstration tour' between 14th and 28th November 1963 (another source says the deployment ended on 4th December). Known as 'Project Australia' the three airplanes deployed to RAAF Amberley near Brisbane, Queensland. One of these also conducted demonstration flights over and static displays at major Australian cities including Canberra, Townsville, Pearce, Edinburgh, Avalon, Sydney, and Darwin. By the sheerest of coincidences, the tour began two weeks prior to Australia's federal elections. The Australian Liberal Party favored the expensive and controversial F-111 deal, so the presence of the B-47s was seen as a means of tacit American support for the government of Prime Minister Sir Robert Menzies in general and the F-111 deal in particular. Officially, however, the visit was to 'assist the RAAF in defining requirements and facilities for possible operations of B-47s,' and to 'enhance the traditionally friendly relations that exist between the two countries and Air Forces.'

The RAF acquired 87 former USAAF B-29s as Washington B.1s. During 1954 General Thomas D White offered a comparable number of B-47s to the RAF, which they politely declined. *Author's collection*

Britain's airborne nuclear deterrent was contingent on bombers such as the Vickers Valiant and the Blue Danube atom bomb, seen in this dummy drop. White proposed that a fleet of B-47s would provide a more immediate capability. *via Terry Panopalis*

This was neither the first proposal to sell B-47s to the RAAF nor was it the first time that B-47s had visited Australia. By 1953 the RAAF was undergoing a critical reevaluation of its mission and capabilities. Fully aware that it could not sustain the type of heavy bombardment that the RAF and USAAF did over Germany or Japan during World War Two, Australian officials instead emphasized the defensive role of fighters as the heart of RAAF airpower in its three main roles of defense of Australia, Cold War commitments, and the defense of Malaya. Nonetheless, there was a notable effort to acquire a modest fleet of bombers capable of flying from 'Darwin to Singapore, and from Singapore to Bangkok with a full bomb load' which would carry atomic weapons to make up for the smaller number of bombers.

Consequently, plans to replace the RAAF's Avro Lincoln bomber included appraisals the following year of the North American A3D Skywarrior, the B-47, and the Canberra, although there was a small contingent of RAAF planners who preferred a larger 'V-bomber,' in particular the Vulcan. The Australian government – with an eye toward local jobs – insisted that the aircraft be built in Australia, which ultimately led to the decision to acquire the Canberra. Air Vice Marshal Sir Alister M Murdoch, who led the international evaluation, further elaborated on why the B-47 was not chosen, saying it was 'too slow, lacks operating height, … has insufficient range, …[was] being taken out of production in June, 1955,' and with a price tag of US$2.5 million apiece, 'the unit costs were very high.'

During 1956 three 9th BW B-47s flew nonstop from Mountain Home AFB to Australia, and later New Zealand, as part of the third annual Operation HANDCLASP (see Appendix IV). They were scheduled to arrive to coincide with the Olympic Games at Melbourne, and were accompanied by KC-97s for refueling and logistics support. At least one RAAF pilot was qualified in the B-47, as Squadron Leader James S Wilson trained at McConnell AFB and remained there from 1956 through 1958 as an instructor pilot.

3960th CSG B-47E 53-1822 was one of three B-47s to visit Australia in 1963. Kangaroo 'zap' marking is barely visible above the brake chute door. The RAAF was unimpressed with the B-47 and instead chose F-4Es pending delivery of its F-111Cs. *via William T Y'Blood*

For the 1963 whirlwind tour, three B-47Es (52-0348, 53-1822, and 53-1845) were accompanied by a KC-135A and led by Brigadier General Harold W Ohlke, the 3rd Air Division (AD) commander. Two (53-1822 and 53-1845) were assigned to the 3960th Combat Support Group (CSG) at Andersen AFB, while the third (52-0348) was from the 9th SAW at Mountain Home AFB on AIR MAIL alert on Guam. Although there are claims that the airplanes received RAAF roundels, these were in fact small 'zap' markings; the airplanes retained their US markings throughout the tour.

Assessments of the tour's impact could not have been more divergent. Writing in *Combat Crew*, SAC's monthly safety magazine, Captain Donald C Goll hailed the 13 flights [a SAC history says 10 flights] as an effective introduction to the B-47's MA-7 radar system and the Ground Proximity Indicator (GPI), especially as the Canberra navigators had no prior experience in radar operation, let alone radar bombing. Missions were flown with an American pilot and navigator along with an Australian pilot and navigator, and included a High-Low-High attack profile. Notable among the missions was a two-ship strike package flown against targets in Sydney. One B-47 flew at high altitude from Central Australia (west to east) and one at low level after a 700nm (1,296km) flight over the ocean (east to west). Sydney air defenses were not warned in advance about the missions. Target for the low-altitude sortie was a 1,500ft (457m) railroad bridge at Hawkesbury. The flight began with a maximum-weight ATO takeoff from RAAF Amberley, followed by an hour's cruise at altitude over the ocean. The B-47 then turned south and descended to a medium altitude and headed toward Sydney. Approximately 400nm (741km) from the target the B-47 descended again, followed by a third descent at a range of 250nm (463km) when the airplane reached its final bomb run altitude of less than 500ft (152m) and then accelerated. The MA-7 bomb/nav system worked as advertised, and after 2 hours 45 minutes of flying at high speed 'on the deck' the deviation at the target was 'negligible.' When the B-47 was 45 seconds from the target it 'popped up' to altitude, and at 20 seconds Squadron Leader Frank Quinn, the RAAF Wing Navigation Officer for 42 Squadron, switched from radar to optics and completed the bombing run. In Goll's words, the systems 'delivered another hit on target, with the able hands of a professional SAC crew on the boxes and on the controls.' He added, 'the reliable and faithful B-47 proved once again that there is still life in the old bird and this one isn't ready just yet for the boneyard.'

The Aussie point of view was notably different. To begin with, senior Australian military officials simply did not want the B-47. Chief of the Air Staff Air Marshal Sir Valston Hancock understood that training the first B-47 crews in the US and achieving full operational capability would not take place until training on the F-111 was starting, would deplete manpower from other units, would

require lengthening runways, and was not even needed as the Canberras could be retained for another five years. Hancock was afforded the opportunity to fly a B-47 from RAAF Amberley to Darwin. In fact, the flight was nearly a disaster – literally. As Wing Commander David Evans, who was in the airplane reported, instead of switching on the water injection, 'Hancock switched it off…We went off the end of the strip and all the Americans watching saw the wing drop and they said "It's gone" because they said that's how they lost a lot of B-47s. Dust came up off the end of the strip…anyhow we finally got up to Darwin.' Whether or not this incident reaffirmed Hancock's negative view of the B-47 remains unknown, but he clearly disliked it. Although it performed 'very well indeed,' he said, 'I dismissed the B-47 very quickly. I said it's no more than a long range Canberra – no damn good to us.' As an RAAF report noted, of the '16 operational requirements listed in the specification, the B-47E failed to meet ten.' The RAAF rejected the B-47 proposal, and the Australian cabinet endorsed this decision on 19th March 1964. The RAAF instead opted for McDonnell Douglas F-4E Phantom IIs as an interim platform pending delivery of the F-111Cs, and the B-47 remained a purely American bomber (excluding the sole example loaned to Canada for testing of the Orenda engine).

A Look Back, A Look Ahead
It would be easy to suggest that the B-47 was an ill-conceived design that never reached its full potential. At the time of its initial development during and immediately after the Second World War, the final design was radically different from the other competitors in the medium jet bomber competition. Almost by default this led to a protracted developmental process, with some six years passing between the first flight of the XB-47 and the first flight of the B-47E, finally resulting in a viable weapon system. Moreover, the airplane was designed and manufactured in a political climate that was colored by the growing fear of communism. Although few US officials, military or civilian, imagined a direct Soviet attack on the United States in 1950, the Soviets and the West clashed on a variety of issues, some of which could easily have led to war between the former allies. The continued presence of Soviet troops in Iran and claims of a planned Soviet invasion of Turkey in 1946, civil strife in Greece and Turkey during 1947 and 1948, the establishment in 1947 of a Polish communist government, the 1948 coup d'état in Czechoslovakia and the Berlin Crisis, the 1949 communist victory in the Chinese civil war and the Soviet detonation of an atomic device, and the 1950 communist invasion of South Korea were all sources of friction, if not potential conflict, between the two leading powers of the post-war world. These led to a distorted sense of urgency that compelled SAC to demand the accelerated delivery of B-47s even if they were

not combat ready. For Curtis LeMay, champion of 1,000-plane raids over Germany and massed B-29 raids over Japan and despite his animus toward the B-47, numbers mattered.

Aside from three books by Lindsay Peacock, Jan Tegler, and Al Lloyd as well as occasional magazine articles, most of which were published well after the end of the Cold War and focused on declassified overflights and peripheral missions by RB-47s, very little has been written about the B-47. There are several reasons for this which reveal much about the B-47's history. To begin with, Boeing never expected much of the airplane. Boeing certainly benefitted from the Air Force's funding but saw the B-47 only as the precursor to the B-52 and the 707 which became Boeing's signature airplanes. Although Bill Cook's *Road to the 707* (as well as those books mentioned above) credits the B-47 for its evolutionary importance, Boeing was never vocal in recognizing the B-47 for its impact of the company's success. The Air Force shared equally in this reluctance to tout the B-47 and its accomplishments. By 2018 many former crewmembers were still reluctant to discuss their missions constrained by non-disclosure agreements signed in the 1950s and 1960s. Despite the handful of world records, newspaper stories, and Congressional budget battles, strict Cold War security meant that amateur photographs of B-47s in operational settings are hard to come by. What few images taken by brave souls willing to risk the wrath of the Air Police have no doubt been tossed into the trash by disinterested sons and daughters (or grandchildren) who have inherited them from now-deceased fliers and maintenance personnel. 'Spotters' seem to have had better luck but even so many of their photographs have disappeared into the inaccessible holdings of private collectors or groups unwilling to share them. Official photos suffered from similar classification restrictions. This book has the only known photograph of a B-47 being loaded with a nuclear weapon, albeit covered by a security drape. Even the National Atomic Museum in Albuquerque, NM, has yet to find such a photo (the picture on page 104 came from an official history of the 376th BW at Barksdale AFB, and censors likely missed it because of the drape over the weapon). Declassification efforts with the US National Archives and Records Administration (NARA) have proven equally unsuccessful in finding additional photographs.

The B-47, like the B-36, has been overlooked as a subject because it 'did not have a war.' Conspicuously absent from Korea or Vietnam, its years on alert hardly constitute the basis for a detailed and captivating operational history. The reconnaissance B-47s certainly faced a hostile enemy, with two shot down and one scrapped after landing. But many readers and authors prefer stories about dogfights and bombing missions, and so far there are no bestseller Clancy-esque novels involving B-47s (although there is Samuel Lockerman's self-published 2003 *Bring Back The B-47*, a curious work in which the lead character champions a movement to bring back the B-47 by the hundreds from the Boneyard while eliminating fighter pilots altogether). Aside from the occasional recycling of magazine articles about Cold War reconnaissance losses even the RB-47s have faded from publication.

An old adage laments that 'the school teacher never gets the credit, just the star pupil.' The B-47 was certainly the teacher in the development of operational tactics and procedures in strategic nuclear warfare, and SAC was the student who benefitted from these many lessons. The successes and failures of the B-47 under LeMay, Power, and the third CINCSAC General John D Ryan paved the way for the successes of the B-52 as both a strategic deterrent and a conventional bomber. The public adulation (and after Vietnam the public opprobrium) went to SAC, not the B-47. Indeed, the B-52 became one of the most conspicuous icons of the Cold War, in large part due to Stanley Kubrick's black comedy *Dr Strangelove, or How I Learned*

The shape of things to come? The B-47 influenced the design of large aircraft, including the B-52 and modern jet airliners. Northrop's YB-49 became the model for the B-2 and the B-21, although its impact on commercial aircraft remains to be seen. *Photo 35585AC USAF*

to Love the Bomb and Stop Worrying. The Stratojet's starring role in the 1955 film *Strategic Air Command* was eclipsed two years later by *Bombers B-52* and the 1963 movie *A Gathering of Eagles*, the latter a showcase of the B-52 and SAC's nuclear readiness mission. Only 744 B-52s were built compared to 2,041 B-47s, but even sheer numbers were insufficient to garner more public attention for the Stratojet.

Finally both the Air Force and Boeing suffered two major embarrassments with the B-47. The Air Force bore tremendous responsibility for allowing early B-47 production to proceed in advance of its development. Boeing was equally unprepared for the new challenges associated with manufacturing the B-47, and the many component suppliers were similarly culpable in not understanding the complexities in designing and building systems that were still largely theoretical when the airplane was first designed. Moreover, the B-47 was a medium bomber assigned to a strategic bombing mission (joining the B-29 and B-50 which SAC had previously redesignated

B-47B 51-2318 was the real star of the movie *Strategic Air Command*, but as with all other B-47s it underwent IRAN following delivery by 305th BW navigator Major Leo I Beinhorn (l to r) and copilot Major William H Hill, 6th AD Commander Brigadier General Kenneth O Sanborn with Boeing test pilots Dick Taylor and Ed Hensley. 51-2318 was scrapped on 20th December 1960. *Photo BW92636 courtesy Boeing*

After an initially tepid public relations effort, Boeing quickly pulled out the stops on getting the B-47 into the public eye.

Top left: Famed reporter and TV news anchor Walter Cronkite joined Captain John S McWilliams (l), Major Frank Wyckoff (c), and Captain Harold Hoffman (r) for an acceptance flight.

Top right: Avid pilot and radio newsman Paul Harvey Aurandt (c – better known as 'Paul Harvey') also enjoyed a B-47 orientation flight.

Bottom, left to right: Barnstormer and racing pilot Roscoe Turner (r) became an advocate for SAC and the B-47, as did Arthur Godfrey. Film and TV star William L 'Hopalong Cassidy' Boyd and fans touted the A-5 tail gun. Miss America 1953 Neva Jane Langley had B-47B 50-0043 named in her honor. *Cronkite Boeing photo BW92481, Neva Jane photo Harold Siegfried, all others courtesy Boeing*

as medium bombers). During the Second World War medium bombers included North American B-25s and Martin B-26s. It would have been inconceivable to assign them the same missions as B-29s or B-24s attacking Tokyo or Ploesti, but that is precisely what SAC did with the B-47. SAC expected the B-47 to function as a strategic bomber and for Boeing to 'make it happen'. The Air Force's willingness to accept substandard airplanes from Boeing reflected a shameful 'anything is better than nothing' acquisition mentality which compelled Boeing to deliver incomplete airplanes, leading to a vicious circle of 'concurrent' production (a lesson ignored decades later in the acquisition of the Lockheed-Martin F-35). Indeed, a Confidential 1969 Pentagon study titled 'Improving the Acquisition Process for

High-Risk Military Electronics Systems' examined 13 'complex weapons systems built…since 1955' and reported that only four – the F-4, F-100, B-52, and AIM-9 Sidewinder air-to-air missile – met or exceeded their performance specifications. At the bottom of the rankings was the B-47, which met its integrated performance requirements only 25% of the time.

The second embarrassment associated with the B-47 was the airplane's structural weakness. Boeing was understandably very sensitive about the MILK BOTTLE program, out of both reputational and litigation considerations. At the time the B-47 was designed, no one fully understood the complexities of fatigue and other stresses associated with highly flexible swept wings and operations at high

Left: Although the MILK BOTTLE modification program was a success, Boeing was caught off guard by the whole structural fatigue issue. Its response became the standard for research and new aircraft development. B-47B 51-2118 undergoes repair at Douglas-Tulsa.

Opposite: The B-47's crew was not only its greatest strength but one of its real vulnerabilities. Launching from alert and then flying 15+ hours on a nuclear strike mission pushed men to their limits. SAC trained to prepare for this hard eventuality, which never transpired. *Both: USAF*

speed and altitude. Moreover, SAC's change from high-altitude operations to low-altitude bombing runs effectively ignored Boeing's early design studies (and confidence) in the airplane. One early study assumed a 4,000-hour life expectancy of the B-47. With an average of eight hours per mission, this meant a total of 500 flights before structural retirement. Given some 73 flights per year, a B-47 would have only a six-year lifespan. Indeed, many B-47s never reached the 4,000-hour mark before retirement. Although the B-52 experienced a similar transition from high- to low-altitude operations, it benefitted directly from the lessons learned in MILK BOTTLE and the B-47 fatigue testing program. B-52Hs still in service in 2018 were delivered in 1960 and 1961, and the 58-year-old jets are slated for re-engining and service through 2040 – an operational life of 80 years. Because of structural difficulties encountered by the B-47, the entire subject of aircraft fatigue and integrity underwent almost as radical a transition as airplanes themselves. The intensified attention and effort that began with the B-47 advanced aircraft design across the entire aerospace industry.

In both cases – concurrent production and changes in operational specifications – the real issue at hand was the ability of the B-47 to perform its mission. Aside from theoretical number crunching by SAC planners or RAND analysts, the opinions of former Stratojet crewmembers remain the most useful measure about the B-47's ability to complete its mission. One crewman believed that given the sheer number of airplanes enough B-47s would have successfully evaded Soviet defenses to strike their assigned targets. He added that few crews would have survived, however, even with planned recovery bases in Iran or Afghanistan. Other crewmembers placed great faith in the ability of Phase V or BLUE CRADLE ECM jets to clear a path for the bomb-laden B-47s to reach their targets, but again the survival of crews would have been problematic. Despite such optimism, it's not altogether clear how realistic these beliefs might be. Launching from Biggs AFB near El Paso, TX, from an alert posture just before bedtime followed by a 14+ hour flight with one or two air refuelings from KC-97s (that might not be available in requisite numbers) then a descent to fly at altitudes less than 500ft (152m) for 2-3 hours followed by a pop-up to deliver a nuclear bomb then a descent and another low-level leg to the next target all while being shot at by SAMs and MiGs and AAA translates to nearly 24 hours without sleep in a pre-apocalyptic holocaust world. Not only does this raise questions about the success rate of a hypothetical B-47 mission, but about what the EWP or SIOP would actually achieve, an issue well beyond the scope of this history but critical to the B-47's role in deterrence as a policy.

What, then, did the B-47 contribute to US and Allied national security, to Strategic Air Command, to the Air Force in general, and to the Boeing Company? As cliché as most single-word answers might be, the Stratojet was simply 'transitional'. In each of these cases, the B-47 served as the evolutionary nexus between a military strategy based on massed ground and naval forces versus a deterrent force based on a strategic nuclear air armada. It was the evolutionary nexus between a largely 'hands off' procurement strategy based on clearly articulated contract requirements versus a highly complex, constantly redefined set of specifications that changed often, sometimes weekly. It was the evolutionary nexus between the design of aircraft based on long-standing, piston-powered straight-wing configurations and 'human' technology versus flexible swept-wing, jet-powered designs that relied on yet-to-be proven electronic equipment for navigation and combat operations.

In addition to its crucial role in these major transitions, the B-47 suffered from a number of other limitations that eventually contributed to other changes in the way both military and civilian aircraft were designed and operated. For example, the shift from World War Two bombers filled with multiple crewmen each

performing a highly specialized tasks to the B-47 crew of just three led to task saturation, cramped quarters, tandem pilot seating, and poor crew coordination. Boeing designed the B-52 with similar pilot seating and no ECM operator, but the lessons of the B-47 compelled LeMay to direct the change to side-by-side pilot arrangement (already demonstrated in the B-47C mockup) and the addition of a dedicated electronic warfare officer. Similarly, the B-47's advanced wing design meant that it could not carry fuel in the wings due to limits in sealing technology and created the undesirable aileron reversal. These issues led Boeing to develop improved sealed wing tanks that allowed the B-52 to use a 'wet' wing and carry more fuel, extending its range. In addition, B-52s used spoilers for lateral control with the added benefit of their dual use as speed brakes, a feature which the B-47 sorely lacked and desperately needed. Finally, the B-47 was limited in its growth potential – there simply was not enough room or load capacity to add more personnel or reasonably carry external stores. Multiple variants of the B-52 attest to the ability to change engines, add mission capability, or carry external stores without sacrificing range and internal weapons capacity.

As it did with the B-52, the B-47 influenced the design of Boeing's famous 367-80 – the Dash 80 – forerunner to both the fleet of 820 KC-135 tankers and other variants as well as more than 1,000 707 and 720 airliners and military versions such as the E-3 Sentry Airborne Warning and Control System (AWACS), E-8 JointSTARS ground-tracking aircraft, and E-6 Take Charge and Move Out (TACAMO) airborne command posts. Configured with a low-mounted swept wing, the Dash 80 used the more conventional landing gear arrangement, with fuel stored in a flexible wet wing and center wing fuselage tank. For the KC-135 and the 707/KE-3 tanker versions, additional fuel tanks were located in the forward and aft lower fuselage. Airliner and cargo variants used this space for luggage and cargo containers. Pylon mounted engines for all of these evolved over time from water-injected turbojets to turbofans, eventually including the CFM-56 high-bypass turbofan in widespread

use by civilian airliners. Each improvement required comparatively little in the way of significant structural modifications, a design feature that reached all the way back to the XB-47.

The need for jet-powered tanker aircraft to refuel the B-47 was the driving factor behind Boeing President Bill Allen's drive to build the KC-135 and its proprietary 'flying boom' refueling system. Despite Lockheed actually winning the design competition for the Air Force's jet tanker, LeMay's intervention and Boeing's success in flying the Dash 80 (versus Lockheed's 'paper plane') resulted in the reversal of this decision and the production of a fleet of tankers, cargo aircraft, reconnaissance variants, and airborne command posts. Indeed, the cramped quarters of the RB-47H profoundly influenced the design of the 10 BIG TEAM RC-135Cs, converted from RC-135Bs.

Aside from the B-47's influence on the structural design of the Dash 80, KC-135, and 707, it had implications for the future operation of jet airliners and homeowners near major airports. From 16th-27th January 1956, 14 airline pilots and engineers attended a B-47 familiarization course at McConnell AFB. Primary purpose of the course was to 'show airline personnel the difference between the operation of piston engine and jet aircraft and to show them the specific problems presented by operation of high speed jets,' with the expectation that these pilots would then define the airlines' training programs. Although the course used the B-47, the intent was to demonstrate the many challenges airline pilots would face as they transitioned to the Boeing 707 and Douglas DC-8. Curriculum included 55 hours of ground instruction in systems, performance, and simulators. Each pilot was checked out in the B-47 and logged approximately 10 hours of flying time.

The B-47's implications for future jet travel extended beyond aircrews. According to a 29th October 1956 article in *Aviation Week*, several 'large movements of B-47s taking off from Hickam AFB, HI'

provoked considerable outcry from Honolulu residents unaccustomed to jet noise. Although departure requirements called for a sharp right turn after takeoff as a noise abatement procedure, the B-47s could not meet this requirement as they needed more speed prior to water injection runout and flap retraction. It would be another 5-10 years before jet airliner noise would become a common complaint by residents near major airports, and many people (especially residents near REFLEX bases in England) got their first 'dose' of jet noise from B-47s.

From the continuous miscues in design, production, and operation of the B-47, Boeing and the Air Force learned invaluable lessons that made the B-52 highly successful both as an airplane and as a nuclear strike platform with true intercontinental capability. SAC especially benefitted from the operational and maintenance lessons learned from the B-47 fiascos, not the least of which was the need to keep aircrew, especially pilots, happy and to recognize the invaluable contributions by the maintenance personnel who worked diligently under great duress to 'keep 'em flying'. Finally Boeing learned the design and production secrets that enabled company president Bill Allen to gamble with confidence the $16 million he risked in 1952 on the development of the Boeing 367-80, which spawned the KC-135 jet tanker and which ultimately introduced the Boeing stable of 707s to 787s, radically altering air travel and the global social, political, economic, and cultural changes that ensued. As such, Boeing Corporate Historian Michael J 'Mike' Lombardi argues that the 'B-47 is the most important airplane Boeing ever built.' Although the B-47 may have indeed been Boeing's 'most important' airplane, it was a qualified disappointment. Nonetheless, its extraordinary legacy as SAC's transitional bomber transcended its many limitations and led directly to the success of the B-52, KC-135, and the ongoing development and production of Boeing jet airliners.

Above: By the time B-52B 53-0376 arrived at Castle AFB the design had already benefitted from the many improvements derived from the B-47 experience. *Photo P16915 courtesy Boeing*

Left: B-47E 53-1965 was among the last B-47s retired, coincidentally, in 1965 when it arrived at MASDC on 20th December. The B-47's sleek lines, deft flying, troubled development, unforgiving handling, and abrupt retirement all contributed to its legacy as well as those of its successors. *Stephen Miller*

Mission-Design-Series (MDS) List

The table which follows reflects the evolution and status of individual B-47s and derivatives. The original Mission-Design-Series (MDS) and block number are shown on the left, followed by the Air Force serial number, Boeing model number, and construction number. Canceled airplanes were not assigned block or construction numbers. The table continues with the roll out date, the first flight date, the MIRR (Material Inspection Receiving Report—proof of delivery) date when the airplane officially became the property of the Air Force, and the flyaway date when the Air Force actually flew the airplane to its first assignment. The next column indicates any subsequent MDS changes. The following column lists the date when the airplane was withdrawn from service with losses due to attrition summarized in full in Appendix II – Attrition.

The final two columns show the date when an airplane was accessioned at the Military Aircraft Storage and Disposition Center (MASDC) at Davis-Monthan AFB, AZ, and when it was stricken off charge there or removed for other duties. The name of this facility changed on several occasions during the time that B-47s were stored there. It initially switched from the 3040th Aircraft Storage Depot (ASD) to the 3040th Aircraft Storage Squadron (ASS), and on 1st June 1956 it became the Arizona Aircraft Storage Branch (AASB). This changed on 1st August 1959 to the 2704th Air Force Storage and Disposition Group (AFSDG), and on 1st February 1965 became the more familiar MASDC.

Beginning 1st January 1965, aircraft assigned to MASDC were given a 5-digit Production Control Number (PCN), sometimes referred unofficially as a 'storage code'. This was a 2-letter identifier

based on the airplane type (for the B-47 it was BB, later expanded to BBA) followed by the sequential arrival number from 001 to 999 (and subsequently blocks of 100, eg, BBA01 to BBA99, BBB01 to BBB99, BBC01 to BBC99 etc). Most B-47s, however, were never assigned a PCN, as most B-47s which transited MASDC were scrapped before this system was introduced. Linking PCNs to specific airplanes after 1st January 1965 has proven problematic. Official records for these early entries are Spartan, at best, and were often incomplete or contradictory. Photos of airplanes with the PCN painted on the nose can be equally confusing: an airplane marked BB79A should in fact be BBA79. The highest known PCN is BBA83 for WB-47E 51-2414, which arrived on 31st October 1969. Had PCNs been assigned retrospectively, which they were not, they would have reached BBG23, accounting for the 1,623 B-47s of all types which passed through MASDC. In addition, MASDC dates for the QB-47Es are incomplete, and (except for 53-4256 and 52-4263) show the dates – if known – when the RB-47Es from which they were converted were originally stored in MASDC. The dates they were removed for conversion have not been verified.

Identifying specific dates for the Out of Service column is a fickle process. The absolute record for any aircraft is the airplane's Air Force Technical Order (AFTO) Form 781 Weight & Balance Sheet. Nearly all of these were destroyed as each airplane was stricken off charge or in subsequent purges of outdated and unneeded documents.

By 1967 there were still hundreds of B-47s awaiting reclamation out of the 1,623 that passed through Davis-Monthan AFB. *USAF photo*

Consequently, the individual airplane record cards from the Air Force Historical Research Agency (AFHRA) have been long considered the 'gold standard' for aircraft data. Whatever their historical legacy, the record cards are frequently 'reconciliation' documents – after-the-fact summaries that combined multiple and occasionally incomplete records with bureaucratic decrees detached from reality to arrive at a convenient date rather than an absolute record. The logistics division at SAC Headquarters (SAC/LG) maintained its own set of record cards for the B-47 fleet. These documents combine both handwritten and typed entries, show frequent erasures, strikeouts, and cryptic symbols known only to SAC/LG personnel long since gone, and are not entirely complete. Not surprisingly, these often conflict with the AFHRA records, as do Boeing documents. For example, Boeing records indicate that B-47B 50-0009 was designated as the sole YB-47F and 50-0040 as the single KB-47G for probe-and-drogue refueling tests. The AFHRA cards do not show these designations (they had no SAC/LG cards as they were never SAC assets) but they are used throughout this book as official given their use by Boeing and in other official Air Force documents.

Gaps in the roll out, first flight, delivery, and flyaway dates reflect the absence of official records. Airplanes built by Douglas-Tulsa and Lockheed-Marietta were tracked separately from those built by Boeing in Wichita. The Douglas-Tulsa records, for example, did not include all of the same dates (such as MIRR) as those maintained by Boeing. Moreover, when Boeing acquired McDonnell Douglas, these records were supposedly stored in St Louis. Repeated efforts to locate these lists have been unsuccessful, and the copy provided to the author years earlier may be the only extant record of Douglas-Tulsa B-47 production, however complete. Similarly, Lockheed-Marietta has been unable to produce its records for the B-47s built at its Georgia facility.

Changes to an airplane's MDS are equally troublesome. SAC/LG cards often list designations that did not appear in the AFHRA cards, and which occasionally changed without apparent reason. B-47B 51-2054 is a salient example. Delivered on 13th June 1952 as a B-47B, it immediately underwent conversion into a YRB-47B by Grand Central, and was designated as such on 21st May 1953. It was subsequently one of two YRB-47Bs which Lockheed-Marietta configured into the ROMAN I configuration, and in November 1954 it was redesignated as an RB-47E (noted only on the SAC/LG card). This MDS obviously conflicted with the existing RB-47E fleet, so this was changed to YRB-47E. After realizing that the basic airframe was a 'B model' rather than an 'E model,' it reverted to a YRB-47B. All three of these changes took place in six weeks' time and appear only on the SAC/LG card. It remained a YRB-47B until 1st March 1955 when it was changed to an RB-47B (the letter 'Y' was crossed out on the SAC/LG card) and acquired the Roman numeral suffix 'I' (written in pencil on the SAC/LG card), rendering it as an RB-47B-I. Six weeks later Soviet MiG-15s shot it down near the Kamchatka Peninsula.

Both the B-47Bs and B-47Es carried Roman numeral suffixes, specifically B-47B-I, B-47B-II, B-47E-I, –II, –III, –IV, and –IVa. These reflected aircraft configurations based on ECM fit, systems, maximum operational weight, and other specifications, and are discussed fully in Chapter 3. Associating a specific serial number with these suffixes is not a particularly meaningful exercise, as an individual airplane could progress through each configuration until it was in the final –IVa configuration. During an Inspect and Repair as Necessary (IRAN) visit a B-47E-I might become a B-47E-III, for example, and during a later visit become a –IV, while a different B-47E-II might go straight to B-47E-IVa. Many of the dates for these changes were recorded only on the AFTO 781 and are no longer available or were never entered on the SAC/LG or AFHRA cards.

B-47B 51-2284 awaits smelting into aluminum ingots in June 1961. It served with the 306th BW, the 321st BW, and the 19th BW. To the left is B-47E 53-2321, which flew with the 2nd BW, 509th BW, and the 40th BW. *USAF photo*

Not all scrapped B-47s ended their days at MASDC. B-47E 52-0281 was abandoned at Elmendorf AFB in 1959 after serving with the 73rd Air Defense Squadron (ADS). *Author's collection*

Following the 1st July 1960 loss of RB-47H 53-4281 to a Soviet MiG-19, SAC changed the MDS of several of its electronic and reconnaissance B-47 variants in August 1961. By deleting the 'B' for bomber SAC sought to emphasize that these airplanes were not armed with bombs and therefor not a threat to the USSR in an effort to reduce (if not eliminate) their vulnerability to attack. The three EB-47E(TT) TELL TWO aircraft were redesignated as E-47Es. RB-47Es became either E-47s or R-47Es, RB-47Hs became R-47Hs, RB-47Ks became R-47Ks, and the three ERB-47Hs became ER-47Hs. None of these changes appear on the AFHRA record cards but appear on technical orders, flight manuals, and in Air Force Regulation (AFR) 66-11, the Air Force manual for MDS designations. Few crewmembers recall seeing these in daily use, and they fooled no one as to the purpose of the airplane. By February 1962 they began reversion to the prior MDS; RB-47Es accessioned to AFSDG were listed as RB-47Es rather than E-47s or R-47s. Similarly, the Phase V ECM B-47Es transitioned from B-47E to E-47E to EB-47E.

Block numbers for the RB-47Ks are somewhat confusing. All 15 of these airplanes were ordered as part of the Block 45 acquisition of the RB-47E, and they were built as RB-47E-45-BWs. After roll out and prior to delivery to SAC, Boeing converted them into RB-47Ks and they received an entirely new block number as RB-47K-1-BWs; both are listed. This also explains why the first flight date is *after* the MIRR date for these airplanes.

Dates used in this table ought to be straightforward using official sources. However, the dates appearing in these original documents are often highly subjective. For example, is it the date the airplane began or finished conversion, the date it arrived at its operational unit after sitting at the depot for a week, the date it arrived at MASDC (say, Friday afternoon) or the date it was logged in (say, Monday morning), or the date someone in an office several months after the fact decided would be the least administrative burden? As much as this book seeks to provide an accurate and definitive reference the source material is itself ambiguous.

MDS and Block Number	Serial Number	Model Number	Const. Number	Roll Out Date	First Flight Date	MIRR Date	USAF Fly Away	New MDS	Out of Service	MASDC Input Date	MASDC Output Date
XB-47-BO	46-0065	450	15972	12 Sep 47	17 Dec 47	29 Nov 48	n/a		31 Dec 53		
	46-0066	450	15973	n/a	21 Jul 48	18 Dec 48	n/a		14 Dec 54		
B-47A-BW	49-1900	450-10-9	4500001	01 Mar 50	25 Jun 50	27 Apr 51	30 Nov 56			28 Feb 58	26 Jun 58
	49-1901	450-10-9	4500002	n/a	n/a	27 Apr 51	15 Nov 56				
	49-1902	450-10-9	4500003	n/a	n/a	27 Apr 51	07 Jun 52		08 Mar 53		
	49-1903	450-10-9	4500004	n/a	n/a	11 May 51	11 May 51	EB-47A	30 Mar 53		
	49-1904	450-10-9	4500005	n/a	n/a	12 Dec 50	13 Dec 50		06 Dec 54		
	49-1905	450-10-9	4500006	n/a	n/a	31 Jan 51	14 Jan 51	EB-47A	30 Dec 57		
	49-1906	450-10-9	4500007	n/a	n/a	13 Apr 51	01 May 51		18 Aug 51		
	49-1907	450-10-9	4500008	n/a	n/a	26 Jul 51	24 Jul 51	EB-47A	06 Dec 54		
	49-1908	450-10-9	4500009	n/a	n/a	25 May 51	25 May 51		09 Jun 55		
	49-1909	450-10-9	4500010	n/a	n/a	06 Mar 51	06 Mar 51	EB-47A	06 Dec 54		
B-47B-1-BW	49-2642	450-11-10	4500011	09 Jan 51	26 Apr 51	26 Apr 51	30 Nov 56	TB-47B	16 Dec 58		
	49-2643	450-11-10	4500012	12 Jan 51	03 Aug 51	31 May 51	15 Nov 56	TB-47B ETB-47B JTB-47B			
	49-2644	450-11-10	4500013	16 Jan 51	12 Aug 51	14 Oct 51	07 Jun 52	TB-47B EB-47B ETB-47B	16 Dec 58		
	49-2645	450-11-10	4500014	18 Jan 51	08 Jul 51	31 Jul 51	31 Jul 51		01 Jan 54 20 Sep 51		
B-47B-5-BW	49-2646	450-11-10	4500015	20 Jan 51	14 Aug 51	10 Oct 51	10 Oct 51	TB-47B	27 Jul 54		
	50-0001	450-11-10	4500016	24 Jan 51	02 Aug 51	28 Aug 51	22 Jul 54	TB-47B	27 Jul 54		
	50-0002	450-11-10	4500017	26 Jan 51	27 Feb 52	31 Mar 52	11 Apr 52	EB-47B JTB-47B TB-47B		04 Dec 58	02 Feb 59
	50-0003	450-11-10	4500018	30 Jan 51	05 Aug 51	22 Sep 51	21 Nov 56	EB-47B ETB-47B JTB-47B TB-47B	16 Dec 58		
	50-0004	450-11-10	4500019	02 Feb 51	28 Aug 51	04 Nov 51	07 Oct 51	EB-47B TB-47B	16 Dec 58		
	50-0005	450-11-10	4500020	05 Feb 51	07 Oct 51	24 Oct 51	27 Oct 51	ERB-47B JRB-47B TB-47B	16 Dec 58		
	50-0006	450-11-10	4500021	08 Feb 51	08 Oct 51	24 Oct 51	26 Oct 51		19 Nov 51		
	50-0007	450-11-10	4500022	10 Feb 51	31 Aug 51	19 Nov 51	n/a		01 Sep 51		
	50-0008	450-11-10	4500023	14 Feb 51	09 Oct 51	22 Oct 51	23 Oct 51	TB-47B	16 Dec 58		
	50-0009	450-11-10	4500024	21 Apr 51	15 Aug 51	17 Oct 51	01 Nov 51	TB-47B YB-47F ETB-47B JTB-47B	31 Dec 58		
	50-0010	450-11-10	4500025	24 Apr 51	25 Jun 51	25 Jul 51	23 Jul 51	TB-47B		12 Jan 60	03 Jan 61
	50-0011	450-11-10	4500026	26 Apr 51	18 Jun 51	13 Jul 51	13 Jul 51	TB-47B	08 Aug 57		
	50-0012	450-11-10	4500027	28 Apr 51	19 Jun 51	03 Jul 51	03 Jul 51	TB-47B	07 Feb 52		
B-47B-10-BW	50-0013	450-11-10	4500028	01 May 51	28 Jun 51	11 Aug 51	14 Aug 51	TB-47B	13 Mar 58		
	50-0014	450-11-10	4500029	03 May 51	07 Aug 51	26 Aug 51	26 Aug 51	TB-47B JTB-47B TB-47B	05 Sep 58		
	50-0015	450-11-10	4500030	04 May 51	08 Jul 51	11 Aug 51	14 Aug 51	TB-47B		05 Feb 60	05 Jan 61
	50-0016	450-11-10	4500031	07 May 51	07 Jul 51	11 Aug 51	14 Aug 51	TB-47B	12 Mar 60		
	50-0017	450-11-10	4500032	09 May 51	25 Jul 51	29 Aug 51	30 Aug 51	EB-47B ETB-47B JTB-47B TB-47B		17 Dec 58	04 May 59
	50-0018	450-11-10	4500033	11 May 51	03 Oct 51	01 Nov 51	02 Nov 51	EB-47B ETB-47B JTB-47B TB-47B		07 Jan 58	01 Oct 58
	50-0019	450-11-10	4500034	14 May 51	30 Aug 51	02 Nov 51	02 Nov 51	TB-47B JTB-47B TB-47B		14 Oct 58	02 Feb 59
	50-0020	450-11-10	4500035	16 May 51	20 Oct 51	15 Nov 51	16 Nov 51	EB-47B UB-47B GB-47B	Oct 63		
	50-0021	450-11-10	4500036	21 May 51	23 Jul 51	14 Aug 51	15 Aug 51	TB-47B	17 Nov 59		
B-47B-10-BW	50-0022	450-11-10	4500037	02 Jun 51	07 Aug 51	31 Aug 51	04 Sep 51	TB-47B	16 Dec 58		
	50-0023	450-11-10	4500038	26 May 51	09 Aug 51	13 Oct 51	15 Oct 51	TB-47B	08 Apr 58		
	50-0024	450-11-10	4500039	04 Jun 51	28 Aug 51	19 Nov 51	n/a		01 Sep 51		
	50-0025	450-11-10	4500040	07 Jun 51	04 Oct 51	16 Oct 51	18 Oct 51	TB-47B		20 Jan 60	03 Jan 61
B-47B-15-BW	50-0026	450-11-10	4500041	15 Jun 51	23 Dec 51	31 Jan 52	31 Jan 52		26 Mar 52		
	50-0027	450-11-10	4500042	15 Jun 51	11 Dec 51	26 Jan 52	30 Jan 52	TB-47B ETB-47B JTB-47B TB-47B		08 Dec 58	01 Jun 59
	50-0028	450-11-10	4500043	19 Jun 51	16 Oct 51	17 Nov 51	27 Nov 51	TB-47B	16 Dec 53		
	50-0029	450-11-10	4500044	21 Jun 51	27 Nov 51	29 Dec 51	22 Jan 52	TB-47B		19 Dec 58	04 May 59
	50-0030	450-11-10	4500045	25 Jun 51	23 Oct 51	23 Nov 51	26 Nov 51	TB-47B		08 Feb 60	06 Jan 61
	50-0031	450-11-10	4500046	22 Nov 51	03 Dec 51	19 Jan 52	23 Jan 52	TB-47B	11 Jun 58		
	50-0032	450-11-10	4500047	29 Jun 51	13 Oct 51	17 Nov 51	26 Nov 51	TB-47B	17 Jun 58		
	50-0033	450-11-10	4500048	06 Jul 51	22 Oct 51	25 Nov 51	27 Nov 51	TB-47B		18 Dec 58	19 May 59
	50-0034	450-11-10	4500049	05 Jul 51	29 Oct 51	17 Dec 51	19 Dec 51	TB-47B	15 Oct 53		
	50-0035	450-11-10	4500050	14 Jul 51	09 Nov 51	28 Dec 51	31 Dec 51		26 Mar 53		
	50-0036	450-11-10	4500051	18 Jul 51	12 Oct 51	14 Nov 51	20 Nov 51	TB-47B		04 Feb 60	05 Jan 61
	50-0037	450-11-10	4500052	16 Jul 51	14 Oct 51	19 Nov 51	20 Nov 51	EB-47B ETB-47B JTB-47B UB-47B GB-47B	21 Sep 65		
	50-0038	450-11-10	4500053	24 Jul 51	21 Oct 51	17 Nov 51	20 Nov 51		11 Apr 52		
	50-0039	450-11-10	4500054	26 Jul 51	13 Nov 51	28 Dec 51	04 Jan 52	TB-47B	24 Dec 57		
	50-0040	450-11-10	4500055	27 Jul 51	06 Nov 51	30 Nov 51	n/a	TB-47B			

MDS and Block Number	Serial Number	Model Number	Const. Number	Roll Out Date	First Flight Date	MIRR Date	USAF Fly Away	New MDS	Out of Service	MASDC Input Date	MASDC Output Date
B-47B-15-BW	50-0040							KB-47G ETB-47B JTB-47B NB-47B		31 May 60	11 Jan 61
	50-0041	450-11-10	4500056	31 Jul 51	23 Oct 51	22 Nov 51	26 Nov 51	TB-47B		14 Jan 60	04 Jan 61
	50-0042	450-11-10	4500057	01 Aug 51	10 Nov 51	28 Dec 51	25 Jan 52	TB-47B		24 Jul 58	15 May 59
	50-0043	450-11-10	4500058	04 Aug 51	27 Nov 51	30 Dec 51	22 Jan 52	TB-47B		13 Jan 60	04 Jan 61
	50-0044	450-11-10	4500059	04 Aug 51	03 Nov 51	10 Dec 51	11 Dec 51	TB-47B		01 Feb 60	04 Jan 61
	50-0045	450-11-10	4500060	01 Aug 51	14 Nov 51	13 Dec 51	15 Dec 51	TB-47B	18 Aug 58		
	50-0046	450-11-10	4500061	04 Aug 51	09 Nov 51	17 Dec 51	26 Dec 51	TB-47B UB-47B GB-47B		09 Dec 58	01 May 59
	50-0047	450-11-10	4500062	04 Aug 51	19 Nov 51	20 Jan 52	22 Jan 52	TB-47B		21 Jan 60	03 Jan 61
	50-0048	450-11-10	4500063	07 Aug 51	03 Dec 51	19 Jan 52	28 Jan 52	TB-47B		16 Dec 58	02 May 59
	50-0049	450-11-10	4500064	09 Aug 51	13 Nov 51	29 Dec 51	22 Jan 52	TB-47B		10 Feb 60	20 Jan 61
	50-0050	450-11-10	4500065	13 Aug 51	07 Nov 51	30 Nov 51	31 Dec 51	TB-47B		19 Jun 59	03 Aug 59
B-47B-20-BW	50-0051	450-11-10	4500066	15 Aug 51	08 Mar 52	30 Apr 52	30 Mar 52	TB-47B		07 Oct 58	02 Feb 59
	50-0052	450-11-10	4500067	20 Aug 51	29 Dec 51	29 Dec 51	29 Dec 51	EB-47B ETB-47B JTB-47B TB-47B		10 Feb 60	12 Jan 61
	50-0053	450-11-10	4500068	21 Aug 51	21 Dec 51	29 Jan 52	11 Feb 52	TB-47B ETB-47B JTB-47B	08 Feb 58		
	50-0054	450-11-10	4500069	23 Aug 51	19 Jan 52	31 Jan 52	31 Jan 52	EB-47B ETB-47B JTB-47B TB-47B	05 Oct 58		
	50-0055	450-11-10	4500070	24 Aug 51	25 Jan 52	08 Feb 52	22 Feb 52	TB-47B		10 Oct 58	01 Jun 59
	50-0056	450-11-10	4500071	27 Aug 51	26 Nov 51	29 Jan 52	31 Jan 52	TB-47B		22 Jan 58	02 Jan 59
	50-0057	450-11-10	4500072	28 Aug 51	23 Dec 51	30 Jan 52	01 Feb 52	TB-47B	07 Jul 59		
	50-0058	450-11-10	4500073	30 Aug 51	08 Feb 52	01 Mar 52	06 Mar 52	TB-47B		04 Sep 58	02 Mar 59
	50-0059	450-11-10	4500074	31 Aug 51	17 Feb 52	31 Jan 52	31 Jan 52	TB-47B	16 Dec 58		
	50-0060	450-11-10	4500075	04 Sep 51	19 Jan 52	20 Feb 52	25 Feb 52	TB-47B		02 Feb 60	09 Jan 61
	50-0061	450-11-10	4500076	06 Sep 51	16 Jan 52	31 Jan 52	31 Jan 52	TB-47B		07 Oct 58	02 Feb 59
	50-0062	450-11-10	4500077	08 Sep 51	19 Jan 52	06 Feb 52	07 Feb 52	JTB-47B TB-47B NTB-47B	01 Apr 67		
	50-0063	450-11-10	4500078	11 Sep 51	25 Jan 52	22 Feb 52	25 Feb 52	TB-47B	16 Mar 54		
	50-0064	450-11-10	4500079	13 Sep 51	24 Jan 52	12 Feb 52	13 Feb 52	TB-47B JTB-47B		01 Sep 61	26 Oct 64
	50-0065	450-11-10	4500080	15 Sep 51	19 Jan 52	10 Feb 52	17 Feb 52		03 Jul 52		
	50-0066	450-11-10	4500081	17 Sep 51	29 Jan 52	25 Jan 52	27 Feb 52	JTB-47B		29 Mar 61	12 May 61
	50-0067	450-11-10	4500082	19 Sep 51	30 Jan 52	14 Feb 52	19 Feb 52	JTB-47B		05 Sep 58	06 Apr 59
	50-0068	450-11-10	4500083	21 Sep 51	04 Feb 52	22 Feb 52	27 Feb 52	TB-47B		15 Feb 60	13 Jan 61
	50-0069	450-11-10	4500084	22 Sep 51	17 Feb 52	12 Mar 52	17 Mar 52	TB-47B ETB-47B		09 Jan 58	09 Nov 58
	50-0070	450-11-10	4500085	25 Sep 51	16 Feb 52	30 Mar 52	27 Mar 52	TB-47B		01 Apr 58	01 Sep 58
	50-0071	450-11-10	4500086	26 Sep 51	16 Feb 52	11 Mar 52	17 Mar 52	TB-47B		07 Jan 58	01 Oct 58
	50-0072	450-11-10	4500087	28 Sep 51	26 Feb 52	20 Mar 52	27 Mar 52	TB-47B		26 Aug 58	Dec 58
	50-0073	450-11-10	4500088	29 Sep 51	18 Feb 52	11 Mar 52	17 Mar 52	TB-47B		08 Apr 58	29 May 58
	50-0074	450-11-10	4500089	02 Oct 51	07 Mar 52	22 Mar 52	27 Mar 52	TB-47B		05 Jun 58	23 Oct 58
	50-0075	450-11-10	4500090	03 Oct 51	28 Feb 52	20 Mar 52	24 Mar 52	TB-47B		16 Sep 58	01 Jun 59
	50-0076	450-11-10	4500091	05 Oct 51	16 Mar 52	16 May 52	21 May 52	TB-47B	18 Dec 57		
	50-0077	450-11-10	4500092	09 Oct 51	16 Mar 52	01 Apr 52	04 Apr 52	EB-47B ETB-47B JTB-47B		05 Sep 58	n/a
	50-0078	450-11-10	4500093	12 Oct 51	18 Mar 52	25 Apr 52	01 May 52	TB-47B		27 Jan 58	01 Oct 58
	50-0079	450-11-10	4500094	13 Oct 51	28 Mar 52	21 May 52	22 May 52	TB-47B		10 Jan 58	02 Dec 58
	50-0080	450-11-10	4500095	16 Oct 51	31 Mar 52	23 Sep 52	25 Sep 52	TB-47B JTB-47B TB-47B	26 May 60		
	50-0081	450-11-10	4500096	17 Oct 51	27 Mar 52	28 Apr 52	01 May 52		22 Jul 52		
	50-0082	450-11-10	4500097	19 Oct 51	n/a	10 Feb 53	10 Feb 52	YB-47C	29 Dec 54		
B-47B-25-BW	51-2045	450-11-10	4500098	24 Oct 51	25 Jan 52	31 Jan 52	31 Jan 52	TB-47B		21 Mar 58	02 Feb 59
	51-2046	450-11-10	4500099	25 Oct 51	05 Apr 52	19 May 52	03 Jun 52	EB-47B XB-47D	15 Aug 60		
	51-2047	450-11-10	4500100	26 Oct 51	10 Apr 52	06 Jun 52	10 Jun 52	JB-47B TB-47B		08 Jan 58	02 Jan 59
	51-2048	450-11-10	4500101	29 Oct 51	14 Apr 52	28 May 52	29 May 52		24 Jun 52		
	51-2049	450-11-10	4500102	31 Oct 51	19 Apr 52	04 Jun 52	10 Jun 52	TB-47B	26 May 60		
	51-2050	450-11-10	4500103	01 Nov 51	03 May 52	29 May 52	03 Jun 52	YRB-47B TB-47B		04 Sep 58	02 May 59
	51-2051	450-11-10	4500104	08 Nov 51	18 Apr 52	21 May 52	22 May 52	TB-47B		19 Nov 57	02 Jan 58
	51-2052	450-11-10	4500105	09 Nov 51	02 Jan 53	04 Feb 53	30 Jan 57	JB-47B TB-47B		29 Jan 58	01 Oct 58
	51-2053	450-11-10	4500106	10 Nov 51	22 Apr 52	20 May 52	21 May 52	TB-47B		22 Jan 58	26 Mar 58
	51-2054	450-11-10	4500107	12 Nov 51	08 May 52	12 Jun 52	13 Jun 52	YRB-47B RB-47E YRB-47E YRB-47B RB-47B-1	18 Apr 55		
	51-2055	450-11-10	4500108	14 Nov 51	03 May 52	03 Jun 52	05 Jun 52	YRB-47B TB-47B		20 Dec 57	23 Sep 58
	51-2056	450-11-10	4500109	15 Nov 51	06 May 52	12 Jun 52	13 Jun 52	YRB-47B TB-47B		07 Dec 57	01 Oct 58
	51-2057	450-11-10	4500110	16 Nov 51	09 May 52	04 Jun 52	06 Jun 52	YRB-47B TB-47B		08 Dec 57	01 Sep 58
	51-2058	450-11-10	4500111	17 Nov 51	21 May 52	02 Jul 52	03 Jul 52	YRB-47B TB-47B		03 Sep 58	02 Mar 61
	51-2059	450-11-10	4500112	20 Nov 51	12 May 52	12 Jun 52	12 Jun 52	TB-47B		29 May 59	12 Aug 59
	51-2060	450-11-10	4500113	21 Nov 51	22 May 52	08 Jul 52	09 Jul 52	YRB-47B TB-47B		13 Jan 58	02 Dec 58
	51-2061	450-11-10	4500114	26 Nov 51	09 May 52	09 Jun 52	11 Jun 52	YRB-47B			

MDS and Block Number	Serial Number	Model Number	Const. Number	Roll Out Date	First Flight Date	MIRR Date	USAF Fly Away	New MDS	Out of Service	MASDC Input Date	MASDC Output Date
B-47B-25-BW	52-2061							TB-47B		27 Apr 59	29 Jun 59
	51-2062	450-11-10	4500115	27 Nov 51	23 May 52	03 Jul 52	08 Jul 52	YRB-47B TB-47B		20 Dec 57	23 Sep 58
	51-2063	450-11-10	4500116	29 Nov 51	21 Jun 52	21 Jun 52	25 Jun 52	YRB-47B TB-47B		12 Nov 57	02 Jan 59
	51-2064	450-11-10	4500117	30 Nov 51	03 Jun 52	27 Jun 52	01 Jul 52	YRB-47B TB-47B		20 Dec 57	01 Oct 57
	51-2065	450-11-10	4500118	03 Dec 51	11 Jun 52	11 Jul 52	15 Jul 52	YRB-47B TB-47B		17 Oct 58	29 Jun 59
	51-2066	450-11-10	4500119	06 Dec 51	06 Jun 52	17 Jul 52	18 Jul 52	YRB-47B TB-47B		02 Sep 58	02 Mar 59
	51-2067	450-11-10	4500120	08 Dec 51	08 Feb 52	26 Feb 52	26 Feb 52	TB-47B		13 Jan 58	04 Dec 58
	51-2068	450-11-10	4500121	11 Dec 51	04 Feb 52	28 Feb 52	29 Feb 52	TB-47B		05 Jun 59	01 Dec 59
	51-2069	450-11-10	4500122	15 Dec 51	16 Feb 52	14 Mar 52	15 Mar 52	TB-47B		19 Jan 59	12 Jan 61
	51-2070	450-11-10	4500123	19 Dec 51	28 Jan 52	25 Feb 52	29 Feb 52	TB-47B		13 Jan 58	02 Dec 58
	51-2071	450-11-10	4500124	20 Dec 51	06 Feb 52	27 Feb 52	28 Feb 52	EB-47B JB-47B TB-47B		15 Jan 58	02 Jan 59
	51-2072	450-11-10	4500125	22 Dec 51	11 Feb 52	15 Mar 52	18 Mar 52	TB-47B		03 Sep 58	02 Mar 59
	51-2073	450-11-10	4500126	26 Dec 51	11 Feb 52	28 Feb 52	28 Feb 52	TB-47B		05 Dec 58	15 Apr 59
	51-2074	450-11-10	4500127	27 Dec 51	09 Feb 52	29 Feb 52	29 Feb 52	TB-47B		19 Mar 58	01 Oct 58
	51-2075	450-11-10	4500128	19 Dec 51	11 Feb 52	18 Mar 52	20 Mar 52	EB-47B JB-47B JTB-47B TB-47B	Feb 60		
	51-2076	450-11-10	4500129	31 Dec 51	08 Feb 52	26 Feb 52	26 Feb 52	TB-47B		11 Dec 57	26 Mar 58
	51-2077	450-11-10	4500130	02 Jan 52	18 Mar 52	19 Mar 52	20 Mar 52	TB-47B	30 Oct 65		
	51-2078	450-11-10	4500131	03 Jan 52	10 Feb 52	01 Mar 52	07 Mar 52	EB-47B JTB-47B TB-47B		12 Jun 59	03 Aug 59
	51-2079	450-11-10	4500132	05 Jan 52	16 Feb 52	19 Mar 52	07 Mar 52	TB-47B		08 Jan 58	03 Nov 58
	51-2080	450-11-10	4500133	07 Jan 52	21 Feb 52	13 Mar 52	14 Mar 52	JB-47B TB-47B		08 Oct 58	02 Feb 59
	51-2081	450-11-10	4500134	08 Jan 52	18 Feb 52	14 Mar 52	15 Mar 52	TB-47B		01 Apr 58	01 Sep 58
B-47B-30-BW	51-2082	450-11-10	4500135	09 Jan 52	07 Mar 52	01 Apr 52	02 Apr 52	TB-47B		01 Sep 58	02 Mar 59
	51-2083	450-11-10	4500136	10 Jan 52	27 Feb 52	26 Mar 52	27 Mar 52	TB-47B		14 Dec 57	01 Oct 58
	51-2084	450-11-10	4500137	12 Jan 52	08 Mar 52	01 Apr 52	02 Apr 52	TB-47B		16 Oct 58	15 Apr 59
	51-2085	450-11-10	4500138	14 Jan 52	26 Feb 52	14 Mar 52	17 Mar 52		19 Mar 53		
	51-2086	450-11-10	4500139	15 Jan 52	28 Feb 52	22 Mar 52	24 Mar 52		06 Jan 55		
	51-2087	450-11-10	4500140	16 Jan 52	29 Feb 52	21 Mar 52	22 Mar 52	TB-47B		15 Oct 58	15 Apr 59
	51-2088	450-11-10	4500141	17 Jan 52	19 Mar 52	01 Apr 52	02 Apr 52	TB-47B		03 Dec 57	26 Mar 58
	51-2089	450-11-10	4500142	18 Jan 52	23 Mar 52	17 Apr 52	17 Apr 52		08 Jan 54		
	51-2090	450-11-10	4500143	19 Jan 52	11 Mar 52	01 Apr 52	02 Apr 52	JTB-47B TB-47B		29 Mar 61	16 May 61
	51-2091	450-11-10	4500144	21 Jan 52	11 Mar 52	27 Mar 52	31 Mar 52	TB-47B		17 Oct 58	02 Feb 59
	51-2092	450-11-10	4500145	22 Jan 52	14 Mar 52	31 Mar 52	01 Apr 52		22 Nov 60		
	51-2093	450-11-10	4500146	23 Jan 52	16 Mar 52	22 May 52	26 May 52		09 Nov 60		
	51-2094	450-11-10	4500147	24 Jan 52	09 Mar 52	28 Mar 52	31 Mar 52		11 Oct 60		
	51-2095	450-11-10	4500148	25 Jan 52	11 Mar 52	01 Apr 52	02 Apr 52		06 Oct 60		
	51-2096	450-11-10	4500149	26 Jan 52	07 Feb 52	13 May 52	15 May 52		13 Oct 53		
	51-2097	450-11-10	4500150	28 Jan 52	08 Mar 52	27 Mar 52	29 Mar 52		22 Dec 60		
	51-2098	450-11-10	4500151	29 Jan 52	18 Mar 52	26 Apr 52	29 Apr 52	UB-47B GB-47B	06 May 64		
	51-2099	450-11-10	4500152	30 Jan 52	09 Mar 52	27 Mar 52	28 Mar 52		03 Mar 60		
	51-2100	450-11-10	4500153	31 Jan 52	19 Mar 52	10 Apr 52	10 Apr 52		10 Dec 54		
	51-2101	450-11-10	4500154	01 Feb 52	11 Mar 52	26 Mar 52	28 Mar 52		12 Jan 60		
	51-2102	450-11-10	4500155	02 Feb 52	18 Mar 52	08 Apr 52	09 Apr 52		06 Aug 57		
	51-2103	450-11-10	4500156	04 Feb 52	25 Mar 52	18 Apr 52	n/a	EB-47B XB-47D	12 Mar 57		
	51-2104	450-11-10	4500157	05 Feb 52	04 Apr 52	12 May 52	14 May 52		13 Mar 58		
	51-2105	450-11-10	4500158	06 Feb 52	27 Mar 52	18 Apr 52	23 Apr 52		22-11-60		
	51-2106	450-11-10	4500159	06 Feb 52	01 Apr 52	19 Apr 52	23 Apr 52			30 Aug 60	30 Jan 61
	51-2107	450-11-10	4500160	08 Feb 52	28 Mar 52	16 Apr 52	17 Apr 52			08 Aug 60	07 Mar 61
	51-2108	450-11-10	4500161	09 Feb 52	24 Mar 02	19 Apr 52	23 Apr 52		03 Mar 60		
	51-2109	450-11-10	4500162	11 Feb 52	07 Apr 52	09 May 52	12 May 52			26 Apr 61	27 Apr 61
	51-2110	450-11-10	4500163	12 Feb 52	27 Mar 52	19 Apr 52	21 Apr 52			13 Jul 60	01 Mar 60
	51-2111	450-11-10	4500164	13 Feb 52	28 Mar 52	01 May 52	03 May 52			29 Sep 60	20 Mar 61
	51-2112	450-11-10	4500165	14 Feb 52	31 Mar 52	30 Apr 52	01 May 52		21 Jun 55		
	51-2113	450-11-10	4500166	16 Feb 52	29 Mar 52	26 Apr 52	28 Apr 52		21 Mar 60		
	51-2114	450-11-10	4500167	15 Feb 52	30 Mar 52	25 Apr 52	25 Apr 52			26 Jan 61	21 Feb 61
	51-2115	450-11-10	4500168	18 Feb 52	30 Mar 52	15 Apr 52	16 Apr 52	WB-47B GB-47B	04 Oct 63		
	51-2116	450-11-10	4500169	19 Feb 52	17 Apr 52	27 May 52	28 May 52		25 Feb 60		
	51-2117	450-11-10	4500170	20 Feb 52	01 Apr 52	21 Apr 52	22 Apr 52			25 Apr 61	10 Feb 64
	51-2118	450-11-10	4500171	21 Feb 52	10 Apr 52	03 May 52	05 May 52			20 Jan 61	18 May 61
	51-2119	450-11-10	4500172	22 Feb 52	01 Apr 52	26 Apr 52	28 Apr 52			10 Jan 61	20 Feb 61
	51-2120	450-11-10	4500173	25 Feb 52	11 Apr 52	13 May 52	15 May 52		20 Mar 63		
	51-2121	450-11-10	4500174	26 Feb 52	07 Apr 52	03 May 52	05 May 52			18 Aug 60	10 Mar 61
	51-2122	450-11-10	4500175	27 Feb 52	15 Apr 52	05 May 52	06 May 52		26 Feb 60		
	51-2123	450-11-10	4500176	28 Feb 52	10 Apr 52	01 May 52	02 May 52		07 Apr 60		
	51-2124	450-11-10	4500177	29 Feb 52	07 Apr 52	29 Apr 52	30 Apr 52			31 May 60	05 Dec 60
	51-2125	450-11-10	4500178	01 Mar 52	07 Apr 52	24 Apr 52	25 Apr 52		31 Jan 61		
	51-2126	450-11-10	4500179	03 Mar 52	08 Apr 52	30 Apr 52	01 May 52		18 Sep 59		
	51-2127	450-11-10	4500180	04 Mar 52	08 Apr 52	28 Apr 52	30 Apr 52			22 Aug 60	14 Mar 61
	51-2128	450-11-10	4500181	05 Mar 52	15 Apr 52	29 Apr 52	30 Apr 52		15 Mar 61		
	51-2129	450-11-10	4500182	06 Mar 52	25 Apr 52	15 May 52	16 May 52		22 Feb 61		
	51-2130	450-11-10	4500183	07 Mar 52	22 Apr 52	15 May 52	16 May 52			08 Jun 61	09 Jan 64
	51-2131	450-11-10	4500184	10 Mar 52	19 Apr 52	13 May 52	15 May 52			29 Mar 61	10 May 61
	51-2132	450-11-10	4500185	11 Mar 52	21 Apr 52	17 Jun 52	18 Jun 52	YRB-47B B-47B		22 Mar 61	16 May 61
	51-2133	450-11-10	4500186	12 Mar 52	28 Apr 52	19 May 52	21 May 52			25 Jun 61	17 Dec 61
	51-2134	450-11-10	4500187	13 Mar 52	18 Apr 52	05 May 52	07 May 52		07 Mar 61		
	51-2135	450-11-10	4500188	14 Mar 52	06 Jun 52	11 Jun 52	12 Jun 52		22 Jan 60		
	51-2136	450-11-10	4500189	15 Mar 52	22 Apr 52	08 May 52	12 May 52			19 May 61	29 Jun 61

MDS and Block Number	Serial Number	Model Number	Const. Number	Roll Out Date	First Flight Date	MIRR Date	USAF Fly Away	New MDS	Out of Service	MASDC Input Date	MASDC Output Date
B-47B-35-BW	51-2137	450-11-10	4500190	17 Mar 52	01 May 52	16 May 52	11 Sep 53		16 Dec 60		
	51-2138	450-11-10	4500191	18 Mar 52	16 May 52	28 May 52	29 May 52		10 Jan 61		
	51-2139	450-11-10	4500192	19 Mar 52	24 Apr 52	19 May 52	21 May 52	YRB-47B B-47B	11 Oct 57		
	51-2140	450-11-10	4500193	20 Mar 52	25 Apr 52	21 May 52	21 May 52			25 Jul 60	24 Feb 61
	51-2141	450-11-10	4500194	n/a	n/a	14 Nov 52	06 Feb 53		09 Mar 60		
	51-2142	450-11-10	4500195	21 Mar 52	24 Apr 52	20 May 52	21 May 52	YRB-47B RB-47B-I		05 Dec 57	20 Jan 61
	51-2143	450-11-10	4500196	24 Mar 52	28 Apr 52	04 Jun 52	06 Jun 52			14 Sep 60	10 Mar 61
	51-2144	450-11-10	4500197	25 Mar 52	01 May 52	22 May 52	23 May 52	YRB-47B B-47B		29 Jun 61	31 Dec 63
	51-2145	450-11-10	4500198	n/a	n/s	n/a	n/a	LM static	n/a		
	51-2146	450-11-10	4500199	26 Mar 52	29 Apr 52	21 May 52	22 May 52			13 Sep 60	13 Mar 61
	51-2147	450-11-10	4500200	27 Mar 52	01 May 52	27 May 52	23 May 52	YRB-47B B-47B	03 Mar 60		
	51-2148	450-11-10	4500201	28 Mar 52	08 May 52	06 Jun 52	09 Jun 52			09 Jun 61	13 Jan 64
	51-2149	450-11-10	4500202	29 Mar 52	06 May 52	05 Jun 52	06 Jun 52	YRB-47B B-47B	03 Mar 60		
	51-2150	450-11-10	4500203	n/a	n/a	08 Dec 52	20 Mar 53			27 Apr 61	06 Jun 61
	51-2151	450-11-10	4500204	31 Mar 52	19 May 52	13 Jun 52	17 Jun 52			21 Jul 60	06 Mar 61
	51-2152	450-11-10	4500205	01 Apr 52	05 May 52	05 Jun 52	06 Jun 52	YRB-47B B-47B UB-47B GB-47B	11 Aug 60		
	51-2153	450-11-10	4500206	02 Apr 52	08 May 52	11 Jun 52	12 Jun 52			26 May 61	07 Jul 61
	51-2154	450-11-10	4500207	03 Apr 52	14 May 52	23 Jun 52	25 Jun 52	YRB-47B B-47B	28 Mar 60		
	51-2155	450-11-10	4500208	n/a	n/a	30 Dec 52	03 Apr 53	EB-47B JB-47B B-47B		28 Aug 68	14 Jan 69
	51-2156	450-11-10	4500209	03 Apr 52	13 May 52	10 Jun 52	11 Jun 52			14 Jun 61	04 Dec 63
	51-2157	450-11-10	4500210	05 Apr 52	15 May 52	07 Jul 52	08 Jul 52	YRB-47B B-47B	26 Jan 60		
	51-2158	450-11-10	4500211	07 Apr 52	19 May 52	13 Jun 52	17 Jun 52			20 Apr 61	25 May 61
	51-2159	450-11-10	4500212	08 Apr 52	16 May 52	11 Jun 52	12 Jun 52	YRB-47B JB-47B B-47B		03 Mar 60	14 Apr 60
	51-2160	450-11-10	4500213	n/a	n/a	16 Jan 53	16 Apr 53	EB-47B JB-47B B-47B DB-47B		03 Jun 60	23 Feb 61
	51-2161	450-11-10	4500214	09 Apr 52	20 May 52	20 Jun 52	23 Jun 52			19 May 61	07 Jul 61
	51-2162	450-11-10	4500215	10 Apr 52	14 May 52	04 Jun 52	06 Jun 52	YRB-47B DB-47B		03 Jun 60	23 Feb 61
	51-2163	450-11-10	4500216	12 Apr 52	22 May 52	18 Jun 52	20 Jun 52	DB-47B	20 May 60		
	51-2164	450-11-10	4500217	14 Apr 52	20 May 52	01 Jun 52	02 Jul 52	YRB-47B DB-47B		02 May 60	06 Apr 61
	51-2165	450-11-10	4500218	n/a	n/a	03 Feb 53	30 Apr 53	DB-47B		09 Jun 60	28 Feb 61
	51-2166	450-11-10	4500219	14 Apr 52	28 May 52	18 Jun 52	25 Jun 52	DB-47B		24 Jun 60	23 Feb 61
	51-2167	450-11-10	4500220	15 Apr 52	20 May 52	21 Jun 52	25 Jun 52	YRB-47B DB-47B		05 Jul 60	05 Jul 60
	51-2168	450-11-10	4500221	16 Apr 52	28 May 52	19 Jun 52	20 Jun 52	DB-47B		07 Jul 60	07 Mar 61
	51-2169	450-11-10	4500222	17 Apr 52	28 May 52	21 Jun 52	25 Jun 52	YRB-47B DB-47B		15 Jul 60	28 Feb 61
	51-2170	450-11-10	4500223	n/a	n/a	19 Feb 53	08 May 53	DB-47B		08 Jul 60	27 Feb 61
	51-2171	450-11-10	4500224	18 Apr 52	30 May 52	26 Jun 52	21 Apr 53	DB-47B		31 May 60	15 Mar 61
	51-2172	450-11-10	4500225	21 Apr 52	02 Jun 52	24 Jun 52	27 Mar 53	DB-47B		29 Apr 60	07 Apr 61
	51-2173	450-11-10	4500226	22 Apr 52	26 May 52	20 Jun 52	21 Jun 52	YRB-47B DB-47B		21 May 60	28 Mar 61
	51-2174	450-11-10	4500227	22 Apr 52	04 Jun 52	07 Jul 52	08 Jul 52	YRB-47B DB-47B		28 Jul 60	23 Feb 61
	51-2175	450-11-10	4500228	n/a	n/a	06 Mar 53	20 May 53	B-47B	28 Mar 56		
	51-2176	450-11-10	4500229	23 Apr 52	03 Jun 52	02 Jul 52	03 Jul 52	DB-47B		13 Jul 60	02 Mar 61
	51-2177	450-11-10	4500230	24 Apr 52	03 Jun 52	01 Jul 52	02 Jul 52	DB-47B	09 Oct 57		
	51-2178	450-11-10	4500231	25 Apr 52	09 Jun 52	08 Jul 52	12 Jul 52	DB-47B		24 Aug 60	01 Mar 61
	51-2179	450-11-10	4500232	26 Apr 52	09 Jun 52	17 Jul 52	18 Jul 52	YRB-47B DB-47B		06 May 60	24 Mar 61
	51-2180	450-11-10	4500233	n/a	n/a	20 Mar 53	28 May 53	DB-47B		25 Apr 60	10 Apr 61
	51-2181	450-11-10	4500234	28 Apr 52	06 Jun 52	08 Jul 52	11 Jul 52	DB-47B	08 May 63		
	51-2182	450-11-10	4500235	29 Apr 52	13 Jun 52	16 Jul 52	18 Jul	DB-47B		26 Jun 60	27 Feb 61
	51-2183	450-11-10	4500236	30 Apr 52	12 Jun 52	14 Jul 52	16 Jul 52	DB-47B		14 Jul 60	02 Mar 61
	51-2184	450-11-10	4500237	01 May 52	12 Jun 52	08 Jul 52	09 Jul 52	YRB-47B DB-47B		21 Jul 60	28 Feb 61
	51-2185	450-11-10	4500238	n/a	n/a	03 Apr 53	16 Jun 53	DB-47B		01 Jun 60	06 Apr 61
	51-2186	450-11-10	4500239	01 May 52	18 Jun 52	14 Jul 52	16 Jul 52	DB-47B		19 Jul 60	03 Mar 61
	51-2187	450-11-10	4500240	02 May 52	19 Jun 52	14 Jul 52	15 Jul 52	YRB-47B DB-47B		17 May 60	11 Apr 61
	51-2188	450-11-10	4500241	05 May 52	13 Jun 52	09 Jul 52	10 Jul 52	DB-47B		02 Aug 60	23 Feb 61
	51-2189	450-11-10	4500242	06 May 52	18 Jun 52	16 Jul 52	18 Jul 52	YRB-47B DB-47B		04 Aug 60	06 Mar 61
	51-2190	450-11-10	4500243	n/a	n/a	16 Apr 53	30 Jun 53	DB-47B		14 May 60	10 Apr 61
	51-2191	450-11-10	4500244	07 May 52	21 Jun 52	23 Jul 52	24 Jul 52	DB-47B		29 Jul 60	23 Feb 61
B-47B-40-BW	51-2192	450-11-10	4500245	08 May 52	20 Jun 52	17 Jul 52	18 Jul 52		02 Mar 57		
	51-2193	450-11-10	4500246	09 May 52	23 Sep 52	14 Jun 52	11 Nov 52			26 Aug 60	02 Mar 61
	51-2194	450-11-10	4500247	12 May 52	21 Jun 52	17 Jul 52	18 Jul 52	YRB-47B B-47B		26 May 61	05 Jul 61
	51-2195	450-11-10	4500248	12 May 52	12 Jun 52	08 Jul 52	09 Jul 52	YRB-47B B-47B		19 May 61	30 Jun 61
	51-2196	450-11-10	4500249	13 May 52	20 Jun 52	16 Jul 52	18 Jul 52			29 Aug 60	09 Mar 61
	51-2197	450-11-10	4500250	n/a	n/a	23 Mar 53	29 May 53		29 Jul 60		
	51-2198	450-11-10	4500251	14 May 52	28 Jun 52	26 Nov 52	26 Nov 52	EB-47B JB-47B UB-47B GB-47B	10 Aug 60		
	51-2199	450-11-10	4500252	15 May 52	21 Jun 52	08 Jul 52	09 Jul 52		22 Nov 58		

MDS and Block Number	Serial Number	Model Number	Const. Number	Roll Out Date	First Flight Date	MIRR Date	USAF Fly Away	New MDS	Out of Service	MASDC Input Date	MASDC Output Date
B-47B-40-BW	51-2200	450-11-10	4500253	16 May 52	12 Sep 52	21 Jun 52	29 Oct 52	JB-47B / B-47B		24 Apr 61	03 Jul 61
	51-2201	450-11-10	4500254	19 May 52	23 Jun 52	17 Jul 52	18 Jul 52	YRB-47B / B-47B		08 Jun 61	03 Mar 64
	51-2202	450-11-10	4500255	20 May 52	25 Jun 52	06 Aug 52	07 Aug 52			14 Dec 60	20 Feb 61
	51-2203	450-11-10	4500256	21 May 52	24 Jun 52	17 Jul 52	18 Jul 52	YRB-47B / B-47B		29 Nov 60	05 Apr 61
	51-2204	450-11-10	4500257	n/a	n/a	14 May 53	10 Jul 53			12 Aug 60	16 Mar 61
	51-2205	450-11-10	4500258	21 May 52	26 Jun 52	23 Jul 52	25 Jul 52	YRB-47B / B-47B		27 Oct 60	03 Apr 61
	51-2206	450-11-10	4500259	22 May 52	16 Sep 52	24 Jun 52	17 Oct 52		25 Jul 58		
	51-2207	450-11-10	4500260	23 May 52	07 Jul 52	06 Aug 52	07 Aug 52	YRB-47B / B-47B	28 Dec 60		
	51-2208	450-11-10	4500261	26 May 52	30 Jun 52	08 Aug 52	11 Aug 52	YRB-47B / B-47B		20 Oct 60	23 Mar 61
	51-2209	450-11-10	4500262	27 May 52	01 Jul 52	08 Aug 52	11 Aug 52	YRB-47B / B-47B		16 Nov 60	06 Apr 61
	51-2210	450-11-10	4500263	n/a	n/a	15 May 53	25 Jun 53			02 Sep 60	15 Mar 61
	51-2211	450-11-10	4500264	28 May 52	01 Jul 52	06 Aug 52	08 Aug 52			25 May 61	10 Jul 61
	51-2212	450-11-10	4500265	29 May 52	17 Sep 52	25 Jun 52	01 Nov 52			16 Sep 60	14 Mar 61
	51-2213	450-11-10	4500266	30 May 52	09 Sep 52	08 Aug 52	11 Aug 52	YRB-47B / B-47B		10 Aug 60	09 Mar 60
	51-2214	450-11-10	4500267	30 May 52	07 Jul 52	07 Aug 52	11 Aug 52	YRB-47B / B-47B		07 Jun 61	24 Jan 64
	51-2215	450-11-10	4500268	02 Jun 52	11 Jul 52	07 Aug 52	08 Aug 52			20 Oct 60	27 Mar 61
	51-2216	450-11-10	4500269	03 Jun 52	09 Jul 52	08 Aug 52	15 Aug 52	YRB-47B / B-47B		21 Nov 60	05 Apr 61
	51-2217	450-11-10	4500270	n/a	n/a	15 Apr 53	09 Jun 53		25 Jun 60		
	51-2218	450-11-10	4500271	04 Jun 52	10 Jul 52	07 Aug 52	08 Aug 52	YRB-47B / B-47B		29 Nov 60	12 Apr 61
	51-2219	450-11-10	4500272	04 Jun 52	15 Jul 52	20 Aug 52	21 Aug 52	YRB-47B / B-47B		30 Nov 60	04 Apr 61
	51-2220	450-11-10	4500273	05 Jun 52	19 Sep 52	23 Jun 52	29 Oct 52		28 Jan 58		
	51-2221	450-11-10	4500274	06 Jun 52	14 Jul 52	08 Aug 52	11 Aug 52	YRB-47B / B-47B		31 May 61	18 Jul 61
	51-2222	450-11-10	4500275	09 Jun 52	16 Jul 52	20 Aug 52	18 Sep 52	EB-47B / JB-47B		29 Jun 60	27 Feb 61
	51-2223	450-11-10	4500276	09 Jun 52	16 Jul 52	18 Aug 52	20 Aug 52	YRB-47B / B-47B		25 Apr 61	31 May 61
	51-2224	450-11-10	4500277	n/a	n/a	03 Jun 53	11 Jun 53			02 Sep 60	10 Mar 61
	51-2225	450-11-10	4500278	10 Jun 52	24 Sep 52	25 Jun 52	01 Nov 52			06 Sep 60	15 Mar 61
	51-2226	450-11-10	4500279	11 Jun 52	12 Jul 52	19 Aug 52	20 Aug 52	YRB-47B	07 Sep 53		
	51-2227	450-11-10	4500280	12 Jun 52	31 Jul 52	27 Aug 52	28 Aug 52			19 Oct 60	20 Mar 61
	51-2228	450-11-10	4500281	12 Jun 52	22 Jul 52	20 Aug 52	21 Aug 52	YRB-47B / B-47B		09 Jun 61	09 Mar 64
	51-2229	450-11-10	4500282	13 Jun 52	21 Jul 52	20 Aug 52	21 Aug 52	YRB-47B / B-47B		21 Nov 60	07 Apr 61
	51-2230	450-11-10	4500283	17 Jun 52	29 Sep 52	27 Jun 52	19 Nov 52			08 Sep 60	14 Mar 61
	51-2231	450-11-10	4500284	n/a	n/a	02 Jun 53	11 Jun 53		13 Oct 55		
	51-2232	450-11-10	4500285	18 Jun 52	04 Aug 52	29 Aug 52	18 Sep 52	EB-47B / B-47B	30 Apr 54		
	51-2233	450-11-10	4500286	18 Jun 52	25 Jul 52	21 Aug 52	26 Aug 52	YRB-47B / B-47B		26 Oct 60	24 Mar 61
	51-2234	450-11-10	4500287	19 Jun 52	03 Oct 52	01 Jul 52	05 Nov 52			12 Sep 60	13 Mar 61
	51-2235	450-11-10	4500288	20 Jun 52	23 Jul 52	27 Aug 52	29 Aug 52	YRB-47B / B-47B		08 Jun 61	24 Jan 64
	51-2236	450-11-10	4500289	21 Jun 52	25 Jul 52	27 Aug 52	28 Aug 52	YRB-47B / B-47B		25 Oct 60	30 Mar 61
	51-2237	450-11-10	4500290	n/a	n/a	30 Jun 53	09 Jul 53			22 Nov 60	20 Mar 61
	51-2238	450-11-10	4500291	21 Jun 52	30 Jul 52	30 Sep 52	09 Jan 52	YRB-47B / B-47B	06 Mar 61		
	51-2239	450-11-10	4500292	23 Jun 52	01 Aug 52	29 Aug 52	16 Sep 52	YRB-47B / B-47B		23 Jun 61	31 Dec 63
	51-2240	450-11-10	4500293	24 Jun 52	03 Oct 52	09 Jul 52	12 Nov 52		28 May 60		
	51-2241	450-11-10	4500294	25 Jun 52	06 Aug 52	27 Aug 52	28 Aug 52	YRB-47B / B-47B		31 May 61	16 Jul 61
	51-2242	450-11-10	4500295	25 Jun 52	05 Aug 52	29 Aug 52	22 Sep 52	YRB-47B / B-47B		16 Dec 60	20 Feb 61
	51-2243	450-11-10	4500296	n/a	n/a	24 Jul 53	06 Aug 53			25 Apr 61	25 May 61
	51-2244	450-11-10	4500297	26 Jun 52	06 Aug 52	27 Aug 52	28 Aug 52	YRB-47B / B-47B		28 Apr 61	22 Jun 61
	51-2245	450-11-10	4500298	30 Jun 52	12 Aug 52	29 Aug 52	23 Sep 52	YRB-47B / B-47B	21 Dec 60		
	51-2246	450-11-10	4500299	01 Jul 52	06 Oct 52	15 Jul 52	01 Nov 52			11 Oct 60	10 Mar 61
B-47B-45-BW	51-2247	450-11-10	4500300	02 Jul 52	25 Aug 52	23 Sep 52	12 Jan 53	YRB-47B / B-47B		14 Jun 61	03 Dec 63
	51-2248	450-11-10	4500301	02 Jul 52	15 Aug 52	22 Sep 52	22 Sep 52	YRB-47B / B-47B		20 Jan 61	21 Feb 61
	51-2249	450-11-10	4500302	03 Jul 52	14 Aug 52	22 Sep 52	23 Sep 52	YRB-47B / B-47B	09 Mar 61		
	51-2250	450-11-10	4500303	07 Jul 52	19 Aug 52	23 Sep 52	13 Jan 53	YRB-47B / B-47B		02 Jun 60	23 Feb 61
	51-2251	450-11-10	4500304	08 Jul 52	15 Oct 52	21 Jul 52	12 Nov 52			01 Sep 60	07 Mar 61
	51-2252	450-11-10	4500305	09 Jul 52	15 Aug 52	23 Sep 52	23 Sep 52	YRB-47B / B-47B	29 Apr 60		
	51-2253	450-11-10	4500306	10 Jul 52	21 Aug 52	25 Sep 52	15 Jan 53	YRB-47B	24 Jul 53		
	51-2254	450-11-10	4500307	10 Jul 52	09 Oct 52	21 Jul 52	12 Nov 52			30 Aug 60	07 Mar 61
	51-2255	450-11-10	4500308	11 Jul 52	20 Aug 52	23 Sep 52	21 Jan 53	YRB-47B / B-47B		08 May 61	13 Jun 61
	51-2256	450-11-10	4500309	14 Jul 52	12 Aug 52	30 Sep 52	23 Jan 53	YRB-47B / B-47B	28 Jan 60		
	51-2257	450-11-10	4500310	15 Jul 52	09 Oct 52	25 Jul 52	21 Nov 52			05 Aug 60	07 Mar 61
	51-2258	450-11-10	4500311	15 Jul 52	26 Aug 52	25 Sep 52	23 Jan 53	YRB-47B / B-47B		15 Dec 61	12 Nov 63
	51-2259	450-11-10	4500312	16 Jul 52	28 Aug 52	25 Sep 52	27 Jan 52	YRB-47B / B-47B		21 Sep 60	16 Mar 61

MDS and Block Number	Serial Number	Model Number	Const. Number	Roll Out Date	First Flight Date	MIRR Date	USAF Fly Away	New MDS	Out of Service	MASDC Input Date	MASDC Output Date
B-47B-45-BW	51-2260	450-11-10	4500313	18 Jul 52	10 Oct 52	29 Jul 52	18 Nov 52			20 Sep 60	21 Mar 61
	51-2261	450-11-10	4500314	18 Jul 52	22 Sep 52	08 Oct 52	30 Jan 53	YRB-47B / B-47B	30 Dec 59		
	51-2262	450-11-10	4500315	21 Jul 52	17 Sep 52	04 Oct 52	22 Oct 52	YRB-47B / B-47B		07 Jun 61	25 Mar 64
	51-2263	450-11-10	4500316	22 Jul 52	10 Oct 52	04 Aug 52	01 Dec 52			31 May 61	17 Jul 61
	51-2264	450-11-10	4500317	23 Jul 52	17 Sep 52	08 Oct 52	20 Oct 52	YRB-47B / B-47B		18 Apr 61	16 Jun 61
	51-2265	450-11-10	4500318	24 Jul 52	13 Oct 52	06 Aug 52	21 Dec 52		22 Mar 57		
	51-2266	450-11-10	4500319	25 Jul 52	19 Sep 52	03 Nov 52	03 Nov 52	YRB-47B / B-47B		07 Jun 61	16 Jun 61
	51-2267	450-11-10	4500320	25 Jul 52	15 Oct 52	06 Aug 52	21 Nov 52	B-47B	02 Jul 53		
	51-2268	450-11-10	4500321	29 Jul 52	18 Sep 52	30 Sep 52	04 Feb 52	YRB-47B / B-47B		20 Apr 61	12 Jun 61
	51-2269	450-11-10	4500322	29 Jul 52	17 Oct 52	08 Aug 52	22 Nov 52			26 Apr 61	02 Jun 61
	51-2270	450-11-10	4500323	29 Jul 52	19 Sep 52	06 Oct 52	23 Oct 52	YRB-47B / B-47B		25 May 61	07 Jul 61
	51-2271	450-11-10	4500324	31 Jul 52	16 Oct 52	12 Aug 52	21 Nov 52			16 Nov 60	04 Apr 61
	51-2272	450-11-10	4500325	01 Aug 52	17 Oct 52	14 Aug 52	01 Dec 52			09 Jun 61	29 Jan 64
	51-2273	450-11-10	4500326	01 Aug 52	22 Oct 52	14 Aug 52	01 Dec 52			22 Sep 60	21 Mar 61
	51-2274	450-11-10	4500327	04 Aug 52	23 Sep 52	11 Oct 52	24 Oct 52	YRB-47B / B-47B	12 Jul 60		
	51-2275	450-11-10	4500328	05 Aug 52	23 Sep 52	07 Oct 52	20 Oct 52	YRB-47B / B-47B		24 Apr 61	25 May 61
	51-2276	450-11-10	4500329	06 Aug 52	27 Oct 52	18 Aug 52	05 Dec 52			26 Sep 60	17 Mar 61
	51-2277	450-11-10	4500330	06 Aug 52	22 Oct 52	19 Aug 52	10 Dec 52			26 Aug 60	02 Mar 61
	51-2278	450-11-10	4500331	07 Aug 52	24 Oct 52	20 Aug 52	23 Nov 52			17 Apr 61	26 Jun 61
	51-2279	450-11-10	4500332	07 Aug 52	24 Oct 52	22 Aug 52	13 Dec 52	EB-47B / JB-47B / B-47B		30 Nov 60	11 Apr 61
	51-2280	450-11-10	4500333	11 Aug 52	24 Sep 52	09 Oct 52	27 Oct 52	YRB-47B / B-47B		19 May 61	29 Jun 61
	51-2281	450-11-10	4500334	12 Aug 52	27 Sep 52	15 Oct 52	24 Oct 52	YRB-47B / B-47B		12 Dec 60	13 Apr 61
	51-2282	450-11-10	4500335	13 Aug 52	28 Oct 52	25 Oct 52	01 Dec 52		23 May 61		
	51-2283	450-11-10	4500336	13 Aug 52	30 Oct 52	26 Aug 52	09 Dec 52			01 Sep 60	09 Mar 61
	51-2284	450-11-10	4500337	14 Aug 52	30 Oct 52	26 Aug 52	02 Dec 52			27 Apr 61	14 Jun 61
	51-2285	450-11-10	4500338	14 Aug 52	01 Oct 52	15 Oct 52	28 Oct 52	YRB-47B / B-47B		12 Dec 60	21 Feb 61
	51-2286	450-11-10	4500339	14 Aug 52	01 Oct 52	15 Oct 52	29 Oct 52	YRB-47B / B-47B	19 Dec 55		
	51-2287	450-11-10	4500340	19 Aug 52	30 Oct 52	02 Sep 52	10 Dec 52			20 Apr 61	20 Jun 61
	51-2288	450-11-10	4500341	20 Aug 52	03 Oct 52	16 Oct 52	20 Oct 52	YRB-47B / B-47B		15 Nov 60	28 Mar 61
	51-2289	450-11-10	4500342	21 Aug 52	31 Oct 52	04 Sep 52	30 Dec 52			22 Nov 60	03 Apr 61
	51-2290	450-11-10	4500343	22 Aug 52	31 Oct 52	04 Sep 52	03 Jan 53			02 Sep 60	09 Mar 61
	51-2291	450-11-10	4500344	25 Aug 52	07 Nov 52	04 Sep 52	20 Dec 52			25 May 61	10 Jul 61
	51-2292	450-11-10	4500345	25 Aug 52	07 Oct 52	30 Oct 52	31 Oct 52	YRB-47B / B-47B		28 Nov 60	11 Apr 61
	51-2293	450-11-10	4500346	26 Aug 52	12 Oct 52	30 Oct 52	05 Oct 53	YRB-47B / B-47B		17 Nov 60	03 Apr 61
	51-2294	450-11-10	4500347	27 Aug 52	31 Oct 52	08 Sep 52	20 Dec 52			24 May 61	30 Jun 61
	51-2295	450-11-10	4500348	28 Aug 52	07 Nov 52	09 Sep 52	13 Dec 52			28 Nov 60	31 Mar 61
	51-2296	450-11-10	4500349	29 Aug 52	13 Nov 52	11 Sep 52	22 Dec 52			23 May 61	11 Jul 61
	51-2297	450-11-10	4500350	29 Aug 52	17 Oct 52	13 Nov 52	14 Nov 52	YRB-47B / B-47B		25 Oct 60	23 Mar 61
	51-2298	450-11-10	4500351	02 Sep 52	17 Nov 52	12 Sep 52	15 Sep 52			19 Oct 60	21 Mar 61
	51-2299	450-11-10	4500352	03 Sep 52	07 Nov 52	15 Sep 52	21 Dec 52			16 Aug 60	10 Mar 61
	51-2300	450-11-10	4500353	04 Sep 52	14 Nov 52	16 Sep 52	13 Jan 53	EB-47B / B-47B		15 Dec 61	06 Nov 63
	51-2301	450-11-10	4500354	04 Sep 52	21 Oct 52	11 Nov 52	12 Nov 52	YRB-47B / B-47B		08 Jun 61	24 Feb 64
B-47B-50-BW	51-2302	450-11-10	4500355	08 Sep 52	14 Nov 52	17 Sep 52	13 Jan 53			31 Aug 60	06 Mar 61
	51-2303	450-11-10	4500356	10 Sep 52	14 Nov 52	19 Sep 52	29 Dec 52			01 Sep 60	08 Mar 61
	51-2304	450-11-10	4500357	10 Sep 52	01 Nov 52	26 Nov 52	31 Oct 52	YRB-47B / B-47B		21 Apr 61	02 Jun 61
	51-2305	450-11-10	4500358	12 Sep 52	17 Nov 52	23 Sep 52	30 Dec 52			28 Apr 61	13 Jun 61
	51-2306	450-11-10	4500359	12 Sep 52	20 Nov 52	25 Sep 52	06 Jan 53			15 Nov 60	04 Apr 61
	51-2307	450-11-10	4500360	16 Sep 52	20 Nov 52	25 Sep 52	10 Jan 53			02 Sep 60	13 Mar 61
	51-2308	450-11-10	4500361	16 Sep 52	20 Nov 52	26 Sep 52	03 Jan 53			10 Aug 60	06 Mar 61
	51-2309	450-11-10	4500362	17 Sep 52	21 Nov 52	27 Sep 52	30 Dec 52		09 Nov 59		
	51-2310	450-11-10	4500363	18 Sep 52	03 Nov 52	01 Oct 52	02 Jan 53			16 Dec 60	20 Feb 61
	51-2311	450-11-10	4500364	22 Sep 52	13 Nov 52	26 Nov 52	18 Dec 52	YRB-47B / B-47B		26 Apr 61	06 Jun 61
	51-2312	450-11-10	4500365	19 Sep 52	07 Nov 52	30 Nov 52	30 Jan 53	YRB-47B / B-47B		18 Oct 60	21 Mar 61
	51-2313	450-11-10	4500366	20 Sep 52	31 Oct 52	26 Nov 52	02 Feb 53	YRB-47B / B-47B		12 Dec 60	13 Apr 61
	51-2314	450-11-10	4500367	24 Sep 52	02 Dec 52	02 Oct 52	13 Jan 53			16 Dec 60	21 Feb 61
	51-2315	450-11-10	4500368	25 Sep 52	02 Dec 52	04 Oct 52	07 Jan 53		20 Mar 61		
	51-2316	450-11-10	4500369	25 Sep 52	05 Dec 52	06 Oct 52	10 Jan 53			27 Apr 61	14 Jun 61
	51-2317	450-11-10	4500370	27 Sep 52	19 Nov 52	31 Dec 52	10 Jan 53		01 Oct 57		
	51-2318	450-11-10	4500371	30 Sep 52	30 Nov 52	29 Dec 52	03 Jan 53		20 Dec 60		
	51-2319	450-11-10	4500372	01 Oct 52	07 Dec 52	29 Dec 52	06 Jan 52			02 Sep 60	08 Mar 61
	51-2320	450-11-10	4500373	01 Oct 52	10 Dec 52	31 Dec 52	06 Jan 53			02 Sep 60	13 Mar 61
	51-2321	450-11-10	4500374	02 Oct 52	06 Dec 52	29 Dec 52	03 Jan 53			20 Apr 61	15 Jun 61
	51-2322	450-11-10	4500375	03 Oct 52	11 Dec 52	31 Dec 52	13 Jan 53			21 Apr 61	19 Jun 61
	51-2323	450-11-10	4500376	06 Oct 52	10 Dec 52	30 Dec 52	06 Jan 53			24 Aug 60	09 Mar 61
	51-2324	450-11-10	4500377	06 Oct 52	11 Dec 52	29 Dec 52	10 Jan 53			10 Dec 60	20 Feb 61
	51-2325	450-11-10	4500378	07 Oct 52	11 Dec 52	30 Dec 52	06 Jan 53		14 Dec 61		
	51-2326	450-11-10	4500379	08 Oct 52	13 Dec 52	23 Jan 53	24 Jan 53			15 Jun 61	10 Dec 63
	51-2327	450-11-10	4500380	09 Oct 52	17 Dec 52	31 Dec 52	10 Jan 53			25 May 61	14 Jul 61
	51-2328	450-11-10	4500381	11 Oct 52	27 Dec 52	12 Feb 53	12 Feb 53	JB-47B / NB-47B		28 Apr 60	13 Apr 61
	51-2329	450-11-10	4500382	12 Oct 52	17 Dec 52	31 Dec 52	16 Jan 53			31 May 61	18 Jul 61
	51-2330	450-11-10	4500383	13 Oct 52	27 Dec 52	23 Jan 53	25 Jan 53			08 Jun 61	29 Jan 64

MDS and Block Number	Serial Number	Model Number	Const. Number	Roll Out Date	First Flight Date	MIRR Date	USAF Fly Away	New MDS	Out of Service	MASDC Input Date	MASDC Output Date
B-47B-50-BW	51-2331	450-11-10	4500384	14 Oct 52	28 Dec 52	29 Jan 53	05 Feb 53			09 Jun 61	13 Jan 64
	51-2332	450-11-10	4500385	15 Oct 52	28 Dec 52	26 Jan 53	31 Jan 53		24 Jan 57	18 Oct 60	17 Mar 61
	51-2333	450-11-10	4500386	16 Oct 52	23 Dec 52	26 Jan 53	30 Jan 53				
	51-2334	450-11-10	4500387	16 Oct 52	28 Dec 52	24 Jan 53	29 Jan 53		01 Feb 59		
	51-2335	450-11-10	4500388	17 Oct 52	23 Dec 52	24 Jan 53	26 Jan 53			21 Apr 61	25 May 61
	51-2336	450-11-10	4500389	21 Oct 52	30 Dec 52	26 Jan 53	30 Jan 53			26 Apr 60	11 Apr 61
	51-2337	450-11-10	4500390	21 Oct 52	03 Jan 53	28 Jan 53	02 Feb 53			24 Apr 61	02 Jun 61
	51-2338	450-11-10	4500391	22 Oct 52	29 Dec 52	24 Jan 53	25 Jan 53			26 Oct 60	28 Mar 61
	51-2339	450-11-10	4500392	23 Oct 52	31 Dec 52	30 Dec 53	05 Feb 53		25 Jan 60		
	51-2340	450-11-10	4500393	23 Oct 52	30 Dec 52	26 Jan 53	30 Jan 53			04 Aug 60	01 Mar 61
	51-2341	450-11-10	4500394	24 Oct 52	05 Jan 53	26 Jan 53	30 Jan 53			09 Jun 61	02 Mar 64
	51-2342	450-11-10	4500395	24 Oct 52	05 Jan 53	27 Jan 53	31 Jan 53			07 Jun 61	18 Feb 64
	51-2343	450-11-10	4500396	28 Oct 52	08 Jan 53	26 Jan 53	02 Feb 53			22 May 61	07 Jul 61
	51-2344	450-11-10	4500397	29 Oct 52	08 Aug 53	26 Jan 53	29 Jan 53		27 Feb 56		
	51-2345	450-11-10	4500398	29 Oct 52	05 Jan 53	25 Jan 53	30 Jan 53			07 Jun 61	11 Feb 64
	51-2346	450-11-10	4500399	30 Oct 52	09 Jan 53	29 Jan 53	30 Jan 53			12 Aug 60	09 Mar 61
	51-2347	450-11-10	4500400	31 Oct 52	09 Jan 53	30 Jan 53	12 Feb 53			22 May 61	07 Jul 61
	51-2348	450-11-10	4500401	31 Oct 52	12 Jan 53	30 Jan 53	12 Feb 53			09 Jun 61	24 Mar 64
	51-2349	450-11-10	4500402	03 Nov 52	11 Jan 53	30 Jan 53	05 Feb 53		05 Feb 58		
	51-2350	450-11-10	4500403	06 Nov 52	09 Jan 53	30 Jan 53	05 Feb 53	JB-47B		26 Aug 58	26 Jan 61
	51-2351	450-11-10	4500404	06 Nov 52	13 Jan 53	30 Jan 53	12 Feb 53			07 Jun 61	18 Jul 61
	51-2352	450-11-10	4500405	10 Nov 52	12 Jan 53	30 Jan 53	06 Feb 53		24 Jan 57		
	51-2353	450-11-10	4500406	10 Nov 52	13 Jan 52	30 Jan 53	05 Feb 53			09 Jun 61	09 Dec 63
	51-2354	450-11-10	4500407	11 Nov 52	24 Jan 53	14 Feb 53	17 Feb 53			17 Apr 61	07 Jun 61
	51-2355	450-11-10	4500408	12 Nov 52	21 Jan 53	13 Feb 53	17 Feb 53			08 Jun 61	31 Jan 64
	51-2356	450-11-10	4500409	13 Nov 52	22 Jan 53	12 Feb 53	12 Feb 53			02 Sep 60	15 Mar 61
B-47E-55-BW	51-2357	450-157-35	4500410	17 Nov 52	12 Feb 53	28 Feb 53	10 Apr 53	EB-47E JB-47E GB-47E	29 Jul 63		
	51-2358	450-157-35	4500411	18 Nov 52	05 Feb 53	28 Feb 53	09 Mar 53	WB-47E		09 Sep 69	18 Sep 69
	51-2359	450-157-35	4500412	20 Nov 52	07 Mar 53	26 Mar 53	15 Mar 56	JB-47E NB-47E		28 Jul 60	03 Feb 61
	51-2360	450-157-35	4500413	19 Nov 52	21 Mar 53	08 Apr 53	09 Apr 53	WB-47E	03 Oct 66		
	51-2361	450-157-35	4500414	20 Nov 52	31 Jan 53	24 Feb 53	28 Feb 53			26 Mar 61	02 May 61
	51-2362	450-157-35	4500415	20 Nov 52	04 Feb 53	25 Feb 53	08 Jul 53	WB-47E		24 Oct 69	12 Nov 69
	51-2363	450-157-35	4500416	21 Nov 52	06 Feb 53	25 Feb 53	14 Mar 53	JB-47E WB-47E		13 Sep 69	18 Sep 61
	51-2364	450-157-35	4500417	24 Nov 52	11 Feb 53	27 Feb 53	07 Mar 53			15 Feb 61	11 May 61
	51-2365	450-157-35	4500418	01 Dec 52	12 Feb 53	27 Feb 53	01 Mar 53		04 Jun 59		
	51-2366	450-157-35	4500419	03 Dec 52	30 Jan 53	27 Feb 53	28 Feb 53	WB-47E	20 Jun 67		
	51-2367	450-157-35	4500420	03 Dec 52	07 Feb 53	25 Feb 53	02 Mar 53			26 Apr 63	25 Sep 67
	51-2368	450-157-35	4500421	01 Dec 52	12 Feb 53	28 Feb 53	07 Mar 53	JB-47E		31 Mar 61	05 May 61
	51-2369	450-157-35	4500422	02 Dec 52	30 Jan 53	24 Feb 53	28 Feb 53	WB-47E		01 Jul 65	18 Jun 69
	51-2370	450-157-35	4500423	03 Dec 52	03 Feb 53	26 Feb 53	02 Mar 53			28 Apr 61	23 Jun 61
	51-2371	450-157-35	4500424	08 Dec 52	12 Feb 53	25 Feb 53	01 Mar 53			03 Jun 60	31 Jan 61
	51-2372	450-157-35	4500425	05 Dec 52	11 Feb 53	25 Feb 53	02 Mar 53			30 Jun 61	24 Mar 64
	51-2373	450-157-35	4500426	05 Dec 52	13 Feb 53	27 Feb 53	05 Mar 53	WB-47E		15 Oct 69	12 Nov 69
	51-2374	450-157-35	4500427	09 Dec 52	16 Feb 53	28 Feb 53	24 Mar 53			19 Apr 61	01 Jun 52
	51-2375	450-157-35	4500428	09 Dec 52	16 Feb 53	27 Feb 53	06 Mar 53	WB-47E		15 Oct 69	12 Nov 69
	51-2376	450-157-35	4500429	12 Dec 52	16 Feb 53	28 Feb 53	05 Mar 53			22 May 62	07 Feb 64
	51-2377	450-157-35	4500430	12 Dec 52	16 Feb 53	27 Feb 53	04 Mar 53		20 Jan 62		
	51-2378	450-157-35	4500431	15 Dec 52	16 Feb 53	28 Feb 53	05 Mar 53			17 May 62	10 Jan 64
	51-2379	450-157-35	4500432	16 Dec 52	17 Feb 53	23 Mar 53	24 Mar 53			11 Jun 62	22 Jan 64
	51-2380	450-157-35	4500433	16 Dec 52	21 Feb 53	30 Mar 53	23 Mar 53	WB-47E		09 Sep 69	18 Sep 69
	51-2381	450-157-35	4500434	18 Dec 52	21 Feb 53	20 Mar 53	27 Mar 53			22 Mar 62	17 Jan 64
	51-2382	450-157-35	4500435	19 Dec 52	20 Feb 53	19 Mar 53	23 Mar 53		06 Aug 54		
	51-2383	450-157-35	4500436	19 Dec 52	07 Mar 53	20 Mar 53	23 Mar 53	WB-47E		03 May 65	18 Jun 69
	51-2384	450-157-35	4500437	19 Dec 52	25 Feb 53	19 Mar 53	23 Mar 53			29 Mar 61	08 May 61
	51-2385	450-157-35	4500438	23 Dec 52	26 Feb 53	20 Mar 53	23 Mar 53	WB-47E		30 Jun 66	18 Jun 69
	51-2386	450-157-35	4500439	28 Dec 52	28 Feb 53	30 Mar 53	23 Mar 53			12 Apr 61	09 May 61
	51-2387	450-157-35	4500440	24 Dec 52	07 Mar 53	23 Mar 53	23 Mar 53	WB-47E	06 Oct 69		
	51-2388	450-157-35	4500441	26 Dec 52	28 Feb 53	23 Mar 53	24 Mar 53			18 May 62	16 Oct 67
	51-2389	450-157-35	4500442	29 Dec 52	n/a	29 Apr 53	n/a		21 Feb 53		
	51-2390	450-157-35	4500443	30 Dec 52	05 Mar 53	19 Mar 53	23 Mar 53	WB-47E		13 Sep 69	18 Sep 69
	51-2391	450-157-35	4500444	31 Dec 52	08 Mar 53	25 Mar 53	27 Mar 53		04 Nov 58		
	51-2392	450-157-35	4500445	02 Jan 53	n/a	29 Apr 53	n/a		21 Feb 53		
	51-2393	450-157-35	4500446	02 Jan 53	25 Mar 53	08 Apr 53	15 Apr 53			01 May 61	20 Jun 61
	51-2394	450-157-35	4500447	02 Jan 53	16 Mar 53	24 Apr 53	29 Apr 53	JB-47E NB-47E		10 Oct 60	17 Apr 61
	51-2395	450-157-35	4500448	06 Jan 53	09 Mar 53	23 Mar 53	27 Mar 53			27 Mar 61	02 May 61
	51-2396	450-157-35	4500449	08 Jan 53	16 Mar 53	30 Mar 53	31 Mar 31	WB-47E		02 Jul 65	18 Jun 69
	51-2397	450-157-35	4500450	07 Jan 53	12 Mar 53	28 Mar 53	28 Mar 53	WB-47E	05 Dec 66		
	51-2398	450-157-35	4500451	08 Jan 53	08 Mar 53	25 Mar 53	30 Mar 53			14 Feb 63	16 Oct 67
	51-2399	450-157-35	4500452	09 Jan 53	16 Mar 53	30 Mar 53	31 Mar 53			15 Mar 61	17 Apr 61
	51-2400	450-157-35	4500453	12 Jan 53	12 Mar 53	30 Mar 53	15 Apr 53	JB-47E	16 Dec 58		
	51-2401	450-157-35	4500454	13 Jan 53	12 Mar 53	28 Mar 53	30 Mar 53			18 May 61	29 Jun 61
	51-2402	450-157-35	4500455	14 Jan 53	14 Mar 53	28 Mar 53	30 Mar 53	WB-47E		12 Sep 69	18 Sep 69
	51-2403	450-157-35	4500456	14 Jan 53	04 Mar 53	18 Jun 53	19 Jun 53			23 May 61	07 Jul 61
	51-2404	450-157-35	4500457	15 Jan 53	07 Mar 53	23 Mar 53	24 Mar 53			07 Feb 63	16 Oct 67
	51-2405	450-157-35	4500458	16 Jan 53	11 Mar 53	26 Mar 53	27 Mar 53			08 Jun 61	26 Aug 63
	51-2406	450-157-35	4500459	16 Jan 53	18 Mar 53	14 Apr 53	12 May 53	WB-47E		10 Sep 69	18 Sep 69
	51-2407	450-157-35	4500460	19 Jan 53	23 Mar 53	08 Apr 53	09 Apr 53			11 May 61	12 Jun 61
	51-2408	450-157-35	4500461	20 Jan 53	16 Mar 53	30 Mar 53	31 Mar 53	WB-47E	30 Jun 65		
	51-2409	450-157-35	4500462	21 Jan 53	17 Mar 53	02 Apr 53	07 Apr 53		20 Apr 61		
	51-2410	450-157-35	4500463	21 Jan 53	13 Mar 53	25 Mar 53	15 Apr 53	JB-47E	15 Apr 59		
	51-2411	450-157-35	4500464	22 Jan 53	17 Mar 53	30 Mar 53	31 Mar 53			31 Jul 62	16 Oct 67
B-47E-60-BW	51-2412	450-157-35	4500465	26 Jan 53	04 Apr 53	30 Apr 53	16 May 53	WB-47E		08 Sep 69	18 Sep 69
	51-2413	450-157-35	4500466	26 Jan 53	01 Apr 53	30 Apr 53	14 May 53	WB-47E		09 Sep 69	18 Sep 69
	51-2414	450-157-35	4500467	27 Jan 53	02 Apr 53	25 Apr 53	02 May 53	WB-47E		31 Oct 69	11 Nov 69
	51-2415	450-157-35	4500468	28 Jan 53	02 Apr 53	25 Apr 53	02 May 53	WB-47E		08 Sep 69	18 Sep 69
	51-2416	450-157-35	4500469	29 Jan 53	04 Apr 53	30 Apr 53	05 May 53		05 Mar 54		
	51-2417	450-157-35	4500470	29 Jan 53	04 Apr 53	25 Apr 53	02 May 53	WB-47E		12 Sep 69	18 Sep 69
	51-2418	450-157-35	4500471	30 Jan 53	09 Apr 53	30 Apr 53	14 May 53			14 Jun 61	02 Apr 64
	51-2419	450-157-35	4500472	05 Feb 53	09 Apr 53	28 Apr 53	02 May 53			10 May 63	16 Oct 67
	51-2420	450-157-35	4500473	02 Feb 53	08 Apr 53	29 Apr 53	06 May 53	WB-47E	10 Nov 63		

MDS and Block Number	Serial Number	Model Number	Const. Number	Roll Out Date	First Flight Date	MIRR Date	USAF Fly Away	New MDS	Out of Service	MASDC Input Date	MASDC Output Date
B-47E-60-BW	51-2421	450-157-35	4500474	03 Feb 53	04 Apr 53	25 Apr 53	02 May 53		06 Nov 56		
	51-2422	450-157-35	4500475	03 Feb 53	13 Apr 53	07 May 53	12 May 53			03 Jun 63	16 Oct 67
	51-2423	450-157-35	4500476	04 Feb 53	03 Apr 53	28 Apr 53	02 May 53			18 May 61	29 Jun 61
	51-2424	450-157-35	4500477	06 Feb 53	13 Apr 53	30 Apr 53	07 May 53			20 Jun 61	16 Dec 63
	51-2425	450-157-35	4500478	06 Feb 53	10 Apr 53	28 Apr 53	02 May 53		07 Apr 57		
	51-2426	450-157-35	4500479	09 Feb 53	15 Apr 53	01 May 53	08 May 53			04 Jun 63	16 Oct 67
	51-2427	450-157-35	4500480	10 Feb 53	10 Apr 53	30 Apr 53	06 May 53	WB-47E		07 Sep 69	18 Sep 69
	51-2428	450-157-35	4500481	10 Feb 53	12 Apr 53	29 Apr 53	14 May 53			19 Apr 63	16 Oct 67
	51-2429	450-157-35	4500482	11 Feb 53	12 Apr 53	29 Apr 53	06 May 53			17 May 63	16 Oct 67
	51-2430	450-157-35	4500483	11 Feb 53	16 Apr 53	30 Apr 53	07 May 53			26 Apr 63	16 Oct 67
	51-2431	450-157-35	4500484	12 Feb 53	02 May 53	27 May 53	29 May 53			07 Jan 63	16 Oct 67
	51-2432	450-157-35	4500485	13 Feb 53	02 May 53	29 May 53	05 Jun 53			06 Jun 62	16 Oct 67
	51-2433	450-157-35	4500486	16 Feb 53	15 Apr 53	29 Apr 53	06 May 53			13 Jul 61	30 Oct 63
	51-2434	450-157-35	4500487	16 Feb 53	21 Apr 53	19 May 53	22 May 53			12 Jun 61	16 Dec 63
	51-2435	450-157-35	4500488	17 Feb 53	20 Apr 53	26 May 53	04 Jun 53	WB-47E		08 Sep 69	18 Sep 69
	51-2436	450-157-35	4500489	18 Feb 53	27 Apr 53	23 May 53	29 May 53			26 May 61	12 Jul 61
	51-2437	450-157-35	4500490	18 Feb 53	25 Apr 53	21 May 53	27 May 53		18 Oct 54		
	51-2438	450-157-35	4500491	19 Feb 53	30 Apr 53	28 May 53	29 May 53			05 Jul 61	18 Nov 63
	51-2439	450-157-35	4500492	23 Feb 53	20 Apr 53	30 Jun 53	03 Jul 53			06 Jun 60	03 Feb 61
	51-2440	450-157-35	4500493	20 Feb 53	25 Apr 53	23 May 53	28 May 53		03 Dec 53		
	51-2441	450-157-35	4500494	23 Feb 53	15 Apr 53	01 May 53	07 May 53			17 Mar 61	17 Apr 61
	51-2442	450-157-35	4500495	24 Feb 53	01 May 53	28 May 53	02 Jun 53		16 May 56		
	51-2443	450-157-35	4500496	24 Feb 53	04 May 53	29 May 53	05 Jun 53			23 May 61	11 Jul 61
	51-2444	450-157-35	4500497	26 Feb 53	01 May 53	27 May 53	02 Jun 53			26 May 61	13 Jul 61
	51-2445	450-157-35	4500498	26 Feb 53	20 Apr 53	22 May 53	27 May 53			07 Jun 61	02 Mar 64
	51-5214	450-157-35	4500499	26 Feb 53	02 May 53	29 May 53	04 Jun 53			24 Mar 61	05 May 61
	51-5215	450-157-35	4500500	27 Feb 53	06 May 53	29 May 53	03 Jun 53			20 Mar 61	31 Mar 61
	51-5216	450-157-35	4500501	02 Mar 53	30 Apr 53	27 May 53	29 May 53			04 Apr 63	16 Oct 67
	51-5217	450-157-35	4500502	03 Mar 53	06 May 53	28 May 53	02 Jun 53			15 Jun 63	16 Oct 67
	51-5218	450-157-35	4500503	04 Mar 53	06 May 53	28 May 53	03 Jun 53	WB-47E		10 Sep 69	18 Sep 69
	51-5219	450-157-35	4500504	04 Mar 53	07 May 53	29 May 53	14 Jun 55	YDB-47E	25 Sep 58		
	51-5220	450-157-35	4500505	05 Mar 53	23 May 53	29 May 53	26 Aug 54	YDB-47E		Dec 59	22 Mar 61
	51-5221	450-157-35	4500506	06 Mar 53	14 May 53	29 May 53	04 Jun 53			23 Apr 64	30 Sep 68
	51-5222	450-157-35	4500507	09 Mar 53	08 May 53	29 May 53	04 Jun 53			16 Mar 61	31 Mar 61
	51-5223	450-157-35	4500508	09 Mar 53	15 May 53	29 May 53	04 Jun 53			21 Jun 61	12 Mar 64
	51-5224	450-157-35	4500509	10 Mar 53	19 May 53	05 Jun 53	11 Jun 53			10 Mar 61	20 Apr 61
	51-5225	450-157-35	4500510	11 Mar 53	22 May 53	24 Jun 53	01 Jul 53			20 Feb 63	16 Oct 67
	51-5226	450-157-35	4500511	12 Mar 53	15 May 53	08 Jun 53	13 Jun 53			31 Mar 61	10 May 61
	51-5227	450-157-35	4500512	12 Mar 53	20 May 53	19 Jun 53	23 Jun 53			31 Aug 60	10 May 61
	51-5228	450-157-35	4500513	13 Mar 53	18 May 53	19 Jun 53	23 Jun 53			30 Sep 60	20 Apr 61
	51-5229	450-157-35	4500514	16 Mar 53	18 May 53	29 May 53	05 Jun 53			31 Jan 63	16 Oct 67
	51-5230	450-157-35	4500515	16 Mar 53	14 May 53	29 May 53	04 Jun 53		05 Oct 56		
	51-5231	450-157-35	4500516	17 Mar 53	22 May 53	23 Jun 53	25 Jun 53			20 Jun 61	02 Apr 64
	51-5232	450-157-35	4500517	18 Mar 53	19 May 53	08 Jun 53	11 Jun 53			26 Apr 61	26 Apr 61
	51-5233	450-157-35	4500518	19 Mar 53	26 May 53	19 Jun 53	23 Jun 53		23 May 61		
	51-5234	450-157-35	4500519	20 Mar 53	01 Jun 53	27 Jun 53	29 Jun 53		08 Jun 61		
B-47E-65-BW	51-5235	450-157-35	4500520	20 Mar 53	29 May 53	23 Jun 53	29 Jun 53		29 Jun 61		
	51-5236	450-157-35	4500521	23 Mar 53	29 May 53	19 Jun 53	24 Jun 53			29 Jun 65	16 Oct 67
	51-5237	450-157-35	4500522	24 Mar 53	29 May 53	23 Jun 53	25 Jun 53		14 Jun 61		
	51-5238	450-157-35	4500523	25 Mar 53	28 May 53	29 Jun 53	01 Jul 53			30 Apr 63	16 Oct 67
	51-5239	450-157-35	4500524	25 Mar 53	01 Jun 53	25 Jun 53	02 Jul 53		18 Feb 60		
	51-5240	450-157-35	4500525	26 Mar 53	27 May 53	29 Jun 53	01 Jul 53			30 Apr 61	10 Jun 61
	51-5241	450-157-35	4500526	27 Mar 53	10 Jun 53	29 Jun 53	03 Jul 53		19 Dec 60		
	51-5242	450-157-35	4500527	30 Mar 53	03 Jun 53	30 Jun 53	09 Jul 53			10 Mar 60	10 Jun 60
	51-5243	450-157-35	4500528	30 Mar 53	02 Jun 53	30 Jun 53	04 Jul 53		01 Jan 60		
	51-5244	450-157-35	4500529	31 Mar 53	15 Jun 53	01 Sep 53	22 Jul 55			25 May 60	10 Feb 61
	51-5245	450-157-35	4500530	01 Apr 53	10 Jun 53	16 Jul 53	18 Jul 53			17 Jan 63	16 Oct 67
	51-5246	450-157-35	4500531	02 Apr 53	27 Jun 53	21 Jul 53	23 Jul 53			12 Oct 62	16 Oct 67
	51-5247	450-157-35	4500532	02 Apr 53	08 Jun 53	30 Jun 53	03 Jul 53			23 May 62	11 Feb 64
	51-5248	450-157-35	4500533	03 Apr 53	04 Jun 53	30 Jun 53	03 Jul 53		08 Oct 59		
	51-5249	450-157-35	4500534	06 Apr 53	05 Jun 53	29 Jun 53	03 Jul 53			08 Jun 60	03 Feb 61
	51-5250	450-157-35	4500535	07 Apr 53	11 Jun 53	30 Jun 53	07 Jul 53			22 Jan 63	16 Oct 67
	51-5251	450-157-35	4500536	07 Apr 53	09 Jun 53	21 Jul 53	31 Jul 53			10 Jul 64	30 Sep 74
	51-5252	450-157-35	4500537	08 Apr 53	11 Jun 53	27 Jul 53	31 Jul 53		10 Jun 54		
	51-5253	450-157-35	4500538	09 Apr 53	12 Jun 53	06 Aug 53	10 Aug 53			10 May 61	30 Jun 61
	51-5254	450-157-35	4500539	10 Apr 53	27 Jun 53	13 Jul 53	30 Jul 53			30 Apr 61	30 Jun 61
	51-5255	450-157-35	4500540	10 Apr 53	26 Jun 53	30 Jun 53	03 Jul 53			12 Mar 63	16 Oct 67
	51-5256	450-157-35	4500541	13 Apr 53	25 Jun 53	30 Jun 53	07 Jul 53			18 Mar 64	30 Sep 68
	51-5257	450-157-35	4500542	14 Apr 53	20 Aug 53	29 Apr 53	02 Sep 53	WB-47E		10 Sep 69	18 Sep 69
RB-47E-1-BW	51-5258	450-158-36	4500543	18 Mar 53	03 Jul 53	30 Jul 53	07 Nov 55	JRB-47E NRB-47E		27 Apr 67	14 Jan 69
	51-5259	450-158-36	4500544	20 May 53	24 Jul 53	31 Jul 53	11 Aug 53			23 Oct 57	01 Jul 60
	51-5260	450-158-36	4500545	18 Jun 53	23 Aug 53	31 Aug 53	23 Sep 53			01 Aug 60	19 Jan 61
	51-5261	450-158-36	4500546	03 Jul 53	24 Aug 53	31 Aug 53	01 Sep 53	JRB-47E		18 Sep 59	12 Jan 61
	51-5262	450-158-36	4500547	20 Jul 53	11 Sep 53	30 Sep 53	03 Oct 53		20 Oct 60		
	51-5263	450-158-36	4500548	29 Jul 53	22 Sep 53	30 Sep 53	09 Oct 53		20 Oct 60		
	51-5264	450-158-36	4500549	06 Aug 53	02 Oct 53	21 Oct 53	23 Oct 53			02 Oct 57	23 Apr 60
RB-47E-5-BW	51-5265	450-158-36	4500550	17 Aug 53	17 Oct 53	29 Oct 53	30 Oct 53			22 Oct 57	23 Apr 60
	51-5266	450-158-36	4500551	25 Aug 53	09 Nov 53	18 Nov 53	25 Nov 53			15 Oct 57	23 Mar 60
	51-5267	450-158-36	4500552	31 Aug 53	12 Oct 53	25 Nov 53	25 Nov 53			16 Oct 57	13 Feb 60
	51-5268	450-158-36	4500553	09 Sep 53	17 Nov 53	30 Nov 53	18 Dec 53			17 Oct 57	25 Mar 60
	51-5269	450-158-36	4500554	16 Sep 53	24 Nov 53	22 Dec 53	23 Dec 53			18 Oct 57	01 Apr 60
	51-5270	450-158-36	4500555	22 Sep 53	17 Nov 53	01 Dec 53	18 Dec 53			24 Oct 57	20 Nov 60
RB-47E-10-BW	51-5271	450-158-36	4500556	28 Sep 53	07 Dec 53	21 Dec 53	23 Dec 53			25 Oct 57	20 Nov 60
	51-5272	450-158-36	4500557	02 Oct 53	09 Dec 53	25 Jan 54	28 Jan 54			14 Oct 57	28 Mar 60
	51-5273	450-158-36	4500558	22 Oct 53	07 Jan 54	20 Jan 54	22 Jan 54			18 Oct 57	04 Apr 60
	51-5274	450-158-36	4500559	08 Oct 53	14 Dec 53	23 Dec 53	23 Dec 53			25 Oct 57	10 Jun 61
	51-5275	450-158-36	4500560	08 Oct 53	15 Dec 53	09 Jan 54	09 Jan 54			14 Oct 57	08 Mar 60
	51-5276	450-158-36	4500561	15 Oct 53	17 Dec 53	08 Jan 54	09 Jan 54			28 Oct 57	18 Apr 60
B-47E-65-BW	51-7019	450-157-35	4500562	15 Apr 53	03 Jul 53	23 Jul 53	24 Jul 53			19 Apr 63	17 Oct 67
	51-7020	450-157-35	4500563	15 Apr 53	02 Jul 53	28 Jul 53	29 Jul 53			15 Jan 63	17 Oct 67
	51-7021	450-157-35	4500564	17 Apr 53	01 Jul 53	23 Jul 53	24 Jul 53	WB-47E		07 Sep 69	18 Sep 69
	51-7022	450-157-35	4500565	17 Apr 53	01 Jul 53	23 Jul 53	25 Jul 53			29 Apr 64	30 Sep 68

MDS and Block Number	Serial Number	Model Number	Const. Number	Roll Out Date	First Flight Date	MIRR Date	USAF Fly Away	New MDS	Out of Service	MASDC Input Date	MASDC Output Date
B-47E-65-BW	51-7023	450-157-35	4500566	20 Apr 53	07 Jul 53	28 Jul 53	29 Jul 53		05 Jan 59		
	51-7024	450-157-35	4500567	20 Apr 53	03 Jul 53	23 Jul 53	25 Jul 53			10 May 63	17 Oct 67
	51-7025	450-157-35	4500568	22 Apr 53	31 Jul 53	18 Aug 53	20 Aug 53			22 Jun 61	12 Mar 64
	51-7026	450-157-35	4500569	21 Apr 53	17 Jul 53	20 Aug 53	24 Aug 53			05 Jun 63	17 Oct 67
	51-7027	450-157-35	4500570	22 Apr 53	10 Jul 53	29 Jul 53	31 Jul 53		26 Sep 62		
	51-7028	450-157-35	4500571	23 Apr 53	17 Jul 53	29 Jul 53	31 Jul 53		18 Mar 60		
	51-7029	450-157-35	4500572	24 Apr 53	18 Jul 53	31 Jul 53	06 Aug 53			12 Aug 60	10 Feb 61
	51-7030	450-157-35	4500573	27 Apr 53	20 Jul 53	29 Jul 53	31 Jul 53			06 Mar 63	17 Oct 67
	51-7031	450-157-35	4500574	28 Apr 53	09 Jul 53	28 Jul 53	30 Jul 53		17 Jul 57		
	51-7032	450-157-35	4500575	29 Apr 53	03 Aug 53	17 Aug 53	20 Aug 53			08 Mar 63	17 Oct 67
	51-7033	450-157-35	4500576	30 Apr 53	15 Jul 53	08 Oct 53	09 Oct 53		12 Feb 55		
	51-7034	450-157-35	4500577	01 May 53	28 Jul 53	25 Aug 53	27 Aug 53			31 May 61	09 Mar 64
	51-7035	450-157-35	4500578	04 May 53	10 Jul 53	31 Jul 53	03 Aug 53		08 Nov 55		
	51-7036	450-157-35	4500579	05 May 53	17 Jul 53	30 Jul 53	03 Aug 53			25 Apr 61	25 Apr 61
	51-7037	450-157-35	4500580	06 May 53	20 Jul 53	31 Jul 53	07 Aug 53			19 Apr 63	17 Oct 67
	51-7038	450-157-35	4500581	07 May 53	11 Aug 53	28 Aug 53	04 Sep 53			18 Feb 63	17 Oct 67
	51-7039	450-157-35	4500582	08 May 53	27 Aug 53	27 Aug 53	27 Aug 53			25 Apr 61	18 Mar 64
	51-7040	450-157-35	4500583	11 May 53	30 Jul 53	20 Aug 53	24 Aug 53			25 Apr 61	31 Mar 64
	51-7041	450-157-35	4500584	12 May 53	15 Jul 53	31 Jul 53	03 Aug 53		06 May 59		
	51-7042	450-157-35	4500585	13 May 53	14 Aug 53	01 Sep 53	04 Sep 53		18 Jul 57		
	51-7043	450-157-35	4500586	14 May 53	24 Jul 53	10 Aug 53	19 Apr 54	JB-47E NB-47E		13 May 60	30 May 60
	51-7044	450-157-35	4500587	15 May 53	04 Aug 53	26 Aug 53	27 Aug 53		03 Nov 65	14 Jul 61	14 Nov 61
	51-7045	450-157-35	4500588	18 May 53	26 Aug 53	22 May 53	07 Oct 53	WB-47E		08 Sep 69	18 Sep 69
	51-7046	450-157-35	4500589	19 May 53	31 Jul 53	29 Aug 53	29 Aug 53		14 Sep 60		
	51-7047	450-157-35	4500590	20 May 53	31 Jul 53	01 Sep 53	01 Sep 53				
	51-7048	450-157-35	4500591	21 May 53	04 Aug 53	18 Aug 53	20 Aug 53	GB-47E WB-47E	15 Apr 64 21 Apr 64		
	51-7049	450-157-35	4500592	22 May 53	10 Aug 53	20 Aug 53	26 Aug 53				
	51-7050	450-157-35	4500593	25 May 53	03 Aug 53	28 Aug 53	31 Aug 53			19 Apr 63	17 Oct 67
B-47E-70-BW	51-7051	450-157-35	4500594	26 May 53	07 Aug 53	20 Aug 53	27 Aug 53			09 Jun 61	17 Feb 64
	51-7052	450-157-35	4500595	27 May 53	04 Sep 53	29 Sep 53	30 Sep 53			22 Apr 61	25 Apr 61
	51-7053	450-157-35	4500596	28 May 53	06 Sep 53	21 Aug 53	24 Aug 53			13 Jun 61	19 Dec 63
	51-7054	450-157-35	4500597	29 May 53	03 Aug 53	20 Aug 53	24 Aug 53			23 Mar 61	11 May 61
	51-7055	450-157-35	4500598	01 Jun 53	14 Aug 53	22 Oct 53	23 Oct 53			27 Apr 61	10 Mar 64
	51-7056	450-157-35	4500599	02 Jun 53	12 Aug 53	11 Sep 53	11 Sep 53			11 Mar 63	17 Jan 64
	51-7057	450-157-35	4500600	03 Jun 53	11 Aug 53	25 Aug 53	27 Aug 53			26 Jun 61	13 Mar 64
	51-7058	450-157-35	4500601	04 Jun 53	13 Aug 53	28 Aug 53	31 Aug 53	WB-47E	12 Oct 69		
	51-7059	450-157-35	4500602	05 Jun 53	19 Aug 53	31 Aug 53	01 Sep 53			29 Jan 63	17 Oct 67
	51-7060	450-157-35	4500603	08 Jun 53	18 Aug 53	10 Sep 53	11 Sep 53		20 Oct 60		
	51-7061	450-157-35	4500604	09 Jun 53	12 Aug 53	11 Sep 53	11 Sep 53			21 Apr 61	26 Apr 61
	51-7062	450-157-35	4500605	10 Jun 53	26 Aug 53	17 Sep 53	18 Sep 53			31 Jul 62	17 Oct 67
	51-7063	450-157-35	4500606	11 Jun 53	21 Aug 53	10 Nov 53	10 Nov 53	WB-47E		13 Sep 69	18 Sep 69
	51-7064	450-157-35	4500607	12 Jun 53	27 Aug 53	21 Sep 53	23 Sep 53			27 Mar 61	04 May 61
B-47E-75-BW	51-7065	450-157-35	4500608	15 Jun 53	28 Aug 53	16 Sep 53	17 Sep 53			28 Apr 61	04 Feb 64
	51-7066	450-157-35	4500609	16 Jun 53	04 Sep 53	26 Oct 53	17 Oct 53	WB-47E	30 Oct 69		
	51-7067	450-157-35	4500610	17 Jun 53	04 Sep 53	17 Sep 53	18 Sep 53			20 Jun 61	19 Mar 64
	51-7068	450-157-35	4500611	18 Jun 53	27 Aug 53	14 Sep 53	16 Sep 53			03 Oct 61	22 Jan 64
	51-7069	450-157-35	4500612	19 Jun 53	24 Sep 53	23 Jun 53	08 Nov 57		13 Jan 59		
	51-7070	450-157-35	4500613	22 Jun 53	04 Sep 53	28 Oct 53	28 Oct 53			15 Aug 60	02 Feb 61
	51-7071	450-157-35	4500614	23 Jun 53	10 Sep 53	19 Oct 53	20 Oct 53		14 Apr 61		
	51-7072	450-157-35	4500615	24 Jun 53	27 Aug 53	16 Sep 53	17 Sep 53			26 Feb 63	17 Oct 67
	51-7073	450-157-35	4500616	25 Jun 53	01 Sep 53	10 Sep 53	11 Sep 53		31 May 55		
	51-7074	450-157-35	4500617	29 Jun 53	08 Sep 53	18 Sep 53	22 Sep 53			12 Jun 61	19 Dec 63
	51-7075	450-157-35	4500618	30 Jun 53	28 Aug 53	04 Sep 53	05 Sep 53			05 Feb 63	17 Oct 67
	51-7076	450-157-35	4500619	01 Jul 53	14 Sep 53	30 Sep 53	01 Oct 53			26 May 61	13 Jul 61
	51-7077	450-157-35	4500620	02 Jul 53	04 Sep 53	18 Sep 53	19 Sep 53			11 Dec 62	31 Oct 63
	51-7078	450-157-35	4500621	03 Jul 53	21 Sep 53	13 Oct 53	14 Oct 53			20 May 64	30 Sep 64
	51-7079	450-157-35	4500622	06 Jul 53	09 Sep 53	07 Oct 53	07 Oct 53			18 Apr 61	16 Jun 61
	51-7080	450-157-35	4500623	07 Jul 53	24 Sep 53	27 Oct 53	27 Oct 53			24 May 63	17 Oct 67
	51-7081	450-157-35	4500624	08 Jul 53	17 Sep 53	05 Oct 53	06 Oct 53	UB-47E GB-47E	30 Apr 64 17 Dec 59		
	51-7082	450-157-35	4500625	10 Jul 53	10 Sep 53	30 Sep 53	02 Oct 53			27 Jun 61	17 Oct 67
	51-7083	450-157-35	4500626	13 Jul 53	16 Sep 53	08 Oct 53	08 Oct 53				
B-47E-5-LM	51-15804	450-157-35	1	n/a	n/a	30 Jul 53	12 Aug 53			30 Apr 63	17 Oct 67
	51-15805	450-157-35	2	n/a	n/a	31 Jul 53	12 Aug 53		01 Jul 59		
	51-15806	450-157-35	3	n/a	n/a	12 Aug 53	01 Sep 53			27 Jun 61	05 Feb 64
	51-15807	450-157-35	4	n/a	n/a	19 Aug 53	01 Sep 53			13 Mar 63	17 Oct 67
	51-15808	450-157-35	5	n/a	n/a	24 Sep 53	09 Oct 53			01 Feb 63	17 Oct 67
	51-15809	450-157-35	6	n/a	n/a	11 Sep 53	23 Sep 53			18 Mar 64	11 Sep 64
	51-15810	450-157-35	7	n/a	n/a	30 Sep 53	21 Oct 53			03 Jun 63	17 Oct 67
B-47E-10-LM	51-15811	450-157-35	8	n/a	n/a	28 Sep 53	07 Oct 53		17 Sep 57		
	51-15812	450-157-35	9	n/a	n/a	30 Sep 53	23 Oct 53			08 Jan 63	17 Oct 67
B-47E	51-15813 to 51-15820	450-157-35 450-157-35	canceled								
RB-47E-10-BW	51-15821	450-158-36	4500627	20 Oct 53	18 Dec 53	22 Jan 54	23 Jan 54			17 Oct 57	22 Jul 63
	51-15822	450-158-36	4500628	22 Oct 53	14 Jan 54	09 Feb 54	10 Feb 54			26 Oct 57	23 Jun 60
	51-15823	450-158-36	4500629	26 Oct 53	13 Jan 54	29 Jan 54	30 Jan 54			24 Oct 57	15 Apr 60
	51-15824	450-158-36	4500630	20 Oct 53	29 Dec 53	13 Jan 54	16 Jan 54			31 Oct 57	20 Jun 60
	51-15825	450-158-36	4500631	28 Oct 53	06 Jan 54	23 Jan 54	23 Jan 54			23 Oct 57	06 Apr 60
	51-15826	450-158-36	4500632	30 Oct 53	13 Jan 54	23 Jan 54	23 Jan 54			19 Oct 57	25 Mar 60
	51-15827	450-158-36	4500633	05 Nov 53	02 Feb 54	18 Feb 54	18 Feb 54			20 Oct 57	29 Mar 60
RB-47E-15-BW	51-15828	450-158-36	4500634	03 Nov 53	19 Jan 54	20 Feb 54	22 Mar 54			30 Oct 57	n/a
	51-15829	450-158-36	4500635	09 Nov 53	14 Jan 54	08 Feb 54	09 Feb 54			14 Oct 57	n/a
	51-15830	450-158-36	4500636	11 Nov 53	23 Jan 54	10 Feb 54	12 Feb 54			31 Oct 57	n/a
	51-15831	450-158-36	4500637	13 Nov 53	23 Jan 54	10 Feb 54	12 Feb 54			28 Oct 57	n/a
	51-15832	450-158-36	4500638	13 Nov 53	23 Jan 54	09 Feb 54	10 Feb 54			25 Oct 57	n/a
	51-15833	450-158-36	4500639	18 Nov 53	27 Jan 54	08 Feb 54	10 Feb 54			24 Oct 57	n/a
	51-15834	450-158-36	4500640	20 Nov 53	03 Feb 54	12 Feb 54	12 Feb 54			30 Oct 57	20 Jun 60

MDS and Block Number	Serial Number	Model Number	Const. Number	Roll Out Date	First Flight Date	MIRR Date	USAF Fly Away	New MDS	Out of Service	MASDC Input Date	MASDC Output Date
RB-47E-15-BW	51-15835	450-158-36	4500641	23 Nov 53	27 Jan 54	12 Feb 54	12 Feb 54			18 Oct 57	16 Mar 60
	51-15836	450-158-36	4500642	30 Nov 53	17 Feb 54	03 Mar 54	05 Mar 54			24 Oct 57	11 Apr 60
	51-15837	450-158-36	4500643	01 Dec 53	01 Feb 54	16 Feb 54	17 Feb 54			25 Oct 57	21 Jul 60
	51-15838	450-158-36	4500644	02 Dec 53	02 Feb 54	16 Feb 54	17 Feb 54			17 Oct 57	16 Mar 60
	51-15839	450-158-36	4500645	04 Dec 53	15 Feb 54	01 Mar 54	05 Mar 54			02 Nov 57	01 Jun 60
	51-15840	450-158-36	4500646	07 Dec 53	15 Dec 53	03 Mar 54	05 Mar 54			19 Oct 57	25 Mar 60
	51-15841	450-158-36	4500647	09 Dec 53	03 Jan 54	18 Feb 54	18 Feb 54			25 Oct 57	01 Jul 60
	51-15842	450-158-36	4500648	11 Dec 53	16 Feb 54	09 Mar 54	02 Apr 53			23 Oct 57	06 Apr 60
	51-15843	450-158-36	4500649	15 Dec 53	18 Feb 54	10 Mar 54	15 Mar 54			31 Oct 57	25 Jul 60
	51-15844	450-158-36	4500650	16 Dec 53	18 Feb 54	26 Mar 54	27 Mar 54			01 Nov 57	25 Jan 61
	51-15845	450-158-36	4500651	18 Dec 53	25 Feb 54	01 Apr 54	02 Apr 54			17 Jun 58	06 Dec 60
	51-15846	450-158-36	4500652	21 Dec 53	23 Feb 54	30 Mar 54	22 Mar 54			04 Nov 57	25 Jan 61
	51-15847	450-158-36	4500653	22 Dec 53	25 Feb 54	15 Mar 54	16 Mar 54			18 Oct 57	21 Mar 60
	51-15848	450-158-36	4500654	28 Dec 53	01 Mar 54	18 Mar 54	22 Mar 54			30 Oct 57	15 Jun 60
	51-15849	450-158-36	4500655	30 Dec 53	23 Feb 54	24 Mar 54	26 Mar 54			23 Jun 58	06 Dec 60
	51-15850	450-158-36	4500656	04 Jan 54	04 Mar 54	17 Mar 54	22 Mar 54			02 Nov 57	02 May 60
	51-15851	450-158-36	4500657	06 Jan 54	05 Mar 54	22 Mar 54	22 Mar 54			26 May 58	18 Jan 61
	51-15852	450-158-36	4500658	08 Jan 54	08 Mar 54	23 Mar 54	26 Mar 54			04 Apr 58	04 Aug 60
	51-15853	450-158-36	4500659	12 Jan 54	11 Mar 54	26 Mar 54	27 Mar 54			04 Apr 58	11 Oct 60
B-47E-75-BW	51-17368	450-157-35	4500660	14 Jul 53	23 Sep 53	15 Oct 53	16 Oct 53		06 Feb 63		
	51-17369	450-157-35	4500661	15 Jul 53	24 Sep 53	20 Oct 53	23 Oct 53			26 May 61	27 Jun 61
	51-17370	450-157-35	4500662	16 Jul 53	16 Sep 53	23 Sep 53	23 Sep 53			07 Jun 61	13 Jan 64
	51-17371	450-157-35	4500663	17 Jul 53	16 Sep 53	07 Oct 53	08 Oct 53			20 Mar 63	17 Oct 67
	51-17372	450-157-35	4500664	20 Jul 53	24 Sep 53	19 Oct 53	21 Oct 53			07 Mar 63	16 Jan 64
	51-17373	450-157-35	4500665	21 Jul 53	18 Sep 53	20 Oct 53	23 Oct 53			06 Mar 63	17 Oct 67
	51-17374	450-157-35	4500666	23 Jul 53	09 Oct 53	06 Nov 53	09 Nov 53			22 Mar 61	10 May 61
	51-17375	450-157-35	4500667	24 Jul 53	22 Sep 53	27 Oct 53	27 Oct 53			29 Mar 61	04 May 61
	51-17376	450-157-35	4500668	27 Jul 53	30 Sep 53	20 Oct 53	23 Oct 53			18 Jan 63	17 Oct 67
	51-17377	450-157-35	4500669	28 Jul 53	24 Sep 53	16 Oct 53	17 Oct 53			07 Jun 61	24 Mar 64
	51-17378	450-157-35	4500670	29 Jul 53	09 Oct 53	09 Nov 53	11 Nov 53			18 Feb 63	17 Oct 67
	51-17379	450-157-35	4500671	30 Jul 53	01 Oct 53	20 Oct 53	30 Oct 53			29 Jan 63	17 Oct 67
	51-17380	450-157-35	4500672	31 Jul 53	29 Sep 53	12 Oct 53	13 Oct 53			01 Jun 61	10 Apr 64
	51-17381	450-157-35	4500673	03 Aug 53	08 Oct 53	05 Nov 53	25 Nov 53			15 Feb 63	17 Oct 67
	51-17382	450-157-35	4500674	05 Aug 53	02 Oct 53	09 Nov 53	18 Dec 53			04 Jan 63	17 Oct 67
	51-17383	450-157-35	4500675	06 Aug 53	02 Oct 53	09 Nov 53	10 Nov 53			08 Jan 63	17 Oct 67
	51-17384	450-157-35	4500676	07 Aug 53	16 Oct 53	10 Nov 53	11 Nov 53			20 Feb 63	17 Oct 67
	51-17385	450-157-35	4500677	10 Aug 53	13 Oct 53	06 Nov 53	09 Nov 53		20 Jul 54		
	51-17386	450-157-35	4500678	23 Jan 54	24 Nov 53	30 Nov 53	04 Dec 53			07 Mar 63	17 Oct 67
B-47E-1-DT	52-0019	450-157-35	43634	n/a	n/a	28 Apr 53	13 Jul 53			14 May 62	17 Oct 67
	52-0020	450-157-35	43635	n/a	n/a	08 May 53	22 Jul 53		19 Apr 61		
	52-0021	450-157-35	43636	n/a	n/a	19 May 53	31 Jul 53			28 Feb 63	17 Oct 67
	52-0022	450-157-35	43637	n/a	n/a	28 May 53	13 Aug 53			29 Mar 61	04 May 61
	52-0023	450-157-35	43638	n/a	n/a	08 Jun 53	21 Aug 53		08 Feb 54		
	52-0024	450-157-35	43639	n/a	n/a	16 Jun 53	28 Aug 53			04 Jun 63	17 Oct 67
	52-0025	450-157-35	43640	n/a	n/a	24 Jun 53	10 Sep 53			08 Mar 63	17 Oct 67
	52-0026	450-157-35	43641	n/a	n/a	01 Jul 53	17 Sep 53			28 Jan 63	17 Oct 67
	52-0027	450-157-35	43642	n/a	n/a	09 Jul 53	25 Sep 53			08 Mar 63	17 Oct 67
	52-0028	450-157-35	43643	n/a	n/a	16 Jul 53	30 Sep 53			14 Jan 63	17 Oct 67
B-47E-5-DT	52-0029	450-157-35	43644	n/a	n/a	22 Jul 53	08 Oct 53		05 Jan 55		
	52-0030	450-157-35	43645	n/a	n/a	29 Jul 53	15 Oct 53			04 Jan 63	17 Oct 67
	52-0031	450-157-35	43646	n/a	n/a	04 Aug 53	21 Oct 53	EB-47L		18 Dec 64	14 Jan 69
	52-0032	450-157-35	43647	n/a	n/a	10 Aug 53	26 Oct 53			16 Feb 63	17 Oct 67
	52-0033	450-157-35	43648	n/a	n/a	14 Aug 53	30 Oct 53	EB-47L		04 Mar 65	13 Dec 68
	52-0034	450-157-35	43649	n/a	n/a	01 Sep 53	04 Nov 53	EB-47L		25 Mar 65	14 Jan 69
	52-0035	450-157-35	43650	n/a	n/a	04 Sep 53	09 Nov 53	EB-47L		26 Feb 65	13 Dec 68
	52-0036	450-157-35	43651	n/a	n/a	10 Sep 53	12 Nov 53			05 Jul 60	09 Feb 61
	52-0037	450-157-35	43652	n/a	n/a	15 Sep 53	17 Nov 53			06 Jul 60	10 Feb 61
	52-0038	450-157-35	43653	n/a	n/a	18 Sep 53	20 Nov 53	EB-47L		26 Mar 65	14 Jan 69
	52-0039	450-157-35	43654	n/a	n/a	23 Sep 53	25 Nov 53			07 Feb 62	17 Oct 67
	52-0040	450-157-35	43655	n/a	n/a	28 Sep 53	30 Nov 53			13 Jun 63	17 Oct 67
	52-0041	450-157-35	43656	n/a	n/a	30 Sep 53	03 Dec 53	EB-47L		30 Nov 64	02 Oct 68
B-47E-10-DT	52-0042	450-157-35	43657	n/a	n/a	05 Oct 53	07 Dec 53			11 Jan 63	17 Oct 67
	52-0043	450-157-35	43658	n/a	n/a	07 Oct 53	10 Dec 53			23 Aug 60	11 May 61
	52-0044	450-157-35	43659	n/a	n/a	12 Oct 53	15 Dec 53			10 Mar 60	24 May 60
	52-0045	450-157-35	43660	n/a	n/a	14 Oct 53	17 Dec 53		28 Feb 55		
	52-0046	450-157-35	43661	n/a	n/a	16 Oct 53	21 Dec 53		16 Mar 55		
	52-0047	450-157-35	43662	n/a	n/a	21 Oct 53	24 Dec 53		26 Sep 60		
	52-0048	450-157-35	43663	n/a	n/a	23 Oct 53	29 Dec 53			11 Apr 61	15 May 61
	52-0049	450-157-35	43664	n/a	n/a	28 Oct 53	31 Dec 53		15 Jan 57		
	52-0050	450-157-35	43665	n/a	n/a	30 Oct 53	06 Jan 54			31 Jul 62	18 Oct 67
	52-0051	450-157-35	43666	n/a	n/a	03 Nov 53	08 Jan 54		03 May 63		
	52-0052	450-157-35	43667	n/a	n/a	05 Nov 53	12 Jan 54			31 Jan 63	18 Oct 67
	52-0053	450-157-35	43668	n/a	n/a	09 Nov 53	15 Jan 54		22 Feb 54		
	52-0054	450-157-35	43669	n/a	n/a	11 Nov 53	19 Jan 54		27 May 55		
	52-0055	450-157-35	43751	n/a	n/a	13 Nov 53	21 Jan 54			08 Mar 63	18 Oct 67
	52-0056	450-157-35	43752	n/a	n/a	17 Nov 53	25 Jan 54			08 Feb 63	18 Oct 67
	52-0057	450-157-35	43753	n/a	n/a	19 Nov 53	27 Jan 54			19 Dec 62	18 Oct 67
	52-0058	450-157-35	43754	n/a	n/a	23 Nov 53	29 Jan 54			08 Feb 63	18 Oct 67
B-47E-15-DT	52-0059	450-157-35	43755	n/a	n/a	25 Nov 53	03 Feb 54	EB-47L		24 Mar 65	14 Jan 69
	52-0060	450-157-35	43756	n/a	n/a	30 Nov 53	05 Feb 54			13 May 64	09 Jul 68
	52-0061	450-157-35	43757	n/a	n/a	02 Dec 53	09 Feb 54	EB-47L		01 Dec 64	02 Oct 68
	52-0062	450-157-35	43758	n/a	n/a	04 Dec 53	11 Feb 54			11 Feb 63	18 Oct 67
	52-0063	450-157-35	43759	n/a	n/a	08 Dec 53	15 Jan 54			07 Jun 61	16 Mar 64
	52-0064	450-157-35	43760	n/a	n/a	10 Dec 53	17 Feb 54			13 Jun 61	31 Mar 64
	52-0065	450-157-35	43761	n/a	n/a	14 Dec 53	19 Feb 54			14 Aug 64	09 Jul 68
	52-0066	450-157-35	43762	n/a	n/a	16 Dec 53	23 Feb 54	EB-47L		30 Nov 64	02 Oct 68
	52-0067	450-157-35	43763	n/a	n/a	18 Dec 53	25 Feb 54	EB-47L		24 Feb 65	13 Dec 68
	52-0068	450-157-35	43764	n/a	n/a	22 Dec 53	26 Feb 54			31 Jan 63	18 Oct 67
	52-0069	450-157-35	43765	n/a	n/a	24 Dec 53	03 Mar 54	EB-47L		01 Dec 64	03 Oct 68
	52-0070	450-157-35	43766	n/a	n/a	29 Dec 53	05 Mar 54		03 Jan 56		
	52-0071	450-157-35	43767	n/a	n/a	31 Dec 53	9-Maar-54	EB-47L		26 Feb 65	13 Dec 68
	52-0072	450-157-35	43768	n/a	n/a	05 Jan 54	11 Mar 54			25 May 61	10 Jul 61

MDS and Block Number	Serial Number	Model Number	Const. Number	Roll Out Date	First Flight Date	MIRR Date	USAF Fly Away	New MDS	Out of Service	MASDC Input Date	MASDC Output Date
B-47E-15-DT	52-0073	450-157-35	43769	n/a	n/a	07 Jan 54	15 Mar 54			29 May 61	19 Mar 68
	52-0074	450-157-35	43770	n/a	n/a	11 Jan 54	17 Mar 54			21 Jan 63	18 Oct 67
	52-0075	450-157-35	43771	n/a	n/a	13 Jan 54	19 Mar 54			26 Apr 63	18 Oct 67
	52-0076	450-157-35	43772	n/a	n/a	15 Jan 54	23 Mar 54			08 Jul 60	07 Feb 61
	52-0077	450-157-35	43773	n/a	n/a	19 Jan 54	25 Mar 54			05 Jun 63	18 Oct 67
	52-0078	450-157-35	43774	n/a	n/a	21 Jan 54	29 Mar 54	EB-47L		01 Dec 64	14 Jan 69
	52-0079	450-157-35	43775	n/a	n/a	25 Jan 54	31 Mar 54			28 Sep 60	10 May 61
	52-0080	450-157-35	43776	n/a	n/a	27 Jan 54	02 Apr 54			22 Jun 61	18 Oct 67
	52-0081	450-157-35	43777	n/a	n/a	29 Jan 54	06 Apr 54	EB-47L		12 Mar 65	13 Dec 68
B-47E-20-DT	52-0082	450-157-35	43778	n/a	n/a	02 Feb 54	08 Apr 54	EB-47L		23 Nov 64	02 Oct 68
	52-0083	450-157-35	43779	n/a	n/a	04 Feb 54	12 Apr 54		25 Nov 54		
	52-0084	450-157-35	43780	n/a	n/a	08 Feb 54	14 Apr 54			12 Feb 65	16 Oct 68
	52-0085	450-157-35	43781	n/a	n/a	10 Feb 54	16 Apr 54			26 May 61	13 Jul 61
	52-0086	450-157-35	43782	n/a	n/a	12 Feb 54	20 Apr 54	EB-47L		24 Feb 65	13 Dec 68
	52-0087	450-157-35	43783	n/a	n/a	16 Feb 54	22 Apr 54			12 Mar 63	18 Oct 67
	52-0088	450-157-35	43784	n/a	n/a	18 Feb 54	26 Apr 54			14 Apr 61	n/a
	52-0089	450-157-35	43785	n/a	n/a	22 Feb 54	28 Apr 54			13 Jan 63	18 Oct 67
	52-0090	450-157-35	43786	n/a	n/a	24 Feb 54	30 Apr 54			13 Jun 60	07 Feb 61
	52-0091	450-157-35	43787	n/a	n/a	26 Feb 54	04 May 54			12 Feb 65	16 Oct 68
	52-0092	450-157-35	43788	n/a	n/a	02 Mar 54	06 May 54		31 Mar 60		
	52-0093	450-157-35	43789	n/a	n/a	04 Mar 54	10 May 54			19 Aug 60	13 Feb 61
	52-0094	450-157-35	43790	n/a	n/a	08 Mar 54	12 May 54			30 Jan 63	18 Oct 67
	52-0095	450-157-35	43791	n/a	n/a	10 Mar 54	14 May 54			03 Jan 63	18 Oct 67
	52-0096	450-157-35	43792	n/a	n/a	12 Mar 54	17 May 54			19 Apr 63	18 Oct 67
	52-0097	450-157-35	43793	n/a	n/a	16 Mar 54	19 May 54			08 Mar 63	18 Oct 67
	52-0098	450-157-35	43794	n/a	n/a	18 Mar 54	21 May 54			05 Feb 63	18 Oct 67
	52-0099	450-157-35	43795	n/a	n/a	22 Mar 54	25 May 54	EB-47L		04 Mar 65	13 Dec 68
	52-0100	450-157-35	43796	n/a	n/a	24 Mar 54	27 May 54			12 Mar 63	18 Oct 67
	52-0101	450-157-35	43797	n/a	n/a	26 Mar 54	28 May 54			12 Apr 63	18 Oct 67
	52-0102	450-157-35	43798	n/a	n/a	30 Mar 54	02 Jun 54		21 Mar 62		
	52-0103	450-157-35	43799	n/a	n/a	01 Apr 54	04 Jun 54			13 Mar 63	18 Oct 67
	52-0104	450-157-35	43800	n/a	n/a	05 Apr 54	08 Jun 54			01 Jun 61	18 Jul 61
	52-0105	450-157-35	43801	n/a	n/a	04 Apr 54	10 Jun 54	EB-47L		24 Mar 65	14 Jan 69
	52-0106	450-157-35	43802	n/a	n/a	09 Apr 54	14 Jun 54			10 Jan 63	18 Oct 67
	52-0107	450-157-35	43803	n/a	n/a	13 Apr 54	14 Jun 54			01 Jun 60	07 Feb 61
	52-0108	450-157-35	43804	n/a	n/a	15 Apr 54	18 Jun 54		17 Nov 59		
	52-0109	450-157-35	43805	n/a	n/a	20 Apr 54	22 Jun 54			24 May 60	30 Jan 61
	52-0110	450-157-35	43806	n/a	n/a	22 Apr 54	24 Jun 54			03 May 60	02 Jun 60
	52-0111	450-157-35	43807	n/a	n/a	26 Apr 54	28 Jun 54			26 Apr 60	03 May 60
B-47E-25-DT	52-0112	450-157-35	43808	n/a	n/a	28 Apr 54	30 Jun 54			14 Apr 60	03 May 60
	52-0113	450-157-35	43809	n/a	n/a	30 Apr 54	02 Jul 54			07 Apr 60	15 May 60
	52-0114	450-157-35	43810	n/a	n/a	04 May 54	07 Jul 54			05 Apr 60	07 Jun 60
	52-0115	450-157-35	43811	n/a	n/a	06 May 54	12 Jul 54		20 Apr 60		
	52-0116	450-157-35	43812	n/a	n/a	10 May 54	14 Jul 54			19 May 60	07 Jun 60
	52-0117	450-157-35	43813	n/a	n/a	12 May 54	19 Jul 54			19 Apr 60	03 May 60
	52-0118	450-157-35	43814	n/a	n/a	17 May 54	21 Jul 54			12 Apr 60	05 May 60
	52-0119	450-157-35	43815	n/a	n/a	19 May 54	23 Jul 54			31 Jul 62	18 Oct 67
	52-0120	450-157-35	43816	n/a	n/a	24 May 54	28 Jul 54			18 May 60	01 Jul 60
	52-0146	450-157-35	44000	n/a	n/a	27 May 54	30 Jul 54		18 Jun 59		
	52-0147	450-157-35	44001	n/a	n/a	01 Jun 54	04 Aug 54			27 Feb 63	18 Oct 67
	52-0148	450-157-35	44002	n/a	n/a	04 Jun 54	09 Aug 54			21 Jan 65	16 Oct 68
	52-0149	450-157-35	44003	n/a	n/a	08 Jun 54	12 Aug 54			03 Feb 66	27 Jan 69
	52-0150	450-157-35	44004	n/a	n/a	11 Jun 54	17 Aug 54			05 Nov 65	23 Oct 68
	52-0151	450-157-35	44005	n/a	n/a	16 Jun 54	20 Aug 54		31 Oct 56		
	52-0152	450-157-35	44006	n/a	n/a	18 Jun 54	25 Aug 54			04 Feb 63	18 Oct 67
	52-0153	450-157-35	44007	n/a	n/a	23 Jun 54	30 Aug 54			13 Feb 63	18 Oct 67
	52-0154	450-157-35	44008	n/a	n/a	29 Jun 54	02 Sep 54	EB-47L		19 Nov 64	02 Oct 68
	52-0155	450-157-35	44009	n/a	n/a	01 Jul 54	08 Sep 54			05 Feb 63	18 Oct 67
	52-0156	450-157-35	44010	n/a	n/a	07 Jul 54	13 Sep 54			31 Jul 62	30 Sep 68
	52-0157	450-157-35	44011	n/a	n/a	12 Jul 54	16 Sep 54			07 Oct 65	23 Oct 68
	52-0158	450-157-35	44012	n/a	n/a	15 Jul 54	22 Sep 54		17 Aug 64		
	52-0159	450-157-35	44013	n/a	n/a	20 Jul 54	27 Sep 54		24 Aug 64		
	52-0160	450-157-35	44014	n/a	n/a	23 Jul 54	30 Sep 54		21 Jul 65		
	52-0161	450-157-35	44015	n/a	n/a	28 Jul 54	05 Oct 54			10 Jan 66	27 Jan 69
	52-0162	450-157-35	44016	n/a	n/a	02 Aug 54	08 Oct 54			18 Jan 66	27 Jan 69
	52-0163	450-157-35	44017	n/a	n/a	05 Aug 54	13 Oct 54			13 May 64	09 Jul 68
	52-0164	450-157-35	44018	n/a	n/a	10 Aug 54	18 Oct 54			10 Feb 65	16 Oct 68
	52-0165	450-157-35	44019	n/a	n/a	13 Aug 54	21 Oct 54			04 Jan 66	27 Jan 69
	52-0166	450-157-35	44020	n/a	n/a	18 Aug 54	26 Oct 54		17 Aug 64		
	52-0167	450-157-35	44021	n/a	n/a	23 Aug 54	29 Oct 54			12 Jan 66	27 Jan 69
	52-0168	450-157-35	44022	n/a	n/a	28 Aug 54	04 Nov 54			26 Jan 66	27 Jan 69
	52-0169	450-157-35	44023	n/a	n/a	31 Aug 54	09 Nov 54			10 Jan 66	27 Jan 69
	52-0170	450-157-35	44024	n/a	n/a	03 Sep 54	12 Nov 54			09 Nov 65	22 Oct 68
	52-0171	450-157-35	44025	n/a	n/a	09 Sep 54	17 Nov 54		26 Feb 65		
	52-0172	450-157-35	44026	n/a	n/a	15 Sep 54	22 Nov 54			31 Jul 62	09 Jul 68
	52-0173	450-157-35	44027	n/a	n/a	20 Sep 54	26 Nov 54			18 Jan 63	18 Oct 67
	52-0174	450-157-35	44028	n/a	n/a	23 Sep 54	31 Nov 54			31 Jul 62	30 Sep 68
	52-0175	450-157-35	44029	n/a	n/a	28 Sep 54	06 Dec 54			31 Jul 62	30 Sep 68
	52-0176	450-157-35	44030	n/a	n/a	01 Oct 54	09 Dec 54			12 Jan 66	27 Jan 69
B-47E-30-DT	52-0177	450-157-35	44031	n/a	n/a	06 Oct 54	14 Dec 54			18 Jun 64	09 Jul 68
	52-0178	450-157-35	44032	n/a	n/a	11 Oct 54	17 Dec 54			23 Jun 64	30 Sep 68
	52-0179	450-157-35	44033	n/a	n/a	14 Oct 54	22 Dec 54		08 May 59		
	52-0180	450-157-35	44034	n/a	n/a	19 Oct 54	28 Dec 54	UB-47E GB-47E	25 Feb 58		
	52-0181	450-157-35	44035	n/a	n/a	22 Oct 54	30 Dec 54		27 Feb 58		
	52-0182	450-157-35	44036	n/a	n/a	27 Oct 54	05 Jan 55			18 Jun 64	11 Sep 68
	52-0183	450-157-35	44037	n/a	n/a	01 Nov 54	10 Jan 55			09 Dec 64	09 Jul 68
	52-0184	450-157-35	44038	n/a	n/a	04 Nov 54	13 Jan 55			07 Oct 65	23 Oct 68
	52-0185	450-157-35	44039	n/a	n/a	09 Nov 54	18 Jan 55		24 Aug 64		
	52-0186	450-157-35	44040	n/a	n/a	12 Nov 54	21 Jan 55		13 Dec 57		
	52-0187	450-157-35	44041	n/a	n/a	17 Nov 54	26 Jan 55			21 Jan 65	16 Oct 68
	52-0188	450-157-35	44042	n/a	n/a	22 Nov 54	31 Jan 55			12 Jun 64	30 Sep 68
	52-0189	450-157-35	44043	n/a	n/a	26 Nov 54	02 Feb 55			07 Oct 65	23 Oct 68
	52-0190	450-157-35	44044	n/a	n/a	01 Dec 54	07 Feb 55			21 Jul 64	11 Sep 68

MDS and Block Number	Serial Number	Model Number	Const. Number	Roll Out Date	First Flight Date	MIRR Date	USAF Fly Away	New MDS	Out of Service	MASDC Input Date	MASDC Output Date
B-47E-30-DT	52-0191	450-157-35	44045	n/a	n/a	06 Dec 54	10 Feb 55			21 Jun 64	09 Jul 68
	52-0192	450-157-35	44046	n/a	n/a	09 Dec 54	15 Feb 55			18 Jan 66	27 Jan 69
	52-0193	450-157-35	44047	n/a	n/a	14 Dec 54	18 Feb 55			10 Jan 66	27 Jan 69
	52-0194	450-157-35	44048	n/a	n/a	17 Dec 54	23 Feb 55			13 Jul 64	09 Jul 68
	52-0195	450-157-35	44049	n/a	n/a	23 Dec 54	28 Feb 55			01 Feb 66	27 Jan 69
	52-0196	450-157-35	44050	n/a	n/a	28 Dec 54	03 Mar 55			07 Mar 63	18 Oct 67
	52-0197	450-157-35	44051	n/a	n/a	04 Jan 55	08 Mar 55			11 Mar 63	18 Oct 67
	52-0198	450-157-35	44052	n/a	n/a	07 Jan 55	11 Mar 55			11 Feb 63	18 Oct 67
	52-0199	450-157-35	44053	n/a	n/a	12 Jan 55	16 Mar 55			03 Feb 66	27 Jan 69
	52-0200	450-157-35	44054	n/a	n/a	17 Jan 55	21 Mar 55	GB-47E	17 Mar 64		
	52-0201	450-157-35	44055	n/a	n/a	20 Jan 55	24 Mar 55			24 Jan 66	27 Jan 69
B-47E-10-LM	52-0202	450-157-35	10	n/a	n/a	09 Oct 53	28 Oct 53			09 Jan 62	18 Oct 67
	52-0203	450-157-35	11	n/a	n/a	09 Oct 53	06 Nov 53			25 Feb 63	18 Oct 67
	52-0204	450-157-35	12	n/a	n/a	26 Oct 53	11 Nov 53	EB-47L		12 Mar 65	14 Jan 69
	52-0205	450-157-35	13	n/a	n/a	21 Oct 53	05 Nov 53		03 Nov 59		
	52-0206	450-157-35	14	n/a	n/a	21 Oct 53	13 Nov 53			19 May 61	05 Jul 61
	52-0207	450-157-35	15	n/a	n/a	30 Oct 53	14 Nov 53			16 Jan 63	18 Oct 67
B-47E-15-LM	52-0208	450-157-35	16	n/a	n/a	11 Nov 53	23 Nov 53			04 Feb 65	24 Oct 68
	52-0209	450-157-35	17	n/a	n/a	19 Nov 53	01 Dec 53			13 Mar 63	19 Oct 67
	52-0210	450-157-35	18	n/a	n/a	24 Nov 53	01 Dec 53			16 May 61	29 Jun 61
	52-0211	450-157-35	19	n/a	n/a	13 Nov 53	24-11-53	EB-47L		18 Dec 64	14 Jan 69
	52-0212	450-157-35	20	n/a	n/a	24 Nov 53	23 Nov 53	EB-47L		26 Mar 65	14 Jan 69
	52-0213	450-157-35	21	n/a	n/a	23 Nov 53	01 Dec 53			03 Apr 61	08 May 61
	52-0214	450-157-35	22	n/a	n/a	07 Dec 53	15 Dec 53	EB-47L		27 May 63	14 Jan 69
	52-0215	450-157-35	23	n/a	n/a	30 Nov 53	15 Dec 53			05 Jul 60	27 Mar 61
	52-0216	450-157-35	24	n/a	n/a	01 Dec 53	17 Dec 53			13 Jan 65	16 Oct 68
	52-0217	450-157-35	25	n/a	n/a	23 Dec 53	07 Jan 54	EB-47L		18 Dec 64	14 Jan 69
	52-0218	450-157-35	26	n/a	n/a	17 Dec 53	31 Dec 53		21 Jan 60		
	52-0219	450-157-35	27	n/a	n/a	31 Dec 53	11 Jan 54			16 Sep 60	12 May 61
	52-0220	450-157-35	28	n/a	n/a	06 Jan 54	16 Jan 54	EB-47L		23 Nov 64	02 Oct 68
B-47E-20-LM	52-0221	450-157-35	29	n/a	n/a	21 Dec 53	25 Feb 54	JB-47E		18 Dec 61	04 Feb 64
	52-0222	450-157-35	30	n/a	n/a	23 Dec 53	31 Dec 53			15 Jun 60	09 Feb 61
	52-0223	450-157-35	31	n/a	n/a	14 Jan 54	01 Feb 54			01 Jun 64	10 Sep 68
	52-0224	450-157-35	32	n/a	n/a	12 Jan 54	25 Jan 54	EB-47L		19 Nov 64	02 Oct 68
	52-0225	450-157-35	33	n/a	n/a	31 Dec 53	16 Jan 54		09 Dec 58		
	52-0226	450-157-35	34	n/a	n/a	16 Jan 54	29 Jan 54			11 Apr 61	15 May 61
	52-0227	450-157-35	35	n/a	n/a	22 Jan 54	06 Feb 54	GB-47E	12 Nov 64		
	52-0228	450-157-35	36	n/a	n/a	28 Jan 54	10 Feb 54			23 Jan 63	19 Oct 67
	52-0229	450-157-35	37	n/a	n/a	03 Feb 54	16 Mar 54		21 Jun 54		
	52-0230	450-157-35	38	n/a	n/a	20 Jan 54	11 Feb 54			15 Oct 65	23 Oct 68
	52-0231	450-157-35	39	n/a	n/a	29 Jan 54	11 Feb 54			21 Jan 63	19 Oct 67
	52-0232	450-157-35	40	n/a	n/a	01 Feb 54	04 Mar 54		09 Dec 59		
	52-0233	450-157-35	41	n/a	n/a	29 Jan 54	11 Feb 54			27 Jan 65	06 Oct 68
	52-0234	450-157-35	42	n/a	n/a	04 Feb 54	08 Mar 54			27 Oct 65	23 Oct 68
	52-0235	450-157-35	43	n/a	04 Jan 54	26 Feb 54	10 Mar 54		15 Apr 58		
B-47E-25-LM	52-0236	450-157-35	44	n/a	n/a	26 Feb 54	22 Mar 54			11 Jun 63	19 Oct 67
	52-0237	450-157-35	45	n/a	n/a	26 Feb 54	16 Jun 54			05 May 60	01 Jul 60
	52-0238	450-157-35	46	n/a	n/a	26 Feb 54	25 Mar 54			26 Apr 63	19 Oct 67
	52-0239	450-157-35	47	n/a	n/a	26 Feb 54	31 Mar 54			14 Mar 63	19 Oct 67
	52-0240	450-157-35	48	n/a	n/a	26 Feb 54	27 Mar 54			23 May 61	29 Jun 61
	52-0241	450-157-35	49	n/a	n/a	22 Mar 54	01 Apr 54		04 Dec 57		
	52-0242	450-157-35	50	n/a	n/a				31 Jan 58		
	52-0243	450-157-35	51	n/a	n/a	31 Mar 54	14 Apr 54			24 May 63	19 Oct 67
	52-0244	450-157-35	52	n/a	n/a	31 Mar 54	08 Apr 54		21 Mar 58		
	52-0245	450-157-35	53	n/a	n/a	31 Mar 54	13 Apr 54			11 Jun 63	19 Oct 67
	52-0246	450-157-35	54	n/a	n/a	31 Mar 54	27 Apr 54			09 Dec 64	09 Jul 68
	52-0247	450-157-35	55	n/a	n/a	31 Mar 54	13 Apr 54		16 Dec 58		
	52-0248	450-157-35	56	n/a	n/a	31 Mar 54	23 Apr 54			17 May 63	19 Oct 67
	52-0249	450-157-35	57	n/a	n/a	31 Mar 54	13 May 54			03 Aug 60	04 Jan 61
	52-0250	450-157-35	58	n/a	n/a	26 Feb 54	14 Apr 54		20 May 59		
	52-0251	450-157-35	59	n/a	n/a	31 Mar 54	22 Apr 54		20 May 59		
	52-0252	450-157-35	60	n/a	n/a	22 Apr 54	04 May 54		18 May 59		
	52-0253	450-157-35	61	n/a	n/a	01 May 54	08 May 54			17 Jun 60	09 Feb 61
	52-0254	450-157-35	62	n/a	n/a	12 Jul 54	20 Jul 54		31 Mar 60		
	52-0255	450-157-35	63	n/a	n/a	30 Mar 54	08 Apr 54		18 May 59		
	52-0256	450-157-35	64	n/a	n/a	01 Apr 54	12 Apr 54		19 May 59		
	52-0257	450-157-35	65	n/a	n/a	12 Apr 54	22 Apr 54			07 Jun 60	13 Feb 61
	52-0258	450-157-35	66	n/a	n/a	14 Apr 54	05 May 54		18 May 59		
	52-0259	450-157-35	67	n/a	n/a	26 Apr 54	09 May 54		30 May 60		
	52-0260	450-157-35	68	n/a	n/a	17 Apr 54	04 May 54			02 Jun 60	13 Feb 61
B-47E-30-LM	52-0261	450-157-35	69	n/a	n/a	08 Apr 54	04 Jun 54			21 Apr 60	06 May 60
	52-0262	450-157-35	70	n/a	n/a	27 Apr 54	05 May 54			04 May 60	01 Jul 60
	52-0263	450-157-35	71	n/a	n/a	19 Apr 54	04 May 54			20 Jun 60	14 Feb 61
	52-0264	450-157-35	72	n/a	n/a	21 Apr 54	04 May 54			17 May 60	01 Jul 60
	52-0265	450-157-35	73	n/a	n/a	01 May 54	10 May 54			28 Mar 60	13 May 60
	52-0266	450-157-35	74	n/a	n/a	04 May 54	17 May 54			05 Aug 60	08 Mar 61
	52-0267	450-157-35	75	n/a	n/a	23 Apr 54	05 May 54			10 May 60	14 Jul 60
	52-0268	450-157-35	76	n/a	n/a	01 May 54	17 May 54		27 May 60		
	52-0269	450-157-35	77	n/a	n/a	01 May 54	08 May 54			22 Jun 60	16 Feb 61
	52-0270	450-157-35	78	n/a	n/a	26 Apr 54	06 May 54			09 Jun 60	14 Feb 61
	52-0271	450-157-35	79	n/a	n/a	27 May 54	08 Jun 54		19 May 60		
	52-0272	450-157-35	80	n/a	n/a	01 May 54	08 May 54			23 Jun 60	16 Feb 61
	52-0273	450-157-35	81	n/a	n/a	07 May 54	19 May 54			04 Apr 61	08 May 61
	52-0274	450-157-35	82	n/a	n/a	12 May 54	21 May 54			14 Jun 60	15 Feb 61
	52-0275	450-157-35	83	n/a	n/a	10 May 54	21 May 54			27 Jun 60	15 Feb 61
	52-0276	450-157-35	84	n/a	n/a	27 May 54	04 Jun 54			08 Jun 60	16 Feb 61
	52-0277	450-157-35	85	n/a	n/a	14 Jun 54	29 Jun 54		10 Feb 56		
	52-0278	450-157-35	86	n/a	n/a	25 May 54	03 Jun 54			28 May 61	17 Jul 61
	52-0279	450-157-35	87	n/a	n/a	27 May 54	02 Jun 54		21 May 59		
	52-0280	450-157-35	88	n/a	n/a	01 Jun 54	09 Jun 54			27 Jan 65	16 Oct 68
	52-0281	450-157-35	89	n/a	n/a	19 Jun 54	06 Jul 54		19 May 59		
	52-0282	450-157-35	90	n/a	n/a	01 Jun 54	11 Jun 54			10 Aug 60	17 Feb 61

MDS and Block Number	Serial Number	Model Number	Const. Number	Roll Out Date	First Flight Date	MIRR Date	USAF Fly Away	New MDS	Out of Service	MASDC Input Date	MASDC Output Date
B-47E-30-LM	52-0283	450-157-35	91	n/a	n/a	07 Jun 54	18 Jun 54		20 May 59		
	52-0284	450-157-35	92	n/a	n/a	09 Jun 54	29 Jun 54		19 Apr 60		
	52-0285	450-157-35	93	n/a	n/a	04 Jun 54	15 Jun 54		24 Sep 54		
	52-0286	450-157-35	94	n/a	n/a	18 Jun 54	06 Jul 54			11 May 60	04 Aug 60
	52-0287	450-157-35	95	n/a	n/a	07 Jun 54	16 Jun 54			12 Apr 60	17 May 60
	52-0288	450-157-35	96	n/a	n/a	12 Jul 54	30 Jul 54			12 May 60	26 Jan 61
	52-0289	450-157-35	97	n/a	n/a	11 Jun 54	22 Jun 54		26 Apr 60		
	52-0290	450-157-35	98	n/a	n/a	11 Jun 54	28 Jun 54		09 Jan 59		
	52-0291	450-157-35	99	n/a	n/a	19 Jul 54	19 Jul 54	EB-47L		01 Dec 64	14 Jan 69
	52-0292	450-157-35	100	n/a	n/a	18 Jun 54	21 Jul 54	EB-47L		24 Mar 65	14 Jan 69
B-47E-35-LM	52-0293	450-157-35	101	n/a	n/a	12 Jul 54	21 Jul 54			09 Feb 66	27 Jan 69
	52-0294	450-157-35	102	n/a	n/a	01 Jul 54	23 Jul 54			20 Jan 66	27 Jan 69
	52-0295	450-157-35	103	n/a	n/a	01 Jul 54	13 Jul 54			17 Aug 60	22 Feb 61
	52-0296	450-157-35	104	n/a	n/a	06 Jul 54	15 Jul 54		19 Aug 61		
	52-0297	450-157-35	105	n/a	n/a	01 Jul 54	19 Jul 54		09 Dec 58		
	52-0298	450-157-35	106	n/a	n/a	09 Aug 54	24 Aug 54	EB-47L		26 Mar 65	14 Jan 69
	52-0299	450-157-35	107	n/a	n/a	01 Jul 54	19 Jul 54			06 Apr 60	13 May 60
	52-0300	450-157-35	108	n/a	n/a	13 Jul 54	27 Jul 54			27 Apr 61	08 Jun 61
	52-0301	450-157-35	109	n/a	n/a	13 Jul 54	28 Jul 54		01 Dec 55		
	52-0302	450-157-35	110	n/a	n/a	30 Jul 54	10 Aug 54			25 Aug 60	09 May 61
	52-0303	450-157-35	111	n/a	n/a	16 Jul 54	09 Aug 54	EB-47L		12 Mar 65	13 Dec 68
	52-0304	450-157-35	112	n/a	n/a	21 Jul 54	04 Aug 54			17 May 60	31 Jan 61
	52-0305	450-157-35	113	n/a	n/a	26 Jul 54	15 Aug 54	EB-47L		26 Feb 65	14 Jan 69
	52-0306	450-157-35	114	n/a	n/a	26 Jul 54	04 Aug 54			18 Apr 61	20 Jun 61
	52-0307	450-157-35	115	n/a	n/a	02 Aug 54	11 Aug 54			13 Apr 60	10 May 60
	52-0308	450-157-35	116	n/a	n/a	02 Aug 54	11 Aug 54	EB-47L		24 Mar 65	14 Jan 69
	52-0309	450-157-35	117	n/a	n/a	10 Aug 54	27 Aug 54	EB-47L		12 Mar 65	14 Jan 69
	52-0310	450-157-35	118	n/a	n/a	18 Aug 54	30 Aug 54			09 Feb 66	27 Jan 69
	52-0311	450-157-35	119	n/a	n/a	10 Aug 54	20 Aug 54			07 Feb 66	27 Jan 69
	52-0312	450-157-35	120	n/a	n/a	01 Sep 54	11 Aug 54			17 Feb 67	30 Sep 68
	52-0313	450-157-35	121	n/a	n/a	04 Aug 54	26 Aug 54			18 Jan 66	27 Jan 69
	52-0314	450-157-35	122	n/a	n/a	05 Aug 54	20 Aug 54			19 Jan 65	16 Oct 68
	52-0315	450-157-35	123	n/a	n/a	13 Aug 54	20 Aug 54			09 Aug 63	30 Sep 68
	52-0316	450-157-35	124	n/a	n/a	17 Aug 54	27 Aug 54			12 Mar 63	30 Sep 68
	52-0317	450-157-35	125	n/a	n/a	01 Sep 54	08 Sep 54			04 Feb 65	16 Oct 68
	52-0318	450-157-35	126	n/a	n/a	16 Aug 54	25 Aug 54			20 Jan 65	16 Oct 68
	52-0319	450-157-35	127	n/a	n/a	02 Sep 54	08 Sep 54			15 Oct 65	23 Oct 68
	52-0320	450-157-35	128	n/a	n/a	03 Sep 54	11 Sep 54		04 Apr 59		
	52-0321	450-157-35	129	n/a	n/a	02 Sep 54	10 Sep 54		27 Mar 64		
	52-0322	450-157-35	130	n/a	n/a	07 Sep 54	22 Sep 54		24 Apr 58		
	52-0323	450-157-35	131	n/a	n/a	07 Sep 54	15 Sep 54			01 Apr 64	11 Sep 68
	52-0324	450-157-35	132	n/a	n/a	03 Sep 54	10 Sep 54			31 Jul 62	19 Oct 67
	52-0325	450-157-35	133	n/a	n/a	13 Sep 54	21 Sep 54			03 Feb 66	27 Jan 69
	52-0326	450-157-35	134	n/a	n/a	07 Sep 54	24 Sep 54			26 Oct 65	23 Oct 68
	52-0327	450-157-35	135	n/a	n/a	01 Oct 54	11 Oct 54			10 Feb 65	16 Oct 68
	52-0328	450-157-35	136	n/a	n/a	n/a	23 Sep 54			07 Oct 65	23 Oct 68
	52-0329	450-157-35	137	n/a	n/a	16 Sep 54	01 Oct 54			13 Jul 64	30 Sep 68
	52-0330	450-157-35	138	n/a	n/a	01 Oct 54	07 Oct 54			22 Apr 64	11 Sep 68
B-47E-40-LM	52-0331	450-157-35	139	n/a	n/a	07 Oct 54	19 Oct 54			08 Jun 64	10 Sep 68
	52-0332	450-157-35	140	n/a	n/a	n/a	23 Sep 54			07 Feb 66	27 Jan 69
	52-0333	450-157-35	141	n/a	n/a	01 Oct 54	08 Oct 54			03 Feb 65	24 Oct 68
	52-0334	450-157-35	142	n/a	n/a	01 Oct 54	08 Oct 54			13 Oct 65	23 Oct 68
	52-0335	450-157-35	143	n/a	n/a	04 Oct 54	08 Oct 54			31 Jul 62	19 Oct 67
	52-0336	450-157-35	144	n/a	n/a	04 Oct 54	12 Oct 54		21 Oct 55		
	52-0337	450-157-35	145	n/a	n/a	04 Oct 54	13 Oct 54			10 Jan 66	27 Jan 69
	52-0338	450-157-35	146	n/a	n/a	04 Oct 54	12 Oct 54			31 Jul 62	19 Oct 67
	52-0339	450-157-35	147	n/a	n/a	11 Oct 54	25 Oct 54		08 Dec 64		
	52-0340	450-157-35	148	n/a	n/a	19 Oct 54	03 Nov 54			12 Jan 65	16 Oct 68
	52-0341	450-157-35	149	n/a	n/a	29 Oct 54	04 Nov 54			19 Oct 64	09 Jul 68
	52-0342	450-157-35	150	n/a	n/a	06 Oct 54	01 Nov 54			07 Jul 64	30 Sep 68
	52-0343	450-157-35	151	n/a	n/a	01 Nov 54	06 Nov 54			14 Jul 64	30 Sep 68
	52-0344	450-157-35	152	n/a	n/a	02 Nov 54	19 Nov 54			18 Jan 65	16 Oct 68
	52-0345	450-157-35	153	n/a	n/a	01 Nov 54	05 Nov 54			01 Mar 63	09 Jul 68
	52-0346	450-157-35	154	n/a	n/a	n/a	09 Nov 54			07 Jan 65	16 Oct 68
	52-0347	450-157-35	155	n/a	n/a	06 Dec 54	17 Dec 54		15 Nov 61		
	52-0348	450-157-35	156	n/a	n/a	10 Nov 54	24 Nov 54			23 Nov 64	09 Jul 68
	52-0349	450-157-35	157	n/a	n/a	12 Nov 54	24 Nov 54			04 Feb 65	16 Oct 68
	52-0350	450-157-35	158	n/a	n/a	18 Nov 54	01 Dec 54			13 Oct 65	23 Oct 68
	52-0351	450-157-35	159	n/a	n/a	05 Nov 54	22 Nov 54			01 Feb 66	27 Jan 69
	52-0352	450-157-35	160	n/a	n/a	04 Nov 54	19 Nov 54			15 Dec 64	11 Sep 68
	52-0353	450-157-35	161	n/a	n/a	03 Nov 54	19 Nov 54			10 Jun 64	09 Jul 68
	52-0354	450-157-35	162	n/a	n/a	24 Nov 54	06 Dec 54			01 Feb 66	27 Jan 69
	52-0355	450-157-35	163	n/a	n/a	01 Dec 54	10 Dec 54			14 Jul 64	30 Sep 68
	52-0356	450-157-35	164	n/a	n/a	19 Nov 54	03 Dec 54			03 Feb 65	16 Oct 68
	52-0357	450-157-35	165	n/a	n/a	01 Dec 54	07 Dec 54			06 Jul 64	30 Sep 68
	52-0358	450-157-35	166	n/a	n/a	07 Dec 54	21 Dec 54			24 Jul 64	09 Jul 68
	52-0359	450-157-35	167	n/a	n/a	01 Dec 54	15 Dec 54			16 Nov 65	23 Oct 68
	52-0360	450-157-35	168	n/a	n/a	02 Dec 54	15 Dec 54			05 Nov 65	23 Oct 68
	52-0361	450-157-35	169	n/a	n/a	07 Dec 54	23 Dec 54			16 Nov 63	09 Jul 68
	52-0362	450-157-35	170	n/a	n/a	16 Dec 54	22 Dec 54			17 Jul 64	11 Sep 68
B-47E-45-LM	52-0363	450-157-35	171	n/a	n/a	03 Jan 55	13 Jan 55			14 Feb 63	19 Oct 67
	52-0364	450-157-35	172	n/a	n/a	06 Dec 54	15 Dec 54			11 Aug 64	11 Sep 68
	52-0365	450-157-35	173	n/a	n/a	03 Jan 55	14 Jan 55			06 Jan 66	27 Jan 69
	52-0366	450-157-35	174	n/a	n/a	10 Dec 54	23 Dec 54		06 Feb 64		
	52-0367	450-157-35	175	n/a	n/a	10 Dec 54	30 Dec 54			21 Oct 64	09 Jul 68
	52-0368	450-157-35	176	n/a	n/a	12 Jan 55	27 Jan 55			20 May 64	09 Jul 68
	52-0369	450-157-35	177	n/a	n/a	03 Jan 55	13 Jan 55		17 Nov 56		
	52-0370	450-157-35	178	n/a	n/a	08 Jan 55	26 Jan 55	JB-47E		05 Jul 67	27 Jan 69
	52-0371	450-157-35	179	n/a	n/a	03 Jan 55	13 Jan 55			05 Aug 64	09 Jul 68
	52-0372	450-157-35	180	n/a	n/a	03 Jan 55	12 Jan 55			13 May 64	10 Sep 68
	52-0373	450-157-35	181	n/a	n/a	07 Jan 55	02 Feb 55			23 Jul 64	09 Jul 68
	52-0374	450-157-35	182	n/a	n/a	11 Jan 55	27 Jan 55			14 Jan 66	28 Jan 69
	52-0375	450-157-35	183	n/a	n/a	08 Jan 55	07 Feb 55			19 Oct 65	23 Oct 68
	52-0376	450-157-35	184	n/a	n/a	14 Jan 55	07 Feb 55			04 Nov 65	23 Oct 68

MDS and Block Number	Serial Number	Model Number	Const. Number	Roll Out Date	First Flight Date	MIRR Date	USAF Fly Away	New MDS	Out of Service	MASDC Input Date	MASDC Output Date
B-47E-45-LM	52-0377	450-157-35	185	n/a	n/a	01 Feb 55	10 Feb 55			26 Jan 66	28 Jan 69
	52-0378	450-157-35	186	n/a	n/a	01 Feb 55	15 Feb 55			24 Mar 64	11 Sep 68
	52-0379	450-157-35	187	n/a	n/a	01 Mar 55	10 Mar 55			16 Dec 64	11 Sep 68
	52-0380	450-157-35	188	n/a	n/a	02 Feb 55	19 Feb 55			12 Feb 63	19 Oct 67
	52-0381	450-157-35	189	n/a	n/a	02 Feb 55	28 Feb 55			26 May 64	09 Jul 68
	52-0382	450-157-35	190	n/a	n/a	02 Feb 55	16 Feb 55			20 May 64	10 Sep 68
	52-0383	450-157-35	191	n/a	n/a	14 Feb 55	02 Mar 55			31 Jul 62	19 Oct 67
	52-0384	450-157-35	192	n/a	n/a	01 Feb 55	23 Feb 55			31 Jul 62	19 Oct 67
	52-0385	450-157-35	193	n/a	n/a	02 Mar 55	22 Mar 55			05 Aug 64	09 Jul 68
	52-0386	450-157-35	194	n/a	n/a	15 Feb 55	02 Mar 55		01 May 55		
	52-0387	450-157-35	195	n/a	n/a	10 Feb 55	28 Mar 55			13 Jul 64	30 Sep 68
	52-0388	450-157-35	196	n/a	n/a	08 Feb 55	02 Mar 55		05 Feb 58		
	52-0389	450-157-35	197	n/a	n/a	01 Mar 55	08 Mar 55	EB-47E JB-47E NB-47E		25 Feb 60	26 Jan 61
	52-0390	450-157-35	198	n/a	n/a	16 Feb 55	09 Mar 55		23 Jul 62		
	52-0391	450-157-35	199	n/a	n/a	03 Mar 55	23 Mar 55			30 Mar 64	11 Sep 68
	52-0392	450-157-35	200	n/a	n/a	03 Mar 55	22 Mar 55			02 Feb 65	16 Oct 68
	52-0393	450-157-35	201	n/a	n/a	02 Mar 55	12 Mar 55			31 Jan 63	19 Oct 67
B-47E-80-BW	52-0394	450-157-35	4500679	11 Aug 53	11 Jan 54	18 Aug 53	25 Mar 54	E-47E EB-47E			
	52-0395	450-157-35	4500680	12 Aug 53	05 Oct 53	13 Oct 53	16 Apr 54	E-47E EB-47E		05 Jan 65	13 Jan 69
	52-0396	450-157-35	4500681	13 Aug 53	22 Jan 54	20 Aug 53	30 Mar 54	E-47E EB-47E		21 May 64	02 Oct 68
	52-0397	450-157-35	4500682	14 Aug 53	11 Feb 54	25 Aug 53	01 Apr 54		02 Aug 55	11 Jun 64	13 Jan 69
	52-0398	450-157-35	4500683	18 Aug 53	28 Jan 54	24 Aug 53	01 Apr 54	E-47E EB-47E		21 Jan 65	13 Jan 69
	52-0399	450-157-35	4500684	19 Aug 53	01 Feb 54	27 Aug 53	02 Apr 54	E-47E EB-47E		21 May 64	02 Oct 68
	52-0400	450-157-35	4500685	20 Aug 53	05 Feb 54	27 Aug 53	01 Apr 54	E-47E EB-47E		05 Jun 64	13 Jan 69
	52-0401	450-157-35	4500686	21 Aug 53	09 Feb 54	28 Aug 53	31 Mar 54	E-47E EB-47E		25 Feb 65	13 Jan 69
	52-0402	450-157-35	4500687	25 Aug 53	08 Feb 54	31 Aug 53	02 Apr 54		23 Oct 58		
	52-0403	450-157-35	4500688	26 Aug 53	09 Feb 54	03 Sep 53	01 Apr 54	EB-47E		15 Dec 64	21 Jun 66
	52-0404	450-157-35	4500689	27 Aug 53	09 Feb 54	04 Sep 53	30 Mar 54			15 Oct 65	23 Oct 68
	52-0405	450-157-35	4500690	28 Aug 53	12 Feb 54	09 Sep 53	31 Mar 54	E-47E EB-47E		25 Feb 65	13 Jan 69
	52-0406	450-157-35	4500691	01 Sep 53	18 Feb 54	08 Sep 53	29 Apr 54	E-47E EB-47E		11 Jun 64	13 Jan 69
	52-0407	450-157-35	4500692	02 Sep 53	23 Feb 54	09 Sep 53	16 Apr 54	E-47E EB-47E		11 Jun 64	13 Jan 69
	52-0408	450-157-35	4500693	03 Sep 53	24 Feb 54	10 Sep 53	14 Apr 54	E-47E EB-47E		03 Dec 64	13 Jan 69
	52-0409	450-157-35	4500694	04 Sep 53	26 Feb 54	14 Sep 53	16 Apr 54	E-47E EB-47E		14 Jan 65	13 Jan 69
	52-0410	450-157-35	4500695	09 Sep 53	26 Feb 54	16 Sep 53	16 Apr 54	E-47E EB-47E	01 Oct 77	11 Feb 65	28 Aug 69
	52-0411	450-157-35	4500696	10 Sep 53	23 Feb 54	17 Sep 53	14 Apr 54	E-47E EB-47E		28 Jan 65	13 Jan 69
	52-0412	450-157-35	4500697	14 Sep 53	01 Apr 54	18 Sep 53	13 Apr 54	E-47E EB-47E	20 Dec 77	17 Feb 65	28 Aug 69
	52-0413	450-157-35	4500698	15 Sep 53	15 Mar 54	22 Sep 53	06 May 54	E-47E EB-47E		09 Jun 64	13 Jan 69
	52-0414	450-157-35	4500699	17 Sep 53	21 Apr 54	04 Nov 53	28 Apr 54	E-47E EB-47E		30 Jul 64	13 Jan 69
	52-0415	450-157-35	4500700	18 Sep 53	05 Mar 54	24 Sep 53	14 May 54	E-47E EB-47E		11 Feb 65	13 Jan 69
	52-0416	450-157-35	4500701	22 Sep 53	04 Mar 54	25 Sep 53	29 Apr 54	E-47E EB-47E		17 Dec 64	13 Jan 69
	52-0417	450-157-35	4500702	23 Sep 53	10 Mar 54	30 Sep 53	19 May 54	E-47E EB-47E		19 May 64	02 Oct 68
	52-0418	450-157-35	4500703	25 Sep 53	09 Mar 54	01 Oct 53	23 Apr 54	E-47E EB-47E		18 Jan 65	13 Jan 69
	52-0419	450-157-35	4500704	28 Sep 53	16 Mar 54	01 Oct 53	14 May 54	E-47E EB-47E		05 Jun 64	13 Jan 69
	52-0420	450-157-35	4500705	29 Sep 53	19 Mar 54	02 Oct 53	07 May 54	E-47E EB-47E		23 Feb 65	13 Dec 68
	52-0421	450-157-35	4500706	30 Sep 53	16 Mar 54	05 Oct 53	04 May 54		14 Jul 55		
	52-0422	450-157-35	4500707	01 Oct 53	01 Apr 54	06 Oct 53	16 Apr 54	E-47E EB-47E		03 Dec 64	13 Jan 69
	52-0423	450-157-35	4500708	05 Oct 53	17 Nov 53	10 Dec 53	23 Apr 54		31 Aug 61		
	52-0424	450-157-35	4500709	05 Oct 53	07 Apr 54	09 Oct 53	28 Apr 54	E-47E EB-47E		21 Jan 65	13 Jan 69
	52-0425	450-157-35	4500710	07 Oct 53	06 Apr 54	12 Oct 53	23 Apr 54	E-47E EB-47E		02 Sep 64	13 Jan 69
	52-0426	450-157-35	4500711	07 Oct 53	08 Apr 54	13 Oct 53	03 May 54	E-47E EB-47E		08 Dec 64	21 Jun 66
	52-0427	450-157-35	4500712	07 Oct 53	07 Apr 54	15 Oct 53	03 May 54	E-47E EB-47E		22 May 64	02 Oct 68
	52-0428	450-157-35	4500713	09 Oct 53	12 Apr 54	16 Oct 53	03 May 54	E-47E EB-47E		18 May 64	02 Oct 68
	52-0429	450-157-35	4500714	17 Oct 53	07 Apr 54	16 Oct 53	03 May 54	E-47E EB-47E		11 Jan 65	13 Jan 69
	52-0430	450-157-35	4500715	13 Oct 53	12 Apr 54	20 Oct 53	03 Mar 54	E-47E EB-47E		01 Feb 65	13 Dec 68
	52-0431	450-157-35	4500716	14 Oct 53	15 Apr 54	02 Nov 53	29 Apr 54	E-47E EB-47E		19 Feb 65	13 Dec 68
B-47E-85-BW	52-0432	450-157-35	4500717	16 Oct 53	07 Dec 53	17 Dec 53	21 May 54			10 Jun 64	10 Sep 68
	52-0433	450-157-35	4500718	19 Oct 53	15 Apr 54	02 Nov 53	14 May 54	E-47E EB-47E		15 Dec 64	13 Jan 69
	52-0434	450-157-35	4500719	21 Oct 53	15 Apr 54	02 Nov 53	14 May 54	E-47E EB-47E		14 Jan 65	13 Jan 69

MDS and Block Number	Serial Number	Model Number	Const. Number	Roll Out Date	First Flight Date	MIRR Date	USAF Fly Away	New MDS	Out of Service	MASDC Input Date	MASDC Output Date
B-47E-85-BW	52-0435	450-157-35	4500720	22 Oct 53	44 may 54	02 Nov 53	21 May 54	E-47E EB-47E	13 Sep 67		
	52-0436	450-157-35	4500721	26 Oct 53	08 Dec 53	17 Dec 53	20 May 54			18 May 64	11 Sep 68
	52-0437	450-157-35	4500722	27 Oct 53	04 May 54	05 Nov 53	18 May 54	E-47E EB-47E		21 May 64	02 Oct 68
	52-0438	450-157-35	4500723	29 Oct 53	04 May 54	12 Nov 53	20 May 54			28 Jul 64	09 Jul 68
	52-0439	450-157-35	4500724	30 Oct 53	11 Dec 53	04 Jan 54	19 May 54		07 Mar 57		
	52-0440	450-157-35	4500725	03 Nov 53	03 May 54	09 Nov 53	18 May 54	E-47E EB-47E		08 Dec 64	21 Jun 66
	52-0441	450-157-35	4500726	04 Nov 53	14 Dec 53	04 Jan 54	18 May 54	E-47E EB-47E		02 Sep 64	13 Jan 69
	52-0442	450-157-35	4500727	06 Nov 53	04 May 54	20 Nov 53	04 Jun 54			29 Jul 64	30 Sep 68
	52-0443	450-157-35	4500728	09 Nov 53	06 May 54	16 Nov 53	22 Jun 54			08 Feb 65	16 Oct 68
	52-0444	450-157-35	4500729	11 Nov 53	12 May 54	01 Dec 53	03 Jun 54			28 Jan 63	19 Oct 67
	52-0445	450-157-35	4500730	12 Nov 53	05 Jan 54	18 Jan 54	29 Oct 54			13 Jan 65	16 Oct 68
	52-0446	450-157-35	4500731	16 Nov 53	11 May 54	01 Dec 53	16 Jun 54	E-47E EB-47E		28 Jan 65	13 Jan 69
	52-0447	450-157-35	4500732	17 Nov 53	12 May 54	01 Dec 53	27 May 54	E-47E EB-47E		09 Jun 64	13 Jan 69
	52-0448	450-157-35	4500733	19 Nov 53	11 May 54	03 Dec 53	03 Jun 54			19 Nov 65	23 Oct 68
	52-0449	450-157-35	4500734	20 Nov 53	11 May 54	07 Dec 53	03 Jun 54			14 Feb 63	19 Oct 67
	52-0450	450-157-35	4500735	24 Nov 53	14 May 54	09 Dec 53	03 Jun 54		02 May 56		
	52-0451	450-157-35	4500736	25 Nov 53	12 May 54	10 Dec 53	26 May 54			13 Feb 63	19 Oct 67
	52-0452	450-157-35	4500737	01 Dec 53	19 May 54	14 Dec 53	26 May 54			02 Jun 64	11 Sep 68
	52-0453	450-157-35	4500738	02 Dec 53	23 Jan 54	28 Jan 54	16 Jun 54			29 Jan 63	19 Oct 67
	52-0454	450-157-35	4500739	04 Dec 53	14 May 54	16 Dec 53	26 May 54	E-47E EB-47E		19 Feb 65	13 Dec 68
	52-0455	450-157-35	4500740	07 Dec 53	27 May 54	18 Dec 53	23 Jun 54			02 Jun 64	11 Sep 68
	52-0456	450-157-35	4500741	09 Dec 53	03 Jun 54	22 Dec 53	17 Jul 54		05 Apr 57		
	52-0457	450-157-35	4500742	10 Dec 53	01 Jun 54	19 Jan 54	19 Jun 54			18 May 64	10 Sep 68
	52-0458	450-157-35	4500743	14 Dec 53	01 Jun 54	04 Jan 54	22 Jun 54		06 Dec 57		
	52-0459	450-157-35	4500744	15 Dec 53	02 Jun 54	06 Jan 54	21 Jun 54		10 Apr 62		
	52-0460	450-157-35	4500745	17 Dec 53	08 Jun 54	29 Dec 53	29 Jun 54		27 Apr 64		
	52-0461	450-157-35	4500746	18 Dec 53	14 Jun 54	29 Dec 53	02 Jul 54			04 Jan 66	13 Jan 69
	52-0462	450-157-35	4500747	21 Dec 53	10 Jun 54	06 Jan 54	12 Jul 54			24 Jun 63	04 Dec 63
	52-0463	450-157-35	4500748	23 Dec 53	10 Jun 54	08 Jan 54	26 Jun 54			11 Feb 65	16 Oct 68
	52-0464	450-157-35	4500749	28 Dec 53	16 Jun 54	08 Jan 54	15 Jul 54			12 Jan 65	16 Oct 68
	52-0465	450-157-35	4500750	30 Dec 53	18 Jun 54	11 Jan 54	15 Jul 54			06 Jan 66	13 Jan 69
	52-0466	450-157-35	4500751	03 Jan 54	17 Jun 54	25 Jan 54	21 Jul 54			14 Aug 66	09 Jul 68
	52-0467	450-157-35	4500752	05 Jan 54	22 Jun 54	25 Jan 54	22 Jul 54	E-47E EB-47E		05 Jun 64	13 Jan 69
	52-0468	450-157-35	4500753	07 Jan 54	22 Jun 54	19 Jan 54	16 Jul 54	E-47E EB-47E		08 Feb 65	13 Jan 69
	52-0469	450-157-35	4500754	08 Jan 54	22 Jun 54	25 Jan 54	22 Jul 54	E-47E EB-47E		09 Jun 64	13 Jan 69
B-47E-90-BW	52-0470	450-157-35	4500755	12 Jan 54	01 Jul 54	25 Jul 54	22 Jul 54		10 Apr 58		
	52-0471	450-157-35	4500756	14 Jan 54	02 Jul 54	25 Jan 54	05 Aug 54	E-47E EB-47E		25 Jan 65	13 Jan 69
	52-0472	450-157-35	4500757	15 Jan 54	30 Jun 54	01 Feb 54	06 Aug 54		01 Feb 63		
	52-0473	450-157-35	4500758	19 Jan 54	21 Jul 54	01 Feb 54	14 Aug 54			31 Jan 66	28 Jan 69
	52-0474	450-157-35	4500759	20 Jan 54	15 Jul 54	01 Feb 54	24 Aug 54			19 Nov 65	22 Oct 68
	52-0475	450-157-35	4500760	22 Jan 54	08 Jul 54	01 Feb 54	29 Jul 54		21 Apr 61		
	52-0476	450-157-35	4500761	25 Jan 54	14 Jul 54	01 Feb 54	29 Jul 54		13 May 64	13 May 64	11 Sep 68
	52-0477	450-157-35	4500762	27 Jan 54	09 Jul 54	02 Feb 54	30 Jul 54		10 Nov 64	10 Nov 64	11 Sep 68
	52-0478	450-157-35	4500763	28 Jan 54	03 Aug 54	05 Feb 54	26 Aug 54			04 Feb 65	16 Oct 68
	52-0479	450-157-35	4500764	01 Feb 54	20 Jul 54	09 Feb 54	14 Aug 54		09 Feb 65	09 Nov 66	23 Oct 68
	52-0480	450-157-35	4500765	02 Feb 54	03 Aug 54	12 Feb 54	28 Aug 54		01 Feb 66	01 Feb 66	28 Jan 69
	52-0481	450-157-35	4500766	04 Feb 54	22 Jul 54	12 Feb 54	18 Aug 54		18 Oct 65	18 Oct 65	23 Oct 68
	52-0482	450-157-35	4500767	05 Feb 54	27 Jul 54	12 Feb 54	30 Jul 54			31 Jul 62	19 Oct 67
	52-0483	450-157-35	4500768	09 Feb 54	27 Jul 54	16 Feb 54	24 Aug 54		19 Nov 65	19 Nov 65	23 Oct 68
	52-0484	450-157-35	4500769	10 Feb 54	30 Jul 54	17 Feb 54	26 Aug 54		23 Nov 65	23 Nov 65	22 Oct 68
	52-0485	450-157-35	4500770	12 Feb 54	24 Jul 54	28 Feb 54	26 Aug 54		18 Jan 66	18 Jan 66	28 Jan 69
	52-0486	450-157-35	4500771	15 Feb 54	29 Jul 54	23 Feb 54	26 Aug 54		01 Feb 66	01 Feb 66	28 Jan 69
	52-0487	450-157-35	4500772	17 Feb 54	03 Aug 54	01 Mar 54	26 Aug 54		03 Feb 66	03 Feb 66	28 Jan 69
	52-0488	450-157-35	4500773	18 Feb 54	03 Aug 54	01 Mar 54	27 Aug 54		07 Jan 65	07 Jan 65	16 Oct 68
	52-0489	450-157-35	4500774	23 Feb 54	12 Oct 54	02 Mar 54	29 Oct 54		26 May 64	26 May 64	10 Sep 68
	52-0490	450-157-35	4500775	24 Feb 54	17 Aug 54	03 Mar 54	19 Sep 54		14 Mar 55		
	52-0491	450-157-35	4500776	26 Feb 54	13 Aug 54	05 Mar 54	25 Sep 54		20 May 59		
	52-0492	450-157-35	4500777	01 Mar 54	18 Aug 54	19 Mar 54	02 Sep 54			05 Nov 65	22 Oct 68
	52-0493	450-157-35	4500778	03 Mar 54	17 Aug 54	19 Mar 54	23 Sep 54			16 Jan 63	19 Oct 67
	52-0494	450-157-35	4500779	04 Mar 54	31 Aug 54	11 Mar 54	30 Sep 54			25 Jan 63	19 Oct 67
	52-0495	450-157-35	4500780	07 Mar 54	20 Aug 54	12 Mar 54	02 Sep 54			10 Feb 65	16 Oct 68
	52-0496	450-157-35	4500781	09 Mar 54	25 Aug 54	15 Mar 54	10 Sep 54			24 Jan 64	30 Sep 68
	52-0497	450-157-35	4500782	11 Mar 54	01 Sep 54	17 Mar 54	25 Sep 54			24 Jul 64	09 Jul 68
	52-0498	450-157-35	4500783	12 Mar 54	28 Aug 54	19 Mar 54	16 Sep 54		14 Jan 60		
	52-0499	450-157-35	4500784	16 Mar 54	31 Aug 54	22 Mar 54	12 Oct 54			21 Jul 64	09 Jul 68
	52-0500	450-157-35	4500785	17 Mar 54	01 Sep 54	23 Mar 54	25 Sep 54		14 Oct 55		
	52-0501	450-157-35	4500786	19 Mar 54	31 Aug 54	25 Mar 54	23 Sep 54			27 Jan 65	16 Oct 68
	52-0502	450-157-35	4500787	22 Mar 54	07 Sep 54	27 Mar 54	29 Sep 54			31 Jul 62	19 Oct 67
	52-0503	450-157-35	4500788	24 Mar 54	09 Sep 54	01 Apr 54	09 Oct 54			06 May 64	10 Sep 68
	52-0504	450-157-35	4500789	25 Mar 54	16 Sep 54	01 Apr 54	07 Oct 54			23 Nov 64	12 Jul 68
	52-0505	450-157-35	4500790	29 Mar 54	16 Sep 54	02 Apr 54	16 Oct 54			20 Feb 63	20 Oct 67
	52-0506	450-157-35	4500791	30 Mar 54	15 Sep 54	06 Apr 54	04 Oct 54			13 Oct 65	23 Oct 68
	52-0507	450-157-35	4500792	01 Apr 54	16 Sep 54	07 Apr 54	28 Sep 54			14 Jan 66	28 Jan 69
B-47E-95-BW	52-0508	450-157-35	4500793	02 Apr 54	27 May 54	24 Jun 54	25 Jun 54			31 Jul 62	30 Sep 68
	52-0509	450-157-35	4500794	06 Apr 54	27 May 54	21 Jun 54	21 Jun 54		23 Mar 59		
	52-0510	450-157-35	4500795	07 Apr 54	26 May 54	25 Jun 54	25 Jun 54	EB-47L		05 Mar 65	13 Dec 68
	52-0511	450-157-35	4500796	09 Apr 54	26 May 54	29 Jun 54	29 Jun 54			12 Feb 63	20 Oct 67
	52-0512	450-157-35	4500797	12 Apr 54	04 Jun 54	24 Jun 54	25 Jun 54			14 Sep 64	11 Sep 68
	52-0513	450-157-35	4500798	14 Apr 54	03 Jun 54	24 Jun 54	25 Jun 54	EB-47L		18 Dec 64	14 Jan 69
	52-0514	450-157-35	4500799	15 Apr 54	04 Jun 54	24 Jun 54	26 Jun 54	JB-47E		06 Sep 66	28 Jan 69
	52-0515	450-157-35	4500800	19 Apr 54	07 Jun 54	23 Jun 54	23 Jun 54			20 Mar 61	15 May 61
	52-0516	450-157-35	4500801	20 Apr 54	19 Jun 54	20 Jul 54	21 Jul 54			08 Feb 63	20 Oct 67
	52-0517	450-157-35	4500802	22 Apr 54	07 Jun 54	27 Jun 54	28 Jun 54			29 Jul 64	30 Sep 68
	52-0518	450-157-35	4500803	23 Apr 54	09 Jun 54	28 Jun 54	28 Jun 54			04 Jan 65	12 Jul 68

MDS and Block Number	Serial Number	Model Number	Const. Number	Roll Out Date	First Flight Date	MIRR Date	USAF Fly Away	New MDS	Out of Service	MASDC Input Date	MASDC Output Date
B-47E-95-BW	52-0519	450-157-35	4500804	27 Apr 54	10 Jun 54	09 Jul 54	10 Jul 54			12 Jan 66	28 Jan 69
	52-0520	450-157-35	4500805	28 Apr 54	17 Jun 54	09 Jul 54	10 Jul 54			13 Jul 64	12 Jul 68
	52-0521	450-157-35	4500806	30 Apr 54	19 Jun 54	07 Jul 54	09 Jul 54			03 Feb 63	20 Oct 67
	52-0522	450-157-35	4500807	03 May 54	16 Jun 54	02 Jul 54	02 Jul 54			15 Feb 65	16 Oct 68
	52-0523	450-157-35	4500808	05 May 54	21 Jun 54	22 Jul 54	23 Jul 54			09 Nov 64	11 Sep 68
	52-0524	450-157-35	4500809	06 May 54	19 Jun 54	29 Jul 54	29 Jul 54			20 Jan 66	28 Jan 69
	52-0525	450-157-35	4500810	10 May 54	19 Jun 54	28 Jul 54	28 Jul 54		26 May 64		
	52-0526	450-157-35	4500811	11 May 54	23 Jun 54	23 Jul 54	27 Jul 54		03 Aug 62		
	52-0527	450-157-35	4500812	13 May 54	28 Jun 54	16 Jul 54	16 Jul 54			27 Oct 65	23 Oct 68
	52-0528	450-157-35	4500813	14 May 54	24 Jun 54	12 Jul 54	15 Jul 54			21 Oct 65	23 Oct 68
	52-0529	450-157-35	4500814	18 May 54	16 Jul 54	19 Aug 54	19 Aug 54			19 Jan 65	16 Oct 68
	52-0530	450-157-35	4500815	19 May 54	28 Jun 54	16 Jul 54	21 Jul 54			16 Nov 65	23 Oct 68
	52-0531	450-157-35	4500816	21 May 54	28 Jun 54	22 Jul 54	23 Jul 54			21 Jan 66	28 Jan 69
	52-0532	450-157-35	4500817	24 May 54	14 Jul 54	19 Aug 54	20 Aug 54			15 Feb 63	20 Oct 67
	52-0533	450-157-35	4500818	26 May 54	16 Jul 54	22 Jul 54	27 Jul 54		12 Jan 61		
	52-0534	450-157-35	4500819	27 May 54	15 Jul 54	29 Jul 54	30 Jul 54		10 Mar 56		
	52-0535	450-157-35	4500820	01 Jun 54	09 Jul 54	06 Aug 54	06 Aug 54		19 Dec 55		
	52-0536	450-157-35	4500821	02 Jun 54	15 Jul 54	06 Aug 54	06 Aug 54		21 Sep 64		
	52-0537	450-157-35	4500822	04 Jun 54	09 Jul 54	06 Aug 54	07 Aug 54			11 Jan 63	20 Oct 67
	52-0538	450-157-35	4500823	07 Jun 54	16 Jul 54	04 Aug 54	04 Aug 54			23 Mar 60	n/a
	52-0539	450-157-35	4500824	09 Jun 54	16 Jul 54	24 Aug 54	25 Aug 54			26 Jan 66	28 Jan 69
	52-0540	450-157-35	4500825	10 Jun 54	21 Jul 54	10 Aug 54	12 Aug 54			07 Feb 66	28 Jan 69
	52-0541	450-157-35	4500826	14 Jun 54	22 Jul 54	30 Aug 54	31 Aug 54			13 Aug 64	11 Sep 68
	52-0542	450-157-35	4500827	15 Jun 54	29 Jul 54	20 Aug 54	20 Aug 54		09 Feb 66		
	52-0543	450-157-35	4500828	17 Jun 54	25 Aug 54	16 Sep 54	16 Sep 54			31 Jul 62	12 Jul 68
	52-0544	450-157-35	4500829	18 Jun 54	05 Aug 54	27 Aug 54	27 Aug 54			08 May 64	12 Jul 68
	52-0545	450-157-35	4500830	22 Jun 54	09 Aug 54	07 Sep 54	08 Sep 54			19 Nov 65	23 Oct 68
B-47E-100-BW	52-0546	450-157-35	4500831	23 Jun 54	02 Aug 54	15 Sep 54	18 Sep 54			21 Sep 64	11 Sep 68
	52-0547	450-157-35	4500832	25 Jun 54	16 Aug 54	27 Aug 54	27 Aug 54			21 Oct 65	23 Oct 68
	52-0548	450-157-35	4500833	28 Jun 54	09 Aug 54	30 Aug 54	31 Aug 54			16 Nov 64	11 Sep 68
	52-0549	450-157-35	4500834	29 Jun 54	20 Aug 54	28 Aug 54	28 Aug 54			15 Jun 64	11 Sep 68
	52-0550	450-157-35	4500835	30 Jun 54	13 Aug 54	30 Aug 54	31 Aug 54			14 Dec 64	11 Sep 68
	52-0551	450-157-35	4500836	02 Jul 54	16 Aug 54	28 Aug 54	01 Sep 54			21 Oct 65	23 Oct 68
	52-0552	450-157-35	4500837	06 Jul 54	23 Aug 54	07 Sep 54	09 Sep 54			23 Nov 64	11 Sep 68
	52-0553	450-157-35	4500838	07 Jul 54	31 Aug 54	27 Aug 54	29 Aug 54		23 Aug 62		
	52-0554	450-157-35	4500839	08 Jul 54	25 Aug 54	10 Sep 54	10 Sep 54		09 Feb 66		
	52-0555	450-157-35	4500840	12 Jul 54	23 Aug 54	01 Sep 54	03 Sep 54			24 Apr 64	10 Sep 68
	52-0556	450-157-35	4500841	13 Jul 54	28 Aug 54	24 Sep 54	24 Sep 54		13 Oct 60		
	52-0557	450-157-35	4500842	14 Jul 54	26 Aug 54	18 Sep 54	18 Sep 54			26 Jan 65	16 Oct 68
	52-0558	450-157-35	4500843	15 Jul 54	26 Aug 54	23 Sep 54	24 Sep 54			26 Mar 63	30 Sep 68
	52-0559	450-157-35	4500844	19 Jul 54	28 Aug 54	17 Sep 54	19 Sep 54			23 Jun 64	30 Sep 68
	52-0560	450-157-35	4500845	20 Jul 54	02 Sep 54	25 Sep 54	28 Sep 54			15 Apr 64	11 Sep 68
	52-0561	450-157-35	4500846	21 Jul 54	03 Sep 54	18 Oct 54	20 Oct 54			27 Feb 63	20 Oct 67
	52-0562	450-157-35	4500847	22 Jul 54	09 Sep 54	25 Sep 54	28 Sep 54		15 Apr 58		
	52-0563	450-157-35	4500848	26 Jul 54	08 Sep 54	12 Oct 54	14 Oct 54		20 Feb 63		
	52-0564	450-157-35	4500849	27 Oct 54	13 Sep 54	23 Sep 54	24 Sep 54			13 Jul 64	10 Sep 68
	52-0565	450-157-35	4500850	28 Jul 54	23 Sep 54	14 Oct 54	15 Oct 54		26 Jun 56		
	52-0566	450-157-35	4500851	29 Jul 54	20 Sep 54	19 Oct 54	20 Oct 54		05 Jan 60		
	52-0567	450-157-35	4500852	02 Aug 54	23 Sep 54	08 Nov 54	09 Nov 54			27 Feb 63	20 Oct 67
	52-0568	450-157-35	4500853	03 Aug 54	20 Sep 54	28 Sep 54	29 Sep 54			20 May 64	12 Jul 68
	52-0569	450-157-35	4500854	04 Aug 54	17 Sep 54	28 Sep 54	29 Sep 54			12 Jan 66	28 Jan 69
	52-0570	450-157-35	4500855	05 Aug 54	24 Sep 54	16 Oct 54	20 Oct 54			02 Feb 65	16 Oct 68
	52-0571	450-157-35	4500856	09 Aug 54	29 Sep 54	16 Oct 54	20 Oct 54			11 Aug 64	11 Sep 68
	52-0572	450-157-35	4500857	10 Aug 54	09 Oct 54	26 Oct 54	27 Oct 54		13 Jul 56		
	52-0573	450-157-35	4500858	11 Aug 54	28 Sep 54	26 Oct 54	27 Oct 54			16 Dec 64	11 Sep 68
	52-0574	450-157-35	4500859	12 Aug 54	09 Oct 54	16 Oct 54	20 Oct 54			07 Jan 65	11 Sep 68
	52-0575	450-157-35	4500860	16 Aug 54	04 Oct 54	14 Oct 54	15 Oct 54			04 Feb 65	16 Oct 68
	52-0576	450-157-35	4500861	17 Aug 54	08 Oct 54	22 Oct 54	26 Oct 54			26 Feb 63	20 Oct 67
	52-0577	450-157-35	4500862	18 Aug 54	09 Sep 54	18 Nov 54	19 Nov 54			26 Oct 65	23 Oct 68
	52-0578	450-157-35	4500863	19 Aug 54	03 Oct 54	21 Oct 54	23 Oct 54			04 Jan 66	28 Jan 69
	52-0579	450-157-35	4500864	23 Aug 54	11 Oct 54	08 Nov 54	08 Nov 54			10 Jul 64	30 Sep 68
	52-0580	450-157-35	4500865	24 Aug 54	10 Oct 54	01 Nov 54	02 Nov 54		04 Oct 55		
	52-0581	450-157-35	4500866	25 Aug 54	15 Oct 54	16 Nov 54	17 Nov 54			23 Jul 64	12 Jul 68
	52-0582	450-157-35	4500867	26 Aug 54	09 Oct 54	21 Oct 54	23 Oct 54			26 Oct 65	23 Oct 68
	52-0583	450-157-35	4500868	30 Aug 54	11 Oct 54	26 Oct 54	27 Oct 54			19 Jun 64	30 Sep 68
B-47E-105-BW	52-0584	450-157-35	4500869	31 Aug 54	20 Oct 54	02 Nov 54	02 Nov 54			31 Jan 66	28 Jan 69
	52-0585	450-157-35	4500870	01 Sep 54	19 Oct 54	09 Dec 54	14 Dec 54			31 Jul 62	30 Sep 68
	52-0586	450-157-35	4500871	02 Sep 54	19 Oct 54	16 Nov 54	18 Nov 54			06 May 64	10 Sep 68
	52-0587	450-157-35	4500872	07 Sep 54	18 Oct 54	02 Nov 54	03 Nov 54			28 Jul 64	12 Jul 68
	52-0588	450-157-35	4500873	08 Sep 54	29 Oct 54	17 Nov 54	17 Nov 54			03 Feb 66	28 Jan 69
	52-0589	450-157-35	4500874	09 Sep 54	28 Oct 54	19 Nov 54	19 Nov 54			06 Jan 66	28 Jan 69
	52-0590	450-157-35	4500875	10 Sep 54	01 Nov 54	11 Nov 54	12 Nov 54			24 Jun 64	30 Sep 68
	52-0591	450-157-35	4500876	14 Sep 54	28 Oct 54	18 Nov 54	19 Nov 54			27 Oct 65	23 Oct 68
	52-0592	450-157-35	4500877	15 Sep 54	05 Nov 54	19 Nov 54	19 Nov 54			28 Jan 66	28 Jan 69
	52-0593	450-157-35	4500878	16 Sep 54	02 Nov 54	17 Nov 54	18 Nov 54			06 Jan 65	16 Oct 68
	52-0594	450-157-35	4500879	17 Sep 54	04 Nov 54	08 Dec 54	10 Dec 54			11 May 64	10 Sep 68
	52-0595	450-157-35	4500880	21 Sep 54	04 Nov 54	11 Nov 54	13 Nov 54		11 Jun 64		
	52-0596	450-157-35	4500881	22 Sep 54	02 Nov 54	08 Dec 54	10 Dec 54			31 Jul 62	12 Jul 68
	52-0597	450-157-35	4500882	23 Sep 54	10 Nov 54	22 Nov 54	24 Nov 54			17 Jun 64	11 Sep 68
	52-0598	450-157-35	4500883	24 Sep 54	11 Nov 54	01 Dec 54	07 Dec 54			20 Jan 66	28 Jan 69
	52-0599	450-157-35	4500884	28 Sep 54	17 Nov 54	06 Dec 54	07 Dec 54			18 Jun 64	30 Sep 68
	52-0600	450-157-35	4500885	29 Sep 54	17 Nov 54	21 Dec 54	22 Dec 54			13 Jul 64	12 Jul 68
	52-0601	450-157-35	4500886	30 Sep 54	16 Nov 54	23 Nov 54	24 Nov 54			17 Jul 64	11 Sep 68
	52-0602	450-157-35	4500887	01 Oct 54	17 Nov 54	01 Dec 54	02 Dec 54			10 Feb 65	16 Oct 68
	52-0603	450-157-35	4500888	05 Oct 54	18 Nov 54	20 Dec 54	21 Dec 54			06 May 64	11 Sep 68
	52-0604	450-157-35	4500889	06 Oct 54	23 Nov 54	22 Dec 54	22 Dec 54			10 Feb 65	16 Oct 68
	52-0605	450-157-35	4500890	07 Oct 54	16 Nov 54	08 Dec 54	10 Dec 54			15 Feb 65	16 Oct 68
	52-0606	450-157-35	4500891	08 Oct 54	19 Nov 54	17 Dec 54	17 Dec 54		21 Oct 59		
	52-0607	450-157-35	4500892	12 Oct 54	02 Dec 54	15 Dec 54	16 Dec 54			15 Feb 65	16 Oct 68
	52-0608	450-157-35	4500893	13 Oct 54	19 Nov 54	16 Dec 54	17 Dec 54			19 Jan 65	16 Oct 68
	52-0609	450-157-35	4500894	16 Oct 54	23 Nov 54	08 Dec 54	17 Dec 54			31 Jul 62	20 Oct 67
	52-0610	450-157-35	4500895	18 Oct 54	03 Dec 54	15 Dec 54	16 Dec 54			23 Jun 64	30 Sep 68
	52-0611	450-157-35	4500896	19 Oct 54	01 Dec 54	22 Dec 54	22 Dec 54			18 Mar 64	20 Oct 67
	52-0612	450-157-35	4500897	21 Oct 54	14 Dec 54	06 Jan 55	07 Jan 55			27 May 64	10 Sep 68
	52-0613	450-157-35	4500898	22 Oct 54	07 Dec 54	07 Jan 55	07 Jan 55			06 Jul 64	30 Sep 68

MDS and Block Number	Serial Number	Model Number	Const. Number	Roll Out Date	First Flight Date	MIRR Date	USAF Fly Away	New MDS	Out of Service	MASDC Input Date	MASDC Output Date
B-47E-105-BW	52-0614	450-157-35	4500899	25 Oct 54	21 Dec 54	19 Jan 55	21 Jan 55			01 Apr 64	11 Sep 68
	52-0615	450-157-35	4500900	26 Oct 54	14 Dec 54	10 Jan 55	12 Jan 55		05 Jan 62		
	52-0616	450-157-35	4500901	27 Oct 54	16 Dec 54	13 Jan 55	13 Jan 55			04 Feb 65	16 Oct 68
	52-0617	450-157-35	4500902	29 Oct 54	16 Dec 54	10 Jan 55	11 Jan 55			11 Jun 64	30 Sep 68
	52-0618	450-157-35	4500903	01 Nov 54	16 Dec 54	20 Jan 55	22 Jan 55			03 Mar 65	16 Oct 68
	52-0619	450-157-35	4500904	02 Nov 54	21 Dec 54	17 Jan 55	21 Jan 55			08 Mar 63	20 Oct 67
	52-0620	450-157-35	4500905	03 Nov 54	16 Dec 54	07 Jan 55	11 Jan 55			16 Jan 63	20 Oct 67
B-47E	52-0621	450-157-35									
	to		canceled								
	52-0684	450-157-35									
RB-47E-20-BW	52-0685	450-158-36	4500906	14 Jan 54	10 Mar 54	05 Apr 54	07 Apr 54	E-47/R-47E RB-47E		13 Sep 61	27 Oct 61
	52-0686	450-158-36	4500907	18 Jan 54	10 Mar 54	02 Apr 54	02 Apr 54			08 Apr 58	17 Jan 61
	52-0687	450-158-36	4500908	20 Jan 54	15 Mar 54	16 Apr 54	17 Apr 54			04 Apr 58	14 Jun 60
	52-0688	450-158-36	4500909	22 Jan 54	16 Mar 54	30 Mar 54	31 Mar 54			23 Jun 58	14 Dec 60
	52-0689	450-158-36	4500910	25 Jan 54	16 Mar 54	02 Apr 54	07 Apr 54			27 May 58	19 Jan 61
	52-0690	450-158-36	4500911	27 Jan 54	22 Mar 54	06 Apr 54	07 Apr 54			30 Jun 58	28 Dec 60
	52-0691	450-158-36	4500912	29 Jan 54	26 Mar 54	15 Apr 54	15 Apr 54			24 Jun 58	13 Dec 60
	52-0692	450-158-36	4500913	02 Feb 54	25 Mar 54	09 Apr 54	13 Apr 54			04 Apr 58	10 Jun 60
	52-0693	450-158-36	4500914	02 Feb 54	25 Mar 54	14 Apr 54	15 Apr 54			24 Jun 58	06 Dec 60
	52-0694	450-158-36	4500915	05 Feb 54	31 Mar 54	15 Apr 54	15 Apr 54			10 Apr 58	n/a
	52-0695	450-158-36	4500916	08 Feb 54	31 Mar 54	15 Apr 54	15 Apr 54			25 Jun 58	13 Dec 60
	52-0696	450-158-36	4500917	09 Feb 54	01 Apr 54	28 Apr 54	04 May 54			27 Jun 58	27 Dec 60
	52-0697	450-158-36	4500918	10 Feb 54	01 Apr 54	15 Apr 54	15 Apr 54			24-Ju-58	n/a
	52-0698	450-158-36	4500919	12 Feb 54	06 Apr 54	21 Apr 54	24 Apr 54			10 Jun 58	03 Jan 61
	52-0699	450-158-36	4500920	16 Feb 54	31 Mar 54	14 Apr 54	14 Apr 54			08 Apr 58	31 Oct 60
	52-0700	450-158-36	4500921	17 Feb 54	07 Apr 54	10 May 54	11 May 54			26 Jun 58	16 Dec 60
	52-0701	450-158-36	4500922	19 Feb 54	15 Apr 54	07 May 54	08 May 54			05 Apr 60	16 Sep 68
	52-0702	450-158-36	4500923	24 Feb 54	15 May 54	04 May 54	06 May 54		21 Oct 59		
	52-0703	450-158-36	4500924	25 Feb 54	15 Apr 54	10 May 54	11 May 54			28 Apr 60	16 Sep 68
	52-0704	450-158-36	4500925	01 Mar 54	19 Apr 54	12 May 54	14 May 54			21 Apr 60	16 Sep 68
	52-0705	450-158-36	4500926	02 Mar 54	19 Apr 54	05 May 54	06 May 54			26 Apr 60	16 Sep 68
	52-0706	450-158-36	4500927	04 Mar 54	20 Apr 54	04 May 54	05 May 54			12 Apr 60	28 Jan 64
	52-0707	450-158-36	4500928	08 Mar 54	26 Apr 54	24 May 54	26 May 54			04 Apr 58	14 Jun 60
	52-0708	450-158-36	4500929	09 Mar 54	26 Apr 54	14 May 54	14 May 54			08 Apr 60	16 Sep 68
	52-0709	450-158-36	4500930	11 Mar 54	26 Apr 54	20 May 54	21 May 54			26 Jun 58	28 Dec 60
	52-0710	450-158-36	4500931	15 Mar 54	04 May 54	20 May 54	21 May 54			07 Apr 58	02 Aug 60
	52-0711	450-158-36	4500932	16 Mar 54	28 Apr 54	19 May 54	19 May 54			27 Apr 60	16 Sep 68
	52-0712	450-158-36	4500933	18 Mar 54	05 May 54	19 May 54	19 May 54			26 Jun 58	16 Dec 60
	52-0713	450-158-36	4500934	19 Mar 54	07 May 54	02 Jun 54	05 Jun 54	E-47/R-47E RB-47E		22 Sep 61	16 Sep 68
	52-0714	450-158-36	4500935	23 Mar 54	17 May 54	09 Jun 54	10 Jun 54			13 Apr 60	30 Jan 64
	52-0715	450-158-36	4500936	24 Mar 54	04 May 54	13 May 54	14 May 54			27 Jun 58	22 Dec 60
	52-0716	450-158-36	4500937	26 Mar 54	11 May 54	01 Jun 54	05 Jun 54		13 Apr 60		
	52-0717	450-158-36	4500938	29 Mar 54	14 May 54	26 May 54	27 May 54			08 Apr 58	n/a
	52-0718	450-158-36	4500939	31 Mar 54	12 May 54	01 Jun 54	05 Jun 54	E-47/R-47E RB-47E		17 Sep 61	16 Dec 61
	52-0719	450-158-36	4500940	01 Apr 54	20 May 54	01 Jun 54	05 Jun 54	E-47/R-47E RB-47E		28 Sep 61	16 Sep 68
RB-47E-25-BW	52-0720	450-158-36	4500941	05 Apr 54	20 May 54	09 Jun 54	10 Jun 54		26 Feb 58		
	52-0721	450-158-36	4500942	06 Apr 54	28 May 54	09 Jun 54	10 Jun 54			12 May 60	25 Feb 64
	52-0722	450-158-36	4500943	08 Apr 54	28 May 54	16 Jul 54	16 Jul 54			30 Oct 57	16 Dec 60
	52-0723	450-158-36	4500944	09 Apr 54	26 May 54	23 Jun 54	24 Jun 54			27 Jun 58	22 Dec 60
	52-0724	450-158-36	4500945	13 Apr 54	26 May 54	22 Jun 54	22 Jun 54			26 May 58	n/a
	52-0725	450-158-36	4500946	14 Apr 54	04 Jun 54	22 Jun 54	22 Jun 54			30 Jun 58	27 Dec 60
	52-0726	450-158-36	4500947	16 Apr 54	04 Jun 54	24 Jun 54	25 Jun 54		25 Sep 58		
	52-0727	450-158-36	4500948	19 Apr 54	08 Jun 54	24 Jun 54	25 Jun 54	E-47/R-47E RB-47E		22 Sep 61	16 Sep 68
	52-0728	450-158-36	4500949	21 Apr 54	10 Jun 54	28 Jun 54	29 Jun 54	E-47/R-47E RB-47E		22 Sep 61	16 Sep 68
	52-0729	450-158-36	4500950	22 Apr 54	10 Jun 54	29 Jun 54	29 Jun 54			17 May 61	16 Sep 68
	52-0730	450-158-36	4500951	26 Apr 54	09 Jun 54	08 Jul 54	08 Jul 54		09 Jan 59		
	52-0731	450-158-36	4500952	27 Apr 54	16 Jun 54	02 Jul 54	02 Jul 54			01 Nov 57	n/a
	52-0732	450-158-36	4500953	29 Apr 54	16 Jun 54	29 Jun 54	29 Jun 54	E-47/R-47E RB-47E		26 Sep 61	21 Jun 66
	52-0733	450-158-36	4500954	30 Apr 54	15 Jun 54	16 Jul 54	16 Jul 54	E-47/R-47E RB-47E		12 Sep 61	16 Sep 68
	52-0734	450-158-36	4500955	04 May 54	19 Jun 54	19 Jul 54	20 Jul 54	E-47/R-47E RB-47E		25 Sep 61	16 Sep 68
	52-0735	450-158-36	4500956	05 May 54	18 Jun 54	19 Jul 54	21 Jul 54	E-47/R-47E RB-47E		19 Sep 61	02 Nov 61
	52-0736	450-158-36	4500957	07 May 54	19 Jun 54	16 Jul 54	17 Jul 54			01 Nov 57	n/a
	52-0737	450-158-36	4500958	10 May 54	24 Jun 54	16 Jul 54	16 Jul 54			04 Nov 57	01 Jun 60
	52-0738	450-158-36	4500959	12 May 54	25 Jun 54	22 Jul 54	23 Jul 54			01 Nov 57	08 Jun 60
	52-0739	450-158-36	4500960	13 May 54	24 Jun 54	13 Jul 54	13 Jul 54			04 Nov 57	01 Jun 60
	52-0740	450-158-36	4500961	17 May 54	29 Jun 54	19 Jul 54	20 Jul 54			07 Nov 57	07 Jun 60
	52-0741	450-158-36	4500962	18 May 54	06 Jul 54	28 Jul 54	29 Jul 54			17 Jan 61	n/a
	52-0742	450-158-36	4500963	20 May 54	07 Jul 54	05 Aug 54	06 Aug 54		25 Mar 55		
	52-0743	450-158-36	4500964	21 May 54	02 Jun 54	22 Jul 54	23 Jul 54	E-47/R-47E RB-47E		28 Aug 61	16 Sep 68
	52-0744	450-158-36	4500965	25 May 54	14 Jul 54	17 Aug 54	19 Aug 54		29 Sep 58		
	52-0745	450-158-36	4500966	26 May 54	08 Jul 54	28 Jul 54	29 Jul 54			23 Jul 61	16 Sep 68
	52-0746	450-158-36	4500967	28 May 54	14 Jul 54	10 Aug 54	12 Aug 54	E-47/R-47E RB-47E		19 Sep 61	02 Nov 61
	52-0747	450-158-36	4500968	01 Jun 54	16 Jul 54	10 Aug 54	11 Aug 54			28 Jul 58	n/a
	52-0748	450-158-36	4500969	03 Jun 54	16 Jul 54	28 Jul 54	29 Jul 54	E-47/R-47E RB-47E		26 Sep 61	16 Sep 68
	52-0749	450-158-36	4500970	04 Jun 54	16 Jul 54	04 Aug 54	04 Aug 54			20 Aug 58	n/a
	52-0750	450-158-36	4500971	08 Jun 54	20 Jul 54	19 Aug 54	20 Aug 54			13 Jun 61	16 Oct 61
	52-0751	450-158-36	4500972	09 Jun 54	19 Jul 54	23 Aug 54	24 Aug 54	E-47/R-47E RB-47E		27 Sep 61	16 Dec 61
	52-0752	450-158-36	4500973	11 Jun 54	26 Jul 52	23 Aug 54	24 Aug 54	E-47/R-47E RB-47E		22 Sep 61	16 Sep 68
	52-0753	450-158-36	4500974	14 Jun 54	27 Jul 54	20 Aug 54	23 Aug 54			19 Sep 58	12 Jan 61

MDS and Block Number	Serial Number	Model Number	Const. Number	Roll Out Date	First Flight Date	MIRR Date	USAF Fly Away	New MDS	Out of Service	MASDC Input Date	MASDC Output Date
RB-47E-25-BW	52-0754	450-158-36	4500975	16 Jun 54	04 Aug 54	20 Aug 54	21 Aug 54		08 Aug 57		
RB-47E-30-BW	52-0755	450-158-36	4500976	17 Jun 54	04 Aug 54	19 Aug 54	21 Aug 54	E-47/R-47E RB-47E		07 Sep 61	16 Sep 68
	52-0756	450-158-36	4500977	21 Jun 54	03 Aug 54	14 Aug 54	15 Aug 54			03 Aug 60	19 Jan 61
	52-0757	450-158-36	4500978	22 Jun 54	30 Jul 54	24 Aug 54	25 Aug 54			02 Aug 60	n/a
	52-0758	450-158-36	4500979	24 Jun 54	04 Aug 54	27 Aug 54	27 Aug 54	E-47/R-47E RB-47E		19 Sep 61	16 Dec 61
	52-0759	450-158-36	4500980	25 Jun 54	10 Aug 54	01 Sep 54	02 Sep 54			26 May 60	16 Sep 68
	52-0760	450-158-36	4500981	29 Jun 54	11 Aug 54	24 Aug 54	25 Aug 54			06 Jun 61	10 Oct 61
	52-0761	450-158-36	4500982	30 Jun 54	24 Aug 54	07 Oct 54	08 Oct 54		01 May 57		
	52-0762	450-158-36	4500983	02 Jul 54	13 Aug 54	02 Sep 54	02 Sep 54			20 May 60	02 Mar 64
	52-0763	450-158-36	4500984	06 Jul 54	19 Aug 54	03 Sep 54	03 Sep 54			25 May 60	24 Jan 64
	52-0764	450-158-36	4500985	08 Jul 54	18 Aug 54	16 Sep 54	16 Sep 54			12 Jun 61	17 Oct 61
	52-0765	450-158-36	4500986	09 Jul 54	26 Aug 54	14 Sep 54	16 Sep 54			02 May 60	27 Mar 64
	52-0766	450-158-36	4500987	13 Jul 54	20 Aug 54	23 Sep 54	23 Sep 54		09 Jan 61		
	52-0767	450-158-36	4500988	14 Jul 54	02 Sep 54	27 Sep 54	28 Sep 54			21 Mar 61	16 Sep 68
	52-0768	450-158-36	4500989	16 Jul 54	27 Aug 54	10 Sep 54	10 Sep 54			10 Mar 61	16 Sep 68
	52-0769	450-158-36	4500990	19 Jul 54	30 Aug 54	21 Sep 54	22 Sep 54	E-47/R-47E RB-47E		17 Apr 62	09 Mar 64
	52-0770	450-158-36	4500991	21 Jul 54	01 Sep 54	24 Sep 54	25 Sep 54		29 Oct 54		
	52-0771	450-158-36	4500992	27 Jul 54	01 Sep 54	23 Sep 54	24 Sep 54	E-47/R-47E RB-47E		12 Sep 61	16 Sep 68
	52-0772	450-158-36	4500993	26 Jul 54	09 Sep 54	27 Sep 54	28 Sep 54			15 May 61	16 Sep 68
	52-0773	450-158-36	4500994	27 Jul 54	09 Sep 54	23 Sep 54	24 Sep 54			18 May 61	16 Sep 68
	52-0774	450-158-36	4500995	29 Jul 54	24 Sep 54	12 Oct 54	13 Oct 54			06 May 60	31 Oct 63
	52-0775	450-158-36	4500996	30 Jul 54	21 Sep 54	12 Oct 54	12 Oct 54	E-47/R-47E RB-47E		20 Sep 61	16 Sep 68
	52-0776	450-158-36	4500997	03 Aug 54	15 Sep 54	25 Sep 54	27 Sep 54	E-47/R-47E RB-47E		29 Sep 61	16 Sep 68
	52-0777	450-158-36	4500998	04 Aug 54	11 Sep 54	28 Sep 54	28 Sep 54	E-47/R-47E RB-47E		12 Apr 62	09 Mar 64
	52-0778	450-158-36	4500999	06 Aug 54	24 Sep 54	11 Oct 54	12 Oct 54	E-47/R-47E RB-47E		22 Sep 61	29 Nov 61
	52-0779	450-158-36	4501000	09 Aug 54	30 Sep 54	15 Oct 54	16 Oct 54			23 May 60	28 Feb 64
	52-0780	450-158-36	4501001	11 Aug 54	09 Sep 54	21 Oct 54	21 Oct 54	E-47/R-47E RB-47E		25 Sep 61	01 Dec 61
	52-0781	450-158-36	4501002	12 Aug 54	28 Sep 54	09 Oct 54	09 Oct 54			09 Jan 61	17 Feb 61
	52-0782	450-158-36	4501003	16 Aug 54	10 Oct 54	18 Oct 54	19 Oct 54			16 May 60	02 Dec 63
	52-0783	450-158-36	4501004	17 Aug 54	04 Oct 54	18 Oct 54	19 Oct 54			10 May 61	16 Sep 68
	52-0784	450-158-36	4501005	19 Aug 54	29 Aug 54	19 Oct 54	20 Oct 54			08 Jun 61	16 Sep 68
	52-0785	450-158-36	4501006	21 Aug 54	08 Oct 54	21 Oct 54	22 Oct 54		30 Nov 55		
	52-0786	450-158-36	4501007	24 Aug 54	09 Oct 54	26 Oct 54	27 Oct 54			11 Oct 60	09 Mar 64
	52-0787	450-158-36	4501008	25 Aug 54	08 Oct 54	14 Oct 54	15 Oct 54			29 May 61	16 Sep 68
	52-0788	450-158-36	4501009	27 Aug 54	09 Oct 54	22 Oct 54	22 Oct 54	E-47/R-47E RB-47E		22 May 62	21 Jun 66
	52-0789	450-158-36	4501010	30 Aug 54	10 Oct 54	18 Oct 54	19 Oct 54			13 Jun 61	16 Sep 68
RB-47E-35-BW	52-0790	450-158-36	4501011	01 Sep 54	15 Oct 54	01 Nov 54	02 Nov 54			19 Apr 61	16 Sep 68
	52-0791	450-158-36	4501012	02 Sep 54	02 Nov 54	23 Nov 54	24 Nov 54			27 Jun 61	18 Oct 61
	52-0792	450-158-36	4501013	07 Sep 54	20 Oct 54	04 Nov 54	05 Nov 54			24 May 60	13 Feb 64
	52-0793	450-158-36	4501014	08 Sep 54	28 Oct 54	15 Nov 54	16 Nov 54			22 May 61	16 Sep 68
	52-0794	450-158-36	4501015	10 Sep 54	27 Oct 54	12 Nov 54	12 Nov 54			16 Jan 61	18 Jan 61
	52-0795	450-158-36	4501016	13 Sep 54	28 Oct 54	22 Nov 54	23 Nov 54			23 Jan 61	16 Sep 68
	52-0796	450-158-36	4501017	15 Sep 54	16 Nov 54	01 Dec 54	01 Dec 54	E-47/R-47E RB-47E		21 Sep 61	17 Nov 61
	52-0797	450-158-36	4501018	16 Sep 54	29 Oct 54	10 Nov 54	12 Nov 54	E-47/R-47E RB-47E		30 Aug 61	27 Mar 64
	52-0798	450-158-36	4501019	20 Sep 54	01 Nov 54	15 Nov 54	16 Nov 54			11 May 60	06 Dec 63
	52-0799	450-158-36	4501020	21 Sep 54	08 Nov 54	18 Nov 54	18 Nov 54	E-47/R-47E RB-47E		28 Sep 61	16 Sep 68
	52-0800	450-158-36	4501021	23 Sep 54	05 Nov 54	01 Dec 54	02 Dec 54	E-47/R-47E RB-47E		22 Sep 61	16 Sep 68
	52-0801	450-158-36	4501022	24 Sep 54	05 Nov 54	18 Nov 54	19 Nov 54	E-47/R-47E RB-47E		22 May 62	16 Sep 68
	52-0802	450-158-36	4501023	28 Sep 54	04 Nov 54	15 Nov 54	16 Nov 54			09 Mar 61	16 Sep 68
	52-0803	450-158-36	4501024	29 Sep 54	10 Nov 54	22 Nov 54	24 Nov 54			06 Apr 61	16 Sep 68
	52-0804	450-158-36	4501025	01 Oct 54	12 Nov 54	08 Dec 54	10 Dec 54			18 May 60	16 Sep 68
	52-0805	450-158-36	4501026	04 Oct 54	11 Nov 54	18 Nov 54	18 Nov 54	E-47/R-47E RB-47E		01 Nov 62	16 Sep 68
	52-0806	450-158-36	4501027	06 Oct 54	16 Nov 54	01 Dec 54	01 Dec 54			10 Jul 61	20 Oct 61
	52-0807	450-158-36	4501028	07 Oct 54	15 Nov 54	23 Nov 54	23 Nov 54	E-47/R-47E RB-47E		22 Sep 61	28 Nov 61
	52-0808	450-158-36	4501029	11 Oct 54	19 Nov 54	08 Dec 54	10 Dec 54	E-47/R-47E RB-47E		25 Sep 61	16 Sep 68
	52-0809	450-158-36	4501030	12 Oct 54	23 Nov 54	03 Jan 55	06 Jan 55	E-47/R-47E RB-47E		25 Sep 61	21 Jun 66
	52-0810	450-158-36	4501031	14 Oct 54	24 Nov 54	21 Dec 54	21 Dec 54	E-47/R-47E RB-47E		25 Sep 61	16 Sep 68
	52-0811	450-158-36	4501032	15 Oct 54	23 Nov 54	15 Dec 54	17 Dec 54	E-47/R-47E RB-47E		21 Sep 61	16 Sep 68
	52-0812	450-158-36	4501033	19 Oct 54	01 Dec 54	21 Dec 54	21 Dec 54	E-47/R-47E RB-47E		07 Sep 61	16 Sep 68
	52-0813	450-158-36	4501034	20 Oct 54	03 Dec 54	03 Jan 55	06 Jan 55			19 May 60	16 Sep 68
	52-0814	450-158-36	4501035	22 Oct 54	02 Dec 54	17 Dec 54	18 Dec 54		27 Jan 60		
	52-0815	450-158-36	4501036	27 Oct 54	08 Dec 54	21 Dec 54	21 Dec 54			17 May 60	16 Sep 68
	52-0816	450-158-36	4501037	28 Oct 54	07 Dec 54	17 Dec 54	17 Dec 54	QB-47E JQB-47E	20 Jun 64		
	52-0817	450-158-36	4501038	01 Nov 54	15 Dec 54	12 Jan 55	14 Jan 55	QB-47E JQB-47E	08 Mar 62		
	52-0818	450-158-36	4501039	04 Nov 54	23 Dec 54	13 Jan 55	14 Jan 55			13 Sep 56	30 Oct 61
	52-0819	450-158-36	4501040	05 Nov 54	12 Dec 54	19 Jan 55	22 Jan 55			19 May 60	16 Sep 68
	52-0820	450-158-36	4501041	09 Nov 54	22 Dec 54	05 Jan 55	07 Jan 55	QB-47E JQB-47E	31 Aug 62		
	52-0821	450-158-36	4501042	12 Nov 54	30 Dec 54	02 Feb 55	07 Feb 55	E-47/R-47E RB-47E		26 Sep 61	16 Sep 68
	52-0822	450-158-36	4501043	16 Nov 54	06 Jan 55	28 Jan 55	07 Feb 55	QB-47E			

MDS and Block Number	Serial Number	Model Number	Const. Number	Roll Out Date	First Flight Date	MIRR Date	USAF Fly Away	New MDS	Out of Service	MASDC Input Date	MASDC Output Date
RB-47E-35-BW	52-0822							JQB-47E	21 Jun 62		
	52-0823	450-158-36	4501044	18 Nov 54	07 Jan 55	21 Jan 55	22 Jan 55	QB-47E JQB-47E	19 Aug 63		
	52-0824	450-158-36	4501045	22 Nov 54	06 Jan 55	19 Jan 55	21 Jan 55		29 Oct 58		
	52-0825	450-158-36	4501046	29 Nov 54	13 Jan 55	11 Feb 55	11 Feb 55			12 Sep 61	16 Sep 68
B-47E-35-DT	52-1406	450-157-35	44090	n/a	n/a	25 Jan 55	30 Mar 55			13 May 64	11 Sep 68
	52-1407	450-157-35	44091	n/a	n/a	28 Jan 55	01 Apr 55			06 Mar 63	20 Oct 67
	52-1408	450-157-35	44092	n/a	n/a	02 Feb 55	06 Apr 55			26 Apr 63	20 Oct 67
	52-1409	450-157-35	44093	n/a	n/a	07 Feb 55	11 Apr 55			11 Jun 63	20 Oct 67
	52-1410	450-157-35	44094	n/a	n/a	10 Feb 55	15 Apr 55			30 Apr 63	20 Oct 67
	52-1411	450-157-35	44095	n/a	n/a	15 Feb 55	20 Apr 55			24 Jan 62	20 Oct 67
	52-1412	450-157-35	44096	n/a	n/a	18 Feb 55	25 Apr 55		04 Mar 64		
	52-1413	450-157-35	44097	n/a	n/a	23 Feb 55	28 Apr 55			15 Apr 64	11 Sep 68
	52-1414	450-157-35	44098	n/a	n/a	28 Feb 55	03 May 55		31 Mar 60		
	52-1415	450-157-35	44099	n/a	n/a	03 Mar 55	09 May 55			10 May 63	20 Oct 67
	52-1416	450-157-35	44100	n/a	n/a	09 Mar 55	12 May 55			10 Apr 64	11 Sep 68
	52-1417	450-157-35	44101	n/a	n/a	14 Mar 55	17 May 55			02 Jun 64	11 Sep 68
B-47E-50-LM	52-3343	450-157-35	202	n/a	n/a	n/a	27 Mar 55			21 Jan 65	16 Oct 68
	52-3344	450-157-35	203	n/a	n/a	n/a	27 Mar 55		02 Jun 59		
	52-3345	450-157-35	204	n/a	n/a	n/a	30 Mar 55			24 Jun 64	12 Jul 68
	52-3346	450-157-35	205	n/a	n/a	n/a	22 Mar 55			08 Jan 65	16 Oct 68
	52-3347	450-157-35	206	n/a	n/a	n/a	30 Mar 55			15 Jan 63	20 Oct 67
	52-3348	450-157-35	207	n/a	n/a	n/a	13 Apr 55			13 Oct 65	23 Oct 68
	52-3349	450-157-35	208	n/a	n/a	n/a	13 Mar 55			29 Jun 64	30 Sep 68
	52-3350	450-157-35	209	n/a	n/a	n/a	17 Mar 55			31 Jul 62	20 Oct 67
	52-3351	450-157-35	210	n/a	n/a	n/a	13 Mar 55			10 Jun 64	12 Jul 68
	52-3352	450-157-35	211	n/a	n/a	n/a	17 Mar 55			24 May 63	20 Oct 67
	52-3353	450-157-35	212	n/a	n/a	n/a	10 Mar 55			25 Jun 64	30 Sep 68
	52-3354	450-157-35	213	n/a	n/a	n/a	24 Mar 55			27 Jun 61	26 Oct 64
	52-3355	450-157-35	214	n/a	n/a	n/a	19 Mar 55			29 Jan 63	20 Oct 67
	52-3356	450-157-35	215	n/a	n/a	n/a	19 Mar 55			05 Jun 61	14 Feb 64
	52-3357	450-157-35	216	n/a	n/a	n/a	27 Mar 55			29 Jun 61	13 Apr 64
	52-3358	450-157-35	217	n/a	n/a	n/a	05 May 55			05 Jun 61	30 Mar 64
	52-3359	450-157-35	218	n/a	n/a	n/a	27 Apr 55			20 Mar 64	12 Jul 68
	52-3360	450-157-35	219	n/a	n/a	n/a	08 May 55		30 Nov 56		
	52-3361	450-157-35	220	n/a	n/a	n/a	19 May 55			31 Jul 62	20 Oct 67
	52-3362	450-157-35	221	n/a	n/a	n/a	04 May 55			24 Jan 63	20 Oct 67
	52-3363	450-157-35	222	n/a	n/a	n/a	09 May 55			13 Jun 63	30 Oct 67
	52-3364	450-157-35	223	n/a	n/a	n/a	25 May 55			17 May 63	30 Oct 67
	52-3365	450-157-35	224	n/a	n/a	n/a	24 May 55			08 Jul 64	30 Sep 68
	52-3366	450-157-35	225	n/a	n/a	n/a	26 May 55			04 Jun 63	30 Oct 67
	52-3367	450-157-35	226	n/a	n/a	n/a	26 May 55			18 Mar 63	30 Oct 67
	52-3368	450-157-35	227	n/a	n/a	n/a	26 May 55			31 Jul 62	30 Oct 67
	52-3369	450-157-35	228	n/a	n/a	n/a	12 Jun 55			03 Jun 63	30 Oct 67
	52-3370	450-157-35	229	n/a	n/a	n/a	05 Jun 55			17 Jun 64	11 Sep 68
	52-3371	450-157-35	230	n/a	n/a	n/a	07 Jun 55		03 Feb 59		
	52-3372	450-157-35	231	n/a	n/a	n/a	14 Jun 55			07 Mar 63	30 Oct 67
	52-3373	450-157-35	232	n/a	n/a	n/a	13 Jun 55			19 Mar 63	30 Oct 67
RB-47E-40-BW	52-3374	450-158-36	4501047	01 Dec 54	21 Jan 55	01 Feb 55	07 Feb 55	E-47/R-47E RB-47E		26 Sep 61	16 Sep 68
	52-3375	450-158-36	4501048	03 Dec 54	24 Jan 55	12 Feb 55	15 Feb 55			13 May 60	16 Sep 68
	52-3376	450-158-36	4501049	08 Dec 54	17 Jan 55	11 Feb 55	11 Feb 55			18 Jun 60	16 Sep 68
	52-3377	450-158-36	4501050	10 Dec 54	25 Jan 55	18 Feb 55	21 Feb 55			16 Jun 60	16 Sep 68
	52-3378	450-158-36	4501051	14 Dec 54	27 Jan 55	21 Feb 55	24 Feb 55			10 Jun 60	16 Sep 68
	52-3379	450-158-36	4501052	17 Feb 55	07 Feb 55	17 Mar 55	18 Mar 55			09 Jun 60	16 Sep 68
	52-3380	450-158-36	4501053	22 Dec 54	31 Jan 55	16 Feb 55	21 Feb 55			14 Jun 60	16 Sep 68
	52-3381	450-158-36	4501054	28 Dec 54	07 Feb 55	01 Mar 55	02 Mar 55			20 Jun 60	16 Sep 68
	52-3382	450-158-36	4501055	03 Jan 55	14 Feb 55	07 Mar 55	09 Mar 55			17 Jun 60	16 Sep 68
	52-3383	450-158-36	4501056	06 Jan 55	01 Mar 55	17 Mar 55	18 Mar 55		09 Jan 59		
	52-3384	450-158-36	4501057	11 Jan 55	08 Feb 55	30 Mar 55	01 Apr 55	E-47/R-47E RB-47E		21 Sep 61	16 Sep 68
	52-3385	450-158-36	4501058	14 Jan 55	07 Mar 55	11 Mar 55	12 Mar 55			06 Jun 60	16 Sep 68
	52-3386	450-158-36	4501059	19 Jan 55	16 Mar 55	30 Mar 55	01 Apr 55			16 Jun 60	16 Sep 68
	52-3387	450-158-36	4501060	24 Jan 55	12 Mar 55	27 Mar 55	01 Apr 55			07 Jun 60	16 Sep 68
	52-3388	450-158-36	4501061	27 Jan 55	22 Mar 55	14 Apr 55	15 Apr 55	E-47/R-47E RB-47E		19 Sep 61	16 Sep 68
	52-3389	450-158-36	4501062	31 Jan 55	23 Mar 55	12 Apr 55	14 Apr 55		24 Mar 59		
	52-3390	450-158-36	4501063	04 Feb 55	30 Mar 55	12 Apr 55	12 Apr 55			09 Jun 60	16 Sep 68
	52-3391	450-158-36	4501064	09 Feb 55	05 Apr 55	14 Apr 55	15 Apr 55	E-47/R-47E RB-47E		19 Sep 61	03 Nov 61
	52-3392	450-158-36	4501065	10 Feb 55	05 Apr 55	15 Apr 55	20 Apr 55			24 Apr 61	16 Sep 68
	52-3393	450-158-36	4501066	15 Feb 55	06 Apr 55	15 Apr 55	15 Apr 55		09 Jan 59		
	52-3394	450-158-36	4501067	18 Feb 55	07 Apr 55	24 Apr 55	27 Apr 55			16 Apr 61	16 Sep 68
	52-3395	450-158-36	4501068	23 Feb 55	08 Apr 55	25 Apr 55	27 Apr 55	E-47/R-47E RB-47E		21 Sep 61	30 Nov 61
	52-3396	450-158-36	4501069	28 Feb 55	14 Apr 55	13 May 55	18 May 55	E-47/R-47E RB-47E		12 Sep 61	13 Nov 61
	52-3397	450-158-36	4501070	02 Mar 55	22 Apr 55	18 May 55	19 May 55	E-47/R-47E RB-47E		13 Sep 61	16 Sep 68
	52-3398	450-158-36	4501071	08 Mar 55	15 Apr 55	03 May 55	04 May 55	E-47/R-47E RB-47E		28 Sep 61	16 Sep 68
	52-3399	450-158-36	4501072	11 Mar 55	26 Apr 55	04 May 55	06 May 55	E-47/R-47E RB-47E		27 Sep 61	16 Sep 68
	52-3400	450-158-36	4501073	17 Mar 55	03 May 55	26 May 55	26 May 55	E-47/R-47E RB-47E		27 Sep 61	16 Sep 68
B-47E-55-LM	53-1819	450-157-35	233	n/a	n/a	13 Jun 55	22 Jun 55			29 Jun 64	30 Sep 68
	53-1820	450-157-35	234	n/a	n/a	07 Jun 55	18 Jun 55			27 Jan 66	28 Jan 69
	53-1821	450-157-35	235	n/a	n/a	08 Jun 55	18 Jun 55			14 Jan 66	28 Jan 69
	53-1822	450-157-35	236	n/a	n/a	28 Jun 55	08 Jul 55			07 Dec 64	11 Sep 68
	53-1823	450-157-35	237	n/a	n/a	14 Jun 55	23 Jun 55			07 Aug 64	11 Sep 68
	53-1824	450-157-35	238	n/a	n/a	22 Jun 55	29 Jun 55			06 Feb 63	30 Oct 67
	53-1825	450-157-35	239	n/a	n/a	n/a	16 Jul 55			12 Feb 66	05 May 66
	53-1826	450-157-35	240	n/a	n/a	04 Jul 55	15 Jul 55			07 Jan 63	30 Oct 67

MDS and Block Number	Serial Number	Model Number	Const. Number	Roll Out Date	First Flight Date	MIRR Date	USAF Fly Away	New MDS	Out of Service	MASDC Input Date	MASDC Output Date
B-47E-55-LM	53-1827	450-157-35	241	n/a	n/a	15 Jun 55	05 Jul 55			07 Aug 63	11 Sep 68
	53-1828	450-157-35	242	n/a	n/a	21 Jul 55	28 Jul 55			11 Mar 64	11 Sep 68
	53-1829	450-157-35	243	n/a	n/a	08 Jul 55	23 Jul 55			04 Jun 64	11 Sep 68
	53-1830	450-157-35	244	n/a	n/a	12 Jul 55	23 Jul 55			18 Jan 63	30 Oct 67
	53-1831	450-157-35	245	n/a	n/a	20 Jul 55	28 Jul 55		05 Feb 56		
	53-1832	450-157-35	246	n/a	n/a	16 Jul 55	25 Jul 55		15 Feb 57		
	53-1833	450-157-35	247	n/a	n/a	18 Jul 55	28 Jul 55			09 Nov 65	23 Oct 68
	53-1834	450-157-35	248	n/a	n/a	01 Aug 55	04 Aug 55			04 Jun 64	11 Sep 68
	53-1835	450-157-35	249	n/a	n/a	20 Jul 55	28 Jul 55			22 Nov 65	22 Oct 68
	53-1836	450-157-35	250	n/a	n/a	20 Jul 55	28 Jul 55			05 Feb 63	30 Oct 67
	53-1837	450-157-35	251	n/a	n/a	08 Aug 55	14 Aug 55			12 Feb 63	30 Oct 67
	53-1838	450-157-35	252	n/a	n/a	04 Aug 55	12 Aug 55			24 Apr 64	11 Sep 68
	53-1839	450-157-35	253	n/a	n/a	10 Aug 55	14 Aug 55			10 Aug 64	12 Jul 68
	53-1840	450-157-35	254	n/a	n/a	04 Aug 55	11 Aug 55			31 Jul 62	30 Oct 67
	53-1841	450-157-35	255	n/a	n/a	11 Aug 55	17 Aug 55			20 Feb 63	30 Oct 67
	53-1842	450-157-35	256	n/a	n/a	16 Aug 55	23 Aug 53			07 Feb 63	30 Oct 67
	53-1843	450-157-35	257	n/a	n/a	26 Aug 55	31 Aug 53			12 Jun 63	30 Sep 68
	53-1844	450-157-35	258	n/a	n/a	01 Sep 55	06 Sep 55			01 Feb 63	30 Oct 67
	53-1845	450-157-35	259	n/a	n/a	23 Aug 55	27 Aug 55			01 Dec 64	11 Sep 68
	53-1846	450-157-35	260	n/a	n/a	01 Sep 55	06 Sep 55			18 Mar 64	11 Sep 68
	53-1847	450-157-35	261	n/a	n/a	02 Sep 55	12 Sep 55		03 Oct 55		
	53-1848	450-157-35	262	n/a	n/a	01 Sep 55	06 Sep 55			14 Jan 63	30 Oct 67
	53-1849	450-157-35	263	n/a	n/a	13 Sep 55	16 Sep 55			03 Aug 64	12 Jul 68
B-47E-60-LM	53-1850	450-157-35	264	n/a	n/a	24 Sep 55	30 Sep 55			16 Mar 64	11 Sep 68
	53-1851	450-157-35	265	n/a	n/a	23 Sep 55	29 Sep 55			26 Mar 64	11 Sep 68
	53-1852	450-157-35	266	n/a	n/a	27 Sep 55	30 Sep 55			10 Aug 64	12 Jul 68
	53-1853	450-157-35	267	n/a	n/a	30 Sep 55	04 Oct 55			10 Jun 64	11 Sep 68
	53-1854	450-157-35	268	n/a	n/a	04 Oct 55	08 Oct 55		30 Sep 63		
	53-1855	450-157-35	269	n/a	n/a	06 Oct 55	08 Oct 55			11 Mar 63	30 Oct 67
	53-1856	450-157-35	270	n/a	n/a	07 Oct 55	10 Oct 55			06 Mar 63	30 Oct 67
	53-1857	450-157-35	271	n/a	n/a	11 Oct 55	14 Oct 55			11 Mar 63	30 Oct 67
	53-1858	450-157-35	272	n/a	n/a	07 Oct 55	10 Oct 55			15 Mar 63	30 Oct 67
	53-1859	450-157-35	273	n/a	n/a	17 Oct 55	19 Oct 55			24 Jan 63	30 Oct 67
	53-1860	450-157-35	274	n/a	n/a	13 Oct 55	17 Oct 55			30 Jan 63	30 Oct 67
	53-1861	450-157-35	275	n/a	n/a	27 Oct 55	01 Nov 55			02 Nov 65	23 Oct 68
	53-1862	450-157-35	276	n/a	n/a	09 Nov 55	16 Nov 55			02 Nov 65	28 Jan 69
	53-1863	450-157-35	277	n/a	n/a	07 Nov 55	10 Nov 55			02 Nov 65	28 Jan 68
	53-1864	450-157-35	278	n/a	n/a	12 Nov 55	21 Nov 55			14 Dec 65	28 Jan 69
	53-1865	450-157-35	279	n/a	n/a	29 Oct 55	03 Nov 55			10 Nov 65	22 Oct 68
	53-1866	450-157-35	280	n/a	n/a	09 Nov 55	16 Nov 55			04 Feb 65	16 Oct 68
	53-1867	450-157-35	281	n/a	n/a	15 Nov 55	21 Nov 55			04 Feb 65	16 Oct 68
	53-1868	450-157-35	282	n/a	n/a	17 Nov 55	22 Nov 55		05 Feb 64		
	53-1869	450-157-35	283	n/a	n/a	15 Nov 55	22 Nov 55			15 Nov 65	23 Oct 68
	53-1870	450-157-35	284	n/a	n/a	23 Nov 55	28 Nov 55			09 Dec 65	28 Jan 69
	53-1871	450-157-35	285	n/a	n/a	13 Dec 55	17 Dec 55			18 Nov 65	28 Jan 69
	53-1872	450-157-35	286	n/a	n/a	28 Nov 55	08 Dec 55			26 Jan 65	16 Oct 68
	53-1873	450-157-35	287	n/a	n/a	13 Dec 55	16 Dec 55			11 Jan 66	28 Jan 69
	53-1874	450-157-35	288	n/a	n/a	06 Dec 55	09 Dec 55			06 Oct 65	23 Oct 68
	53-1875	450-157-35	289	n/a	n/a	02 Dec 55	10 Dec 55			12 Oct 65	23 Oct 68
	53-1876	450-157-35	290	n/a	n/a	12 Dec 55	17 Dec 55			19 Oct 65	23 Oct 68
	53-1877	450-157-35	291	n/a	n/a	03 Jan 56	06 Jan 56			04 Nov 65	23 Oct 68
	53-1878	450-157-35	292	n/a	n/a	22 Dec 55	30 Dec 55			12 Oct 65	23 Oct 68
	53-1879	450-157-35	293	n/a	n/a	05 Jan 56	12 Jan 56			19 Oct 65	23 Oct 68
	53-1880	450-157-35	294	n/a	n/a	20 Dec 55	23 Dec 55			04 Nov 65	28 Jan 69
B-47E-65-LM	53-1881	450-157-35	295	n/a	n/a	23 Dec 55	30 Dec 55	E-47E EB-47E		08 Feb 65	13 Dec 68
	53-1882	450-157-35	296	n/a	n/a	03 Jan 56	11 Jan 56			02 Feb 65	16 Oct 68
	53-1883	450-157-35	297	n/a	n/a	01 Feb 56	08 Feb 56	E-47E EB-47E		15 Dec 64	21 Jun 66
	53-1884	450-157-35	298	n/a	n/a	12 Jan 56	19 Jan 56			02 Dec 65	28 Jan 69
	53-1885	450-157-35	299	n/a	n/a	09 Jan 56	13 Jan 56			03 Mar 65	16 Oct 68
	53-1886	450-157-35	300	n/a	n/a	13 Jan 56	20 Jan 56		08 Nov 60		
	53-1887	450-157-35	301	n/a	n/a	12 Jan 56	20 Jan 56			18 Jan 66	28 Jan 69
	53-1888	450-157-35	302	n/a	n/a	01 Feb 56	04 Feb 56			15 Nov 65	28 Jan 69
	53-1889	450-157-35	303	n/a	n/a	08 Feb 56	10 Feb 56	E-47E EB-47E		11 Feb 65	13 Jan 69
	53-1890	450-157-35	304	n/a	n/a	08 Feb 56	10 Feb 56			02 Dec 65	23 Oct 68
	53-1891	450-157-35	305	n/a	n/a	21 Feb 56	28 Feb 56		24 Oct 57		
	53-1892	450-157-35	306	n/a	n/a	01 Mar 56	07 Mar 56			13 Dec 65	28 Jan 69
	53-1893	450-157-35	307	n/a	n/a	22 Feb 56	01 Mar 56			30 Nov 65	28 Jan 69
	53-1894	450-157-35	308	n/a	n/a	14 Feb 556	20 Feb 56			20 Oct 65	23 Oct 68
	53-1895	450-157-35	309	n/a	n/a	01 Mar 56	09 Mar 56			13 Dec 65	28 Jan 69
	53-1896	450-157-35	310	n/a	n/a	19 Mar 56	27 Mar 56			08 Oct 65	23 Oct 68
	53-1897	450-157-35	311	n/a	n/a	09 Mar 56	16 Mar 56			19 Mar 65	16 Oct 68
	53-1898	450-157-35	312	n/a	n/a	16 Mar 56	23 Mar 56			10 Nov 65	28 Jan 69
	53-1899	450-157-35	313	n/a	n/a	19 Mar 56	26 Mar 56			18 Nov 65	23 Oct 68
	53-1900	450-157-35	314	n/a	n/a	16 Mar 56	21 Mar 56	E-47E EB-47E		18 Jan 65	13 Jan 69
	53-1901	450-157-35	315	n/a	n/a	02 Apr 56	13 Apr 56			16 Feb 65	16 Oct 68
	53-1902	450-157-35	316	n/a	n/a	02 Apr 56	09 Apr 56			02 Mar 65	16 Oct 68
	53-1903	450-157-35	317	n/a	n/a	04 Apr 56	10 Apr 56			15 Nov 65	28 Jan 69
	53-1904	450-157-35	318	n/a	n/a	02 Apr 56	04 Apr 56			30 Nov 65	28 Jan 69
	53-1905	450-157-35	319	n/a	n/a	12 Apr 56	19 Apr 56		27 Nov 61		
	53-1906	450-157-35	320	n/a	n/a	10 Apr 56	13 Apr 56			18 Feb 65	16 Oct 68
	53-1907	450-157-35	321	n/a	n/a	19 Apr 56	27 Apr 56			10 Dec 65	28 Jan 69
	53-1908	450-157-35	322	n/a	n/a	02 May 56	11 May 56			01 Dec 65	24 Oct 68
	53-1909	450-157-35	323	n/a	n/a	01 May 56	11 May 56			03 Mar 65	21 Oct 68
	53-1910	450-157-35	324	n/a	n/a	01 Jun 56	05 Jun 56			29 Oct 65	24 Oct 68
	53-1911	450-157-35	325	n/a	n/a	01 May 56	15 May 56			09 Mar 65	21 Oct 68
B-47E-70-LM	53-1912	450-157-35	326	n/a	n/a	01 May 56	04 May 56			30 Apr 65	21 Oct 68
	53-1913	450-157-35	327	n/a	n/a	15 May 56	23 May 56			08 Oct 65	24 Oct 68
	53-1914	450-157-35	328	n/a	n/a	23 May 56	29 May 56			03 Feb 66	28 Jan 69
	53-1915	450-157-35	329	n/a	n/a	08 May 56	16 May 56	E-47E EB-47E		23 Feb 65	13 Dec 68

MDS and Block Number	Serial Number	Model Number	Const. Number	Roll Out Date	First Flight Date	MIRR Date	USAF Fly Away	New MDS	Out of Service	MASDC Input Date	MASDC Output Date
B-47E-70-LM	53-1916	450-157-35	330	n/a	n/a	01 Jun 56	08 Jun 56			04 Nov 65	24 Oct 68
	53-1917	450-157-35	331	n/a	n/a	01 Jun 56	07 Jun 56			18 Feb 65	21 Oct 68
	53-1918	450-157-35	332	n/a	n/a	05 Jun 56	08 Jun 56			13 Apr 66	27 May 66
	53-1919	450-157-35	333	n/a	n/a	28 Jun 56	03 Jul 56			15 Feb 65	21 Oct 68
	53-1920	450-157-35	334	n/a	n/a	25 Jun 56	29 Jun 56			11 Feb 66	18 May 66
	53-1921	450-157-35	335	n/a	n/a	27 Jun 56	03 Jul 56			05 Feb 66	28 Jan 69
	53-1922	450-157-35	336	n/a	n/a	02 Jul 56	10 Jul 56			30 Nov 65	24 Oct 68
	53-1923	450-157-35	337	n/a	n/a	03 Jul 56	13 Jul 56			02 Dec 65	28 Jan 69
	53-1924	450-157-35	338	n/a	n/a	10 Jul 56	17 Jul 56			09 Dec 65	28 Jan 69
	53-1925	450-157-35	339	n/a	n/a	19 Jul 56	26 Jul 56			08 Oct 65	28 Jan 69
	53-1926	450-157-35	340	n/a	n/a	24 Jul 56	31 Jul 56			22 Jan 66	28 Jan 69
	53-1927	450-157-35	341	n/a	n/a	31 Jul 56	27 Aug 56			07 Dec 65	28 Jan 69
	53-1928	450-157-35	342	n/a	n/a	23 Jul 56	28 Jul 56			02 Nov 65	24 Oct 68
	53-1929	450-157-35	343	n/a	n/a	03 Aug 56	09 Aug 56	E-47E EB-47E		17 Feb 65	13 Dec 68
	53-1930	450-157-35	344	n/a	n/a	02 Aug 56	09 Aug 56	E-47E EB-47E		21 Jan 65	13 Jan 69
	53-1931	450-157-35	345	n/a	n/a	13 Aug 56	17 Aug 56		11 Jun 58		
	53-1932	450-157-35	346	n/a	n/a	15 Aug 56	23 Aug 56			04 Mar 65	21 Oct 68
	53-1933	450-157-35	347	n/a	n/a	13 Aug 56	21 Aug 56		25 Oct 56		
	53-1934	450-157-35	348	n/a	n/a	16 Aug 56	27 Aug 56			19 Oct 65	24 Oct 68
	53-1935	450-157-35	349	n/a	n/a	31 Aug 56	21 Sep 56			08 Mar 65	21 Oct 68
	53-1936	450-157-35	350	n/a	n/a	21 Sep 56	29 Sep 56			21 Mar 66	05 May 66
	53-1937	450-157-35	351	n/a	n/a	27 Sep 56	09 Oct 56			09 Feb 66	28 Jan 69
	53-1938	450-157-35	352	n/a	n/a	28 Sep 56	03 Oct 56			06 Jan 66	29 Jan 69
	53-1939	450-157-35	353	n/a	n/a	29 Sep 56	10 Oct 56			26 Jan 65	21 Oct 68
	53-1940	450-157-35	354	n/a	n/a	13 Sep 56	26 Sep 56	E-47E EB-47E		01 Dec 64	13 Jan 69
	53-1941	450-157-35	355	n/a	n/a	27 Sep 56	05 Oct 56			04 Mar 65	21 Oct 68
	53-1942	450-157-35	356	n/a	n/a	02 Oct 56	09 Oct 56	E-47E EB-47E		11 Jan 65	13 Jan 69
B-47E-75-LM	53-1943	450-157-35	357	n/a	n/a	14 Sep 56	26 Sep 56			07 Dec 65	29 Jan 69
	53-1944	450-157-35	358	n/a	n/a	09 Oct 56	15 Oct 56			06 Oct 65	24 Oct 68
	53-1945	450-157-35	359	n/a	n/a	01 Oct 56	06 Oct 56	E-47E EB-47E		25 Jan 65	13 Jan 69
	53-1946	450-157-35	360	n/a	n/a	11 Oct 56	23 Oct 56			23 Oct 65	24 Oct 68
	53-1947	450-157-35	361	n/a	n/a	10 Oct 56	18 Oct 56			01 Dec 65	24 Oct 68
	53-1948	450-157-35	362	n/a	n/a	27 Oct 56	31 Oct 56			10 Dec 65	29 Jan 69
	53-1949	450-157-35	363	n/a	n/a	17 Oct 56	23 Oct 56			18 Nov 65	24 Oct 68
	53-1950	450-157-35	364	n/a	n/a	07 Nov 56	13 Nov 56			18 Nov 65	29 Jan 69
	53-1951	450-157-35	365	n/a	n/a	06 Nov 56	14 Nov 56			08 Dec 65	29 Jan 69
	53-1952	450-157-35	366	n/a	n/a	14 Nov 56	21 Nov 56			15 Nov 65	24 Oct 68
	53-1953	450-157-35	367	n/a	n/a	12 Nov 56	19 Nov 56			10 Nov 65	29 Jan 69
	53-1954	450-157-35	368	n/a	n/a	09 Nov 56	21 Nov 56			20 Oct 65	24 Oct 68
	53-1955	450-157-35	369	n/a	n/a	27 Nov 56	03 Dec 56			14 Dec 65	29 Jan 69
	53-1956	450-157-35	370	n/a	n/a	28 Nov 56	04 Dec 56			25 Mar 65	21 Oct 68
	53-1957	450-157-35	371	n/a	n/a	29 Nov 56	05 Dec 56			07 Dec 65	24 Oct 68
	53-1958	450-157-35	372	n/a	n/a	27 Nov 56	06 Dec 56			03 Mar 65	21 Oct 68
	53-1959	450-157-35	373	n/a	n/a	19 Dec 56	27 Dec 56			09 Dec 65	29 Jan 69
	53-1960	450-157-35	374	n/a	n/a	06 Dec 56	17 Dec 56			13 Dec 65	29 Jan 69
	53-1961	450-157-35	375	n/a	n/a	18 Dec 56	07 Jan 56			30 Nov 65	29 Jan 69
	53-1962	450-157-35	376	n/a	n/a	29 Dec 56	10 Jan 57			08 Dec 65	29 Jan 69
	53-1963	450-157-35	377	n/a	n/a	29 Dec 56	12 Jan 57	E-47E EB-47E		19 Feb 65	13 Dec 68
	53-1964	450-157-35	378	n/a	n/a	30 Dec 56	12 Jan 57			02 Dec 64	12 Jul 68
	53-1965	450-157-35	379	n/a	n/a	29 Dec 56	08 Jan 57			14 Dec 65	29 Jan 69
	53-1966	450-157-35	380	n/a	n/a	09 Jan 57	18 Jan 57	E-47E EB-47E		28 Jan 65	13 Jan 69
	53-1967	450-157-35	381	n/a	n/a	12 Jan 57	23 Jan 57			10 Nov 65	24 Oct 68
	53-1968	450-157-35	382	n/a	n/a	18 Jan 57	28 Jan 57	E-47E EB-47E		11 Jan 65	13 Jan 69
	53-1969	450-157-35	383	n/a	n/a	12 Feb 57	16 Feb 57	E-47E EB-47E		05 Jan 65	13 Jan 69
	53-1970	450-157-35	384	n/a	n/a	23 Jan 57	04 Feb 57			09 Dec 65	29 Jan 69
	53-1971	450-157-35	385	n/a	n/a	31 Jan 57	07 Feb 57			23 Nov 65	29 Jan 69
	53-1972	450-157-35	386	n/a	n/a	12 Feb 57	16 Feb 57			18 Jan 66	29 Jan 69
B-47E	53-1973 to 53-2027	450-157-35 450-157-35	canceled								
B-47E-35-DT	53-2028	450-157-35	44149	n/a	n/a	17 Mar 55	20 May 55			21 Jan 65	21 Oct 68
	53-2029	450-157-35	44150	n/a	n/a	22 Mar 55	25 May 55			08 Feb 66	23 Apr 66
	53-2030	450-157-35	44151	n/a	n/a	25 Mar 55	31 May 55			05 Jan 66	29 Jan 69
	53-2031	450-157-35	44152	n/a	n/a	30 Mar 55	06 Jun 55			05 May 64	10 Sep 68
	53-2032	450-157-35	44153	n/a	n/a	04 Apr 55	09 Jun 55			16 Nov 65	29 Jan 69
	53-2033	450-157-35	44154	n/a	n/a	07 Apr 55	14 Jun 55			27 Oct 65	24 Oct 68
	53-2034	450-157-35	44155	n/a	n/a	13 Apr 55	17 Jun 55			26 Mar 64	11 Sep 68
	53-2035	450-157-35	44156	n/a	n/a	18 Apr 55	22 Jun 55		21 Jan 59		
	53-2036	450-157-35	44157	n/a	n/a	21 Apr 55	28 Jun 55			11 Aug 64	11 Sep 68
	53-2037	450-157-35	44158	n/a	n/a	27 Apr 55	30 Jun 55			12 Feb 66	29 Apr 66
	53-2038	450-157-35	44159	n/a	n/a	02 May 55	06 Jul 55		17 Aug 64		
	53-2039	450-157-35	44160	n/a	n/a	05 May 55	12 Jul 55			20 Feb 64	11 Sep 68
	53-2040	450-157-35	44161	n/a	n/a	10 May 55	15 Jul 55			05 May 64	10 Sep 68
B-47E	53-2041 to 53-2089	450-157-35 450-157-35	canceled								
B-47E-40-DT	53-2090	450-157-35	44436	n/a	n/a	16 May 55	20 Jul 55			10 Jun 64	11 Sep 68
	53-2091	450-157-35	44437	n/a	n/a	19 May 55	26 Jul 55		24 May 57		
	53-2092	450-157-35	44438	n/a	n/a	25 May 55	29 Jul 55			31 Jul 62	30 Sep 68
	53-2093	450-157-35	44439	n/a	n/a	01 Jun 55	04 Aug 55			31 Jul 62	30 Oct 67
	53-2094	450-157-35	44440	n/a	n/a	07 Jun 55	10 Aug 55			20 Feb 63	31 Oct 67
	53-2095	450-157-35	44441	n/a	n/a	13 Jun 55	16 Aug 55			11 Aug 64	11 Sep 68
	53-2096	450-157-35	44442	n/a	n/a	17 Jun 55	22 Aug 55			27 May 64	10 Sep 68

MDS and Block Number	Serial Number	Model Number	Const. Number	Roll Out Date	First Flight Date	MIRR Date	USAF Fly Away	New MDS	Out of Service	MASDC Input Date	MASDC Output Date
B-47E-40-DT	53-2097	450-157-35	44443	n/a	n/a	23 Jun 55	26 Aug 55		10 Jan 63		
	53-2098	450-157-35	44444	n/a	n/a	29 Jun 55	02 Sep 55			08 Jun 64	11 Sep 67
	53-2099	450-157-35	44445	n/a	n/a	06 Jul 55	09 Sep 55			14 Jan 65	21 Oct 68
	53-2100	450-157-35	44446	n/a	n/a	12 Jul 55	16 Sep 55			22 May 64	20 Oct 68
	53-2101	450-157-35	44447	n/a	n/a	19 Jul 55	22 Sep 55			16 Apr 64	11 Sep 68
	53-2102	450-157-35	44448	n/a	n/a	25 Jul 55	28 Sep 55			13 May 64	10 Sep 68
	53-2103	450-157-35	44449	n/a	n/a	29 Jul 55	05 Oct 55			08 Jan 65	21 Oct 68
B-47E-45-DT	53-2104	450-157-35	44450	n/a	n/a	04 Aug 55	12 Oct 55	JB-47E NB-47E		07 Nov 74	13 Jul 79
	53-2105	450-157-35	44451	n/a	n/a	11 Aug 55	18 Oct 55			19 Feb 63	31 Oct 67
	53-2106	450-157-35	44452	n/a	n/a	17 Aug 55	24 Oct 55			12 Feb 63	31 Oct 67
	53-2107	450-157-35	44453	n/a	n/a	23 Aug 55	31 Oct 55			07 Jan 63	31 Oct 67
	53-2108	450-157-35	44454	n/a	n/a	30 Aug 55	04 Nov 55	JB-47E	27 Aug 56	23 Jan 63	31 Oct 67
	53-2109	450-157-35	44455	n/a	n/a	06 Sep 55	10 Nov 55			08 Dec 65	29 Jan 69
	53-2110	450-157-35	44456	n/a	n/a	12 Sep 55	16 Nov 55		18 Jun 61		
	53-2111	450-157-35	44457	n/a	n/a	16 Sep 55	22 Nov 55			26 Feb 65	21 Oct 68
	53-2112	450-157-35	44458	n/a	n/a	23 Sep 55	30 Nov 55			11 Oct 65	29 Jan 69
	53-2113	450-157-35	44459	n/a	n/a	29 Sep 55	06 Dec 55			28 Jan 66	29 Jan 69
	53-2114	450-157-35	44460	n/a	n/a	05 Oct 55	12 Dec 55			06 Jan 66	29 Jan 69
	53-2115	450-157-35	44461	n/a	n/a	11 Oct 55	16 Dec 55			11 Oct 65	29 Jan 69
	53-2116	450-157-35	44462	n/a	n/a	18 Oct 55	22 Dec 55			01 Feb 66	29 Jan 69
	53-2117	450-157-35	44463	n/a	n/a	24 Oct 55	30 Dec 55				
B-47E-50-DT	53-2118	450-157-35	44464	n/a	n/a	28 Oct 55	05 Jan 56			17 Nov 65	24 Oct 68
	53-2119	450-157-35	44465	n/a	n/a	04 Nov 55	11 Jan 56		16 Jan 62		
	53-2120	450-157-35	44466	n/a	n/a	10 Nov 55	17 Jan 56			10 Dec 65	29 Jan 69
	53-2121	450-157-35	44467	n/a	n/a	16 Nov 55	23 Jan 56	E-47E EB-47E		01 Feb 65	13 Dec 68
	53-2122	450-157-35	44468	n/a	n/a	23 Nov 55	27 Jan 56			03 Nov 65	24 Oct 68
	53-2123	450-157-35	44469	n/a	n/a	30 Nov 55	02 Feb 56			08 Oct 65	24 Oct 68
	53-2124	450-157-35	44470	n/a	n/a	06 Dec 55	09 Feb 56	E-47E EB-47E		10 Dec 64	21 Jun 66
	53-2125	450-157-35	44471	n/a	n/a	13 Dec 55	15 Feb 56			02 Feb 65	21 Oct 68
	53-2126	450-157-35	44472	n/a	n/a	19 Dec 55	21 Feb 56	E-47E EB-47E		14 Jan 65	13 Jan 69
	53-2127	450-157-35	44473	n/a	n/a	23 Dec 55	28 Feb 56	E-47E EB-47E		01 Feb 65	13 Dec 68
	53-2128	450-157-35	44474	n/a	n/a	30 Dec 55	06 Mar 56	E-47E EB-47E		10 Dec 64	21 Jun 66
	53-2129	450-157-35	44475	n/a	n/a	06 Jan 56	12 Mar 56		11 Jun 59		
	53-2130	450-157-35	44476	n/a	n/a	12 Jan 56	19 Mar 56			17 Nov 65	24 Oct 68
	53-2131	450-157-35	44477	n/a	n/a	19 Jan 56	23 Mar 56	E-47E EB-47E		10 Dec 64	21 Jun 66
B-47E-55-DT	53-2132	450-157-35	44478	n/a	n/a	25 Jan 56	30 Mar 56			01 Dec 65	29 Jan 69
	53-2133	450-157-35	44479	n/a	n/a	31 Jan 56	05 Apr 56	E-47E EB-47E		01 Dec 64	21 Jun 66
	53-2134	450-157-35	44480	n/a	n/a	07 Feb 56	11 Apr 56	E-47E EB-47E	05 Feb 63		
	53-2135	450-157-35	44481	n/a	n/a	13 Feb 56	17 Apr 56			08 Dec 64	21 Jun 66
	53-2136	450-157-35	44482	n/a	n/a	17 Feb 56	23 Apr 56	E-47E EB-47E	22 Sep 59		
	53-2137	450-157-35	44483	n/a	n/a	24 Feb 56	26 Apr 56	E-47E EB-47E		03 Dec 64	13 Jan 69
	53-2138	450-157-35	44484	n/a	n/a	01 Mar 56	04 May 56	E-47E EB-47E		23 Feb 65	13 Dec 68
	53-2139	450-157-35	44485	n/a	n/a	07 Mar 56	10 May 56			05 Mar 65	21 Oct 68
	53-2140	450-157-35	44486	n/a	n/a	14 Mar 56	16 May 56			09 Mar 65	21 Oct 68
	53-2141	450-157-35	44487	n/a	n/a	20 Mar 56	22 May 56			03 Nov 65	24 Oct 68
	53-2142	450-157-35	44488	n/a	n/a	26 Mar 56	29 May 56			29 Nov 65	24 Oct 68
	53-2143	450-157-35	44489	n/a	n/a	02 Apr 56	05 Jun 56			18 Jan 66	30 Jan 69
	53-2144	450-157-35	44490	n/a	n/a	06 Apr 56	11 Jun 56			22 Jan 66	30 Jan 69
B-47E-60-DT	53-2145	450-157-35	44491	n/a	n/a	12 Apr 56	18 Jun 56			08 Nov 65	30 Jan 69
	53-2146	450-157-35	44492	n/a	n/a	19 Apr 56	14 Jun 56			29 Nov 65	30 Jan 69
	53-2147	450-157-35	44493	n/a	n/a	25 Apr 56	19 Jun 56			22 Nov 65	22 Oct 68
	53-2148	450-157-35	44494	n/a	n/a	01 May 56	02 Jul 56			22 Nov 65	22 Oct 68
	53-2149	450-157-35	44495	n/a	n/a	08 May 56	03 Jul 56			22 Nov 65	30 Jan 69
	53-2150	450-157-35	44496	n/a	n/a	14 May 56	09 Jul 56			01 Nov 65	24 Oct 68
	53-2151	450-157-35	44497	n/a	n/a	18 May 56	12 Jul 56			29 Nov 65	30 Jan 69
	53-2152	450-157-35	44498	n/a	n/a	25 May 56	19 Jul 56			08 Nov 65	24 Oct 68
	53-2153	450-157-35	44499	n/a	n/a	01 Jun 56	01 Aug 56			23 Oct 65	24 Oct 68
	53-2154	450-157-35	44500	n/a	n/a	07 Jun 56	03 Aug 56			28 Oct 65	24 Oct 68
	53-2155	450-157-35	44501	n/a	n/a	14 Jun 56	07 Aug 56			01 Nov 65	24 Oct 68
	53-2156	450-157-35	44502	n/a	n/a	20 Jun 56	08 Aug 56			23 Oct 65	24 Oct 68
	53-2157	450-157-35	44503	n/a	n/a	26 Jun 56	23 Aug 56			05 Jan 66	30 Jan 69
B-47E-65-DT	53-2158	450-157-35	44504	n/a	n/a	03 Jul 56	04 Sep 56			14 Oct 65	24 Oct 68
	53-2159	450-157-35	44505	n/a	n/a	10 Jul 56	06 Sep 56			17 Nov 65	30 Jan 69
	53-2160	450-157-35	44506	n/a	n/a	16 Jul 56	10 Sep 56		12 Jul 63		
	53-2161	450-157-35	44507	n/a	n/a	23 Jul 56	19 Sep 56			07 Dec 65	30 Jan 69
	53-2162	450-157-35	44508	n/a	n/a	27 Jul 56	21 Sep 56			20 Jan 66	30 Jan 69
	53-2163	450-157-35	44509	n/a	n/a	02 Aug 56	01 Oct 56			06 Oct 65	24 Oct 68
	53-2164	450-157-35	44510	n/a	n/a	09 Aug 56	03 Oct 56	E-47E EB-47E		25 Jan 65	13 Jan 69
	53-2165	450-157-35	44511	n/a	n/a	16 Aug 56	11 Oct 56			08 Nov 65	30 Jan 69
	53-2166	450-157-35	44512	n/a	n/a	21 Aug 56	12 Oct 56			01 Nov 65	30 Jan 69
	53-2167	450-157-35	44513	n/a	n/a	28 Aug 56	19 Oct 56			05 Feb 66	30 Jan 69
	53-2168	450-157-35	44514	n/a	n/a	04 Sep 56	01 Nov 56	E-47E EB-47E		17 Feb 65	13 Dec 68
	53-2169	450-157-35	44515	n/a	n/a	10 Sep 56	05 Nov 56		21 Feb 61		
	53-2170	450-157-35	44516	n/a	n/a	17 Sep 56	07 Nov 56			03 Nov 65	30 Jan 69
B-47E-110-BW	53-2261	450-157-35	4501074	04 Nov 54	21 Dec 54	19 Jan 55	22 Jan 55			08 Jan 65	21 Oct 68
	53-2262	450-157-35	4501075	08 Nov 54	20 Dec 54	12 Jan 55	12 Jan 55			29 Apr 64	11 Sep 68
	53-2263	450-157-35	4501076	09 Nov 54	20 Dec 54	14 Jan 55	15 Jan 55			15 Apr 64	10 Sep 68
	53-2264	450-157-35	4501077	10 Nov 54	21 Dec 54	17 Jan 55	21 Jan 55			27 May 64	10 Sep 68
	53-2265	450-157-35	4501078	11 Nov 54	29 Dec 54	27 Jan 55	28 Jan 55			26 Feb 63	31 Oct 67

MDS and Block Number	Serial Number	Model Number	Const. Number	Roll Out Date	First Flight Date	MIRR Date	USAF Fly Away	New MDS	Out of Service	MASDC Input Date	MASDC Output Date
B-47E-110-BW	53-2266	450-157-35	4501079	12 Nov 54	23 Dec 54	02 Feb 55	06 Feb 55			15 Feb 63	31 Oct 67
	53-2267	450-157-35	4501080	15 Nov 54	23 Dec 54	12 Jan 55	13 Jan 55		19 Aug 58		
	53-2268	450-157-35	4501081	17 Nov 54	28 Dec 54	03 Feb 55	09 Feb 55			24 Jan 63	31 Oct 67
	53-2269	450-157-35	4501082	17 Nov 54	28 Dec 54	14 Jan 55	15 Jan 55			29 Jul 64	12 Jul 68
	53-2270	450-157-35	4501083	19 Nov 54	05 Jan 55	27 Jan 55	28 Jan 55			21 Jul 64	30 Sep 68
	53-2271	450-157-35	4501084	22 Nov 54	06 Jan 55	21 Jan 55	21 Jan 55			29 Jan 65	21 Sep 68
	53-2272	450-157-35	4501085	23 Nov 54	10 Jan 55	09 Feb 55	10 Feb 55			28 Jan 63	31 Oct 67
	53-2273	450-157-35	4501086	24 Nov 54	07 Jan 55	06 Feb 55	06 Feb 55			29 Jan 65	21 Oct 68
	53-2274	450-157-35	4501087	29 Nov 54	11 Jan 55	10 Feb 55	10 Feb 55			28 Jan 63	31 Oct 67
	53-2275	450-157-35	4501088	30 Nov 54	10 Jan 55	14 Feb 55	15 Feb 55		18 Aug 64		
	53-2276	450-157-35	4501089	02 Dec 54	11 Jan 55	14 Feb 55	15 Feb 55	JB-47E	22 May 57		
	53-2277	450-157-35	4501090	02 Dec 54	12 Jan 55	24 Feb 55	19 Mar 55		15 Apr 55		
	53-2278	450-157-35	4501091	06 Dec 54	13 Jan 55	11 Feb 55	12 Feb 55			26 Jun 64	30 Sep 68
	53-2279	450-157-35	4501092	09 Dec 54	28 Jan 55	21 Feb 55	22 Feb 55		11 Feb 66		
	53-2280	450-157-35	4501093	09 Dec 54	25 Jan 55	23 Feb 55	02 Sep 55	JB-47E	Oct 67		
	53-2281	450-157-35	4501094	09 Dec 54	20 Jan 55	19 Feb 55	19 Feb 55	YB-47J	09 Apr 59		
	53-2282	450-157-35	4501095	13 Dec 54	28 Jan 55	19 Feb 55	19 Feb 55	JB-47E	12 Sep 57		
	53-2283	450-157-35	4501096	13 Dec 54	01 Feb 55	17 Mar 55	19 Mar 55			31 Jul 62	31 Oct 67
	53-2284	450-157-35	4501097	15 Dec 54	28 Jan 55	25 Feb 55	26 Feb 55			30 Jan 63	31 Oct 67
	53-2285	450-157-35	4501098	16 Dec 54	04 Feb 55	26 Feb 55	01 Mar 55			31 Jul 62	31 Oct 67
	53-2286	450-157-35	4501099	20 Dec 54	07 Feb 55	25 Feb 55	25 Feb 55			11 Feb 66	17 May 66
	53-2287	450-157-35	4501100	21 Dec 54	04 Feb 55	24 Feb 55	25 Feb 55			08 Jul 64	30 Sep 68
	53-2288	450-157-35	4501101	23 Dec 54	04 Feb 55	26 Feb 55	02 Mar 55			31 Jul 62	31 Oct 67
	53-2289	450-157-35	4501102	27 Dec 54	08 Feb 55	11 Mar 55	12 Mar 55			05 May 64	10 Sep 68
	53-2290	450-157-35	4501103	29 Dec 54	11 Feb 55	18 Mar 55	19 Mar 55			03 Aug 64	12 Jul 68
	53-2291	450-157-35	4501104	30 Dec 54	09 Feb 55	09 Mar 55	10 Mar 55			26 Feb 63	31 Oct 67
	53-2292	450-157-35	4501105	04 Jan 55	11 Feb 55	02 Mar 55	03 Mar 55			08 Jul 64	30 Sep 68
	53-2293	450-157-35	4501106	05 Jan 55	01 Mar 55	24 Mar 55	26 Mar 55			05 Nov 65	30 Jan 69
	53-2294	450-157-35	4501107	07 Jan 55	14 Feb 55	08 Mar 55	10 Mar 55			21 Oct 65	24 Oct 68
	53-2295	450-157-35	4501108	10 Jan 55	21 Feb 55	16 Mar 55	18 Mar 55			25 Feb 63	31 Oct 67
	53-2296	450-157-35	4501109	12 Jan 55	25 Feb 55	15 Mar 55	16 Mar 55		26 May 64		
B-47E-115-BW	53-2297	450-157-35	4501110	13 Jan 55	04 Mar 55	25 Mar 55	26 Mar 55			08 Jul 64	30 Sep 68
	53-2298	450-157-35	4501111	17 Jan 55	09 Mar 55	28 Mar 55	29 Mar 55			09 Nov 65	24 Oct 68
	53-2299	450-157-35	4501112	18 Jan 55	04 Mar 55	25 Mar 55	26 Mar 55			16 Nov 65	30 Jan 69
	53-2300	450-157-35	4501113	20 Jan 55	08 Mar 55	27 Mar 55	29 Mar 55			23 Jan 63	31 Oct 67
	53-2301	450-157-35	4501114	21 Jan 55	16 Mar 55	07 Apr 55	08 Apr 55		10 Oct 56		
	53-2302	450-157-35	4501115	25 Jan 55	16 Mar 55	23 Apr 55	23 Apr 55			19 Mar 64	11 Sep 68
	53-2303	450-157-35	4501116	26 Jan 55	11 Mar 55	07 Apr 55	08 Apr 55			06 Feb 63	31 Oct 67
	53-2304	450-157-35	4501117	28 Jan 55	11 Mar 55	25 Mar 55	26 Mar 55		07 Feb 56		
	53-2305	450-157-35	4501118	01 Feb 55	18 Mar 55	04 Apr 55	05 Apr 55			12 Feb 63	31 Oct 67
	53-2306	450-157-35	4501119	03 Feb 55	18 Mar 55	08 Apr 55	08 Apr 55			07 Jan 66	30 Jan 69
	53-2307	450-157-35	4501120	07 Feb 55	18 Mar 55	29 Mar 55	31 Mar 55			23 Apr 64	10 Sep 68
	53-2308	450-157-35	4501121	08 Feb 55	22 Mar 55	12 Apr 55	12 Apr 55			15 Jan 66	30 Jan 69
	53-2309	450-157-35	4501122	11 Feb 55	28 Mar 55	25 Apr 55	27 Apr 55			31 Jul 62	31 Oct 67
	53-2310	450-157-35	4501123	14 Feb 55	25 Mar 55	13 Apr 55	14 Apr 55			01 Feb 66	30 Jan 69
	53-2311	450-157-35	4501124	11 Feb 55	28 Mar 55	26 Apr 55	27 Apr 55			23 Jul 64	12 Jul 68
	53-2312	450-157-35	4501125	17 Feb 55	30 Mar 55	13 Apr 55	14 Apr 55			01 Feb 66	30 Jan 69
	53-2313	450-157-35	4501126	21 Feb 55	01 Apr 55	26 Apr 55	27 Apr 55			27 Oct 65	24 Oct 68
	53-2314	450-157-35	4501127	24 Feb 55	04 Apr 55	26 Apr 55	28 Apr 55			01 Apr 64	11 Sep 68
	53-2315	450-157-35	4501128	25 Feb 55	20 Apr 55	11 May 55	11 May 55	EB-47E / E-47E / EB-47E(TT)		30 Nov 67	13 Jan 69
	53-2316	450-157-35	4501129	01 Mar 55	15 Apr 55	12 May 55	13 May 55	EB-47E / E-47E / EB-47E(TT)		29 Nov 67	13 Jan 69
	53-2317	450-157-35	4501130	03 Mar 55	20 Apr 55	13 May 55	14 May 55			29 Jun 64	12 Jul 68
	53-2318	450-157-35	4501131	07 Mar 55	25 Apr 55	17 May 55	18 May 55			29 Jan 65	21 Jul 68
	53-2319	450-157-35	4501132	09 Mar 55	22 Apr 55	01 Jun 55	01 Jun 55		02 Apr 59		
	53-2320	450-157-35	4501133	10 Mar 55	28 Apr 55	18 May 55	19 May 55	EB-47E / E-47E / EB-47E(TT)	03 Apr 65		
	53-2321	450-157-35	4501134	15 Mar 55	27 Apr 55	19 May 55	19 May 55			08 Jan 63	31 Oct 67
	53-2322	450-157-35	4501135	16 Mar 55	28 Apr 55	21 May 55	21 May 55			02 Jun 64	11 Sep 68
	53-2323	450-157-35	4501136	21 Mar 55	03 May 55	25 May 55	27 May 55			19 Mar 64	11 Sep 68
	53-2324	450-157-35	4501137	22 Mar 55	29 Apr 55	20 May 55	20 May 55			15 Jun 64	11 Sep 68
	53-2325	450-157-35	4501138	25 Mar 55	09 May 55	24 May 55	26 May 55			22 May 64	12 Jul 68
	53-2326	450-157-35	4501139	29 Mar 55	11 May 55	25 May 55	26 May 55			19 Feb 63	31 Oct 67
	53-2327	450-157-35	4501140	30 Mar 55	10 May 55	13 Jun 55	13 Jun 55			19 May 64	10 Sep 68
	53-2328	450-157-35	4501141	05 Apr 55	12 May 55	01 Jun 55	03 Jun 55			31 Jul 62	31 Oct 67
	53-2329	450-157-35	4501142	07 Apr 55	13 May 55	08 Jun 55	10 Jun 55	EB-47L		25 Mar 65	14 Jan 69
	53-2330	450-157-35	4501143	11 Apr 55	16 May 55	15 Jun 55	18 Jun 55			31 Jul 62	30 Sep 68
	53-2331	450-157-35	4501144	14 Apr 55	11 May 55	08 Jun 55	10 Jun 55		02 May 61		
B-47E-120-BW	53-2332	450-157-35	4501145	15 Apr 55	31 May 55	01 Jul 55	01 Jul 55			02 Jan 63	31 Oct 67
	53-2333	450-157-35	4501146	19 Apr 55	20 May 55	10 Jun 55	10 Jun 55			11 Mar 64	11 Sep 68
	53-2334	450-157-35	4501147	22 Apr 55	02 Jun 55	28 Jun 55	29 Jun 55			31 Jul 62	31 Oct 67
	53-2335	450-157-35	4501148	26 Apr 55	01 Jun 55	22 Jun 55	22 Jun 55			02 Jan 63	11 Sep 68
	53-2336	450-157-35	4501149	28 Apr 55	07 Jun 55	29 Jun 55	29 Jun 55			13 May 64	12 Jul 68
	53-2337	450-157-35	4501150	02 May 55	08 Jun 55	11 Jul 55	12 Jul 55			08 Jun 64	11 Sep 68
	53-2338	450-157-35	4501151	05 May 55	09 Jun 55	21 Jun 55	22 Jun 55			06 Jul 64	30 Sep 68
	53-2339	450-157-35	4501152	09 May 55	17 Jun 55	22 Jul 55	25 Jul 55			17 Jun 64	30 Sep 68
	53-2340	450-157-35	4501153	12 May 55	16 Jun 55	12 Jul 55	12 Jul 55			09 Mar 64	11 Sep 68
	53-2341	450-157-35	4501154	16 May 55	20 Jun 55	15 Jul 55	15 Jul 55			02 Jun 64	11 Sep 68
	53-2342	450-157-35	4501155	19 May 55	23 Jun 55	14 Jul 55	14 Jul 55			15 Jul 64	30 Sep 68
	53-2343	450-157-35	4501156	25 May 55	05 Jul 55	27 Jul 55	28 Jul 55			14 May 64	12 Jul 68
	53-2344	450-157-35	4501157	31 May 55	07 Jul 55	29 Jul 55	30 Jul 55			15 Feb 63	11 Sep 68
	53-2345	450-157-35	4501158	02 Jun 55	16 Oct 56	14 Jun 55	14 Jun 55	DB-47E / JDB-47E	10 Mar 59		01 Dec 59
	53-2346	450-157-35	4501159	07 Jun 55	02 Nov 56	14 Jun 55	14 Jun 55	DB-47E / JDB-47E		20 Oct 60	22 Mar 61
	53-2347	450-157-35	4501160	08 Jun 55	19 Jul 55	23 Aug 55	23 Aug 55	JB-47E / B-47E	24 Feb 61		
	53-2348	450-157-35	4501161	13 Jun 55	03 Aug 55	25 Aug 55	26 Aug 55			22 Jun 64	30 Sep 68
	53-2349	450-157-35	4501162	17 Jun 55	26 Jul 55	08 Sep 55	10 Sep 55			12 May 64	10 Sep 68
	53-2350	450-157-35	4501163	23 Jun 55	04 Aug 55	07 Sep 55	08 Sep 55			27 Feb 64	11 Sep 68
	53-2351	450-157-35	4501164	29 Jun 55	05 Aug 55	25 Aug 55	26 Aug 55			16 Feb 65	21 Oct 68

MDS and Block Number	Serial Number	Model Number	Const. Number	Roll Out Date	First Flight Date	MIRR Date	USAF Fly Away	New MDS	Out of Service	MASDC Input Date	MASDC Output Date
B-47E-120-BW	53-2352	450-157-35	4501165	07 Jul 55	12 Aug 55	26 Aug 55	26 Aug 55			04 Mar 64	11 Sep 68
	53-2353	450-157-35	4501166	13 Jul 55	15 Aug 55	26 Aug 55	26 Aug 55			19 May 64	10 Sep 68
	53-2354	450-157-35	4501167	20 Jul 55	22 Aug 55	14 Sep 55	19 Sep 55			26 Aug 62	11 Sep 68
	53-2355	450-157-35	4501168	25 Jul 55	24 Aug 55	22 Sep 55	23 Sep 55			23 Nov 65	30 Jan 69
	53-2356	450-157-35	4501169	29 Jul 55	02 Sep 55	05 Oct 55	05 Oct 55			15 Feb 65	21 Oct 68
	53-2357	450-157-35	4501170	04 Aug 55	08 Sep 55	05 Oct 55	06 Oct 55			06 Nov 64	11 Sep 68
	53-2358	450-157-35	4501171	08 Aug 55	12 Sep 55	20 Oct 55	22 Oct 55			16 Feb 65	21 Oct 68
	53-2359	450-157-35	4501172	12 Aug 55	14 Sep 55	13 Oct 55	15 Oct 55			18 Jan 66	30 Jan 69
	53-2360	450-157-35	4501173	18 Aug 55	20 Sep 55	06 Oct 55	06 Oct 55			20 Jan 66	30 Jan 69
	53-2361	450-157-35	4501174	22 Aug 55	27 Sep 55	02 Nov 55	02 Nov 55			18 Dec 64	11 Sep 68
	53-2362	450-157-35	4501175	24 Aug 55	28 Sep 55	07 Dec 55	08 Dec 55			29 Nov 65	22 Oct 68
	53-2363	450-157-35	4501176	26 Aug 55	04 Oct 55	08 Nov 55	09 Nov 55		03 Jun 64		
	53-2364	450-157-35	4501177	30 Aug 55	06 Oct 55	10 Nov 55	16 Nov 55			03 Mar 65	21 Oct 68
	53-2365	450-157-35	4501178	01 Sep 55	07 Oct 55	02 Nov 55	03 Nov 55		19 Aug 63		
	53-2366	450-157-35	4501179	06 Sep 55	12 Oct 55	07 Nov 55	08 Nov 55		27 Jul 64		
	53-2367	450-157-35	4501180	08 Sep 55	11 Oct 55	01 Nov 55	02 Nov 55			12 Feb 66	05 May 66
B-47E-125-BW	53-2368	450-157-35	4501181	12 Sep 55	20 Oct 55	08 Nov 55	09 Nov 55			02 Dec 64	11 Sep 68
	53-2369	450-157-35	4501182	15 Sep 55	21 Oct 55	24 Jan 56	25 Jan 56			03 Nov 65	22 Oct 68
	53-2370	450-157-35	4501183	19 Sep 55	21 Oct 55	09 Nov 55	10 Nov 55			26 Jan 66	30 Jan 69
	53-2371	450-157-35	4501184	21 Sep 55	27 Oct 55	07 Dec 55	08 Dec 55			24 Feb 65	21 Oct 68
	53-2372	450-157-35	4501185	22 Sep 55	01 Nov 55	21 Nov 55	23 Nov 55			24 Feb 65	21 Oct 68
	53-2373	450-157-35	4501186	26 Sep 55	03 Nov 55	01 Dec 55	02 Dec 55			29 Oct 65	24 Oct 68
	53-2374	450-157-35	4501187	28 Sep 55	04 Nov 55	23 Nov 56	23 Nov 55			25 Feb 65	21 Oct 68
	53-2375	450-157-35	4501188	03 Oct 55	08 Nov 55	22 Nov 55	23 Nov 55			03 Feb 66	30 Jan 69
	53-2376	450-157-35	4501189	05 Oct 55	09 Nov 55	13 Dec 55	15 Dec 55			14 Oct 65	24 Oct 68
	53-2377	450-157-35	4501190	06 Oct 55	15 Nov 55	13 Dec 55	13 Dec 55			28 Jan 66	30 Jan 69
	53-2378	450-157-35	4501191	11 Oct 55	10 Nov 55	16 Dec 55	20 Dec 55			06 Oct 65	24 Oct 68
	53-2379	450-157-35	4501192	12 Oct 55	18 Nov 55	16 Dec 55	16 Dec 55			22 Nov 65	30 Jan 69
	53-2380	450-157-35	4501193	14 Oct 55	21 Nov 55	08 Dec 55	08 Dec 55			06 Jan 66	30 Jan 69
	53-2381	450-157-35	4501194	18 Oct 55	23 Nov 55	21 Dec 55	22 Dec 55			17 Nov 65	24 Oct 68
	53-2382	450-157-35	4501195	20 Oct 55	29 Nov 55	13 Dec 55	13 Dec 55			20 Jan 66	30 Jan 69
	53-2383	450-157-35	4501196	21 Oct 55	09 Dec 55	12 Jan 56	12 Jan 56	E-47E EB-47E		18 Jan 65	13 Jan 69
	53-2384	450-157-35	4501197	27 Oct 55	07 Dec 55	27 Dec 55	28 Dec 55			04 Jan 66	30 Jan 69
	53-2385	450-157-35	4501198	28 Oct 55	14 Dec 55	12 Jan 56	12 Jan 56		27 Dec 65		
	53-2386	450-157-35	4501199	01 Nov 55	15 Dec 55	28 Dec 55	29 Dec 55			25 Oct 65	24 Oct 68
	53-2387	450-157-35	4501200	03 Nov 55	21 Dec 55	19 Jan 56	20 Jan 56			04 Mar 65	21 Oct 68
	53-2388	450-157-35	4501201	07 Nov 55	22 Dec 55	17 Jan 56	20 Jan 56	E-47E EB-47E		17 Dec 64	21 Jun 66
	53-2389	450-157-35	4501202	09 Nov 55	28 Dec 55	20 Feb 56	21 Feb 56			31 Jan 66	30 Jan 69
	53-2390	450-157-35	4501203	11 Nov 55	03 Jan 56	19 Jan 56	20 Jan 56			01 Nov 65	24 Oct 68
	53-2391	450-157-35	4501204	15 Nov 55	29 Dec 55	16 Jan 56	19 Jan 56			09 Feb 66	24 Jun 66
	53-2392	450-157-35	4501205	17 Nov 55	29 Dec 55	17 Jan 56	19 Jan 56			18 Feb 65	21 Oct 68
	53-2393	450-157-35	4501206	21 Nov 55	04 Jan 56	14 Jan 56	14 Jan 56			08 Nov 65	30 Jan 69
	53-2394	450-157-35	4501207	22 Nov 55	04 Jan 56	25 Jan 56	30 Jan 56			06 Dec 65	30 Jan 69
	53-2395	450-157-35	4501208	28 Nov 55	13 Jan 56	24 Jan 56	23 Jan 56		07 Mar 57		
	53-2396	450-157-35	4501209	29 Nov 55	05 Jan 56	19 Jan 56	25 Jan 56			28 Oct 65	24 Oct 68
	53-2397	450-157-35	4501210	01 Dec 55	09 Jan 56	23 Jan 56	25 Jan 56			07 Dec 65	24 Oct 68
	53-2398	450-157-35	4501211	02 Dec 55	18 Jan 56	04 Feb 56	11 Feb 56		02 Dec 64		
	53-2399	450-157-35	4501212	06 Dec 55	19 Jan 56	16 Feb 56	18 Feb 56			23 Nov 65	30 Jan 69
	53-2400	450-157-35	4501213	07 Dec 55	20 Jan 56	08 Feb 56	11 Feb 56			28 Oct 65	24 Oct 68
	53-2401	450-157-35	4501214	09 Dec 55	20 Jan 56	22 Feb 56	25 Feb 56	E-47E EB-47E		04 May 64	12 May 66
	53-2402	450-157-35	4501215	12 Dec 55	24 Jan 56	14 Feb 56	15 Feb 56	E-47E EB-47E		25 May 64	02 Oct 68
B-47E-130-BW	53-2403	450-157-35	4501216	14 Dec 55	26 Jan 56	15 Feb 56	18 Feb 56	E-47E EB-47E		23 Apr 64	12 May 66
	53-2404	450-157-35	4501217	15 Dec 55	31 Jan 56	14 Feb 56	18 Feb 56	E-47E EB-47E		04 May 64	12 May 66
	53-2405	450-157-35	4501218	19 Dec 55	27 Jan 56	22 Feb 56	24 Feb 56			10 Dec 65	30 Jan 69
	53-2406	450-157-35	4501219	20 Dec 55	01 Feb 56	17 Feb 56	19 Feb 56	E-47E EB-47E		28 May 64	02 Oct 68
	53-2407	450-157-35	4501220	22 Dec 55	03 Feb 56	25 Feb 56	01 Mar 56	E-47E EB-47E		07 Apr 64	12 May 66
	53-2408	450-157-35	4501221	23 Dec 55	03 Feb 56	28 Feb 56	01 Mar 56	E-47E EB-47E		04 May 64	12 May 66
	53-2409	450-157-35	4501222	28 Dec 55	07 Feb 56	25 Feb 56	29 Feb 56			09 Feb 66	30 Jan 69
	53-2410	450-157-35	4501223	29 Dec 55	17 Feb 56	02 Mar 56	09 Mar 56	E-47E EB-47E		28 May 64	02 Oct 68
	53-2411	450-157-35	4501224	03 Jan 56	16 Feb 56	16 Mar 56	17 Mar 56	E-47E EB-47E		15 Apr 64	12 May 66
	53-2412	450-157-35	4501225	04 Jan 56	17 Feb 56	06 Mar 56	09 Mar 56	E-47E EB-47E		11 May 64	12 May 66
	53-2413	450-157-35	4501226	06 Jan 56	22 Feb 56	21 Mar 56	24 Mar 56	E-47E EB-47E		25 May 64	02 Oct 68
	53-2414	450-157-35	4501227	09 Jan 56	22 Feb 56	12 Mar 56	17 Mar 56			06 Dec 65	30 Jan 69
	53-2415	450-157-35	4501228	11 Jan 56	23 Feb 56	16 Mar 56	17 Mar 56			02 Dec 65	22 Oct 68
	53-2416	450-157-35	4501229	12 Jan 56	21 Feb 56	19 Mar 56	20 Mar 56			26 Feb 65	21 Oct 68
	53-2417	450-157-35	4501230	16 Jan 56	24 Feb 56	02 Apr 56	04 Apr 56			03 Mar 65	21 Oct 68
	53-4207	450-157-35	4501231	17 Jan 56	27 Feb 56	07 Mar 56	09 Mar 56	E-47E EB-47E		25 May 64	13 Jan 69
	53-4208	450-157-35	4501232	19 Jan 56	27 Feb 56	02 Apr 56	04 Apr 56		17 Feb 59		
	53-4209	450-157-35	4501233	20 Jan 56	29 Feb 56	21 Mar 56	23 Mar 56		06 Apr 56		
	53-4210	450-157-35	4501234	24 Jan 56	01 Mar 56	19 Mar 56	20 Mar 56	E-47E EB-47E		30 Apr 64	12 May 66
	53-4211	450-157-35	4501235	25 Jan 56	01 Mar 56	23 Mar 56	26 Mar 56			08 Jan 66	30 Jan 69
	53-4212	450-157-35	4501236	27 Jan 56	05 Mar 56	23 Mar 56	26 Mar 56		26 Nov 58		
	53-4213	450-157-35	4501237	30 Jan 56	12 Mar 56	22 Mar 56	26 Mar 56		07 Dec 65		
	53-4214	450-157-35	4501238	01 Feb 56	14 Mar 56	03 May 56	04 May 56	E-47E EB-47E		11 May 64	03 Oct 69
	53-4215	450-157-35	4501239	02 Feb 56	14 Mar 56	17 Apr 56	20 Apr 56	E-47E EB-47E		28 May 64	02 Oct 68
	53-4216	450-157-35	4501240	06 Feb 56	20 Mar 56	11 Apr 56	13 Apr 56			23 Oct 65	25 Oct 69
	53-4217	450-157-35	4501241	07 Feb 56	16 Mar 56	11 Apr 56	12 Apr 56			05 Mar 65	22 Oct 69
	53-4218	450-157-35	4501242	09 Feb 56	16 Mar 56	03 Apr 56	05 Apr 56		19 Jul 62		

MDS and Block Number	Serial Number	Model Number	Const. Number	Roll Out Date	First Flight Date	MIRR Date	USAF Fly Away	New MDS	Out of Service	MASDC Input Date	MASDC Output Date
B-47E-130-BW	53-4219	450-157-35	4501243	11 Feb 56	20 Mar 56	03 Apr 56	04 Apr 56			26 Feb 65	21 Oct 68
	53-4220	450-157-35	4501244	14 Feb 56	16 Mar 56	11 Apr 56	12 Apr 56	E-47E EB-47E		15 Apr 64	12 May 66
	53-4221	450-157-35	4501245	15 Feb 56	20 Mar 56	13 Apr 56	13 Apr 56	E-47E EB-47E		11 May 64	03 Oct 69
	53-4222	450-157-35	4501246	17 Feb 56	23 Mar 56	11 Apr 56	12 Apr 56			05 Mar 65	22 Oct 69
	53-4223	450-157-35	4501247	20 Feb 56	22 Mar 56	12 Apr 56	13 Apr 56			09 Mar 65	25 Oct 69
	53-4224	450-157-35	4501248	22 Feb 56	26 Mar 56	13 Apr 56	14 Apr 56			08 Mar 65	22 Oct 69
	53-4225	450-157-35	4501249	23 Feb 56	28 Mar 56	20 Apr 56	25 Apr 56			13 Dec 65	30 Jan 69
	53-4226	450-157-35	4501250	27 Feb 56	03 Apr 56	02 May 56	09 May 56		07 Mar 63		
	53-4227	450-157-35	4501251	28 Feb 56	05 Apr 56	15 May 56	16 May 56			17 Dec 64	12 Sep 69
	53-4228	450-157-35	4501252	01 Mar 56	09 Apr 56	18 May 56	22 May 56			20 Oct 65	25 Oct 69
	53-4229	450-157-35	4501253	02 Mar 56	06 Apr 56	30 Aug 56	30 Aug 56	E-47E EB-47E		30 Apr 64	12 May 66
	53-4230	450-157-35	4501254	06 Mar 56	10 Apr 56	04 May 56	09 May 56		27 Jul 56		
	53-4231	450-157-35	4501255	07 Mar 56	10 Apr 56	17 Jul 56	17 Jul 56			14 Oct 65	24 Oct 68
	53-4232	450-157-35	4501256	09 Mar 56	16 Apr 56	21 May 56	22 May 56			06 Jan 66	30 Jan 69
	53-4233	450-157-35	4501257	12 Mar 56	17 Apr 56	24 Aug 56	28 Aug 56			25 Oct 65	25 Oct 69
	53-4234	450-157-35	4501258	14 Mar 56	18 Apr 56	22 May 56	23 May 56			25 Oct 65	25 Oct 69
	53-4235	450-157-35	4501259	15 Mar 56	20 Apr 56	22 May 56	23 May 56		17 Nov 56		
	53-4236	450-157-35	4501260	19 Mar 56	24 Apr 56	18 May 56	19 May 56			02 Mar 65	22 Oct 69
	53-4237	450-157-35	4501261	20 Mar 56	01 May 56	24 May 56	26 May 56			14 Jan 66	30 Jan 69
	53-4238	450-157-35	4501262	22 Mar 56	02 May 56	31 May 56	01 Jun 56	JB-47E		12 Mar 64	12 Sep 69
	53-4239	450-157-35	4501263	23 Mar 56	08 May 56	12 Jun 56	13 Jun 56			12 Jan 66	30 Jan 69
	53-4240	450-157-35	4501264	27 Mar 56	09 May 56	29 May 56	01 Jun 56			25 Oct 65	25 Oct 69
	53-4241	450-157-35	4501265	28 Mar 56	11 May 56	31 May 56	01 Jun 56			26 Jan 66	30 Jan 69
	53-4242	450-157-35	4501266	30 Mar 56	11 May 56	30 Aug 56	30 Aug 56	E-47E EB-47E		17 Dec 64	13 Jan 69
	53-4243	450-157-35	4501267	02 Apr 56	14 May 56	06 Jun 56	08 Jun 56			01 Feb 66	30 Jan 69
	53-4244	450-157-35	4501268	04 Apr 56	14 May 56	15 Jun 56	18 Jun 56		04 Jan 61		
RB-47E-45-BW	53-4245	450-158-36	4501269	18 Mar 55	05 May 55	02 Jun 55	06 Jun 55	E-47/R-47E RB-47E		13 Sep 61	12 May 66
	53-4246	450-158-36	4501270	24 Mar 55	03 May 55	20 May 55	24 May 55	E-47/R-47E RB-47E		01 Sep 61	12 May 66
	53-4247	450-158-36	4501271	28 Mar 55	04 May 55	20 May 55	24 May 55			02 Jun 60	18 Jan 61
	53-4248	450-158-36	4501272	01 Apr 55	10 May 55	23 May 55	26 May 56	QB-47E JQB-47E	18 Aug 60	11 Feb 58	n/a
	53-4249	450-158-36	4501273	04 Apr 55	05 May 55	01 Jun 55	03 Jun 55			03 Jun 60	30 Jan 61
	53-4250	450-158-36	4501274	08 Apr 55	11 May 55	09 Jun 55	10 Jun 55	XQB-47E QB-47E JQB-47E	12 Jan 61		
	53-4251	450-158-36	4501275	12 Apr 55	17 May 55	02 Jun 55	03 Jun 55			04 May 60	30 Jan 61
	53-4252	450-158-36	4501276	18 Apr 55	23 Sep 55	09 Jun 55	10 Jun 55			01 Jun 60	11 Jan 61
	53-4253	450-158-36	4501277	21 Apr 55	25 Sep 55	14 Jun 55	14 Jun 55	QB-47E JQB-47E	07 Feb 62	29 Sep 58	n/a
	53-4254	450-158-36	4501278	25 Apr 55	06 Jun 55	24 Jun 55	27 Jun 55			30 Mar 60	13 Jan 61
RB-47E-45-BW	53-4255	450-158-36	4501279	29 Apr 55	08 Jun 55	23 Jun 55	27 Jun 55	QB-47E JQB-47E	28 Sep 61	13 Feb 58	n/a
	53-4256	450-158-36	4501280	04 May 55	10 Jun 55	06 Jul 55	08 Jul 55	QB-47E JQB-47E	10 Aug 68	20 Aug 68	02 Jan 70
	53-4257	450-158-36	4501281	06 May 55	14 Jun 55	05 Jul 55	06 Jul 55	JRB-47E NRB-47E	n/a	n/a	n/a
	53-4258	450-158-36	4501282	10 May 55	17 Jun 55	12 Jul 55	13 Jul 55	QB-47E JQB-47E	17 Aug 61	17 Feb 58	n/a
	53-4259	450-158-36	4501283	13 May 55	20 Jun 55	18 Jul 55	18 Jul 55	QB-47E JQB-47E	23 May 61	24 Sep 58	n/a
	53-4260	450-158-36	4501284	18 May 55	27 Jun 55	19 Jul 55	21 Jul 55	JRB-47E NRB-47E		28 Apr 61	23 Oct 61
	53-4261	450-158-36	4501285	20 May 55	27 Jun 55	19 Jul 55	21 Jul 55	JRB-47E NRB-47E	29 Dec 65		
	53-4262	450-158-36	4501286	24 May 55	29 Jun 55	19 Jul 55	21 Jul 55	JRB-47E		04 Feb 60	17 Aug 60
	53-4263	450-158-36	4501287	27 May 55	07 Jul 55	12 Aug 55	12 Aug 55	QB-47E JQB-47E		22 Aug 68	02 Jan 70
	53-4264	450-158-36	4501288	01 Jun 55	08 Jul 55	27 Jul 55	29 Jul 55	XQB-47E QB-47E JQB-47E	22 Mar 62		
RB-47E-45-BW RB-47K-1-BW	53-4265	450-158-36	4501289	03 Jun 55	26 Oct 55	16 Jun 55	13 Dec 55	RB-47K R-47K RB-47K		06 Jun 63	03 Oct 69
	53-4266	450-158-36	4501290	09 Jun 55	23 Nov 55	17 Jun 55	21 Dec 55	RB-47K R-47K RB-47K		11 Jun 63	03 Oct 69
	53-4267	450-158-36	4501291	14 Jun 55	08 Dec 55	17 Jun 55	26 Jan 56	RB-47K R-47K RB-47K		11 Jun 63	03 Oct 69
	53-4268	450-158-36	4501292	16 Jun 55	16 Dec 55	20 Jun 55	07 Jan 56	RB-47K R-47K RB-47K		13 Jun 63	03 Oct 69
	53-4269	450-158-36	4501293	21 Jun 55	20 Dec 55	24 Jun 55	26 Jan 56	RB-47K R-47K RB-47K		13 Jun 63	03 Oct 69
	53-4270	450-158-36	4501294	24 Jun 55	28 Dec 55	05 Jul 55	13 Jan 56	RB-47K R-47K RB-47K GRB-47K	18 Jun 63		

MDS and Block Number	Serial Number	Model Number	Const. Number	Roll Out Date	First Flight Date	MIRR Date	USAF Fly Away	New MDS	Out of Service	MASDC Input Date	MASDC Output Date
RB-47E-45-BW RB-47K-1-BW	53-4271	450-158-36	4501295	27 Jun 55	05 Jan 56	05 Jul 55	13 Feb 56	RB-47K R-47K RB-47K		06 May 64	03 Oct 69
	53-4272	450-158-36	4501296	01 Jul 55	18 Jan 56	06 Jul 55	13 Feb 56	RB-47K R-47K RB-47K GRB-47K	18 Jun 63		
	53-4273	450-158-36	4501297	05 Jul 55	25 Jan 56	08 Jul 55	26 Mar 56	RB-47K R-47K RB-47K		06 May 64	03 Oct 69
	53-4274	450-158-36	4501298	08 Jul 55	27 Jan 56	12 Jul 55	28 Feb 56	RB-47K R-47K RB-47K		12 May 64	03 Oct 69
	53-4275	450-158-36	4501299	12 Jul 55	03 Feb 56	15 Jul 55	29 Feb 56	RB-47K R-47K RB-47K		06 May 64	03 Oct 69
	53-4276	450-158-36	4501300	15 Jul 55	10 Feb 56	20 Jul 55	28 Feb 56	RB-47K R-47K RB-47K		12 May 64	03 Oct 69
	53-4277	450-158-36	4501301	19 Jul 55	15 Feb 56	01 Aug 55	28 Feb 56	RB-47K R-47K RB-47K		13 May 64	14 Jan 69
	53-4278	450-158-36	4501302	22 Jul 55	28 Feb 56	01 Aug 55	23 Mar 56	RB-47K R-47K RB-47K		13 May 64	14 Jan 69
	53-4279	450-158-36	4501303	27 Jul 55	29 Feb 56	03 Aug 55	26 Mar 56	RB-47K R-47K RB-47K	27 Sep 62		
RB-47H-1-BW	53-4280	450-172-51	4501304	02 Feb 55	21 Jun 55	26 Jul 55	24 Jul 56	R-47H RB-47H		25 May 67	18 Jun 69
	53-4281	450-172-51	4501305	09 Mar 55	21 Jun 55	27 Jul 55	02 Aug 55	JRB-47H RB-47H	01 Jul 60		
	53-4282	450-172-51	4501306	09 Mar 55	22 Jun 55	11 Aug 55	11 Aug 55	R-47H RB-47H		29 Mar 67	18 Jun 69
	53-4283	450-172-51	4501307	23 Mar 55	24 Jun 55	05 Aug 55	05 Aug 55		10 Feb 56		
	53-4284	450-172-51	4501308	31 Mar 55	29 Jun 55	04 Aug 55	05 Aug 55	R-47H RB-47H		30 Jun 67	18 Jun 69
	53-4285	450-172-51	4501309	06 Apr 55	29 Jun 55	05 Aug 55	05 Aug 55	R-47H RB-47H		14 Jul 65	18 Jun 69
	53-4286	450-172-51	4501310	13 Apr 55	12 Jul 55	05 Aug 55	05 Aug 55	R-47H RB-47H		25 Oct 65	18 Jun 69
	53-4287	450-172-51	4501311	20 Apr 55	14 Jul 55	14 Sep 55	15 Sep 55	R-47H RB-47H		15 Mar 67	18 Jun 69
	53-4288	450-172-51	4501312	27 Apr 55	18 Jul 55	08 Sep 55	08 Sep 55	R-47H RB-47H		21 Jul 65	18 Jun 69
	53-4289	450-172-51	4501313	03 May 55	22 Jul 55	08 Sep 55	08 Sep 55	R-47H RB-47H		20 Oct 65	18 Jun 69
	53-4290	450-172-51	4501314	11 May 55	26 Jul 55	02 Sep 55	02 Sep 55	R-47H RB-47H	28 Apr 65		
	53-4291	450-172-51	4501315	17 May 55	08 Aug 55	02 Sep 55	07 Sep 55	R-47H RB-47H		05 Jan 67	18 Jun 69
	53-4292	450-172-51	4501316	23 May 55	15 Aug 55	13 Sep 55	14 Sep 55	R-47H RB-47H		20 Oct 65	18 Jun 69
	53-4293	450-172-51	4501317	26 May 55	16 Aug 55	02 Sep 55	06 Sep 55	R-47H RB-47H		06 Oct 65	18 Jun 69
	53-4294	450-172-51	4501318	06 Jun 55	23 Aug 55	12 Sep 55	13 Sep 55	R-47H RB-47H		31 Mar 67	18 Jun 69
	53-4295	450-172-51	4501319	10 Jun 55	23 Aug 55	15 Nov 55	15 Nov 55	R-47H RB-47H		05 Jan 67	18 Jun 69
	53-4296	450-172-51	4501320	16 Jun 55	25 Aug 55	15 Sep 55	16 Sep 55	R-47H RB-47H		29 Dec 67	15 Jul 68
	53-4297	450-172-51	4501321	13 Jun 55	30 Aug 55	12 Oct 55	12 Oct 55	R-47H RB-47H	11 Nov 62		
	53-4298	450-172-51	4501322	22 Jun 55	30 Aug 55	15 Nov 55	16 Nov 55	R-47H RB-47H		11 Aug 65	18 Jun 69
	53-4299	450-172-51	4501323	28 Jun 55	31 Aug 55	03 Oct 55	05 Oct 55	R-47H RB-47H	27 Jun 66		
	53-4300	450-172-51	4501324	30 Jun 55	02 Sep 55	03 Oct 55	05 Oct 55	R-47H RB-47H		08 Dec 65	18 Jun 69
	53-4301	450-172-51	4501325	06 Jul 55	22 Sep 55	10 Oct 55	11 Oct 55	R-47H RB-47H		23 Mar 67	18 Jun 69
	53-4302	450-172-51	4501326	11 Jul 55	20 Sep 55	03 Oct 55	05 Oct 55	R-47H RB-47H		30 Jun 67	18 Jun 69
	53-4303	450-172-51	4501327	14 Jul 55	10 Oct 55	21 Oct 55	21 Oct 55	R-47H RB-47H		25 May 67	18 Jun 69
	53-4304	450-172-51	4501328	18 Jul 55	30 Sep 55	02 Nov 55	02 Nov 55	R-47H RB-47H		17 Nov 65	18 Jun 69
	53-4305	450-172-51	4501329	21 Jul 55	28 Sep 55	07 Oct 55	07 Oct 55	R-47H RB-47H		13 Oct 65	18 Jun 69
	53-4306	450-172-51	4501330	26 Jul 55	29 Sep 55	04 Oct 55	05 Oct 55	R-47H RB-47H		25 Aug 65	18 Jun 69
	53-4307	450-172-51	4501331	02 Aug 55	04 Oct 55	11 Oct 55	11 Oct 55	R-47H RB-47H		06 Jul 65	18 Jun 69
	53-4308	450-172-51	4501332	10 Aug 55	13 Oct 55	22 Nov 55	23 Nov 55	R-47H RB-47H		04 Feb 66	18 Jun 69
	53-4309	450-172-51	4501333	11 Aug 55	24 Oct 55	09 Nov 55	15 Nov 55		29 Apr 60		

MDS and Block Number	Serial Number	Model Number	Const. Number	Roll Out Date	First Flight Date	MIRR Date	USAF Fly Away	New MDS	Out of Service	MASDC Input Date	MASDC Output Date
RB-47H	53-4310 to 53-4321	450-172-51 450-172-51	canceled								
B-47E-135-BW	53-6193	450-157-35	4501334	05 Apr 56	15 May 56	11 Jun 56	13 Jun 56			28 Jan 66	30 Jan 69
	53-6194	450-157-35	4501335	09 Apr 56	15 May 56	13 Jun 56	14 Jun 56			14 Jan 66	30 Jan 69
	53-6195	450-157-35	4501336	10 Apr 56	16 May 56	07 Jun 56	11 Jun 56			01 Feb 66	30 Jan 69
	53-6196	450-157-35	4501337	12 Apr 56	18 May 56	13 Jun 56	14 Jun 56			03 Feb 66	30 Jan 69
	53-6197	450-157-35	4501338	13 Apr 56	21 May 56	21 Jun 56	23 Jun 56			18 Oct 65	24 Oct 68
	53-6198	450-157-35	4501339	17 Apr 56	24 May 56	14 Jun 56	14 Jun 56		01 Feb 57		
	53-6199	450-157-35	4501340	18 Apr 56	28 May 56	18 Jun 56	20 Jun 56			08 Jan 66	30 Jan 69
	53-6200	450-157-35	4501341	20 Apr 56	29 May 56	14 Jun 56	18 Jun 56			26 Jan 66	30 Jan 69
	53-6201	450-157-35	4501342	23 Apr 56	05 Jun 56	21 Jun 56	21 Jun 56			14 Oct 65	24 Oct 68
	53-6202	450-157-35	4501343	25 Apr 56	04 Jun 56	02 Jul 56	03 Jul 56			09 Feb 66	24 May 66
	53-6203	450-157-35	4501344	26 Apr 56	06 Jun 56	26 Jun 56	26 Jun 56			18 Oct 65	24 Oct 68
	53-6204	450-157-35	4501345	30 Apr 56	08 Jun 56	05 Jul 56	06 Jul 56		28 Feb 58		
	53-6205	450-157-35	4501346	01 May 56	11 Jun 56	19 Jul 56	19 Jul 56			21 Jan 66	31 Jan 69
	53-6206	450-157-35	4501347	03 May 56	13 Jun 56	03 Jul 56	05 Jul 56		19 Aug 63		
	53-6207	450-157-35	4501348	04 May 56	18 Jun 56	03 Jul 56	05 Jul 56			05 Feb 66	26 May 66
	53-6208	450-157-35	4501349	08 May 56	20 Jun 56	17 Jul 56	18 Jul 56			05 Jan 66	31 Jan 69
	53-6209	450-157-35	4501350	09 May 56	23 Jun 56	17 Jul 56	18 Jul 56			28 Jan 66	31 Jan 69
	53-6210	450-157-35	4501351	11 May 56	25 Jun 56	13 Jul 56	13 Jul 56	JB-47E	12 Apr 62		
	53-6211	450-157-35	4501352	15 May 56	29 Jun 56	18 Jul 56	18 Jul 56		06 Jul 62		
	53-6212	450-157-35	4501353	16 May 56	02 Jul 56	01 Aug 56	03 Aug 56			13 Jan 66	31 Jan 69
	53-6213	450-157-35	4501354	21 May 56	03 Jul 56	26 Jul 56	27 Jul 56			18 Oct 65	24 Oct 68
	53-6214	450-157-35	4501355	23 May 56	10 Jul 56	25 Jul 56	25 Jul 56			13 Jan 66	31 Jan 69
	53-6215	450-157-35	4501356	25 May 56	11 Jul 56	08 Aug 56	08 Aug 56		10 Feb 59		
	53-6216	450-157-35	4501357	29 May 56	13 Jul 56	27 Jul 56	27 Jul 56			26 Jan 66	31 Jan 69
	53-6217	450-157-35	4501358	01 Jun 56	16 Jul 56	03 Aug 56	07 Aug 56			12 Jan 66	31 Jan 69
	53-6218	450-157-35	4501359	05 Jun 56	19 Jul 56	10 Aug 56	13 Aug 56	JB-47E		20 Jan 66	31 Jan 69
	53-6219	450-157-35	4501360	07 Jun 56	20 Jul 56	08 Aug 56	08 Aug 56			11 Oct 65	24 Oct 68
	53-6220	450-157-35	4501361	11 Jun 56	23 Jul 56	13 Aug 56	14 Aug 56			05 Feb 66	31 Jan 69
	53-6221	450-157-35	4501362	13 Jun 56	26 Jul 56	20 Aug 56	21 Aug 56			18 Oct 65	24 Oct 68
	53-6222	450-157-35	4501363	14 Jun 56	30 Jul 56	16 Aug 56	16 Aug 56			03 Feb 66	31 Jan 69
	53-6223	450-157-35	4501364	18 Jun 56	31 Jul 56	24 Aug 56	29 Aug 56			05 Jan 66	31 Jan 69
	53-6224	450-157-35	4501365	21 Jun 56	01 Aug 56	06 Sep 56	06 Sep 56			08 Dec 65	31 Jan 69
	53-6225	450-157-35	4501366	25 Jun 56	02 Aug 56	12 Sep 56	12 Sep 56			08 Jan 66	31 Jan 69
	53-6226	450-157-35	4501367	27 Jun 56	06 Aug 56	23 Aug 56	23 Aug 56			12 Jan 66	31 Jan 69
	53-6227	450-157-35	4501368	28 Jun 56	07 Aug 56	11 Sep 56	12 Sep 56		12 Aug 60		
	53-6228	450-157-35	4501369	03 Jul 56	09 Aug 56	21 Sep 56	21 Sep 56			28 Oct 65	24 Oct 68
	53-6229	450-157-35	4501370	06 Jul 56	09 Aug 56	10 Sep 56	11 Sep 56		29 Oct 57		
	53-6230	450-157-35	4501371	10 Jul 56	13 Aug 56	05 Sep 56	06 Sep 56		15 May 62		
	53-6231	450-157-35	4501372	12 Jul 56	16 Aug 56	11 Sep 56	11 Sep 56			23 Nov 65	31 Jan 69
	53-6232	450-157-35	4501373	13 Jul 56	20 Aug 56	17 Sep 56	18 Sep 56			29 Oct 65	24 Oct 68
	53-6233	450-157-35	4501374	17 Jul 56	21 Aug 56	17 Sep 56	18 Sep 56			22 Jan 66	31 Jan 69
	53-6234	450-157-35	4501375	20 Jul 56	22 Aug 56	13 Sep 56	17 Sep 56	E-47E EB-47E		25 Feb 65	13 Jan 69
	53-6235	450-157-35	4501376	24 Jul 56	24 Aug 56	24 Sep 56	25 Sep 56			12 Feb 66	12 May 66
	53-6236	450-157-35	4501377	24 Jul 56	28 Aug 56	09 Oct 56	12 Oct 56			08 Mar 65	21 Oct 68
	53-6237	450-157-35	4501378	30 Jul 56	29 Aug 56	24 Sep 56	24 Sep 56			10 Feb 66	13 Apr 66
	53-6238	450-157-35	4501379	01 Aug 56	04 Sep 56	19 Sep 56	19 Sep 56			29 Oct 65	31 Jan 69
	53-6239	450-157-35	4501380	03 Aug 56	07 Sep 56	02 Oct 56	03 Oct 56			11 Oct 65	24 Oct 68
	53-6240	450-157-35	4501381	07 Aug 56	11 Sep 56	17 Oct 56	18 Oct 56		14 Jan 58		
	53-6241	450-157-35	4501382	09 Aug 56	16 Sep 56	01 Oct 56	01 Oct 56			08 Jan 66	31 Jan 69
	53-6242	450-157-35	4501383	13 Aug 56	14 Sep 56	03 Oct 56	05 Oct 56			24 Feb 65	21 Oct 68
	53-6243	450-157-35	4501384	15 Aug 56	20 Sep 56	15 Oct 56	17 Oct 56			29 Oct 65	24 Oct 68
	53-6244	450-157-35	4501385	17 Aug 56	03 Oct 56	23 Oct 56	24 Oct 56		22 Jan 65		
ERB-47H-1-BW	53-6245	450-172-51	4501386	30 Aug 56	16 Jul 57	12 Sep 56	23 Dec 57	ER-47H ERB-47H		07 Sep 67	14 Jan 69
	53-6246	450-172-51	4501387	07 Sep 56	17 Oct 57	12 Sep 56	19 Dec 57	ER-47H ERB-47H		09 Jan 67	14 Jan 69
RB-47H-1-BW	53-6247	450-172-51	4501388	14 Sep 56	03 Dec 56	16 Jan 57	18 Jan 57	R-47H RB-47H		27 Oct 65	18 Jun 69
	53-6248	450-172-51	4501389	20 Sep 56	04 Dec 56	16 Jan 57	17 Jan 57	R-47H RB-47H	27 Oct 62		
ERB-47H-1-BW	53-6249	450-172-51	4501390	22 Sep 56	30 Oct 57	01 Oct 56	23 Dec 57	ER-47H ERB-47H		11 Jan 67	14 Jan 69
B-47E	53-6250 to 53-6531	450-157-35 450-157-35	canceled								

Attrition Summary

By any account the B-47 was an extraordinary airplane. Newspapers enthusiastically described it as 'SAC's first swept-wing jet-powered atom bomber.' Headlines boasted of its speed, calling it the 'the 660mph jet bomber.' From Seattle to Savannah, from Florida to Fairford, from Renton to Ramey, nearly every B-47 flight set some kind of speed record. Only supersonic fighters could outpace the B-47. Indeed, pilots routinely described the Stratojet as 'nimble', handling like a fighter. But SAC was not a fighter command and its pilots were not fighter pilots. In the B-47's early days they had flown B-17s or B-24s or B-29s in the Second World War, straight-winged, piston-powered lumbering leviathans, culminating in the mammoth B-36. Airspeeds averaged 200KIAS (370kph), allowing pilots plenty of time to anticipate what to do next. Flight engineers monitored the many complex systems on B-29s, B-50s, and B-36s, allowing pilots to focus on flying the airplane, especially during critical phases of flight such as approach and landing. SAC and its fliers, maintenance personnel, and planners were ill prepared for the radical design of the B-47 and the changes it portended. Nor were they prepared for the vagaries of early jet engine spool-up times or reliability. Swept-wing aerodynamics, especially approach-speed stall characteristics, were profoundly different. Mixing jet bomber operations with piston-powered tankers proved to be a dangerous (and occasionally fatal) combination. The B-47 lacked both speed brakes and any fuel dump capability. For pilots, these many different factors meant that flying the B-47 was a complex and unforgiving exercise in momentum management rather than traditional stick-and-rudder skills. The result was a loss rate that reached a peak of one B-47 crash every two weeks and earned it the notorious reputation of 'One a Day in Tampa Bay.'

By the Numbers
In 1951, the first year of B-47 operations, five B-47s were lost. There were only 11 B-47s in service that year, however, amounting to a staggering 45.5% loss rate. In 1960, the safest year of B-47 operations prior to their final retirement in 1967, this rate dropped to only 1.36 percent, with 16 aircraft destroyed out of 1,178 B-47s in service. Comparing the B-47's annual loss rate over its entire 17 year operational history to the loss rate over a similar period of its successors is illuminating. During the first 17 years of KC-135 operations, the worst KC-135 annual loss rate was in 1960 (coincidentally the B-47's best year) with five losses from a fleet of 431, some 1.16%. It was not simply the novelty of B-47 performance that contributed to these crashes. During its 17 years of service, 14 B-47s were lost with each having fewer than 100 total flying hours. Indeed, the fewest hours accumulated was on B-47E 53-4209, delivered to the Air Force on 23rd March 1956 (six years after the first B-47B was handed over, long enough to have ironed out any teething issues), which crashed on 6th April (just two weeks after delivery) with only 21 hours and 20 minutes of total flying time.

Overall, 237 Stratojets were destroyed, compared to 46 KC-135s and 56 B-52s in the same 17-year period (over 60 years, only 78 KC-135s and 78 B-52s have been lost). Compared to its jet-powered peers in SAC, the B-47 had a significantly worse safety record,

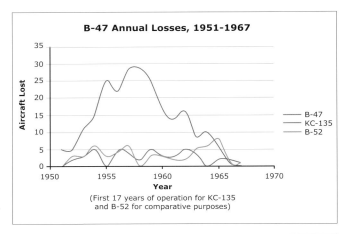

B-47 Annual Losses, 1951-1967

(First 17 years of operation for KC-135 and B-52 for comparative purposes)

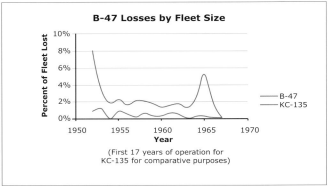

B-47 Losses by Fleet Size

(First 17 years of operation for KC-135 for comparative purposes)

averaging 13.9 losses per year versus 1.3 losses per year each for the KC-135 and the B-52. For a third of its operational lifetime, B-47 losses exceeded 20 per year, nearly two a month. SAC could ill afford to sustain these losses in airframes, fliers, and confidence its strategic bomber fleet. By the numbers, the B-47 was a dangerous airplane.

A Time of Secrecy
Trying to make sense of these losses has proven troublesome. These accidents occurred at a time when any crash and its causes were considered national secrets. Losses due to design or materiel failure revealed physical limits and flaws in the airplane, manufacturing process, and the logistics chain. Losses due to human error or operational mismanagement revealed fundamental flaws in the ability of SAC leaders or crewmembers to plan and execute an operational war order. Keeping these incidents quiet, if not secret, kept both potential enemies and the American public in the dark. It is certainly understandable to preclude any adversary from learning about the B-47's weaknesses, but it is surprising to think about the need for SAC to keep these events out of the public eye. SAC, the Air Force, and America's senior leadership were banking on the B-47 as the primary strike aircraft for deterring an attack against the United States or its allies through the credibility of a swift and sure nuclear

retaliation. A compromised airplane not only weakened this capacity, but cost vast sums of money to design, build, procure, operate, and repair. MILK BOTTLE is a good example, making front-page headlines in the *New York Times* – 'Defect Is Found In B-47 Bombers; Modification Set; Planes, Mainstay of SAC, Show Structural Flaws in Low-Level Flight'. Americans' confidence in their defense strategy and the prudent expenditure of their tax dollars was too valuable a commodity to undermine with detailed reports in the national media about B-47 crashes. In an environment where limited tax dollars were the source of fierce inter-service rivalries, the US Army and Navy would be only too pleased to cite each B-47 crash as proof that scarce resources were better spent elsewhere on proven weapons such as soldiers and aircraft carriers. Moreover, accidents in England and North Africa raised legitimate concerns among local residents about the safety of the airplane.

Physical Limitations

Perhaps what is most remarkable about these many B-47 losses is simply the inherent danger in flying the Stratojet. Jet engines were still in their adolescence and spool-up times were horrendous, leaving crews without airspeed and energy just when they needed it to stay alive. The bicycle landing gear led to pilot-induced oscillations (PIO – or 'porpoising') during landing, usually with only two 'lose-lose' options: cut the power and ride it out or 'pour on the coal' and hope to fly it out. Both situations produced their share of fatal accidents. Crosswinds, too, made takeoffs and landings a risky affair. The B-47, as with the U-2, often flew in the 'coffin corner,' where it was only a few knots above its low-speed stall and a few knots below its high-speed buffet. Aileron reversal ran counterintuitive to a half century of pilot stick-and-rudder skills. Without speed brakes the B-47 was so aerodynamically clean that it was nearly impossible to slow down, leading to overstresses and structural failures in flight and runway overruns on takeoff and landing. Although it handled like a fighter, formation flying was always dangerous. Refueling behind the slow KC-97 led to spins and loss of control. As with any other jet in this era, pilots especially had to think ahead of the airplane given its speed, turn radius, and other flight parameters. Flying a B-47 with the same mental frame of reference as flying a B-50 could be, and occasionally was, fatal. Many of the crashes described here would today be listed as 'CFIT – controlled flight into terrain' as distracted crews failed to pay attention and 'fly the jet,' ending up striking the ground. There was no way to dump fuel (although the drop tanks could be jettisoned), so crews in abnormal or emergency situations had to continue flying to burn fuel to lower the landing weight (and hence lower the landing speed to a safer degree), needlessly exposing them to danger longer than necessary. Ejection seats – once they were finally incorporated – often failed to work, were improperly rigged or installed, or (especially for the navigator) could not provide safe egress in a 'low and slow' environment. Even something as simple as the canopy proved lethal. There were 38 canopy related incidents or accidents. Of these, 26 happened in flight and a similar number

involved complete separation of the canopy from the airplane. Eight crewmen – including the first B-47 fatality – were killed by canopy loss or improper design in XB-47 46-0065, B-47B 50-0065, and B-47E 52-0277.

Organizational Constraints

As an organization SAC hardly tolerated incidents and accidents; paradoxically SAC contributed to and even increased their frequency. Crews worked long hours before flying, usually long-duration missions across multiple time zones or halfway around the globe. Despite medical awareness of circadian rhythms, crews flew day and night sorties with too little respect for the effect of sleep disruption on flight performance. Maintenance and support crews routinely worked 12-18 hour shifts, sometimes weeks straight in preparation for Operational Readiness Inspections (ORIs) or REFLEX deployments. Improperly fueled airplanes or incorrect records of fuel loads contributed to several fatal accidents. SAC was strictly a 'by the book' organization, and occasionally crews made poor decisions by blindly adhering to generic guidance in situations not previously considered 'acceptable' by engineers or operations planners safe at home. The B-47 Dash One, the flight manual, begins with a smiling cartoon clergyman and a caption written in Old English script saying 'read and heed for This is the Word' (the Biblical analogy should not be missed). 'The instructions in this manual are designed to provide for the needs of a crew inexperienced in the operation of these airplanes. This book provides the best possible operating instructions under most circumstances, but it is a poor substitute for sound judgment. Multiple emergencies, adverse weather, terrain, etc, may require modification of the procedures contained herein.'

Despite this caveat that should have allowed crews to think for themselves, any variation from the canonical Dash One usually meant a grilling in front of the squadron or wing commander, whose career hinged on absolute safety and that meant absolute obedience and conformity. Spot crews could lose their promotions (and pay) if they deviated from established procedures. Standardization and evaluation board (Stanboard) crews were always ready to armchair quarterback or second-guess a crewmember's performance. Check rides, planned or no-notice, were always certain to create unique, unheard of circumstances. Reviewing the list of crew fatalities of these many accidents, for example, there is a surprising number of evaluator navigators who, confined to a web sling rather than an ejection seat, perished while on check rides. Moreover, given the pioneering nature of the B-47 and its operations, even highly seasoned crewmembers often had little practical experience that could form the basis of 'sound judgment'.

Crews equally viewed the Command Post as a hazard to safety. Justified or not, Command Post controllers often held the reputation of being weak fliers, stuck behind the console because they could not hack it in the air. In many cases this is an unfair characterization, as the controllers (many of whom were non-rated) often relayed, rather than came up with, specific orders from senior wing officials. Nonetheless, the Command Post was often viewed as the 'enemy,' and at least three B-47s (51-2206, 51-7035, and 53-2097) were lost either directly or incidentally to poor decisions made by Command Post officials. During the early 1960s, for example, a B-47E from Plattsburgh AFB was on a night flight over Florida when the crew learned that severe weather and heavy snow had shut down Plattsburgh AFB. Regardless, the Command Post ordered the crew to return to Plattsburgh AFB where the controller would *then* make a decision about a divert base for landing. Several hours later and now over Plattsburgh AFB, the crew suggested Hunter AFB, GA, which had clear weather and a forecast for more of the same. The Command Post, however, directed the crew to divert to Lockbourne

read and heed for
𝔗𝔥𝔦𝔰 𝔦𝔰 𝔱𝔥𝔢 𝔚𝔬𝔯𝔡

CLOSE CALLS

Not all B-47 accidents resulted in a destroyed airframe or loss of life. One of the more unusual ones happened on 12th November 1953 when B-47B 51-2114 ran out of fuel on the way to Tinker AFB. The weather was below minimums at all alternates and its fuel was soon exhausted. Lacking ejection seats, the crew elected to land wheels-up in an Oklahoma wheat field. There was very little damage and instead of disassembling the airplane and trucking it to Tinker, OCAMA elected to fly the airplane out. It was raised with jacks and airbags, the gear was lowered, and the airplane was towed to a nearby small airport four miles away with the necessary modifications to fences, ditches, terraces and power lines. The minimal damage to the airplane was repaired on site, the weight reduced to 106,700 lb (48,398kg), and a crew flew the aircraft the 70nm (130km) to Tinker AFB after a harrowing takeoff from a 2,000ft (610m) runway! The flight was made without retracting the landing gear. OCAMA estimated that this rather creative method of recovery saved $1,500,000.

OCAMA photo

AFB, OH, which was then in the midst of a blizzard with the forecast anticipating multiple inches of snow and poor visibility. The crew protested, but the Command Post would not budge. Moreover, given the bad weather along the planned route of flight, there would be no tanker to provide additional fuel. Arriving over Lockbourne AFB, the airfield was below minimums, forcing the crew to orbit. The airplane had little fuel remaining, so the AC made a life- and career-defining decision to fly a GCA approach and, if they were lucky enough to make it to the runway, they would land. If not, they would execute a missed approach, climb, and eject. As the AC passed through the decision height on the approach in blinding snow and darkness he saw nothing, but pressed his luck and continued to descend, hopeful that the runway, and not trees or buildings, lay in his path. At perhaps 50ft (15m) above the ground the AC saw a white runway light pass by the right side, and then another, and another – but were they on centerline or to the left of the runway? With little choice other than ejecting the AC pulled the power and the airplane settled on the runway. Eventually a Follow Me truck found them and led them to the ramp. Ultimately safety-of-flight issues were left to the discretion of the AC, but few junior fliers were willing to argue with the Wing Commander for disobeying a Command Post directive.

Virtual Reality

There are many reasons why crews put up with these high-risk airplanes, dangerous circumstances, and 'damned if you do, damned if you don't' consequences. For nearly all of those who flew or maintained or supported the B-47, the most compelling was a real belief that the United States was at war, a cold war, with the Soviet Union. The risks they took were the same kind of risks they would willingly face in a shooting war, which for many of them was only a decade earlier. Actor Jimmy Stewart, as Colonel 'Dutch' Holland in *Strategic Air Command*, tells his disgruntled wife, played by June Allyson, that he and SAC are 'in a kind of war' and he expects her to make the same sacrifices as she would have when he flew B-29s in combat against Japan. Although clearly a healthy dose of SAC 'party line,' the movie accurately portrays the very real and honestly held belief among SAC crews and personnel that their efforts deterred war – nuclear war – with the Soviet Union and its communist cousins in the People's Republic of China and Eastern Europe, and preserved the freedoms enjoyed by the Western world. It should come as no surprise, then, that B-47 crews would argue, as did Boeing test pilot Bob Robbins, that 'it is hard…to imagine the sustained fear of nuclear war which gripped the world in the 1950s.' The 'B-47 served as the lynchpin of America's strategic defense,' and SAC's 'fleet of B-47s with their nuclear power absolutely could not be stopped,' presenting the Soviets with 'such obvious power that they wouldn't start anything.' Yet these same crewmen recalled 'I didn't love the B-47. I considered it an adversary that would have killed me if I had given it a chance.' The Stratojet was 'simply an airplane you couldn't fool with…it could bite you in a minute.'

Four hundred and ninety nine men, women, and children paid the ultimate price that the B-47 demanded for its role in strategic deterrence. With a few exceptions, their names have been intentionally omitted from the summaries that follow. Their anonymous sacrifice, however, must never be forgotten and should long be remembered as the price of freedom.

Key

Serial, MDS
Home Unit
Incident Date, Location, and Total Hours (where known)

n.b. This section lists those airplanes removed from service as a consequence of unplanned causes such as accidents or combat, or were intentionally destroyed in flight such as the QB-47s (described in Chapter 7). It does not include airplanes which were administratively scrapped, reclaimed, or converted to ground instructional duties, which are otherwise accounted for in the MDS Table in Appendix I.

Table A2-1. **Attrition by Date**

Serial	MDS	Date	Attrition Location	Remarks
49-1906	B-47A	18 Aug 51	Wichita Mid-Continent AP, KS	Stalled during landing at Wichita
50-0007	B-47B	01 Sep 51	Wichita Mid-Continent AP, KS	Mid-air collision with B-47B 50-0024 during formation test flight
50-0024	B-47B	01 Sep 51	Wichita Mid-Continent AP, KS	Mid-air collision with B-47B 50-0007 during formation test flight
49-2645	B-47B	20 Sep 51	Eielson AFB, AK	Fire during ground fueling for USSR overflight mission
50-0006	B-47B	19 Nov 51	Edwards AFB CA	Crashed after takeoff on a routine test flight
50-0026	B-47B	26 Mar 52	Kirtland AFB, NM	Stalled during ATO take-off
50-0038	B-47B	11 Apr 52	MacDill AFB, FL	Fuel mismanagement led to six-engine failure, landed short in Tampa Bay
51-2048	B-47B	24 Jun 52	Edwards AFB, CA	Stalled during touch-and-go landing
50-0065	B-47B	03 Jul 52	Myakka City, FL	Loss of canopy incapacitated pilots
50-0081	B-47B	22 Jul 52	Marianna, FL	Apparent spin and over-g on recovery led to in-flight break up; engine fell on house
51-2389	B-47E	21 Feb 53	Wichita Mid-Continent AP, KS	Caught fire from burning adjacent B-47E 51-2392
51-2392	B-47E	21 Feb 53	Wichita Mid-Continent AP, KS	Fire due to static discharge during ground fueling; fire spread to B-47E 51-2389
51-2085	B-47B	19 Mar 53	Wichita Mid-Continent AP, KS	Bounced during landing and pilot lost control
50-0035	B-47B	26 Mar 53	Wichita Mid-Continent AP, KS	Control failure during simulated 3-engine out on one side go-around
51-2267	B-47B	02 Jul 53	RAF Upper Heyford, UK	Stalled during final turn for crosswind landing and struck railroad embankment
51-2253	YRB-47B	24 Jul 53	Lockbourne AFB, OH	Stalled during touch-and-go landing
51-2226	YRB-47B	07 Sep 53	Lockbourne AFB, OH	Loss of control during touch-and-go landing; ground looped off the runway
51-2096	B-47B	13 Oct 53	March AFB, CA	Loss of control following touch-and-go landing
50-0034	TB-47B	15 Oct 53	Pinecastle AFB, FL	Stalled during touch-and-go landing
51-2440	B-47E	03 Dec 53	Reddington Pass, AZ	Disintegration of #4 engine caused bomb bay fuel fire during air refueling
50-0028	TB-47B	16 Dec 53	Pinecastle AFB, FL	Stalled during touch-and-go landing
51-2089	B-47B	08 Jan 54	Wichita AFB, KS	Aircraft struck an embankment during an excessively low visual approach
52-0023	B-47E	08 Feb 54	RAF Upper Heyford, UK	Undershot approach and struck trees in Stoke Wood
52-0053	B-47E	22 Feb 54	Hunter AFB, GA	Fuel hose failure during ground refueling led to uncontrolled fire
51-2416	B-47E	05 Mar 54	Davis-Monthan AFB, AZ	Lost power on takeoff and stalled
50-0063	TB-47B	16 Mar 54	Wichita AFB, KS	Mid-air collision with B-47B 51-2092 while practicing low approaches
51-2232	EB-47B	30 Apr 54	Kirtland AFB, NM	Stalled on approach and landed short, shearing off aft landing gear
51-5252	B-47E	10 Jun 54	Oujda, Morocco	Lost control after air refueling, stalled and entered unrecoverable spin
52-0229	B-47E	21 Jun 54	Townsend, GA	Ignition of fuel vapors in bomb bay tank caused in-flight explosion
51-17385	B-47E	20 Jul 54	RAF Fairford, UK	Landed 8 miles short after excessive descent rate and deviation from localizer
51-2382	B-47E	06 Aug 54	RAF Fairford, UK	Overrotated on takeoff and stalled
52-0285	B-47E	24 Sep 54	Smoky Hill AFB, KS	Landing chute failure and defective brakes led to overshoot in ditch
51-2437	B-47E	18 Oct 54	Davis-Monthan AFB, AZ	Bounced during landing and pilot lost control
52-0770	RB-47E	29 Oct 54	Olathe, KS	Rudder failure led to loss of control
52-0083	B-47E	25 Nov 54	RAF Lakenheath UK	High and fast on GCA caused overshoot
51-2100	B-47B	10 Dec 54	Oulmes, French Morocco	Fuel starvation in bad weather and unable to find the base
52-0029	B-47E	05 Jan 55	Gulf of Mexico	Mid-air collision with B-47E 51-7066 during air refueling
51-2086	B-47B	06 Jan 55	Braman, OK	Unauthorized aerobatics at low level
51-7033	B-47E	12 Feb 55	Big Sandy Lake, SK, Canada	Engine disintegration during flight led to uncontrollable fire
52-0045	B-47E	28 Feb 55	Lake Charles AFB, LA	Stalled during night weather instrument approach; possible aileron obstruction
52-0490	B-47E	14 Mar 55	Ben Guerir AB, French Morocco	Pilot distracted by seat malfunction, stalled on landing
52-0046	B-47E	16 Mar 55	North, SC	Fuel starvation following weather divert
52-0742	RB-47E	25 Mar 55	El Paso IAP, TX	Stalled during tailwind landing following weather divert
53-2277	B-47E	15 Apr 55	Kindley AB, Bermuda	Crashed from unknown cause into Castle Harbour after takeoff
51-2054	RB-47B-I	18 Apr 55	Kamchatka Peninsula, USSR	Shot down by Soviet MiG-15s east of Petropavlovsk
52-0386	B-47E	01 May 55	RAF Fairford, UK	Stalled on crosswind takeoff
52-0054	B-47E	27 May 55	Lincoln AFB, NE	Aircraft hit construction equipment after brake chute failure and poor braking
51-7073	B-47E	31 May 55	Barksdale AFB, LA	Stalled during takeoff due to excessive aft CG from improper fuel load
51-2112	B-47B	21 Jun 55	Pinecastle AFB, FL	Cockpit heat and smoke required heavyweight landing but brake chute failed
52-0421	B-47E	14 Jul 55	Barksdale AFB, LA	Crashed during takeoff, cause unknown
52-0397	B-47E	02 Aug 55	RAF Upper Heyford, UK	Gear collapsed after aborted takeoff due to smoke in cockpit
53-1847	B-47E	03 Oct 55	Tatum, NM	Excessive recovery during unusual attitude led to in-flight breakup
52-0580	B-47E	04 Oct 55	Galva, KS	False engine fire warning led crew to believe the left wing was on fire
51-2231	B-47B	13 Oct 55	March AFB, CA	Descended and struck terrain during flap retraction following takeoff
52-0500	B-47E	14 Oct 55	NAS Atlanta, GA	Landed short after approach to wrong airfield
52-0336	B-47E	21 Oct 55	Misawa AB, Japan	Stalled during takeoff due to improper engine power setting
51-7035	B-47E	08 Nov 55	Marlin, TX	Inflight explosion due to structural failure; possible crew physiological issues
52-0785	RB-47E	30 Nov 55	Lockbourne AFB, OH	Compressor stall during go-around due to asymmetric power
52-0301	B-47E	01 Dec 55	Smoky Hill AFB, KS	Exploded during ground maintenance, cause not known
51-2286	B-47B	19 Dec 55	Tampa, FL	Mid-air collision with B-47E 52-0535
52-0535	B-47E	19 Dec 55	Tampa, FL	Mid-air collision with B-47B 51-2286
52-0070	B-47E	03 Jan 56	Amarillo AFB, TX	Stalled during practice ILS and hit a telephone pole
53-1831	B-47E	05 Feb 56	Walker AFB, NM	Multiple emergencies during takeoff, stalled, hit power station
53-2304	B-47E	07 Feb 56	Hunter AFB, GA	Trim failure after maintenance caused uncontrollable roll following engine loss
52-0277	B-47E	10 Feb 56	Westmoreland, KS	Loss of canopy incapacitated pilots
53-4283	RB-47H	10 Feb 56	Ellsworth AFB, SD	Crashed due to pilot fatigue and improper takeoff calculations
51-2344	B-47B	27 Feb 56	Whiteman AFB, MO	Crashed after takeoff due to unknown cause, hitting a farmhouse
52-0534	B-47E	10 Mar 56	Mediterranean Sea	Disappeared during let-down for aerial refueling
51-2175	B-47B	28 Mar 56	McConnell AFB, KS	Bomb bay tank boost pump overheated and exploded after takeoff
53-4209	B-47E	06 Apr 56	Ceresco, NE	Failure of aft fuselage from undetermined cause
52-0450	B-47E	02 May 56	Lincoln AFB, NE	Crashed during a GCA approach
51-2442	B-47E	16 May 56	English Channel	Uncontrolled fire in #6 engine due to oil starvation
52-0565	B-47E	26 Jun 56	Smoky Hill AFB, KS	Failure to follow missed approach procedures and struck terrain
52-0572	B-47E	13 Jul 56	Smoky Hill AFB, KS	Aborted takeoff after refusal speed and failed to stop in remaining runway
53-4230	B-47E	27 Jul 56	RAF Lakenheath, UK	Loss of control during touch-and-go; crashed into nuclear weapon storage igloo
51-5230	B-47E	05 Oct 56	March AFB, CA	Catastrophic failure of #1 engine after takeoff
53-2301	B-47E	10 Oct 56	Hunter AFB, GA	Landed short during GCA approach
53-1933	B-47E	25 Oct 56	Lake Charles AFB, LA	Improper takeoff and abort procedures

Serial	MDS	Date	Attrition Location	Remarks
52-0151	B-47E	31 Oct 56	March AFB, CA	Improper go-around procedures failed to establish positive rate of climb
51-2421	B-47E	06 Nov 56	Hobart, OK	Crashed during jet penetration, cause unknown
52-0369	B-47E	17 Nov 56	Lincoln AFB, NE	Struck by F-80C 44-85284 landing on the taxiway
53-4235	B-47E	17 Nov 56	Lincoln AFB, NE	Struck by F-80C 44-85284 landing on the taxiway
52-3360	B-47E	30 Nov 56	Port Arthur, Canada	Aileron failure led to spin
52-0049	B-47E	15 Jan 57	Homestead AFB, FL	Crashed after cockpit fire during approach
51-2332	B-47B	24 Jan 57	Isle of Pines, Cuba	Mid-air collision with B-47B 51-2352 during air refueling
51-2352	B-47B	24 Jan 57	Isle of Pines, Cuba	Mid-air collision with B-47B 51-2332 during air refueling
53-6198	B-47E	01 Feb 57	Atlantc Ocean near MA	Crashed during jet penetration, cause unknown
53-1832	B-47E	15 Feb 57	Walker AFB, NM	Destroyed by ground fire, cause unknown
51-2192	B-47B	02 Mar 57	March AFB, CA	Improper engine fire procedure on takeoff
52-0439	B-47E	07 Mar 57	Lake Charles AFB, LA	Destroyed by ground fire from B-47E 53-2395
53-2395	B-47E	07 Mar 57	Lake Charles AFB, LA	Ground fire caused by failed boost pump; also destroyed adjacent EB-47E 52-0439
51-2265	B-47B	22 Mar 57	Pinecastle AFB, FL	Crashed after takeoff, possibly trying to avoid severe weather
52-0456	B-47E	05 Apr 57	Lincoln AFB, NE	Loss of control during a crosswind landing
51-2425	B-47E	07 Apr 57	Ka'ala Mt, O'ahu, Hawai'i	Struck terrain at night after improper jet penetration
52-0761	RB-47E	01 May 57	Pittsburgh, TX	Loss of control during night IMC refueling
53-2091	B-47E	24 May 57	Arnett, OK	Loss of control avoiding severe weather
51-7031	B-47E	17 Jul 57	Dyess AFB, TX	Stalled during takeoff due to improper fuel load
51-7042	B-47E	18 Jul 57	Shaffer, NV	Loss of control during air refueling and exploded
51-2102	B-47B	06 Aug 57	Whiteman AFB, MO	Bounced during landing causing ground loop
52-0754	RB-47E	08 Aug 57	Forbes AFB, KS	Stalled and dragged right wing during landing
53-2282	JB-47E	12 Sep 57	Bastrop, LA	Aileron control failure during IMC led to loss of control
51-15811	B-47E	17 Sep 57	Gulf of St Lawrence	Loss of aileron control led to a spin
51-2317	B-47B	01 Oct 57	Homestead AFB, FL	Improper abort procedure led to aircraft running of the end of the runway
51-2177	DB-47B	09 Oct 57	Winter Park, FL	Inflight structural failure due to over-G flight
51-2139	B-47B	11 Oct 57	Homestead AFB, FL	Failed takeoff due to flat tire
53-1891	B-47E	24 Oct 57	Lake Charles AFB, LA	Destroyed in ground fire caused by failed boost pump
53-6229	B-47E	29 Oct 57	Falun, KS	Loss of control during a LABS training mission
52-0241	B-47E	04 Dec 57	Eglin AFB, FL	Loss of control during a LABS training mission
52-0458	B-47E	06 Dec 57	Barksdale AFB, LA	Aborted takeoff for unknown cause and failed to stop
52-0186	B-47E	13 Dec 57	Duluth AP, MN	Lost control during GCA 3-engine approach
50-0076	TB-47B	18 Dec 57	Mt Palomar, CA	Off course during VOR approach, struck Mt Palomar observatory
53-6240	B-47E	14 Jan 58	Hunter AFB, GA	Landed short in the unpaved overrun
51-2220	B-47B	28 Jan 58	Pinecastle AFB, FL	Gear failed on second landing following hard impact short of threshold
52-0242	B-47E	31 Jan 58	Sidi Slimane AB, Morocco	Burned after rear wheel shattered during COCO alert taxi
51-2349	B-47B	05 Feb 58	Savannah, GA	Mid-air collision with F-86L 52-10108, landed; w/o 27 Mar 58
52-0388	B-47E	05 Feb 58	San Miguel Island, CA	Disappeared during a HAIRCLIPPER mission
50-0053	JTB-47B	08 Feb 58	Westover AFB, MA	Stalled during intentional 5-engine takeoff
52-0720	RB-47E	26 Feb 58	Lancaster, OH	Unexplained loss of control
52-0181	B-47E	27 Feb 58	Biggs AFB, TX	Fuel starvation after weather divert from Schilling AFB
53-6204	B-47E	28 Feb 58	RAF Greenham Common, UK	Destroyed by fuel tanks dropped from B-47E 53-6216
50-0013	TB-47B	13 Mar 58	Tulsa, OK	Wing failure during unusual attitude training; 2nd MILK BOTTLE crash
51-2104	B-47B	13 Mar 58	Homestead AFB, FL	Wing failure after ATO takeoff; 1st MILK BOTTLE crash
52-0244	B-47E	21 Mar 58	Avon Park Bombing Range, FL	Wing failure during pop-up maneuver; 3rd MILK BOTTLE crash
52-0470	B-47E	10 Apr 58	North Collins, NY	Inflight explosion due to structural failure; 4th MILK BOTTLE crash
52-0235	B-47E	15 Apr 58	MacDill AFB, FL	Wing failure after takeoff into thunderstorm; 5th MILK BOTTLE crash
52-0562	B-47E	15 Apr 58	Pease AFB, NH	Prematurely airborne during takeoff, improper fuel setting
52-0322	B-47E	24 Apr 58	Goose Bay, Labrador, Canada	Lose of altitude during climb phase, settled into Goose Bay
50-0031	TB-47B	11 Jun 58	McConnell AFB, KS	Loss of control during crosswind landing
53-1931	B-47E	11 Jun 58	West Hills, VT	Loss of orientation during instrument approach, hit high terrain
51-2206	B-47B	25 Jul 58	McCoy AFB, FL	CG imbalance due to fuel loss, unrecoverable spin
53-2267	B-47E	19 Aug 58	Follet, TX	Inflight break-up due to fuel pump explosion
51-5219	YDB-47E	25 Sep 58	Baltimore, MD	Bounced on landing, ground looped, gear collapsed; w/o 20 Oct 58
52-0726	RB-47E	25 Sep 58	Forbes AFB, KS	Stalled during flare and dragged left wing during backseat student landing
52-0744	RB-47E	29 Sep 58	Little Rock AFB, AR	Bounced during landing and stalled
52-0402	B-47E	23 Oct 58	Lockbourne AFB, OH	CG too far aft for flight due to improper fuel load, stalled after takeoff
52-0824	RB-47E	29 Oct 58	Pine Bluff, AR	Stalled and spun during simulated two-engine out approach
51-2391	B-47E	04 Nov 58	Dyess AFB, TX	ATO explosion and uncontrolled fire during takeoff
51-2199	B-47B	22 Nov 58	Loring AFB, MA	Stalled during takeoff when #6 engine support pin sheared, engine pivoted downward
53-4212	B-47E	26 Nov 58	Chennault AFB, LA	ATO bottle exploded while on the ground leading to an uncontrolled fire
52-0247	B-47E	16 Dec 58	MacDill AFB, FL	Ruptured hydraulic line led to wing fire after takeoff
51-7023	B-47E	05 Jan 59	Plattsburgh AFB, NY	Dragged wing during crosswind takeoff
52-2035	B-47E	21 Jan 59	Plattsburgh AFB, NY	Hit terrain while on final approach
52-3371	B-47E	03 Feb 59	Little Rock AFB, AR	Crashed during approach
53-6215	B-47E	10 Feb 59	Goose Bay IAP, Labrador, Canada	Engine failure during takeoff
53-4208	B-47E	17 Feb 59	Marietta, GA	Crashed during test flight, cause not known
52-3389	RB-47E	24 Mar 59	Morrilton, AR	Engine explosion and wing fire during flight
53-2319	B-47E	02 Apr 59	Mountain Home AFB, ID	Structural failure during emergency landing after engine fire and loss
52-0320	B-47E	04 Apr 59	Davis-Monthan AFB, AZ	Struck high terrain during night IMC approach
51-7041	B-47E	06 May 59	MacDill AFB, FL	Destroyed following an aborted takeoff
52-0179	B-47E	08 May 59	Hunter AFB, GA	Aborted takeoff due to W/A loss and overran the runway
52-0491	B-47E	20 May 59	Schilling AFB, KS	Hard landing, folding the forward landing gear aft
52-3344	B-47E	02 Jun 59	Winchester, CA	Crashed during GCA approach
51-2365	B-47E	04 Jun 59	Hunter AFB, GA	Landed on taxiway instead of runway following engine loss, ran into a ditch
53-2129	B-47E	11 Jun 59	Hunter AFB, GA	#6 engine exploded, tearing off 14 feet of wing; uneconomical to repair
51-15805	B-47E	01 Jul 59	Atlantic Ocean near Lajes, Azores	Improper fuel management led to aft CG and spin after air refueling
51-2126	B-47B	18 Sep 59	Bergstrom AFB, TX	In-flight engine explosion but landed safely; w/o 13 Nov 59
53-2136	B-47E	22 Sep 59	Pease AFB, NH	#4 engine turbine failed causing uncontrollable fire in bomb bay
51-5248	B-47E	08 Oct 59	Lincoln AFB, NE	Crashed during ATO take-off

Serial	MDS	Date	Attrition Location	Remarks
52-0606	B-47E	21 Oct 59	Dobbins AFB, GA	Brake chute failed, braking failed and airplane overran runway
52-0702	RB-47E	21 Oct 59	Lake of the Ozarks, MO	Spin during stall demonstration
52-0205	B-47E	03 Nov 59	Gulf of Mexico	Inflight fire between engines # 4 and 5
50-0021	TB-47B	17 Nov 59	Windsor, MO	Excessive nose-down trim caused abrupt pitch down during climb on missed approach
51-7082	B-47E	17 Dec 59	James Bay, Ontario, Canada	Mid-air collision with F-102A 56-1473
51-2261	B-47B	30 Dec 59	Torrejon AB, Spain	Crashed during takeoff, cause not known
51-5243	B-47E	01 Jan 60	Plattsburgh AFB, NY	Aft gear collapsed rupturing aft fuel tank while on alert; w/o 13 Jan 60
52-0566	B-47E	05 Jan 60	Hugoton, KS	Hit tanker prop wash and entered an inverted spin after air refueling
52-0498	B-47E	14 Jan 60	Eielson AFB, AK	Crashed while maneuvering for tower fly by to check landing gear
52-0814	RB-47E	27 Jan 60	Torrejon AB, Spain	Landed short, bounced, uneconomical to repair; w/o 10 Mar 60
51-7028	B-47E	18 Mar 60	MacDill AFB, FL	Landing gear collapsed on touchdown after complete DC failure
52-1414	B-47E	31 Mar 60	Little Rock AFB, AR	Overstressed during recovery from unusual attitude
52-0716	RB-47E	13 Apr 60	Perrin, MO	Disintegrated after flying into a thunderstorm
53-4309	RB-47H	29 Apr 60	Topeka, KS	Crashed during approach due to disorientation
51-2240	B-47B	28 May 60	McCoy AFB, FL	#3 engine exploded during ground maintenance, aircraft burned and later scrapped
53-4281	RB-47H	01 Jul 60	Barents Sea near Kola Peninsula	Shot down by Soviet MiG-19
51-2274	B-47B	12 Jul 60	Lake Okeechobee, FL	Engine disintegrated during flight
53-6227	B-47E	12 Aug 60	Plattsburgh AFB, NY	Landed short and burned
51-7047	B-47E	14 Sep 60	Atlantic Ocean	Mid-air collision with B-47E 53-1967 250nm W of Ireland
52-0047	B-47E	26 Sep 60	MacDill AFB, FL	Loss of control due to engine explosion, crashed in Tampa Bay
52-0556	B-47E	13 Oct 60	Whiteman AFB, MO	Struck ground during GCA approach
53-1886	B-47E	08 Nov 60	Lockbourne AFB, OH	Stalled during takeoff with two engines as reduced power
53-4244	B-47E	04 Jan 61	Pease AFB, NH	Stalled during takeoff
52-0766	RB-47E	09 Jan 61	McConnell AFB, KS	Stalled during touch-and-go climbout
52-0533	B-47E	12 Jan 61	Mt Palomar, CA	Autopilot malfunction after takeoff
53-2169	B-47E	21 Feb 61	Bowling Green, KY	Loss of control during night refueling in bad weather
53-2347	B-47E	24 Feb 61	Hurley, WI	Sheared pin during pull up allowed engine to drop on low level route
51-2315	B-47B	20 Mar 61	Bunker Hill AFB, IN	Engine exploded; deemed uneconomical to repair, w/o 3 Apr 61
52-0475	B-47E	21 Apr 61	Little Rock AFB, AR	Destroyed following ground loop during landing
53-2331	B-47E	02 May 61	Hurley, WI	Loss of control exiting low-level route
53-4259	QB-47E	23 May 61	Eglin Field #3, FL	Ran off runway during ground controlled landing
53-2111	B-47E	18 Jun 61	Lincoln AFB, NE	Stalled during takeoff due to engine fire
52-0296	B-47E	19 Aug 61	Las Animas, CO	Engine disintegration led to catastrophic fire and structural failure
52-0423	B-47E	31 Aug 61	Lockbourne AFB, OH	Ran off the end of the runway on takeoff
52-0347	B-47E	15 Nov 61	Lincoln AFB, NE	Pilot suffered heart attack during initial climb
53-1905	B-47E	27 Nov 61	Plattsburgh AFB, NY	Excessive sink rate on final approach due to 3 engines out, attempted go-around
52-0615	B-47E	05 Jan 62	March AFB, CA	Stalled during takeoff
53-2119	B-47E	16 Jan 62	Wright Peak, NY	Hit high terrain in bad weather descending to low-level training flight
51-2377	B-47E	20 Jan 62	Skiatook, OK	Anti-ice duct failure led to ignition of fuel vapors and explosion
52-0817	QB-47E	08 Mar 62	Gulf of Mexico	Split-S into water from 4,000 feet
53-4264	QB-47E	22 Mar 62	Gulf of Mexico	Drone destroyed after unable to recover from left bank
52-0459	B-47E	10 Apr 62	Collegport, TX	Structural failure during aerobatic flight
53-6230	B-47E	15 May 62	Whiteman AFB, MO	Caught fire during ground pre-flight and exploded
53-6211	B-47E	06 Jul 62	Bird City, KS	Structural failure while dealing with engine explosion
53-4218	B-47E	19 Jul 62	Des Moines AP, IA	Landed short during weather divert in thunderstorms and low fuel
52-0390	B-47E	23 Jul 62	Emigrant Peak MT	Descended below minimum safe altitude for low-level training
52-0526	B-47E	03 Aug 62	Pease AFB, NH	Fuel line broke during takeoff causing loss of power
52-0553	B-47E	23 Aug 62	Near Smith's Ferry, ID	Descended below minimum safe altitude for low-level training
51-7027	B-47E	26 Sep 62	MacDill AFB, FL	Crashed after takeoff into Tampa Bay after engine fire
53-4279	RB-47K	27 Sep 62	Forbes AFB, KS	Engine failure during takeoff
53-6248	RB-47H	27 Oct 62	Kindley AB, Bermuda	Stalled after takeoff due to improper water/alcohol solution
53-4297	RB-47H	11 Nov 62	MacDill AFB, FL	Stalled during takeoff
53-2097	B-47E	10 Jan 63	McConnell AFB, KS	Loss of control while attempting an emergency landing
53-2134	B-47E	05 Feb 63	RAF Greenham Common, UK	Stalled during go-around in snow storm due to asymmetric thrust
52-0563	B-47E	20 Feb 63	Comfrey, MN	Structural failure exiting low level route
53-4226	B-47E	07 Mar 63	Lincoln AFB, NE	Fuselage fire from ATO during takeoff
52-0051	B-47E	03 May 63	Yellowstone National Park, ID	Mid-air collision with KC-135A 60-0342 during air refueling
53-2160	B-47E	12 Jul 63	Zaragosa AB, Spain	Overran runway during heavyweight emergency landing
53-2365	B-47E	19 Aug 63	Irwin, IA	Mid-air collision with B-47E 53-6206
53-6206	B-47E	19 Aug 63	Irwin, IA	Mid-air collision with B-47E 53-2365
52-0823	QB-47E	19 Aug 63	Eglin AFB, FL	Ran off runway during ground controlled landing and into traffic on a nearby road
51-2420	WB-47E	10 Nov 63	Lajes AB, Portugal	Fuel starvation on final due to bad weather
53-1868	B-47E	05 Feb 64	Plattsburgh AFB, NY	Landed short; w/o 8 March 1964
52-0366	B-47E	06 Feb 64	Mountain Home AFB, ID	Stalled after takeoff in fog
52-0321	B-47E	27 Mar 64	Little Rock AFB, AR	Exploded shortly after takeoff due to ATO fire
51-7049	WB-47E	21 Apr 64	Eielson AFB, AK	Stalled during takeoff
52-0525	B-47E	26 May 64	RAF Upper Heyford, UK	Struck on the ground by B-47E 53-2296; w/o 27 Jun 64
53-2296	B-47E	26 May 64	RAF Upper Heyford, UK	Limited control during landing, striking B-47E 52-0525
53-2363	B-47E	03 Jun 64	Lincoln AFB, NE	Engine fire during takeoff, aborted and burned
53-2366	B-47E	27 Jul 64	Lincoln AFB, NE	Failed to accelerate during night takeoff and crashed
53-2398	B-47E	02 Dec 64	Plattsburgh AFB, NY	Failure of forward main landing gear during landing; w/o 13 Jan 65
52-0339	B-47E	08 Dec 64	Newington, NH	Stalled during takeoff due to loss of control, possibly due to icing or improper CG
52-0171	B-47E	26 Feb 65	Atlantic Ocean off Newfoundland	Mid-air collision with KC-135A 63-8882 during air refueling
53-2320	EB-47E(TT)	03 Apr 65	Incirlik, Turkey	Crashed during landing in severe crosswinds
53-4290	RB-47H	28 Apr 65	Yokota AB, Japan	Attacked by DPRK MiG-17s, landed at Yokota AB, scrapped
52-0160	B-47E	21 Jul 65	Pease AFB, NH	Belly landing after gear malfunction; w/o 8 Aug 65
51-2077	TB-47B	30 Oct 65	NAS Pt Mugu, CA	Insufficient power during go-around and struck runway
53-4261	NRB-47E	29 Dec 65	Holloman AFB, NM	Crashed during takeoff
51-2397	WB-47E	05 Dec 66	Ramey AB, PR	Stalled during touch-and-go landing
51-2366	WB-47E	20 Jun 67	Clark AB, Philippines	Damaged beyond repair during movement attempt following collapsed front gear

49-1906 B-47A
WIBAC, Wichita Mid-Continent Airport, KS
18th Aug 1951, Wichita Mid-Continent Airport, KS, TH: 269:55
This B-47A crashed following a test flight. Investigation revealed that the airplane lost an excessive amount of airspeed prior to touch down. The airplane stalled and dragged the right wing. The aft gear collapsed, the airplane ground looped, and engines, struts, outrigger gear, and the tail turret separated from the airplane. The crew survived.

49-2645 B-47B
3200th Photo Test Squadron, Eglin AFB, FL
20th September 1951, Eielson AFB, AK
This airplane was scheduled to fly the first B-47 reconnaissance overflight of the USSR, and was configured with a bomb-bay camera pod similar to the one installed on the YRB-47B. Following a local familiarization flight, the aircraft underwent ground servicing in preparation for the overflight mission. During single-point refueling the primary float shutoff switch for the forward tank was intentionally by-passed to allow the maximum amount of fuel in the forward tank. The secondary shutoff valve failed to stop the fuel, causing it to flow out of the vent line. This excess fuel was ignited by a C-22 ground power unit, and the airplane burned to destruction.

50-0006 B-47B
6510th ABW, Edwards AFB, CA
19th November 1951, Near Edwards AFB, CA, TH: 43:05
The airplane made a 180° left turn some 8-10 miles (13-16km) following a normal takeoff, climbing to approximately 3,000ft (914m). It then began a gentle, descending left turn, which abruptly steepened into an almost vertical dive into the ground at 300-350KIAS. The two pilots and crew chief on board perished. Cause of the accident was never determined.

50-0007 B-47B
WIBAC, Wichita Mid-Continent Airport, KS
1st September 1951, Near Wichita Mid-Continent Airport, KS
B-47Bs 50-0007 and 50-0024 were being flown in close formation at 2,000ft (610m) to visually determine if the landing gear on one airplane was fully down and in the locked position. While in formation, the lower B-47B climbed into the tail section of the upper aircraft. Both broke apart and crashed immediately. None of the four Boeing crewmen aboard the two airplanes survived.

50-0013 TB-47B
3520th CCTW, McConnell AFB, KS
13th March 1958, Tulsa, OK
This was a routine training sortie for a student crew. During the second practice unusual attitude (a descending 30° right bank), the crew heard a 'crack.' Unable to determine its origin, the crew continued the mission, practicing steep turns. During the second 45°-bank turn, the pilots heard a second 'crack' or 'muffled explosion' and the airplane shuddered violently. The student pilot in the front seat immediately noticed flames below and ahead of his left foot. He began the ejection sequence, and as the canopy separated the cockpit was engulfed in flames. The IP in the back seat bailed out manually while the now-uncontrollable airplane was inverted. The pilot in the navigator's seat did not attempt to egress the airplane and perished. Investigation revealed that the left wing failed at butt line 35 due to existing fatigue cracks. This was the second MILK BOTTLE crash.

50-0021 TB-47B
4347th CCTW, McConnell AFB, KS
17th November 1959, Windsor, MO
This was a training sortie with the IP in the front seat and a student copilot under the instrument hood in the back seat. During climb out after a GCA approach to Whiteman AFB, MO, the elevator trim tab and trim wheel locked due to excessive nose down trim. Despite considerable manual effort by the pilots to keep the nose up, the airplane pitched down abruptly at an altitude of 3,000ft (915m). It crashed near vertically some 450 yards (411m) from an elementary school, killing the crew of four.

50-0024 B-47B
WIBAC, Wichita Mid-Continent Airport, KS
1st September 1951, Near Wichita Mid-Continent Airport, KS
B-47Bs 50-0007 and 50-0024 were being flown in close formation at 2,000ft (610m) to visually determine if the landing gear on one airplane was

49-1906 was the only B-47A lost despite the type being used heavily in early test duties. *Author's collection*

fully down and in the locked position. While in formation, the lower B-47B climbed into the tail section of the upper aircraft. Both broke apart and crashed immediately. None of the four Boeing crewmen aboard the two airplanes survived.

50-0026 B-47B
4925th TG (Atomic), Kirtland AFB, NM
26th March 1952, Kirtland AFB, NM, TH: 23:00
During an ATO takeoff the left wing dropped and the nose began to rise steeply. At a maximum altitude of 100ft (30m) the airplane was in a 75° left bank and 45° degrees nose high, some 55° degrees to the left of the runway heading. The airplane developed a 30° sink angle with the nose approximately 20° up. Fire on impact burned the fuselage from the aft section to the forward wheel well. The crew of three perished, and no cause was determined.

50-0028 TB-47B
3540th CCTW, Pinecastle AFB, FL
16th December 1953, Pinecastle AFB, FL, TH: 172:05
While performing touch-and-go landings, the student pilot lost control of the aircraft while it was on the runway. He pulled it abruptly back up into the air where it stalled. The airplane cartwheeled and crashed. All four crewmen died.

50-0031 TB-47B
3520th CCTW, McConnell AFB, KS
11th June 1958, McConnell AFB, KS
Following a night GCA approach, the student pilot transitioned from the GCA to a visual final approach for a full-stop landing. The student pilot held the landing attitude with left wing low to compensate for crosswind. Upon touchdown the airplane ballooned and drifted to the right, and the student applied power and tried to level the wings. At this point the IP retarded all throttles and attempted to get the airplane safely back onto the runway. The right wing tip, #6 engine, and right outrigger gear dragged in the earth next to the runway, after which the main gear and other outrigger struck the sod. The main gear then collapsed, the fuselage broke in half, and the airplane was destroyed. The crew escaped without injury.

50-0034 TB-47B
3540th FTW, Pinecastle AFB, FL
15th October 1953, Pinecastle AFB, FL
On the eighth touch-and-go landing, the student IP allowed the aircraft to stall, dragging the left wing. The crash killed the student IP, but the IP and observer survived.

TB-47B 50-0035 in ATC markings. *Author's collection*

50-0035 B-47B
3520th CCTW, Wichita Mid-Continent Airport, KS
26th March 1953, Wichita Mid-Continent Airport, KS, TH: 697:00 hours
During a low-altitude go-around simulating three engines out on one side, loss of the right aileron power control unit (PCU) superimposed an actual emergency upon the one being simulated. The aircraft was uncontrollable under the combined conditions, and sufficient altitude was not available for recovery. All three crewmembers perished.

50-0038 B-47B
369th BS, 306th BW, MacDill AFB, FL
11th April 1952, Tampa Bay, FL, TH: 212:00 hours
While on the downwind leg for a full stop landing, the airplane experienced a simultaneous 'flame-out' on all six engines. Attempts to restart the engines failed and the aircraft ditched approximately 3,750ft (1,143m) short of the runway in 9ft (3m) of water in Tampa Bay with gear and flaps down. The airplane was destroyed but the crew of three survived.

50-0053 JTB-47B
ARDC, Wright-Patterson AFB, OH
8th February 1958, Westover AFB, MA
Due to bad weather at Wright-Patterson AFB, the airplane diverted to Westover AFB. It experienced multiple engine start problems at Westover AFB, leading to the cancelation of two attempts to return. On 8th February the #6 engine had a starter malfunction, so the AC requested (but erroneously believed he received) permission for a 5-engine takeoff and flight back to Wright-Patterson AFB. The airplane was defueled to 135,000 lbs (61,235kgs) for the takeoff. It became airborne 5,200ft (1,585m) down the runway in a nose-high right bank (toward the inoperative engine). Some 2,000ft (610m) further down the runway the crew began flap retraction and the airplane continued to climb steeply as the right bank increased. The airplane stalled in a 45° right bank at an altitude of 250ft (76m) and crashed between two B-52 hangars 1,450ft (442m) from the runway centerline. All three crew were killed. Investigation revealed that the fuel weight was incorrectly determined, the decision to take off using 5 engines was inappropriate, and pilot takeoff technique was improper.

50-0063 TB-47B
3520th CCTW, Wichita AFB, KS
16th March 1954, Near Wichita AFB, KS, TH: 602:55 hours
While practicing low approaches on the Forbes AFB radio range, this TB-47B collided with another B-47B. The three crew of the TB-47B perished, but B-47B 51-2092 landed safely.

50-0065 B-47B
367th BS, 306th BW, MacDill AFB, FL
3rd July 1952, Near Myakka City, FL, TH: 131:40
Approximately 10 minutes after takeoff, the airplane dove into the ground 32nm (59km) SSE of MacDill AFB, killing the crew of three. Probable cause of this accident was that the canopy came off in flight, incapacitating the pilots, causing the airplane to enter a dive and crash.

50-0076 TB-47B
320th BW, March AFB, CA
18th December 1957, Near Mt Palomar Observatory, CA
The airplane was cleared for a VOR penetration in IMC and instructed to advise crossing the VAIL intersection turning inbound on the approach. The crew reported VAIL and asked radar approach control (RAPCON) to verify their position, but RAPCON did not see them. The airplane then struck the 6,000ft (1,828m) Mt Palomar several hundred yards between the main observatory housing the 200-inch (508cm) telescope and the observatory containing the 48-inch (122cm) Schmidt telescope (which sustained structural damage), killing the TB-47B crew of nine. The crew was from the 15th AF Headquarters staff, including a highly experienced senior officer and IP with 1,300 hours instructing in B-47s. Investigation revealed that the aircraft was 8nm (15km) off course and 5,500ft (1,676m) below the minimum safe altitude.

50-0081 B-47B
369th BS, 306th BW, MacDill AFB, FL
22nd July 1952, Near Marianna, FL, TH: 67:05
The airplane descended from cruise altitude in a tight spiral or spin. At approximately 7,000ft (2,134m) the airplane appeared to regain control, but the fuselage broke into two sections and a fireball ensued. A falling engine

The damaged vertical stabilizer of TB-47B 51-2092 following its midair collision with TB-47B 50-0063. *Author's collection*

destroyed a home and badly injured the two occupants. Burning fuel covered a large area and, tragically, killed two children ages 5 and 3. The crew of four also perished. Investigation revealed that the fuselage break-up was due to 'excessive g loading,' likely induced during the attempted recover from the uncontrolled descent, for which no cause was determined. Although there was evidence of fire prior to ground impact, it could not be determined if the fire occurred before or after disintegration of the airplane.

51-2048 B-47B
6510th ABW, Edwards AFB, CA
24th June 1952, Edwards AFB, CA, TH: 23:50 hours
On the third touch-and-go landing, the airplane apparently stalled a 'considerable' distance above runway. The aircraft then struck the runway tail first, breaking the fuselage at station 861. Just before leaving runway, the forward section of the fuselage turned 180° and continued backwards to its final resting place. The aft section continued down the runway facing forward. Both sections were subsequently destroyed by fire. The crew escaped without injury.

51-2054 RB-47B-1
26th SRW, Lockbourne AFB, OH
18th April 1955, Northern Pacific Ocean near the Kamchatka Peninsula
This RB-47B-I was one of two modified to the ROMAN I configuration with a 100-inch (254cm) focal length camera installed. It departed Eielson AFB on 17th April on an Operation SEASHORE mission along the Kamchatka Peninsula and Kurile Islands to a point 100nm (185km) north of Hokkaido, Japan, and then return. The airplane was reported missing when it did not return. The first public announcement of the loss said merely that the airplane and crew 'vanished while on a long-distance flight over the North Pacific [Ocean]. A search was started in murky weather,' and ended on 23rd April with negative results. The crew of Major Lacie C Neighbors, Captain Robert N Brooks, and Captain Richard E Watkins perished, and no cause was established.
The true nature of this incident was publicly revealed in 1992 when Russian President Boris Yeltsin provided US investigators with documents on this and other Soviet-American aerial encounters. The RB-47-I was attacked and shot down over international waters 32nm (59km) east of Cape Kronotski by two Soviet *V-VPO* MiG-15 *Fagots* flown by pilots 'Korotkov and Sazhin.' Soviet documents show the attack occurred between 1125L and 1127L on 18th April (this would have been 17th April in the United States, accounting for variations in the date of the loss). At the time, US officials had no idea that the RB-47B-I had in fact been shot down, only that it was unaccounted for. The Soviets monitored the US search-and-rescue efforts, but refused to point out that the search was in the wrong place to avoid culpability. Three Soviet submarines were detected in the area where the RB-47B-I in fact crashed, but US forces were unaware of their actual purpose of searching for debris.

51-2077 TB-47B
FEWSG, Douglas Aircraft, Tulsa, OK
30th October 1965, NAS Pt Mugu, CA

Unable to see the runway due to fog, the crew elected to abort a nighttime GCA and go around. Rapid throttle movement caused the three left engines to stall, and the jet struck the runway with the #1 engine. Fire crews attempted to extinguish the blaze on #1, but in doing so their foam spray pushed burning fuel toward the fuselage, which caught fire, consuming the aircraft. The crew of three evacuated with minor injuries.

51-2085 B-47B
3520th CCTW, Wichita Mid-Continent Airport, KS
19th March 1953, Wichita Mid-Continent Airport, KS, TH: 83:00 hours

During landing the front gear hit first, causing the airplane to bounce an estimated 20ft (6m) into the air. On the second bounce the front gear again hit the runway first, and the airplane began to 'porpoise' severely on subsequent bounces. It finally broke apart some 3,500ft (1,067m) from the initial point of contact. The crew of three escaped. The accident investigation board attributed the crash to improper landing technique.

51-2086 B-47B
3520th CCTW, McConnell AFB, KS
6th January 1955, Braman, OK, TH: 919:15

During a day VFR flight to re-qualify an instructor pilot, witnesses reported that the airplane appeared to perform two high-speed aileron rolls at an altitude of approximately 5,000ft (1,524m). After the second roll the airplane lost altitude while in a left bank, leveled, banked to the right, and then crashed with a 70° nose-down angle slightly inverted. The investigation board found that the airplane was out of control with engines at low power, was structurally sound prior to impact, and the crash was the result of either intentional unauthorized aerobatics or an uncontrollable maneuver resulting from an attempt to recover from extremely high speed. In either case, the ailerons were determined to be ineffective due to the high speed. The crew of three perished.

51-2089 B-47B
3520th CCTW, Wichita AFB, KS
8th January 1954, Wichita AFB, KS, TH: 427:30

During a pattern training mission, the tower requested the airplane make a 360° turn for pattern spacing. When the airplane rolled out on final approach, it was at 1,800ft (549m) but descending rapidly. The student copilot warned the IP that the approach was too low. The IP applied power but the airplane struck an embankment 1,180ft (360m) from the end of the runway. The landing gear and both inboard engine pylons separated from the aircraft, which bounced and finally came to a stop 600ft (183m) from the point of initial contact. The IP and a student pilot in the observer's seat perished, but the student copilot in the back seat survived. Investigation determined that the approach was too low, although turbulence may have been a contributing factor.

51-2096 B-47B
33rd BS, 22nd BW, March AFB, CA
13th October 1953, March AFB, CA, TH: 83

Following an air refueling training mission, this B-47B returned to March AFB for touch-and-go practice. The airplane crashed during the takeoff portion of the third touch-and-go, but the cause was not determined. All three crewmembers were killed.

51-2100 B-47B
445th BS, 321st BW, Pinecastle AFB, FL
10th December 1954, Oulmes, French Morocco, TH: 455:10 hours

This B-47B was en route from Pinecastle AFB to RAF Lakenheath via Sidi Slimane AB on a SILVER CUP deployment. Upon arriving in the vicinity of Sidi Slimane AB, the crew could not locate the base and became lost due to an unreliable VOR and radio compass, an inoperative radar system, darkness, and a broken cloud ceiling at 4,500ft (1,372m). Out of fuel, the pilot informed Sidi Slimane AB they would bail out (the airplane lacked ejection seats). The crew chief, observer, and copilot bailed out at 5,000ft (1,524m) in a mountainous area 50nm (93km) south of the base near Oulmes and were rescued by Berber tribesmen. The AC then placed the airplane in a 10° left bank, engaged the autopilot, stowed the control column, and bailed out successfully. He noted that all 12 fuel boost pump 'no pressure' lights were illuminated. Despite this, the airplane orbited for an additional 30 minutes

before striking a ridge and disintegrating. The accident investigation remains classified.

51-2102 B-47B
340th BW, Whiteman AFB, MO
6th August 1957, Whiteman AFB, MO

The copilot was completing a jet penetration with a GCA approach to a planned touch-and-go landing. Two miles (3.7km) from the end of the runway the AC directed the copilot to take over visually but continue to utilize GCA guidance. The airplane crossed the threshold 60ft (18m) in the air and leveled off at 10-20ft (3-6m). The copilot lowered the nose in an attempt to land and the forward gear hit hard, causing a bounce. The AC then took control but the right wing and the #6 engine dragged the ground, causing a ground loop. The airplane burst into flames. The AC and copilot were able to evacuate despite receiving severe burns, but both the navigator and evaluator navigator perished.

51-2104 B-47B
379th BW, Homestead AFB, FL
13th March 1958, Homestead AFB, FL

The airplane made an ATO departure at 172,682 lb (78,327kg) gross weight. After takeoff the AC called the command post to report their takeoff time. Immediately thereafter the airplane began to break up, and the airplane was engulfed in fire. The crew of four was killed. Investigation revealed that the left wing failed at the inboard root section at butt line 35, caused by a 9in (23cm) fatigue crack in the lower aft center section skin which was the result of an instantaneous overload placed on the airplane during some previous flight. TB-47B 50-0013 also crashed on 13th March; they were the first two of five accidents leading to the MILK BOTTLE structural modifications.

51-2112 B-47B
447th BS, 321st BW, Pinecastle AFB, FL
21st June 1955, Pinecastle AFB, FL, TH: 645:00 hours

After takeoff on a routine training mission, the navigator discovered smoke in the crawlway to the bomb bay. Unable to locate the cause, he returned to his station but inadvertently left the crawlway and cabin pressure doors open, allowing smoke and heat to enter the main cabin. Cockpit temperatures reached 200°F (93°C), and smoke obscured the instrument panels. The AC declared an emergency and descended for landing. The brake chute deployed but shredded. Realizing that he could not stop, the AC attempted a ground loop but the forward gear collapsed as the aircraft left the runway. The airplane was destroyed by fire and all four crew survived. Investigation determined that a hot air duct was not properly connected, but indicated that the primary cause of the accident was the failure of the brake chute during the heavy weight, high-speed landing.

51-2126 B-47B
4347th CCTW, McConnell AFB, TX
18th September 1959, Bergstrom AFB, TX

During air refueling the #5 engine exploded, engulfing the right wing in flame. The crew made an emergency landing at Bergstrom AFB. All five on board survived. The airplane was deemed uneconomical to repair and was written off on 13th November 1959.

51-2139 B-47B
379th BW, Homestead AFB, FL
11th October 1957, Homestead AFB, FL

This B-47B (call sign *Derby 39*) was the last airplane in a flight of four scheduled to deploy from Homestead AFB to Wheelus AB, Libya, as part of Operation DARK NIGHT. Once on the runway the crew notified the tower that the right outrigger tire appeared flat. The tower directed the crew to hold its position while awaiting maintenance to evaluate the tire. Shortly thereafter the crew announced they would attempt the takeoff with the tire 'as is.' The takeoff was normal until the 6,000ft (1,829m) point when sparks appeared in the vicinity of the right outrigger gear. The crew reduced – then reapplied – power and became airborne in a nose high, right wing low attitude. It struggled to gain altitude, striking a dike 1,466ft (447m) beyond the end of the runway, began to break up and burn, and continued another 2,500ft (762m) before impact. All four crewmembers were killed. The investigation revealed that the outrigger tire was flat at the beginning of the takeoff roll, reducing the airplane's ability to accelerate properly. When the crew reduced power it deactivated the water alcohol thrust augmentation, and the remaining alcohol level was too low to restart the system. The airplane was carrying an unarmed 'open pit' nuclear weapon. The weapon core and its carrying case were recovered intact and only slightly damaged by the heat. Approximately one-half of the weapon remained and all its major components were recovered but damaged.

51-2175 B-47B
3520th CCTW, McConnell AFB, KS
28th March 1956, McConnell AFB, KS, TH: 1,014:15 hours

According to a US Navy pilot witness, about 2 minutes after takeoff the B-47B began a left turn and experienced a fire and explosion in the bomb bay fuel tank, leading to structural breakup. The three crewmen and two civilians on the ground were killed. Investigation revealed there was insufficient fuel in bomb bay tank to cover the overheating boost pump, leading to arcing and explosive detonation (a problem that remained for KC-135s in the years ahead).

51-2177 DB-47B
321st BW, Pinecastle AFB, FL
9th October 1957, Winter Park, FL

The sortie was planned as a two-hour local mission and instrument check for Colonel Michael N W McCoy, the 321st Bombardment Wing Commander. Also on board was Royal Air Force (RAF) Group Captain John Woodroffe, commander of the RAF Vickers Valiant bomber detachment visiting Pinecastle AFB for the annual SAC bombing competition. Witnesses report the DB-47B was at 1,500ft (457m) and at high speed when it began a turn. The bank angle rapidly reached nearly 90°, white smoke or fuel vapors appeared at the wing root, and the airplane disintegrated. All four on board, including McCoy, Woodroffe, and LtCol Charles Joyce, Wing Deputy Commander for Operations, and Maj Vernon D Stuff, were killed. Investigation revealed that the lower fuselage longeron exceeded designed g limits and failed. On 7th May 1958 Pinecastle AFB was renamed McCoy AFB in honor of Colonel McCoy.

51-2192 B-47B
320th BW, March AFB, CA
2nd March 1957, March AFB, CA, TH: 1,103:55 hours

This B-47 departed March AFB as the second airplane in a four-ship cell. At 350ft (107m) altitude the airplane began to roll left. The roll continued through nearly 360°, striking the ground in a slight wing-low attitude. The airplane was destroyed by impact and fire, killing all four crewmen. Investigation revealed the #1 and #2 engines were at idle RPM and the fire shutoff switch for #1 had been pulled. The AC may have shut down the #1 engine using the fire shutoff switch just after rotating but incorrectly retarded the #2 throttle. Jet wash may have contributed to the extreme roll rate.

51-2199 B-47B
321st BW, McCoy AFB, FL
22nd November 1958, Loring AFB, ME

During takeoff the airplane became airborne in an unusually nose-high attitude. It then started a right turn, began to lose altitude, and crashed 940ft (287m) to the right of the runway centerline and 10,400ft (3,170m) from the start of the takeoff roll. All four crewmen on board were killed. Investigation failed to determine a conclusive cause for the crash. Most probably the loss or failure of the aft mount pin on the #6 engine allowed the engine to pivot downward – it had no power at the time of impact – causing an asymmetric thrust situation at a critical phase of flight.

B-47B 51-2206 visits RAF Brize Norton. *Photo HS5664 courtesy Boeing*

51-2206 B-47B
321st BW, McCoy AFB, FL
25th July 1958, McCoy AFB, FL

During flight the airplane required excessive nose up trim (4 units), and the AC confirmed the aft fuel tank showed empty. The crew followed the appropriate fuel management procedures, and was able to reduce the trim to 2.5-3.0 units nose up, which the copilot determined to be within landing limits. Passing Hunter AFB the crew discussed the problem with the SAC Command Post there, which assured them they had mitigated the problem and it was safe to continue. Upon initial contact the McCoy SAC Command Post agreed, but directed the crew to configure at 25,000ft (7,620m) and slow to approach speed to determine safe handling characteristics. After lowering the gear and flaps the airplane became uncontrollable, entering a spin. The crew managed to recover the airplane. When they reapplied power the airplane once again went into a spin. Passing 14,000ft (4,267m) the AC directed the crew to evacuate. The three primary crewmembers ejected and the fourth man on board safely bailed out. Cause of the fuel imbalance was not determined.

51-2220 B-47B
321st BW, Pinecastle AFB, FL
28th January 1958, Pinecastle AFB, FL

The copilot was flying a GCA to a planned touch-and-go. The tower crew observed the aircraft abnormally high about one mile from the runway but the B-47 then went abruptly low as the approach continued. The touchdown was severe at a point 882ft (269m) short of the threshold. The AC took control of the aircraft and initiated a go-around, requesting fire equipment as he believed the forward gear tires had blown on impact. The subsequent landing was normal, but as the aircraft passed the 5,000ft (1,524m) point the tower observed sparks and the airplane swerved to the left, ran off the runway, and burst into flame. Crewmembers safely departed the aircraft but neglected to shut down the engines or turn off power. The fire chief completed the shutdown. The investigation revealed that the forward gear partially collapsed into the bomb bay on the hard landing, and completely collapsed on the final landing.

51-2226 YRB-47B
324th SRS, 91st SRW, Lockbourne AFB, OH
7th September 1953, Lockbourne AFB, OH: TH: 66:30 hours

Following a fly-by at the 1953 Dayton Air Show, the airplane returned to Lockbourne AFB. After a diving, unstable approach, the right wingtip struck the runway with 30° of bank 1,275ft (389m) down the runway. The main gear sheared off the airplane when it hit the ground 2,050ft (625m) down the runway. It came to rest at a point 2,800ft (853m) and 375ft (114m) to the right of the runway. The airplane caught fire and was destroyed. The crew evacuated through the canopy opening and the navigators' escape hatch. Investigation revealed that the pilot turned prematurely from downwind to base leg, was high on final approach, and in an effort to descend quickly, had pulled the power to idle without sufficient consideration to spool-up time. In addition, the pilot failed to account for existing wind conditions.

51-2231 B-47B
441st BS, 320th BW, March AFB, CA
13th October 1955, March AFB, CA, TH: 641:55

This airplane crashed into hills three minutes after takeoff from March AFB in reduced visibility of one mile in haze. The accident investigation board did not determine a probable cause, although it concluded that the airplane had been allowed to descend during flap retraction. All four on board, including a chaplain, were killed.

51-2232 EB-47B
4925th TG, Kirtland AFB, NM
30th April 1954, Kirtland AFB, NM, TH: 146:55 hours

The airplane stalled on final approach and landed short of the runway at Kirtland AFB. The aft main gear struck a street curb, an 8ft (2.4m) fence, and rising terrain, causing it to collapse. The rear of the fuselage was destroyed by fire. There were no fatalities.

51-2240 B-47B
321st BW, McCoy AFB, FL
28th May 1960, McCoy AFB, FL
The #3 engine exploded during ground operations, severely damaging the airplane and starting a fire. The airplane was deemed uneconomical to repair and recommended for salvage on 2nd June 1960.

51-2253 YRB-47B
3rd SRS, 26th SRW, Lockbourne AFB, OH
24th July 1953, Lockbourne AFB, OH, TH: 31:55 hours
     During the fifth touch-and-go landing, the airplane appeared to land normally but bounced slightly and touched down again close to the right side of the runway. Power was applied – then abruptly cut – then rapidly reapplied as it slid to the right off the runway onto the grass. Now at full power, it bounced into the air as it crossed an intersecting runway but dragged the #6 pod and right outrigger gear. The airplane spun 90° to the right, slid across a drainage ditch, and exploded. All three crewmembers were fatally injured.

51-2261 B-47B
19th BW, Homestead AFB, FL
30th December 1959, Torrejón AB, Spain
     This B-47B was the second of three B-47Bs returning to Homestead AFB following a REFLEX deployment. Weather at departure time was 5 miles visibility with fog over the first third of the runway. The takeoff of the mishap airplane was normal until it reached an altitude of 200ft (61m) when it began a gradual descending right turn until it crashed 1.75nm (3.2km) from the departure end of the runway. All four crewmen were killed. Cause of the crashed was never determined.

51-2265 B-47B
321st BW, Pinecastle AFB, FL
22nd March 1957, Pinecastle AFB, FL, TH: 458:00
     The airplane crashed some 3 minutes after takeoff, killing all four crewmen. There were thunderstorms in the vicinity and the AC may have been turning to avoid a storm cell. At the time of the crash the engines were operating at high RPM.

51-2267 B-47B
368th BS, 306th BW, MacDill AFB, FL
2nd July 1953, RAF Upper Heyford, TH: 275:05
     Following a training sortie from RAF Fairford, the airplane planned to land at RAF Upper Heyford 'for a ground training mission in conjunction with special weapons' (none was carried during the flight). Witnesses report that the airplane appeared to fly a tighter than normal downwind and base leg, as compared to the two B-47s that preceded it. To align with the runway, the airplane reached 60°-75° of bank and entered an accelerated stall. The pilot recovered but again stalled the aircraft trying to clear a hedgerow, striking the ground tail turret first. The airplane began to disintegrate as it slid through a railway embankment. All four crewmen perished.

51-2274 B-47B
19th BW, Homestead AFB, FL
12th July 1960, Lake Okeechobee, FL
     After air refueling the #5 engine exploded due to turbine wheel disintegration, followed by failure of the #4 engine. The crew abandoned the airplane; all three survived their landing in the Florida Everglades.

51-2286 B-47B
93rd BS, 19th BW, Pinecastle AFB, FL
19th December 1955, Near Tampa, FL, TH: 827:50
     B-47E 52-0535 experienced smoke in the cockpit after takeoff from MacDill AFB, as well as shut down of the #1 engine due to an engine overspeed. In preparation for landing, the crew lowered the gear but experienced a significant vibration. The crew asked for a visual inspection. B-47B 51-2286 was in the area and provided the visual check, reporting that everything appeared normal. While maneuvering in close proximity behind B-47E 52-0535, the pilot of B-47B 51-2286 required excessive back force on the elevators due to downward jet wash from the B-47E. Passing beneath the B-47E this jet wash dissipated and the pilot of 51-2286 could not release the backpressure fast enough, climbing abruptly into B-47E 52-0535. The collision killed everyone on both airplanes.

51-2315 B-47B
305th BW, Bunker Hill AFB, IN
20th March 1961, Bunker Hill AFB, IN
     During takeoff the #6 engine exploded, severing 16ft (4.9m) of the right wing. Captain John W Schwartz (AC), Captain Edwin L Waldo and First Lieutenant James Melaney (CPs), and Major Clyde D Jordan (N) successfully landed the airplane at Bunker Hill AFB. The B-47 was deemed uneconomical

to repair and it was written off on 3rd April 1961, and is now on static display at Grissom AFB, IN.

51-2317 B-47B
19th BW, Homestead AFB, FL
1st October 1957, Homestead AFB, FL
     The AC aborted the takeoff because the airspeed was 5KIAS below planned speed. The copilot cut engines #1, 2, 5, and 6 and deployed the approach and brake chutes. As the airplane neared the end of the runway at 40KIAS, the AC attempted to turn the airplane onto the taxiway but could not. The AC directed the copilot to retract the landing gear, but the copilot's shoulder harness inertia reel locked and he could not reach the switches. The AC overrode the gear retraction system and they collapsed rearward in the soft ground off the runway. The crew egressed safely. Investigation determined that the approach chute was not deployed and the brake chute failed either because the copilot pulled the jettison handle or the chute was improperly installed.

51-2332 B-47B
19th BW, Homestead AFB, FL
24th January 1957, Isle of Pines, Cuba, TH: 1,176:00
     During a cell air refueling B-47B 51-2352 was connected to a KC-97 tanker with B-47B 51-2332 in formation off to the right. Confusion over proper position of another tanker in the cell caused the tanker lead to transmit 'clear the refueling track.' B-47B 51-2352 followed its tanker as the KC-97 cut in front of B-47B 51-2332 and the bombers collided. The AC of 51-2352 ejected but the remaining bomber crewmen perished.

51-2344 B-47B
340th BW, Whiteman AFB, MO
27th February 1956, Whiteman AFB, MO
     About 3 minutes after takeoff the airplane disintegrated and crashed, striking a farmhouse about 15nm (28km) NE of Whiteman AFB. Witnesses reported that the airplane's flight path was very erratic and it appeared to be flying at a relatively low airspeed. All on board were killed, and two occupants of the farmhouse were reportedly injured. Cause of the accident could not be determined.

51-2349 B-47B
28th BS, 19th BW, Homestead AFB, FL
5th February 1958, Near Savannah, GA
     At approximately 0030 North American F-86L 52-10108 *Gold 01* from the 444th Fighter Interceptor Squadron (FIS) collided in mid-air with this B-47B during a unit simulated combat mission (USCM) near Savannah, GA. The B-47B was carrying a single Mk15 Mod 0 'open pit' nuclear weapon (without capsule). The crew of *Ivory 02*, Major Howard Richardson (AC), First Lieutenant Robert Lagerstrom (CP), and Captain Leland Woolard (N), conducted a handling check with gear and flaps extended, 'cleaned up,' and then headed for Hunter AFB as a suitable divert field. Given that the runway at Hunter AFB was undergoing construction and the 7,600lbs (3,447kg) of additional weight of the Mk15 meant a faster approach and landing speed than might otherwise be safe, the crew elected to jettison the Mk15 in the Atlantic Ocean.
     The crew released the weapon several miles from the mouth of the Savannah River in Wassaw Sound off Tybee Beach and then proceeded to Hunter AFB, where they landed safely. Despite a search lasting through 16th April 1958, the weapon was not found, although nearly 60 years later a contentious private search effort continues in an effort to locate the weapon (including a spurious web site declaring its discovery). Major Richardson was awarded the Distinguished Flying Cross and the other two crewmembers received Air Force Commendation Medals. The B-47B was removed from service on 27th March 1958. The F-86 pilot, Clarence A Stewart, also survived the accident.

51-2352 B-47B
19th BW, Homestead AFB, FL
24th January 1957, Isle of Pines, Cuba, TH
     During a cell air refueling B-47B 51-2352 was connected to a KC-97 tanker with B-47B 51-2332 in formation off to the right. Confusion over proper position of another tanker in the cell caused the tanker lead to transmit 'clear the refueling track.' B-47B 51-2352 followed its tanker as the KC-97 cut in front of B-47B 51-2332 and the bombers collided. The AC of 51-2352 ejected but the remaining bomber crewmen perished.

51-2365 B-47E
308th BW, Hunter AFB, GA
4th June 1959, Hunter AFB, GA

The day prior to the accident a fire developed in the tail cone of the #5 engine and it was ostensibly repaired. On the day of the accident, the AC performed an engine check and all appeared normal. Shortly after takeoff smoke appeared in the aft portion of the #5 engine and the crew shut it down. Smoke then appeared in the forward section, and the crew elected to land immediately at 136,000 lbs (61,689kg) gross weight. However, the AC made a normal landing on a 5,500ft (1,676m) taxiway parallel to the main runway, was unable to stop in the available distance, and ran off into a drainage ditch where the airplane exploded and burned. Three crewmen were killed and one survived.

51-2366 WB-47E
57th WRS, Hickam AFB, HI
20th June 1967, Clark AB, Philippines

After a routine ARC LIGHT support mission while deployed to Det 2, 57th WRS at Clark AB, the crew was unable to lower the front landing gear. Following a smooth landing and safe crew egress, ground personnel began the process of clearing the aircraft from the runway. According to a member of the crash crew who operated the recovery equipment, a senior wing staff officer directed that the airplane be moved using equipment appropriate for a smaller airplane. As a result, the narrower metal sling and cables cut deeply into the fuselage through the wings to the spar, and effectively severed the inboard pylons. At this point the airplane was no longer repairable and was scrapped on 9th November 1967.

51-2377 B-47E
306th BW, MacDill AFB, FL
20th January 1962, Skiatook, OK

The airplane was returning from the Douglas modification center at Tulsa, OK. Prior to entering overcast during the climbout the crew turned on the exterior surfaces anti-icing switches. Shortly thereafter the crew felt a thump and heard a loud noise, and the airplane banked slightly and pitched down slightly. The crew recovered the airplane easily, although there were vibrations in the rudder pedals, and the crew continued their climb to cruise altitude. At level off there was an explosion and the airplane pitched down steeply. Unable to recover, the three crewmen ejected. The airplane then disintegrated and crashed. Cause of the accident was failure of the anti-ice duct which led to ignition of fuel vapors in the aft fuel cell.

51-2382 B-47E
656th BS, 68th BW, Lake Charles AFB, LA
6th August 1954, RAF Fairford, TH: 170:20

During takeoff from RAF Fairford the pilot over-rotated the aircraft into a nose-high attitude, causing it to stall and crash near Radcot Lock, some 3nm (5.6km) from RAF Fairford. The crew of four was killed. Rescuers were delayed reaching the crash site because a fire truck overturned while racing to the scene, blocking traffic. This was the second 68th BW B-47E lost during this deployment, with 51-17385 crashing on 20th July.

51-2389 B-47E
USAF, Wichita Mid-Continent Airport, KS
21st February 1953, Wichita Mid-Continent Airport, KS

During ground refueling of B-47E 51-2392 a fuel fire erupted, possibly the result of static discharge due to improperly grounded refueling equipment. Fire spread to adjacent B-47E 51-2389 which was damaged beyond repair, and 51-2392 was completely destroyed. Neither airplane ever flew, although the USAF had accepted both with a planned delivery date of 29th April 1953. Boeing retained 51-2389 (nicknamed *Ole Smoky*) and used it as a test 'lab' throughout B-47 production.

Top left: B-47B 51-2315 shown landing at Bunker Hill AFB after the #6 engine exploded and tore off 16ft (4.9m) of the right wing.
Author's collection

Above left: B-47B 51-2344 seen on initial delivery to the 22nd BW at March AFB on 29th January 1953. *USAF photo*

Top right: B-47B 51-2352 collided with B-47B 51-2332, resulting in the loss of both airplanes. Note B-2 turret with 0.50 caliber guns. *USAF photo*

Right: B-47E 51-2389 suffered smoke and fire damage from B-47E 51-2392 (background) which was destroyed. Subsequently 51-2389, known as *Ole Smoky*, served as a Boeing ground test airframe that never flew.
Photo BW60236 courtesy Boeing

51-2391 B-47E
12th BS, 341st BW, Dyess AFB, TX
4th November 1958, Dyess AFB, TX

The B-47 alert force at Dyess AFB was scheduled for a JULIET alert launch of eight EWP aircraft (including nuclear weapons) at 0920 on 4th November 1958 to participate in a BIG SICKLE mission. The first three B-47s of 'Red Cell' launched without incident, but the fourth airplane experienced a misfired ATO bottle while it was still on the runway. The flames spread rapidly until the entire airplane behind the aft wheel well was fully engulfed. The crew did not hear a tower transmission warning them of the fire, and the airplane became airborne about 7,200ft (2,195m) down the runway. Now aware of the expansive fire the crew turned the airplane to the right, and passing 200ft (61m), ejected. Three crewmen survived, but the crew chief – without an ejection seat – perished in the crash. The remaining four aircraft aborted their launch. Investigation revealed that an ATO bottle exploded on ignition, rupturing either fuel lines or an aft fuel cell and starting an uncontrollable fire. The high explosives in the nuclear weapon detonated on impact, forming a crater 35ft (11m) deep, but there was no radioactive contamination.

51-2392 B-47E
BMAC, Wichita Mid-Continent Airport, KS
21st February 1953, Wichita Mid-Continent Airport, KS

During ground refueling of B-47E 51-2392 a fuel fire erupted, possibly the result of static discharge due to improperly grounded refueling equipment. Fire spread to adjacent B-47E 51-2389 which was damaged beyond repair, and 51-2392 was completely destroyed. Neither airplane ever flew, although the USAF had accepted both with a planned delivery date of 29th April 1953. Boeing retained 51-2389 (nicknamed *Ole Smoky*) and used it as a ground test 'lab' throughout B-47 production.

51-2397 WB-47E
53rd WRS, Ramey AB, PR
5th December 1966, Ramey AB, PR
Crashed during a touch-and-go landing with no fatalities.

51-2416 B-47E
358th BS, 303rd BW, Davis-Monthan AFB, AZ
5th March 1954, Davis-Monthan AFB, AZ, TH: 239:25

The airplane was scheduled to deploy from Davis-Monthan AFB to RAF Greenham Common, UK. Following what appeared to be a normal takeoff the airplane dipped sharply to the right at approximately 100ft (30m), then leveled the wings. It continued to climb to 200ft (61m) when the pilot appeared to initiate a gear-up, flaps-down emergency landing. Touchdown was smooth at a point 8,100ft (2,469m) from start of takeoff roll, but the #6 engine caught something and spun the aircraft 180° to the right. It slid an additional 885ft (270m) before stopping. The entire wreckage was consumed in an intense fire, and the crew of four perished. Investigators believed that the airplane lost power on one or more engines on the right side.

51-2420 WB-47E
55th WRS, McClellan AFB
10th November 1963, Lajes AB, Azores, Portugal

The airplane was returning to the United States when it lost all navigational equipment due to a power failure. Cloud cover prevented the navigator from

WB-47E 51-2420 at Lajes AB after departing the runway following a deadstick landing. *USAF photo*

using celestial navigation, and the crew became lost. They requested a radio direction finding (DF) steer from Lajes AB, but instead followed an erroneous TACAN signal which put them further off course. A second DF steer got them to Lajes AB, but they ran out of fuel 1,775ft (541m) short of the runway. The airplane was destroyed but there were no casualties.

51-2421 B-47E
96th BW, Altus AFB, OK
6th November 1956, Hobart, OK, TH: 1,164:20

The crew acknowledged clearance for a jet penetration after passing the Hobart VOR. The airplane crashed while turning inbound, killing all four crewmen. Cause of the accident is unknown.

51-2425 B-47E
96th BW, Altus AFB, OK
7th April 1957, Ka'ala Mountain, O'ahu, Hawai'i, TH: 1,225:40

During a redeployment flight from Andersen AB, Guam, the #1 engine fire warning light illuminated about 1 hour from Wake Island. There was no other indication of fire but the engine was properly shut down and the crew planned to divert to Hickam AFB, O'ahu, Hawai'i. The crew did not have the correct letdown chart for the VOR approach, so Honolulu Approach Control transmitted the instructions verbally. The AC repeated them but said a 'right penetration turn' instead of the correct 'left penetration turn.' Approach Control challenged the error but did not receive an acknowledgement. The crew had earlier reported problems with their radios, and may not have heard this challenge. The airplane began the penetration and made the incorrect right turn, crashing at 0405 AM 50ft (15m) below the 2,650ft (808m) summit of Ka'ala Mountain on O'ahu. All four on board were killed.

51-2437 B-47E
359th BS, 303rd BW, Davis-Monthan AFB, AZ
18th October 1954, Davis-Monthan AFB, AZ, TH: 568:45

While performing practice landings, the copilot pulled back sharply on the control column as the airplane neared the ground. The AC was able to regain control of the airplane and attempted to re-establish the landing attitude, but the copilot jammed the throttles to 100% and the aircraft crashed. The AC and crew chief survived, but the copilot was killed (there was no navigator on the flight).

51-2440 B-47E
360th BS, 303rd BW, Davis-Monthan AFB, AZ
3rd December 1953, Reddington Pass, AZ, TH: 237:50

Following multiple practice contacts with a KC-97, B-47 51-2440 went to a second KC-97 from Smoky Hill AFB. After the second contact the tanker boom operator reported fire on the inboard side of #4 engine nacelle. The B-47E performed an emergency breakaway but the fuel spray caused a fireball to engulf the B-47, although there was no explosion. The crew shut down engines #4 and 5, but the airplane crashed with four fatalities. Investigation revealed a severe fire fed by the bomb bay fuel tank was caused by disintegration of the #4 engine turbine wheel which was flung into the bomb bay. This weakened the aircraft which then disintegrated.

51-2442 B-47E
97th BW, Biggs AFB, TX
16th May 1956, English Channel near Lands End

After the airplane left the parking apron at RAF Upper Heyford for a routine training sortie the crew chief noticed a puddle of oil beneath the #6 engine area. He alerted the tower to hold the airplane and advised the base maintenance section. A maintenance officer and two maintenance personnel failed to find any evidence of an oil leak and the airplane was cleared for takeoff. After leveling at cruise altitude of 33,500ft (10,211m), the crew noted the #6 oil pressure to be low, followed by an unusual noise and a drop in oil pressure to zero. The crew shut down the engine; a jolt ensued and a fire erupted in the #6 engine. The AC headed back toward the base but directed the navigator to eject. He survived and was picked up by the French trawler *Jean Taburel*. Only an oil slick and the copilot's body were found floating in the English Channel some 12nm (22km) SW of Land's End and 6nm (11km) S of Wolf Rock, Cornwall. The navigator reported that the AC had also ejected, but his body was never found. Unsubstantiated media reports have suggested that the airplane was carrying a nuclear weapon, but the accident and wing records for this deployment remain classified. Investigation revealed that the airplane experienced an uncontrolled fire in the #6 engine due to oil starvation.

51-5219 YDB-47E
Air Materiel Command, Patrick AFB, FL
25th September 1958, Martin Company Airport, Baltimore, MD,

During landing on the 8,100ft (2,469m) runway the airplane touched down in the first third of available runway, bounced twice, and finally settled on the runway with just 3,000ft (914m) remaining. Braking would not stop the airplane, so the AC initiated a ground loop. The forward main gear failed, vfollowed by the outrigger gear. The three crewmembers evacuated safely. The airplane was written off on 20th October 1958.

51-5230 B-47E
22nd BW, March AFB, CA
5th October 1956, March AFB, CA, TH: 1,116:00

Approximately 2 minutes 20 seconds after an 0732 takeoff the airplane crashed in an inverted dive some 12nm (22km) SE of March AFB, killing the crew of three. The accident investigation determined the cause to be failure of the #1 engine followed by abrupt seizure and high torque load leading to failure of the aft engine mount pin, causing the airplane to enter an accelerated yaw.

51-5243 B-47E
380th BW, Plattsburgh AFB, NY
1st January 1960, Plattsburgh AFB, NY

The airplane was on ground alert configured with a nuclear weapon and ATO. Following a previous alert exercise, the crew chief did not properly insert the ground safety pin in the aft gear. During a subsequent alert exercise on 1st January, when power was applied to the aircraft the landing gear relay failed, commanding retraction of the aft gear, and the down-lock pin popped out. The aft fuselage settled to the ground, breaking at the 861 bulkhead and rupturing the aft fuel tank. The storm drains were frozen shut so the spilled fuel pooled over the alert ramp. The remaining aircraft on alert taxied clear of the Christmas Tree. Miraculously, none of the spilled fuel ignited. The mishap airplane was written off on 13th January 1960. Interestingly, the AC on this airplane was also the AC on B-47E 53-1967 which suffered a mid-air collision with B-47E 51-7047 on 14th September 1960.

51-5248 B-47E
307th BW, Lincoln AFB, NE
8th October 1959, Lincoln AFB, NE

The airplane crashed during an ATO takeoff. All four aboard were killed.

51-5252 B-47E
66th BS, 44th BW, Lake Charles AFB, LA
10th June 1954, Near Oujda, Morocco, TH: 304:10

During a night air refueling at 20,000ft (6,096m), the B-47 was at a high angle of attack and slow speed to maintain position behind the slower KC-97. The B-47 stalled to the left, and attempted a split-s recovery, but this led to an accelerated stall and spin to the left. The copilot and navigator ejected, but the AC perished. Investigation revealed the cause of accident was failure of the AC to account for post-air refueling yaw.

After its Rascal test duties YDB-47E 51-5219 crashed on 25th September 1958. *USAF photo*

Unusually, the SAC 'Milky Way' on B-47E 51-5230 extends over part of the crew entry hatch. *USAF photo*

51-7023 B-47E
380th BW, Plattsburgh AFB, NY
5th January 1959, Plattsburgh AFB, NY

During a crosswind takeoff the left wing dropped. The AC overcorrected with an aggressive roll to the right, requiring a larger roll to the left, allowing the left wing to strike the ground. The airplane exploded, killing one. Three others survived.

51-7027 B-47E
306th BW, MacDill AFB, FL
26th September 1962, MacDill AFB, FL

The airplane crashed shortly after takeoff from MacDill AFB following a fire in the #2 engine. All three crewmen ejected over Tampa Bay, but the navigator was killed.

51-7028 B-47E
306th BW, MacDill AFB, FL
18th March 1960, MacDill AFB, FL

During a functional check flight following replacement of four engines and the left flaperon, the airplane lost all DC power. The crew decided to land, and the copilot used the emergency landing gear extension procedures to lower the gear in the absence of DC power. The left outrigger gear would not lower, but by rocking the wings the gear eventually extended. The airplane touched down in a nose-high attitude about 1,300ft (396m) down the runway, but the aft gear collapsed approximately 2,700ft (823m) farther down the runway. The airplane swerved violently to the left and the front main gear collapsed. Engines #3 and #4 could not be shut down, but there was no fire. All three crewmen survived.

51-7031 B-47E
341st BW, Dyess AFB, TX
17th July 1957, Dyess AFB, TX

The airplane had been previously configured with an Emergency War Plan (EWP) fuel load and the external wing tanks were scheduled to be defueled prior to its next sortie. However, the excess fuel was not removed, and the airplane attempted to takeoff in an overloaded condition. During takeoff the water alcohol system failed or was turned off, and the airplane was unable to gain altitude, crashing moments after becoming airborne. All four crewmen were killed, including the crew chief who made the erroneous maintenance form entry that the wing tanks had been defueled.

51-7033 B-47E
9th BS, 22nd BW, March AFB, CA
12th February 1955, Big Sandy Lake, Saskatchewan, Canada, TH: 602:35 hours

This jet was on a polar training flight from March AFB to Thule AB, Greenland, and then back to March AFB. After the first air refueling, the #4 engine stuck at approximately 70% RPM, but after some corrective action appeared to resume full range of performance. After the second refueling en route between Thule AB and March AFB, the #2 engine fuel boost pump failed. Shortly thereafter engines #4 and 5 exploded, with the fire quickly spreading to the fuselage. The crew initiated a dive to extinguish the flames. During the rapid descent the airplane exploded and broke into three sections, crashing in Saskatchewan 378nm (700km) NW of Winnipeg, Manitoba, Canada [interestingly, the impact site was 38nm (70km) SE of the location where U-2A 56-6717 would make an emergency landing on 15th March 1960]. Three crewmembers parachuted to safety, but the navigator was killed, still at his position on impact. Cause of the accident was improper use by the aircraft commander of the engine stall prevention (ESP) switch, which stalled and damaged the #4 engine during the first refueling.

51-7035 B-47E
341st BS, 97th BW, Biggs AFB, TX
8th November 1955, Marlin, TX, TH: 559:40

During a night training mission the AC advised the Biggs AFB Command Post that the oil pressure on #5 engine had dropped. The Command Post directed him to continue the mission but to report further difficulties. The crew later gave a position report over Waco, TX, with no indication of problems. The airplane exploded in flight some 4.5nm (8.3km) S of Marlin, TX, and all three crewmembers were killed. The accident investigation board determined that the airplane experience structural failure due to high speed from a dive or dive recovery. Carbon monoxide discovered in the post-mortem may have disabled the crew and contributed to why they were in a steep descent.

51-7041 B-47E
306th BW, MacDill AFB, FL
6th May 1959, MacDill AFB, FL

The airplane was destroyed following an aborted takeoff, killing the copilot. The three other crewmen survived.

51-7042 B-47E
22nd BW, March AFB, CA
18th July 1957, Shaffer, NV

This airplane was #3 in a four-ship formation for night mass refueling mission. With thunderstorms in the area, the KC-97s were forced to climb to 19,500ft (5,944m) to remain above the bad weather, slowing the formation to 163KIAS. Approximately two minutes after the #3 tanker began its climb the remainder of the cell noticed a brilliant flash and B-47E 51-7042 broke up and crashed into a mountain 8nm (15km) W of Shaffer, NV. All four crew were killed. The investigation suggests that the #6 engine stalled at the reduced climb speed behind the KC-97. Given the turbulence and IMC conditions, the B-47 may have yawed abruptly and severely and the AC lost control, overstressing the airplane.

51-7047 B-47E
380th BW, Plattsburgh AFB, NY
14th September 1960, Atlantic Ocean

Three Plattsburgh B-47Es were on a REFLEX deployment to RAF Brize Norton, UK. Approximately 250nm (463km) west of Shannon, Ireland, the copilot of B-47E 51-7047 asked the crew of B-47E 53-1967 to maneuver close to the mishap airplane to film a home movie of the other airplane (call signs *Holt 53* and *Holt 63*). The right wingtip and #6 engine of B-47E 53-1967 struck B-47E 51-7047, which became uncontrollable and crashed into the Atlantic Ocean. B-47E 53-1967 was able to divert to Shannon IAP where it landed with the #6 engine dangling beneath the wing. The crew of 51-7047 perished.

In a sad and unusual epilogue to this event, unverified reports arose that at least one of the crewmen of 51-7047 survived the crash. Aircraft and ships reported seeing red and green flares the following day, and a wing tank was discovered floating on the surface. According to one claim, the surviving crewman was picked up by a Soviet submarine and interned in a prison camp. No evidence has been found to corroborate this assertion. Coincidentally, the AC on 53-1967 was the AC on B-47E 51-5243 which broke apart on alert on 1st January 1960.

51-7049 WB-47E
Det 1, 55th WRS, Eielson AFB, AK
21st April 1964, Eielson AFB, AK

During takeoff roll the airplane hit a slight rise in the middle of runway, causing the airplane to bounce. The inexperienced AC attempted to pull the airplane into the air prematurely where it stalled, causing it to crash. Although badly burned, the AC and copilot survived. The three remaining crewmembers were killed.

51-7073 B-47E
353rd BS, 301st BW, Barksdale AFB, LA
31st May 1955, Barksdale AFB, LA, TH: 600:40

During takeoff the airplane rotated into an abnormally nose-high attitude, reaching 60° pitch. At approximately 700ft (213m) the airplane stalled and crashed 9,600ft (2,926m) from start of takeoff and 1,400ft (427m) right of the runway centerline. The four crewmembers were killed. The accident investigation revealed that the center of gravity (cg) of 41.7% exceeded the aft limit due to a faulty fuel quantity indicator system. There should have been an additional 11,300 lbs (5,126kgs) of fuel in the forward main tank to maintain proper cg.

51-7082 B-47E
384th BW, Little Rock AFB, AR
17th December 1959, James Bay, Ontario, Canada

The mishap B-47E was third in a flight of three B-47Es participating in an ECM training run. F-102A 56-1473 from the 438th FIS was completing a ground-assisted visual intercept on the second B-47E when it struck B-47E 51-7082, severing its tail section. Two B-47E crewmen survived, but two others and the F-102A pilot perished.

WB-47E 51-7049 crashed at Eielson AFB. USAF photo

B-47E 51-7082 collided with F-102A 56-1473 over Canada.
Author's collection

51-15805 B-47E
367th BS, 306th BW, MacDill AFB, FL
1st July 1959, Atlantic Ocean near Lajes, Azores.

Following air refueling the crew began a turn to avoid bad weather. Three minutes later the crew reported trouble and were bailing out. Three crew perished, but the navigator survived. Investigation revealed that as a result of the heavy post-air-refueling weight and slow airspeed necessary to refuel from the KC-97, the B-47 stalled during the turn and entered an inverted spin. The AC was able to recover from the spin, but entered a second spin from which recovery was not possible. Investigation revealed that the cg was likely too far aft as the result of improper fuel management, making the airplane unstable and compromising the ability to recover from a stall or spin. Further inquiry revealed that it was common practice among B-47 pilots to assume that, with auxiliary tanks full, the cg would be within limits if the amount of fuel in the aft main tank did not exceed the amount in the forward main by more than 3,000 lb (1,361kg). Indeed, many pilots considered this differential to be ideal. Investigation demonstrated that if this aircraft took on fuel in this manner, the cg at completion of refueling would have been 2.2% aft of the allowable limit for flight above 20,000ft (6,096m).

51-15811 B-47E
380th BW, Plattsburgh AFB, NY
17th September 1957, Gulf of St Lawrence between Nova Scotia and Newfoundland

While returning from a mission the crew experienced difficulty in controlling the airplane. Even with both the AC and CP working together, the airplane rolled repeatedly up to 60° bank. All efforts failed to overcome the problem, including recycling the power controls and lowering the landing gear. After descending from 37,000ft (11,278m) to 21,000ft (6,401m) and entering an overcast layer while remaining uncontrollable, the AC ordered the crew to eject. The copilot was rescued from his raft in the Gulf of St Lawrence, but the AC and navigator were never found.

51-17385 B-47E
51st BS, 68th BW, Lake Charles AFB, LA
20th July 1954, Near College Farm, UK, TH: 229:10

B-47E 51-15811 gets a washdown while with the 22nd BW at March AFB. It was lost following its reassignment to the 380th BW. *USAF photo*

While on a night GCA approach to RAF Fairford this B-47E deviated to the right of the final approach course and descended below the glide slope. Weather at the time was 900ft (274m) overcast with visibility of 7nm (13km). The airplane crashed 7.5nm (13.9km) from the end of the runway and 1.5nm (2.8km) right of the extended centerline, near College Farm. Three of the four crewmembers survived; the navigator was killed when thrown clear of the fuselage while still strapped into his ejection seat. This was one of two 68th BW B-47Es lost during this deployment (the other was 51-2382). The accident investigation determined that the pilot failed to correct the airplane's descent well below the glide slope.

52-0023 B-47E
2nd BS, 22nd BW, March AFB, CA
8th February 1954, RAF Upper Heyford, UK, TH: 184:25

During a pre-dawn approach in night VFR conditions, the airplane was well below its final approach altitude. When the pilot turned on the landing lights he saw trees ahead, pulled up abruptly, and stalled the airplane. It struck 58ft (17.7m) trees at Stoke Wood, dropped the right wing, cartwheeled, and exploded approximately 1.5nm (2.8km) from the end of the runway at RAF Upper Heyford. All four on board perished. Investigation revealed the pilot was directed to fly a left-hand visual pattern but instead flew a right-hand visual pattern and was 500ft (152m) too low. Moreover, the pilot's altimeter read 29.52 inches of mercury instead of the correct 29.62 which was properly set on the copilot's altimeter. This caused the pilot to believe he was not too low, and the copilot failed to challenge the improper altitude.

52-0029 B-47E
68th BS, 44th BW, Lake Charles AFB, LA
5th January 1955, Gulf of Mexico, TH: 473:15

B-47E 52-0029 collided in mid air with B-47E 51-7066 during air refueling. All four crewmembers on 52-0029 perished. The other B-47 was heavily damaged but landed safely, although the navigator ejected and was never found.

52-0045 B-47E
52nd BS, 68th BW, Lake Charles AFB, LA
28th February 1955, Lake Charles AFB, LA, TH: 379:25

The airplane began a jet penetration for a night GCA approach, with weather of 600ft (183m) overcast and 10nm (19km) visibility. Some 3nm (5.6km) from the end of the runway the B-47 deviated to the left, followed by a 5° heading change to the right. The right turn continued and the airplane descended rapidly, crashing into four houses and a trailer park 6nm (11km) N of the base. All three crew were killed, as well as two residents of the trailer park. Investigation revealed that the #2 engine was inoperative, and the airplane stalled during the GCA approach in heavy turbulence. In addition, tools were found inside the aileron bus drum compartment, which contributed to limited aileron effectiveness in controlling the airplane.

52-0046 B-47E
308th BW, Hunter AFB, GA
16th March 1955, North, SC, TH: 460:25

The crew made five night GCA attempts to land in low cloud and fog at Hunter AFB. With the approach end of the runway obscured by fog and the airplane low on fuel, the crew diverted to Charleston AFB, SC, where the weather was 500ft (152m) ceiling with 2nm (3.7km) visibility and fog. Prior to reaching Charleston AFB it ran out of fuel and the AC ordered the crew to bail out, which they did safely. The abandoned airplane glided for 40nm (74km), crashing near North, SC.

52-0047 B-47E
306th BW, MacDill AFB, FL
26th September 1960, MacDill AFB, FL

During climb out from MacDill AFB the left outboard engine exploded and the airplane began an uncontrollable roll to the right. The pilots ejected as the airplane rolled through 120° and the navigator waited to eject through 270°. All landed safely in Tampa Bay. The two US Coast Guard (USCG) helicopters sent to rescue the B-47 crewmen also crashed. Ultimately the six B-47 and USCG crewmen were rescued by a father and son in their small boat, which ran aground. The crewmen got out and pushed the boat to safety. A second USCG helicopter carrying four rescue personnel also went down following mechanical problems, but the crew of four were picked up by a USCG patrol boat. A fourth B-47 crewman was scheduled to fly this mission but was ordered to get off the aircraft just prior to engine start. Without an ejection seat, his flight surely would have been fatal.

52-0049 B-47E
379th BW, Homestead AFB, FL
15th January 1957, Homestead AFB, FL

After takeoff the landing gear did not show a positive up and locked indication. The Command Post directed the crew to extend the gear and remain in the local area to burn off fuel for landing. After 2.5 hours the crew began their approach. On the downwind leg the AC declared an emergency due to fire in the lower compartment. While turning to the base leg, the canopy separated or was jettisoned, severing 2ft (0.6m) of the left horizontal stabilizer (the Dash One warns not to jettison the canopy below 180 or 190KIAS, depending on canopy style, to avoid hitting the vertical stabilizer). The navigator then ejected at about 1,000ft (305m) altitude. Witnesses reported flames in the cockpit area as the crew attempted to continue the approach. At about 300ft (91m) the AC bailed out over the side of the fuselage. The airplane entered a steep dive and near vertical bank and crashed. All four of the crew were killed in the crash or attempting to egress the airplane. Investigation revealed the fire was caused by failure of a hot air duct in the crawlway.

52-0051 B-47E
9th SAW, Mountain Home AFB, ID
3rd May 1963, Near Yellowstone National Park, ID

During air refueling the B-47 pilot requested that 462nd SAW KC-135A 60-0342 slow to 265KIAS. Consequently, the B-47 under ran the KC-135 and the B-47's left wing struck the KC-135's right wing. The B-47 entered a flat spin, crashing near Yellowstone National Park. The KC-135 recovered safely at Mountain Home AFB. The B-47 copilot ejected and survived some 40 hours in deep snow until rescued. The three remaining B-47 crewmembers died.

52-0053 B-47E
49th BS, 2nd BW, Hunter AFB, GA
22nd February 1954, Hunter AFB, GA

The aircraft exploded on the flight line during refueling. A maintenance man was attempting to escape by walking down the spine of the fuselage but, unfortunately, slipped, fell into the surrounding fire, and perished. Investigation revealed that a fuel hose failed near the hydrant connection spilling fuel onto the ground and into the refueling pit. Fire emanated from the pit destroying the aircraft.

52-0054 B-47E
370th BS, 307th BW, Lincoln AFB, NE
27th May 1955, Lincoln AFB, NE, TH: 473:15

During landing the brake chute deployed but did not blossom. With poor braking response on the wet runway, the AC realized that the airplane would roll off the end of the runway. He then attempted to steer the airplane onto the taxiway at the end of the runway. The airplane slid sideways into a construction area, the inboard engines and both outrigger gear were torn away, and the forward gear collapsed. The crew escaped serious injury, but the airplane was deemed beyond economical repair and scrapped

52-0070 B-47E
96th BW, Altus AFB, OK
3rd January 1956, Amarillo AFB, TX, TH: 680:18

During an ILS approach, witnesses observed this B-47E to be low and in a near stall condition as it passed the outer marker. The crew applied power but the airplane settled to the ground with the left wing low. As the crew leveled the wings the airplane hit a telephone pole and the airplane crashed about 2nm (3.7km) SW of the base, killing all three aboard.

52-0083 B-47E
65th BS, 43rd BW, Davis-Monthan AFB, AZ
25th November 1954, RAF Lakenheath, UK, TH: 238:15

The airplane was high and fast on a GCA approach. It landed successfully but ran off the far end of runway. The AC, copilot, and crew chief escaped through the canopy opening and the navigator escaped through the broken nose.

52-0151 B-47E
22nd BW, March AFB, CA
31st October 1956, March AFB, CA, TH: 824:40 hours

After a failed GCA and a failed visual approach at March AFB with visibility limited to 2nm (3.7km) in fog, the crew attempted a third GCA approach. The AC called the runway in sight but at 150ft (46m) altitude the

TEE TOWN B-47E 52-0160 was written off after a landing gear malfunction. *Author's collection*

airplane entered fog and the pilot lost sight of the runway. The AC initiated a go-around but struck the ground 246ft (75m) left of centerline and 2,000ft (610m) past the runway threshold. It became airborne again but finally crashed 7,500ft (2,286m) beyond the initial impact point. Although crash crews rescued all four crewmembers, the navigator died of his injuries the following day. Investigation revealed the pilot failed to maintain GCA guidance during the approach, and during the go-around did not establish a positive rate of climb.

52-0160 B-47E
509th BW, Pease AFB, NH
21st July 1965, Pease AFB, NH

The landing gear failed to retract after takeoff. The crew completed four aerial refuelings while attempting to fix the problem but finally determined it was unsolvable. The crew burned off fuel and made a belly landing on a well-foamed runway after a seven-hour mission. The crew escaped without injury. The airplane was written off on 8th August 1965.

52-0171 B-47E
100th BW, Pease AFB, NH
26th February 1965, Atlantic Ocean

The airplane was returning from Torrejón AB, Spain, to Pease AFB, and was scheduled to refuel second from 379th BW KC-135A 63-8882. Witnesses reported the B-47 maneuvered laterally beneath and forward of the KC-135A only a minute after the first receiver had disconnected. The right wing of the B-47 struck the left wing of the KC-135, and both exploded and crashed into the Atlantic Ocean some 220nm (407km) S of Cape Race, Newfoundland, Canada, and some 700nm (1,296km) east of Dow AFB, ME. There were no survivors from either airplane.

52-0179 B-47E
429th BS, 2nd BW, Hunter AFB, GA
8th May 1959, Hunter AFB, GA

Following loss of water/alcohol augmentation, the pilot aborted the takeoff but ran off the runway. The airplane was destroyed. There were no fatalities.

52-0181 B-47E
40th BW, Schilling AFB, KS
27th February 1958, Biggs AFB, TX

Bad weather at Schilling AFB forced the crew to divert to Walker AFB, NM. En route the crew determined they lacked the fuel to continue and instead chose to divert to Biggs AFB, TX. By choosing to fly a standard radar approach the crew used more fuel than necessary and the aft and center main fuel tanks were empty during the turn to final. Shortly thereafter all 12 fuel empty lights illuminated and the airplane experienced complete power failure and total darkness 1,100ft (335m) above the terrain. The crew raised the gear for a belly landing. The airplane touched down in sand dunes and slid straight ahead. The navigator was killed when the nose section broke up, but the three remaining crewmembers survived.

52-0186 B-47E
98th BW, Lincoln AFB, NE
13th December 1957, Duluth AP, MN

The #1 engine fire warning light illuminated, and the pilot noticed what appeared to be smoke coming from the left wing. The pilot declared an emergency. He then shut down all three engines on the left side. Once cleared for a GCA approach the airplane overshot the inbound course by 5nm (9.3km) but stalled and crashed while attempting to return to course. All three crewmen were killed. Investigation revealed no evidence of in-flight fire. The #1 engine fire warn light had malfunctioned, and the 'smoke' was aerodynamic vapor condensation. Taken together these led the AC to mistakenly believe that the wing was on fire.

52-0205 B-47E
306th BW, MacDill AFB, FL
4th November 1959, Gulf of Mexico

A fire erupted between the #4 and #5 engines. The crew bailed out at 11,000ft (3,353m) over the Gulf of Mexico. Three crewmen were lost but the navigator was rescued.

52-0229 B-47E
49th BS, 2nd BW, Hunter AFB, GA
21st June 1954, Townsend, GA, TH: 142:30

Fuel vapors ignited in the bomb bay during flight, producing a series of explosions causing the airplane to crash 3nm (5.6km) WSW of Townsend, GA. All four crewmembers on board were killed.

52-0235 B-47E
306th BW, MacDill AFB, FL
15th April 1958, MacDill AFB, FL

After becoming airborne the airplane disappeared into the low clouds and acknowledged an air traffic control clearance. It then crashed some 13nm (24km) from the end of the runway, killing all four crewmen. Investigation determined that the right wing failed as the result of a fatigue crack, exacerbated by the severe gust loads associated with the local severe turbulence during takeoff. Weather at takeoff time was forecast at 600ft (183m) broken, cloud tops to 20,000ft (6,096m), visibility of 10nm (18.5m), scattered thunderstorms in the vicinity with heavy rain and gusty winds on the runway. Although the official cause of the crash was materiel failure, SAC was critical of the lack of command supervision in allowing the airplane to take off directly into thunderstorms associated with reported tornadoes, and argued that the wing would not have failed except under these extreme conditions. This was the fifth MILK BOTTLE crash.

52-0241 B-47E
367th BS, 306th BW, MacDill AFB, FL
4th December 1957, Eglin AFB, FL

The airplane disintegrated while performing a LABS delivery on the Eglin AFB bombing range, killing the crew of three.

52-0242 B-47E
368th BS, 306th BW, MacDill AFB, FL
31st January 1958, Sidi Slimane AB, Morocco

This alert-configured B-47E was making a simulated takeoff during a Coco alert exercise. When the airplane reached approximately 30KIAS the left rear wheel casing failed, allowing the tail to strike the runway and rupture a fuel tank. The airplane caught fire but the crew managed to egress safely. The airplane was carrying a single fully operable Mk36 Mod 1 TN nuclear weapon. Fire crews fought the fire for the recommended maximum of ten minutes and then evacuated the area, anticipating detonation of the weapon's high explosive components. This detonation did not occur but the fire burned for some seven hours, destroying the airplane and a 100ft (30m) section of runway. Base residents were evacuated. An Air Force report warned 'contamination of the wreckage was high, but that of the surrounding area was low.' In the wake of this accident, Coco exercise alerts were temporarily suspended and all B-47 wheels were checked for defects. A 31st January 1958 TOP SECRET Department of State memorandum noted that 'the less said about the Moroccan incident the better,' and that no public statement be made to avoid providing 'large opportunities for Soviet propaganda.' The US ambassador to Morocco was authorized at 'his discretion to inform the King or a senior official regarding the incident, including the fact that a nuclear weapon was involved, but this would be for the confidential information of the senior Moroccan officials.'

52-0244 B-47E
306th BW, MacDill AFB, FL
21st March 1958, Avon Park Bombing and Gunnery Range, FL

This B-47E had just completed three bombing runs involving low-level 'pop-up' tactics. The AC requested and completed a fourth high-speed, low-altitude pass by the range control tower, which he then followed with an aggressive left-hand climb and a concurrent 'watch this' radio transmission. The right wing failed at wing station 555 and separated from the airplane

followed by an in-flight explosion and total destruction of the airplane, killing all four crewmembers. This was the third MILK BOTTLE crash.

52-0247 B-47E
367th BS, 306th BW, MacDill AFB, FL
16th December 1958, Tampa Bay, FL

About three minutes after takeoff a ground observer reported seeing a wing fire on the mishap B-47E. The AC discussed options with air traffic control, but many of these transmissions were 'stepped on' by other routine departure transmissions, including those to the three other B-47s in the flight. After six minutes the mishap B-47 switched to MacDill AFB Tower frequency to coordinate an immediate return to land. Approximately 10nm (18.5km) from the runway the airplane crashed into Tampa Bay, killing all four aboard. The investigation revealed that the right aileron PCU flex hydraulic return line pulled loose from its coupling just prior to takeoff, allowing hydraulic fluid to pool in the wing and drain into the canoe fairing above # 6 engine. The heat generated by the engine during takeoff and climb ignited the fluid. The ensuing fire caused complete failure of the PCU hydraulic pressure line and the aileron cable pulley. The aileron cable slipped from the damaged pulley, causing complete loss of aileron control during turn onto final approach.

52-0277 B-47E
310th BW, Smoky Hill AFB, KS
10th February 1956, Westmoreland, KS, TH: 578:00

The airplane was on a local radar acceptance test flight with weather of 2,600ft (792m) overcast and 15nm (28km) visibility with two cloud decks at 12,000ft (3,658m) and 25,000ft (7,620m). Eyewitnesses observed the airplane descending out of the bottom of the overcast on a southeasterly heading in a shallow turn. The bank angle increased until impact in a near-vertical right bank near Westmoreland, KS. All four crewmen were killed. Investigation suggested that the canopy came off during flight, incapacitating the AC. The copilot took control but may have experienced spatial disorientation induced by instrument meteorological conditions, leading to loss of control.

52-0285 B-47E
379th BS, 310th BW, Smoky Hill AFB, KS
24th September 1954, Smoky Hill AFB, KS, TH: 60:15

After landing the crew deployed the brake chute but it failed to blossom. Worn brake pads reduced the effectiveness of the brakes, so the airplane failed to slow and ran off the runway. The AC attempted a wide-radius ground loop to slow the airplane, but did not see a ditch that broke the fuselage aft of the wing root. The airplane then burned to destruction. All three crewmen egressed safely.

52-0296 B-47E
303rd BW, Davis-Monthan AFB, AZ
19th August 1961, Los Animas, CO

Immediately following release of a large practice weapon the #3 engine turbine wheel failed. The sheared parts penetrated the fuselage causing an intense fire, leading to failure of the upper right fuselage longeron and complete breakup. The airplane crashed 15nm (27.8km) SE of Los Animas, CO, killing two of the four crewmembers.

52-0301 B-47E
310th BW, Smoky Hill AFB, KS
1st December 1955, Smoky Hill AFB, KS

The airplane exploded on the ground during maintenance; further details unknown.

52-0320 B-47E
43rd BW, Davis-Monthan AFB, AZ
4th April 1959, Davis-Monthan AFB, AZ

The airplane hit a ridge in the Santa Rita Mountains 19nm (35km) from Davis-Monthan AFB while making a night instrument approach, killing all three crewmen.

52-0321 B-47E
384th BW, Little Rock AFB, AR
27th March 1964, Jacksonville, AR

During takeoff an ATO bottle exploded, setting fire to the aft fuselage. This led to an in-flight explosion severing the tail section. The airplane crashed about 15nm (28km) E of the base, killing the crew of four and two children on the ground.

52-0322 B-47E
98th BW, Lincoln AFB, NE
24th April 1958, Goose Bay, Labrador, Canada

The airplane was second in a five-ship flight returning to Lincoln AFB after a REFLEX deployment. Departure weather was 300ft (91m) broken, 800ft (244m) overcast, visibility 5nm (9.3km) in light rain and fog. Approximately two minutes after takeoff the airplane crashed into Goose Bay, killing two of the crew. The AC survived the crash and evacuated the burning wreckage after it came to rest on the ice of Goose Bay. Investigation revealed improper climb technique by the pilot, allowing the airplane to lose altitude during the climb phase.

52-0336 B-47E
5th BS, 9th BW, Mountain Home AFB, ID
21st October 1955, Misawa AB, Japan, TH: 306:15

The airplane was fourth in a five-ship cell departure. During takeoff the airplane appeared to over rotate, the left wing dropped, and then the airplane stalled. Three crewmen survived, but the navigator was killed. The investigation revealed that the #5 engine would not produce full power, and the AC forced the airplane into the air 7KIAS below unstick speed.

52-0339 B-47E
100th BW, Pease AFB, NH
8th December 1964, Newington, NH

During a pilot upgrade flight the airplane completed a normal takeoff roll but rapidly increased its climb angle until it stalled. The airplane crashed on centerline 6,500ft (1,981m) from the departure end of the runway. All four crewmembers were killed. Investigation determined the cause as pilot error with possible contributing factors of malfunctioning or iced Q-spring and/or possible cg problem due to improper fuel loading procedures.

52-0347 B-47E
98th BW, Lincoln AFB, NE
15th November 1961, Lincoln AFB, NE

The airplane crashed 2nm (3.7km) after takeoff, killing the crew of four. Investigation suggested that the AC suffered a heart attack leading to loss of control at a critical phase of flight.

52-0366 B-47E
9th SAW, Mountain Home, ID
6th February 1964, Mountain Home, ID

An instructor pilot and an inexperienced copilot took off in fog and indefinite ceiling with 1/2nm (0.9km) visibility. Witnesses reported the airplane breaking out of the fog at an altitude of 150ft (46m) in a nose-high, wings level attitude but with a high sink rate. The airplane crashed 3,000ft (914m) from the departure end of the runway. All four crewmen were killed. Investigators believed that the sun shining through the fog created a glare that made it difficult for the pilot to see or interpret his flight instruments.

52-0369 B-47E
98th BW, Lincoln AFB, NE
17th November 1956, Lincoln AFB, NE

The pilot of 173rd FIS, Nebraska Air National Guard, Lockheed F-80C 44-85284 mistook a taxiway for the runway and ran into two parked B-47Es, 52-0369 and 53-4235. All three airplanes were destroyed. The F-80 pilot and two B-47 ground crew were killed. In November 1957 First Lieutenant Robert J Cox from the 371st BS received the Soldier's Medal for saving an airman's life during the disaster and for preventing further damage to other aircraft.

52-0386 B-47E
359th BS, 303rd BW, Davis-Monthan AFB, AZ
1st May 1955, RAF Fairford, UK, TH: 86

During takeoff the airplane would not accelerate above 142KIAS, so the AC aborted the takeoff. Witnesses reported that the airplane appeared to become airborne briefly in an extreme attitude, forcing the airplane to stall. The airplane exited the departure end of the runway and bounced through a 10ft (3m) ditch. The airplane then slid 480ft (146m) on just the aft main and left outrigger gear before coming to rest near College Farm and being destroyed by fire when the bomb bay tank ruptured. The crew of three escaped serious injury. Investigation revealed incorrect operation of the elevator trim tab system and failure to follow crosswind takeoff procedures.

52-0388 B-47E
22nd BW, March AFB, CA
5th February 1958, near San Miguel Island, CA

This airplane disappeared during a HAIRCLIPPER low-level training mission near San Miguel Island, CA, some 39nm (72km) off the coast of Santa Barbara at 1756 PST. No trace of the airplane or its three crewmembers was found. It is believed that the airplane was attempting a LABS maneuver but lost control.

52-0390 B-47E
96th BW, Dyess AFB, TX
23rd July 1962, Emigrant Peak, MT

After air refueling the airplane proceeded to the OIL BURNER low-level route entry fix and received clearance to continue. Weather was reported as scattered clouds with unlimited visibility. For some unknown reason the crew descended below the minimum published altitude of 15,000ft (4,572m) and struck Emigrant Mountain 2,000ft (610m) below the 10,921ft (3,329m) peak. The crash killed all four crewmen and started a forest fire.

52-0397 B-47E
512th BS, 376th BW, Barksdale AFB, LA
2nd August 1955, RAF Upper Heyford, UK, TH: 500:15

During takeoff roll the crew of this BLUE CRADLE B-47E experienced smoke in the cockpit. The AC aborted the takeoff, but determined he could not stop in the remaining 3,300ft (1006m) and shut off four engines and deployed the drag chute, but a main tire blew. He then attempted to turn the airplane onto a taxiway which doubled as a road. It was congested with traffic, and the jet veered off the side of the runway shearing the forward gear. A small fire erupted but was contained. All crewmen egressed safely. Investigation revealed that the AC improperly stowed his ejection seat initiator safety pins by hanging them from his headrest rather than placing them in the appropriate storage bag. During takeoff roll acceleration caused the metal pins to come in contact with the exposed #5 terminal strip on the back of the copilot's instrument panel, causing a short circuit and producing smoke in the cockpit. In addition to improper stowage of the ejection seat pins, the accident board found that the AC had failed to follow proper abort procedures. OCAMA determined the airplane to be beyond economical repair and it was stricken from service on 30th November 1955.

52-0402 B-47E
376th BW, Lockbourne AFB, OH
23rd October 1958, Lockbourne AFB, OH

Planned takeoff distance was 6,900ft (2,103m) for this BLUE CRADLE EB-47E trim coordination flight. After 4,000ft (1,219m) the forward gear became airborne, and the airplane was fully airborne in an extreme nose-high attitude at the 5,000ft (1,524m) point. As the airplane passed 6,000ft (1,829m) it was 300ft (91m) high. At that point the crew jettisoned the canopy; the airplane stalled and crashed 7,500ft (2,286m) from the start of the takeoff roll and 960ft (292m) to the left of the runway. All three crewmen were killed. Investigation revealed that due to faulty fuel gauges and improper ground fueling technique the forward main fuel tank had 8,000 lb (3,629kg) less fuel than indicated. The cg at takeoff was approximately 39.9% mean aerodynamic chord (MAC). The aft cg limit for flight is 35% MAC.

52-0421 B-47E
376th BW, Barksdale AFB, LA
14th July 1955, Barksdale AFB, LA, TH: 345:25

This BLUE CRADLE airplane was lead of the second flight of 15 airplanes deploying from Barksdale AFB to RAF Upper Heyford. It was a dark night with no moon, and the crew made no transmissions after the normal takeoff roll. About three minutes after takeoff the airplane crashed in a slight right bank and at high speed, killing all four crewmen aboard. The accident investigation found that the #4 engine was shut down, but was otherwise unable to determine a cause for this crash.

52-0423 B-47E
376th BW, Lockbourne AFB, OH
31st August 1961, Lockbourne AFB, OH

This BLUE CRADLE B-47E ran off the end of the runway on initial takeoff and was consumed by fire. There were no fatalities. Witnesses reported that the airplane appeared to attempt takeoff with the brake chute deployed, but this may have been part of the abort process.

52-0439 B-47E
376th BW, Barksdale AFB, LA
7th March 1957, Lake Charles AFB, LA

A boost pump failure in B-47E 53-2395 resulted in a fire that completely destroyed that airplane. Fuel from the ruptured tanks spread to BLUE CRADLE B-47E 52-0439, which was badly damaged, and into water drainage lines causing fires as far as 1.3nm (2.4km) away. The hulk of 52-0439 was used for training and eventually scrapped.

52-0450 B-47E
98th BW, Lincoln AFB, NE
2nd May 1956, Lincoln AFB, NE, TH: 692:28

The crew aborted their mission after 1.5 hours due to faulty radar and returned to Lincoln AFB to practice GCA approaches. At a distance of 3.5nm (6.5km) from the end of the runway on the seventh approach the airplane disappeared from the GCA radar scope. The airplane was destroyed by impact and fire, and all four crewmen were killed. The investigation blamed the crash on the 'copilot's misjudgment of altitude and distance while on final approach and the [AC] not monitoring the flight instruments while the copilot was flying the airplane.'

52-0456 B-47E
98th BW, Lincoln AFB, NE
5th April 1957, Lincoln AFB, NE, TH: 836:05

During approach the pilot used 10° of bank to correct for crosswind, and the airplane crossed the threshold at 30ft (9.1m). Shortly after the flare a strong wind gust caused the right wing to drop. Despite full-left aileron, full left rudder, and increased power to engines #4, 5, and 6, the right wingtip struck the ground 2,675ft (815m) down the runway. The airplane yawed to the right, shearing the right outrigger gear, and both main gear collapsed. The airplane came to rest 1,470ft (448m) from initial impact and 135° clockwise from the landing direction. The airplane was destroyed by fire, but the crew escaped.

52-0458 B-47E
352nd BS, 301st BW, Barksdale AFB, LA
6th December 1957, Barksdale AFB, LA

The crew aborted the takeoff during a rainstorm. The brake chute deployed, failed to blossom fully, and then collapsed. The airplane ran off the end of the runway, the main gear collapsed, and the airplane burst into flames, killing all four on board. The accident board determined that the abort was initiated with 8,400ft (2,560m) of runway remaining, but could not determine the reason for the abort or why the airplane failed to stop. It is possible the engines were not fully at idle or the airplane experienced hydroplaning which reduced braking effectiveness.

52-0459 B-47E
384th BW, Little Rock AFB, AR
10th April 1962, Collegeport, TX

During the en route cruise portion of a scheduled training mission, the AC decided to fly a series of 'lazy eight' aerobatic maneuvers. He lost control of the airplane, and it broke up in flight. The airplane crashed 2nm (3.7km) S of Collegeport, TX, killing the AC and navigator; the copilot survived.

The remains of B-47E 52-0458 near the end of the runway at Barksdale AFB. *USAF photo*

52-0470 B-47E
376th BW, Lockbourne AFB, OH
10th April 1958, North Collins, NY

The airplane was 1.5nm (2.8km) behind a tanker when the B-47E exploded in flight, crashing near Niagara Falls, NY. All four crewmen were killed. Cause of the accident was attributed to structural failure. This was the fourth MILK BOTTLE crash.

52-0475 B-47E
384th BW, Little Rock AFB, AR
21st April 1961, Little Rock AFB, AR

During landing the airplane experienced a ground loop, ran off the runway, and was destroyed by fire.

52-0490 B-47E
305th BW, MacDill AFB, FL
14th March 1955, Ben Guerir AB, French Morocco, TH: 291:20

This airplane was deploying from MacDill AFB to Ben Guerir AB, French Morocco. During final approach the AC was distracted by his seat, which had already bottomed out twice. Due to this inattention the AC allowed the airplane to stall, dropping violently onto the runway, collapsing the main landing gear and the outrigger gear, and causing the navigator to suffer a compression fracture of his vertebra. The main gear failed completely within 300ft (91m) of initial contact, and the airplane came to rest some 1,000ft (305m) later without the landing gear, the two inboard engine pods, and pieces of the fuselage. The crew egressed through the open canopy; the aircraft was consumed by fire.

52-0491 B-47E
40th BW, Schilling AFB, KS
20th May 1959, Schilling AFB, KS

After an extremely hard landing the forward landing gear folded aft and collapsed. The aircraft departed the runway and was destroyed. There were no fatalities.

52-0498 B-47E
40th BW, Schilling AFB, KS
14th January 1960, Eielson AFB, AK

The airplane had taken off to return to Schilling AFB following a REFLEX deployment to Eielson AFB when the landing gear indicator showed an intermediate position. Due to ice fog in the area, the AC requested GCA assistance to provide vectors for a fly-by of the tower to inspect the gear. While maneuvering, the airplane crashed, killing the navigator and crew chief. The AC and copilot survived.

52-0500 B-47E
364th BS, 305th BW, MacDill AFB, FL
14th October 1955, Near NAS Atlanta, GA, TH: 468:10

While on a ferry flight from MacDill AFB to Dobbins AFB, GA, the AC mistook NAS Atlanta (now Peachtree-DeKalb Airport) for Dobbins AFB, and headed there in error. The navigator saw an airfield on his radarscope and, unaware that it was the wrong field, directed the AC to NAS Atlanta. Realizing his mistake at the last minute, the AC attempted to go around, but the airplane struck the ground. This sheared the left outrigger and aft main gear, as well as rupturing the aft fuel cell. The airplane was destroyed in the ensuing fire but the crew escaped. Interestingly, the abandoned fuselage was discovered during an expansion project for Atlanta's Hartsfield-Jackson Atlanta IAP.

52-0525 B-47E
509th BW, Pease AFB, NH
26th May 1964, RAF Upper Heyford, UK

B-47E 52-0525 was cocked for alert launch and was damaged on the ground by the crash of B-47E 53-2296. There was no damage to the nuclear weapon on board. Estimates to repair the airplane included 1,800 man-hours with depot-level skills. With plans to remove B-47s from service this was deemed unacceptable and was subsequently written off on 27th June 1964.

52-0526 B-47E
509th BW, Pease AFB, NH
3rd August 1962, Pease AFB, NH

A fuel line broke on takeoff resulting in a loss of power causing the airplane to crash. All three crewmen perished.

52-0533 B-47E
22nd BW, March AFB, CA
12th January 1961, Near Mt Palomar, CA

Crashed 23 minutes after takeoff about 5nm (9.3km) from the Mt Palomar Observatory. The crew safely egressed the airplane, but one crewmember died when he struck a tree. Cause of the accident was an autopilot malfunction.

52-0534 B-47E
369th BS, 306th BW, MacDill AFB, FL
10th March 1956, Mediterranean Sea

This B-47E was one of a flight of four in a deployment from MacDill AFB to Sidi Slimane AB, Morocco. In preparation for the second aerial refueling the flight descended from cruise altitude through a solid cloud deck to the planned refueling altitude of 14,000ft (4,267m), some 500ft (152m) beneath the bottom of the cloud deck, with poor visibility. B-47E 52-0534, call sign *Inkspot 59*, never made contact with its KC-97. The crew may have become disoriented during the descent and experienced an unusual attitude from which they failed to recover, crashing into the sea. On board the airplane were two capsules of nuclear weapons material in carrying cases. An exhaustive search failed to locate the aircraft, its weapons capsules, or its crew.

52-0535 B-47E
369th BS, 306th BW, MacDill AFB, FL
19th December 1955, Near Tampa, FL

B-47E 52-0535 experienced smoke in the cockpit after takeoff from MacDill AFB, and also shut down the #1 engine due to an engine overspeed. In preparation for landing, the crew lowered the gear but experienced a significant vibration. The crew asked for a visual inspection. B-47B 51-2286 was in the area and provided the visual check, reporting that everything appeared normal. While maneuvering in close proximity behind B-47E 52-0535, the pilot of B-47B 51-2286 required excessive back force on the elevators due to downward jet wash from the B-47E. Passing beneath the B-47E this jet wash dissipated, and the pilot of 51-2286 could not release the backpressure fast enough and climbed abruptly into B-47E 52-0535. The collision killed everyone on both airplanes.

52-0553 B-47E
303rd BW, Davis-Monthan AFB, AZ
23rd August 1962, Near Smith's Ferry, ID

Following night cell air refueling the airplane proceeded to the OIL BURNER low-level route entry point. Reported weather was clear with 30nm (56km) visibility. The crew was cleared for a SHORT LOOK LARGE CHARGE simulated bomb release. Three minutes later another B-47 reported an explosion and fire. The mishap airplane crashed wings-level in a slight descent at the 6,830ft (2,082m) level of a 7,091ft (2,161m) mountain. Published minimum altitude for the route segment was 9,500ft (2,896m). All three of the Select crew perished.

52-0556 B-47E
340th BW, Whiteman AFB, MO
13th October 1960, Whiteman AFB, MO

The airplane crashed and burned during a GCA approach to Whiteman AFB. All four crewmen survived.

52-0562 B-47E
509th BW, Walker AFB, NM
15th April 1958, Pease AFB, NH

During takeoff roll the airplane became airborne after 7,000ft (2,134m), then settled back onto the runway. The airplane again became airborne at the planned 9,000ft (2,743m) point, climbed steeply in a nose-high attitude to approximately 400ft (122m), then stalled and crashed, killing all four crewmen. The investigation determined that the fuel panel was not set properly for takeoff, and was instead configured according to wing policy for heavy weight taxi operations to adjust the center of gravity. In the mishap configuration the airplane experienced a slight loss in acceleration, but not enough to cause the crash. Simulations showed that despite the loss in acceleration the crew attempted to take off at least 8KIAS below minimum takeoff speed, failed to use all available runway, and then climbed out too steeply.

52-0563 B-47E
98th BW, Lincoln AFB, NE
20th February 1963, Comfrey, MN

After departing the IRON HORSE low-level route an outboard engine mount failed. The airplane crashed near Comfrey, MN. All four on board were killed.

52-0565 B-47E
40th BW, Smoky Hill AFB, KS
26th June 1956, Smoky Hill AFB, KS, TH: 667:40

After a night training mission the airplane was inbound on a jet penetration to Smoky Hill AFB. The AC canceled the Instrument Flight Rules (IFR) clearance and proceeded on course using Visual Flight Rules (VFR). Due to reduced visibility the crew executed a go around, and made a left turn at 700ft (213m) in altitude after passing the runway and disappeared into an intense dust storm. The airplane crashed and burned in a wheat field 4.5nm (8.3km) from the base. All three crewmen were killed. The investigation determined that the crew failed to follow missed approach procedures and flew into terrain. Disorientation and severe weather may have been contributing causes.

52-0566 B-47E
40th BW, Schilling AFB, KS
5th January 1960, Hugoton, KS

Following air refueling the B-47E flew into the KC-97's prop wash. It stalled, entered an inverted spin, and crashed. Three crewmen were killed and one ejected successfully and survived.

52-0572 B-47E
40th BW, Smoky Hill AFB, KS
13th July 1956, Smoky Hill AFB, KS, TH: 679:05

Just prior to becoming airborne the right forward tire failed, and the AC aborted the takeoff. Both aft main tires failed and the airplane continued off the overrun, down sloping terrain, striking a drainage ditch 1,400ft (427m) from the end of the runway. The airplane was destroyed by impact and fire, killing all four crewmembers. Investigation revealed that the AC aborted the takeoff well past the calculated refusal point, some 200ft (61m) short of the planned takeoff distance and with only 3,300ft (1,006m) of runway remaining, far too short for an abort stop.

52-0580 B-47E
25th BS, 40th BW, Smoky Hill AFB, KS
4th October 1955, Galva, KS, TH: 303:10

Following air refueling the #1 fire engine light illuminated, and the crew determined that a fire was spreading rapidly along the left wing. The AC ordered the crew to bail out, but the copilot and navigator's ejection seats failed. They, along with the instructor navigator, bailed out through the bomb bay. The AC ejected at the last minute with the airplane in a steep left bank while nose down. All survived without serious injury. The airplane crashed near Galva, KS. Investigation revealed that the fire warning system had malfunctioned, and the AC ordered an unnecessary bailout without assessing the situation.

52-0606 B-47E
96th BW, Dyess AFB, TX
21st October 1959, Dobbins AFB, GA

After completing a GCA, the airplane touched down, bounced, and then landed again. The brake chute detached without opening and wheel braking failed to stop the airplane. It then crossed 1,100ft (305m) of soft overrun and plunged down a 20ft (6.1m) ravine. The airplane was destroyed by fire but the crew of four escaped safely.

52-0615 B-47E
22nd BW, March AFB, CA
5th January 1962, March AFB, CA

The pilot forced the airplane into the air prematurely. It stalled and crashed, killing all three aboard.

52-0702 RB-47E
90th SRW, Forbes AFB, KS
21st October 1959, Lake of the Ozarks, MO

The airplane entered a spin during a stall demonstration and was unable to recover. It crashed at Possum Hollow, near the Lake of the Ozarks, 18nm (33km) SE of Versailles, MO. Two crewmen were killed. Two survived – one landed in the lake and another landed in telephone lines.

52-0716 RB-47E
90th SRW, Forbes AFB, KS
13th April 1960, Perrin, MO

Early during this training sortie the airplane experienced a malfunction in the aileron boost hydraulic power. With all other conditions nominal the crew continued the flight, but during air refueling the aileron control system failed completely. The crew discontinued air refueling and aborted the mission. Without a navigator on board to recommend an avoidance course, the pilot flew directly into a thunderstorm where, coupled with the lack of adequate aileron control, the airplane stalled, entered a spin, and disintegrated. Two crewmen died, but the crew chief and one other crewman survived.

52-0720 RB-47E
26th SRW, Lockbourne AFB, OH
26th February 1958, Lancaster, OH

The airplane was returning to Lockbourne AFB and initiated a jet penetration. One minute after passing the VOR the airplane crashed 6nm (11km) S of Lancaster, OH, killing all four crewmen. Investigation revealed that the airplane struck the ground in a 60° dive and was structurally intact. The crew may have become disoriented in an unusual attitude or was distracted, leading to a high-speed dive from which it was impossible to recover.

52-0726 RB-47E
90th SRW, Forbes AFB, KS
25th September 1958, Forbes AFB, KS

The student copilot in the back seat had completed a GCA approach and transitioned to a visual approach to complete the landing. During the flare, which was excessively nose high, the airplane rolled sharply to the left and the #1 engine, left outrigger gear, and aft main gear struck the runway. The airplane continued to the left off the runway, hitting terrain which sheared off the left engine pod and the forward main gear. There were no fatalities. The investigation board determined that the IP had failed to recognize an unsafe situation and did not intervene soon enough to prevent the accident.

52-0742 RB-47E
320th SRS, 90th SRW, Forbes AFB, KS
25th March 1955, El Paso IAP, TX, TH: 255:25

Upon returning from Lake Charles AFB to Forbes AFB, the Command Post directed the crew to divert to Walker AFB, NM, due to ice on the runway at Forbes AFB. En route the AC decided to land instead at Biggs AFB, TX. When the visibility at Biggs AFB decreased to 1/2nm (0.9km) with blowing dust, the AC elected to land instead at nearby El Paso IAP. The airplane crashed into a home approximately 1/2nm (0.9km) from the end of the runway while turning final, killing all three crewmen. The accident investigation found that tailwind on final led to improper landing pitch and caused the airplane to stall. The board also argued that lack of crew rest was a contributing factor to the crash, as was the Command Post's decision to divert to Walker AFB, bypassing other suitable B-47 bases.

52-0744 RB-47E
70th SRW, Little Rock AFB, AR
29th September 1958, Little Rock AFB, AR

During the third touch-and-go landing the airplane landed on the front gear 2,000ft (610m) down the runway, bounced, recovered, and then became airborne again at approximately 5,000ft (1,524m). The airplane was in a nose-high attitude which became increasingly extreme as it banked and turned to the right. It stalled and crashed 9,400ft (2,865m) from the approach end of the runway and 1,200ft (366m) to the right of the runway centerline. The crew of four was killed.

52-0754 RB-47E
90th SRW, Forbes AFB, KS
8th August 1957, Forbes AFB, KS

Following two successful back-seat student pilot touch-and-go landings, the third student approach resulted in a nose-high attitude prior to the flare. About 200ft (61m) from the end of the runway the right wing dropped and the airplane struck the unpaved overrun nose-high in 10-15° of right bank. The airplane rolled 4,800ft (1,463m) down the runway where the #6 engine began to burn, igniting fuel spilling from the ruptured aft main tank. The crew safely egressed the airplane, which was completely destroyed.

52-0761 RB-47E
70th SRW, Little Rock AFB, AR
1st May 1957, Pittsburgh, TX, TH: 804:55

During a night mass air refueling mission the crew was attempting its second contact with its KC-97. As the first contact was unsuccessful, the crew elected to use the manual/emergency override method to hold the boom in place. The tanker experienced a fuel pump problem, so the RB-47 remained in contact rather than disconnect. The flight entered clouds, and about 3

minutes later the RB-47 reported that it was taking fuel. As the two aircraft moved in and out of the clouds, the RB-47 began to sway from side to side. Eventually the RB-47 reached some 90° of left bank with its right wing in the tanker prop wash, causing a brute-force disconnect. The RB-47 entered a spin. At 7,000ft (2,134m) above ground level (AGL) the AC ordered the crew to eject, which they did. The three primary crewmembers survived, but the fourth man on board perished, unable to egress the airplane because of the spin forces. The airplane crashed near Pittsburgh, TX.

52-0766 RB-47E
4347th CCTW, McConnell AFB, KS
9th January 1961, McConnell AFB, KS

Following a touch-and-go landing, the airplane assumed an unusually nose-high attitude. It climbed briefly, banked abruptly to the right, and then cartwheeled on the airfield. All three crewmen were killed.

52-0770 RB-47E
319th SRS, 90th SRW, Forbes AFB, KS
29th October 1954, Olathe, KS

Following a night departure from Forbes AFB the aircraft climbed through an 8,000ft (2,438m) overcast. As the crew completed their cockpit checks, the airplane entered a high-speed descending left-hand spiral. Passing 460KIAS both pilots attempted to recover using full opposite aileron and rudder, but this only aggravated the wing-down condition (aileron reversal) and the airplane became uncontrollable. The AC ejected successfully, but the remaining three crewmen were killed. The aircraft crashed 10nm (18.5km) from Olathe, KS. Investigation revealed the rudder failed leading to the initial upset.

52-0785 RB-47E
3rd SRS, 26th SRW, Lockbourne AFB, OH
30th November 1955, Lockbourne AFB, OH, TH: 395:40

After takeoff the airplane experienced failure of the rudder/elevator PCU due to a sheared pump motor gear. The crew burned off fuel to a suitable landing weight and began an approach. The jet was too high so the AC initiated a go around. As he applied power the airplane went into a steep left bank. The AC retarded the throttles and the aircraft struck the ground 520ft (158m) to the left and 2,700ft (823m) short of the end of the runway. There was no fire and all aboard survived the accident. Investigation determined that asymmetric power and compressor stall caused the airplane to go into the left bank during the go around.

52-0814 RB-47E
3970th CSG, Torrejón AB, Spain
27th January 1960, Torrejón AB, Spain

During final approach the airplane landed short of the runway, bounced, and then landed on the runway. All crewmembers egressed safely. The airplane was uneconomical to repair and was written off on 10th March 1960.

52-0817 QB-47E
3205th Drone Squadron, Eglin AFB
8th March 1962, Gulf of Mexico

This drone rolled inverted and attempted to recover by performing a split-s maneuver 4,000ft (1,219m) above the Gulf of Mexico, but was too low and crashed into the water.

58-0823 QB-47E
3205th Drone Squadron, Eglin AFB
19th August 1963, Eglin AFB, FL

Unable to land at Field #3 due to thunderstorms, the airplane diverted to the main runway at Eglin AFB. The airplane 'burst into flames on initial contact' with the runway, then veered off the runway during landing and came to rest on the Eglin Parkway, a major road parallel to the runway. It struck two cars, killing two of the occupants and injuring another.

52-0824 RB-47E
70th SRW, Little Rock, AR
29th October 1958, Pine Bluff, AR

This was a scheduled pilot upgrade sortie, and the crew was conducting low approaches on the VOR while practicing two-engine failure procedures. Witnesses report that at approximately 1/4nm (0.46km) from the end of the runway the airplane stalled and enter a right-hand spin. Although the airplane appeared to recover, it resumed spinning, making nearly two revolutions prior to ground impact, killing all three crewmembers.

52-1414 B-47E
545th BS, 384th BW, Little Rock AFB, AR
31st March 1960, Little Rock, AR

During climb out 10 minutes after initial takeoff from Little Rock AFB, the copilot was monitoring SAC HF radio traffic when he realized the airplane was in a very steep bank around 15,000 feet. He retarded the throttles and alerted the AC, who was flying the jet. The AC pulled up the nose and leveled the wings aggressively and the airplane disintegrated. Debris fell on two housing areas some two miles apart, destroying seven houses and damaging others. The copilot survived, but five others were killed including three crewmen and two civilians on the ground.

52-3344 B-47E
22nd BW, March AFB, CA
2nd June 1959, Winchester, CA

This airplane crashed 11nm (20km) S of March AFB while on approach. Three crewmen were killed with one survivor.

52-3360 B-47E
32nd BS, 301st BW, Lake Charles AFB, LA
30th November 1956, Near Sea Gull Lake, Ontario, Canada

The airplane was participating in an Operational Readiness Inspection (ORI) mission. Prior to the first scheduled air refueling the aileron power control hydraulic system pressure began to drop. The emergency pump restored pressure to normal and the flight continued for an additional 5 hours. Shortly thereafter the main hydraulic system experienced total failure, and aileron power control circuit breakers popped. About 10 minutes later the airplane entered a shallow right bank. The AC disengaged the autopilot but, even with the help of the copilot, could not stop the bank from increasing. At 60-70° of bank at 35,000ft (10,668m) the AC ordered the crew to eject. The airplane crashed near Sea Gull Lake, 50 miles northeast of Port Arthur, Ontario, Canada. Only the AC survived; the three other crewmembers perished. Investigation determined the primary cause of the accident to be a locked aileron power control shuttle valve.

Official records make no reference to weapons on board B-47E 52-3360, but the airplane almost certainly carried one (or at least the components). An 8th November 1956 TOP SECRET letter from the US Department of State requested permission from the Canadian government for 72 B-47s to operate in Canadian airspace from 29th-30th November as part of Operation ROADBLOCK, an 'XYZ mission' associated with carrying nuclear weapons or components during an ORI. Half of these airplanes were so equipped. The 91st SRW RB-47E AC who located the crash site reported he was told to 'find the remains of the aircraft *and the weapons on board*' [emphasis added]

52-3371 B-47E
384th BW, Little Rock AFB, AR
3rd February 1959, Little Rock AFB, AR

The airplane crashed 25nm (46km) NE of Little Rock AFB while on approach. The impact left a 30ft (9m) deep crater in the swampy wooded area where the airplane went down, killing all three crewmen.

52-3389 RB-47E
70th SRW, Little Rock AFB, AR
24th March 1959, Morrilton, AR

The #6 engine exploded during flight and the wing caught fire. Captain Keith L Thrash, the AC, received the Distinguished Flying Cross for his part in enabling the first successful bailout of five crewmen from a B-47. The aircraft crashed into Petit Jean Mountain near Morrilton.

53-1831 B-47E
715th BS, 509th BW, Walker AFB, NM
5th February 1956, Walker AFB, NM, TH: 160:00

Immediately after takeoff the #4 engine began to overspeed and the landing gear failed to retract completely. The crew recycled the landing gear, raised the flaps below minimum flap speed, and retarded the #4 engine. The airplane entered a low-speed buffet and stalled, settling to the ground. The jet slid about 1.7nm (3.14km) before striking a high-tension transformer station and stopping 3nm (5.6km) from the end of the runway. The crew of four survived the accident. Investigation revealed that recycling the landing gear led to increased drag, and that the crew prematurely raised the flaps leading to the stall.

53-1832 B-47E
509th BW, Walker AFB, NM
15th February 1957, Walker AFB, NM

The airplane exploded during ground refueling and was destroyed by fire. One person (believed to be the crew chief) perished.

53-1847 B-47E
63rd BS, 43rd BW, Davis-Monthan AFB, AZ
3rd October 1955, Tatum, NM, TH: 35:15

The airplane took off from Davis-Monthan AFB as third in a cell on an IFR clearance, but with an inoperative attitude gyro for the aircraft commander. Approximately 5 minutes after refueling the airplane entered weather and the copilot believed that his attitude gyro failed as well. The airplane entered a descending right spiral, leading to an aggressive recovery effort where the crew felt several jolts (which the copilot believed were due to terrain impact) and fire broke out in the forward fuselage. The copilot egressed the airplane, but the AC and navigator were killed in the ensuing crash. The accident investigation determined that the lower right fuselage longeron broke due to excessive control forces during the attempted recovery.

53-1868 B-47E
380th BW, Plattsburgh AFB, NY
5th February 1964, Plattsburgh AFB, NY

The airplane landed short, shearing off engines #3, 4, and 6. It was written off on 8th March 1964.

53-1886 B-47E
419th BS, 301st BW, Lockbourne AFB, OH
8th November 1960, Lockbourne AFB, OH

Takeoff roll was nearly 2,000ft (610m) longer than planned. The airplane (a Phase V B-47E) reached an altitude of 100ft (30m) when the right wing dropped and the airplane crashed inverted 520ft (158m) off the right side of the runway, 12,500ft (3,810m) from the start of the takeoff roll. All five on board were killed. Investigation revealed that at impact the #4 engine was operating at 40-50% rpm and the #6 engine was operating at 5-10% rpm, but the board offered no explanation or cause.

53-1891 B-47E
44th BW, Lake Charles AFB, LA
24th October 1957, Lake Charles AFB, LA

The airplane caught fire during maintenance as mechanics changed a boost pump and was destroyed.

53-1905 B-47E
100th BW, Pease AFB, NH
27th November 1961, Plattsburgh AFB, NY

The airplane exited the HANGOVER Low Level Training Route missing the rear end of the #4 engine and with the #6 engine shut down due to icing. The crew elected to divert to Plattsburgh AFB for an emergency landing. Prior to descent, the aft mounting pin on the #1 engine failed, leaving the engine hanging at an angle beneath the wing. As the airplane broke of out the weather on final approach, the #2 engine failed. After extending the gear for landing the airplane had insufficient power to continue flying, so the AC retracted the gear and attempted to go around. The sink rate was too high and the airplane hit trees 1nm (1.9km) short of the runway. Three of the four crewmen were killed.

53-1931 B-47E
96th BS, 2nd BW, Hunter AFB, GA
11th June 1958, West Hills, VT

While en route on a REFLEX deployment from Hunter AFB to RAF Brize Norton, the flight of three diverted to Plattsburgh AFB. The first two B-47Es in the flight completed the VOR penetration and approach to Plattsburgh AFB without incident. The mishap airplane (call sign *Oatmeal 51*) began the VOR penetration but did not follow the published approach. Radar approach control could not positively identify the B-47E, and the crew could not ascertain their actual position. At one point the ground radar had the airplane some 7nm (13km) NNE of Plattsburgh AFB while the B-47E navigator had them 30nm (56km) away. Fearful that the B-47E was too low and in danger of hitting high ground, the ground controller directed the crew to climb to 5,000ft (1,524m) and follow a southerly course to clear high terrain. The crew acknowledged this transmission. Shortly thereafter the airplane hit high ground in the Cold Hollow Mountains 35nm (65km) NE of Plattsburgh near West Hills, VT, killing all four crewmen. At impact the airplane was in a near vertical left bank, nose down, with the flaps and gear configured for approach and landing. The investigation determined that the crew became disoriented resulting in loss of aircraft control.

53-1933 B-47E
44th BW, Lake Charles AFB, LA
25th October 1956, Lake Charles AFB, LA, TH: 88:15
The crew attempted to takeoff without water alcohol and failed to accelerate sufficiently. After 8,500ft (2,591m) of takeoff roll the AC aborted the takeoff, but the airplane continued off the end of the runway striking the ILS localizer building and a drainage ditch, breaking up and burning. All four on board were killed. The investigation determined the refusal distance to be 5,000ft (1,524m), and was unable to determine why water alcohol was not used or why the takeoff was improperly aborted. The runway was 10,701ft (3,262m) long, so the airplane had only 2,200ft (671m) to stop.

53-2035 B-47E
509th BW, Pease AFB, NH
21st January 1959, Plattsburgh AFB, NY
The airplane hit terrain short of the runway during approach.

53-2091 B-47E
43rd BW, Davis-Monthan AFB, AZ
24th May 1957, Arnett, OK
The AC elected to fly the most direct route from Tulsa, OK, to Davis-Monthan AFB despite the weather forecast of heavy to extreme turbulence, hail, and tornadoes for the route. After passing Oklahoma City the aircraft encountered severe thunderstorms and the AC chose to climb over the top rather than go around them, eventually leveling at 38,500ft (11,735m) but still in the clouds and severe weather. Thinking better of this plan, the AC began a 20° left bank and asked the copilot to get a weather avoidance clearance. At this time both pilots' attitude indicator failed. Unable to maintain aircraft control, the AC ordered the crew to eject. The AC and the navigator survived.

53-2097 B-47E
307th BW, Lincoln AFB, NE
10th January 1963, McConnell AFB, KS
After diverting to McConnell AFB on 9th January due to bad weather at Lincoln AFB, five 307th BW B-47s were directed to fly missions from McConnell AFB. Crews protested this order as the weather at McConnell AFB was poor and getting worse. Nonetheless, the Command Post prevailed and 53-2097 was the first to depart at 2204L. Within four to five minutes the airplane became uncontrollable and the crew attempted to make an emergency landing. Two crewmen ejected safely, but the AC maneuvered the airplane away from a populated area and perished in the ensuing crash. Investigation revealed the Q-spring iced over, resulting in loss of control of the airplane.

53-2111 B-47E
307th BW, Lincoln AFB, NE
18th June 1961, Lincoln AFB, NE
During takeoff roll a fire erupted in the #6 engine. The airplane became airborne but stalled, falling to the right and crashing some 2,950ft (899m) from the end of the runway. The copilot successfully ejected but the remaining three crewmen died.

53-2119 B-47E
380th BW, Plattsburgh AFB, NY
16th January 1962, Wright Peak, NY
After descending to enter the HANGOVER Low Level Training Route, the airplane struck Wright Peak just below the 4,580ft (1,396m) top. The four crewmen perished. Investigation revealed that due to inclement weather and high winds, the airplane had wandered some 30 miles off course. With the bad weather conditions the crew was unable to see the high terrain.

53-2129 B-47E
308th BW, Hunter AFB, GA
11th June 1959, Hunter AFB, GA
The #6 engine exploded, destroying 14ft (4.3m) of the right wing. The airplane was deemed uneconomical to repair and written off on 1st July 1959.

53-2134 B-47E
307th BW, Lincoln AFB, NE
5th February 1963, RAF Greenham Common, UK
The *City of Lincoln* was attempting to land at RAF Greenham Common during a snowstorm with significant crosswind. The crew initiated a go-

around due to misalignment with the runway because of the crosswinds, but the #6 engine did not accelerate. The resulting asymmetric thrust caused the right wingtip to drag. At this point the copilot ejected but received fatal injuries due to a malfunctioning ejection seat, which caused significant damage to the aircraft controls that ran along the spine of the airplane. The AC was able to get the airplane onto the ground, although it was ultimately destroyed. The three remaining crewmen survived.

53-2136 B-47E
100th BW, Pease AFB, NH
22nd September 1959, Pease AFB, NH
The #4 engine turbine disintegrated over Anticosti Island, Quebec. The AC decided to return to Pease AFB, a distance of 506nm (937km), and landed safely. There were no fatalities. Nonetheless, the airplane was deemed uneconomical to repair and it was written off on 9th November 1959 at Pease AFB.

53-2160 B-47E
98th BW, Lincoln AFB, NE
12th July 1963, Zaragosa AB, Spain
The airplane departed Zaragosa AB, Spain, to return to Lincoln AFB, NE. Climbing through 20,000ft (6,096m) the airplane experienced rapid and progressive loss of all six electrical generators, resulting in total loss of electrical power. The crew returned to Zaragosa AB, extended the landing gear via the emergency system, and opted for an immediate heavy weight no-flap landing. During a planned low approach the fuel feed to the engines on the right side dropped due to reduced-flow gravity feed, causing an abrupt loss of power and compelling the crew to land rather than make a low approach. Touchdown weight was 175,000lb (79,379kg), there was no rudder-elevator power control, no anti-skid, and the brake chute failed at the 180KIAS touchdown speed. The airplane was unable to stop on the runway and ran off the departure end where it was destroyed. One crewman was killed. The investigation found that the AC landed the airplane in a configuration that only optimal performance of braking devices would have stopped the airplane on the runway, and should instead have burned fuel at altitude to allow a lighter and safer landing weight.

53-2169 B-47E
301st BW, Lockbourne AFB, OH
21st February 1961, Bowling Green, KY
The pilot lost control of this Phase V airplane at 15,000ft (4,572m) during a night air refueling in marginal weather conditions. Four crewmen were killed, but the navigator survived.

53-2267 B-47E
97th BW, Biggs AFB, TX
19th August 1958, Follet, TX
Passing 32,000ft (9,754m) to avoid thunderstorms, the AC noticed a bright flash over his right shoulder, heard a loud 'crack,' the airplane pitched downward abruptly, and the canopy separated. The elevator moved freely and the airplane was unresponsive in pitch. The AC ordered the crew to evacuate; three survived, but the crew chief perished. Investigation determined that an aft fuel pump likely exploded, causing structural failure and the resulting break up.

53-2277 B-47E
3200th TG, Eglin AFB, FL
15th April 1955, Kindley AB, Bermuda
The airplane crashed on takeoff for reasons unknown, killing the crew of three. One body was recovered from Castle Harbour.

Phase V B-47E 53-2169 was lost during air refueling. *Author's collection*

Loss of control claimed JB-47E 53-2282. *Author's collection*

53-2282 JB-47E
3245th TG, Eglin AFB, FL
12th September 1957, Bastrop, LA

The airplane was on an automatic astrotracking mission while ferrying personnel to Edwards AFB, CA. Just prior to entering IMC near Jackson, MS, the aileron power control unit failed. After entering the clouds and disconnecting the autopilot and aileron power controls, the AC attempted to maneuver clear of the severe weather. After 45° of heading change the airplane pitched up violently and went out of control. Despite multiple efforts to regain control, the AC ordered the crew to bail out. The airplane crashed near Bastrop, LA.

53-2296 B-47E
509th BW, Pease AFB, NH
26th May 1964, RAF Upper Heyford, UK

The airplane (call sign *Taboo 40*) crashed while landing, the result of failure of the right elevator PCU. Three crewmen from 53-2296 survived, but the navigator perished during rescue efforts. Debris from the crash struck B-47E 52-0525 which was parked on Alert Hardstand #43. It was cocked on alert and carried a nuclear weapon, but this was not damaged by the debris.

53-2301 B-47E
2nd BW, Hunter AFB, GA
10th October 1956, Hunter AFB, GA

After a practice refueling sortie with an IP and two student pilots, the airplane began a GCA approach to Hunter AFB. At 500ft (152m) altitude the IP in the back seat directed the student pilot in the front seat to take over visually and continue the approach. At 3/4nm (1.4km) from the end of the runway GCA observed the aircraft to go below the glide path and notified the pilot. Despite this warning the airplane struck the ground and broke up along the runway. There were no fatalities.

53-2304 B-47E
2nd BW, Hunter AFB, GA
7th February 1956, Hunter AFB, GA, TH: 327:00

During a trim coordination test flight the trim motors would not correct a wing-heavy condition. While performing a touch-and-go, the airplane entered a right yaw and the right wingtip struck the ground. The airplane reached approximately 35° of right bank before crashing. It was destroyed by fire, and the AC received major injuries. The cause was believed to be loss of one or more engines on right side.

53-2319 B-47E
43rd BW, Davis-Monthan AFB, AZ
2nd April 1959, Mountain Home AFB, MT

The airplane experienced loss of #4 engine and a fire in #5. The fire was extinguished and the airplane diverted to Mountain Home. On approach the #5 engine broke loose and wedged between the drop tank and the wing leading edge. The crew could not maintain control and the airplane crashed eight miles short of the runway. All four crewmen were killed.

53-2320 EB-47E(TT)
38th SRS, 55th SRW, Forbes AFB, KS
3rd April 1965, Incirlik AB, Turkey

Following a classified reconnaissance mission the crew orbited Incirlik AB, unable to land due to out-of-limit crosswinds. Running out of fuel, the crew attempted to land but ballooned after touchdown and crashed. Two of the five crewmen perished.

53-2331 B-47E
40th BW, Forbes AFB, KS
2nd May 1961, Hurley, WI

The airplane had completed a practice low-level bomb run under intermittent instrument conditions. During the pull up the airplane went out of control, experiencing two abrupt nose-up and nose-down cycles. It crashed at 0245 some 10nm (19km) SE of Hurley, WI. Two crewmen perished and two survived. Spatial disorientation due to flashing anti-collision lights in night instrument conditions may have contributed to the accident. This was the second 40th BW B-47E to crash near Hurley in three months, as B-47E 53-2347 was lost on 24th February 1961.

53-2347 B-47E
660th BS, 40th BW, Forbes AFB, KS
24th February 1961, Hurley, WI

The crew was practicing a low-level bomb run. During the climb-out the radar plot showed that the airplane vacillated left, then right, of the plotted course and then struck the ground near Hurley, WI, killing all four crewmen. Investigation revealed that the #1 engine aft support pin failed and that the #1 engine departed the airplane prior to the impact.

53-2363 B-47E
307th BW, Lincoln AFB, NE
3rd June 1964, Lincoln AFB, NE

The airplane was third in a night three-ship MITO. At approximately 3,500ft (1,067m) from the start of the takeoff roll the tower reported fire coming from the left inboard nacelle. The crew aborted and stopped 4,000ft (1,219m) later. The crew of three evacuated but two received minor injuries. Oddly enough, the crew shut down all the engines except those in the burning nacelle, and #4 ran at idle RPM until fire consumed the available fuel. Investigation revealed materiel failure of the #3 engine compressor section, and resulted in the installation of engine stall warning indicators throughout the B-47 fleet.

53-2365 B-47E
310th BW, Schilling AFB, KS
19th August 1963, Irwin, IA

Two B-47s (53-2365 and 53-6206) planned to fly formation through the navigation and refueling portion of a BAR NONE mission. In violation of SAC regulations, they agreed to fly in a loose formation at the same altitude and accomplish celestial navigation while maintaining visual separation. Prior to starting celestial observation, the two B-47s collided, crashing near Irwin, IA. Two of the six crewmen were killed.

53-2366 B-47E
307th BW, Lincoln AFB, NE
27th July 1964, Lincoln AFB, NE

The airplane failed to accelerate during takeoff and crashed, killing the crew of four.

53-2395 B-47E
44th BW, Barksdale AFB, LA
7th March 1957, Lake Charles AFB, LA

A boost pump failure in B-47E 53-2395 resulted in a fire that completely destroyed that airplane. Fuel from the ruptured tanks spread to BLUE CRADLE B-47E 52-0439, which was also destroyed, and into water drainage lines causing fires as far as 1.3nm (2.4km) away.

53-2398 B-47E
380th BW, Plattsburgh AFB, NY
2nd December 1964, Plattsburgh AFB, NY

After a normal landing and brake chute deployment, the airplane experienced significant vibrations, rapidly becoming severe. The forward main landing gear collapsed at approximately 90KIAS. The crew egressed without injury. The airplane was written off on 13th January 1965. Investigation determined that materiel failure allowed the landing gear support structure to fail.

53-4208 B-47E
307th BW, Lincoln AFB, NE
17th February 1959, Marietta, GA

The airplane crashed while on a test flight from Lockheed-Marietta. The crew of three, including a civilian Lockheed test pilot, was killed. The cause is not known.

53-4209 B-47E
307th BW, Lincoln AFB, NE
6th April 1956, Ceresco, NE, TH: 21:20

An explosion of unknown origin caused the airplane to break into three main sections shortly after takeoff. The airplane crashed near Ceresco, NE, and all four crewmen were killed. The cause of the crash was never determined.

53-4212 B-47E
44th BW, Chennault AFB, LA
26th November 1958, Chennault AFB, LA

An ATO bottle exploded on the ramp leading to total destruction of this B-47E and killing one. The single nuclear weapon on board was destroyed; there was no explosion and contamination was limited to the immediate vicinity of the fire.

53-4218 B-47E
307th BW, Lincoln AFB, NE
19th July 1962, Des Moines AP, IA

Due to severe thunderstorms and low fuel, the crew elected to divert to Des Moines AP, an approved evacuation airport. Due to local construction, however, there were no approach lights. The airplane landed short in the construction area and made contact with the runway lip which sheared off the forward main gear. The airplane came to rest off the runway and was partially destroyed by fire. All four crewmen survived.

53-4226 B-47E
307th BW, Lincoln AFB, NE
7th March 1963, Lincoln AFB, NE

The airplane crashed on takeoff due to fuselage fire from ATO. All four crewmembers ejected or bailed out, but the AC died when his ejection seat failed. The remaining three crewmembers survived.

53-4230 B-47E
307th BW, Lincoln AFB, NE
27th July 1956, RAF Lakenheath, UK, TH: 87:10

During the fourth touch-and-go at RAF Lakenheath the airplane began to porpoise and the AC attempted a go around. However the right wing tip struck the ground and the aircraft crashed into a nuclear weapons storage igloo about 1,000ft (305m) beyond the perimeter taxiway on the south side of Lakenheath Hill, killing all the crew, including a maintenance technician on board to evaluate the recent repair of the radar system.

This was a particularly sensitive accident (which by coincidence was recorded by a USAF camera crew) producing a BROKEN ARROW nuclear incident. Three Mk VI atomic weapons were affected. Although they lacked their fissile core, each had some 8,000 lb (3,629kg) of high explosive (HE) as part of their trigger mechanism. No detonation occurred, but one USAF general warned that had there been an HE explosion then a large portion of eastern England would have become a 'desert' due to the dispersal of radioactive material.

A TOP SECRET memo to General LeMay noted that the 'bomb disposal officer says [it was] a miracle that one mark six with exposed detonators sheared didn't go.' Fire crews focused their efforts on containing the blaze to cool the weapons, meriting an 'investigation to warrant decorating firemen.' The damaged weapons and components were eventually returned to the Atomic Energy Commission (AEC).

53-4235 B-47E
307th BW, Lincoln AFB, NE
17th November 1956, Lincoln AFB, NE

The pilot of 173rd FIS, Nebraska Air National Guard, Lockheed F-80C 44-85284 mistook a taxiway for the runway and ran into two parked B-47Es, 52-0369 and 53-4235. All three airplanes were destroyed. The F-80 pilot and two B-47 ground crew were killed. In November 1957 First Lieutenant Robert J Cox from the 371st BS received the Soldier's Medal for saving an airman's life during the disaster and for preventing further damage to other aircraft.

53-4244 B-47E
100th BW, Pease AFB, NH
4th January 1961, Pease AFB, NH

The airplane was second in a three-ship MITO takeoff. Approximately 8,000ft (2,438m) down the runway witnesses reported sparks coming from the right side of the airplane. The airplane became airborne but failed to climb, striking the ground 246ft (75m) past the end and 661ft (201m) left of the runway. All four crewmen were killed. Investigation revealed that the sparks were caused by the right wing tip and #6 engine nacelle striking the runway. This could only have occurred if the airplane was in a right bank of at least 18.5° and an angle of attack (AoA) of 13.5°. The B-47 begins to buffet at 9.8° AoA, so the airplane was already in a stall when the witnesses saw the sparks.

53-4259 QB-47E
3205th Drone Squadron, Eglin AFB, FL
23rd May 1961, Eglin AFB, Field #3, FL

This QB-47E ran off the runway during a ground-controlled landing. It was written off on 24th July 1961.

53-4261 NRB-47E
ASD, AFSC, Wright-Patterson AFB, OH
29th December 1965, Holloman AFB, NM

While deployed to Holloman AFB to fly 'radar target missions,' the airplane crashed on takeoff, killing two crewmen. It was written off on 27th January 1966.

QB-47E 53-4259 was destroyed when it ran off the runway.
Author's collection

NRB-47E 53-4261 at Wright-Patterson AFB on 29th October 1965, two months before its crash at Holloman AFB. *Photo by Stephen Miller*

53-4264 QB-47E
3205th Drone Squadron, Eglin AFB, FL
22nd March 1962, Gulf of Mexico

The QB-47E entered a left bank and did not respond to commands to level the wings. The airplane was intentionally destroyed.

53-4279 RB-47K
55th SRW, Forbes AFB, KS
27th September 1962, Forbes AFB, KS

During the takeoff roll engine #6 failed just prior to S$_1$. The crew initiated abort procedures, including deploying the drag chute. The airplane became briefly airborne approximately 7,800ft (2,377m) down the runway and turned to the right, quickly contacting the ground, sliding some distance, and burning. The crash killed all four crewmen on board.

53-4281 RB-47H
343rd SRS, 55th SRW, Forbes AFB, KS
1st July 1960, Barents Sea

The airplane was on a CASTLE GATE peripheral ELINT mission and was in international airspace over the Barents Sea some 50nm (93km) from Soviet airspace. The RB-47H picked up an 'escort' of a 206th Air Division, 171st *GvIAP* MiG-19 *Farmer* flown by Vasily Polyakov. Suddenly the MiG-19 began firing, and RB-47H copilot Captain F Bruce Olmstead returned fire. Damage to the left wing of the RB-47H rendered it uncontrollable and AC Major Willard G Palm ordered the crew to abandon the airplane. Palm, Olmstead, and navigator Captain John R McKone ejected; Palm succumbed to the frigid waters but Olmstead and McKone were rescued by a Russian fishing trawler. Electronic Warfare Officers Major Eugene E Posa and Captains Oscar L Goforth, and Dean D Phillips perished, possibly unable to eject from the out-of-control airplane.

53-4283 RB-47H
55th SRW, Forbes AFB, KS
10th February 1956, Ellsworth AFB, SD, TH: 94:20

The airplane diverted to Ellsworth AFB due to bad weather at Forbes AFB. After some 36 hours, the airplane was ready for departure. Given the high field elevation at Ellsworth AFB (3,280ft/1,000m MSL – compared to Forbes AFB at 1,078ft/329m MSL) and the full fuel load, the AC knew that the takeoff would be heavy but planned to burn some fuel during taxi. The airplane had slow acceleration during the takeoff run and experienced a stall to one of the left engines after passing 200ft (61m) altitude. It then struck a hill and crashed approximately 4,100ft (1,250m) from the end of the runway. All six crewmen perished. The accident investigation board determined the cause of the accident to be pilot fatigue (the AC had 3.5 hours of sleep prior to the flight) and inadequate takeoff planning, including incorrect computation of takeoff data.

53-4290 RB-47H
55th SRW, Forbes AFB, KS
28th April 1965, Yokota AB, Japan

During a routine ELINT mission this RB-47H came under attack by two MiG-17s from the Democratic People's Republic of Korea (DPRK). The attack began at 33,000ft (10,058m) and continued for some six minutes as the crew maneuvered to avoid damage, before entering a cloud deck at

RB-47H 53-4283 on the ramp at Boeing-Wichita prior to initial delivery. *Photo 92802 courtesy Boeing*

16,000ft (4,877m). The RB-47H sustained major damage, but copilot First Lieutenant Hank Dubuy, Jr, returned fire. Gunfire from the MiG-17s ruptured the RB-47H's rear fuel tanks which shifted the center of gravity forward. The crew managed to return to Yokota AB, Japan. Due to the forward cg, they successfully landed the airplane without flaps, tricky under even normal circumstances. The crew, including LtCol Hobart D Mattison (AC), First Lieutenant Henry E "Hank" Dubuy (CP), Captain Robert A Rogers (N), Captain Robert C Winters (EWO), First Lieutenant George V Back (EWO), and First Lieutenant Joel J Lutkenhouse (EWO), escaped injury. A USAF 3rd Air Division history reported that according to classified intelligence sources, Dubuy's gunfire hit one of the MiG-17s which then crashed, making him the only B-47 crewmember to shoot down an enemy airplane.

53-4297 RB-47H
343rd SRS, 55th SRW, Forbes AFB, KS
11th November 1962, MacDill AFB, FL

During the Cuban Missile Crisis the airplane departed MacDill AFB at a weight of 183,000 lb (83,007kg). After a normal takeoff, the airplane entered

SILVER KING RB-47H 53-4290 on the ramp at Yokota AB after being attacked by DPRK MiG-17s. *USAF photo*

RB-47H 53-4297 was lost during the October 1962 Cuban Missile Crisis. In this image it carries the unpainted nose radome. *Author's collection*

an extreme nose-high attitude, climbed steeply to 200ft (61m) and the left wing dropped. The crew leveled the wings but the airplane descended rapidly in a stalled attitude, contacting the ground to the left of the runway centerline in a right-wing-low, nose up attitude. All three crewmen were killed. No cause was ever determined.

53-4309 RB-47H
55th SRW, Forbes AFB, KS
29th April 1960, Topeka, KS

During a radar approach to Forbes AFB the AC acknowledged a left turn to a heading of 130°, and 30 seconds later the airplane crashed into a hay meadow 10nm (18.5km) E of Topeka at a steep angle. All three crewmen were killed. Cause of the accident is believed to be either a failed pilot's attitude indicator or spatial disorientation.

53-6198, B-47E
350th BS, 100th BW, Pease AFB, NH
1st February 1957, Atlantic Ocean near Gloucester, MA, TH: 315:25

The crew began a jet penetration from 38,000ft (11,582m) over the Boston VOR. Approximately 12 minutes into the penetration Air Traffic Control (ATC) canceled the clearance and gave priority to a B-47E experiencing radio difficulty at higher altitude. About 10 minutes later B-47E 53-6198 crashed into the Atlantic Ocean 11nm (20.4km) E of Gloucester, MA, killing the crew of four. Only the copilot's body was recovered, who had successfully ejected but succumbed to the elements or drowned. Cause of the crash was not determined. Subsequently a trophy was named in honor of Captain Orrin Snyder, the Evaluator Navigator on board, and was awarded to the most outstanding navigator of the quarter at Pease AFB.

53-6204 B-47E
310th BW, Lincoln AFB, NE
28th February 1958, RAF Greenham Common, UK

B-47E 53-6216 (call sign *Granville 20*) was making a heavyweight takeoff from RAF Greenham Common when it experienced a fire in engines #2 and #3 accompanied by wing overheat conditions. To avoid crashing, the AC notified the tower he was going to jettison the two 1,700gal (6,435 liters) external fuel tanks in the designated on-base drop area parallel and adjacent to the runway. The tower directed him to the designated on-base drop area parallel and adjacent to the runway. The AC lost visual contact with the runway and requested assistance from the tower in finding the drop area, and the B-47E was not in the proper position when the tower told the AC to jettison the tanks from an altitude of 8,000ft (2,438m) onto a small plot of land, hardly a precise undertaking. Consequently, one tank fell onto a hangar and the other hit 65ft (20m) behind B-47E 53-6204 which was being prepared for flight. The crew chief of 53-6204, a maintenance man, and a 307th FMS fuel truck driver were killed, and 53-6204 was destroyed. B-47E 53-2154 sustained minor damage but recovered safely. The resulting fire burned for 16 hours and took over a millions gallons of water to extinguish. As a result of this accident, SAC changed from its US-style flight line clustering of aircraft to wide dispersal while deployed to British bases.

Anti-nuclear activists claimed that the explosion involved a '1.1 megaton B28 thermonuclear free-fall bomb' in 53-6204, and alleged that the nuclear weapon experienced a conventional explosion, releasing radioactive material, including powdered uranium and plutonium oxides [with at least 10 to 20 grams found up to 8nm (15km) away]. As late as 1996 the American and British governments denied that a nuclear accident took place, citing as evidence a University of Southampton study which showed 'no increase at RAF Greenham Common over the presence of naturally occurring uranium.' Conversely, activists point to another scientific study by the British Atomic Weapons Establishment (AWE) at Aldermaston which detected contaminated fallout in 1960. Other critics dismiss the claim of a nuclear incident by noting that the B28 was not in use at that time at either RAF Greenham Common or with the 307th BW at Lincoln AFB, where the destroyed airplane was based, but errant nomenclature does not disprove the presence of some other type of nuclear weapon. At this point, however, evidence that a nuclear accident took place remains unconvincing.

53-6206 B-47E
310th BW, Schilling AFB, KS
19th August 1963, Irwin, IA

Two B-47s (53-2365 and 53-6206) planned to fly formation through the navigation and refueling portion of a BAR NONE mission. In violation of SAC regulations, they agreed to fly in a loose formation at the same altitude and accomplish celestial navigation while maintaining visual separation. Prior to starting celestial observation, the two B-47s collided, crashing near Irwin, IA. Two of the six crewmen were killed.

53-6211 B-47E
310th BW, Schilling AFB, KS
6th July 1962, Bird City, KS

While preparing for a simulated bomb release at FL320, the crew observed 50ft (15m) flames emanating from engines #2 and 3. The AC ordered the crew to bail out, which the copilot did. The AC and navigator remained with the airplane as the AC attempted to deal with the emergency. Descending past 12,000ft (3,658m), the airplane broke up into three sections and crashed near Bird City, KS, killing the two remaining crewmen. Investigation revealed that a bearing failed in the #2 engine, causing the turbine wheel to disintegrate and strike the #3 engine, leading to its failure. While attempting to address the engine failure, the AC probably overstressed the airplane causing the breakup.

53-6215 B-47E
310th BW, Schilling AFB, KS
10th February 1959, Goose Bay IAP, Labrador, Canada

The airplane crashed after losing an engine on takeoff at Goose Bay IAP, Labrador, killing two crewmen.

53-6227 B-47E
380th BW, Plattsburgh AFB, NY
12th August 1960, Plattsburgh AFB, NY

Landed short of the runway, striking a 24in (61cm) lip to the runway. The crew escaped with minor injuries.

53-6229 B-47E
310th BW, Schilling AFB, KS
29th October 1957, Falun, KS

The airplane stalled and entered an unrecoverable spin while on a LABS training mission, crashing near Falun, KS, 18nm (33km) from Schilling AFB. One crew member survived, but subsequently died of his injuries.

53-6230 B-47E
340th BW, Whiteman AFB, MO
15th May 1962, Whiteman AFB, MO

The airplane was loaded with 10,000gal (37,854 liters) of fuel in preparation for a training mission when a fire erupted. The airplane was covered with foam and the fire appeared to under control. As firefighters were soaking the interior of the bomb bay with foam, a sudden explosion engulfed two dozen firemen within 100ft (30m) of the airplane. The flight crew of three and the two crew chiefs survived, but four firefighters were killed and 18 others hospitalized for burns and injuries.

53-6240 B-47E
2nd BW, Hunter AFB, GA
14th January 1958, Hunter AFB, GA

Following a night training mission the airplane began a high-altitude penetration from the Savannah VOR to Hunter AFB for a ground-controlled approach (GCA). The crew discontinued the GCA at minimums and continued the approach visually. The aircraft touched down 1,157ft (352m) short of the runway threshold in an area excavated for construction. When the aircraft contacted the lip of the runway the forward gear folded into the bomb bay and the outrigger gear sheared. There was no fire and the crew escaped safely. The investigation revealed that the construction had left a 1,300ft (396m) unlighted area where the threshold had been displaced and may have caused the pilot to become disoriented, landing short. There were no fatalities.

53-6248 RB-47H
55th SRW, Forbes AFB, KS
27th October 1962, Kindley AB, Bermuda

This BABY BONNET sea search mission was part of events associated with the Cuban Missile Crisis. The airplane accelerated slowly during takeoff and used all 9,600ft (2,926m) of runway before becoming airborne. It flew an additional 2,650ft (808m) prior to crashing in a right-wing-low attitude on a steep shoreline at Ferry Beach, St George's Island. All four crewmen were killed. Investigation revealed the airplane had been serviced with improperly prepared water alcohol solution. Normal solution was 28%, but the mishap airplane had only 12% alcohol, reducing the available thrust for takeoff.

Retirements

Table A3-1. **Static Display**

Serial	MDS	Date	Location	Comments
46-0066	XB-47	14 Dec 54 Sep 16	Octave Chanute Aerospace Museum, Rantoul, IL Air Force Flight Test Center Museum, Edwards AFB, CA	Displayed as '2278' as flown by 1Lt James Obenauf To be restored as 46-0065 prior to its first flight
49-1901	B-47A	Jan 80	Pima Air & Space Museum, Tucson, AZ	Nose section only, recovered from New Mexico Institute of Mines, Socorro, NM. USN asset
50-0062	NTB-47B	01 Apr 67 07 Aug 97	Florence Air & Space Museum, Florence, SC National Museum of the Mighty Eighth Air Force, Pooler, GA	Museum closed
50-0074	TB-47B	1992	March Field Air Museum, Riverside, CA	Cockpit only – used in the movie *Strategic Air Command*. Transferred to March Field Museum from the Tallmantz Aircraft collection. Other sources inaccurately report that Lockheed-Marietta built the simulated cockpit and it was never part of an actual airplane.
51-2075	TB-47B	Feb 60	Air Force Flight Test Center Museum, Edwards AFB, CA	Incomplete airframe used as radar and photographic target on Edwards AFB bomb range
51-2120	B-47B	20 Mar 63	Whiteman AFB, MO	Never assigned to SAC, direct to MATS
51-2207	B-47B		Lincoln AFB, NE	Scrapped
51-2315	B-47B	03 Apr 61	Grissom Air Museum, Grissom AFB, IN	
51-2360	WB-47E	Jun 67 Oct 02	New England Air Museum (NEAM), Windsor Locks CT Hill Aerospace Museum, Ogden, UT	Wfu 3 Oct 66 but retained at McClellan AFB until delivered to NEAM Undergoing restoration
51-2387	WB-47E	06 Oct 69 29 Jun 05	Oklahoma City State Fairgrounds, Oklahoma City, OK Kansas Aviation Museum, Wichita, KS	
51-7066	WB-47E	30 Oct 69	Museum of Flight, Seattle, WA	On loan from the National Museum of Naval Aviation
51-7071	B-47E	14 Apr 61	Hightower Park, Altus, OK	*City of Altus*
52-0166	B-47E	17 Aug 64 17 Jun 86	NAWS China Lake, CA Castle Air Museum, Atwater, CA	The last B-47 flight
52-0410	EB-47E	20 Dec 77 1990	Pease AFB, NH South Dakota Air and Space Museum, Ellsworth AFB, SD	Relocated to Ellsworth AFB in 1990 Components used to restore RB-47H 53-4299 at NMUSAF, remains sold for scrap 4 Apr 15
52-0412	EB-47E	01 Oct 77	Dyess Linear Air Park, TX	Ex USN; displayed as '24120'
52-0595	B-47E	11 Jun 64	Little Rock AFB, AR	
52-1412	B-47E	27 May 64	Strategic Air Command and Space Museum, Ashland, NE	
53-2104	NB-47E	12 Jul 79	Pueblo Weisbrod Aircraft Museum, Pueblo, CO	
53-2135	EB-47E	21 Jun 66	Pima Air & Space Museum, Tucson, AZ	Marked as 376th BW BLUE CRADLE aircraft but is actually a 301st BW Phase V Capsule aircraft
53-2275	B-47E	18 Aug 64 Jan 68	NAWS China Lake, CA March Field Air Museum, Riverside, CA	
53-2276	JB-47E	03 Jun 70	Eighth Air Force Museum, Barksdale AFB, LA	
53-2280	JB-47E	Oct 67 Aug 13	National Museum of the US Air Force, Dayton, OH National Museum of Nuclear & Science History, Albuquerque, NM	
53-2385	B-47E	27 Dec 65	Plattsburgh IAP, Plattsburg, NY	*Pride Of The Adirondacks*
53-4213	B-47E	12 Jul 65 18 Jul 88	Mid-Continent Airport, Wichita, KS McConnell AFB, KS	
53-4257	NRB-47E	Jun 68 12 Sep 86	Confederate Air Force Museum, Harlingen, TX Charles B Hall Air Park, Tinker AFB, OK	
53-4296	RB-47H	30 Apr 76	Air Force Armament Museum, Eglin AFB, Valparaiso, FL	Originally displayed with F-111 nose radome; restored with nose from B-47E 51-5251 received 4 Sep 79. This was one of four 55th SRW RB-47Hs that participated in the HOME RUN overflights of the USSR in 1956.
53-4299	RB-47H	27 Jun 66 20 Jun 05	Salina, KS National Museum of the US Air Force, Dayton, OH	Relocated to NMUSAF in 1998 Restored with parts from EB-47E 52-0410 at Ellsworth AFB
53-6244	B-47E	22 Jan 65	17th BW HQ, Wright-Patterson AFB, OH	Destroyed on fire dump at Wright-Patterson AFB, OH 1977

XB-47 46-0066 was very nearly scrapped when the Octave Chanute Museum closed in 2016. Boeing and other groups graciously financed its relocation to the AFFTC Museum at Edwards AFB, where it will be restored to appear as 46-0065 on the day of its first flight on 17th December 1947. *Photo by William J Simone*

NTB-47 50-0062 was never a SAC asset. It was originally assigned to ATC for training at Wichita and then to APGC at Eglin AFB. Note residual test infrared sensor under the nose. *Photo by Augustine Letto*

A sad end for TB-47B 51-2075 on the bomb range at Edwards AFB. Fortunately it will be used for parts in the restoration of XB-47 46-0066. *Photo by William Simone*

The nose section of B-47A 49-1901 is hoisted aboard a trailer in preparation for movement to the Pima Air & Space Museum. Internal structure is notable, including the wing locating pins at the top. *Photo by Rhodes Arnold*

WB-47E 51-2360 was damaged by a tornado on 3rd October 1979. A C-5 transported it from New England to the Hill AFB Aerospace Museum where it is undergoing restoration. *Photo courtesy New England Air Museum*

After many years on pylons at the Oklahoma State Fairground, WB-47E 51-2387 was moved to the Kansas Aviation Museum in 2005. It suffered tornado damage on 14th April 2012, as seen here, and awaits restoration. *Author photo*

B-47E 51-7071 at a public park in Altus, OK, bears the incorrect serial '520413' and an oversized fuselage insignia. Why this number was used has not been determined. *Author photo*

The final flight of any B-47 variant was B-47E 52-0166 *Spirit* from NAWS China Lake to Castle AFB on 17th June 1986. It was flown by Major General John D Moore and Lieutenant Colonel Dale Wolf. *Author's collection*

Former BLUE CRADLE EB-47E 52-0410 served as a US Navy ECM testbed (note fairing on lower fuselage forward of landing gear) before being displayed at Pease AFB in 509th BW markings. When Pease AFB closed the jet was transferred to Ellsworth AFB and used for parts in the restoration of RB-47H 53-4299. *Photo by Terry Panopolis*

Top left: Following its retirement from the US Navy in 1977 as an ECM testbed, BLUE CRADLE EB-47E 52-0412 ended up at Linear Air Park, Dyess AFB. It was towed into position in 1978 and has since had the name *City of Abilene* removed. *USAF photo*

Top right: Undergoing restoration at the Strategic Air Command and Aerospace Museum, B-47E 52-1412 served as a standard bomber with the 301st BW. *Author photo*

Right: NB-47E 53-2104 made one of the final B-47 flights on 12th July 1979 to the Pueblo Weisbrod Aircraft Museum. It carried the civil registration N1045Y. The SAC 'Milky Way' is definitely nonstandard. *Author photo*

Below: EB-47E 51-2135 is the only Phase V capsule ECM aircraft still in existence. It appears here in the markings of the 376th BW which operated only 3 of the type through 1959, after which they were reassigned to the co-located 301st BW. *Author photo*

Left: One of the best maintained B-47 displays is 53-2385 at Plattsburgh IAP, although the tail band is strictly nonstandard. *Pride of the Adirondacks* served with the 380th BW and is among the jets flown by the author's father. *Author's collection*

Right: The effects of weather, birds, and vandalism prompted the 1988 move of B-47E 53-4213 to McConnell AFB. Now restored, it is displayed behind former KC-135A 55-3118. *Author photo*

Below: NRB-47E served at Wright-Patterson AFB prior to its retirement to the Confederate Air Force Museum. The salt air led to considerable corrosion, leading to its relocation to the Charles B Hall Air Park at Tinker AFB in this nonstandard paint scheme. *Author photo*

Above left: RB-47H 53-4296 retired to the Air Force Armament Museum at Eglin AFB in 1976 while retaining the F-111 nose used during its test days with Autonetics. The nose section of B-47E 51-5251 was grafted onto 53-4296 (seen here) and later painted black to better represent the RB-47H. *Author's collection*

Above: After 40 years of exposure to the elements at Salina, KS, RB-47H 53-4299 was transferred to the NMUSAF where it was meticulously restored and now resides in a display hangar, a fitting tribute to the crews who flew clandestine – and dangerous – reconnaissance missions. *Author's collection*

Upper left: 53-6244 was the last B-47E delivered by Boeing-Wichita. As the B-47s were retired, 53-6244 was chosen to represent the fleet at the Air Force Museum where it arrived on 22nd January 1965. *Author's collection*

Left: When the Museum relocated to Wright Field, 53-6244 was left behind and displayed in front of the 17th BW HQ. Sadly, it ended up on the fire dump leaving NMUSAF without an operational B-47E. *Author's collection*

APPENDIX IV

Records and Special Achievements

It should not be surprising that the new jet-powered B-47 promptly established records for speed and endurance, especially when undertaken with aerial refueling. A 4-5 hour trans-Atlantic flight, for example, easily broke existing piston-powered flight times for airplanes in a similar weight class. What is surprising is that few of the B-47's records were sanctioned by the Fédération Aéronautique Internationale (FAI) or its US subsidiary the National Aeronautics Association (NAA). Consequently, most of the 'records' listed here are unofficial. Moreover, many of the records were eclipsed immediately by other B-47s, especially those achieved during the mass deployments to and from the United Kingdom.

SAC was of two minds in publicizing these achievements. Obviously they attracted favorable attention, particularly during highly publicized events such as the General Electric (GE) Trophy Race. This built support for SAC's mission and the funding of additional SAC airplanes and infrastructure in Congressional budgets, many of which were highly contentious. Conversely the flights revealed the operational capabilities of SAC's new bomber. Knowing how fast the B-47 could fly enabled an adversary to determine how long it would take to reach its target and even the weight of its weapons, especially when combined with one or more aerial refuelings. SAC also tended to make any public announcements in the *New York Times* or other newspapers somewhat ambiguous. Often the only person named was the aircraft commander, a disappointing slight to the other crewmembers who made the flight possible. Serial numbers were never mentioned and have been determined only by careful scrutiny of photographs accompanying news bulletin or from declassified unit histories. Some dates are imprecise, as many early records were announced months after the fact and then mentioned only by month.

These historical challenges aside, both Boeing and SAC crews were eager to show the world that the future of strategic airpower was the jet bomber. The B-47 pioneered this future through its record-setting flights, many of which may never be recorded.

Competition and Awards

The B-47 made its debut appearance in the 1953 navigation and bombing competition, popularly known as 'Bomb Comp', held that year at Davis-Monthan AFB, when seven B-47 wings each sent two crews. A B-36 crew won the competition, with the two best B-47 performances achieving ninth and tenth place and the remaining five B-47 units all at the bottom. A single YRB-47B competed at the annual reconnaissance meet at Ellsworth AFB. During the 1954 competition at Barksdale AFB 15 B-47 wings took part, but again a B-36 crew won the overall best performance award. A B-47 crew from the 305th BW delivered a fourth-place finish. The 55th SRW and 91st SRW entered RB-47Es in the reconnaissance competition at Fairchild AFB but failed to beat RB-36 units.

A crew from the 93rd BW at Castle AFB, CA, flew the *City of Merced* to win SAC's 1955 Bombing and Navigation Competition. It was the first time a jet bomber had won the annual meet, scoring 853 out of 1,000 possible points. The crew included aircraft commander Major Horace C Taylor, copilot Major Martin A Speiser, and observer Major José L Holguin. CINCSAC General LeMay was

Major Horace C Taylor (AC), Major José L Holguin (N), and Major Martin A Speiser flew the *City Of Merced*. They won the Best B-47 Crew award and the Wing Navigation Trophy. *Photo USAF*

on hand to award the crew their trophy, as well as pin on their 'spot promotion' to Lieutenant Colonel. LeMay told the participants, 'Remember a few years ago when we got B-47s there was a lot of yacking that you couldn't bomb accurately from a B-47? This year's competition proves otherwise.' To be fair, the B-47's earlier critics were right and LeMay had to move a lot of mountains to make the B-47 fully mission capable, but he was right when he effectively announced that the B-47's time had come. In addition, a B-47 crew from the 320th BW won the Fairchild Trophy (awarded to the outstanding bomb unit in the combined fields of bombing and navigation), beating out 22 other wings.

SAC's five RB-47E wings were the only competitors in the reconnaissance competition. The 91st SRW received the Paul T Cullen Trophy, awarded for the unit that contributes the most to the Air Force's photo and signals intelligence collection effort. The 91st SRW won the Cullen Trophy again the following year. The 1956 bombing and reconnaissance competitions were held at Lockbourne AFB, but the 27 participating B-47 wings were again bested by the B-36s from the 11th BW.

The 1957 bombing competition at Pinecastle AFB was marred by the loss on 9th October of DB-47B 51-2177, killing the flamboyant 321st BW Commander Colonel Mike McCoy and visiting Royal Air Force (RAF) Group Captain John Woodroffe, as well as the remaining crewmembers (see Appendix II). The base was renamed McCoy AFB on 7th May 1958. Perhaps fittingly, the 321st BW B-47s won all the major events, including the Fairchild Trophy. RB-47Es from the 26th SRW won the reconnaissance competition. The following year B-47 units won the top three slots in the bombing and navigation competition, and the 306th BW won the coveted Fairchild Trophy, an honor that went to B-47s of the 307th BW in 1959.

By 1960 the B-47's dominance at Bomb Comp came to an end as a B-52 unit won the Fairchild Trophy. Only two B-47 wings took part in the competition held at Bergstrom AFB, TX. The 1965 competition was the last year in which B-47s took part, without notable results.

The 321st BW won both the Fairchild Trophy and the McCoy Trophy in the 1957 Competition. It was represented by two Stratojets, *City of Winter Park* and *City of Orlando*. *Author's collection*

The 341st BW received the Wing Bombing Trophy at the 1958 Bomb Comp. B-47E 53-2031, *City Of Abilene*, displays the flags of countries visited following its win. *Author's Collection*

Bomb Comp included other events such as Loading Equipment Judging that recognized the effort by maintenance and other personnel. By the 1960 competition at Bergstrom AFB, seen here, B-52s overshadowed the B-47s including 53-1858 of the 68th BW, 51-2361 also of the 68th BW, 52-0312 from the 321st BW, and 52-0584 from the 303rd BW. *Photo USAF*

Table A4-1. **Records and Special Achievements**

Date	MDS	Serial	Crew	Notes
08 Feb 49	XB-47	46-0065	Maj Russell E Schleeh, Maj Joe Howell	Moses Lake to Andrews AFB, 2,289nm in 3:46 hrs, 607.2mph
18 May 51	XB-47	46-0066	Maj Robert W Halliday, Maj James E Bauer, Lt John T Jurcyk	Hickam AFB to Edwards AFB, 2,600nm, 5:50 hrs, 445.7mph. Original plan was Hickam AFB to Bolling AFB
09 Aug 51	B-47B	n/a	LtCol Patrick D Fleming, Maj H V Leonhardt, MSgt J H Brown	Eielson AFB to Wichita, 2,800nm, 5:36 hrs, 500mph
20 Sep 51	B-47B	49-2645	Col Richard C Neely, Col J G Foster, Capt D J Haney	First B-47 flight over North Pole, Eielson AFB to Eielson AFB
13 Mar 52	B-47B	n/a	Ed Hartz, Lew Wallick, Ed Sullivan	Wichita to Wichita, 7,000nm, 14:57 hrs, 468mph, Boeing crew
23 Mar 52	B-47B	50-0004	LtCol Russell E Schleeh, Capt Leonard P Farrell, MSgt Chester E Lee, Robert A Jackson	Edwards AFB to Edwards AFB, 12,025nm 24:01 hrs, 500.6mph, 3 air refuelings, dropped a dummy 10,000 lb bomb en route
Apr 52	B-47B	51-2137	n/a	Albuquerque (Kirtland AFB) to Wichita 794mph average over a 30 minute segment of flight
16 Jun 52	B-47B	51-2254	Capt Ken Juhne, Lt John Wade, Capt William B Hopkins	MacDill AFB to MacDill AFB, 12,000nm, 25:19 hrs, 473mph, *Dinero al Contado*
29 Sep 52	B-47B	n/a	Maj James E Bauer, Maj George T Matis, Capt Charles J Gilmore	Travis AFB to Hickam AFB, 2,463nm, 4:52 hrs, 500mph
21 Nov 52	B-47B	n/a	BGEN Frederic E Glantzberg, Maj James E Bauer, Capt Charles J Gilmore	Hickam AFB to Travis AFB, 2,434nm, 4:22 hrs, 565mph
19 Feb 53	B-47B	n/a	Capt Guy Fender, Capt David J Haney, Maj R A Christenson	First refueling over North Pole
07 Apr 53	B-47B	n/a	Col Michael N W McCoy, LtCol G P Birdsong, Jr, LtCol Michael Berkowitz	Limestone AFB to RAF Brize Norton 3,120nm, 5:38 hrs, 553.8mph, 1st flights to England, 306th BW
07 Apr 53	B-47B	n/a	LtCol Benny Close, LtCol Loyd Griffin, LtCol Lawrence Grant	Limestone AFB to RAF Brize Norton 3,120nm, 5:38 hrs, 553.8mph, 1st flights to England, 306th BW

Date	Type	Serial	Crew	Details
05 Jun 53	B-47B	n/a n/a n/a	Capt Kenneth P Kuhn Maj Horace B Reeves Maj M H Fitchke	Limestone AFB to RAF Fairford, 3,120nm, 5:36 hrs, 555mph. SAC records indicate that two B-47Bs set this record but do not specify which of the three 306th BW crews listed here were responsible
07 Jun 53	B-47B	n/a	n/a	Limestone AFB to RAF Fairford, 3,120nm, 5:22 hrs, 581mph, 306th BW
28 Jul 53	B-47B	n/a	LtCol James Smith, LtCol Don Frank, Maj Gene Dawson	Limestone AFB to RAF Fairford, 3,120nm, 4:45 hrs, 656mph, 306th BW
28 Jul 53	B-47B	n/a	Col Elliott Vandevanter, Jr, LtCol Robert Michie, Maj William Richards, Jr	Goose Bay to RAF Fairford, 2,403nm, 4:03 hrs, 569.8mph. A SAC source shows 4:14 hrs, 2,480nm, and 586mph, 306th BW
28 Jul 53	B-47B	n/a	Capt Robert D Carlstrom	Limestone AFB to RAF Fairford, 3,120nm 5:22 hrs, 581mph, 306th BW
28 Jul 53	B-47B	n/a	n/a	12,000nm in 24 hrs, 500mph during a 306th BW flight from the UK to North Africa to the UK
04 Aug 53	B-47B	n/a	Col Elliott Vandevanter, Jr, LtCol Robert Michie, Maj William Richards, Jr	RAF Fairford to MacDill AFB, 4,450nm, 9:53 hrs, 454 mph
04 Aug 53	B-47B	n/a	LtCol James Smith, LtCol Don Frank, Maj Gene Dawson	RAF Fairford to Savannah (Hunter AFB), 4,151nm, 9:26, 440mph
04 Sep 53	B-47B	n/a	Col Michael N W McCoy	RAF Fairford to MacDill AFB, 4,450nm, 9:13 hrs, 508.8 mph
06 Sep 53	B-47B	51-2287	Col G P Birdsong	RAF Fairford to MacDill AFB via Dayton, OH, 12:15 as 'the longest operational jet flight'
05 Nov 53	B-47B	n/a	Maj H B Howard	Limestone AFB to RAF Fairford, 3,120nm, 4:43 hrs, 661mph, 305th BW
14 Dec 53	B-47B	n/a	Col William E Creer	RAF Fairford to MacDill AFB, 4,480nm, 8:53 hrs, 504.3mph, 305th BW
23 Dec 53	B-47B	n/a	Capt Russell Bishop	Limestone AFB to RAF Upper Heyford, 2,970nm, 4:34 hrs, 650.5mph, 22nd BW
16 Jun 54	n/a	n/a	n/a	MacDill AFB to MacDill AFB, 12,000nm, 25:19 hrs, 473mph
21 Jun 54	B-47E	51-7062 51-7065 51-7071	MGEN Walter C Sweeney, Jr, Maj W A Price, Maj Arnold Sipes, Maj R L Kennedy, Col W F Coleman, Capt R B Carlson, Capt J E Mcue, Lt B W Cooper, Col W R Smith, Maj Raymond A Siebert, Lt Thomas J Fiden, Lt R E Carrigan	First Trans-Pacific Jet Crossing, March AFB to Yakota AB, 6,670nm, 15 hrs, 22nd BW
03 Jul 54	B-47E	51-7062 51-7065 51-7071	MGEN Walter C Sweeney, Jr, Maj W A Price, Maj Arnold Sipes, Maj R L Kennedy, Col W F Coleman, Capt R B Carlson, Capt J E Mcue, Lt B W Cooper, Col W R Smith, Maj Raymond A Siebert, Lt Thomas J Fiden, Lt R E Carrigan	Return trip from Yokota AB; The leg from Guam to Hawai'I was a record, 22nd BW
29 Jul 54	RB-47E	n/a	Boeing pilots Rodney M Randall, Maurice Norum	Wichita to Oklahoma City (Tinker AFB), 157nm, 15 min 20 secs, 622mph, Boeing crew
06 Aug 54	B-47E	n/a	373rd BS crew: Capt Donald L Keplinger (AC), 1LT Donald A Lutz (CP), 1LT Alfred H Guidotti (N), and LtCol Vernon A Kammack (IP) 375th BS crew: Capt Glenn W Stockton (AC), 1LT John R Terpening (CP), Capt Oscar A Bernhoff (N), and Capt James M Watson, Jr (IP)	2 of 4 B-47Es completed non-stop round-trip simulated strike from Hunter AFB to French Morocco, 10,000nm in 25:23 hrs and 24:40 hrs. For this the crews received the 1954 Mackay Trophy. This was the first mission to fly across the Atlantic, simulate a strike on foreign targets, and return to home base in the US, reflecting SAC's bomber capability.
16/18 Nov 54	n/a	n/a	n/a	USAF announcement of 17,000nm flight in 35 hrs, 486mph, no further details
17 Nov 54	YRB-47B	51-2062	Col David A Burchinal, Maj Pat H Earhart, Capt Steve Franko, Maj Forrest A McCoy	21,163 miles, Sidi Slimane to RAF Fairford (twice due to inclement weather, 9 aerial refuelings), 47:35 hrs, 445 mph, 43rd BW
28 Feb 55	n/a	n/a	n/a	March AFB to Hunter AFB, 2,000nm, 3:19 hrs, 641mph
04 Sep 55	B-47B	51-2314	Maj Leonard J (Red) Stevens (AC), Major Freedman (Jim) Weedman (CP), Capt. Glenn Fornes (N).	March AFB to Philadelphia, GE Trophy Race, 320th BW, 2,337nm at 589mph, 443rd BS/320th BW
02 Sep 56	B-47E	51-5232	Maj Joseph Schreiber	Bermuda to Oklahoma City (Tinker AFB), GE Trophy Race, 1,900nm, 3:08, 601mph, 22nd BW 21.3 seconds ahead of LtCol John C Lewis in second place 301st BW, and 3rd place B-47 310th BW
Nov 56	B-47E	n/a	9th BS: LtCol Charles B Phippen (AC), 1LT Rollie Jones (N), LtCol Joseph J O'Hara (CP); 5th BS: Maj Willaim Brown (AC), Major Stephen Constant (CP), Capt John B Owen (N); 99th BS: Major Charles R Hardy (AC), Major Manus Murtha (CP), Capt Jimmy S Lassetter (N)	Three B-47s from the 9th BW flew 8,300nm from Mountain Home AFB to Australia and New Zealand in conjunction with the 1956 Olympic Games in Melbourne, Australia. Hailed as the 'longest point-to-point excursion ever performed by SAC jet bombers'
25 Jan 57	JB-47E	52-0514	Maj Mont Smith, Lt Hayden Y Grubbs, Capt Charles F Hawkins, W/O James J Lansford	March AFB to Hanscom AFB, 2,650nm, 3:47 hrs, 715mph (max speed 750mph), *Jet Streamers*
09 Mar 57	JB-47E	52-0514	Maj Merle Henderson	Seattle to Savannah (Hunter AFB), 2,800nm, 4:18 hrs, 665 mph, *Jet Streamers*
28 May 57	B-47E	n/a	n/a	Nonstop flight over 47 hrs 35 min
28 May 57	B-47E	51-2379	Capt Robert E Sheridan, 1LT J L Mombrea, Capt Frank R Beadle, Sgt E W Smith	Three Capitols Air Race over Madrid, Rome and Paris, 2,346nm 4:12 hrs, 558mph, sponsored by GE, flown by 529th BS, 380th BW
10 Aug 57	B-47E	n/a	BGEN James V Edmundson, LtCol Leslie E Gaskins, 1LT Robert L Yarbrough, Maj Leon M Burgess	Andersen AB to Sidi Slimane AB Morocco, 11,450nm, 22:50 hrs, 520mph, 321st BW
30 Nov 59	JB-47E	n/a	Anthony (AC, rank unknown)	Jet Endurance Record Wright-Patterson AFB to Wright-Patterson AFB, 39,000nm, 80:36 hrs, 484mph, possibly a test flight associated with an improved-comfort ejection seat trial

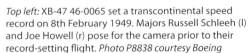

Top left: XB-47 46-0065 set a transcontinental speed record on 8th February 1949. Majors Russell Schleeh (l) and Joe Howell (r) pose for the camera prior to their record-setting flight. *Photo P8838 courtesy Boeing*

Above: During the return flight following XB-47 46-0066's participation in the GREENHOUSE atomic tests, Major James Bauer (l), Major Robert Halliday (c), and Lieutenant John Jurcyk (r) set the speed record for Hickam AFB to Edwards AFB. *Author's collection*

Top right: The first Stratojet to overfly the North Pole was B-47B 49-2645 flown by Colonel Richard Neely (l), Colonel J G Foster (c), and Captain D J Haney (r). It was intended to overfly the USSR but burned to destruction shortly after this picture was taken. *USAF*

Right: B-47B 51-2254 set an endurance record on 16th June 1952 of more than 25 hours over 12,000nm. Nicknamed *Dinero al Contado* (*Cash Money* in Spanish), the record-setting crew returned it to Boeing-Wichita for subsequent upgrades. From left to right are Captain Ken Juhne (AC), Captain William Hopkins (N), William Speer (Boeing), and Lieutenant John Wade (CP). *Author's collection*

Top left: The 306th BW's record-setting deployment in June 1953 from MacDill AFB to RAF Fairford included a stop at Limestone AFB. Colonel G P Birdsong (r) joins Major Roger Chafee (l) and Lieutenant Colonel W K Greer (c) in watching the B-47s arrive at Limestone AFB. Birdsong, the 369th BS Commander, was Colonel Michael McCoy's copilot during the first record-setting flight on 7th April. *Photo BW90079 courtesy Boeing*

Top right: A surprisingly chipper Major General Walter Sweeney is welcomed after his 15-hour flight in B-47E 51-7062 from March AFB to Yokota AB. During the return trip the three B-47s set a record for the leg from Guam to Hawai'i. *USAF Photo*

Right: Commemorative envelope carried aboard 46-0066 during its 18th May 1951 record flight shows 'Washington DC' – the intended destination – inked over. Why it landed instead at Edwards AFB has not been verified. *Author's collection*

Below: Commemorative envelope carried on the 6th September 1953 flight from RAF Fairford to MacDill AFB. Other 'jet operational' missions would soon eclipse this flight in duration. *Author's collection*

Above: B-47E 51-7065, 51-7062, and 51-7071 on the ramp at Yokota AB following their record-setting flight from March AFB on 21st June 1954. *USAF Photo*

Right: 308th BW Commander Colonel John Batjer (far left) greets the 373rd BS crew that shared the 1954 Mackay Trophy. From left to right are Captain Don Keplinger (AC), Lieutenant Colonel Vernon Cammack (spare pilot), First Lieutenant Alfred Guidotti (N), and First Lieutenant Donald Lutz (CP). *USAF photo via George Culley*

Left: A crew from the 375th BS shared the 1954 Mackay Trophy 308th BW crew. From left to right are Colonel John Batjer, 308th BW Commander, Captain Glenn Stockton (AC), First Lieutenant John Terpening (CP), Captain Oscar Bernhoff (N), and Captain James Watson (spare pilot). *USAF photograph via George Culley*

Below: In what was ballyhooed as a 47+ hour weather divert between the UK and North Africa and back again, 43rd BW crew Colonel David Burchinal (AC), Major Forrest McCoy (N), Captain Stephen Franco (CP), and Major Pat Earhart (spare pilot) covered 21,163nm in YRB-47B 51-2062. Burchinal later admitted that he actually planned the flight as an experiment in 20+ hour sorties. *Author's collection*

Above: B-47s won the prestigious GE Trophy on three occasions, the first in 1955 for a flight from March AFB to Philadelphia. From left to right are Captain Glenn Fornes (N), Colonel Robert Miller (320th BW Commander), Major Leonard 'Red' Stevens (AC), Lieutenant Colonel Richard Hoban (443rd BS Commander), Major Freedman 'Jim' Weedman (CP), and Brigadier General Charles B Westover, 12th AD Commander. *Photo via Douglas Weedman*

Below: National Aeronautics Association timers Bertram Rhine (l) and Clyde Barnett (r) get an earful of noise as they start the clock while 51-2314 starts its early morning takeoff roll from March AFB. *USAF photo*

Above: The 1956 GE Trophy went to a 22nd BW crew commanded by Major Joseph Schreiber flying B-47E 51-5232.

Right: Special markings applied to 51-5232 following its successful speed run. *Both photos author's collection*

Above: JB-47E 52-0514 *The Jet Streamers* set two records on 25th January 1957 from March AFB to Hanscom AFB, and on 9th March 1957 from Seattle to Savannah while conducting high-altitude jet-stream research. *Photo by Howard Henry*

Right: B-47E 51-2379 won the 'Three Capitols' Air Race on 28th May 1957. The crew, from left to right, included Captain Robert Sheridan (AC), First Lieutenant J L Mombrea (CP), Captain Frank Beadle (N), and Sargent E W Smith (CC). *Author's collection*

Glossary

AAB — Army Air Base
AAF — Army Air Force or Army Air Field
AASB — Arizona Aircraft Storage Branch
AB — air base
ABNCP — airborne command post
AC — alternating current aircraft commander
ACRES — Airborne Communication Relays
ACRP — Airborne COMINT Reconnaissance Program
ACRS — Airborne Communication Relay Squadron
AD — Air Division
ADC — Air Defense Command
ADGP — Air Delivery Group
ADS — Air Defense Squadron
AEC — Atomic Energy Commission
AF — Air Force
AFB — Air Force Base
AFFTC — Air Force Flight Test Center
AFHRA — Air Force Historical Research Agency
AFLC — Air Force Logistics Command
AFSC — Air Force Systems Command
AFSDG — Air Force Storage and Disposition Group
AFSS — Air Force Security Service
AFTAC — Air Force Technical Applications Center
AFTO — Air Force Technical Order
AGL — above ground level
AI — airborne intercept [radar]
AMA — Air Materiel Area
AMC — Air Materiel Command
AoA — angle of attack
AP — Airport
APGC — Air Proving Ground Command
ARDC — Air Research and Development Command
ARE — atmospheric research equipment
AREFS — Air Refueling Squadron
ASD — Aeronautical Systems Division or Aircraft Storage Depot
ASIP — Aircraft Structural Integrity Program
ASS — Aircraft Storage Squadron
ATC — Air Training Command or air traffic control
ATO — assisted takeoff
AUXCP — auxiliary command post
AWE — Atomic Weapons Establishment
AWS — Air Weather Service
BDV — Boeing-Douglas-Vega
BL — butt line
BMAC — Boeing Military Airplane Company
BMEWS — Ballistic Missile Early Warning Systems
BNS — bombing-navigation system
BO — Boeing-Seattle
BS — Bombardment Squadron or body station
BTWT — Boeing Transonic Wind Tunnel
BW — Bombardment Wing or Boeing-Wichita
C — Celsius
CAA — Civil Aeronautics Authority
CC — crew chief
CCTS — Combat Crew Transition School (later Combat Crew Training Squadron)
CCTW — Combat Crew Training Wing
CE — crew engineer
CENTAUX — Central Auxiliary Command Post
CENTO — Central Treaty Organization
CFIT — controlled flight into terrain
cg — center of gravity
CIA — Central Intelligence Agency
CINCPAC — Commander-in-Chief, Pacific
CINCSAC — Commander-in-Chief, Strategic Air Command
cm — centimeter
COMINT — communications intelligence
COMTAC — Commander, Tactical Air Command
CONUS — Continental United States
CP — copilot
cps — cycles per second

CRM — crew resource management
D — Democrat
DASA — Defense Atomic Support Agency
DC — direct current
DCS — Drag Control System
Det — Detachment
DEFCON — Defense Condition
DEW — Distant Early Warning
DF — direction finding
DoD — Department of Defense
DPRK — Democratic People's Republic of Korea [North Korea]
DS — Drone Squadron
DT — Douglas-Tulsa
E — Execution time/hour
EAM — Emergency Action Message
EASTAUX — East Auxiliary Command Post
ECI — Electronic Communications, Inc
ECM — electronic countermeasures
EGT — exhaust gas temperature
ELGE — emergency landing gear extension
ELINT — electronic intelligence
ERCS — Emergency Rocket Communication System
ESP — engine stall prevention switch
EW — electronic warfare or electronic warfare officer or early warning
EWO — Emergency War Order or electronic warfare officer
EWP — Emergency War Plan
ExComm — Executive Committee
F — Fahrenheit
FAA — Federal Aviation Agency
FAI — Fédération Aéronautique Internationale
FE — flight engineer
FEAF — Far Eastern Air Forces
FIS — Fighter Interceptor Squadron
FM — frequency modulated
FOD — foreign object damage
fpm — feet per minute
ft — feet
FTW — Flight Training Wing
FY — fiscal year
gal — gallon
GCA — ground-controlled approach
GCAC — Grand Central Aircraft Corporation
GCI — ground controlled intercept
GE — General Electric
GFE — government-furnished equipment
GFP — government-furnished property
GIUK — Greenland-Iceland-United Kingdom
GPI — ground position indicator
GPL — General Precision Laboratories
gpm — gallons per minute
GTOW — gross takeoff weight
HASP — High Altitude Sampling Program
HE — high explosive
HF — high frequency
HQ — headquarters
hr — hour
HRR — high-resolution radar
IAP — International Airport
ICBM — intercontinental ballistic missile
ICCS — interim camera control system
IFF — Identification – Friend or Foe
IFR — Instrument flight rules
IG — Inspector General
ILS — instrument landing system
IMC — image motion compensation
IMP — Improved Maintenance Program
in — inch
IN — instructor navigator
IP — instructor pilot or initial point
IR — infrared
IRAN — inspect and repair as necessary
JATO — jet assisted takeoff
JCS — Joint Chiefs of Staff
JP — jet propellant
JRC — Joint Reconnaissance Center
KIAS — knots indicated air speed
kg — kilogram
km — kilometer

kN — kilonewtons
kph — kilometers per hour
kt — kiloton
KTAS — knots true air speed
kVA — kilovolt ampere
l — liter
L — local time
LABS — Low Altitude Bombing System
lb — pound
lbf — pound-force
LG — logistics [SAC/LG]
LM — Lockheed-Marietta
LORAN — Long Range Navigation
LRDP — Long Range Detection Program
LUSTY — Luftwaffe Secret Technology
m — meter
MAC — Military Airlift Command or mean aerodynamic chord
MARS — mid-air retrieval system
MASDC — Military Aircraft Storage and Disposition Center
MASINT — measurement and signature intelligence
MATS — Military Air Transport Service
Mc — Megacycles
MCGS — Microwave Command Guidance System
MDS — Mission-Design-Series
MET — Meteorological (System)
MEZ — Military Emergency Zone
MiG — Mikoyan i Gurevich
MIRR — Material Inspection Receiving Report
MIT — Massachusetts Institute of Technology
MITO — minimum interval takeoff
Mk — Mark
ml — milliliter
mm — millimeter
MO — meteorological officer
mph — miles per hour
mpm — meters per minute
MRT — military rated thrust
MSL — mean sea level
Mt — megaton
N — navigator
n/a — not available
NAA — National Aeronautics Association
NACA — National Advisory Committee on Aeronautics
NAF — Numbered Air Force
NALS — National Alternative Landing Site
NAS — Naval Air Station
NATO — North Atlantic Treaty Organization
NAWS — Naval Air Weapons Station
NCA — National Command Authorities
NEAC — North East Air Command
NEAM — New England Air Museum
NHRP — National Hurricane Research Project
nm — nautical mile
NMUSAF — National Museum of the US Air Force
NORAD — North American Air Defense Command
nr — near
NSC — National Security Council
NUDINT — nuclear detonation intelligence
O — observer
O&M — operations and maintenance
OAT — outside air temperature
OCAMA — Oklahoma City Air Materiel Area
OL — operating location
OpOrd — operational order
ORI — Operational Readiness Inspection
P — pilot
PACCS — Post Attack Command and Control System or Post Attack Command and Control Squadron
PAF — Pakistan Air Force
PIO — pilot-induced oscillation
PCN — Production Control Number
PCU — power control unit
PDB — President's Daily Brief
PDM — programmed depot maintenance
PHOTINT — photographic intelligence

PHS — Public Health Service
PIO — pilot-induced oscillation
PPI — plan position indicator
PPM — precision parameter measurements
PRC — People's Republic of China (Red China)
psi — pounds per square inch
QRC — quick reaction capability
qt — quart
RADC — Rome Air Development Center
RAF — Royal Air Force
RAMP — Radiation Monitoring Program
RAPCON — Radar Approach Control
RATO — rocket assisted takeoff
RBS — radar bomb scoring
RFP — request for proposal
RoC — Republic of China (Taiwan)
rpm — revolutions per minute
RS — Reconnaissance Squadron
RSO — reconnaissance system operator
SAAMA — San Antonio Air Materiel Area
SAC — Strategic Air Command
SAD — Strategic Aerospace Division
SAFE — semi-automatic ferret equipment
SAM — surface-to-air missile
SENSINT — sensitive intelligence
SEO — special equipment operator
SIGINT — signals intelligence
SIOP — Single Integrated Operational Plan
SLAR — side-looking airborne radar
SLBM — sea-launched ballistic missile
SMAMA — Sacramento Air Materiel Area
SOI — signal of interest
SRW — strategic reconnaissance wing
SS — Support Squadron
SSADS — Soviet Semi-automatic Air Defense System
SSB — single side band
SW — strategic wing
TAC — Tactical Air Command
TACAN — tactical aerial navigation
TDY — temporary duty
TELINT — telemetry intelligence
TEMCO — Texas Engineering and Manufacturing Company
TG — Test Group
TH — total hours
TO — Technical Order
TRAP — Terminal Radiation Program
TS — Training Squadron
UCCS — universal camera control system
UHF — ultra-high frequency
UK — United Kingdom
UN — United Nations
US — United States
USA — United States of America
USAAF — United States Army Air Force
USAF — United States Air Force
USAFE — United States Air Forces – Europe
USCG — United States Coast Guard
USCM — Unit Simulated Combat Mission
USSR — Union of Soviet Socialist Republics
V — volt
VFR — visual flight rules
VHF — very high frequency
VOR — very high frequency omnidirectional radio
WADC — Wright Air Development Center
WESTAUX — West Auxiliary Command Post
WFNA — white fuming nitric acid
wfu — withdrawn from use
WIBAC — Wichita Boeing Airplane Company
w/o — written off
WRAMA — Warner-Robins Air Materiel Area
WRM — war reserve materiel
WRS — Weather Reconnaissance Squadron
WS — Weather Squadron or wing station
Z — zulu time (Greenwich Mean Time/Universal Coordinated Time)
ZI — Zone of the Interior

Index